Welsh Castle Builders

Welsh Castle Builders

The Savoyard Style

John Marshall

PEN & SWORD
HISTORY

First published in Great Britain in 2022 by
Pen & Sword History
An imprint of
Pen & Sword Books Ltd
Yorkshire – Philadelphia

ISBN 978 1 39908 548 9

A CIP catalogue record for this book is
available from the British Library.

Typeset by Mac Style
Printed in the UK by CPI Group (UK) Ltd, Croydon, CR0 4YY.

Pen & Sword Books Limited incorporates the imprints of Atlas,
Archaeology, Aviation, Discovery, Family History, Fiction, History,
Maritime, Military, Military Classics, Politics, Select, Transport,
True Crime, Air World, Frontline Publishing, Leo Cooper, Remember
When, Seaforth Publishing, The Praetorian Press, Wharncliffe
Local History, Wharncliffe Transport, Wharncliffe True Crime
and White Owl.

For a complete list of Pen & Sword titles please contact

PEN & SWORD BOOKS LIMITED
47 Church Street, Barnsley, South Yorkshire, S70 2AS, England
E-mail: enquiries@pen-and-sword.co.uk
Website: www.pen-and-sword.co.uk

Or

PEN AND SWORD BOOKS
1950 Lawrence Rd, Havertown, PA 19083, USA
E-mail: Uspen-and-sword@casematepublishers.com
Website: www.penandswordbooks.com

Contents

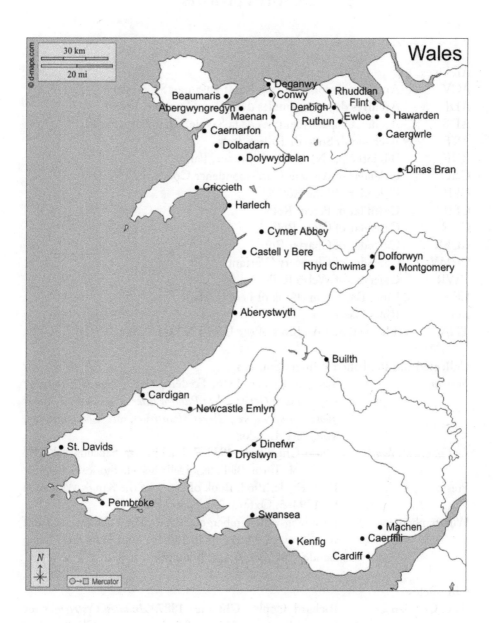

Abbreviations

Archives

ACV	Archives cantonales vaudoises, Lausanne, Switzerland
ADI	Archives départementales de l'Isère, Grenoble, France
ADS	Archives départementales de la Savoie, Chambéry, France
AST	Archivio di Stato di Torino, Italy
BNF	Bibliothèque Nationale de France, Paris
CAC	Calendar of Ancient Correspondence Concerning Wales
CFR	Calendar of Fine Rolls
CPR	Calendar of Patent Rolls
CCR	Calendar of Close Rolls
CChR	Calendar of Charter Rolls
CChW	Calendar of Chancery Warrants
CWR	Calendar of Welsh Rolls.
LF	Liber Feodorum (Book of Fees (Fiefs))
RG	Rôles Gascons
TNA	The National Archives of the UK (TNA)

Collected and Published Primary Sources

Fœdera	Thomas Rymer. 1816. Fœdera, *Conventiones, Litteræ, et Cujuscunque Generis Acta Publica Inter Reges Angliæ et alios quosvis Imperatores, Reges, Pontifices, bel Communitates.* Volume 1, London.
La Finanza Sabauda	Mario Chiaudano. 1933-7. La Finanza Sabauda nel XIII sec. 3 Vols Turin. Biblioteca Della Società Storica Subalpina.
Prests	E. B. Fryde. 1962. Book of prests of the King's Wardrobe for 1294-5. Oxford: Clarendon Press.
Wurstemberger	J. Ludwig Wurstemberger. 1856-9. Peter der Zweite, Graf von Savoyen, Markgraf in Italien, Sein Haus und Seine Lande. Vols 1-4. Berne: Stæmpfle.

Chronicles

Ann. Cestrienses	Richard Copley Christie. 1887. *Annales Cestrienses*: or Chronicle of the Abbey of St Werburg at Chester. The Record Society.
Ann. Dunstable	Henry Richards Luard, 1864 *Annales Monastici* Vol III. *Annales Prioratus Dunstaplia* London: Longmans, Green, Reader and Dye.

Ann. Trevet	Thomas Hog. 1845. F. Nicholai Triveti, de ordine frat. *Praedicatorum, Annales.* English Historical Society.
Brut	*Brut y Tywysogion,* or the Chronicle of the Princes: 1955. Red Book of Hergest Version, ed. and trans. by T. Jones, History and Law Series, 16 Cardiff: Cardiff: University of Wales Press.
Chron. Gloucester	William Alldis Wright, 1887. The Metrical Chronicle of Robert of Gloucester, Part II. London, HMSO.
Chron. Guisborough	Walter of Guisborough. 1848. *Chronicon domini Walteri de Hemingburgh* Vols 1 & 2. London.
Chron. Lanercost	Herbert Maxwell. 1913. The Chronicle of Lanercost, 1272–1346.
Chron. Langtoft	Thomas Wright. 1868. The Chronicle of Pierre de Langtoft: In French Verse from the Earliest Period to the Death of King Edward I. Vol II.
Chron. Majora Eng	John Allen Giles translation. 1852–3. Matthew Paris's English History Vols 1–3. Henry G. Bohn. London.
Chron. Majora Lat	Latin text. *Matthæi Parisiensis.* 1880. *Chronica Majora.* Vols 1–5. Ed. Henry Richards Luard. London: Longmans, Green, Reader and Dye.
Chron. Osney	Henry Richards Luard, 1869. *Annales Monastici* Vol IV. *Annales Monasterii de Oseneia.* London: Longmans, Green, Reader and Dye.
Chron. Thomas Wykes	Henry Richards Luard. 1869. *Annales monastici* Vol IV *Chronicon vulgo dictum chronicon Thomae Wykes* (1066–1289). London: Longmans, Green, Reader and Dye
Chron. Worcester	Henry Richards Luard. 1864. *Annales Monastici: Annales de Wigornia.* London: Longmans, Green, Reader and Dye.
Flores Historiarum	Henry Richards Luard. 1890. *Flores Historiarum.* Volume III. London: for HMSO by Eyre and Spottiswoode.
Giraldus Cambrensis	*Giraldus Cambrensis,* 1146?–1223?, George F. (George Frederic) Warner, James Francis Dimock, and John Sherren Brewer. *Giraldi Cambrensis Opera.* London: Longman & co.; [etc., etc.], 1861–91.
Hist. Anglicana	Chronicles and Memorials of Great Britain and Ireland, 1859, Bartholomæi de Cotton, *Monachi Norwicensis, Historia Anglicana.*

A Note on Names

It was normal in previous years to anglicize the names of people and places of other lands for English-speaking readers, thus Welsh Dafydd became David and francophone Jacques became James; similarly place names like Conwy became Conway and Caernarfon became Carnarvon. In deference to the people involved in this story and modern readers who are by now more used to place names expressed in local languages, we will use names, as far as is reasonably possible, with which they would have self-identified, that is called themselves. The main protagonist of the story is known today in the UK as Master James of St George, but he is referred to in thirteenth-century English primary sources (when not done so in Latin) by the name of his mother tongue, Mestre Jakes de Seint George. Therefore, we will use the closest thing we have to *Mestre Jakes de Seint George*, the name he himself used, the modern French rendering of Maître Jacques de Saint Georges. Accordingly, Edward's right-hand man, rendered variously in English as Otto de Grandson and Otto de Grandisono will be restored to his francophone Othon de Grandson, his brother from William of Grandison to Guillaume de Grandson, John of Bonvillars to Jean de Bonvillars, William of Cicon to Guillaume de Cicon, Peter of Savoy to Pierre de Savoie and so on. Similarly, with Eleanor de Provence we will use the Provençal form of her name which she herself used in correspondence, Alianor. Similarly for Eleanor de Castile we will use the Castilian Leonor for Eleanor – if only to better distinguish all these Eleanors.

For place names, particularly relevant in Wales, will use Welsh names, not anglicized versions. When quoting directly from previous authors who used anglicized or latinized versions of these names we will quote the authors directly.

A Note on Money

The main money in use in Savoy, France and the British Isles, and so the substance of this book was *livre*, *sol* and *denari*, varying in value by the issuing mints' silver content. In Latin this would be expressed as *libra*, *solidus* and *denarius*, rendered in French as *livre*, *sou*, *denier* and lastly rendered into English as pounds, shillings and pence – shortened in all three languages as l, s and d.

- No *libra*, *livre*, pound or *solidus*, *sou* or shilling coins were ever issued, they were simply a convenient accounting form.
- There were twelve (12) *denarius*, *denier* or pence in one (1) *solidus*, *sou or shilling*.
- There were twenty (20) *solidus*, *sou* or shillings in one (1) *libra*, *livre* or pound.
- And so, there were 240 *denarius*, *denier* or pence in one (1) *libra*, *livre* or pound.
- A further accounting form in use in England was the mark which represented two-thirds of a pound, and so thirteen (13) shillings and four (4) pence or 160 pence.

To help, on occasion, to give some meaning to quoted numbers, we have used the UK National Archives Currency converter. This has been done as a helpful guide and is in no way intended to be a statement of fact. The converter can be found online at www.nationalarchives.gov.uk/currency-converter/, hereinafter abbreviated as TNA currency converter.

Medieval scribes, both in England and Savoy, expressed numbers, such as money, in Roman Numerals. However, we should note that they usually broke the "iv" rule, using iiii instead. Furthermore the last i is often rendered as a j to make numbers easier to read, hence four would be rendered as iiij. You will see numerous examples of this in the latin original texts, found most usually in the endnotes and appendices of this book.

Without Whose Help …

A stranger in a strange land, I am indebted to the help of many in the preparation of this book. In no particular order: Jean-Luc Rosset whose patient explanation of medieval Latin, of its origins and differences from classical Latin was quite simply invaluable. Monsieur Rosset is the source of much of the Latin translation from primary sources used in the coming chapters, which revealed a good deal of the human story of the dry accounting texts.

Thanks to Justin Favrod, a notable Swiss historian himself, the current owner of the Château de Saint-Prex, for allowing access to the castle built by Jean Cotereel. It was a rare privilege to sit in a window seat that may well have been utilised by the young Maître Jacques de Saint Georges.

Thanks to France Terrier, the former director of the museum of the Château de Yverdon, for allowing a thorough examination of the donjon tower at Yverdon. It was particularly satisfying to accompany her, along with other Swiss heritage guardians, to north Wales where we visited together the castles of Flint, Conwy, Harlech and Beaumaris. The discovery at Flint of a twin for the castle of Yverdon, provided an omega to the alpha.

Thanks to Joël Berchten, intendant du château de Lucens, who along with historian, Monique Fontannaz, provided access to the private castle at Lucens, and together we discovered 'something most unusual in the attic'.

Thanks also to the helpful contributions of those at Cadw in north Wales, of Kate Roberts and Chris Wilson who guided us around the castles in their care. Particularly though, the help of Siân Roberts for her insights at Harlech, and liaison with Cadw.

Thanks to Monsieur Guy Mattrat of Vanclans, France, who assisted in finding the three remaining steps that constitute all that is left of the Château de Cicon, origin of the *Famille de Cicon*.

Thanks also to the owner of the Chateau de Grilly, Monsieur Jean-Jacques Piquet, for allowing access to his home, the origin of the *Famille de Grailly*. Also thanks to Monsieur Jean-Claude Gafner, intendant de la Cathédrale de Lausanne for providing access to the renowned western porch window and the cathedral's *triforium*. Also, thanks to Chris George and Mireille Rosselet-Capt for their help with Welsh forms, literature and mythology.

Thanks to my son, Sean, for spending his holidays in Switzerland delving deep into the byways to seek out long-gone castles in the undergrowth, and for adding his own insight to the developing story. Neither of us had any thought of this book, when visiting Conwy Castle, as we'd done many times previously, in 2014. Which brings me to a thank-you to my late father, who was responsible more than most for my interest in history, and a first visit to the castles of north Wales back in 1968, when aged just four years I first set eyes upon Rhuddlan Castle.

And lastly, and mostly, thanks to my partner, Mary-Claude Dennler, without whose many hours of patience and fortitude trekking the wilds of the Viennois, the archives in Lausanne, Chambéry, Grenoble, and Kew, and castles too numerous to mention, this book would simply not have been possible. Her particular help in trying to make sense of Old French texts should be noted.

Notable Savoyards in England

The Comital Family

Pierre II de Savoie (1203–68), Count of Savoy

The seventh son of Count Thomas I de Savoie and Marguerite de Genève, uncle to Queen Alianor de Provence of England and so great-uncle to King Edward I of England. He was likely born in Susa. In January 1236, Alianor de Provence, Pierre's niece, married King Henry III of England. On 20 April 1240, Peter was given the Honour of Richmond by Henry III who invited him to England about the end of the year, and knighted him on 5 January 1241 when he became known popularly as Earl of Richmond, although he never assumed the title of earl, nor was it ever given to him in official documents. From 1241–2 he was Castellan of Dover Castle and Keeper of the Coast. In February 1246 he was granted land between the Strand and the Thames, where Peter built the Savoy Palace in 1263, on the site of the present Savoy Hotel. It was destroyed during the Peasants' Revolt of 1381. When Pierre's nephew, Count Boniface of Savoy, died without heirs in 1263, he became Count of Savoy and largely withdrew from English affairs.

Alianor de Provence (1223–4–25 June 1291), Queen of England

The sister of Marguerite de Provence, Queen of France, Sanchia de Provence, Queen of the Romans and Béatrice de Provence, Queen of Naples. Born in Aix-en-Provence or Brignoles, she was the second daughter of Ramon Berenguer V, Count of Provence (1198–1245) and Béatrice de Savoie (1198–1267), the daughter of Thomas I de Savoie and his wife Marguerite de Genève. She was well educated as a child, and developed a strong love of reading. Her three sisters also married kings. Like her mother, grandmother and sisters, Alianor was renowned for her beauty. She was a dark-haired brunette with fine eyes. Although she was completely devoted to her husband, and staunchly defended him against the rebel Simon de Montfort, 6th Earl of Leicester, she was disliked by the Londoners. Responsible for introducing many Savoyards to the English court.

Sanchia de Provence (1225–9 November 1261), Queen of the Romans

A sister to Queen Alianor de Provence of England, sister-in-law of King Henry III of England and King Louis IX of France, aunt to King Edward I of England, wife to 1st Earl Richard of Cornwall, King of the Romans.

Guillaume de Savoie (unknown–1239), Bishop Elect of Valence
A son of Thomas I de Savoie and Marguerite de Genève, another uncle of Queen
Alianor de Provence of England and so great-uncle to King Edward I of England.
When already a Dean of Vienne, he was elected Bishop of Valence in 1224. He
negotiated the weddings of Queens Marguerite and Alianor de Provence and was
an adviser to Henry III of England. Between his religious roles and his family
relations, his influence was noted from London to Rome.

Boniface de Savoie (1217–18 July 1270), Archbishop of Canterbury
A son of Thomas I de Savoie and Marguerite de Genève, yet another uncle of
Queen Alianor de Provence of England and so great-uncle of King Edward I
of England. He is not to be confused with his nephew, and fellow member of
the House of Savoy, Count Boniface de Savoie, the son of Amédée IV. Boniface
was the Prior of Nantua in 1232 along with holding the bishopric of Belley in
Savoy. After the marriage of his niece, Alianor de Provence, to King Henry III
of England, Henry attempted to have Boniface elected Bishop of Winchester, but
was unable to get the cathedral chapter to elect Boniface. On 1 February 1241,
he was nominated to the see of Canterbury, and was enthroned at Canterbury
Cathedral on 1 November 1249. He clashed with his bishops, with his nephew-by-
marriage, and with the papacy, but managed to eliminate the archiepiscopal debt
which he had inherited on taking office. During Simon de Montfort's struggle
with King Henry, Boniface initially helped Montfort's cause, but later supported
the king. After his death in Savoy, his tomb became the object of a cult, and he was
eventually beatified in 1839.

Philippe I de Savoie (1207–16 August 1285), Archbishop of Lyon then Count of Savoy
The eighth son of Thomas I de Savoie and Marguerite de Genève, once more,
another uncle of Queen Alianor de Provence of England and so great-uncle of
King Edward I of England. Philippe was born in Aiguebelle in Savoy. His family
prepared him for a clerical career. He followed his brother Guillaume as Dean of
Vienne and Bishop elect of Valence. In 1244, Pope Innocent IV fled from Rome,
and Philip convinced his brother, Amédée IV, Count of Savoy, to let the Pope pass
through Savoy. Philippe escorted the Pope to Lyon, and then remained with him
to ensure his safety. Pope Innocent ensured Philippe's election as Archbishop of
Lyon in 1245. When, against expectations, Philippe became the next heir for the
County of Savoy, he gave his church offices up and married Adelaide, Countess
Palatine de Bourgogne, on 12 June 1267. He became Count of Savoy in 1268, and
in 1272 he also acquired Bresse.

Amédée V de Savoie (4 September 1249–16 October1323), Count of Savoy
A son of Thomas, Count of Flanders, and household knight of King Edward I
of England. Married to Sibylle de Baugé, bringing Bresse into Savoy. With the
English army at Montgomery in 1277 in the First Welsh War before leading the

English army that relieved the siege of Rhuddlan in 1282 in the Second Welsh War. A son, Edward, born in 1284 and named after Edward I of England, would go on to be Conte Edward de Savoie in 1323.

Louis I de Vaud (1249–1302), Baron de Vaud

Son of Thomas, Count of Flanders, and household knight of King Edward I of England and Dean of St Martin Le Grand in London. His barony was created at the time of the succession of his brother Amédée V as Count of Savoy with the help of Queen Alianor de Provence of England and King Edward I of England.

Savoyard Knights

Sir Othon de Grandson (1238–1328), Seigneur de Grandson

Othon was the most prominent of the Savoyard knights in the service of Edward I, King of England. He was a close personal friend of Edward, a career diplomat and envoy of the Crown. The son of Pierre, Lord of Grandson, the young Othon travelled to England, probably in the company of Pierre II de Savoie around 1252, certainly not later than 1265. There he entered the service of King Henry III and by 1267 was placed in the household of the Lord Edward. By 1267 he had been knighted, and in 1271, he accompanied his lord on the Ninth Crusade, where he served at Acre. Returning to England, he was a key household knight of King Edward I in his campaigns in Scotland and Wales, where he served as Justiciar of North Wales, based at Caernarfon Castle from 1284 to 1294. In 1278 he was served as Lieutenant of Gascony, along with Robert Burnell, Bishop of Bath and Wells, hiring Jean de Grailly as Seneschal and laying the foundations of the Treaty of Amiens (1279) which returned the Saintonge and Agenais to the Crown. During the second invasion of Wales in 1282–3, he narrowly escaped death at the battle of Moel-y-don before, in April 1283, taking the town of Harlech at the head of 560 infantry. He was appointed governor of the Channel Islands and in 1290 appointed a bailiff for each of the bailiwicks of Guernsey and Jersey, giving them civil powers to administer the islands.

Sir Jean de Bonvillars (Unknown–1287), Constable of Harlech Castle

Likely son of Sir Henri de Bonvillars, châtelain for Pierre II de Savoie at the Château de Rue. He was brother-in-law to Othon de Grandson. Knight of King Edward I's household and deputy Justicier of North Wales to Othon de Grandson from 1284 to 1287. On 2 April 1277, he was bearer of a letter to Othon de Grandson who was besieging Dolforwyn Castle. He was at Chester in September 1277. Revisited Savoy in 1278, was at Evian on 22 March 1279. With Othon de Grandson in Wales in 1282 when latter was commanding forces based on Montgomery. In 1283 he was sent to Wales, in 1284 he was described as Othon de Grandson's Knight Companion. He oversaw the construction of Conwy Castle. Constable of Harlech Castle from 1285 to his death by drowning, probably during siege of

Dryslwyn in south Wales, between July and November 1287. Married to Agnès de Bevillard (likely sister of Othon de Grandson) who held on to the Constable of Harlech role until succeeded by Maître Jacques de Saint Georges in 1290.

Sir Guillaume de Cicon (Unknown–1310–11), Constable of Conwy Castle
From Cicon near Vanclans, fifteen miles (twenty-four kilometres) north of Pontarlier in the Jura. Introduced to King Edwards service by Othon de Grandson. First mentioned 13 November 1276 when he came to England with a message from Othon de Grandson to King Edward I. With the army in south Wales in 1277. Constable of Rhuddlan Castle between February 1282 and May 1284 including the period of the Siege of Rhuddlan. First Constable of Conwy Castle from its construction until his death in 1310 or 1311.

Sir Pierre de Champvent (Unknown–circa 1303), Steward to King Henry III and Chamberlain of the Royal Household to Edward I
Son of Henri de Champvent and Helviz, brother of Guillaume and Othon de Champvent, both Bishops of Lausanne, a cousin of Othon de Grandson. Steward to King Henry III, he was knighted in 1259, serving as a knight of the royal household, then in 1269 Sheriff of Gloucestershire and Constable of Gloucester Castle. Later under Edward I he was again a steward before becoming a chamberlain of the Royal Household to King Edward I. Fought in the Welsh wars, and later in Scotland.

Sir Gerard de St Laurent (Unknown–1282), Constable of Flint Castle
With King Edward I and Othon de Grandson on crusade, in Acre from 1271 to 1272. One of King Edward I's inner circle. Fought in the First Welsh War. First Constable of Flint Castle from 1277 to 1281. Died in 1282 possibly in the Welsh attack on the castle. Had been in Chillon during the 1260s.

Sir Jean de Grailly (Unknown–1301), Seneschal of Gascony
Jean was born at Grilly near Gex on the shores of Lac Léman in the County of Savoy. He probably travelled to England during the reign of Henry III of England in the entourage of Pierre II de Savoie. In 1262, he was already a knight in the household of Prince Edward, the king's heir and future King Edward I of England. In 1263, he had attained the status of a counsellor to the young prince. He was made Edward's Seneschal in Gascony from 1278. In 1279, Jean travelled to Amiens and to England to negotiate the Treaty of Amiens, which ended the state of war between Edward of England and Philip III of France and returned the Agenais to English control. Jean de Grailly eventually fell short of funds for his activities, since his expenses need approval from the Exchequer before he could receive his salary. He took to exploitation and illegal exactions from the peasants, whose complaints eventually reached the ears of Edward I. He was removed from office sometime between June 1286 and Spring 1287. Led a French force alongside the English led by Othon de Grandson at the Fall of Acre in 1291.

Jean Cosyn (possibly de Gofyn or Gousyn or de Grandson), Squire
A *cosyn* or cousin of Othon de Grandson, he was a squire in the service of King Edward I of England, assigned in 1283 as being jointly responsible for Harlech during early construction and prior to the appointment of its first Constable, Jean de Bonvillars. Noted again in 1304.

Ebal II de Mont (circa 1230–68), Constable of Windsor Castle
Born as a younger son of Ebal I de Mont and his wife, Béatrice, Ebal II was first noted in 1237. Better known in English records as Ebulo de Montibus, Ebal II de Mont had travelled to England by 1246. A household steward and knight of King Henry III of England granted much land in England. By 1256 he was part of the Savoyard circle of the Lord Edward (possibly steward), later King Edward I. A witness for King Henry at the Mise of Amiens, where he swore for the king's good conduct in accepting King Louis XIVs arbitration. Left England with Queen Alianor and Pierre II de Savoie and active in attempting to raise an army loyal to the Crown. Rewarded for his loyalty by being made Constable of Windsor Castle.

Ebal IV de Mont (unknown – circa 1317), Constable of Stirling and Edinburgh castles
Son of Ebal II de Mont and Joan de Bohun, a Savoyard servant of King Henry III of England, whose family hailed from Mont-sur-Rolle in the Pays de Vaud above Lac Leman. Ebal II had been latterly the Constable and Governor of Windsor Castle from 1266. Ebal IV began as a squire in the service of King Edward I of England, assigned with Jean Cosyn de Grandson as being jointly responsible for Harlech from 1283, during early construction and prior to the appointment of its first Constable, Jean de Bonvillars. He was close to Leonor de Castile, married Lady Elizabeth de Clinton possibly through her intervention. Fought in Scotland in 1300 and obtained land there. Later he became Constable of Stirling and Edinburgh castles.

Pierre d'Estavayer (unknown–1322), Lord of Tipperary
Nephew of Othon de Grandson, in the service of King Edward I as a household knight. Given the Lordship of Tipperary in 1290 by his uncle with whom he served at Acre in 1291. His brother, Guillaume d'Estavayer, became Archdeacon of Lincoln in 1290.

Sir Arnold de Montagny
Another kinsman of Othon de Grandson in the service of the English crown.

Savoyard Clerics

Pierre d'Aigueblanche (Unknown–1268), Keeper of the Wardrobe then Bishop of Hereford
Born at Aigueblanche, of the *famille de Briançon*, Lords of Aigueblanche, in Savoy, he was initially a clerk to Guillaume de Savoie and came to England with the wedding party of Alianor de Provence. He entered the service of King Henry III,

becoming first Keeper of the Wardrobe in February 1240 then Bishop of Hereford in 1241. As a diplomat and envoy, he was in regular employment by the English crown, he helped to arrange the marriage of Earl Richard of Cornwall to Sanchia de Provence and later the Lord Edward to Leonor of Castile. He became embroiled in King Henry's attempts to acquire the kingdom of Sicily for Henry's son Edmund. During the anti-Savoyard period of the Second Barons' War, he was arrested briefly in 1263 by the said barons, before being mostly restored to his lands after the Battle of Evesham.

Guillaume de Champvent (circa 1239–1301), Bishop of Lausanne
Son of Henri de Champvent and Helviz, brother of Pierre de Champvent, in the household of both King Henry III and Edward I of England, also brother of Othon de Champvent, also Bishop of Lausanne.

Gerard de Vuippens (circa 1260–5–17 March 1325), Bishop of Lausanne
Son of Ulrich de Vuippens and Agnès de Grandson, sister of Othon de Grandson, he was accordingly his nephew. Moved to England to become firstly a sub-deacon at the Priory of St Leonard in Stamford, then a pastor at Greystoke in Cumberland. He went on to become a sub-deacon in Richmond and canon at York before taking on a key diplomatic role with King Edward I during the difficult negotiations with King Philippe IV of France over Gascony. Left England to become firstly Bishop of Lausanne from 1301 until 1309 when he moved on to become the Bishop of Basel until his death in 1325.

Savoyard Builders, Masons and Artisans

Maître Jacques de Saint Georges, Master of the King's Works in Wales
He is documented as the son of a Master stonemason, Jean, very likely to be identified as Jean Cotereel, the master of works for the Cathedral of Lausanne and town of Saint-Prex. His recorded work in Savoy includes castles ar Yverdon, Voiron, La-Côte-Saint-André, Saint-Laurent-du-Pont and Saint-Georges-d'Espéranche in addition to works at Romont, Gümmenen, Salins, Châtel Argent, Montmelian and likely Chillon. But his worldwide renown is a product of the work he carried out in north Wales for King Edward I of England, the UNESCO-listed castles of Caernarfon, Harlech, Conwy and Beaumaris, plus Aberystwyth, Flint and Rhuddlan and amongst other likely works at Caergwrle, Denbigh, Dolywyddelan and Criccieth. He came to England with his wife Ambrosia, where they were later joined by their likely son, Giles.

Master Giles de Saint Georges
He is likely the son of Maître Jacques de Saint Georges and Ambrosia, noted as building the Tower at Saxon for Count Philippe I de Savoie before moving to England and being recorded at Aberystwyth and Harlech.

Tassin de Saint Georges

He is also a likely son of Maître Jacques de Saint Georges and Ambrosia, also noted as building, with his brother, the Tower at Saxon for Count Philippe I de Savoie, but unlike his brother remained in Savoy. A stonemason he is noted for works at Falavier, Treffort and Saint-André amongst others.

Jean Francis

A stonemason, but never described as a master mason, he is first recorded as working for Jean de Mézos at Conthey and Saillon both for Pierre de Savoie, also likely at Brignon as part of the same works. He is later noted as working again for, the now Count Pierre II de Savoie at Chillon, before moving to England. Working for Maître Jacques de Saint Georges, he is recorded at Conwy, where he built the Mill Gate of the castle walls, before last being recorded at Beaumaris, a career of spanning some forty years. It is most likely the affinity of Conwy's town walls with those at Saillon that is attributable to Jean Francis.

Adam Boynard

He is first noted as 'Beynardus, King of the Ribalds' at Saxon, working for Giles and Tassin de Saint-George before moving to Wales and working for Maître Jacques de Saint Georges at Harlech. He stayed in Harlech, becoming a burgess of the town, before enduring the siege of 1294 during the Madog rebellion.

Albert de Menz

A stonemason, likely from Le Mintset formerly Menze near Martigny-Combe in Valais, not far from La Bâtiaz. He is recorded as building a number of features at Harlech, including a chimney and window mullions.

Guillaume Seyssel

A mason, almost certainly from the town of Seyssel on the Rhône between Geneva and the Lac du Bourget, recorded as working at Conwy alongside Jean Francis.

Gillot de Chalons

A mason, his likely origin would either be Chalon-sur-Saône in the Franche-Comté (in the late thirteenth century a part of Savoy) or more likely Chalon, Isère, just eighteen miles (twenty-nine kilometres) south-west of Saint-Georges-d'Espéranche in the Viennois. He most likely worked at Rhuddlan, where a tower carried his name for a while, before moving on to Conwy.

Stephen the Painter

A painter of English or Savoyard origins, he is noted as carrying out various assignments in Savoy and England. Notably at Chillon and Saint-Laurent-du-Pont in Savoy and later in Wales, the King's Chamber at Rhuddlan Castle. His work is undocumented at Chillon but survives, his work is documented at Saint-Laurent-du-Pont and Rhuddlan but does not survive.

Guy de Vercors
A stonemason from the Vercors Massif above Grenoble, in what was the Dauphiné adjacent to Savoy. He is recorded as working alongside Maître Jacques de Saint Georges at both Montmelian and Saint-Georges-d'Espéranche before moving to Wales and being recorded as working again at Rhuddlan.

Jean Picard
A stonemason recorded as working at Conwy, his family name remains a common one to this day in the Pays de Vaud.

Master Manasser de Vaucoulers
Not a Savoyard, but one who found employment in England as a result of links with Geoffrey de Geneville. He is recorded as working at Caergwrle with Maître Jacques de Saint Georges before going on to be responsible for the castle ditch at Caernarfon, where he became a town bailiff.

Prologue

It was a cold November morning in the year of our Lord 1307 as an old man walked along the hillside, making his way past the grazing sheep toward a hilltop from which he could take in the view. Stumbling a little, he arrived at the crest and rested upon his walking stick; the cold wind was blowing in from the Irish Sea once more. He looked out at the vista before him, to his right he could see the estuary of the River Dee, behind it the Wirral peninsula where he'd heard that the Vikings had made their home centuries before. The cold Irish Sea wind blew hard against the old man's face as he surveyed the horizon. On a clear day he could see for thirty miles, but today was grey and the clouds scudded in from the murky sea. Turning to his left, he knew, behind these foothills that were now his, lay the wilds of Snowdonia. The old man closed his eyes and memories began to flood back like water overflowing a cup. Sure, these Welsh mountains could be fearsome indeed, but he remembered the view from the Petit Saint-Bernard, as the Tarentaise and Savoy and the Viennois lay open toward the horizon, over 7,000 feet below. He pursed his lips; he could still taste the wine of the Viennois and the warm breezes coming up the Rhône. Memories of the lakes and mountains of his early years, these Welsh hills had become his home now, but he smiled to himself when he remembered his real home. For the old man was not Welsh, or even English; the old man was from far-off Alpine Savoy. He remembered the hills, the mountains, the Great Lake ... ah, the Great Lake, he'd worked on a castle there once. A marvellous, beautiful castle by the Great Lake, the castle at Chillon. He smiled to himself at the thought, of how building castles had brought him so far from home.

For the old man was none other than Jacques de Saint-Georges, Maître Jacques de Saint Georges, the English had called him. He chuckled to himself at how these Norman English mangled his language, but they had paid him well and given him a blank canvas upon which to paint the dreams he'd had as a young man back in distant Savoy where it all began. As he turned his back to the north-westerly wind, he made his way back to the Manor House at Mostyn, given to him by his friend, and began to turn his thoughts back to the beginnings of his long journey to north Wales.

As the old man settled by the warming fire, he reflected that he was all alone now; his one-time patron, King Edward, had passed away, his good friend from Savoy, the knight Othon de Grandson, had lately returned to his lands, and sadly, so sadly, his loving wife Ambrosia had passed.

Thoughts turned to the day, to events, that had brought him so far, and the meeting that had brought them together, that beautiful day in southern France, in the year of Our Lord 1273. The trumpets blew and the heralds cried for the arrival of visitors from afar, on their way home from taking the Cross and Crusade ... what a time it was.

Chapter One

This story will be of Welsh Castle Builders: The Savoyard Style, for the old man was from the County of Savoy. But where and what is Savoy, it's not easy to find on the map, many have written of it as French, or Italian, or Swiss, but it is none of these, it is Savoy.

The County of Savoy had grown from the wreckage of a number of post Roman Empire kingdoms that had established their rule of the mountainous lands of the Jura and Alps. Originally the Francs had dominated, conquering the First Kingdom of Burgundy in 534 only to see what had become by then the Carolingian Empire divided into three by the Treaty of Verdun in 843. The westernmost kingdom would become West Francia and later still France, the easternmost kingdom ultimately the German lands of the Holy Roman Empire. But the Middle Kingdom would be Lotharingia, named after its founder. This Middle Kingdom would itself be divided north from south, and it is the southernmost lands that stretched from the Jura by way of the Alps to Provence and the azure sea which will concern us. The lower kingdom has been known by a number of names; the Kingdom of Arles, the Kingdom of Arles and Vienne, the Arelat and lastly the name we shall use, the Second Kingdom of Burgundy. Geographically it encompassed mostly the course of the River Rhône, ethnically it was a Romance kingdom, linguistically it spoke what we now call Arpitan in the mountains and a form of Occitan further south. This Second Kingdom of Burgundy remained independent until 1033 when it was absorbed into the Empire, the dying last King of Burgundy, Rudolf III, sent his crown and regalia to Konrad. It was henceforth generally accepted that the Emperor was King of three Kingdoms, of Germany, of Italy and of Burgundy. The Kingdom failed ultimately for want of a centralised state, Saracen incursion and the failure of Rudolf III to provide an heir. Into the power vacuum of the failed Second Kingdom of Burgundy strode the Savoyards.

Savoy is a land of lakes and tall mountains, towering peaks and glistening blue waters; set amidst the Alpine passes, it sits astride the ancient routes from the balmy Mediterranean lands of the classical world to the colder, darker world of the north. The name Savoy, in French *Savoie*, Italian *Savoia*, comes from the Latin *Sapaudia* – which came from a Celtic name for the *Pays de Sapins* – Land of the Fir Trees.[1] Mountain passes were the raison d'être of Savoy, the source of its wealth and therefore the very essence of its being. The Grand Saint-Bernard, the Petit Saint-Bernard, the Mont Cenis – these were the routes of pilgrims to Rome since classical antiquity, the Via Francigena.[2] The mountain passes lead, quite literally, to heaven, not so much passes as cracks in the mountain wall that separates Italy from Europe. If you needed to travel between where men spoke French and where men spoke Italian, then you needed to travel through the lands of the Savoyards.

Savoy stretched across the Western Alps, in an arc from the Mediterranean to the Gotthard central massif of what is now Switzerland, a fief bounded by the territorially expansive Kingdom of France to the west and north-west, and by the quarrel between Holy Roman Emperors and Popes to the north, south and east. There was contrast between the fertile lands of Provence, the Rhône Valley, the Pays de Vaud and the high mountain passes covered for much of the year in snow and ice. Whatever the fertility of the land, it is noted throughout for its stunning natural beauty, vineyards producing the most wonderful wines, pasture supporting livestock in abundance; it might be said of Savoy that it encompassed a garden of Eden.

In the thirteenth century and before, the County of Savoy was a fief of the Holy Roman Empire – it was not to become a Duchy until 1310[3] – the empire that, in the view of Voltaire, was neither holy, nor Roman, nor an empire[4] – therefore the Count of Savoy was a vassal of the Hohenstaufen Holy Roman Emperor also King of Burgundy, but as Voltaire might have understood, that gave the Count a high degree of latitude for movement and independence. This means, for example, a Count of Savoy would be able to develop his own international foreign policy and alliances independent to a large extent of imperial policy. So, within the titular Kingdom of Burgundy, itself within the empire, emerging counties enjoyed considerable freedom. By example, Provence, to the south-west, went so far as to leave the empire in 1246, when acquired by the Angevins.[5]

So as we've seen Burgundy had been independent until 1033 when it was absorbed into the empire. By then it was generally accepted that the emperor was king of three kingdoms: of Germany, of Italy and of Burgundy.[6] Counts and Ccunties had grown in the declining Carolingian state. *Comes*, companions of the emperor, had been granted lands in return for service in place of paid officials and administrators – the beginnings of feudality.[7] So it was with Savoy; the founder of the House of Savoy was Humbert I de Savoie. He was granted lands as a reward for service, in Maurienne, the Aosta Valley and the Upper Rhône Valley (or Valais) by the emperor Konrad II when he'd inherited Burgundy in 1033.[8] Humbert I became the first Count of Savoy, and thus the land granted to him became the County of Savoy. These imperial grants to a loyal supporter secured key passes through the Alps, controlling trade between Italy and Western Europe, which would be the core of Savoy power for centuries.

Count Thomas I de Savoie was the Count of Savoy from 1189 until 1233. He was named for the murdered Archbishop of Canterbury, Thomas Becket. In May 1195, he gathered a group of knights and lay in wait for Marguerite de Geneva (daughter of the Count of Geneva), who was being transported to France for her forthcoming marriage to King Philippe II Auguste. Marguerite was by all accounts a beauty of some distinction, no doubt she would have to have been to embolden a Count of Savoy to attempt the kidnap of a future Queen of France. So struck so assuredly

2

by cupid's bow, the Count and his knights hid themselves in the Albarine Valley for the beauteous Marguerite to pass. Upon kidnap, Marguerite went willingly with the count the short distance to the little parish church at Rossilon in the Cluse de Hopitâux by the fast-flowing Furans, where the two were immediately made count and countess. Their family comprised no less than at least eight sons and two daughters, perhaps more. In order of appearance Marguerite would give birth to the boys: Amédée at Montmélian in 1197, Humbert circa 1198, Aymon circa 1200, Guillaume circa 1201, Thomas at Montmélian in 1202, Pierre at Susa in 1203, Philippe at Aiguebelle in 1207, and Boniface at the Château de Sainte-Hélène du Lac circa 1207; and the girls: Béatrice circa 1205 and Marguerite circa 1212. Giving birth to the Savoyard dynasty, was for Marguerite no doubt, a full-time occupation.

The County of Provence[9] bordered Count Thomas of Savoy's lands to the south; it was the fabled land of the troubadours, of wine, song and courtly love. The beauty of the landscape attracted these roving players who gave the county the title by which it was known across Europe – the Land of Song. Thomas was looking for a southern ally in his fights to secure more land in the Piedmont and to support his rivalry with the County of Albon; therefore, the marriageability of his daughter Béatrice came to the fore. The Fourteen-year-old Count of Provence, Ramon Berenguer[10] was bewitched by the beauty of 12-year-old Béatrice (Figure 1.0). They married not long after the betrothal, thus uniting the ruling families of Savoy and Provence.

The ongoing Albigensian Crusade against the Cathars in southern France had taken their toll on Ramon's resources, as had a growing family. It had not taken long for a family to appear, sons not surviving long, before a string of daughters was born by Béatrice for the Count of Provence: Marguerite was born in 1221, Alianor in 1223, Sanchia in 1228 and lastly Béatrice, probably in 1231.[11] The girls spent their childhood moving between the principle castle at Tarascon on the River Rhône, midway between Arles and Avignon, and the summer residence at Aix-en-Provence, and also at Ramon's newly built castle at Brignoles, built in the year of Alianor's birth;[12] daughters of such fame that Dante Alighieri would later write of them in his *The Divine Comedy: Paradise Canto IV*. Ramon and Béatrice had appointed troubadour and poet Romeo de Villeneuve as their tutor.[13] Dante encountered Justinian in the sphere of Mercury, who described Romeo de Villeneuve as 'the shining light' responsible for their good fortune in life, saying:

> Four daughters had Count Ramon Berenguer,
> Each of them a Queen, thanks to Romeo,
> This man of lowly birth, this pilgrim soul.[14, 15]

With their grandmother Marguerite de Geneva, and mother Béatrice de Savoie[16] being noted for their charm and beauty, we can't be entirely astonished that the four daughters growing to maidenhood in the Land of Song and courtly love would become the most eligible young ladies in Christendom. Matthew Paris did not spare the eulogies, later, in 1254, describing their mother Béatrice as Niobe and suggesting that 'among the female sex throughout the world, no other mother could boast of such illustrious fruit of the womb as could she in her daughters'.[17] Not surprising then, either that very soon the crowned heads and hearts of Europe would come a calling in Provence.

Marriage with Provence brought the House of Savoy closer within the gravitational pull of one of the era's defining struggles, that between two French families, for the soul of France, the Capetian rulers of France and Plantagenet rulers of England. The Plantagenets still held much of southern and western France. So, it would be no surprise that a King of England, Duke of Aquitaine might seek the hand of a Provençal lady. For, King Henry III of England, the prize would be the second-eldest daughter, Alianor. The negotiations began in June 1235, not so much with the Count of Provence, but also with two of the uncles of the bride,[18] Amédée and Guillaume de Savoie.[19] Henry reminded them that earlier his father John had been betrothed to a lady of the House of Savoy, Alais, daughter of Humbert III in 1173.[20] Now was a time to begin the alliance of England and Savoy anew – an alliance of mutual interest against the strength of the expansionist Capetian regime,[21] confirmed by letters of 22 June 1235.

And so it was that the County of Savoy became linked with the Kingdom of England, when the beauteous young Alianor became betrothed to Henry. Alianor was crowned amid much pomp and circumstance at Westminster Abbey on 20 January 1236.[22] England had once more a King Henry and a Queen Eleanor on the throne. Matthew Paris, related a dazzling ceremony of 'nuptial festivities' of 'flags and banners' and 'wonderful devices', of citizens 'dressed out in their ornaments' and of a 'splendid ceremony',[23] the choir singing *Christus vincit, Christus regnat, Christus, Christus imperat,* imploring the Almighty to give good health and long life to the Queen of the English.[24]

Soon England was rejoicing in the birth of a son to King Henry and Queen Alianor – that thing to which all monarchies of the time aspired above all others – a royal baby, an heir, born on the night of 17 June 1239.[25] The young prince was to be the first King of England since 1065 to carry an English name, named for the saintly penultimate Anglo-Saxon King of England, Edward the Confessor. Perhaps we shouldn't be entirely surprised by Henry's veneration of Edward, obviously because they shared a sincere piety, but also because Henry was the first English king since Edward's time to be raised exclusively in England.[26] Edward would be a break with the recent past for the French-speaking Anglo-Norman Plantagenets – harking back to an earlier age, an English King of England, a new Arthur.

Firstly, Alianor had brought her uncle, Guillaume de Savoie, to London;[27] he'd been heavily involved in arranging her marriage to Henry and had become his chief counsellor.[28] But Guillaume had died, probably murdered whilst away in Rome.[29] Then Henry had managed to get another uncle, Boniface de Savoie, raised to the see of Canterbury. But it would be a visit by a further uncle, Thomas,

Count of Flanders, that would be the catalyst in bringing the greatest Savoyard influence to London: yet another uncle, Pierre de Savoie.

Pierre de Savoie, lately struggling with matters in Savoy,[30] had indeed been distracted, as Eugene Cox said, by riches elsewhere. Much before Boniface had been confirmed as Archbishop of Canterbury or even set foot in England, Pierre had responded to his brother Thomas, Count of Flanders' advice that preferment awaited in England for those Savoyards prepared to serve King Henry – the famous chronicler Paris disapproved.[31]

Henry's benevolence toward his uncle soon flowed, too freely for Matthew Paris to abide happily in St. Albans. Pierre received from Henry the Honour of Richmond,[32] an 'Honour' being a lucrative collective estate, but wisely did not use the title Earl for himself.[33] In time many more garlands would be hung around the neck of the queen's uncle, amongst the most lucrative being the Honour of the Eagle, the lands of Lewes, Pevensey and Hastings on England's strategic south coast. There would be a palace too, Henry granting Pierre land by the Strand, where the name lives on as the Savoy Hotel. Richmond had previously been held by his late brother Guillaume, so this was perhaps merely keeping it in the family. The Honour of Richmond comprised a vast and wealthy landholding of 199 manors in 1086, centred upon the 'good castle, fair and strong' built by the Breton, Alan Rufus, on land granted to him by William the Conqueror.[34] The land was centred on a goodly portion of what is now North Yorkshire, called Richmondshire, with the castle of Richmond at its heart, but also valuable land scattered across the length and breadth of eastern England, in Lincolnshire, Cambridgeshire, Norfolk and Suffolk.[35] The Honour of Richmond was worth some £1,200[36] annually to Pierre de Savoie; in modern terms that's £875,000.[37] An example of how the interests of the Savoyard brothers might line up can be found in the port of Boston in Lincolnshire: it was attached to the Honour of Richmond by what was known as the Richmond Fee. By the time of Pierre's acquisition of the honour, Boston was handling over a third of England's wool exports, much of it from Yorkshire estates including Pierre's, to destinations such as Flanders. The Count of Flanders had been, since 1237, Pierre's brother Thomas, and since 1239 Thomas had recognized Henry as his suzerain. Around a quarter of Pierre's entire Honour of Richmond income came from Boston, some £333 or nearly a quarter of a million pounds in today's terms.[38] So we have wool grown on Savoyard estates shipped through a Savoyard port to a Savoyard land to be woven into expensive tapestries and sell throughout Europe – good business!

Pierre de Savoie used his influence and status in England to grow his influence and status in Savoy, especially his landholding and number of subject vassals. Pierre went on to widen his net of vassalage to encompass many families of the Pays de Vaud.[39]

One of the most important to our story will be the *famille de Grandson*; the castle at Grandson lay toward the southernmost point of Lac Neuchâtel, on the northern bank, in the shadow of the Jura. The castle itself had been constructed on a rectangular ridge of glacial moraine overlooking the lake. Ebal IV had been Lord of Grandson until his death in 1235; his fief also included Belmont and La Sarraz. He had been granted the lands by Emperor Frederick Barbarossa 'to build in the territory of the Noires-Joux, houses, villages, villages and castles, without any other reserve than that of immediate suzerainty of the empire'.[40] Ebal had divided his lands amongst his first three sons,[41] Henri receiving Champvent (only five miles from Grandson), Girard getting La Sarraz and finally Pierre inheriting Grandson itself. Pierre de Grandson and Henri de Champvent had been friends of Pierre de Savoie (with his links to England) since at least 1234 and had both acted on his behalf in the region.[42] Cousins would be born in the castles of Champvent and Grandson, whom Pierre de Savoie would take to England and all would play a key part in the service of the English crown, Othon son of Pierre[43] and Pierre son of Henri.[44] We're not certain of Othon's date of birth, but Swiss academics have speculated with some accuracy the year 1238 or soon thereafter,[45] making him around the same age as England's Prince Edward.[46]

And so the two young cousins, Othon de Grandson and Pierre de Champvent, travelled the road northward through the Jura and Burgundy to England and fortune, very soon after their fathers became vassals of Pierre de Savoie. The move followed Pierre's usual modus operandi of extending his influence in the Pays de Vaud: approaching a family in need of money and protection with the offer of same in return for becoming his vassal. Part of the deal would be the chance for the new vassals' children to enjoy advancement in England, using Pierre's royal patronage. This acquisition of allodial[47] tenure as a means of extended fiefdom began in France during the tenth century, spread south of the Loire in the eleventh and would now be practised by the Savoyard in Vaud.[48]

Bernard Andenmatten describes this acquisition of Vaudoise nobility as vassals of Savoy as solving 'the problems of a small aristocracy badly in need of money.'[49],[50] The Savoyards were growing rich and influential through their possession of the alpine passes, but the nobles of Vaud lacked this advantage. David Carpenter had estimated that between 1236 and 1272 lands in England were granted to thirty-nine Savoyards, and additionally forty received money pensions, but more plausibly Swiss historian Jean-Pierre Chapuisat, recorded more than 300 names enjoying English largesse;[51] Pierre often took with him the second-eldest male child, those who would not inherit being a perennial problem in the days of primogeniture.

A good example would be young Ebal II de Mont, second son of Ebal I de Mont and his wife Béatrice who held the castle at Mont-le-Grand,[52] today's Mont-sur-Rolle on the road from Lausanne to Geneva above Lac Léman.[53] The eldest son, Henri stood to (and indeed did) inherit the family castle; Ebal was taken to England by Pierre, along with Grandson and Champvent to go into service with the English court, Champvent becoming a steward in Henry III's household from 1256.[54] Othon de Grandson, as an eldest child, was perhaps a noted exception.

Pierre would call by the castles of Grandson and Champvent en route from Savoy to England, over late-night firelight stirring the boys with tales of potential daring do if they were to come north with him – it's certainly an attractive picture.[55] The cousins' arrival in England was not documented; we can only attach an approximate date for Grandson, that he was probably in England at some point in the 1250s,[56] perhaps by 1252. We have a number of clues toward the date, firstly noting that the Lord of Grandson became a likely vassal of Pierre de Savoie by 1251.[57] We see their fathers, Henri de Champvent and Pierre de Grandson, amongst Pierre de Savoie's entourage, witnessing charters at this time.[58] Which leads us to the second clue: in the summer of 1252 Henry III agreed for a pension to be paid to Pierre de Grandson, though the reason for the grant is unspecified. That the grant of a pension appears on the same page as a gift to English-based Savoyard Ebal II de Mont of two bucks from the royal forest and that both appear beneath Pierre de Savoie cannot be unconnected.[59]

King Edward in later years, referring back to Othon de Grandson's arrival in England, when later bestowing Lordship of the Channel Islands upon him on 25 January 1277, to 'Otonis … on account of his intimacy with the king, and his long and faithful service, from an early age'.[60] Edward's dating of his friendship with Othon to his 'early childhood' would suggest during at least his minority when coming to England, and so perhaps at least before 1255.[61] Sara Cockerill, in her biography of Leonor de Castile, ventured 1247, and for lack of evidence to the contrary this is as good a date as any.[62] The key element in dating the age of the relationship between Edward and Othon is *primeva etate nostra* or French *depuis notre tout jeune âge* and English 'from our earliest years'. So, we can see that young Othon de Grandson went immediately into Prince Edward's household and service; they would be lifelong, faithful friends.[63] Edward himself later gave toy castles and siege engines to his sons to play with as boys,[64] and it is not too far a leap of the imagination to suggest that he did so because he'd had them himself. We can therefore further hypothesize that Edward and Othon played these games together as boys, sieges of castles, heroic battles – except for Edward and Othon these childhood games would begin a lifetimes journey of adventures together, they would besiege real castles, build grand castles, fight heroic defences together – all of the adventures that medieval boys might wish for. Whilst we cannot be certain of the year of Grandson's move to England, we can be more certain that his cousin, Pierre de Champvent, had arrived by 1252. On 20 June 1252 Champvent was being given five marks to buy a horse by Henry III of England.[65] Champvent went into Henry's service as a steward – a decade later Henry referred 'to his beloved and faithful Peter de Chauvent'.[66]

Both Othon and Pierre would be joined in England, at some stage, by their brothers, both named Guillaume. Guillaume de Champvent would pursue a career in the church, becoming dean of St Martin-le-Grand in London in 1262, ultimately becoming Bishop of Lausanne. Grandson would be joined in England later by his younger brothers, Guillaume and Henri.[67] Guillaume de Grandson was born in 1262, and would be placed into the household of the Lord Edward's younger brother, Edmund Crouchback, Earl of Lancaster, who had been born in

1245. So, the two brothers in the service of the two brothers. Henri de Grandson, like his cousin Guillaume de Champvent would pursue a church career ending in the Bishopric of Lausanne. The wider *famille de Grandson* would also see much of England, particularly a network of cousins and in-laws, including the Bonvillars, Estavayers and Vuippens. The seeds of Savoyard influence sewn by the comital family were being widely expanded upon by the Grandson clan.

Another young Savoyard taken to England by Pierre at this time was Jean de Grailly, from the Château de Grilly, overlooking the shores of Lac Léman between Gex and Divonne. Jean would serve the English crown for some time, mostly overseas, but for now, like Othon, he was placed into Edward's service. Pierre's offer of riches in England even went so far as the Champagne region of France, where he recruited young Geoffrey de Joinville, brother of Saint Louis's biographer Jean de Joinville. Geoffrey would become known in England as Geoffrey de Geneville. The link between Champagne and Savoy was the younger brother of both Geoffrey and Jean, Simon de Joinville, who was Lord of Gex, within Pierre's lands above Lac Léman, close to Geneva. It is within this period that we see a proliferation of documents in England sealed by the Savoyard coterie around Pierre: all royal stewards and servants, the aforementioned Pierre de Champvent and Ebal II de Mont[68] but also Imbert Pugeys[69] and Imbert de Montferrand.[70] Queen Alianor had taken great care to surround her prized asset, the heir to the throne, with Savoyards – Edward's household was largely from Savoy, including the aforesaid Ebal II de Mont and Geoffrey de Geneville.[71] Huw Ridgeway described the Savoyards surrounding Edward as an 'embryonic colonial service';[72] no wonder Matthew Paris wasn't happy.

Edward's main source of revenue as a boy (1244–54) was the Honour of Eu, Eu being a coastal town in the extreme north of Normandy. A list of names of its custodians is revealing: Bernard de Savoie (1244–7), Pierre de Geneva (1247–9) and Pierre de Savoie himself (1249–54).[73] A 1252 issue of the charter granting Gascony to Edward carries this annotation: *'Ista carta missa fuit Petro de Sabaudia'* or 'This charter has been sent to Peter of Savoy.'[74] Cox wrote of the degree to which Pierre de Savoie was leading the cordon that surrounded Queen Alianor and Prince Edward, and so controlling the kingdom, describing Pierre as 'a kind of regent for his great-nephew'.[75] It became normal, not only for such acts to be witnessed by the Savoyard, but copies to be sent for safe keeping to Pierre's archives, some of which have survived to the care of the UK National Archive.[76] A kind of regent are strong words indeed, but given Henry's perceived weakness and perhaps the threat of his Lusignan half-brothers, it helps us to understand Alianor's defence of her personal and the wider Savoyard position, and also the hostility of natives such as Matthew Paris. Pierre de Savoie held the wardship of the heir to the English crown; Edward was in the words of Carpenter 'the rock on which Savoyard fortunes were founded'.[77]

If we want to understand how much of a Savoyard rock Edward was, we need to go no further than his escape from Montfortian custody in early 1265, during the hiatus between the battles of Lewes and Evesham, in the Second Baronial War that would engulf England. When Edward escaped custody to plot Montfort's downfall at Evesham, it was to Ludlow Castle that he went. For lovers of a good plot, Ludlow was the home of Geoffrey de Geneville, who'd married its heiress, Maude de Lacy. Lacy had been previously married to another protégé of Pierre de Savoie, Pierre de Genève. As we said earlier, Geneville was the younger brother was Simon de Joinville, Lord of Gex. Yet the lordship of Gex was a fief of the now Count Pierre II de Savoie. The plot was likely orchestrated from Flanders by Alianor and Pierre, based with a largely Savoyard invasion army that never came. Also with Alianor and Pierre in this abortive invasion force were also a number of notable Savoyards temporarily exiled from England, including influential Pierre de Champvent and Ebal II de Mont.[78] Edward securing the defeat of Montfort himself rather than by a foreign invasion being a wiser course to take. It should come as no surprise that it would be to a Savoyard-held castle in England that Edward went upon his escape; the Savoyards had protected their investment.

Chapter Two

Six years earlier, in 1259, Pierre de Savoie had been furthering his interest in the Pays de Vaud when he met with Richard, King of the Germans, at Mere Castle (Dorset) in December, gaining approval for the acquisition of Gummenen[1] and Yverdon. On his return to Vaud, he purchased, for 500 *livres Viennois*, the *seigneurie* of Yverdon, which was described in the sale as encompassing 'a watercourse, with a mill and fishing rights, twenty *livres* of land, a *péage* and a "certain man"'.[2] Thus enters our story the *Villeneuve* of Yverdon, where Pierre de Savoie will build a castle, beginning the recorded career of the future builder of the castles of north Wales. The very beginning of the career of Maître Jacques de Saint Georges is a direct consequence of the career of Pierre de Savoie in England.

A little earlier, in 1258, he had purchased the fief of Rue from the Count of Geneva, another *seigneurie* in the region of Moudon and Romont that would strengthen his hold in the region north of Lausanne. First châtelain for Pierre at Rue was Henri de Bonvillars,[3] whose son Jean would marry into the Grandson family and become heavily influential in English affairs in the coming decades.[4] The *famille de Bonvillars* had been involved with the *famille de Grandson* for some time, having together witnessed charters in the twelfth century.[5]

To know who would build castles for Pierre in Savoy and later for Edward in Wales, we are indebted to their accountants for the answer, as they kept records of payments made to the builders and artisans – meticulous records of who did what, what they were paid, and when. It is from these accounts, many of which survive in Savoyard archives, now kept in Turin, Chambéry and elsewhere, and English ledgers held at the National Archive in Kew, that we can trace the story of the great castles in Wales. It is upon these primary sources that much of our story will be based.

Accounts for Pierre de Savoie for 1261 relate that 'Maître Jean the mason ... came from his home to Yverdon' working upon the castle there with 'his son Maître Jacques'. The latter was sick during some of this time, both working under the auspices of the 'custodian' Pierre Mainier.[6]

A further entry for the much later period of 1265–7 suggests Maître Jacques is no longer working with his father;[7] one last entry relating to the castle at Yverdon is dated to the period 1 April 1269 to 15 August 1269 and is simply: 'Maître Jacques the mason, ten *livres*.'[8]

And so we meet *Magistro Jacobo* or Maître Jacques as he would have been known in Yverdon, and his father Maître Jean – but who were they and where had they come from? There was a Maître Jean Cotereel[9] who had built the great cathedral at Lausanne[10] and, from 1234,[11] the fortified burgh of Saint-Prex (Figure 1.1) where he became castellan.[12] Jean Cotereel was the son of the previous architect at Lausanne Cathedral,[13] and of English ancestry,[14] and likely the father of Maître Jacques.[15] That Maître Jacques de Saint Georges was the son of two generations of architects, and that they may well have been of English origin is to join together the theories of Bony, Grandjean, Wilson and Taylor, but is there strong evidence to support joining their theories together?

Amongst the problems we have, are the lack of personal records, birth and death certificates with which we are most familiar today. Furthermore, the habit of attaching surnames or family names had not yet fully evolved – it was more common to attach their job title or place of birth as a family name. For these reasons it is impossible to prove with empirical proof this statement; however, we can perhaps pass a lower test, that of reasonable doubt.

The name Cotereel gives rise to the interesting idea that Jean Cotereel may well have been of English ancestry, which given the theory that he is to be identified as the father of Maître Jacques, suggests that in the years before the Savoyards came to England, the English had come to Savoy. The name is unknown in the Pays de Vaud and Savoy;[16] its origins lay in Normandy and thence to England.[17] Bony, Grandjean and most recently Wilson have pointed to the undoubted English architectural styles of the Notre-Dame de Lausanne linking it to Canterbury.[18] This plausibly constructs an English ancestry for Maître Jacques which may well answer some of the questions raised as to his absorption of styles from the Anglo-Norman milieu.

The parental link between the first anonymous English architect and Jean Cotereel is documented in the Lausanne cartulary. But the parental link between Cotereel and Jacques rests on the notion that Jean Cotereel is to be identified as the same Maître Jean documented in Savoyard archives as building Yverdon, the known father of Maître Jacques.

Firstly, we have two facts which are made clear from the record: the first name and the occupation of the two men – they were both Johns and both master builders.[19] Secondly, we can also establish that their lifespans were broadly aligned, we know that Maître Jean of Yverdon disappears from the archival records from the year 1265. Whereas for Maître Jean of Saint-Prex the archives show that he is no longer living by the year 1268. We can also say that in the early part of the 1260s they are both very much alive and can be found in the Savoyard records, both with their names attached to castles under construction, at Yverdon in May 1261 and at Saillon between 24 June 1261 and 2 February 1262 – both times in the pay of Pierre de Savoie.[20]

Therefore, we can say that the approximate years of death may well be the same – the lack of a death certificate will never permit definitive proof, but the archival records support a suggestion that they may well be one and the same man. So, we have two men who have the same name, the same occupation and who die around the same time. Another piece of circumstantial positive evidence is the 1234 grant of land to Jean Cotereel at Saint-Prex, that refers to an eldest son.[21] This infers that not only did the two men share a name, a profession, a likely death year – but also shared the blessings of a son. There is a tantalizingly human piece of potential evidence, that the Jean of Saint-Prex is the Jean of Yverdon – that is that Saint-Prex lies on the *Via Jacobi*, that runs from Lake Constance to Geneva by way of Saint-Prex. What could be more natural in the pious thirteenth century than for Jean to name his eldest son Jacques? It is entirely impossible to be certain, but nevertheless when one adds the circumstantial evidence together, perhaps it is the final piece of the jigsaw.

Taylor goes on to point to evidence in the architectural ground plan of the *ville-neuve* at Yverdon, which bears many similarities with that of Saint-Prex: that is, a small walled town, with water defences, a castle in one corner and three main internal thoroughfares. What he doesn't do is point to the fact that these attributes of Saint-Prex and Yverdon could also be attached to towns in distant north Wales – to Conwy and Beaumari, to some degree, also be attached. Taylor pointed out the link between Saint-Prex and Yverdon, Keith Lilley that between Conwy and Beaumaris, we can connect them by adding the similitude between the concept of the town plan of Yverdon with that at Conwy thus creating a chain of towns linked by the career of Maître Jacques de Saint Georges.[22] So, given these Maître Jacques connections, that Jean Cotereel is known to have been responsible for Saint-Prex, the prima-facie evidence is of the built environment of four towns in Vaud and Wales pointing to a connection.

A further architectural link was one we found deep in the cellar of the castle at Saint-Prex, a feature that will become common throughout the castles built during the life of Maître Jacques. The castle at Saint-Prex is much changed; only an original tower remains. However, beneath the new works there survives the original cellar, which is part-divided by a doorway beneath a shallow segmented head with no keystone. We will find this feature later at Yverdon, Chillon, Saint-Georges, Harlech and Beaumaris.

However, one possible objection could be that the work at Yverdon was carried out under the auspices of a man identified as Pierre Mainier. Surely the architect of the great cathedral in Lausanne would not be working beneath another on a project like the castle at Yverdon? What this leads us to is a need to understand the hierarchy within thirteenth-century building works, and the Latin terms used to describe those involved by the accountants of the time. It had been thought that Pierre Mainier was the architect of Pierre de Savoie's works in Savoy; he was described as 'the real architect and military engineer of Peter II' and 'The general master of works of the count' by Albert Naef and those that followed.[23] This was an orthodoxy that Taylor quite correctly challenged.[24]

There are a number of terms applied by the clerks in Savoy, and in England too, that have been commonly misinterpreted. Some clarification would be helpful. Firstly a word applied to Mainier, '*custos*' which can be most simply translated as 'one who takes care of' or 'one who is guardian'.[25] Then we have '*clerico*', which for the thirteenth century didn't quite mean clerk as we understand the word, but rather, outside of the ecclesiastical world, a 'learned or literate man'.[26] *'Magistro'* would be simply translatable as 'master', which again in our thirteenth century context would mean a 'title for a man of high rank or learning'.[27] Moving on we have the more specific descriptions of *'cementario'*, *'lathomo'* and *'carpentario'* – the first two are essentially synonyms for stonemason or builder, the last the origin of our word carpenter.

Pierre Mainier is described as *'clerico domini'*[28] and *'custodis operum domini'*[29] and *'magistri ... custodis operum domini'*[30] – he is described first as a 'man of learning' then as the 'guardian of his lord's works' and lastly as 'a man of learning and rank who is guardian of his lord's works'. To underline the sense of 'guardian' of *'custos operacionum'* or *'custodis operum domini'*,[31] it is similar to that of *'custos ville'* when used to describe a lord's representative in a new town.[32] Blondel had associated *'custos operum domini'* with 'directing the construction of the entire castle at Yverdon'.[33] Latin scholars confirm that *'custodis'* in classical Latin did not signify a 'builder" What is more, Pevsner, a contemporary of Blondel, was noting that *'operarius'* nearly always indicates 'the clerk of the works and not the architect'.[34] The *'custos operum domini'* was indeed analogous to William of Louth, described as being Edward I's *'custodis de garderoba regis'*.[35]

We can contrast this with Jean Francis at Saillon, who is described as *'Francisco cementario'*,[36] more simply as Jean Francis the builder, and Master Jean at Yverdon, who is described as *'magistri Iohannis cementarii'* or 'Master John the builder with rank'.[37] Far from being a 'chief architect' Mainier was a civil servant, not a craftsman, a counter of numbers, not a builder of castles. The precise relationships are best evidenced by an English exchequer request for information from 1296, where master masons Jacques and Walter are clearly identified as equal to but differing from the clerks Walter of Winchester and Hugh of Leominster, for Beaumaris and Caernarfon works – the latter being addressed as *'clerico custodibus operacionum'* and *'clerico custodibus castri Regis et ville de ...'* respectively.[38] Douglas Knoop and G. P. Jones set out this relationship between those responsible for building design and building finance: 'Normally on important works ... a master mason and a treasury official ... were associated ... The king's master mason had authority mainly, no doubt, over the workmen and actual building work while his colleague was chiefly concerned with finance.'[39] Pierre Mainier in Savoy, as would William de Perton, Roger de Belvoir, Hugh of Leominster and Walter of Winchester later in England, performed the vital task of assembling the finance on site for Maître Jacques and his father to build castles.

So, armed with this understanding of the Latin terms used by the Savoyard scribes, we can understand why Taylor discounted Albert Naef's and Louis Blondel's earlier idea that Pierre Mainier had been *'Le véritable architecte et ingénieur militaire de Pierre II.*[40] Blondel, whilst accurately charting the Gascon connection with Savoy, had originally missed the related English connection,[41] until later recognizing the 'remarkable' work undertaken by Taylor – they went on to collaborate profitably.[42] More recently, the works of Jean-Pierre Chapuisat and others, have described Mainier as 'not a man or art' but a 'clerk'.[43]

Specifically, for us Taylor realized that the Maître Jean of Yverdon had from the financial archival record the same pay, therefore equal billing with Pierre Mainier. The pay allotted, for those constructing the castle at Yverdon was twelve *sol* per week for Maître Jean and ten *sol* six *den* for Maître Jacques.[44] To give some context, Maître Jean's weekly salary would take a regular skilled tradesman two months to earn.[45] This evidence would largely satisfy the objection to a former creator of the cathedral in Lausanne being reduced in rank to create Yverdon – clearly he had not.[46]

Lastly, an obstacle in identifying Maître Jean of Yverdon with Jean Cotereel of Saint-Prex was Blondel describing the former as being as a mason 'who comes from Yverdon'. However, we can quite simply dismiss this objection by remembering that the 1261 account for Yverdon had said, 'Maître Jean the mason from the day when he came from his home to Yverdon.' Clearly this confirms that, if Maître Jean was at the time of the construction 'from Yverdon' then at that time he was not living there, thus we lose this particular obstacle.[47]

In summary, Taylor suggested that Maître Jean of Yverdon may well be Jean Cotereel.[48] I would put it more strongly: the chances that there were two Johns, both masons, both expiring at the same time, both having sons, and constructing towns as similar as Saint-Prex and Yverdon and (a son building similarly at Conwy and then Beaumaris) – well, these chances begin to stretch to it being unlikely they were not the same man. In other words, Maître Jean Cotereel of Saint-Prex is likely to have been the father of Maître Jacques de Saint-Georges; that it is likely the 'family business' so to speak, constructing, not only a part of the great cathedral at Lausanne but also the great castles of north Wales.

Taylor goes on to construct three generations of a family tree for this collection of architectural geniuses. He identifies Maître Jean, his son Maître Jacques, and in turn his sons Maître Giles and Maître Tassin.[49] So, we can add to our story the birth to Maître Jean and his wife a son, Jacques, between the years 1230 and 1235 – this being a number of years before King Henry III of England married Alianor de Provence; thus were the events that shaped the life of Maître Jacques happening unbeknownst to him in a far-off land when he was but yet an infant. Jacques was married to Ambrosia at the age of 25, so postulates Taylor, meaning they married 'not later than' 1254 – around the same time that his future patron Edward would marry Leonor de Castile. In what Taylor calls 'controlled conjecture' we find the idea that Tassin was born in 1255 and Giles two years later – the year in which Richard, Earl of Cornwall became King of the Romans.[50] So, by the year 1261, in which construction begins on Pierre de Savoie's castle at Yverdon, we have a father and son, Maître Jean and Maître Jacques – the latter with a young wife and two sons, Tassin and Giles. The evidence for a family group of Jacques, Ambrosia, Tassin and Giles can never be certain, but nonetheless the evidence is, for the thirteenth century, strong.[51]

The castle Maître Jean and his apprenticed son Jacques began to construct for Pierre de Savoie at Yverdon was what we now call a classic *Carré Savoyard*. Although it was of simple design and relatively cheap to construct, it incorporated all the latest military technology learned by Europeans in fighting the crusades. '*Carré*' implies a square design, with a tower upon each corner. But, unlike earlier Savoyard design, it follows the latest trend in having round towers, not square. The curved walls made it harder for siege towers to be placed effectively against them, but also easier for them to deflect projectiles hurled against them by trebuchets and mangonels. In Roman times Vitruvius had said:

> The towers must be round or polygonal. Square towers are sooner shattered by military engine, for the battering ram pounds their angles to pieces; but in the case of the round towers, they do no harm, being engaged, as it were, in driving wedges to their centre.[52]

Traditionally castles had also employed a central stronghold within the curtain walls, called by the English a keep and the French a *donjon*. The *Carré Savoyard* dispensed with this central stronghold and instead built it into the fabric of the curtain walls, by constructing one of the four towers of greater circumference and taller than the others. The fourth larger tower was in some way separated from the castle itself to some extent, allowing it to be used in extremis as a stronghold of last resort, the advantage being that the tower could add to the immediate defensive strength of the castle at minimal cost. Later, designs would begin to incorporate a gatehouse into a *donjon*, but for the *Carré Savoyard* it was the fourth tower. The source for the design is an adaptation of the French castles constructed for Philippe Auguste, such as at Dourdan.[53] The Anglo-French world had developed the round tower, and castle without a central keep in response to the latest siege engine technology and use of mining, as the Plantagenets and Capetians made war one upon the other. Whether these ideas of round towers and lack of a central *donjon* came from Arabic or Byzantine Outremer, and in particular Armenia, or was a case of parallel development to meet a similar threat, is unclear.[54]

As we shall see it has been suggested that gatehouses in Savoy were not as sophisticated as those being constructed across the Channel in England.[55] Whilst it is true to say that a twin-towered gatehouse as seen by Pierre de Savoie at Pevensey was not used in his castle at Yverdon, it is not true to say that great care was not taken in protection of the main entrance to the castle. At Yverdon, toward the castle from across the river (which acted as a moat) to the left, protection was afforded by the guards' tower. This arrangement had been used previously at Romont and provided a supply of troops for the gate, along with the ability to pour fire upon anyone wanting to gain unwanted entry. Having crossed the river by way of a bridge, one was then met with an outer gate, protected by a drawbridge and a wooden hourd directly above the gate. Once through the gate, one was forced into a ninety-degree turn to be met by another gate set into an inner curtain wall complete with wall walk. Once through, one had to negotiate stairs before another drawbridge protected the inner gate – all this whilst in the field of fire of the guard tower. Mottaz had suggested, 'barbican'[56] but archaeology has found no evidence of this. Nonetheless, the gate at Yverdon was well protected.[57] Maître Jean and Maître Jacques evidently faced some difficulty in enclosing the curtain walls, on a flat watery site.[58] As a first castle to be built, Yverdon provided some difficulty and would prove a valuable apprenticeship for the young Maître Jacques. This ability to construct upon difficult wet ground would later prove invaluable at Flint and Beaumaris in north Wales.

Pierre, meanwhile, obtained in August 1260 temporal authority in Lausanne,[59] and a war that summer with the Bishop of Sion extended Savoyard power down the Valais. The peace settlement saw him take three castles from the bishop, including, at the foot of the Grand Saint-Bernard Pass, Martigny – the same Martigny that had served as a great Roman centre of power sitting astride the main route between North and South Europe. A substantial portion of the Bishop of Sion's rich wine-growing lands passed to Pierre. Whilst the new castle at Yverdon began to take shape close by the lake, Pierre completed his stranglehold of the region by purchasing, in August 1263, the péage of nearby Grandson.[60] The deed of 31 August 1263, survives in an unlikely source, in the records of the British House of Lords;[61] it records the names of the Grandson clan and Othon's absence, presumably in England.[62]

Now nobody passed from the Swiss plateau, from Neuchâtel, from Bern or from Lausanne, without payment at Les Clées, Yverdon or Grandson – Pierre de Savoie, later nicknamed the *'Petit Charlemagne'*, had Vaud and the wider region in his grip. The extensive building by Pierre, before and after his succession as Count in 1263, is evidence of the need to constrain his main opponent to his east – the Bishop of Sion. Accordingly, new Savoyard castles or towers had also been built recently at Conthey[63] and Brignon (1257–8),[64] Saillon (1261)[65] and would be rebuilt at La Bâtiaz near Martigny (1265). The imposing La Bâtiaz had been built for the bishop and had been taken besieged by Pierre in 1259; he'd acquired it by pledge in 1260 and would then add the circular central *donjon* tower.[66] Brignon and Conthey were virtually on either side of the bishop's front door; the castles were a serious provocation to the Bishop of Sion and the people of the Upper Valais. Interestingly, the border between the Upper and Lower Valais still runs where Pierre drew it, at Conthey.

Saillon's town walls, wandering up the hillside, had first piqued Taylor's interest in Savoy, reminding him of Conwy in north Wales (Figure 1.2). They reminded him with good reason, as Savoyard mason Jean Francis, who would later move to Wales with Maître Jacques before building the town walls of Conwy, was involved in both the construction of Conthey and Saillon. At the latter we know that he was not only paid for his work in raising the tower seventy feet into the air but was additionally paid by Pierre with two robes.[67] The small town of Saillon is located on the north bank of the Rhône, just eight miles upstream from Martigny and an ideal location to police the Bishop of Sion. The small town was walled itself; in addition to the tower, design work for the latter was allocated to Gascon mason Jean de Mézos[68] to 'settle the form of the tower'.[69, 70] Before there would be a Savoyard mason in the service of the English king there would be a mason in the service of the English king who would then serve the Count of Savoy – his name was this Jean de Mézos. Mézos lay on the *Via Campino* to Santiago de Compostela around midway between Bordeaux and Bayonne. Since medieval scribes could not settle on an agreed spelling of his name, we will fall back on using the modern Mézos for want of an alternative.

Mézos had previously been described as a *'magistri ingeniatorum'* for King Henry III, working in the English territory of Gascony. He was the more senior of the *ingeniators*[71] involved in the siege of Benauges in 1253;[72] with fellow Gascon and engineer Master Bertram, they assembled the two mangonels hurling rocks at the castle[73] that was later given to Savoyard Jean de Grailly. His work for Henry, encamped at Loupiac,[74] laying siege to the Gascon rebels, saw him ennobled at Bordeaux in 1254 by the English king, and he is referred to thereafter as *'dominus'*.[75] Whilst in Gascony he worked with Master Bertram who would later labour alongside Maître Jacques in north Wales. Master Bertram had first appeared in the written record as *'Magistro Bertrando de Saltu, ingeniatori'* in 1248,[76] Saltu being Sault-de-Navailles.[77]

Also, at Benauges he would have met Ebal II de Mont, who was a Savoyard steward of Henry III. In 1254 Ebal was given charge of Benauges,[78] before returning to England by way of Paris where he's allotted the task of acquiring *'objets précieux'* for Edward to be offered at the Shrine of Saint Edward in Westminster.[79] The 'English' army in Gascony had a distinct Savoyard flavour; Blondel identified over ninety *'représentants de familles nobles'* of *'Savoie, du Genevois, de la Tarentaise, du Bugey, de la Franche-Comté, du Pays de Vaud … et du Val d'Aosta'* amongst Henry's army in the Gascon rolls, with Jean de Châtillon, Reynaud d'Orbe, Jean Grossi and Guillaume de Pesmes knighted, amongst others.[80]

It is, no doubt, Pierre de Savoie's significant involvement in Gascony that now leads him to employ his nephew's engineer, Jean de Mézos, back in Savoy. He is first known to have moved to the service of Pierre in 1261.[81] It's possible that reference to 'masters' coming from beyond the Jura to repair dykes on the Rhône in the Chablais may refer to Mézos amongst others;[82] however, to remove any doubt, the castellan at Chillon then recorded him citing the tower at Saillon.[83] Later, in 1266–7, we first find Jean de Mézos working alongside Maître Jacques at Yverdon, key evidence in establishing the relationship between the two.[84]

The key to understanding Jean de Mézos's role at Saillon is the word *'supervidendum'*. By the thirteenth century this was often written as *'supervis'*, from which the English word 'supervise' originates, and the French *'superviser'*. Medieval Latin took the word from *'super'*, meaning 'over' and *'videre'*, meaning 'to see'. Under the supervision of Mézos, day-to-day construction at Saillon was assigned to a *'Franciscus cementarius'*, or 'Francis the builder'. As we saw earlier some Swiss sources continue to misattribute the tower to Pierre Mainier, misunderstanding the difference between one who builds and one who pays the bills.[85]

If, sadly, Conthey is almost no longer with us, then Saillon, at least, remains to this day a delightfully medieval island, possessed of peace, charm and idyll and its Bayart Tower a landmark. If we can attribute Anglo-Norman architectural influence in Savoy to Maître Jean, then we can now trace the influence of Gascony (then an English possession) to the arrival of Jean de Mézos. It would be this blending of the architectural heritage of England and Gascony with the lessons learned on crusade that would influence the building style of the young Maître Jacques. As we have seen, Mézos was working alongside Jacques from his first project at Yverdon. The seniority between Mézos and Jacques is most obviously shown by Mézos's knightly status, but also by the Savoyard archives for the digging of a well at the Château de Melphe at Salins-les-Thermes in the Tarentaise in 1266–7. The castle, newly acquired by the County of Savoy, guarded the long valley of the Isère that winds its way towards the strategic Petit Saint-Bernard Pass and access to the Aosta Valley and Italy.[86] Jean de Mézos is described as 'dictating' works, including those of Maître Jacques.[87]

There was much work for Mézos and Jacques to do for Pierre de Savoie, was now engaged in a major castle-building programme. At Martigny,[88] the Château de la Bâtiaz guarded the entrance to the Grand Saint-Bernard as it meets the valley of the Rhône. It sits high above the town on a suitably rocky outcrop, affording perfect views not only toward the entrance to the Grand Saint-Bernard, but also down the Rhône Valley and Sion – another perfect castle site.

New building work was also undertaken at Romont (1260), guarding the approach to Lausanne from the north; it too had long been a Savoyard power base[89] – the 'Petit Charlemagne' was digging in.[90] The main castle (*Grand Donjon*), with a typical Savoy square floorplan, had been completed much before 1260. The further military work was a second castle with a round tower, formerly known as the '*Petit Donjon*', but now known as '*La tour à Boyer*', which may have been built around 1250–60. There is some doubt as to the precise age. Taylor suggested perhaps even 1274/5,[91] and we do have an archival mention for Maître Jacques for Romont in 1275[92] and other primary source evidence for 1274/5.[93] Perhaps works were begun in the earlier period and modified later.

Jean de Mézos, '*ingénieur*', may well have been responsible for another castle built by the Léman, at Rolle. The *Castrum de Ruello* was built by the Lords of Mont to rival Saint-Prex and Aubonne. It was built for Ebal III de Mont, the son of Henri de Mont, himself the eldest brother of Ebal II de Mont who had left for England with Pierre II de Savoie, there to become a loyal servant of King Henry and eventually Constable of Windsor Castle. Rolle Castle, meanwhile, eventually taken over by the Savoyard, had the newly fashionable round towers. Furthermore, whereas Saint-Prex and Les Clées had square towers, those at Yverdon, Saillon and Rolle, begun after 1259/60 and the arrival of Jean de Mézos, would be round.

We say 'believed' for Jean de Mézos and his building of Rolle, because the building records are likely to have perished in 1802 when Vaudois peasants burned papers in connection with the French Revolution. Similarly, peasants stormed Le

Sarraz, Champvent, Yverdon, Grandson and many more, extinguishing much that would have been useful to twenty-first-century historians. We are lucky that much of the records kept by the Count of Savoy had by this time reached Turin and relative safety.

Architectural historian Nicola Coldstream has queried the origins of Maître Jacques' building and design skills, looking for sources in England.[94] However, we affirm that the true source of his ability to construct in stone would be both his father, Maître Jean, to whom he was apprenticed at Yverdon from 1261, and Jean de Mézos. The essential skills of construction would no doubt have passed from the father, but the finer points of more advanced castle architecture, emanating from the Anglo-French world, and possibly Outremer and Armenia before that, came most likely via the 'dictating' of the Gascon, Jean de Mézos.[95]

There is one other in this Anglo-Gascon Savoyard milieu we ought to briefly mention, if only to illustrate the connectedness of this triangle. Master Arnaud was a clerk who held senior position within Pierre de Savoie's court in Savoy, and is mentioned in connection with multiple building works, including at Chillon.[96] It should be of little surprise that he'd previously been in the employ of Pierre's sister, Béatrice de Savoie, the Countess of Provence (mother to Queen Alianor de Provence and hence mother-in-law of Henry III). Furthermore, it then should come as little surprise that like Jean de Mézos he'd previously been employed by the English crown in Gascony.[97]

On 16 or 17 May 1268, Pierre II, Count of Savoy, the 'Petit Charlemagne,' passed from this life at Pierre-Châtel. He was laid to rest, where he lies to this day, beside his brothers at Hautecombe Abbey, by the beautiful Lac Bourget.[98] Pierre de Savoie was one of the key players of his times, the thirteenth century. He'd begun his career as a canon of Geneva and ended it as Earl of Richmond, Baron of Vaud, Faucigny and Chablais, Lord-protector of Morat and Bern, Count of Savoy and Marquis of Italy. His intimate relationship with England is perhaps his greatest legacy. Our view of this legacy has been tainted somewhat by English contemporary chronicler Matthew Paris, a monk described by Christopher Tyerman as being 'suspicious' and 'xenophobic'.[99] We should begin to look past this partial witness who could see little good in anything 'foreign'. Pierre left a deep and lasting legacy in England. For Pierre it was who introduced so many of his fellow countrymen to England. If we want to see Pierre de Savoie's legacy we must go no further than Caernarfon and see the castle there, for it would be in the next generation that the legacy would bear fruit, in men like Othon de Grandson, who'd been brought to England by Pierre, and in Maître Jacques de Saint-Georges who was soon brought to England by Othon. Without Pierre de Savoie, King Henry III's son Edward I would not have been able to call upon the array of Savoyard knighthood and castle-building genius that was to mark his reign. Pierre's legacy is, as he himself would have wished, split between Savoy and Britain, at Chillon and at Caernarfon – just as he'd split his life between the two.

In the summer of 1268, the baton in both Savoy and England had or was about to be passed to a new generation. In Savoy, Pierre's younger brother Philippe took over the reins; in England, an ageing King Henry worked hard to complete his Westminster Abbey, before leaving the kingdom to his son, the Lord Edward. The loyal Savoyard servant of Henry, Ebal II de Mont, died some time between 14 February and 1 April as Constable of Windsor Castle. The executor of his will was appropriately Alianor de Provence.[100] His son Ebal IV de Mont was now a household squire of the Lord Edward; the baton was indeed passing to a new generation. With Philippe as Count, the centre of gravity within Savoy moved from the Léman and the Alpine passes west toward the lower Rhône Valley and Lyon.

In 1270, the Lord Edward, along with his Savoyard household knights, Othon de Grandson, Guillaume de Grandson and Jean de Bonvillars, left to join the crusade of King Louis IX of France to rescue Outremer from the Mamluk Baibars.

The crusade, restricted largely to sorties from the crusader outpost of Acre, would not be a success.

Just before or during his return Edward would have learned of the passing of his Uncle Richard, King of the Romans and erstwhile 'Bad Miller' of Lewes. Richard, Earl of Cornwall, perhaps the richest man in all Europe, had died at Berkhamsted on 2 April 1272; he was buried alongside his wife Sanchia de Provence at the beautiful Hailes Abbey in the Cotswold hills.

Worse, that autumn of 1272, King Henry III, who'd been gravely ill in February 1271, grew weaker yet. The great and the good gathered around him, including his wife of thirty-six years, Alianor de Provence. Henry passed away from the kingdom he'd kept together for fifty-six years later that day.

'Le Roi est mort, longue vie au Roi.' So passed the days of King Henry III, who bequeathed his son a more secure kingdom than his father had given to him – and surely that is the ultimate test of any monarch. Henry had been born into the chaos of his father John's reign; he'd been crowned at the tender age of just 10 in Gloucester not Westminster and yet it would be the great, beautiful, soaring Westminster Abbey that he'd lavished so much devotion upon that he would leave his nation. His last resting place was indeed the abbey that became his epitaph in stone, his burial there on 20 November 1272.

Henry received in his own time, and for most of the centuries since, criticism from Englishmen of his favour to his family from Savoy, but the seeds sewn in his reign would soon bear fruit for his son.

Chapter Three

It was as Edward was sailing back from Acre to Sicily that he became king; upon landing at Trapani he learned of his father's death, inheriting from his father the throne of England. It was a double blow for Edward because he also learned of the death of his son, John. Edward's return to England would be a long and circuitous journey; he did not make at once for London, indicating that he was secure in his succession, a luxury not afforded earlier in the century to his father.

Edward had begun to make recourse to a new way of funding royal expenses: the Riccardi and other merchants of Lucca in Italy. In the coming twenty years they would be crucial in providing the liquidity to fund his conflicts in Wales and Gascony, not to mention the capital outlay for an unprecedented royal castle-building programme. Before 1272, English kings had made some use of Italian bankers, particularly in papal relations, but Edward was about to take that to another level, and to begin with to fund his expenses on crusade and incurred on on his way home. Loans would be granted against customs revenue, providing a ready and continuous availability of liquidity.[1]

At Westminster, in April 1275, Parliament would pass a tariff on wool exports. The proposal for this came from Edward's treasurer, Joseph de Chauncy, a hospitaller Edward had met in Acre, who took up an idea of the Italian merchant Poncius de Ponto.[2] By agreement the customs were collected directly from Italian merchants in the ports. The income from customs, which until 1279 amounted to about £10,000 annually, was directly offset against the debts the Crown had owed to the Italian merchants. This in effect gave Edward what might now be described as a current account with an overdraft facility with his Italian bankers. Edward could call upon immediate loans irrespective of whether the accumulated income from customs could at that point bear the request; in the words of the English archives the Riccardi were called upon to provide liquid cash 'out of royal funds or their own'.[3] In fact, we know that for the crusading period and the coming First Welsh War, 1272 until 1279, their excess payments are listed as £23,000[4] and the period 1290–4 as £18,924,[5] essentially an overdraft facility much used by its holder. We do not know precisely when Edward came to a definite agreement with the Riccardi di Lucca, but it was most likely during his time in Acre and may have been consolidated during his journey through Italy.

The Riccardi di Lucca were amongst the new breed of Italian merchants who had evolved from so called 'caravan merchants', travelling to buy and sell in the markets north of the Alps, to 'sedentary merchants', who made use of a network of agents to carry on business on their behalf. These merchants had moved from buying and selling to finance, to support the increasing north–south payments in Europe generated by the wool trade, the crusades and papal relations – precisely the needs that drew them into Edward's orbit.[6]

The Riccardi family partnership was the foremost of the Luchesse merchant associations and founded as a simple partnership with joint and unlimited liability.[7] These partnerships were relatively new in their scope and breadth, growing out of father and son associations to take in many outside the immediate family, as was the case with the Riccardi. This ability to outgrow the family led to an increase in both business acumen and capital and saw a significant rise to prominence from the 1250s onwards.[8] Perhaps the key individual on the Italian side of the relationship was the interestingly named Lucasio Natale, who appears in the English records as 'Luke de Luk' and his 'merchants of Lucca';[9] his partner at the London end was Orlandino da Pogio. Edward wasn't the first English king to make use of their services; his father Henry had bought fine cloths and ecclesiastical vestments from them in June 1245[10] – but the son would deal far more in raising finance for war than buying priestly robes. Richard Kaeuper notes well, that 'if the label of capitalist is to be applied to any group of men in early European history, the Riccardi must be included'.[11] Michael Prestwich estimated the bill for the ninth crusade as £100,000 – over £70 million in today's money.[12]

We can also add that it was not only to Edward and the Crown that the Riccardi of Lucca would be bankers, but also to key members of his retinue who rode back with him through Italy that summer of 1273. Othon de Grandson also 'held an account' with the Riccardi. He was so well known to them that they familiarly referred to him as 'Messer Otto' in correspondence. He was not only a link to the English crown, but also to the *famille de Grandson* more widely.[13] Another Riccardi customer travelling back with Edward would be Anthony Bek, the future Bishop of Durham and key servant of Edward. Indeed, we can say that both key negotiators of what would be the Treaty of Aberconewey of 1277 were Riccardi account holders, as was the Crown, account holders of the bank that financed the coming Welsh Wars.[14] In the summer of 1279, the auditors of the annual accounts prepared by the Riccardi for Edward were listed as Robert Burnell, Joseph de Chauncy, Jean de Vesci, Othon de Grandson, Anthony and Thomas Bek[15] – the king's inner circle.[16] Jean de Vesci was a one-time ward of Pierre de Savoie and husband to the Savoyard, Agnès de Saluzzo.[17] During the baronial war he had been a Montfortian. The chronicler Thomas Wykes[18] describes the mercy shown to the one-time rebel who then became a lifelong servant to the king and lifelong friend and comrade of Othon de Grandson.

Meanwhile, returning from crusade, Edward firstly made his way toward the new pope and Orvieto, before travelling north-east across the never-ending Apennines until they came across the *Via Emilia*, the former Roman road that cut straight across Italy in a north-westerly direction from Rimini toward the Alps. Edward was recorded as having been entertained at the episcopal palace of Reggio Emilia on 20 May. His route continued through Emilia Romagna to Parma and then the great city of Milan. Leaving Milan, and on to Turin and behind it the wall around Italy, that is the Alps, which would have grown ever higher in Edward's eyes as he made for the Mont Cenis. The reason for the Mont Cenis route is that it was a mountain pass controlled by his Savoyard great-uncle Philippe, and led to Savoy. In 1246,[19] the English Crown had come to the overlordship of a number of Savoyard castles and towns: Avigliana and Bard, and the towns of Saint-Maurice d'Agaune[20] and Susa together with the palace there – Edward would receive homage from Philippe for them on his way home to England. The acquisition by Henry of castles in the far away alps has been much criticised by commentators since, but would soon lead to consequences unseen in 1246 and which would prove to be fundamental to the reign of Henry's son and his realm. When Edward arrived at Rivoli, on the road to Susa, he entered Savoyard territory. The majestic castle, at Rivoli, afforded elevated views across Turin to its front and the Alps they'd need to cross to its rear. The Savoyard castellan at Rivoli sent two messengers to meet Edward, who was presented with gifts of wine and food. Philippe's bailiff at Montmélian brought ten oxen, fifty-nine lambs and twenty-nine geese ready for a royal feast and escorted him on into Savoy.[21]

Travelling toward the setting sun they rested at the Castello di San Giorio di Susa, dominating the valley at midway point toward the pass, and noted its unusual merlons topped each by three finials, a striking design they would later replicate in north Wales.[22] Susa had been the birthplace of Edward's great-uncle Pierre de Savoie some seventy years earlier; he would be conscious of now entering the lands of his mother's family. Once along the narrowing Val di Susa they began to climb the Mont Cenis Pass. Edward, accompanied by Leonor of Castile, and their baby daughter Joan of Acre, crested the mountains into Savoy. A young Edward had married Leonor in her father's kingdom at Burgos back on 1 November 1254, and she had gone with him on crusade. Along with the couple came the brothers Othon de Grandson and Guillaume de Grandson, Othon's chief household knight Jean de Bonvillars, Jean de Vesci, Robert de Tibetot (future justiciar of west Wales), Payn de Chaworth and Roger de Clifford[23] and household knights including Richard de Brus. The royal party came down the Mont Cenis Pass[24] on 7 June,[25] arriving at Saint-Georges d'Espéranche on 18 June 1273.[26] The marriage to Leonor is important in the story of Wales, since Leonor's half-brother, Alfonso X of Castile, who had contacted the marriage, naturally insisted that his new relative, the Lord Edward, be invested in sufficient funds to maintain his half-sister, some 10,000 marks or £6,666 was stipulated. Accordingly, Henry had granted his son, not only the rich lands of Gascony, but also the royal lands in Wales and Ireland, including the disputed four *cantrefi* of the Perfeddwladd – in 1254, Edward and Wales come into close contact for the first time.[27]

The extent of Philippe's County of Savoy can be measured by a progress he made in the summers of 1271 and 1272, whilst his grandnephew was still busy crusading. Such a progress would have involved a travelling retinue of cooks, bakers, kitchen and bed-chamber servants, marshals to attend to the horses and forgers to make new shoes for them, and lastly a continual flow of messengers riding to and fro from the main travelling party – similarly with Edward travelling through Italy. He set out in the summer of 1271 from an unfinished Château de Saint-Georges-d'Espéranche (Figure 1.3) on 10 August, heading east-south-east across the gently wooded Viennois.[28] By the 12th, he was at La Côte-Saint-André, the castle sitting on its softly sloping hillside and commanding key trade routes from the Dauphiné to the south-east.[29] Then, on 14 August, he'd entered the mouth of the Isère Valley at Voiron, his castle dominating the approach.[30] To the south-east down the Val d'Isère lay Grenoble, the capital of the Savoyard rivals in the Dauphiné. So on from Voiron, heading north-easterly, he entered the ravine-strewn mountains of the Chartreuse massif[31] and by the 19th had reached Saint-Laurent, later to become Saint-Laurent-du-Pont with the addition of its bridge.[32] En route to Saint-Laurent he may well have visited the nearby castle at Les Échelles, the onetime fief of his late sister Beatrice, mother of four queens and the late King Henry's mother-in-law.

By 24 August Philippe had come down from the Chartreuse and skirted Lac Bourget to reach Aix, across the lake from the Savoyard-founded monastery which would become their family necropolis: Hautecombe Abbey. To continue north-eastward would have taken him to Annecy, but this would have meant entering the lands of the Count of Geneva, so instead a south-easterly route to the later Savoyard capital of Chambéry where he arrived on 26 August.[33] At Chambéry he met an important vassal, Humbert de Seyssel, Lord of Aix, who held important lands around Lac Bourget.[34] Trouble in the Aosta Valley required then an easterly journey, rejoining the Isère Valley to Montmélian where he passed on 6 September. Then up the steeply sided Tarentaise Valley past Aigueblanche, the birthplace of the Bishop of Hereford, and to the bottom of the Petit Saint-Bernard Pass at Bourg-Saint-Maurice where he arrived on 16 September.[35] He'd thankfully arrived at the foot of the pass before the winter snows would have made passage impossible over the summit of 7,178 feet (2,188 metres). The near-vertical ascent from Bourg-Saint-Maurice is today made via nearly thirty subsequent hairpin bends as the road zigzags its way upward to the summit, almost ascending a wall. A journey in 1271 on horseback or in carriages would have been incredibly difficult. The 16–18 September transit of the Petit Saint-Bernard Pass was made before descending deep into the Aosta Valley to join the Dora Baltea torrent on its way from Mont Blanc to the Po, the white mountain now looming over their shoulders until they reached Châtel Argent on 21 September, and Aosta itself on 22 September.[36]

Once business there was concluded, Philippe swung north over the mountains, following the tributary of the Dora Baltea, the Buthier, up to the Grand Saint-Bernard Pass, this even higher than the wall only just crossed at 8,100 feet (2,469 metres). Not so much as a pass than a tiny crack in the top of a mountainous barrier, and yet this had long been a key international route. Claudius and Julius Caesar had passed this way with armies bound for Britain and Gaul, followed centuries later by the pilgrims in the other direction to Rome, for this way was the *Via Francigena*. He may well have made offerings for safe passage at the monastery at the summit dedicated to Saint Bernard himself before beginning the descent into the Valais.[37]

On 2 November, the comital party arrived at the old legionary town of Martigny, dominated by its castle of La Bâtiaz, turning eastward into the Rhône Valley to Conthey, where he arrived on 4 November, passing Saillon on the 3rd.[38] Backtracking to Saint-Maurice and its famous monastery and bridge over the Rhône on the 6th, he reached the castle at Aigle on 9 November. Now as the valley widened and travelling westward into the sun, he passed Pierre's new town of Villeneuve before reaching the great family castle of Chillon on 10 November.[39] Chillon had been the preferred residence of the counts of Savoy before Philippe's reign. He visited, but he was happier down closer to Lyon, amongst the sunny vineyards of the Viennois, at his new palace-castle of Saint-Georges-d'Espéranche. Whilst at Chillon, he met up with the bishops of Lausanne (Jean de Cossonay) and Geneva (Aymon de Cruseilles), along with a key ally and vassal on his northern frontier, the Count of Gruyère.[40]

Taylor made much of the similitude of the windows at Chillon to those later built at Harlech, he and Chapuisat going so far as to measure them and find them a very close match. This is, however, evidence of Savoyard builders common to both constructions, not necessarily of the same architect. Whilst Taylor pointed to a record from 1266–7 of a *Jacquetto de Sancto Jorio* working at Chillon,[41] and there is certainly much evidence of Maître Jacques being at Chillon,[42] there is no primary source evidence for him actually being paid to work there. We do have evidence of Jean Francis being paid to work there,[43] but it is my view that the *Jacquetto de Sancto Jorio*[44] is unlikely to have been the same as the *Magistro Jacobi cementarii* recorded at Yverdon also during 1266–7.[45] This does not make it impossible that Jacques worked on Chillon, indeed it is likely he did; it is just that there is no written evidence. The much-vaunted windows could equally be a standard Savoyard type, known to Jacques or brought to Wales by men such as the documented Jean Francis.

Meanwhile, after a short stay, Philippe crossed the still waters of the Léman to its southern shore, where he spent Christmas at Evian from 22 December – a marathon journey, showing the vast contrasts of his lands. Whilst in the Valais he'd concluded a fresh treaty with the ever-troublesome Bishop of Sion, whilst at Chillon another with the Bishop of Lausanne – these bishoprics continuing to be a thorn in Savoy's side.[46] Whilst Philippe remained at Evian a while, he called his chatelains from Vaud, the Valais and the Chablais to him for a meeting on 2 February 1272. Records show the grain, oil, wine, spices, candle wax, parchment and medications required for his stay at Evian. The wines came from the Lavaux across the lake (now UNESCO-protected vineyards) but also from Rolle, Aigle,

Villeneuve, Moudon, Cossonay and Lutry – a medieval court consumed a whole lot of wine.

Setting out later that year, his sojourn would see him up at Romont on 24 July, crossing the Gros-de-Vaud to be at Yverdon on 25 August where he met up with the future Bishop of Lausanne, Guillaume de Champvent, brother of Pierre de Champvent and Jacques de Grandson, Lord of Belmont, another younger brother of Othon de Grandson.[47] The links between the comital family of Savoy and the wider *famille de Grandson* (which included the Grandsons and the Champvents) remain central to an understanding of the web of Anglo-Savoyard relations at this time. As Philippe arrived in Yverdon, the castle built for his late brother Pierre by Jean de Mézos and Maître Jacques, the status and whereabouts of the *famille de Grandson* in August 1272 was:

Othon de Grandson	With the Lord Edward, future Justiciar of North Wales
Guillaume de Grandson	With the Lord Edward, future Deputy Justiciar.
Henri de Grandson	Whereabouts unknown, future Pastor of Greystoke in Cumberland.
Jacques de Grandson	Meeting with Philippe de Savoie, Lord of Belmont
Agnès de Grandson	Widowed wife of Ulrich de Vuippens
Gerard de Vuippens	Son of Agnès, future Pastor of Greystoke in Cumberland and Bishop of Lausanne
Pierre de Champvent	With Henry III as Steward, future King's Chamberlain
Guillaume de Champvent	Meeting with Philippe de Savoie, Dean of St Martins-le-Grand in London, future Bishop of Lausanne

One can imagine that a meeting between the House of Savoy and members of the *famille de Grandson* would entail much interesting detail that is sadly lost to us. But we might usefully speculate that a recent meeting with the incumbent Bishop of Lausanne, the aged Jean de Cossonay and now Guillaume de Champvent brought from London, might just include a Savoyard/Grandson interest in the see of Lausanne when we remember that the very next year Champvent will be appointed bishop. Finally, Philippe's progress ended at Les Clées on the well-trodden road to Burgundy and England in the Pays de Vaud on 31 August.[48]

Savoy encompassed much of the current French departments of Ain and Isère, and all Haute Savoie and Savoie, much of the Swiss canton of Valais, all of Vaud, and the Italian regions of the Valle d'Aosta and Piedmont. But we should note, Savoy had no large urban centres at this time: Geneva and Annecy remained the fief of the Count de Geneva, Lausanne the Bishop of Lausanne and Lyon the Archbishop of Lyon. But what the Savoyards did control was not only access to these urban centres, their trade routes, but also, vitally, the frighteningly high passes between France and Italy which were the key artery of Europe.

It had been along yet another of these arteries that Edward and his entourage had journeyed that June of 1273. Travelling westward from Turin toward the mountains and the Mont Cenis pass, their route took them via Aiguebelle to Montmélian and Chambéry.[49] Their destination was the castle of Saint-Georges-d'Espéranche, then under construction for Philippe as a new palatial residence,[50] given his departure from the comforts of the see of Lyon. Saint-Georges-d'Espéranche lies in the rolling hill country above the plain of the River Rhône, some twelve and a half miles (twenty kilometres) south-east of Lyon, but nine miles (fifteen kilometres) north-east of Vienne. The hilly uplands above the Rhône, very much like England, were rich in woodland, which made them rich in game – ideally suited to a thirteenth-century count and ideally suited to a young would-be king in search of some good hunting after the hot deserts of the Levant. For Edward and the English in his entourage, they provided a first taste of home.

Philippe had lived pretty much all his life in and around Lyon and had no intention of moving to Chillon by Lac Léman as Pierre had done, so at Saint-Georges-d'Espéranche he had decided to build a new palace for himself and his new bride. He'd acquired the seigneurial rights whilst Archbishop of Lyon in 1242, but we have no record of a castle earlier than 1270.[51] There was a visit by Edmund Crouchback from England, in early August 1271, en route to the Holy Land.[52] Virtually nothing remains of the castle today, just the lower parts of one tower, but we can thank a Citizen Chabord[53] for a colour-wash plan (Figure 1.4) made of the castle in 1794 and preserved in the Archives de l'Isère. Saint-Georges was of a square outline, a *Carré Savoyard*, with a curtain wall surrounded by a revetted moat, with towers at each corner, of apparently the same size, largely aesthetic and octagonal in shape.[54] An accompanying report by Chabord adds that the curtain walls were some five feet thick and surrounded a great courtyard. He describes the building as '*vaste*', and that towards the top of the four octagonal towers were some embrasures.[55] The chief architect for Philippe was *Majistro Jacobo lathomo*, who maintained a house in Saint-Georges.

Can we take this to be the same man as the *Majistri Jacobi*, working with his father Jean at Yverdon, from 1260, for Pierre de Savoie? Taylor certainly thought so, despite the almost complete lack of archival records for Saint-Georges-d'Espéranche's construction (thanks to the French revolutionaries),[56] he found the evidence in a combination of architecture and archive, or archaeology and history. There is little remaining of Philippe's castle (and Yverdon has subsequently been much changed), but what remained in Taylor's time allowed him to make a measurement of windows and compare them to originals at Chillon and Yverdon, also an assessment of shallow latrine shafts at Saint-Georges and Yverdon – they closely matched (Figure 1.5).[57] Swiss architectural historians now view the Yverdon shallow latrine shaft as a much more recent addition, however this does not invalidate Taylor since the location and form is so close to that at Saint-Georges, and could easily have been a later rebuild not a new build. Indeed, as we shall see later the shallow latrine shaft design employed by a Maître Jacques would become something of his signature, being employed not only with these castles in Vaud and the Viennois but also later in Wales. The windows, with their shallow segmented head, lacking a keystone, are also somewhat of a speciality. We find them in the windows at Harlech, Beaumaris, Yverdon and Saint-Georges but also tellingly we found them in the cellar of the castle at Saint-Prex – the castle which may have been the childhood home of Maître Jacques (Figure 1.6). For Yverdon, we say 'remained' because the original windows in the western elevation which Taylor measured and compared with bricked-up remnants at Saint-Georges were lost to us when Yverdon was later renovated – thankfully, we have Taylor's records and publication.[58]

But, perhaps the key evidence is not architectural but archival, we now know for certain something that Taylor appears not to have written of, that Maître Jacques lived at Saint-Georges. A will in the Turin archive records the death of the castellans of Susa in the house of Maître Jacques.[59] So, we have the Viennois castle being built by a man with a closely similar name as the Vaudois, for the same patron and his successor, with the same architectural style, who is known to have lived in the Viennois castle – as far as history allows us we can say that Saint-Georges-d'Espéranche was built by the same man who had built the castle at Yverdon or in Taylor's words 'by a common hand'. Taylor remained in no doubt, and confirms the evidence of the Savoyard Archive in Turin, that 'records do at least show beyond question that Count Philip's principal court architect or master mason was a *Magister Jacobus lathomus*, and that … this Maître Jacques had a supervisory responsibility over all the count's building works'.[60] Swiss historian Daniel de Raemy goes further, describing the castle in the Viennois as 'the first masterpiece entirely conceived by the mason-architect Jacques de St Georges'.[61] In other words, the castle at Saint-Georges is the first work that can be solely and entirely attributed to the man who would take its name.[62] For it would be that the English would come to know *Magistro Jacobo lathomo* as Maître Jacques de Saint Georges. Today the village of Saint-Georges honours the builder of its castle with a Rue Maître Jacques, the village after which perhaps the greatest architect-mason of the Middle Ages took his name.[63]

At Saint-Georges-d'Espéranche on 25 June 1273, Philippe did his homage for the aforementioned castles of 1246, to the yet uncrowned king of England[64] and entertained his great-nephew to a tremendous feast – at which we are almost certain Edward would have been introduced to the one-time master mason for Pierre de Savoie now in the employ of Philippe de Savoie, Maître Jacques. This meeting has been rightly identified as pivotal in Edward's life, and in the history of England and Wales: here the young Edward came face to face with the man who would build castles for him. It's tempting to imagine what the conversation might have been. Edward had, on his travels, seen Louis IX's magnificent crusader port of Aigues-Mortes with its great circular tower, he'd seen the complex and state-of-the-art crusader castles in Outremer; now here he was with the master mason constructing a new palace-castle for his great-uncle Philippe, Count of Savoy. Edward was almost certainly impressed by the scale of Jacques' work, that he was embarking upon the simultaneous construction of no less than four castles for Philippe – at Voiron, La-Côte-St-André, St-Laurent-du-Pont as well as Saint-Georges.[65] In the coming years, Edward would be in great need of a supervisory master mason who could deliver multiple castles in double quick time. An interesting echo of the works found by Edward in the Viennois that summer of 1273 would later be found in Wales. The castles of Voiron, La-Côte-St-André and St-Laurent-du-Pont all had, as was the fashion, round towers whereas Saint-Georges, as the palace, had octagonal towers – can we see in the ruins in France the prototype for Caernarfon? It's an intriguing thought that the genesis of one of history's most spectacular castles may well have been formed in the minds of Edward and Jacques on 25 June 1273 in the sun of a Viennois afternoon.[66]

Whilst at the 'Chastel Seint George', Philippe took the homage of a recalcitrant local lord, Guillaume I de Tournon, whose castle sat between Vienne and Valence, at a key position on the Rhône, now Tournon-sur-Rhône. Philippe took advantage of Edward's presence to have him, and his knights witness the homage: perhaps a touch of medieval name-dropping to include the illustrious grandson of his sister Béatrice de Savoie, the 'Roy d'Engleterre'. Listed amongst the witnesses are, of course, the ever-present Jean de Vesci and Othon de Grandson.[67] Once more we should note that in the thirteenth-century francophone world, there was nothing unusual in the witnessing, by a knight from Northumbria, a knight from Vaud, of the homage of a knight from the Viennois to the Count of Savoy and Burgundy. Ominously, as Edward indulged in the medieval spectacle of a homage to Philippe by Guillaume, on the same page of the Fœdera[68] there is noted a restraint, issued in Edward's name in London to a recalcitrant vassal in Britain, Llywelyn ap Gruffydd, not to build a castle near Montgomery.[69] Storm clouds were gathering, even if those in the Viennois did not quite yet know it.

However, for Edward, Jacques and Othon, Caernarfon lay in the future. Following the feast, Othon de Grandson took his leave of Edward for a while, returning to his home by Lac Neuchâtel for the first time in many years, and Edward continuing with the main party through France toward Paris. The royal party arrived in the French capital on 17 July 1273,[70] so that he could pay homage to the new French king, Philippe III, for Gascony.[71] It would then be to Gascony, not England, that Edward would first turn his horse toward. The complex interweaving of feudal relationships between French kings, the French nobility, English kings who were also themselves French nobles and lastly Princes of Wales would give rise to continual dispute and warfare in the coming centuries.

It was only in April 1274, that Edward and Leonor finally set out once more for England but, even then, by the overland route through France, not the quicker sea voyage. On the way they took the opportunity to visit Leonor's mother, Jeanne, in Ponthieu. For those that imagine, in the light of events that would happen

Britain, that Edward on becoming king immediately set out upon the conquest of Wales and Scotland, a satisfactory explanation needs to be found of the nearly two years that Edward and Leonor spent in returning to London. Papal affairs, family affairs with the Montforts, family affairs with the Savoyards, paying homage for and suppressing a revolt in Gascony, family affairs in Ponthieu, all seem to have taken a precedence over English affairs: a slow passage through Rome, Padua, Bologna, Milan, Turin, the Viennois, Paris, Orleans, Limoges, Saintes, Bordeaux, Bayonne, Bordeaux, Limoges and Paris before ever reaching the English Channel and setting eyes upon England once more – an England they'd last seen as Portsmouth receded into the distance that late August nearly four years earlier, an England where Henry was still king.

Meantime, Grandson had been given leave of Edward for a while and made his way toward Lac de Neuchâtel; his route back to Grandson took him over the Col de la Faucille and along the Vallée de Joux, then as now remote from the lands around Lac Léman. As the one-time crusader knight made his way alongside Lac de Joux, he may well have contemplated his life since leaving for England as a boy. He was returning this way to visit the Abbaye de Joux and its abbot, Jean de Bretigny. One can easily imagine thanks for his safe deliverance from the Holy Land were offered to his ancestors entombed within the walls of the great familial abbey.

Whilst Grandson had been with Edward and Philippe at Saint-Georges, news had reached them that the Bishop of Lausanne, Jean de Cossonay was no more. The new bishop would be none other than Guillaume de Champvent, brother of Pierre de Champvent, the same Champvent that had for many years until the king's recent demise been a loyal steward to Henry III in London. Guillaume de Champvent was also Othon's first cousin, as the Grandson family had separated a generation earlier into the Lords of Grandson and of Champvent. Since the bishopric was the greatest landowner in Vaud, the see had been the cause of past struggles and indeed trebuchets firing toward the bishop's palace. It was most helpful that a Grandson would now sit upon the bishop's throne. The new Bishop of Lausanne had previously spent much time in England, being a dean of St Martin Le Grand[72] in London from 1262 until his elevation to the bishopric, and he had also been a sub-dean at York Minster.[73] His influence at court in 1262 is evidenced by his joining the Savoyard witness list for a charter relating to Alianor's dowry.[74] Upon his move to Lausanne, Edward would appoint Louis, the son of Thomas II and future Baron de Vaud, to the vacant dean's position at St Martin.[75]

His *cathedra* or seat would be the great cathedral at Lausanne that was nearing completion, the work of Jean Cotereel and his anonymous father, Cotereel being the man believed to be the late father of Maître Jacques. Grandson had been joined on this family business by his cousin, Pierre de Champvent, from England in April 1274.[76] Whilst Pierre stayed awhile in Vaud, attending the consecration of Lausanne Cathedral on 20 October 1275,[77] in the presence of Pope Gregory X and Rudolph of Hapsburg, Othon returned to England to be with Edward not long after his coronation in August 1274; we know they were at Northampton together in November 1274.[78] The need to be in Vaud, attending to family business, and balancing that with the need to be in England, illustrates the difficult choices made by Savoyards. Indeed, the visit to Northampton saw the renewal, following his homage of June 1273, of Philippe's pension for what has been described as the 'English Savoyard lands'.[79] On Edward's business, Grandson returned to Savoy, and the Viennois to spend Christmas of 1274 at Saint-Georges-d'Espéranche, no doubt with Philipe.

Once the Christmas festivities were done in the Viennois, Othon de Grandson then spent the following two years engaged upon much diplomatic work for Edward relating to Gascony and its neighbouring territories. Such cross-Channel journeys would, no doubt, have been unpleasant, uncomfortable and not a little dangerous to undertake. His journeys would make him familiar with the dangers and pleasures of the open road. Indeed, his cross-Channel sojourns became so frequent he evidently became so well known by the men of Dover that when Thomas Salekyn, a boatman there, 'feared that he would lose the house which he was alleged to have built on the common soil, it was to his "very dear lord, and it please him friend, Sir Otho de Granson [sic]" that he appealed for protection'.[80]

Crossing the Channel with Grandson on one mission would also be his brother, Henri de Grandson, to whom Edward granted two years protection on 26 May 1276. Henri travelled to the far north of Edward's realm to take up a position as parson of the church in Greystoke in the county of Cumberland.[81] The church at Greystoke had been recently built in 1255, some features from Henri's time remain still. The rood beam bridging the chancel arch is oldest item in the church, and carries floral emblems representing the wounds of Christ. The ancient choir stalls in the chancel have some well-preserved misericords (carved shelf underneath the seat). In 1278, Henri moved south once more to take up the see of Verdun, from his recently deceased brother, Gerard de Grandson,[82] Verdun then not yet in France but a prestigious prince bishopric within the Holy Roman Empire.

The position of Othon de Grandson at court was now so significant that his friend Edward would reward him with, in November 1275, the title 'Keeper of the Isles of *Gernesye* [Guernsey] and *Gereseye* [Jersey]'.[83] The Vaudois knight would be an absentee keeper, nevertheless, and as further reward, he would be granted the islands for life in 1277.

Whilst Edward and Leonor returned to England by way of Paris and Gascony, and Othon returned to the Lac de Neuchâtel, Philippe and Maître Jacques got on with the business of building castles in the Viennois. It was in the Savoyard enclave, surrounded by the rival Dauphiné,[84] close to Vienne and Lyon, that Philippe had chosen to base himself, at Saint-Georges-d'Espéranche, a seigneurie acquired in 1242.[85] At Saint-Georges he built a *ville neuve*, a new town; it's thought that the 'Saint-Georges' part of the name came from the sainted George, Archbishop of Vienne, whose relics had been hidden in the locale during a Saracen raid.[86] The

'Espéranche' name came from es-Péranche named for a local stream, so we have the new town of the relics of Saint Georges by the Péranche stream.[87] But the enclave, like all enclaves, was always under perceived or actual threat, not least by the Dauphin, who still laid claim to the region. Accordingly, castles would need to be constructed to reinforce Savoyard hegemony. Whilst Saint-Georges was under construction, Philippe would begin building or rebuilding three other castles, work taking place simultaneously: these would be at La-Côte-Saint-André, at Voiron and at Saint-Laurent-du-Pont.[88] To undertake the construction of these castles simultaneously was a tremendous undertaking on the part of Philippe and his Master of Works, Jacques. The financial and logistical strain would be apparent in the twenty-first century, let alone the thirteenth century – yet build the castles they did.

So, Philippe had for many years been active in the furthering of Savoyard interests in the Viennois to the south-east of Lyon and Bresse to the north-east. This furthering of interest would eventually take the form of territorial expansion, which would ultimately require new castles or repairs and modifications to existing ones. Philippe also continued the administrative reforms of his late brother, Pierre, and we have both to thank for the improved accounting and record-keeping in Savoy. The combination of this renewed castle building and improved record-keeping would result in the best record we have for Maître Jacques in Savoy.

The surviving Savoyard archives record the movements of Maître Jacques in the years following the meeting with Edward at Saint-Georges d'Espéranche.[89] Sadly, by the Treaty of Lyon, the building accounts for Saint-Georges itself passed to France and were destroyed by revolutionaries on 29 November 1793.[90] However, the records retained in Savoy (Turin and Chambéry) do survive and a full listing of these records is provided in the appendix, along with other key primary sources. The record is not necessarily a full account of his movements over these years –it's certainly not the medieval equivalent of a time-card, more a list of expense claims – but it does give us a flavour of his movements and hence responsibilities.

Of particular interest in these records are the names of some of the builders who will go on to build castles in Wales. It is necessary here to clarify the job title applied to Maître Jacques in the Savoyard archives: *lathomo*. This designation can be read as a work-derived name, in the same way as the author Ken Follet ascribed the name 'Tom Builder', in his novel *Pillars of the Earth*, to the man who began the fictional cathedral. In the same way *Magistro Jacobo lathomo* becomes Maître Jacques the mason/stone carver/builder. If we are under any doubt as to his home base, it is supplied by the scribe at Evian (18 March 1274) who records that *'Magistro Jacobo lathomo'* is *'redeundo ad Sanctum Georgium'*, helpfully telling us that he is returning home to Saint-Georges-d'Espéranche; which despite the itinerant life of a master mason looks to have been his home in 1274 – certainly that's where Edward had met him in June 1273. Later, the accountant at Voiron (28 June 1274) gives an insight into his life when describing a payment as 'for keeping his land'. It's tempting to imagine that Count Philippe has given up to Maître Jacques a small portion of land upon which he can have someone grow food.

Relating to his work at Saint-Laurent-du-Pont, another peculiar (to modern eyes) reference in the archives is to '*desertum*', which we can literally translate as 'desert'. There are many geographic features in Savoy and the Viennois but certainly there was no desert – a wider translation is 'wilderness' or 'sparsely populated place' or even 'vacated space'. The clerk in Saint-Georges d'Espéranche was referring to the land above Voiron toward and including Saint-Laurent-du-Pont, and the Massif de la Chartreuse.[91] We can see from the appellation '*Sanctum Laurencium*' that the medieval bridge that gave the future village its name, Saint-Laurent-du-Pont, had yet to be built – Saint-Laurent was yet to be a du-Pont.

The scribe at La Rochette gives us a wonderful insight into the daily life of a medieval master mason. Maître Jacques had acquired a '*roncino*' or packhorse whilst in the Aosta Valley for transporting something over the Petit Saint-Bernard Pass to La Rochette where he was then paid. Jacques had been working on the count's castle in the Val d'Aosta at Châtel Argent; a trek over the 7,000-feet Petit Saint-Bernard Pass would have seen him to Chambéry and eventually back to the Viennois. Such a trek, an endless series of hairpin bends today and steep descent to Bourg-Saint-Maurice and the Tarentaise is not easy; with horse and accompanying packhorse in tow it suggests once more the mason was not a stranger to long and arduous journeys.

Travelling with him in 1274–5, we find *Iohanni de Maso* and *Johannis de Massout*, both almost certainly referencing the same Sir Jean de Mézos, under whose leadership he'd worked before at Yverdon in 1266–7[92] and Salins in 1267–8.[93] As we've noted before, Mézos was an *ingeniator*,[94] an engineer of Gascon origin, ennobled by Henry III in 1254.[95] Henry had introduced Mézos to Pierre de Savoie at the siege of Benauges in 1253, Mézos subsequently moved from Henry's employ to Pierre's. The *ingeniator* was well acquainted with the construction practices of Gascony, in summary of the wider Anglo-Norman world.

The underappreciated link between the Anglo-Norman building sphere and the Savoyard was, then, Jean de Mézos. This connection partly explains the spread of round towers and lack of a central *donjon* to Savoy, and ultimately perhaps, the castles of north Wales. Swiss historian Louis Blondel dates the arrival of *donjons circulaires* or round towers in Savoy from the arrival of Mézos.[96] To suggest that the castles in Wales that would come are 'not Savoyard but Anglo-French'[97] is to misunderstand the process by which 'Anglo-French' castle-building ideas were transmitted from Gascony to Savoy thence to Wales by the medium of firstly Jean de Mézos and then Maître Jacques. It cannot be said that the Savoyard castles lacked sophistication as they were built entirely to a more restrictive comital budget, rather than an extravagant royal budget, and for a different purpose which they entirely fulfilled: the castles of Gascon Mézos, being alpine sentry posts rather than an instrument of royal conquest.

The last entry, in the Savoyard archive, is from Bourg-en-Bresse but is, sadly, undated. It appears on the roll for the year commencing 1 March 1277 and may relate to Maître Jacques. During his last years in Savoy, Jacques appears to have been much employed in Bresse, which, given that these are his last fully documented works before Wales, are of interest to us. The Lord of Bresse had been a title granted by Philippe to his nephew Amédée. Bresse had come into Savoyard hands with Amédée's marriage by the Bishop of Geneva, amid much fanfare, at the Château de Chillon on 5 July 1272, to Sybille de Baugé. Sybille was the daughter of Guy II, the seignur de Bourg et Baugé, hence the title passing to Amédée. Philippe had engineered the acquisition over some decades by aligning the interests of the Savoyards with Sybille's family, eventually gaining the prize of the betrothal of Sybille to Amédée.[98] Bourg-en-Bresse, or fortified city in Bresse, and Bâgé-le-Châtel, or the castle in Bâgé[99] were the centres of power within the seigniorage of Bourg and Baugé. Bâgé-le-Châtel had been the ancient capital; the Savoyard moved it to the more easily defendable bastion of Bourg. The rich, fertile, flat plain of Bresse extends from the wetlands of the Dombes in the south to the River Doubs in the north, and from the River Saône eastward to the Jura Mountains. At the western base of the Jura sits Bourg-en-Bresse. Amédée and Sybille installed themselves in Bresse, receiving the homage of the locals; those who refused were reduced to paying homage by physical force. It would be in Bresse that Jacques would spend much time in 1274 and 1275.

At Châtillon-les-Dombes, now called Châtillon-sur-Chalaronne, halfway along the road from Bourg-en-Bresse to Lyon, the local seigneury had built a fine castle, where centuries earlier the Romans had built fortifications by a bend in the River Chalaronne. Amédée found the castle to be of considerable strategic interest. Moreover, the size of the buildings allowed him to hold marvellous receptions there, aided no doubt by restoration work carried out by Maître Jacques.

Taylor believed it was very possible that the 1277 entry in Bresse was the last record. A journey by the *lathomi* or mason, from Bourg-en-Bresse to Saint-Georges-d'Espéranche in the Savoyard archive might relate to the mason who'd begun work under his father seventeen years earlier at Yverdon and was now finishing his work for the Counts of Savoy before travelling to England to begin work for Edward. Taylor does not seem to have been aware, nor many of those writing since, of a last will and testament dated 8 December 1277 that would appear to confirm this *lathomi* as Maître Jacques and that Saint-Georges was indeed his home until moving to England. Jean Bertrand de Canusco, passing away at Saint-Georges, wrote his testament '*in domo Magistri Jacobo Lathomi*'. Confirmation of his having a *domo* in Saint-Georges only strengthens the acquisition in England of toponymic name *de Sancto Georgio* and the case of Giles and Tassin de Saint Georges being his children. This overlooked primary source is evidence of his living at Saint-Georges and being part of the Savoyard comital court.[100]

These last entries in the Savoyard archives for 1277 represent the only primary sources we have for Maître Jacques between September 1275 and

March 1278, which constitute a missing three years, or two building seasons in his life. Following on from the June 1273 meeting with Edward and Othon de Grandson at Saint-Georges-d'Espéranche, Edward returned (eventually) to England, Othon was given leave to return to Savoy as his cousin, Guillaume de Champvent, had recently become Bishop of Lausanne.[101] It is this latter development which may fill in those missing years as we shall return to later. But with Othon in Savoy, and Jacques certainly in Bresse and then also Savoy, Edward returned to an expectant England, but one where troubling winds had begun to blow.

Chapter Four

Edward arrived in England, eventually, in the summer of 1274, having made his way from Savoy via Paris but also by way of Gascony, there to put the affairs of the troubled duchy to rights. His slow voyage home from the Holy Land is strongly indicative that, unlike his father's, and despite the recent baronial war, his succession to the throne was secure and uncontested. By now Edward was 33 years of age, and a kingdom lay before him as he landed at Dover on 2 August 1274 and surveyed the great castle before him. Things had changed a good deal since he'd last seen it four years earlier. Edward had left England a prince, he now returned a king.

Edward and his party made their way to London, where on 19 August 1274 he was crowned King of England. Contemporary historian Nicholas Trivet paints a word picture of Edward for us:

> In build he was handsome and of great stature, towering head and shoulders above the average . . . his brow was broad, and the rest of his face regular, though a drooping of the left eyelid recalled his father's expression.[1]

Sadly, unlike the crowning of his mother, Alianor de Provence, we do not have a richly embroidered chronicle of the coronation. Edward proceeded from the Palace of Westminster to the Abbey by way of a specially built covered walkway. He would have progressed to the Abbey behind the sword *Curtana*, first used at his mother's coronation in 1236.[2] His brother Edmund had wanted to carry the sword, but by his absence from the coronation this wasn't apparently to be.[3] The essential elements of the coronation service used for Edward could be traced back to the crowning of King Edgar, who had become the first King of All England at Bath in 973 AD. At Edward's coronation there would have been the aforesaid procession, an oath or promise, anointing and investiture followed by the Mass.[4] At the time of unction, anointing with holy oil, we can assume the words of 'Zadok the Priest' were said or sung, since they have been used at every coronation since Edgar's:

> Zadok the Priest, and Nathan the Prophet anointed Solomon King.
> And all the people rejoiced and said:
> God save the King! Long live the King!
> May the King live for ever,
> Amen, Alleluia.

The most sacred part of the ceremony was, and still is, the anointing of the king with holy oil, the unction. Carried out as suggested by Zadok the Priest and Nathan the Prophet on Solomon himself, this was God turning Edward from a mere mortal into God's anointed ruler of England, in the words given by Shakespeare to Richard II: 'Not all the water in the rough rude sea Can wash the balm off an anointed king' – and so it was firmly believed in 1274.

Along with the acclamations, as with his father and mother of the *Laudes Regiæ*, '*Christus vincit! Christus regnat! Christus imperat! Christus vincit! Christus regnat! Christus imperat!*' or 'Christ conquers! Christ reigns! Christ commands! Christ conquers! Christ reigns! Christ commands!'[5]

The Coronation Feast, or at least some of the menu, has survived: there were '60 oxen and cows, 60 swine, 2 fat boars, 60 live sheep, 3,000 capons and hens and 40 bacon pigs'.[6] For Edward the battles of Lewes, Evesham and Acre might have been behind him, but far greater tests awaited.

We also know of one salient point in the abbey ceremony itself: apparently when the Archbishop of Canterbury, Robert Kilwardby,[7] placed the crown upon his head, Edward immediately removed it, declaring before the assembled great and good of the kingdom that he would only replace it once the lands lost to the Crown by his father had been recovered – this new king it seemed was bent upon restoring the kingly authority he perceived had been lost in his father's time. Perhaps Edward had in mind a generality of lands, recalling the carefully worded homage he'd recently made before the King of France, but very more likely he had in mind lands lost during the civil war to men like Llywelyn ap Gruffydd, who now rejoiced in the name Prince of Wales. Edward's appanage included the four cantrefs: Rhuddlan was mentioned by name, as was Builth, all of these lands now in the possession of Llywelyn.[8] And worse, a notable absentee at his coronation that August day in Westminster Abbey was the aforesaid Llywelyn ap Gruffydd, Prince of Wales – it was an absence that had not gone unnoticed by the new king.[9]

At first Edward got on with setting the government of his new kingdom as he would wish it; on 21 September, he replaced Walter de Merton as Lord Chancellor with loyalist Robert Burnell.[10] Robert Burnell, like Othon de Grandson, was of the same age as Edward, and like the Savoyard a long and loyal servant, companion and friend.[11] Burnell had remained loyal to Edward throughout the Montfortian rebellion and was rewarded with being made Archdeacon of York in December 1270. He'd remained in England whilst Edward was away on crusade – like Grandson, Robert Burnell was a man Edward could trust. The first witnesses to a charter of Edward's patronage were: Thomas de Clare, Jean de Vesci, Othon de Grandson and Robert de Tibetot[12] – all these men had been on crusade with Edward. If Pierre de Savoie had been a veritable witnesser of forty five charters of the English Crown. In 1252 during Henry's reign, then the thirty-two out of thirty-seven charters that would be issued by Edward up to 1290 and witnessed by Grandson mark him as a close second in terms of Savoyard influence in England.[13] It was not their rank that marked them out, but their loyalty; it would be a distinction that Edward had learned from the reign of his father and it would mark the way in which he would rule.

But, meanwhile, trouble was brewing. On 3 November 1274, Llywelyn ap Gruffydd, the Prince of Wales, was asked to come to the king at Shrewsbury to do the homage required of him by treaty.[14] Llywelyn ap Gruffydd was the son of Gruffydd ap Llywelyn Fawr who fell ignominiously whilst attempting escape from the Tower of London, and so the grandson of Llywelyn Fawr,[15] albeit an illegitimate grandson. Following his father's untimely end, he defeated his brothers, Dafydd and Owain, at the Battle of Bryn Derwin in 1255 to claim ascendancy within the House of Gwynedd.[16] He had become a growing thorn in the side of the late Henry and now of Edward. We cannot be certain of when this Llywelyn was born, or indeed where; we cannot even be certain of who his mother was – but we can be certain that he had for all his life been attempting to live up to the name of his grandfather Llywelyn Fawr.[17]

The Treaty of Montgomery, seven years earlier in 1267, had not only granted Llywelyn title as Prince of Wales,[18] but also accorded him suzerainty over all other Welsh rulers, and had robbed Edward personally of his appanage land in Wales. What's more, it had created a dangerous source of conflict, for the native Welsh princes now owed allegiance to the Prince of Wales. But the native Welsh princes were not the only rulers of Wales – there were the Marcher lords for all to contend with. The Marcher lords occupied Welsh land outside the Kingdom of England, and owed allegiance not to the Prince of Wales but to the King of England. The Marcher lords held lands along much of the Welsh border with England, but also held most of south Wales, Glamorgan and Pembroke. Llywelyn himself held Gwynedd, now extending from the Llyn peninsula all the way to Deeside and down the western coast, as far as the Dovey estuary. His vassals held Powys and Ceredigion, meaning that a cocktail of warring interests held Wales, with ultimately the Prince of Wales and the Marcher lords subject to Edward. The Treaty of Montgomery did not provide the basis for a peaceful settlement of Wales. As the Lord Edward became King of England, trouble began to brew on his western border, and perhaps his coronation declaration showed and that he was determined to meet the threat. His father Henry had stayed his hand with the last Prince of Wales, Dafydd ap Llywelyn Fawr, when the Welshman reneged on earlier treaties. Henry had not invaded Gwynedd when he'd had every right, showing leniency instead; his son had learned that to be a king you had to defend your *majesté*.[19] Not only was Edward resolved to claw back his lands lost to Llywelyn, so too were the Marcher lords who would throw oil onto the fire – war threatened.

Contravening the express wishes of the government in London, Llywelyn had recently set about consolidating his hold over Powys with the construction of a castle in the Upper Severn Valley at Dolforwyn, beginning in 1273, around the time Edward was visiting Count Philippe's castle under construction at Saint-Georges in the Viennois. But Dolforwyn was no palace; whilst it lacked entirely the military sophistication of the Savoyard castles, it was nonetheless a dagger held toward Edward's kingdom and the county of Shropshire in particular.

The strategically important Montgomery and the nearby Ceri hills had been the flashpoint of an earlier confrontation between Llywelyn Fawr and a young Henry III in 1228.[20] Dolforwyn Castle was only four miles (six kilometres) away and obviously threatening Montgomery Castle,[21] the very venue of the treaty of 1267. The regency government had attempted to prevent the castle's construction, across from the River Severn at Abermule. On 23 June 1273, they issued an 'inhibition of his [Llywelyn] erecting a castle at Abrunol, near the castle of Montgomery ... so that the king may not be compelled to apply his hand otherwise to this'.[22]

Another castle as a source of conflict was that built by Marcher Lord, Gilbert de Clare, Earl of Gloucester, at Caerffili, built from 1268 to consolidate his rule in Glamorgan. The lordship of Glamorgan had been cut out of the Welsh Kingship of Morgannwg by the Normans, who'd first extended their interests into the lands of Welsh-speakers after their conquests of the lands of the English. Robert fitz[23] Hamo had established Norman rule, with his chief castle at Cardiff, from his lands in nearby Gloucestershire. After a period of royal custody, the lordship of Glamorgan passed into the hands of the Clare family[24] in 1217. But the Earls of Gloucester had only established their rule in lowland Morgannwg. They began to extend into the upland areas of the rivers Rhymney and Taff from 1246, bringing them closer toward Brecon and the southern extremities of Llywelyn ap Gruffydd's nascent principality of Wales. Clare rule had been extended to the commote of Glyn Rhondda and Meisgyn in 1246, Afan in 1247 and lastly Senghennydd in 1267.

Gwynedd had not extended its rule hitherto to south Wales, but Llywelyn was bent now upon this path, something Gilbert de Clare was equally bent upon resisting. The move into Senghennydd, nearly twenty years after the earlier extensions, was likely made following moves by Llywelyn into the area.[25] The Treaty of Montgomery had failed to define the relationship between Llywelyn and Gilbert; the latter would have felt a growing threat from the north. Caerffili Castle, where the Rhymney begins a great bend in Senghennydd, was the response to the Welsh threat. On 13 October 1270, Llywelyn burned the construction site to the ground, but on 1 June 1271 building was renewed,[26] with a castle so strong that the Marcher Lord's authority was firmly established over Glamorgan. 'Giant' Caerffili, as described by a Welsh chronicle,[27] was built as a magnificent concentric ring fortress, upon a small island and surrounded by artificial lakes. Its scope and grandeur were no doubt not lost upon Edward, neither more importantly was its ability to successfully mark the authority of its builder upon the surrounding land.

North of Glamorgan lay Brecon, only recently, in 1263, brought into the lands of Llywelyn. When Humphrey de Bohun, who would succeed his elderly grandfather as Earl of Hereford in 1275, sought to restore his lands in Brecon, there would be more trouble. The Treaty of Montgomery had reserved Brecon for Llywelyn and to the Welsh prince this encroachment was a clear breach of the treaty. In the summer of 1273, it was a transgression formalized when the regency government (Henry having died, Edward not having returned) referred to Brecon as 'the land of Humphrey de Bohun'. Welsh historian R. R. Davies notes: 'These individual confrontations in the March need not have led to a more general breakdown of Anglo-Welsh relations … Yet their cumulative effect, especially as the years passed, was to create in Llywelyn's mind a suspicion that there was an orchestrated attempt to undermine his hard won gains.'[28] If there had been an 'orchestrated attempt to undermine' Llywelyn, it seems that it had not lain with King Henry in his dying days, nor with his son Edward fighting Mamluks at Acre, but perhaps with the regency government and one of mutual interest, between the Marchers Clare, Bohun and Mortimer.

Llywelyn sat upon an uncertain perch in Gwynedd: whilst there was a strong sense of Welsh identity, there was not yet a Welsh polity and so there were Welshmen who did not necessarily accept the overlordship of Gwynedd. Cracks, in terms of loyalty to Llywelyn, began to appear in Brecon and Deheubarth.[29] Both his brother Dafydd ap Gruffydd and Gruffydd ap Gwenwynwyn of Powys had been with Llywelyn when he'd challenged Clare at Caerffili – both men may have begun to doubt the fight Llywelyn was picking. Llywelyn's retreat from Glamorgan in the face of the Marcher Lord was perhaps the beginning of the end for Llywelyn, not Edward's return from the Holy Land. Welsh historian J. Beverley Smith suggests wryly, that when he 'abandoned the siege of Caerffili and withdrew' that 'he was unable to arrest that withdrawal until he stood on the frontiers of Snowdon itself'.[30]

And so, we will soon have a new king who'd learned that perceived weakness in the face of opposition on behalf of his father led to civil war – a new king eager to assert his kingly dignity. And we have a native Prince of Wales, becoming ever suspicious of this new English king and eager to assert his own authority in the face of a perceived undermining of his position.

The Treaty of Montgomery was never meant to be a permanent solution to Anglo-Welsh relations; historian of the Welsh Wars John. E. Morris described it as 'rather a truce than a peace'.[31] If a truce, it was ineffective: its less-than-precise definitions of what was owed by whom and for what meant that, in the climate of mutual suspicion prevalent in the early 1270s, the provisions of the treaty began to fall apart. In Llywelyn's troubled mind, he began to think of a way in which he could leverage the support of Edward in his disputes with Mortimer, Clare and Bohun. That leverage appeared to be withholding the tribute owed by him to the Crown. But in doing so, he was breaching a treaty with the Crown. And remember this was a crown not yet placed upon Edward's head when Llywelyn began to withhold the payments, even prior to Edward's return in February 1274.[32]

The regency government, as recorded in the Closed Rolls[33] for Edward's reign, began immediately, in December 1272, to display anxiety that Llywelyn was withholding treaty commitment payments.[34] Despite their 1272 request, no payment was forthcoming. Llywelyn was linking the lack of tribute payments with the failure of the Crown to contain the Marcher Lords. But how could the ailing Henry, a regency government and the absent Edward have been able to contain Clare, Bohun and Mortimer? With the failure to maintain payments, the Treaty of Montgomery was in trouble, with Edward and Llywelyn set upon a collision course. By attempting to use the withdrawal of these payments to influence the actions of an uncrowned king, Llywelyn was catastrophically misjudging Edward. Importantly, we can see that the quarrel that ended with the First Welsh War in 1277 was not of Edward's making, he being at the time being most decidedly out of the country. In summary, Beverley Smith agrees that it was the confluence of a worsening position in the Marches, alongside an absence of influence from Westminster that saw the deterioration of Anglo-Welsh relations between 1267 and 1276, saying that it was not 'something that dated from Edward's accession'.[35]

Llywelyn's paranoia would not have been helped, nor his position strengthened by a plot to assassinate him in early 1274. It had been arranged that Owain ap Gruffydd ap Gwenwynwyn would come with armed men on 2 February to carry out the assassination but were thwarted by a snowstorm. Llywelyn did not discover the full details of the plot until Owain confessed to the Bishop of Bangor. The plot implicated Llywelyn's brother Dafydd ap Gruffydd, who upon its discovery, in November 1274, fled to England and a sanctuary provided by Edward. The plotters also included the leading family of Powys Wenwynwyn: Gruffydd ap Gwenwynwyn, his wife Hawise and aforesaid son Owain. The plot laid bare the weakness of Llwelyn's position amongst Welshmen, particularly the rift within his own family and between Gwynedd and Powys. Llywelyn's expanded influence in Wales had always been built upon less than secure ground, evidenced by the necessity of taking hostages to guarantee agreements with lesser Welsh princes: Maerdudd ap Rhys back in 1261, many in mid Wales in 1271 and Gruffydd ap Gwenwynwyn now in 1274 had been coerced in this way.[36] So the plotters added further poison to the deteriorating relationship between the Prince of Wales and the King of England, by increasing Llywelyn's internal paranoia. The harbouring of Dafydd ap Gruffydd and Gruffydd ap Gwenwynwyn by Edward has been offered by some as an excuse for Llywelyn not to pay homage to Edward. This might be true of 1275–6, but it cannot be said to apply to the first requests, and particularly that of the regency government for him to come to Rhyd Chwima in 1272. His continuing refusals to take an oath of fealty and pay homage due to his liege Lord, Edward, began a downward spiral in Anglo-Welsh relations, that would march irrevocably to war.

Rhyd Chwima in 1272, is a watershed moment in the build-up to the First Welsh War. Barely eleven days after Henry had passed away, and long before any internal Welsh conspiracy, the regency government issued, in Edward's absence, an order for Llywelyn to come to Rhyd Chwima. This was the ford of the River Severn near Montgomery, where traditional Anglo-Welsh meetings were held, and here Llywelyn was asked to pay due homage to Edward.[37] It is remarkable that this order appears on page two of Edward's Calendar of Close Rolls,[38] only the third order of his government, and one issued in his absence. Llywelyn had not been summoned to leave Wales, but to come the traditional meeting place of Rhyd Chwima. Those appointed to receive the homage on Edward's behalf, the abbots of Dore and Haughmond,[39] waited all day by the banks of the Severn. No one came, they waited and eventually left.

When Edward returned and was crowned in August 1274, the lack of Llywelyn's presence and homage would have been keenly felt by a new king who'd seen the dignity of this father's reign compromised so often. But the failure, from the aforesaid order onward, to obey no less than five summons to attend Edward to do homage and give fealty was foolhardy and disastrous for Gwynedd – the leopard would exact revenge upon this slight against his honour. If fealty was 'the glue that held feudal society together'[40] then Edward had no choice but to defend his position. Edward noted to the Pope, regarding Llywelyn, that 'in order to receive his homage and fealty' in August 1276: 'we had so demeaned our royal dignity (*regiam dignitatem*) as to go to the confines of his land'. Edward was referring to a visit to Chester in 1275, when an attempt had been made to get Llywelyn to come to pay the due homage in June 1275.[41] If ever there was a king conscious, because of the many challenges to his father's dignity, of his own *regiam dignitatem*, then it was this king. At Chester, the chronicler of the monastery there noted with dismay Llywelyn's 'contempt' for Edward by not coming to pay homage.[42] Edward had been in Cheshire awaiting his Prince of Wales since late August; his presence at Macclesfield is noted on 24 August. He was at Chester to take Llywelyn's homage on 3 and 4 September, where he paced up and down awaiting the Welshman. However, he waited in vain – no Llywelyn. Edward went up to Birkenhead, on the nearby Wirral peninsula for a few days and on his return on 10 September, still no sign of Llywelyn.[43]

Yet another mandate, this time to Westminster, followed on 10 September;[44] however, Llywelyn again failed to show. Oddly, he still proclaimed a peace had been made to his people in Wales and levied a new tax to renew payments of monies owed to Edward. Since this is entirely at odds with his known failure to attend at Chester, and the above renewed summons to Westminster, we can only assume this was a pretext on Llywelyn's part and that he was, in fact, now preparing for war.[45]

Perhaps worse still for Edward: following the death, in the spring of 1275 of his Aunt Eleanor, wife of his slain uncle and one-time enemy, Simon de Montfort, their daughter, his cousin Eleanor, was married to none other than Llywelyn ap Gruffydd. The Prince of Wales and Eleanor de Montfort were married by proxy: he was in Wales, she in France.[46] So, here now for Edward was Llywelyn marrying the daughter of one-time rebel and man he'd fought at Lewes and had brutally slain at Evesham. Edward had last visited his aunt and the young Eleanor in an act of reconciliation, just two years earlier; so much for family reconciliations. The Plantagenet family was not famed for its even temper and patience, that by ignoring an order to refrain from castle building, with a breach of the Treaty of

Montgomery, by refusal to pay Edward homage and give due fealty[47] and lastly marriage to the daughter of Edward's and his late father's greatest enemy, then we can imagine that Llywelyn was trying that temper and patience beyond breaking point. The very last thing the new king wanted, especially after the peaceful uncontested succession, was a resurrection of a Montfortian faction. This raised the spectre of another civil war.

The two ships carrying Eleanor, her brother Amaury and their entourage, sailing off the south coast of England, were captured just off the Scilly islands by sailors from the port of Bristol. Buried beneath the boards of the ship was found the banner of the *famille de Montfort*. The chronicler of Guisborough, writing later, would attribute the breakdown as having been brought to a head by 'Llywelyn, Prince of Wales' that he 'had taken himself a wife, daughter of Lord Simon de Montfort'.[48] In a marriage union between the Montfort family and the House of Gwynedd, the relationship betwixt king and prince had reached breaking point. And yet there had been another futile attempt to bring Llywelyn to the king.[49]

However this stillborn attempt at peace would in part by stymied by an empty chair in that traditional source of mediation, Rome. The then papal legate, Ottobuono, who'd done so much to write the Treaty of Montgomery in 1267, had come to the papacy as Adrian V. Sadly he would be in no position to create a new peace between Edward and Llywelyn, as he left Rome in August to escape the heat, retreating to Viterbo, where he suddenly fell ill and died on 18 August 1276. As there would be a succession of four popes in 1276,[50] Rome was to be of little use as an intermediary this time.

This last attempt at bringing Llywelyn to pay due homage looks to have been the straw that broke the camel's back, for the order now went out to Edward's Gascon *ingeniator*, Bertram, to travel to the forests of Kingsclere and Burghfield, on the Hampshire/Berkshire border, to choose and fell timber appropriate for the construction of siege engines.[51] The timber was to be hauled to Caversham where the Sheriff of Berkshire and Oxfordshire was to arrange for it to be shipped down the Thames to the Tower of London.[52] The order to ship the timber was just twenty-four hours on from Llywelyn's latest failure to show, 26 April 1276. The drums of war were beginning to beat.[53]

However, Parliament had sat between 6 May and 3 June at Westminster, with no action yet taken. But, when Parliament sat once more at Westminster from 29 September, Edward arriving on 19 October, this time, there would be a response to Llywelyn's provocations. The king's patience finally snapped, Edward declaring Llywelyn ap Gruffydd, the Prince of Wales, to be a 'rebel' and 'disturber of his peace' on 12 November 1276. The English Closed Rolls listed, impatiently, Llywelyn's failures to pay the due homage to Edward, who would 'go against Llywelyn as his rebel and disturber of his peace'.[54]

One can hear the impatience of the Plantagenet king rising with every line. Despite last-minute protestations from Llywelyn, the Church declared he and his supporters to be excommunicate, and the principality placed under interdict.

So had war been inevitable? Perhaps Edward's coronation declaration suggests so, but equally there is a weight of evidence that Edward tried to avoid war. The failure to expand the Treaty (truce) of Montgomery into a lasting peace settlement, upon which the future of Anglo-Welsh relations could be built, was perhaps the starting point. The personalities of both Llywelyn, paranoid and wanting to hold what he'd gained, and Edward, proud and wanting to regain what he felt the Crown had lost – suggest an inevitable outcome. Llywelyn must have known the consequences of his failures to pay homage. He himself had acted against Maredudd ap Rhys Gryg of Deheubarth for such a breach, imprisoning him at Criccieth Castle.[55] That the Treaty of Montgomery built into the peace a tribute due to the Crown that the Prince of Wales would find difficult to meet, and made no account of Marcher lords seeking redress – meant the treaty (truce) set up the pathway to conflict.

From the standpoint of the twenty-first century, it seems obvious that England and Gwynedd were set from an early point after Montgomery for war, but it didn't seem like that at the time. Given Edward's leisurely return from his crusade, it seems that Wales was a long way from his thoughts. But when he did arrive back in England, Llywelyn would soon push his way up the young king's consciousness until the point he was left with little option but to declare him a rebel beyond the king's peace, a dangerous place to be in the thirteenth century. Prestwich is in no doubt that 'it was Llywelyn's attitude, not Edward's, that explains why war broke out in 1276'.[56]

So, some 200 years since Duke William set foot amongst the English, a reckoning had long been brewing between the Anglo-Norman state, born in 1066 and the descendants of the Britons who had long resisted English incursions into their mountainous lands; such a reckoning now beckoned. Edward gathered to himself an army to invade Wales, an army larger than any seen in the British islands since the time of his ancestor, Duke William. Anglo-Norman kings, Edward's ancestors, had made incursions into Wales: they had made punitive raids, they had encouraged their nobles to establish semi-independent fiefs in the Marches, but now Edward prepared with all the thoroughness of a man about a business he knew well. His crusade to the Holy Land had been still born for lack of resources and planning; his father's incursions into Wales had also been found wanting and he was not to make that mistake this time. This time the remaining lands of the Britons would be brought to heel.

Chapter Five

Instructions for the invasion of Wales were issued from Westminster on 13 November 1276. There would be three armies invading Wales. Firstly, William de Beauchamp, 9th Earl of Warwick, was dispatched to garrison Chester in the North. Roger de Mortimer, a man with land to reclaim, was sent to his base at Montgomery on the Severn to secure the counties of Shropshire, Staffordshire and Herefordshire adjacent to mid Wales. Lastly, Payn de Chaworth, Lord of Kidwelly, a crusading companion of Edward's, was sent to south and west Wales.[1] His loyal Savoyard friend Othon de Grandson having been recalled from sunnier climes, went to Montgomery to join the push into central Wales. As the winter let hold of its chilly grasp the opening moves were made, the first target being Llywelyn's new castle at Dolforwyn. Shortly before 8 March 1277, Master Bertram headed from London for the six-day journey to Montgomery, along with crossbowmen and miners, to prepare a siege, there to rendezvous with Grandson.[2] Master Bertram was an *ingeniator* of Gascon origin, who, as we saw, had been long in the service of the Crown, working with Jean de Mézos before his move to Savoy.

Othon de Grandson joined the banner of Henri de Lacy, Earl of Lincoln and great-grandson of Amédée IV de Savoie, and the central army in Shropshire, commanding a troop of knights in January 1277. Edward had, late in 1276, sent to France for war horses, seventy-five being noted as passing through the French port of Wissant.[3] Morris suggested the final number received was more than 100 in total.[4] Grandson himself caused two destriers[5] and thirty mounted crossbowmen to be brought from Gascony, where he'd spent much recent time, also by way of Wissant in France.[6] When a medieval army mustered, it involved a lot of work over many days, lists to be made of the men, pay agreed and arms to be procured. Some 200,000 crossbow bolts were ordered from the Forest of Dean. Edward meant business; he'd learned in the failed crusade and before that preparation was everything. Marcher Lord Roger de Mortimer was accompanied by Henri de Lacy, who had twenty-five knights under his command, divided amongst eight bannerets.[7] Henri de Lacy himself had six knights and twenty-three troopers, Jean de Vesci had four knights and ten troopers, Othon de Grandson, a banneret, had also four knights and ten troopers, smaller numbers were divided amongst Guillaume de Leyburn, Robert FitzRoger, Jean de Vaux, Geoffrey de Lucy and lastly Jean de Bohun. Grandson had been assigned to Lacy's command; the other knights owed him feudal obligation – Grandson did not.

Henri de Lacy, 3rd Earl of Lincoln, was himself descended from a Count of Savoy, and so related to his king by common Savoyard ancestry. His mother was

Alésia de Saluce,[8] the daughter of Béatrice de Savoie, who in turn was the daughter of Count Amédée IV de Savoie – thus making Henri a great-grandson of the Savoyard. Edward, meanwhile, was the son of Alianor de Provence, herself a daughter of another Béatrice de Savoie who was a sister of the same Count Amédée IV de Savoie. Such were the intricate ways in which the ruling families of Savoy and England were interrelated in the thirteenth century.

This force pushed up the Upper Severn to the castle at Dolforwyn – recently and provocatively constructed by Llywelyn and menacing the border – and laid siege to the castle. Othon de Grandson was not the only Savoyard invading Llywelyn's lands in the spring of 1277; indeed, the invasion of Wales might be said to have more than just a hint of Savoy. Whilst Othon was amongst those laying siege to Dolforwyn, a messenger came to him on 3 April 1277: it was Jean de Bonvillars.[9] Jean was Othon's brother-in-law, married to Othon's sister Agnès.[10] Bonvillars was (and still is) a small village just over three miles (five kilometres) north of Grandson by the Lac de Neuchâtel. Bonvillars' father, Henri, had been chatelain at Rue for Pierre de Savoie until 1266. His brother, Henri de Bonvillars, a Cluniac dean responsible for the convent at the beautiful Romanesque monastery of Payerne, across the Lac de Neuchâtel, was later to come to England to be prior of Bermondsey, and later, its mother priory at Wenlock, in Shropshire,[11, 12] just across the border from Dolforwyn.[13] Nonetheless, on that April morning at Dolforwyn, it was Jean de Bonvillars who was galloping up to the knights laying siege to the castle.

Earlier, another messenger between Edward and Othon had been yet a further Savoyard, Guillaume de Cicon.[14] We first hear of Guillaume de Cicon in an archival reference dated 13 November 1276, the very day following Edward's declaration of Llywelyn as an outlaw.[15] This would have been the time Othon was away on Edward's business in Gascony and shows Guillaume de Cicon as a messenger from Othon to Edward. He was a knight from Cicon in the Franche-Comté de Bourgogne, then attached to Savoy by marriage of Alix, Countess of Burgundy, to Philippe, Count of Savoy. Cicon lies around twenty miles (thirty kilometres) to the north of Pontarlier, by the village of Vanclans. Today, extraordinarily little remains of the castle, just several stone steps, but the House of Cicon had been long in Burgundian history. The castle was held for the bishopric of Besançon by the Maison de Cicon from the eleventh century. The arms of the family that Cicon would have born into Wales was a black horizontal band across a field of yellow. Pontarlier would be one of the towns, along with the nearby Château de Joux, that Count Othon IV would pay homage for to Edward, in 1281,[16] in the same way that Philippe had paid homage for Savoyard castles in 1273. Such were the interests of both Savoy and Franche-Comté bound up with the Plantagenet monarchy of England. A recent ancestor, Othon de Cicon, had been with the Fourth Crusade that had sacked Constantinople in 1204 and founded a fiefdom on the island of Euboea at Karystos. The Latin-Greek origins of Cicon will become fundamental to the castles in Wales, particularly at Caernarfon.

Along with Grandson, Bonvillars and Cicon was Gerard de Saint-Laurent, a knight who had also served with Edward on crusade in the Holy Land, in 1271–2. Gerard received arrears of wages, including a payment for a horse during his time at Acre, and expenses totalling seventy-two marks.[17] Taylor thought that his name might relate to Saint-Laurent-en-Grandvaux, in the Jura.[18] However, Chapuisat records a family of this name in Lausanne earlier in the century, these St Laurents providing officers for the Bishops of Lausanne and taking their name from a quarter in the city. Today the baroque Eglise Saint Laurent lies at the heart of the Saint Laurent quarter of Lausanne.[19] These four knights, as we shall see later, go on to fulfil key positions for Edward in Wales: Grandson as Justiciar of North Wales, Bonvillars, Cicon and Saint-Laurent as constables of Harlech, Rhuddlan, Conwy and Flint. We will return to focus on each knight as we see their differing impacts on these castles of north Wales in turn.

However, that is as yet for the future. In the meantime, we have the siege of Dolforwyn, a siege that ended with its surrender on 8 April 1277. The builders had not yet fully completed the castle and it lacked something vital for its defence: a water supply. The Welsh had neglected to dig a well and so very quickly ran out of water. The fallen stronghold was left in the possession of Edward's Welsh ally Gruffydd ap Gwenwynwyn of Powys, allowing him to fully regain control of Powys Wenwynwyn.[20] Indeed, Gruffydd ap Gwenwynwyn had been instrumental in bringing many Welshmen over to Edward's cause. Prestwich describes the First Welsh War as, in part 'a civil war in Wales',[21] given the many Welshmen who fought on Edward's side, Gruffydd ap Gwenwynwyn and Dafydd ap Gruffydd being perhaps the most notable. The extent to which we should not treat Wales and Gwynedd as synonyms is evidenced by the number of Welshmen serving with the royal armies of the First Welsh War: some 9,000 of 15,000 men. As Adam Chapman also said, the war 'was as much a conflict between Welshmen, as much as it was a conflict between Welsh and English'.[22]

With the fall of Dolforwyn, Llywelyn's position in mid Wales proved untenable; by May he had vacated Brecon. Also, by 3 May, Henri de Lacy and Roger de Mortimer had moved the forty miles (sixty-four kilometres) on to Builth, where Mortimer had once been constable.[23] Builth had been specifically a part of his appanage, so Edward immediately instructed them to begin reconstruction of his castle destroyed by the Welsh prince seventeen years earlier in 1260. In the south Payn de Chaworth had been making good progress, bringing Deheubarth back to the king's allegiance, helped by local lords like Gruffydd ap Maredudd of Ceredigion and Rhys ap Maredudd (son of the imprisoned Maredudd ap Rhys Gryg) of Ystrad Tywi and thus gaining, much without a fight. By 16 May 1277, Chaworth was able to list those who would come to Edward at Worcester to pay due homage: the aforementioned, plus Rhys Wyndod, also from Ystrad Tywi, and Rhys Fychan ap Rhys Maelgwn and Cynan ap Maredudd also from Ceredigion. This swift collapse of Llywelyn's authority over and control of Welsh lordships, as established by the Treaty of Montgomery, is a marker of the First Welsh War.

Henri de Lacy's attackers had caused some damage at Dolforwyn; it seems likely that siege engines such as trebuchets had been employed, since stone balls have been subsequently discovered in and around the castle. The castle was by Savoyard and recent English standards a rather basic affair. There was no powerful gatehouse or flanking mural towers, so the attacking force was able to sack the small nearby town and set up those siege engines to good effect. The latest castle-building developments of the thirteenth century had not yet reached Welshmen.[24] A Cadw artist's impression of 2002 by Ivan Lapper shows the small town alight, a trebuchet knocking lumps out of the curtain wall and the castle itself on fire.[25] The square *donjon* bears the scars of Master Bertram's siege engines to this day. As had fallen Benauges in 1253 so had fallen Dolforwyn in 1277 to Master Bertram's artillery. The primitive nature, by thirteenth century standards, of the castle built by Llywelyn at Dolforwyn is further evidenced that the repairs carried out following the siege have outlasted the original work.[26] Jean de Bonvillars arrived at Dolforwyn on 3 April 1277 with a message for Othon de Grandson and gave likely rise to a reply.[27]

The *Calendar of Ancient Correspondence Concerning Wales* by Sir John Goronwy Edwards, published in 1935, interprets the letter to Edward:[28]

> The sender reports that they laid siege to the castle of Dolvoreyn [sic] on the Wednesday in Easter Week [31 March 1277] … Informs the king that when the castle comes into his hands – *il auera mester de grant amendement* – it will need much repair. Wherefore there will be need of some man who will take these matters in hand, and will loyally employ the king's money. For if the sender employs Master Bertram for the work, he fears that Master Bertram will devise too many things, and perhaps the king's money will not be so well employed as it needs to be. Asks the king's will in this matter. Thanks the king for the letter sent by the hand of John de Bevilar, which was of great assistance, for the sender's force looks like the force of a great lord and this cannot be done without money.[29]

Edwards suggests that the Earl of Lincoln might be the letter's author, but his index also lists Grandson as a potential source.[30] In addition to Edwards', perhaps ambiguous, attribution of either, Henri de Lacy or Othon de Grandson, several writers have variously suggested a number of potential authors.[31] Discounting Tanquerey, who'd suggested Roger de Mortimer, as he misidentifies the date and recipient, what reasons do we have to suppose it was Grandson rather than Lacy?

Firstly, the extreme familiarity of the greeting '*A sun tres cher seignur saluz*', which translates as 'To my very dear Lord, *Salut!* (Warmest greetings)'. Both Othon and Henri were members of Edward's household – Othon having been brought to England as a boy by Pierre de Savoie, and Henri educated at court. Both men went on to serve Edward for many years, but Edward and Othon, as contemporaries, had in effect been raised together since boyhood, whereas Henri was over ten years their junior. Secondly, the original letter carried by Bonvillars from Edward to Dolforwyn was to Othon, and the reply is immediate, which implies a receipt and return. Thirdly, all the men with the Earl of Lincoln were the 'king's men'; they were his vassals, except Othon[32] who was very much Edward's special friend. It may seem natural for Edward to write to Othon. Othon, as Edward's lifelong friend and confidant, would appear to have a greater interest in the protection of the king's purse than the young Earl of Lincoln, and greater access to a solution, namely the hiring of a better mason. Certainly, we can know in what esteem Grandson was held by Edward at this point: in March 1278, he'd described him as someone who could 'do his will ... better and more advantageously' than 'others about him', as well as 'if he himself were to attend to the matters in person'.[33] Othon de Grandson, along with Robert Burnell, was, perhaps, the man Edward trusted above all others to act on his behalf. Taylor points out that other letters from the Earl of Lincoln are formally dated with the regnal year – this one is not.[34] Then also, we have the certification of the wages for Master Bertram at Dolforwyn being *par la veue sire Otes de Grauntson*' – 'by the wish of Sir Othon de Grandson'.[35] But perhaps the best evidence is that the archive records that in August it was again Othon showing a particular interest in castle-building – this time, as we will see, at Flint. Prestwich agreed, writing, 'Taylor plausibly argued [the letter] was from Othon de Grandson' before confirming 'Othon's influence was important in the choice that Edward made of the Savoyard Maître Jacques de Saint Georges'.[36]

Given all of this, it is most likely that Grandson was the author of the letter. It is this letter that is the 'smoking gun' which gives rise to what happens next. King Edward I summons the Master Mason he'd been introduced to in Saint-Georges, in June 1273, Maître Jacques. Dolforwyn Castle has been described as the 'last Welsh castle', given its native Welsh construction. The coming Welsh castles would all be Savoyard.

But, in the Welsh wars, the siege of Dolforwyn was a border preliminary; the real task of subduing Llywelyn and Gwynedd would now begin. Edward's initial feudal muster required a rendezvous at Worcester in July 1277,[37] followed by a division of his forces for a twin-pronged assault on Gwynedd. A smaller force, perhaps 200 men, were to come from the south, starting in Carmarthen. The main force would travel west from the old Roman city of Chester, along the coast and the four *cantrefi*, to the Conwy and Gwynedd. Payn de Chaworth would command the southern army, the Earl of Warwick the northern. With Payn would be the king's brother, Edmund, Earl of Lancaster, and with Warwick would be the king himself. Edward had prepared well: he had arranged for the ships of the Cinque Ports to sail and meet him at Chester, a circuitous voyage indeed from the Channel.

That summer, as the ships docked, and horseman rode into the city from the south-east, Chester thronged with voices and the sound of military preparation not seen since the legions had departed. One can only imagine the cries of the knights, their squires, the foot soldiers, the sailors amidst the usual panoply of merchants, innkeepers and citizens of Chester. The twice-weekly markets at St Peter's church and the abbey would have been overwhelmed by the travelling host. Some 700 sailors would have joined an army of nearly 3,000, English voices mixing with Savoyard and Gascon. Chester's normal trade with Wales would have been interrupted by the newcomers, but more than made up for by their demands for corn at Eastgate, fish from the Dee estuary and meat from the cattle grazed on Saltney marsh from the assembling army. The smell of woodsmoke, the sound of clanging from blacksmiths re-shoeing warhorses, fixing coats of mail, fashioning crossbow bolts and arrows and tellingly sharpening swords – the sounds of an army preparing to invade would have carried across the Dee floating on the wind to the Welsh. Edward arrived at Chester from Worcester, by way of Shrewsbury, on 15 July 1277, aware that his army would soon exhaust the supplies available, and that the feudal obligation to serve owed to him by much of his army was time limited. Just one week after his arrival by the Dee, on or about 21 July 1277, Edward and his army moved west.

Some 2,576 men, including 120 from Lancashire, 100 archers from Macclesfield, Cheshire, 640 men from Staffordshire and Shropshire and 1,000 foot spearmen and archers from Cheshire gathered their arms and began the invasion of Llywelyn's lands. Along with them went Dafydd ap Gruffydd and the 220 men of his bodyguard – Welshmen. So, along with the English infantry were Welshmen, Savoyard knights, Gascon crossbowmen – this was very much a multinational force of many tongues, the infantry largely speaking English and Welsh, the cavalry largely Norman-French, Arpitan and Occitan. The army marched beneath no English flag, since no English flag was yet in use, the army marched behind the king's banner. Edward's banner was three golden lions *passant guardant* (three golden lions on a red field); the banner had been brought into use by his great-uncle Richard Cœur de Lion and represented the Kingdom of England, the Duchies of Normandy and Aquitaine. The lion had long been an emblem of the Anglo-Norman kings, and the lions were now marching across the Dee toward Wales. Behind the three lions came the yellow band and six yellow crosslets on a red field of the Earl of Warwick, the three red chevrons on a yellow field of Red Gilbert, Earl of Gloucester, the blue and yellow chequerboard of Jean de Warenne, Earl of Surrey, the three red *coquilles St Jacques* crossed diagonally across blue white stripes of Othon de Grandson, the white *coquille St Jacques* atop a black cross on yellow background of Jean de Grailly, the three golden *caveçons* beneath a red lion of Geoffrey de Joinville,[38] the black cross on a yellow field of Jean de Vesci – the full colourful panoply of Anglo-Norman, Savoyard and even French heraldry glinting in the summer sun as they progressed across the Dee and followed the three lions into Wales. In 1300, *The Song of Caerlaverock* gave us a description of a later campaign, but its imagery of 'many a beautiful pennon fixed to a lance', the sound of 'neighing horses' and of wagons loaded with 'provisions, and sacks of tents and pavilions' paints the picture we need.[39]

Davies writes of the army: 'It was a remarkable display of the capacity of the nascent nation-state to mobilize its resources for a coordinated and centralized war-effort.'[40] Finance for the expedition came, of course, from the Riccardi of Lucca. Thomas Bek's Wardrobe accounts for the year 20 November 1276 to 20 November 1277 show a receipt of £22,476 (equivalent today circa £16.5 million), against a war commitment of £20,220. The following year, 20 November 1277 to 20 November 1278 shows a receipt of a further £18,233 (today over £13 million).[41] Morris calculated the cost of the war to be £23,149, the total Riccardi receipts for these years amounting to £40,709. We can be clear: without the Riccardi di Lucca this 'coordinated and centralized war-effort' would have been very difficult to achieve. Edward's army would be something relatively new in Britain as it was formed of many paid professionals rather than just the customary feudal host; for this he had the liquid resources of the Riccardi. Sure, there would be the feudal host, but now the king needed a more competent group of men-at-arms who might be able to provide extended service with greater technical expertise, such as the crossbowmen – what we would call a professional army.[42]

Edward had seen his father's expeditions into Wales founder upon the rock of Welsh resistance but compounded by a lack of preparation upon the part of the English. Faced with the sheer power of the Anglo-Norman war machine, the Welsh had fallen back upon the natural defences offered by their mountainous lands, fallen back upon hit-and-run guerrilla warfare. They had descended upon English columns advancing into Wales with cries and missiles emerging from the mists of the mountains only to disappear when a number of the attacking knights and soldiers lay dead and wounded. The Welsh had perfected the weapon of being the wasp that continually stings the dog until, maddened, it runs for cover.

But this time it would be different: marching into Wales, Edward would have passed the site of the Battle of Ewloe, where his grandfather Henry had come to grief at the hands of another Welsh prince, Owain Gwynedd, in 1157.[43] Henry had been defeated by ambush in a densely wooded valley, which no doubt influenced Edward cutting his forest road deep into Wales. The Welsh had built a castle at Ewloe, commanding the road from England, but apparently and perhaps sensibly, given what had happened at Dolforwyn, had abandoned it prior to the invasion.

For with Edward's army that summer of 1277 marched new warriors – armies of woodcutters, carpenters, diggers and masons. Edwards counted no fewer than five hundred woodcutters dedicated to the forest road, accompanied by over two thousand others destined to build castles. Add Chapter Two Endnote to J. G. Edwards. 1951. The Building of Flint. The Flintshire Historical Society XII: 12. A peak of 500 woodcutters in the week from 2 August 1277 and a peak of 2,057 others in the week from 9 August 1277. Edward had learned the lessons of previous campaigns, and indeed of his ill-fated crusade. As early as June, Lucasio and the Riccardi were ordered to pay forty marks to Robert de Belvero and William de Perton, that they might collect masons and carpenters 'as many as [they] can get and in whatsoever works or service they may be, and to conduct them whither'.[44]

Firstly, the army made for Flint, on the Welsh side of the Dee, where Edward decided it would be useful to build an initial stronghold from which to proceed along the coast. The chronicler Thomas Wykes described the land between Chester and the lands of Llywelyn as *'silva tantæ densitatis et amplitudinis'*, that is a 'dense forest of great size'.[45] Just over a thousand years earlier the Romans had similarly advanced into the Teutoburg Forest of Germany and been annihilated by Germanic tribes in tactics similar to those now employed by the Welsh. But 1277 was not AD 9, Edward was no Publius Quinctilius Varus: he had brought with him those 1,800 axemen and proceeded to build himself a clear road along the coast as he went. So, the army moved slowly into Wales to the sound of axes ripping into wood and trees falling. To any Welshmen within hearing, this must have sounded like a monster was coming to devour Wales.

By 25 July the army had hacked its way through to Flint, where it paused to build the planned advance headquarters, from which to move farther along the coast.[46] Edward chose the Flint site rather than occupying native Ewloe Castle, since Flint could be resupplied by sea, whereas Ewloe could not – an example of the king's intention to make recovery of the four *cantrefi* permanent. Following the war, Edward was described as granting land to the brothers of Llywelyn, Dafydd and Owain, as being 'in the camp of the Flint near Basingwerk'.[47] Basingwerk was the site of a Cistercian abbey just under five miles (eight kilometres) farther down the coast. According to legend, the name Flint came as an English corruption of the Latin word *'fluentum'*, meaning stream. But this legend takes no note of the archival records, where two later entries in the Calendar of Welsh Roles[48] point elsewhere: on 3 December 1277, Flint is referred to as *'Le Chaylou'*,[49] and on 18 January 1278 it is referred to as *'Le Cayllou'*.[50] The modern French word for a small pebble or stone is *caillou*; therefore, we can see that the scribes in Shrewsbury and Westminster translated the word *'flint'* into French, and that *'flint'* referred to 'stone' or 'rock', not a corruption of 'stream'. Whilst the area around the Flint site is marshy and wet, the castle itself would be built upon a small stone platform – a Flint – hence the name.

Construction soon began on the small stone platform, or more accurately perhaps, the land surrounding it. We have reference to a payment made, upon the recommendation of none other than Othon de Grandson, on 10 August, to build a palisade around the works there, to better defend the builders from Welsh attacks.[51] As we noted earlier, that it is Othon de Grandson ordering construction work at Flint which adds further credence to the belief that he is the author of the letter to Edward written at Dolforwyn. Morris describes the building works at Flint that summer: 'A strong post was thus made, though the works were but yet temporary and of wood, for there was no time to prepare stone.'[52] Others have, to a greater or lesser degree, made claims for something more solid begun in the four months that remained of the 1277 building season.[53] Edwards reasonably deduced from pay accounts, at Chester then Flint, that work at Flint had begun by "about 21 July [1277], thus making the building season a short 14 to 15 weeks.[54] By analysis of the building records, Edwards pointed to three stages of construction, a first stage in 1277, a second from 1278 to 1280 and then a third to completion in 1286. For 1277 a determined start does seem to have been made, albeit one where payments for carpenters and diggers far outweigh those for stonemasons.[55] Morris set the scene of the defence at Flint that summer: 'Imbert, with his crossbows, and the Macclesfield archers, had the post of honour in defending the works.'[56] What we are seeing here at Flint in July and August 1277 is analogous to a movie portrayal of the US Cavalry constructing a fort deep in hostile 'Indian territory'. Morris added: the purchase of great numbers of quarrels means that there was plenty to do in the way of beating off the Welsh.'[57] The army was much in need of a palisade, as prescribed by Grandson, and arrows for the archers. Flint was, that summer, the frontline of the invasion of Wales. Taylor confirms that the workers and works at Flint were 'treated as a military unit and placed under a knight'.[58] The Welsh chroniclers are also clear in their description of the works at Flint, recording that Edward 'fortified a court in Flint, with huge ditches around it'.[59]

So, who were the Welsh the army encountered in Wales that summer? Firstly, we need to say that the Welsh fought on both sides, that the English army had many Welsh voices within it. Adding to its substantial Savoyard contingent, this English army, in addition to speaking many dialects of French, spoke an awful lot of Welsh. Edward had recruited many Welsh soldiers from the Marches, men from Gwerthrynion, Maelienydd, Elfael, Builth, Radnor and Brecon.[60] Beverley Smith goes on to give us their names, these Welsh captains of the English army: Meurig ap Llewelyn of Brecon, Ifor ap Gruffydd of Elfael, Einion ap Madog of Builth, all led by Hywel ap Meurig of Radnor.[61] This Welsh army under Hywel ap Meurig amounted to some 2,700 footmen raised in Brecon and Radnor. Hywel ap Meurig had been passing intelligence of Llywelyn's castle at Dolforwyn to Edward since before the war.[62] But what did these Welsh soldiers look like? Christopher Rothero paints a vivid picture of 'migrant tribesmen, half warriors, half farmers'.[63] A Welsh chieftain would not have differed much from his ancestors who fought the Roman legions, equipped perhaps with a round wooden shield in the like of a Saxon or a Viking, rudimentary segmented armour around his upper body and armed with sword and spear. His ancestors had succumbed to the Roman, but not the Saxon and not entirely to the Norman. Gerald of Wales, writing a century earlier, gives us a description of 'mobile and lightly armed' men, who wore 'no armour at all' and 'who always prefer to do battle on rough terrain'. He went on to describe soldiers who would not take prisoners, but 'cut off their heads' and rather than taking captives for ransom 'massacre them'.[64] Around 1300 a Flemish observer spoke of soldiers whose 'weapons were bows, arrows and swords' and 'javelins' but who 'never saw them wearing armour'.[65] They were, as Churchill admiringly described them, 'hardy and unsubdued'[66] and 'valiant Ancient Britons'.[67] They belonged to what R. R. Davies called a 'heroic society'.[68]

In the south Edward's younger brother, Edmund Crouchback, Earl of Lancaster, had joined Payn de Chaworth and taken command of the southern army. They faced much less in the way of obstacles than the northern army and by 25 July had reached Aberystwyth from Carmarthen. On 1 August, within a week of arrival, on the mid Welsh coast they began to build a castle.[69] The castle was begun by the mouth of the Rheidol and originally named in contemporary records as Lampader or Lampadarn.[70] Edward had given prior approval for a quick beginning of work to Master Henry of Hereford.[71] The wider West Country this time provided the source for the labour: 120 masons and 120 carpenters from Somerset, Dorset and Wiltshire, soon followed by a barrel of some 6,000 nails, indicating that, like at Flint, the early works were of wood. They came by way of Bristol, thence by boat to Carmarthen, then on into mid Wales.

What was created at Aberystwyth was a concentric castle of a very flattened lozenge shape, with the main entrance being a great twin-towered gatehouse on the eastern side. Work was concentrated into the first three years of the build, the 1277–9 building seasons. The great gatehouse will be of interest as we go on, possibly being the means of a transmission of its type from Caerffili to Harlech, as Malcolm Hislop has plausibly suggested.[72]

Meanwhile in the north, Edward, on 16 August, renewed his drive into Wales from Flint. He left behind him there a garrison under the command of Reginald de Grey, with orders to protect and defend both Flint and the forest road. Edward was carefully attending to his lines of communication. The works underway, from 25 July, at Flint, were left with *ingeniator* Master Richard of Chester[73] along with some 720 *fossatores* or diggers, 330 carpenters, 320 woodsmen, 200 masons, twelve smiths and lastly ten charcoal burners.[74] The stonemasons from Lincolnshire, Nottinghamshire and Leicestershire[75] appear to have been under Master Thomas of Grantham, but with Master Richard in overall charge. Reginald de Grey was protecting this work along with Robert de Tatesdale, Aymer de St Amand, Alex de Balliol, John d'Eyvil, Roger de la Zouche and no less than sixty-seven accompanying troopers. Master Richard appears for the first time in the archive that summer of 1277 at Flint and has been the subject of an excellent re-examination of his contribution by historian Rick Turner.[76] He is almost certainly the effective Master of Works at Flint for 1277 and into 1278, but this does not mean he was the designer of the castle, as we shall see.[77]

So, with work at Flint begun and the forest road protected, the axemen began again the work of clearing a road to the west, a road wide enough apparently for a man to loose an arrow from one side to the other. The road now gorging itself upon the Welsh forest has been described, perhaps with little exaggeration, as being wide enough to accommodate four modern three-lane motorways.[78] Within a week, around 19 August, the army had progressed forward to Rhuddlan, one time Saxon and then Norman township on the River Clwyd and only a few miles downstream from the cathedral town of St Asaph. Henry III had preferred the nearby hilltop position of Dyserth for his castle, but as with Flint, Edward considered resupply by sea a key requirement. The king had learned from Llywelyn's destruction of his father's castles in Wales that in time of revolt the ability to quickly resupply a garrison was vital in its defence.

Rhuddlan first appears in history, in 796 when King Offa of Mercia won a battle by the Clwyd and later it's thought that Edward the Elder had founded a Saxon *burh* at Rhuddlan back in 921, although the precise location is unknown. The conquest and reconquest of the region is shown again as by 1063 it had once more become a part of the lands of Gruffydd ap Llywelyn, Prince of Gwynedd, only for him to lose it and his palace there burned by Earl Harold – the same Harold who would soon lose his life and England to the Normans. Literally Rhuddlan, named Roelent in the 1086 Domesday Book, meant 'red bank', which described the colour of the soil making up the banks of the River Clwyd. What was then at Rhuddlan was a small Norman settlement protected by a motte and bailey castle, built by Robert de Rhuddlan in 1073.[79] Later, in 1258, a Dominican friary had been founded.[80] Edward lodged, during his time at Rhuddlan, with the Dominicans, a record of payment for which survives, along with a donation towards the glazing of their church – always an expensive thing in the Middle Ages.[81] The next year, Edward ordered that the prior and his friars at Rhuddlan should have wood from the forest and fish from the river and be able to 'grind freely at the king's mill there at the king's will'.[82] Rhuddlan commanded a bridging point of the Clwyd, but in addition to the coastal route east–west from the Dee to the Conwy, it sat at the head of Clwyd Valley and its route inland to Denbigh and Ruthun. The Normans had thought this a good place for a castle, and likewise Edward, although he would build a little way from the original fortress.

The evolution of castle design, between the eleventh and thirteenth century, can be easily seen from the story of the castles in and around Rhuddlan: the Norman motte and bailey, Henry III's at Dyserth and then Edward's again at Rhuddlan. Originally, it was thought enough to place a castle high atop an artificial hill or mound: the motte. Then, as these castles fell, grew the need to build on higher ground to take advantage of nature's rocky outcrops as at Dyserth. But, as these higher placed castles proved vulnerable to a sustained siege, then a coastal location seemed to offer the chance of resupply. Though Rhuddlan was not by the sea, Edward and Jacques would bring the sea to Rhuddlan. There is no record of work commencing in 1277 at Rhuddlan beyond the planning stage, and what Taylor called a 'veritable army of diggers'.[83] That Edward should want to build a castle at Rhuddlan is unsurprising: not only was it a key point on the road from Chester to the Conwy, but '*Rothelan*' was specifically named way back in 1254, when Edward was a boy, as being his own, in his appanage.

Another week of westward cutting and hacking through the forest finally found Edward and his army, of now 15,000 men, by the wide expanse of the Conwy estuary. He had recovered the four *cantrefi* lost to Llywelyn, but the Prince of Wales retreated to the mountain vastness of Snowdonia and a position by Penmaenmawr. Henry III had constructed a castle at Deganwy in 1245, as the frontline of the realm, but this had been destroyed by Llywelyn in 1263. Edward had no intention of playing into the prince's hands and attempting a river crossing and frontal assault on the Welsh mountain strongholds. He had something considerably more effective in mind: he meant to starve Llywelyn into submission.

The four *cantrefi* recovered, work underway at Flint and planned for Rhuddlan, the forest road from the Dee to the Conwy secure, now Edward gathered a force, under Othon de Grandson and Jean de Vesci, of 2,000 foot and horse, collected by the Cinque Ports fleet at the Great Orme. Some 360 harvesters were also taken to the island, along with the army.[84] Anglesey was the Welsh breadbasket, it was where Llywelyn grew the wheat that would feed his people for the long winter ahead.[85] The force landed with the fields still full of unharvested cereal. The corn was harvested, but to English, not Welsh granaries; for Llywelyn it was a grievous blow. Welsh cattle were gathered from upland areas above Flint and Rhuddlan to feed Edward's army;[86] there would be no repetition of previous English armies in Wales failing for lack of supplies.

By the late summer of 1277 Llywelyn had Edward to his front, across the Conwy, with a large army that had confiscated the four *cantrefi* from him. To his right and rear was Edmund Crouchback and his southern army at Aberystwyth, to his left he had another English army under Vesci and Grandson – and worst of all he had lost his grain supply. There was much of Caesar's conquest of Gaul and Alesia about the campaign. With Llywelyn playing the unfortunate role of Vercingetorix to Edward's Caesar, it was the methodical subjugation of an enemy by resource denial. Clausewitz many centuries later spoke of the need 'to take possession of his [the enemy] material and other sources of strength, and to direct our operations against the places where most of these resources are concentrated'. Edward was following Caesar and foreshadowing Clausewitz.[87] He had invaded the principality and, unlike those that had come before, he had taken careful, methodical steps to slowly pin Llywelyn against his mountain home and encircle him in a chain-mailed vice without the resources to resist – it was as they say game, set and match.

Llywelyn made it known that he was prepared to submit to Edward – he had little choice. Edward could have pressed on and destroyed the Welsh prince, but he chose quite deliberately not to. The bad weather of autumn was coming, a frontal assault on Llywelyn would be costly and time consuming, and most tellingly he had the Welsh prince where he wanted him. Peace made sense for Edward too. Accordingly, the banner of the three lions retired from the Conwy to the Dominican friary at Rhuddlan on 12 September 1277, to await formal negotiations of a peace.

The English commissioners who negotiated what became known as the Treaty of Aberconwy[88] were Antony Bek, Robert de Tibetot and none other than Othon de Grandson – the Savoyard had been at the siege of Dolforwyn, instrumental at Flint, helped seize the Welsh harvest and now was a key negotiator of the peace. Anthony Bek, like Grandson, was a veteran of Edward's crusade and would later be rewarded with the Bishopric of Durham. Likewise, Tibetot had accompanied Edward on crusade and would be rewarded with being appointed Justiciar of

South Wales. The commissioners were authorized to negotiate on behalf of the king on 2 November and crossed the Conwy to Aberconwy Abbey. The quiet of the Cistercian abbey provided a backdrop for the weeklong negotiations, Bishop Anian of St Asaph acting as mediator, and the abbot acting, as in the past, for Llywelyn, along with his emissaries Tudur ap Ednyfed and Goronwy ap Heilin.[89]

A perhaps unusual transaction occurred at this time. Financiers of the war, the Riccardi, had followed Edward's army into north Wales. Orlandino da Pogio was one of their number. During or immediately after negotiations at the abbey of Aberconwy the Riccardi undertook to buy fleeces from the abbot and got a safe conduct to transport twenty sacks of wool back to Chester. The Riccardi were clearly not ones to let a war get in the way of a good business opportunity.[90]

The Treaty of Aberconwy was agreed on 9 November 1277, the treaty was sealed by Llywelyn on the same day and ratified by Edward on 10 November at Rhuddlan. That day Llywelyn had crossed the Conwy to make his way to Rhuddlan to finally pay a homage to the king, homage asked of the Welsh prince by the Severn in 1272. He would have knelt before Edward, kissed his hand and given the oath of fealty. The terms of the peace were indeed Carthaginian: the four *cantrefi* would once more belong to the King of England. Thus, the continual passing of the Perfeddwlad between the Plantagenets and Gwynedd in the thirteenth century ended with Edward in possession of what had been his appanage. In a little over sixty years, it had been taken by his grandfather John in 1211, lost again to Llywelyn Fawr in 1216, retaken from Dafydd by Henry in 1247, granted to Edward in 1254, retaken by Llywelyn ap Gruffydd in 1264 and now lastly retaken by Edward – truly the middle country. Two of the *cantrefi* would be temporarily leased to Llywelyn's wayward and unreliable brother Dafydd – these being Rhufoniog (centred on Denbigh) and Dyffryn Clwyd (centred on Ruthun). The coastal and strategically vital *cantrefi* of Rhos and Tegeingl, Edward retained for himself. Llywelyn would have to travel to England, to London, to swear fealty to Edward after firstly having done so at Rhuddlan. Although Llywelyn could still style himself Prince of Wales, the majority of the Welsh nobility would now be Edward's vassals, not Llywelyn's. Lastly and by no means least, Llywelyn was required to pay the sum of £50,000[91] as a fine for his disobedience – although this was soon remitted.[92] Dafydd was given the two *cantrefi*, and recognition would be given also to the rights of Owain Goch and Rhodri – Edward was imposing his peace between the brothers ap Gruffydd. Llywelyn was made to release Owain Goch from imprisonment; he would live out his life, the next five years probably, on the Llyn peninsula. The vanquished of Bryn Derwin in 1255 had finally achieved a restitution of sorts, courtesy of Edward. As a footnote, Llywelyn was after all allowed to marry the daughter of Simon de Montfort, the ceremony taking place at Worcester in 1278. In the end, Llywelyn paid homage to Edward and swore an oath of fealty. One is bound to ask at this point what he had gained from not doing so at Rhyd Chwima five years earlier. His subsequent actions had lost him the four *cantrefi*, his suzerainty of all but Gwynedd and a good deal of blood and treasure.

Llywelyn ap Gruffydd was again what he had originally been, and in Edward's mind, what he should always remain – Edward's man. Perhaps a sign that, for Edward, the Welsh matter was now considered concluded was his dispatch in the early months of 1278 of Othon de Grandson once more to Gascony.[93] Having ended Llywelyn's disobedience, Edward paid renewed attention to something he might have considered more important than Gwynedd: the stability of Gascony and the return to him of lost adjacent ancestral lands.

Upon first returning to England as king in 1274, Edward had begun his first castle works at that great royal castle at the centre of kingly power, the Tower of London. His father had expanded the castle greatly from its Norman origins, spending £9,000 (the equivalent of £4.8 million today), but had left the work incomplete – and what is more, the gatehouse had collapsed.[94] Matthew Paris had told of a gateway collapsing on the evening of the Feast of Saint Georges (23 April 1240) to be partially rebuilt but collapsing again just a year later. The tale emphasizes the care needed in raising fortifications in the thirteenth century, and the importance of preparation, good materials and above all the right masons be recruited.[95] Edward sought the completion of the castle into the concentric fortress that is still much visible today. A new outer wall, a new moat, a new water gate and lastly a new outer gate complete with barbican involved much work. Edward employed the services of Flemish Master Walter in surrounding the castle with its large new moat, which measured some 160 feet across (49 metres). The new impressive moat even went so far as to help feed the garrison when stocked with pike.[96] Edward learned the necessity of employing just the right man for the job – Master Walter was an 'expert moat-builder'.[97] Chief mason was Robert of Beverley,[98] who had undertaken much work for Henry at Westminster Abbey.[99]

In 1271, Master Robert became the Surveyor of the Royal Works at the Tower of London, the castles of Windsor, Rochester and Hadleigh, and the manors of Guildford, Kempton and Havering. He designed the Byward and Middle towers of the Tower of London, complete with their beautiful internal vaults. Robert was a consummate architect and in his effigy of Henry III he is partly responsible for our image of the king. Alongside Beverley, Edward seems to have brought a mason with him from the Holy Land, Brother John of Saint Thomas of Acre. The creation of the enlarged concentric walled Tower of London cost Edward £21,000, more than double the expenditure there of his father. The work took eleven years to complete, from 1275, the year after his coronation and before the Welsh wars, until 1286, after both Welsh wars. Prestwich suggests that Robert of Beverley would have been the more obvious choice as builder of the castles in Wales, but he was tied up in the works in London, and unlike the Savoyard, Maître Jacques, he had no proven record in constructing a number of castles simultaneously.[100] So with Master Robert and Master Walter, along with Brother John, being fully employed in London, the resources of the King's Works would be fully occupied. Edward would need to call upon additional resources for what he had in mind for Wales. Edward was beginning works at Aberystwyth, Builth and Flint, and in light of the Treaty of Aberconwy, he now planned the largest at Rhuddlan. Gwynedd would be surrounded by castles, and to build himself many castles in double quick time he knew exactly whom to call upon. What happens next is certain; Edward brought to England, all the way from Savoy, the man who'd been building castles for the Count, a man whose talents it is almost certain Edward was well aware of.

Coldstream has held: 'It is difficult to see how Edward I could possibly could have predicted that the ugly duckling at work in Savoy would turn into the swan of Wales.'[101, 102] However, before indulging in a critique of the castles of Savoy, we would do well to recall Hugh Kennedy's observation of similarly simple designs in Outremer: 'They were small and simple because they were built to accommodate small and not particularly wealthy households.'[103] That is they were built to a limited budget for a specific purpose, and met that purpose so well they mostly survive to this day. Indeed, as Blondel noted, castle design in Savoy was conservative. As he rightly said, 'they were naturally defended by their position' and had been built on 'sheer rocks and promontories' with 'steep slopes' – that is they *had* been conservative until the arrival of Jean de Mézos in the mid-century, who brought with him the more advanced Anglo-Norman building ideas of Gascony.[104] As Blondel then said: 'It is by this route, passing through the possessions of the English crown, that new forms of military art have come to us [Savoy].'[105] It is then also a matter of record that Edward did indeed bring Maître Jacques to England. Whilst Coldstream helpfully acknowledges that working for a king, rather than working for a count, might afford a mason more scope in which to work, her remark could be seen as unjustly pejorative. The criticism is perhaps especially unfair since so little remains of the Viennois castles built in the 1270s, particularly at Saint-Georges-d'Espéranche itself – the castle that had been visited by Edward. What little remains there, the octagonal tower, does seem to point to more than what she dismissed as 'building' and more toward what Pevsner called 'architecture'.[106]

What is certain is that Edward saw the architecture, since he hired its builder. If Edward was to encircle Wales, in the way that Caesar had castrated Vercingetorix with wooden walls at Alésia, then he would now need stone walls, he would need castles. If ever there is a single testimony to Edward's thorough, ruthless, determined approach to the age-old English problems in Wales then it is the massive castles constructed there. In the winter of 1277, the call went from England to Savoy, the King of England required the services of the Count of Savoy's builder of castles.

Chapter Six

We last heard of Maître Jacques in September of 1275, buying a packhorse in the Val d'Aosta and working for Count Philippe in the Viennois, but then the archival records in Savoy fall silent. No primary source archival evidence for his activities in 1276 and 1277 have survived the ravages of time. Which leads us to conclude that he was no longer in the pay of Philippe, but there is beginning to be evidence, albeit architectural, contextual and circumstantial, that he may well have been in the pay of the *famille de Grandson* before moving to England in 1278.

Sadly, as with a good deal of the castles in Vaud, building and rebuilding records do not survive for the Château de Grandson. However, through dendrochronology we can date the timbers used, and for Grandson they were felled in the autumn and winter of 1277–8 and autumn and winter of 1279–80. This means that construction began after Maître Jacques left for Wales in the winter and spring of 1277–8.[1] This does not mean, however, that he did not lay out the scope of works before his departure, leading to speculation as to his involvement. Swiss architectural historian Daniel de Raemy noted that the 'exodus of the Savoyard workforce' to Wales 'begins' just as the work on the castle at Grandson began, but that 'one can imagine' Maître Jacques was responsible for the general design.[2] There is certainly the suggestive triangular arrow loops common to Saint-Georges-d'Espéranche and Rhuddlan that can also be found at the Château de Grandson – although we cannot be certain of the circumstances surrounding their addition to Grandson. Were they the design work of Maître Jacques? Or simply the later addition of masons who'd previously worked in Wales? When writing the text for the guidebook for the Château de Grandson, Annick Voirol Reymond wrote, based upon her understanding of de Raemy: 'The conception of Othon's fortress [Grandson] is probably the work of the famous Jacques de Saint-Georges, who may have been the master of the works until 1278.'[3] But for Grandson the precise nature of who built what and when remains uncertain.

However the works at the Château de Grandson were not the only building projects undertaken for the family in the years after 1275. A cousin of Othon de Grandson, Guillaume de Champvent, the brother of English-based Pierre de Champvent, became Bishop of Lausanne in 1273. With his appointment to the Bishopric of Lausanne, Guillaume would be the first of three consecutive bishops who had previously spent time in England, before coming to the episcopacy between 1273 and 1313, the following two being Girard de Vuippens and Othon de Champvent.[4] The first of this anglicized triumvirate soon realized his castle at

Lucens (Figure 1.7), approximately twenty miles (thirty kilometres) across the hills from Grandson, required work. He had constructed for himself, from 1275, a large circular tower, set into and projecting from the northern wall of the castle.[5] De Raemy found the same arrow slit similitude to Saint-Georges-d'Espéranche that he had found at Grandson.[6] Vaudoise historian Monique Fontannaz also found architectural links with Grandson, but also with what would be built later in north Wales, writing: 'Its parapet is lightly corbelled, constituting the first example of this type in the region ... before ... Grandson (1277–80) ... which are found in great number in Wales.'[7] It is also very possible that we find in the subsequently added (1311–12)[8] roof space of the *grand donjon* tower at Lucens, something replicated a few years later by Tassin de Saint Georges for Count Philippe at Falavier and something that would evolve into the turrets later built from the towers of Conwy.[9] What de Raemy describes as a *'guette'*, literally a 'watch' or 'lookout', is hidden mostly from view, and extends from the top of the tower on the inward side of its circumference. De Raemy describes the *guette* surviving today as the 'partially preserved ... remains of the lookout', confirming that what we see today is less than the as built condition.[10] The parapet of the tower was, and is, reached by a spiral staircase. Fontannaz confirms that the *guette* was built before the tower was roofed in 1311–12. The *guette*, squared at its base, becomes circular in its barrel, before reaching its possibly truncated form above the roofline – we may have, at Lucens and Falavier, the genesis of what Prestwich called the 'watch turrets' of Conwy.[11]

De Raemy writes that the works at Grandson and Lucens were undertaken by those of close relationship with Savoy.[12] But this is evidence of artisans from the Viennois, not necessarily the direction of Maître Jacques. However, in what Taylor might have described as 'controlled conjecture', we can say the works at Grandson and Lucens certainly fits the nature of those hitherto and subsequently ascribed to Maître Jacques. If he had been involved in the Pays de Vaud, then the work would have required the simultaneous direction of works of some twenty miles (thirty kilometres) distant, as had been the case in the Viennois and would be the case in Wales. Furthermore, Yverdon, the first Maître Jacques castle, and between Grandson and Lucens, was having work undertaken on its *'grande tour'*, work directed, according to de Raemy 'without doubt under the direction of Maître Jacques de Saint Georges..[13] So, three simultaneous works underway in Vaud, look to carry his 'signature' of multiple projects.

That Lucens and Grandson were both in the care of the wider *famille de Grandson* would give us a common patron for the works. The lack of archive evidence for the work, and also Maître Jacques' 'missing' three years in primary sources is explainable by the almost complete loss of records at Lucens and Grandson, attributable to the Bernese invasion of Vaud in 1536. The conflict between the Bishop of Lausanne and the House of Savoy, that had for example given rise to the town of Saint-Prex, had abated with the death of Jean de Cossonay. Now that the see was in the hands of the *famille de Grandson*, there would be a temporary thaw in relations. For Jacques to have worked for the *famille de Grandson*, the opportunity would have been necessary for Othon de Grandson to discuss his employment with both his cousin, Guillaume de Champvent, the mason himself, and his patron, Count Philippe. We do indeed have two opportunities for such discussions – firstly, during Grandson's leave of absence from Edward of 1273–4, when he returned to Vaud, the Savoyard accounts place Maître Jacques at Chillon and Cossonay in June 1274.[14] Secondly, Grandson was at the Christmas festivities of 1274 at Saint-Georges d'Espéranche, when he was noted as a guest of Philippe.[15] One must observe at this point that it may not be entirely coincidental that the absence of Maître Jacques from Savoyard records begins in 1275, the year in which construction of the great *donjon* tower at Lucens is known to have begun. So, notwithstanding de Raemy's critique of the late thirteenth-century works at Grandson, it is possible that in the 1275–7 period Maître Jacques was directing works for the *famille de Grandson* at both Lucens and Grandson. The architectural evidence at both Grandson and Lucens, the sudden absence from Savoyard accounts, the fit with the known historical context of his work and the presence of Othon de Grandson at key moments in the Viennois and Vaud certainly are strongly suggestive.

We cannot pass lightly over the possible significance of the architecture surviving within the roof space of the *donjon* at Lucens. Coldstream had described a 'lower standard of construction in Savoy' and that in Savoy we might find an 'ugly duckling' and in Wales a 'swan'.[16] Perhaps it would be more accurately described as a progression. At Yverdon we find simple towers, at Lucens[17] an addition of a watch turret to the tower, and finally at Conwy fully fledged decorative watch turrets[18] atop the towers suggesting he had then moved to the services of the English court and to Wales.

There is one more intriguing piece of the jigsaw, which sadly lacks primary sources. Marcel Grandjean dated the western window of Lausanne Cathedral to around 1275, during the episcopacy of Guillaume de Champvent.[19] Arnold Taylor drew attention to the remarkable likeness of this three-lancet window beneath three oculi to the similar treatment of the eastern hall window of Conwy Castle.[20] Given the possibility discussed here that Maître Jacques may well have worked for Champvent at Lucens, the question is are both windows the work of Maître Jacques de Saint Georges?

Whilst we cannot be certain of Jacques' whereabouts in Savoy in 1277, given the absence of primary source material, we can be certain he was not there in 1278, because the evidence suggests he had then moved to the services of the English court and to Wales. A journey undertaken from the Viennois to England would today by road be quite some enterprise. In the thirteenth century it was time consuming, exhausting and potentially dangerous. Jacques' route from Saint-Georges-d'Espéranche would have taken him, most likely, by way of Vienne and/or Lyon then Burgundian territory and Dijon and then the Kingdom of France, either Auxerre, Paris and Rouen for the Channel or Reins and Saint-Omer. Once across the Channel he may well have made for London before joining the king in Gloucestershire by way of the old Roman road, Akeman Street. This journey of between 600 and 700 miles would have taken over a month to complete. A fast messenger with relief horses en route could make fifty miles a day, but the average for one man and his horse was closer to just twenty miles. For the most part the ride would have taken advantage of the Roman roads still in existence some thousand years after their construction, riding from one town to the next. The journey would have been dangerous, since the roads were not patrolled for the most part, travellers usually electing to take to the road in numbers – and this may also have been true for Jacques, who may have made the journey accompanied by fellow castle builders. Riding would have proved expensive as well as dangerous, since passage by most towns and bridges required the payment of tolls at the *péage*, a technique by which the Savoyard had long since acquired much wealth. Passage across the Channel would have been hopefully achieved in a day by medieval cog but was not for the feint hearted. So, over a month after leaving the sunny Viennois, he would have found himself on the deck of a little cog rolling in the sea off the English coast. Like many before him he would have viewed this as a journey to the end of the known world, the coast shrouded in mist, the land under permanent clouds. Following the call of King Edward, this was, no doubt, a tremendous opportunity for Jacques to work with a wealthy and powerful patron, but one must wonder at his feelings seeing the French coast recede behind him and at the home for the rest of his life appearing above the horizon. No doubt, as the seagulls circled the little vessel, he had much time to contemplate his past and the future to come.[21]

Upon arrival at the English court, then processing through Gloucestershire, he would have met at least one fellow Savoyard, Amédée de Savoie, who would later succeed Philippe, his former patron, as the Count of Savoy. Specifically, Amédée was at court between 2 April and 23 April.[22] But he would have also met for the first time in his life the full majesty of a royal court, the full dazzle of royal power. Jacques had previously been in the employ of Pierre de Savoie, before he'd been Count, and of his brother Count Philippe I de Savoie, but this was entirely of a different magnitude: he'd been summoned to the presence of God's anointed King of England. Was he nervous? We will never know, but his career was about to take off.

The Pipe Rolls[23] for 1278 introduce us to Maître Jacques in England; they describe him, firstly as an 'engineer', going firstly in April 'for ordering the castles in Wales',[24] then after a return to court, as an 'engineer' and a 'mason' going to more specifically 'visit the castles of Flint and Rhuddlan'.[25] This is another key piece of primary source evidence upon which the role of Flint and Rhuddlan begins to hang, because it immediately places him directly at both castle sites. Those that diminish his role at Flint, or indeed Rhuddlan, need to find an explanation for what the scribe meant by "Visitandum castra de flint et Rothelan" other than the obvious one. The scribe records his presence at court for seventeen days prior to 8 April, which would mean he had been with Edward's court since at least 22 March 1278. If one imagines a messenger had left England after the Treaty of Aberconwy, ratified by Edward on 10 November 1277, then we can imagine him travelling to Savoy with a request for the master mason's services arriving just before Christmas 1277. Given the need to respond to and prepare for a journey to England, we can equally imagine a departure from Savoy sometime late in January or February 1278. One might ponder whether Jacques met up with Grandson en route, given that the latter left England for Gascony in February. Both may well have travelled via Paris and or the Channel ports, but if so, such a meeting is lost to history.

At Rhuddlan, it's most likely Jacques would have met another fellow Savoyard that summer of 1278: Guy de Vergers. The English archive records payments to a man recorded in Savoy as Guy de Vercors,[26] a man who'd been with Jacques at Montmélian in 1271 and working at Saint-Georges-d'Espéranche in 1275.[27, 28] It would be surprising perhaps if Jacques was the only Savoyard called by Edward to north Wales. He will be the first of many artisans we will meet in north Wales who'd previously built castles for the Counts of Savoy.

The archival record for Jacques at the court of King Edward from 22 March is entirely consistent with him being summoned following the Treaty of Aberconwy. An arrival at court at this time would have found Jacques joining Edward at Down Ampney in Gloucestershire, seven miles to the south-east of Roman Cirencester, the royal party having recently moved there from nearby Quenington.[29] At Quenington Edward and Leonor had been staying at the twelfth-century preceptory, enjoying no doubt the hospitality of the Knights Hospitaller; at Down Ampney they had availed themselves of the new Manor House there. It is no doubt in this short period that King Edward briefed his new master mason on the Welsh War and his need for castles at Aberystwyth, Builth, Flint and Rhuddlan. When the court had reached Edington in Somerset on 8 April, the scribe not only pays Jacques for the seventeen days since his arrival at court, but for the coming twenty-nine days he will be away in Wales. In other words, Jacques arrived Down Ampney, 22 March 1278, was briefed by Edward, and was dispatched from Edington to Wales on or about 8 April 1278 to see at first hand the sites where preparation for castle building had begun the previous summer. Taylor notes that Jacques received 'a daily wage of 1s., an additional subsistence allowance of 1s. being paid to him when absent on official business "*extra curiam*".[30]

It has been suggested that Maître Jacques was little more than a clerk in the king's pay, and that he arranged for castles to be built by others, but one is bound to say the archives suggest otherwise. In his time Taylor critiqued W. D. Simpson, who held firstly that the Savoyard was 'a civil servant, not an architect' before retracting somewhat to say he was a 'practical master mason of high professional status'.[31] More recently some have taken Simpson's earlier view, suggesting a 'project manager',[32] John R. Kenyon writing, 'today, however, many would concur with Simpson and prefer to think of Master James as the man who implemented and oversaw the King's great design, instead of being the designer or architect of the buildings.'[33] But this is to ignore key primary sources, including, in 1278 of the verb '*ordinandum*',[34] of which Pevsner could find only one passage in the whole of Europe where the term referred to 'a patron or his representative merely supervising a building job'.[35] It is also to ignore, that whilst, in 1291, holding the title '*magister operacionum regis in Wallia*' he could still at the same time be described as '*Magistro Jacobo de sancto Georgio cementario nostro in Wallia*' or 'our builder in Wales' and, in 1302, as '*Mestre Jakes de seint Jorge le Machoun*' or 'the Mason'.[36] At no time in Savoy or England were the words '*custos*' or '*clerico*' ever used in his regard, as they had been, for example, to Pierre Mainier, Hugh of Leominster and Walter de Wynton.[37] Maître Jacques had indeed skills we might attribute today to a project manager, but he was always, first and foremost, a master mason, a builder of castles.

Christopher Wilson writing *The Gothic Cathedral* (1990) shed light upon the evolving ability of a master mason developing the dual role of architect and what we might call a project manager, writing: 'architects of major projects were liberated from the need to be constantly present at a single site, and if their work was particularly in demand, they became able to commute between several sites.'[38]

The use of drawings in the construction of cathedrals, and by extension, castles, is further evidenced by the surviving manual of architectural drawings made by French contemporary, Villard de Honnecourt, which survive in the Bibliothèque de France in Paris. His depiction of the cathedral of Reims is taken from an architectural drawing rather than from live observation.[39] Wilson seems to be describing the evolution of the Maître Jacques of Yverdon to the Maître Jacques of the Viennois, managing multiple sites, to the Maître Jacques of Wales, managing multiple major sites perfectly. Here we have a master mason who makes the transition described by Wilson exactly. Rather than a mere implementer of King's designs, as suggested by Kenyon, we have a master mason who has become so 'in demand' in his art that he can employ the new techniques of scale drawing to manage multiple sites. Sadly, no such drawings have survived to provide conclusive proof, but the multiple site management has, as has the consistent description of Jacques as a master mason. The precise nature of Maître Jacques' role can be found, as Taylor suggested himself, in the primary sources available.

Jacques, in the records of 1278, is consistently referred to as '*Magistro Jacobo Ingeniatori*', so in order to better understand his role we must appreciate what the writer of the rolls had in mind by ascribing the title '*Ingeniatori*'.[40] The word '*ingeniator*' had been applied to both Master Bertram and Jean de Mézos. It means 'military engineer', but one also given to not only designing siege engines, but also building works, architect, contractor and superintendent.[41]

Our word 'architect' has its origin in the Greek '*arkhi*' meaning chief and '*tektōn*' meaning 'builder'; this Greek word had reached Rome,[42] but had yielded by the Middle Ages to a variety of terms: '*magister*', '*cementario*', '*lathomo*', '*ingeniator*' and '*mason*'.[43] In using '*magister*', meaning 'man eminently or perfectly skilled in something' and '*ingeniator*', meaning 'designer and constructor of fortifications and weapons', our scribe was reasonably clear in his meaning.[44] Indeed, '*ingeniator*' comes from the Latin '*ingeniare*' meaning to create, generate, contrive, devise, and *'ingenium'*, literally meaning 'cleverness'.[45] This absence of the term architect reflected a greater weight being applied to the patron of works (such as Edward) than to the realizer of his requests (such as Jacques), the oft-quoted anonymity of the medieval architect. At a salary of two shillings per day, King Edward was paying for someone who could realize his ambition in stone.

After *'ingeniator'*, there is the key phrase is *'ad ordinandum opera castrorum'* or 'ordering the works of the castles', and the key word is *'ordinandum'*. Indeed, upon this word, hangs to a great extent, Jacques' reputation as an 'architect' erecting 'architecture' that has been challenged of late – Vitruvius had written *'Architectura autem constat ex ordinatione'*, 'Architecture depends on order'.[46] *'Ordino'* is the root word for *'ordinandum'* and can be defined in a number of ways: to 'adjust' or 'regulate', to 'compose', to 'ordain' or 'appoint' and lastly to 'arrange', 'order' or 'set in order'.[47] Coldstream, critical of Taylor's attribution of design skills to the Savoyard, equivocated, suggesting that this record held the only 'hint of a design process' on the part of Maître Jacques, but citing Pevsner, added that 'This term is interpreted to mean design, but it can also mean setting out,' having earlier accepted that 'This term can cover matters of design.'[48] Indeed, it can cover matters of design, Pevsner had summarized his position as 'it can be maintained that whenever the term[s] … "ordinatio" … are found, they may be said to allude to architectural designing and planning and not to purely clerical work.'[49] So, did the scribe mean to say explicitly or implicitly 'design'? – that the term is used only once is not problematic, since Jacques could only take over works once 'setting them in order'? I think the scribe is clear: to set in order, to take over the order of the castles, including modification to the design if found necessary. In the historical context the meaning is unambiguous – to set in order includes elements of design. *'Ordinandum'* used in this context by the English scribe upon the dispatch to Wales of Maître Jacques is another key piece of primary-source evidence that cannot be dismissed lightly.

We should also note that the scribe uses *'castrorum'*, which is the genitive plural of *'castra'*. Clearly the scribe is writing of 'castles' not 'a castle' – so the scribe is suggesting visits to both Flint and Rhuddlan not just Rhuddlan as some have supposed. both Flint and Rhuddlan not just Rhuddlan as some have supposed. The Wardrobe accounts all fit the description of a man being sent to oversee totality of the works in Wales. If we are to follow those who seek to minimize the affairs of Jacques in Wales, then we must find a way to explain *'ad ordinandum opera castrorum'* in a way other than the obvious one, that Edward sent Jacques to Wales in the spring of 1278 to supervise the construction of both his castles in north Wales.

The salary of two shillings per day gives us a lead into the time spent away, since as mentioned the salary was doubled whilst away from court. So, the April payment covers a period from 23 March until 8 April with the king at court, followed by twenty-nine days in Wales, that is up to 7 May. The 20 May payment included seven days in Wales and a further eight days back at court. It is possible, therefore, from the archive, to construct a journey to and from '*Wallie*' from 8 April until 14 May, some thirty-six days in total. We can reasonably assume from these accounts that Jacques joined Edward in Wiltshire, was briefed for a time and was then sent on a mission to Wales to view the sites under construction for himself before reporting back to Edward.

Accompanying Jacques on his visit to the works in Wales may well have been Pierre le Burguynun or Peter the Burgundian. We have an entry in the archive, immediately preceding that for Maître Jacques, of a payment to Peter of twenty-one shillings and nine pence, for precisely the same dates as those for Jacques' entry. Interestingly, Pierre had been one of three engineers working in Gascony for Henry in 1254, the others being Master Bertram and Sir Jean de Mézos. We have all three, Pierre, Bertram and Jean, working at some time with Maître Jacques – a veritable Anglo-Savoyard-Gascon triangle of masons.[50] We can glimpse the lives of these much-travelled masons and the dangers they experienced on the thirteenth-century open road by Pierre's loss of a horse whilst in the king's service.[51]

What might Jacques have found on his trip to Wales of just over a month, the scribe does not help by giving us a list of the '*castorum*' or castles to be reviewed, but we do know that Aberystwyth, Builth, Flint and Rhuddlan were under construction in the spring of 1278. It would have been impossible to review all four sites in the one trip, so we might reasonably assume he visited just two sites – but which two?

Work at Flint was under the direction of Master Richard of Chester, Rhuddlan under the long-time servant of the Crown, Master Bertram, Builth in the charge of Master Henry, and work at Aberystwyth was paused until restarting on 29 June. The most advanced of the works underway was at Builth, in mid Wales, where work had begun in May 1277 and had, therefore, one full building season completed. Builth had been the site of a Norman castle taken by Llywelyn in the summer of 1260 when he was at the height of his powers. Llywelyn had destroyed the castle, and in rebuilding it, Edward was systematically restoring what he saw as personally his. '*Buelt*' [Builth] had after all, like Rhuddlan, been specifically granted to him, by name, by his father as a part of his appanage.[52]

For April 1278, the archives record that building at Builth was still at winter levels, which means that the second building season had yet to commence. By winter levels we mean a dozen men clearing earth from the quarry and bringing stone and sand to site in readiness for the building season to come.[53] Should Jacques have visited Builth, which is by no means certain, in the spring or summer of 1278 on his assessment visit to Wales, then he would have seen little more than the reported '*magnum palicium*' or 'large palisade' of forty-nine perches[54] (270 yards or nearly 247 metres) in length, built to defend the builders from hostile Welsh action.[55] This palisade, or at least the wood from it, may well have been gifted the following year to Roger de Mortimer, the nearby Marcher Lord. With the war safely concluded, the constable at Builth was ordered by Edward to make a 'gift' of the '*bretach*' to Mortimer.[56] Within the palisade would have stood temporary wooden buildings: a chapel, a hall, a kitchen and a smithy. Rough stone for the construction was arriving from the nearby 'Black quarry', whilst the finer freestone was coming the twenty miles (thirty-two kilometres) from Clifford and Cusop.[57] It's often thought that building a castle was an exclusively male occupation, and mostly it was, but as the women working today at Guédelon show, women could and did join construction teams. At Builth, the records give the name of one such woman, Gwladus Talgard, a hodwoman, whom Spurgeon suggested may have been a native of Talgard in 'Brycheiniog' or Brecon.[58] If so, we should adjust our picture of English castle-building in Wales to include not only Welsh men, but women too. Builth would never conform to the form of the castles built elsewhere in the Welsh wars, and is now entirely gone from sight above ground. Without much in the way of castle remaining today, we can get some picture of the rising castle at Builth from the archives, which describe the building work undertaken between 1277 and 1280 as 'of a great tower', 'one stone wall and six turrets … [a] drawbridge and two great towers', a 'bailey' and an 'outer bailey'.[59] Therefore, despite no surviving stonework above ground, thanks to this description and together with extant earthworks, we can reasonably imagine the castle. It would have contained a great tower, a greater and a lesser bailey, protected by a curtain wall with six turrets, a twin-towered gatehouse including a turning bridge-style drawbridge across a surrounding moat. Since Llywelyn is most unlikely to have destroyed the structure atop the Norman motte, then it's likely to think that the 'magne turris' sat on the motte. The original Norman horseshoe-shaped bailey, beneath the motte, had been divided into two by a new bailey ditch that bisected the original, the smaller lesser bailey most likely falling into disuse. Much speculation has been conducted into whether the 'fossatum' or ditch was a water-filled moat. Despite the marshy nature of the ground, it has now been confirmed that it was indeed a dry ditch.[60]

What was begun in May 1277 would not be completed until August 1282, when work at Builth was suspended. The total cost of the castle would be £1,626, a comparatively modest sum as the earthworks from the previous castle could be reused. The yearly breakdown gives us an idea of the pace of the work: for 1277 £433.16s.11d, for 1278 £262.7s.7d, for 1279 £197.14s.8d, for 1280 £239.4s.1d, also for 1280 £303.12s.2d and lastly for 1282 £148.3s.3d. As Edwards, the author of this breakdown points out, these numbers are not meant to be 'free from error' but to give an idea of the speed of construction – something we can summarize as a larger initial outlay, as can be expected, followed by a slow but not precipitate levelling-down of expenses.[61] The garrison at Builth, under Hywel ap Meurig, a Welshman loyal to Edward, amounted to nine troopers and forty foot soldiers.[62]

With evidence unclear of a visit to Builth and with work paused at Aberystwyth, I think it is far more likely that the trip made by Jacques to Wales that spring would have been to the two more critical works at Flint and Rhuddlan.[63] The castles on the coast road protected the best route from England into Wales, a route known to invaders from Suetonius Paulinus to Edward's great-grandfather Henry II and his father Henry III. The castles visited by Jacques would become the cornerstone of English authority in Wales and, therefore, we can assume they were the works visited.

He would have ridden to Chester, most likely by the old Roman roads of Fosse Way and Watling Street. Just ten miles (sixteen kilometres) to the north-west of the old Roman city of Deva, still on the English side of the Dee, was the site of a quarry at Nesshead from which sandstone was being quarried for use in Wales, and also available was the harder millstone gritstone. A castle would require a mix of such hard stone to stiffen the walls to withstand siege weapons, much as we now use steel to stiffen concrete. Perhaps Jacques visited en route to the Welsh sites in order to see for himself the material being used. Perhaps he made straight for the newly created forest road to the marshy ground by the Dee which comprised the site of what would become the castle at Flint. Along the forest road Jacques would have noted the plentiful immediate supply of Cheshire and Flintshire oaks with which to build castles. Oak from the forest would be able to supply him with wood for the roof timbers and battens to hang the roof tiles upon. Whilst riding he would also have been aware of the ready supply of sand, both from Nesshead and the Welsh coast itself, important for making mortar, clay for the roof and floor tiles. Colossal quantities of sandstone would be required; in comparison the builders in the twenty-first century at Guédelon in France estimated their requirement as 10,000 cubic metres – for a castle of similar scope as Flint, but far less than the plans for Rhuddlan.[64] It would have seemed to him that nature itself was abundant in supplying the needs of the English king he now served – this was excellent castle-building country. Edward had already chosen the sites for his castles, so the first task of a castle builder, choosing a site with a suitable water supply, would not concern him. Nor would the equally important task of choosing a defensible position; that too had been Edward's decision the summer earlier.

As he approached Flint, he would have been able to see the estuary of the River Dee to his right, a wide expanse of shifting sands, with the flatlands of the Wirral peninsula and England beyond, and to his left would have risen the Clwydian Range of hills. He would have reflected that the flattened site would place no constraints upon the design of a castle. Arriving at Flint, he would have found a site by the Dee estuary cleared of trees and obstructions, newly constructed earthworks – a double bank and ditch to protect the camp which would later be drawn in 1610 by John Speed,[65] a town growing up for which a market had just been proclaimed,[66] a wooden palisade for protection and other wooden construction – but as yet not much in the way of a castle.

An interesting account from 1277 noted financial penalty applied, even then, for 'defective labour'.[67] At least one gang of diggers having been pressed into service may have looked resentfully at the Savoyard paymaster riding into their midst but continued moving the earth as was their lot. The archive for the 1278 building season that was yet to come show that some £830 would be spent at Flint, whereas some £3,160 would be expended at Rhuddlan; furthermore, of the Flint expenditure the largest outlay would be £485 for diggers and £176 for carpenters. Taylor notes that 'Mason's work [at Flint] amounted to only £53 (compared with £1,267 at Rhuddlan) and was limited to preparing stone in the quarry across the Dee at Nesshead for revetting the castle ditch'.[68] Therefore, in April 1278, Flint was seen as the secondary task at hand, the primary task being the castle at Rhuddlan, which I think Jacques would have visited quickly having familiarized himself with Flint.

Riding further along the freshly cleared forest road, Jacques would have come to Rhuddlan by the River Clwyd, further inland than the works underway down the coast at Flint. Arriving at Rhuddlan, he would have appreciated the more elevated position offered over and above that at Flint, the Clwydian hills now to his rear, the winding River Clwyd to his immediate front, set in a wide flat fertile valley and the hills of the Denbigh moors beyond. At both Flint and Rhuddlan the Savoyard would have heard the unfamiliar cries of seagulls and smelt the unmistakable sea air; this was a distant land far from home.

Edward had already decided in 1277 to site the new castle a little downstream of the original Norman motte and bailey built for Robert de Rhuddlan.[69] Riding into the work camp, Maître Jacques would have observed work beginning on site huts or lodges and a site office, for which Master Bertram had received finance in March.[70] That spring a beginning had been made on the earthworks for the new castle, but it would have been immediately apparent to Jacques that resupply of the future castle by sea would necessitate work on the River Clywd to make it navigable for shipping. If Jacques had been aware of the subtleties of the native English language, he would have heard at Flint and Rhuddlan ditchers and diggers from Yorkshire, Lincolnshire, Lancashire, Warwickshire and Leicestershire. Conversing with the masons, he'd have heard the dulcet tones of men from Lincolnshire, Nottinghamshire, Gloucestershire, Oxfordshire, Shropshire, Staffordshire, Leicestershire and Warwickshire.[71]

Edward would no doubt have briefed Jacques that it was at Rhuddlan he intended his principal administrative centre, a castellated borough, to be built; in order to maintain royal control henceforth in the four cantrefi, there would be no recurrence of Llywelyn's destruction of his father's castle at nearby Dyserth. Whilst at Shrewsbury in December last, Edward had appointed Nicholas Bonel as 'his surveyor of his works at Le Chaylou [Flint] and at Rothelan'.[72] But then Bonel's principal concern seems to have been the acquisition of tenants for new towns at Flint and Rhuddlan, so perhaps he sought out too those masons directly responsible for the castle works.[73] At Flint, Jacques may have spent time too with Master Richard of Chester and at Rhuddlan with Master Bertram. One wonders what Master Richard, a man local to Flint, made of the Savoyard visitor. At Rhuddlan too, the Gascon Master Bertram, a man long used to the senior position at court and close to what we now might call retirement, may have wondered of the man who would be his successor in that role. Perhaps he may have recalled that Jacques had recently worked with fellow Gascon Jean de Mézos in Savoy, a man he well knew from his days in Gascony. It is very possible, however, that Bertram had even left Rhuddlan long before the arrival of Jacques from Savoy. During the last weeks of the 1277 building season, it is one of his assistants helping the carpenters at Rhuddlan, not Bertram himself,[74] and we have records of his being paid expenses at the Tower of London dated 17 April 1278, just ten days after Jacques had set out from Edington on 7 or 8 April. Sadly, there are no records that survive of any encounters they may have had.[75]

Armed with a feeling for the sites and the work required to realize Edward's ambition, Jacques returned to the royal court by 15 May 1278. Whilst Jacques had been away in Wales, the court had moved to and spent Easter at Glastonbury. And thus, striding purposefully into our story steps the king of legend, Arthur. There is much debate, beyond the scope of this book, of the historical Arthur, a Celtic legend from what we used to call the Dark Ages. Whatever the debate, we can say that Edward believed a king called Arthur had once ruled a Kingdom of Britannia, or at least, if he did not actually believe, then it suited his purpose to believe. The legendary King Arthur ruled what had been the Roman Province of Britannia once the Romans had left the island. Given that Britannia incorporated the lands not only now referred to as England but also of Wales, one can imagine that Arthur might prove a useful precedent for a king of England wanting to rule Wales. Furthermore, if one was to add the land of the Celts to one's kingdom of the English, what better legend to add to the canon of the English but the legendary Arthur – in other words to co-opt the mythical leader of the Britons, now the Welsh?[76] The legend could add genuine legitimacy to his overlordship of Wales.

Arthur mania had been rampant amongst the French-speaking world, of which Plantagenet England was a part, since Geoffrey of Monmouth had written *De gestis Britonum or Historia regum Britanniae* in the eleventh century.[77] It relates the purported history of Britain, from its first settlement by Brutus, a descendant of the Trojan hero Aeneas, to the death of Cadwallader in the seventh century, taking in Julius Caesar's invasions of Britain, two kings, Leir and Cymbeline, later immortalized by William Shakespeare, and one of the earliest developed narratives of King Arthur. The Normans had long been interested in the 'back story' of the island they had conquered in 1066, an interest that spread widely throughout France and even to the Castilian home of Edward's wife Leonor. Indeed, it was the twelfth-century French writer Chrétien de Troyes who added Lancelot and the Holy Grail to the story, beginning the genre of Arthurian romance that became such a significant strand of medieval literature. In these French stories, the narrative focus often shifts from King Arthur himself to other characters, such as various Knights of the Round Table. The romance of knights in shining armour lives to this day as testimony to the potency of the myth. Perhaps in Edward's mind too was the element of the myth that suggested Arthur was 'Once and Future King', that in Britain's hour of need Arthur would awake and come riding from Avalon to drive away the danger. Another myth recounted by Geoffrey of

Monmouth in the Arthur tale, related to Merlin, told of a Red Dragon, taken to be Wales, fighting the White Dragon, taken to be the English, after much struggle and many reverses the Red Dragon being eventually triumphant. Edward would no doubt have known the story, and perhaps wanted to lay this dragon to rest. What we can say is that Edward, whilst not himself Arthur manic, would have been fully conversant with the myths and sought to co-opt and appropriate them for his purposes that Easter in Somerset.

According to legend Arthur had passed from this life to Avalon, and the monks of Glastonbury Abbey decided in 1190 that their monastery was indeed founded upon the legendary isle. Chronicler Gerald of Wales had written: 'What is now known as Glastonbury was, in ancient times, called the Isle of Avalon.'[78] The monks there said they had discovered a massive tree-trunk coffin and a lead cross bearing the inscription, 'Here lies entombed the renowned king Arthur in the island of Avalon.'[79] Now of course monks were notorious in medieval Europe for finding relics that would generate revenue for their abbeys in the way of pilgrims. More likely is that a fire at the abbey in 1184 necessitated the raising of funds for repairs, but nonetheless the thirteenth century believed the word of men of God such as the venerable monks of Glastonbury. So, the court, King Edward, Queen Leonor, Thomas Bek, the king's treasurer, Henri de Lacy, fresh from his exploits in Wales and Amédée de Savoie decamped from Bruton to Glastonbury at Easter 1278.[80]

Two days after Easter, a large, hushed crowd gathered in the spring twilight for a ceremony before the high altar of the abbey. With great reverence, and no little eye for the theatrical, they exhumed the remains of Arthur and his queen, Guinevere. The coffins were raised and carefully set to one side, the lead cross removed to reveal the once and future king and his queen. The disinterred remains were kept for a later and a grander reburial, Edward carefully wrapping the remains of Arthur in silk, Leonor likewise for Guinevere. The dramatic ceremony was designed to be a powerful reminder to the Welsh that the Plantagenet dynasty were Arthur's heirs, that their cultural identity was now a part of the Plantagenet whole, that Britannia was in the process of being reunited.

The Wardrobe accounts show that Jacques stayed at court but a brief time, just the week from 15 until 22 May, before returning to Wales. This time the scribe is more specific in terms of describing his destinations in Wales writing: 'ad visitandum castra de flint et Rothelan' or 'in order to visit the castles of Flint and Rhuddlan'.[81] One can imagine that the return to court would have been to report to Edward an assessment of the works underway before returning for an extended sojourn, the entry for 18 June indicating that further reference to the court could be made by a servant without necessitating another return.[82]

The accounts for the summer building season of 1278 indicate most strongly that the major effort undertaken that year was at Rhuddlan rather than Flint. A comparison of the accounts for the period from November 1277 to March 1279 show that whilst £3,160 was spent at Rhuddlan, only a sum of £830 was expended on Flint. For comparison the other works underway that summer in Wales needed £679 for Aberystwyth and just £262 for Builth.[83] Further analysis of what these sums were spent on reveals yet more: at Flint for example, £485 went on diggers, £176 on carpenters and only £53 on the work of masons – whereas along the coast at Rhuddlan a sum of £1,267 went to the masons. Clearly 1278 saw a concentration of work at Rhuddlan, which was undoubtedly the principal site.[84] Additionally, some £965 went to the diggers, £710 for transporting material and only £30 for the material itself.[85] So whilst the work at Rhuddlan included considerably more in terms of masonry work than at Flint, it shared the requirement for a large outlay on diggers, something one might expect to see in the early months of castle construction. However, it also illustrates the colossal work underway at Rhuddlan in diverting the channel of the River Clwyd to allow the new castle to be resupplied by sea – the canalization of the river. Building accounts refer to '*fossa maris*' or a sea ditch and digging 'a great ditch in which the port leads from the sea until the castle'.[86] Additionally they would build a ditch and palisade around the works of the new town at Rhuddlan, as they had at Flint, a common practice.[87] The '*fossatores*' or diggers included a large contingent from the fens, the wetland areas of the Wash – some 300 men from 'parts of New Holland', led at *Rhuddlan* by Master William of Boston and at Flint by Master William of March, supervised by Master Richard the Enginee.[88] They were extremely experienced in the drainage of fenland areas and seem to have been specifically recruited with drainage work at Flint and more importantly the new Clwyd canal in mind. Edward and the men working for him knew what they were about – this was a model logistical exercise. The English were rebuilding Wales itself, moving the very rivers themselves in order to ensure that their presence would now be a permanent one.[89]

The major works that summer and into the autumn, the remainder of the summer building season, were then those of moving earth. The building season would see the giant task of moving the river at Rhuddlan, but clearly the significant expenditure on the work of masons implies stones beginning to be laid upon stones. One can imagine therefore that whilst the scribe described Jacques as '*visitandum*' both '*Flint et Rothelan*', much of his time would be spent at Rhuddlan, and he was most likely based there, shuttling between the sites as he had done previously in the Viennois between Saint-Georges-d'Espéranche, La Côte-Saint-André, Voiron and Saint-Laurent-du-Pont. The masons on site, Master Richard of Chester at Flint and perhaps Master Bertram at Rhuddlan would have had what Taylor describes as 'local control' but the guiding hand must surely have passed to Maître Jacques. If not, then why bring him all the way from the Viennois, why dispatch him to Wales, why describe him as '*ordinandum opera castrorum*'?

Rhuddlan is a concentric walled castle, as was the fashion coming from Outremer, the outer wall affording some protection against siege engines for the inner wall. The very first castle Jacques had been engaged on, Yverdon, was similarly of a concentric nature, although the outer wall is now lost to us. The inner wall was a quadrilateral diamond, in effect a slightly flattened *Carré Savoyard*, round towers at each corner, but two of them replaced by twin-towered gatehouses (Figure 1.8). It has been suggested that Maître Jacques had either not seen or not constructed such gatehouses before. The twin-towered gatehouse was a relatively new innovation in castle building, and single-towered protection was still the norm in Savoy.[90] The entrance had been well known as a weak point in a castle's defences. Most obviously, cutting an opening into an otherwise strong curtain wall to gain entrance in good times might also be used by an enemy in less happy times.

Thoughts turned to ways in which a weakness could be turned into a strength. Two solutions evolved: firstly, a complex of obstacles surrounded by defending mural or flanking towers, and secondly a castle where the keep was moved to envelop the gateway as an integral part of the wall. The first application of the twin-towered gatehouse in England had been at Dover Castle in the late twelfth century.[91] The Warenne family had incorporated a gatehouse into their town defences at Castle Acre in Norfolk at the turn of the twelfth/thirteenth centuries – Jean de Warenne would later be a part of Edward's entourage in Wales. The Castle Acre gatehouses had incorporated portcullises, or sliding grills, into their design. Montgomery Castle, in the Welsh Marches, built by Hubert de Burgh in the ten years following 1224 had used a gatehouse flanked by twin towers to strengthen its defences. Around 1220, Pevensey Castle would first benefit from a gatehouse, before having new walls attached to the new feature by Pierre de Savoie in the years before 1254.[92] Contemporaneously with Pevensey would be another Welsh Marcher castle, this time high above the Cheshire Plain at Beeston. The second of these ideas first appeared just prior to Jacques' arrival in England; Gilbert de Clare had added a massive gatehouse to his new castle at Caerffili, built between 1268 and 1271. This gatehouse 'on steroids' echoed that built by his father at Tonbridge in Kent.[93] Edward would, himself, have been familiar with Tonbridge, if not from his father's taking of the castle before the Battle of Lewes in 1264, then certainly from his visit there in August 1274 just prior to his coronation.[94] The gatehouses built for Richard de Clare and his son Gilbert de Clare at Tonbridge and Caerffili are a whole new departure from the gatehouses seen thus far and were in every sense essentially *donjons* serving as gatehouses: taking the weakest point of the castle and making it essentially its strongest point by depositing an enormous *donjon* over the gate. R. Allen Brown disliked the term 'keep gatehouses', but as built for the Clare family and replicated at Harlech and Beaumaris, it is difficult to describe them otherwise.[95] They provided extensive castle accommodation, encompassing living chambers and chapels, but also ensured that an attacker seeking to gain entrance to the castle gate would be met by the surest deadly force. The Tonbridge gatehouse is one of the earliest examples of the form. In Tonbridge and Caerffili we see perhaps the father and grandfather of the design that Master Jacques would later employ to good effect at Harlech and Beaumaris – but for now Rhuddlan would be a simpler affair.[96] [97]

So, whilst the twin-towered gatehouse was, as yet, unknown in Savoy, it would be familiar to Jacques' erstwhile patron, Pierre de Savoie, as well as to the knights with Edward such as Warenne and Gilbert de Clare. The gatehouses constructed at Rhuddlan would not yet match the architectural heights of Caerffili, but it would mark a significant advance for Maître Jacques. Rhuddlan would have two massive drum-shaped towers on two corners flanking the gateways to the castle. The overall scope of the castle design would be of a concentric pattern, a dry moat surrounding an outer wall, with square towers, the last of which by the Clwyd would be named Gilot's Tower. The name is likely for its Savoyard builder, Giles or Gillot de Chalons, who'd worked with Jacques in the Viennois; we'll meet him again at Conwy. Protected by this outer wall would be an outer ward before an inner curtain wall. The inner curtain wall, surrounding the inner ward, would be the castle's key defence and form a slightly flattened square or lozenge shape. Looking from the River Clwyd each corner would have a tower, but the nearest left and farthest right towers would be doubled and surround gateways – the West and East gatehouses. The design represents an adaptation of the traditional *Carré Savoyard* that would have been well known to Maître Jacques – save for the flattened shape and the doubling-up of two of the towers to form gatehouses. In keeping with Jacques' Savoyard castles and the thirteenth-century fashion, there would be no central *donjon*.[98]

But there is something in the criticism of Coldstream when she says the gatehouses at Rhuddlan are 'less advanced', but perhaps not when she goes on to dismiss them as 'an amateurish first effort by Master James' but closer to the mark when earlier attributing them to Master Bertram.[99] Taylor had already suggested, with some plausibility, that the gatehouses, in their conception, may well have been the work of the Gascon rather than the work of Maître Jacques. The castles of Culzac and Blanquefort[100] are suggested as the last works of Master Bertram in Gascony before moving to England. Sadly, we have no primary sources that can confirm or deny the idea, and more recently Marc Morris has been critical of the theory, but it would help to explain 'the feeling' that the gatehouses and towers at Rhuddlan are of a different nature to those later built at Conwy, Harlech and Beaumaris.[101]

It therefore may or may not be true of Maître Jacques that he had neither built nor seen a twin-towered gatehouse. But we should remember that his first patron, Pierre de Savoie, had owned a castle with such a structure at Pevensey, and we should also remember his mentor had been Jean de Mézos who had worked alongside Master Bertram in Gascony. Nevertheless. on arrival at Rhuddlan, he could also have quickly grasped the idea from the works begun by Master Bertram. This suggestion by Taylor would both explain the 'less advanced' works at Rhuddlan, whist also reminding us of the triangular Anglo-Savoyard-Gascon relations of key players in our story – Master Bertram who went from Gascony to England, Jean de Mézos who went from Gascony to Savoy and lastly Maître Jacques who went from Savoy to England.

In September 1278, King Edward and Queen Leonor themselves came to spend a week at Rhuddlan as part of an autumnal royal progress, moving from Windsor via the Welsh Marches. Edward coming to Rhuddlan is why we see no further recall to court for Jacques: the court came to him. Undoubtedly Edward would have met with Jacques once more to discuss the finer points of the final designs for Flint and Rhuddlan. As we have suggested earlier, the choice of site would have been Edward's, almost certainly too, much of the actual design of the castles; Edward was after all the patron. At some stage Edward may well have suggested the Constance Tower he'd seen at Aigues-Mortes as a design model he'd like to incorporate at Flint, or perhaps Jacques modified a classic *Carré Savoyard* design accordingly for the final form of Flint. The eventual castle at Flint would look remarkably like Yverdon Castle, the first Jacques had constructed, with the *donjon* tower greatly upsized à *la* Aigues-Mortes (Figures 1.9 & 2.0). Rhuddlan too takes on the look of a *Carré Savoyard*, except at two of the corners where there would be double not single towers and they'd form the gatehouse. Rhuddlan followed Caerffili in having the benefit of concentric rings of defence: an outer revetted wide ditch protecting a curtain wall complete with mural towers, which in turn protected the not-quite-square castle within.

However, dissenting voices have pointed to the lack of separation between the *donjon* tower and castle at Yverdon.[102] But, as if to illustrate the difficulty in assessing architectural evidence, Swiss historian de Raemy disagrees; in his detailed plan of Yverdon[103] he reveals a castle much modified by the Bernese from its original form. The great tower does not appear to fit well with the adjoining structures, implying separation. Furthermore, the current outer curtain walls are not the thirteenth-century outer walls: originally outer and inner walls protected the castle, so we cannot be certain of how the outer walls related to the towers. However, the concept of the great tower at Yverdon and Flint and the way they both related to the rest of the castle are markedly similar – they provided both strength and ultimately a last point of refuge. The isolation of the *donjon* at Yverdon is not of the magnitude of Flint, but then neither is the tower circumference. An impartial observer can clearly see to this day the family resemblance. As Allen Brown agreed, we can safely say the design concept of each castle in terms of its defence is identical, and that the castle at Flint can also be said to be an evolution of that at Yverdon. [104]

There have been other dissenting voices, including Perfect, who suggested that the claim for Maître Jacques as designer of Flint was 'a false claim'.[105] Whilst Perfect correctly said that Maître Jacques does not appear in the Flint accounts until 1280, we have seen that his pay came from the Royal Wardrobe accounts and were not attributed to the castle. Furthermore, what she calls a 'full building season' in 1277 was nothing of the sort – being little more four months of ditch digging and the creation of palisade works. Furthermore, the scribe was quite clear in his 1278 entries[106] that Maître Jacques was sent by Edward to both Flint and Rhuddlan.[107] In questioning the role Jacques played in north Wales, she preferred to elevate the works of Master Richard of Chester. It is not, however, to denigrate the undoubted contribution he made to recognize that a hierarchy clearly existed in terms of castle design and construction, and that the archives clearly point to Maître Jacques as the apex of that hierarchy. Turner is right to remind us that Master Richard was primarily a carpenter not a master mason.[108] With all of this in mind it is difficult to support Perfect's bold assertion.

It has also been suggested by Perfect[109] and more recently by Hislop[110] that the architectural style of Flint can be explained by direct reference to Aigues-Mortes. However, Keith Lilley[111] was less sure and the comparison was described by Taylor as 'facile' since there is no equivalence for its interior.[112] We simply have no primary-source evidence to support either theory.

What's certain is that both Flint and Rhuddlan would be built with rounded not squared towers and no central square *donjon*. In building Flint and Rhuddlan, Jacques did not simply arrive 'off the boat' with a ready-made standard design. He consulted extensively with Edward and others, notably fellow Savoyards amongst the household knights, on at least three occasions in 1278, thus the final form owing as much to Edward as Jacques. But Jacques did arrive in England with something Edward had great need of: an ability to construct castles, but especially an ability to construct multiple castles on different sites simultaneously.

Whilst sceptical of Jacques' architectural prowess, Coldstream did at least acknowledge him as a 'consummate organizer ... over a vast area and difficult terrain'.[113] Something of an understatement. Having undertaken the journey, by car, from the Viennois past the Massif de la Chartreuse into the winding Tarentaise Valley, climbing the twenty-two hairpins of the descriptively named 7,178-feet Petit Saint-Bernard Pass down into the Aosta Valley just as Jacques did when travelling to Châtel Argent in 1275, I can confirm that the area is more than vast, the terrain not just difficult, but onerous.

Edward ended the year releasing Eleanor de Montfort from her captivity and attending her wedding to Llywelyn at the great cathedral in Worcester. In keeping with the Treaty of Aberconwy of November 1277, the affairs for the First Welsh War were concluded – save for the construction of the castles. There in the winter of 1278–9 *Magistro Jacobo Ingeniatori* would while away the short Welsh winter days planning the 1279 building season to come.

But we must be sure that the '*Magistro Jacobo Ingeniatori*' that appears in our Wardrobe accounts in England for 1278 is one and the same man as the '*Magistro Jacobo lathomo*' that appears in the Savoyard accounts of Philippe I de Savoie for the Viennois in 1275 or indeed the '*Jacobi filii*' and '*Jacobo lathomo*' of the Yverdon accounts for Pierre II de Savoie for 1261 and 1269. We have been charting the story of a man from Yverdon by Lac de Neuchâtel to the works in the Valais for Pierre, to works in the Viennois for Philippe until we finally reach the beginnings of works for King Edward I in Wales; we must now address the evidence for this Jacobo, and this Jacques, being the same builder of castles.

Chapter Seven

Firstly, we must acknowledge that we may never prove empirically that the three men referred to in the archives at Yverdon, the Viennois and north Wales are the same man – to put it plainly we have no birth, marriage or death certificates with which to confirm identity. Worse, we have no offers of employment or conditions of employment, not even a job description. However, it may well be possible to apply a lower test of identity, that is to prove beyond all reasonable doubt that they are one and the same. If we can accept 'beyond reasonable doubt', then what is the evidence supporting a claim of common identity?

Given the lack of these primary-source documents that might confirm the identity, we must rely upon other means. Firstly, as historians, we have the historical context within which the life of Maître Jacques was set. We have seen already the deepening relationships between the House of Savoy and the English monarchy that began even before Jacques' birth. We read of the marriage of Alianor de Provence to King Henry III and the subsequent exodus of Savoyards of noble and less noble birth to England. That one of the key individuals brought to London by his niece Alianor was Pierre de Savoie is perhaps crucial, for it was Pierre de Savoie who had been Jacques' first patron in the building of the castle at Yverdon in 1261. We have then immediately established a direct link between the English royal family and Maître Jacques, through Pierre II de Savoie. We have also read of the deep links between the *Famille de Grandson* and Pierre de Savoie in Vaud, and the intimate service provided by the Grandsons to the Crown. What's more, Jacques went on to work for Pierre's brother and successor, Philippe de Savoie, upon the passing of Pierre. He was therefore a key employee of successive Counts of Savoy, who we must remember were uncles of Queen Alianor. Therefore, the historical context would certainly point to Savoy as a potential source for Maître Jacques' origins, something that originally led Arnold Taylor to Switzerland in search of Maître Jacques. A link by way of Pierre and Philippe would explain a knowledge of the Savoyard master mason by the English, but the meeting of the summer of 1273 at Saint-Georges-d'Espéranche between the Lord Edward and Count Philippe I de Savoie gives us an almost certain actual meeting and direct contact.

Then, of course, we do have the primary sources that confirm we have a '*Magistri Jacobi*'[1] in Savoy and a '*Magistro Jacobo*' in England, both undertaking the same work, that is building castles. Furthermore, within a short while of '*Magistri Jacobi*' disappearing from the Savoyard records we have '*Magistro Jacobo*'[2] appearing in the English accounts. At no time after 1275 does '*Magistri Jacobi*' again appear in the records for the Counts of Savoy, at no time before 1278 does a '*Magistro Jacobo*' appear in the English records – very strong circumstantial evidence.

There is further strong evidence from the primary sources: the English scribes begin to describe Maître Jacques as Maître Jacques de Saint Georges. Recalling that the last entry for '*Magistri Jacobi*', of 8 December 1277, in Savoy, confirmed his having a '*domo*' in '*sanctum georgium de esperenchis*'; we then find nearly three years later that accounts at Rhuddlan to 3 November 1280 are compiled '*per visum ac testimonium Magistri Jacobi de Sancto Georgio*'. Family names were uncommon in the Middle Ages so it would be normal to either attach an occupational epithet as in '*Lathomo*' or a geographic moniker as in '*de Sancto Georgio*'. That Jacques never acquired a toponymic surname whilst based in Savoy would not invalidate an acquisition of one in England – it is simply that his work in the Viennois had by now acquired such fame that the scribe was now happier using '*de Sancto Georgio*' instead of '*Lathomo*' or '*Ingeniator*'.

For historians then, the primary sources and historical context do establish a plausible background for supposing the same identity: we have in Pierre de Savoie and the meeting of the summer of 1273 a means by which the English knew of the Savoyard mason. But is there any architectural or archaeological evidence to suppose a common identity? Taylor was certain that there was considerable such evidence, to suppose that we are indeed dealing with the same castle builder. Taylor, on his trips to the Alps found the following features common to those he knew so well in Wales: latrine projections of the shaft and corbelled variety, window embrasures and styles, fully centred arches and the unified nature of the groups in Savoy and Wales.[3]

We should now take some time to review the architectural evidence brought to us by Arnold Taylor. I have taken the time and had the considerable pleasure in visiting all the key Savoyard castle sites in question: Yverdon, Chillon, Grandson, Champvent, Estavayer, Lucens, Moudon, Rue, Romont, La Bâtiaz, Conthey, Saillon, Brignon, Saxon, Châtillon-sur-Chalaronne, Cicon, Gummenen, Saint-Georges-d'Espéranche, La Côte-Saint-André, Voiron and Saint-Laurent-du-Pont. So was Taylor accurate in his reportage?

Firstly, in terms of the unified group, I can confirm that the much-destroyed sites in the Viennois do indeed all show evidence of having had round towers. At La Côte-Saint-André the castle was largely destroyed by later building, but the brick base of one tower did survive and is round. Voiron is also largely destroyed and buried beneath undergrowth, but a sole remaining tower is also round. At Saint-Laurent-du-Pont there is almost no evidence whatsoever that a castle ever existed on the site, save a plaque to the effect that sits in the church foyer now occupying the grounds. But there is no evidence of a square tower and so we must conclude that we have no reason to dispute Taylor's assertion that in 1274 three rounded-tower castles were under construction. At Saint-Georges-d'Espéranche there is one tower remaining, and as Taylor suggests, it is indeed octagonal. Therefore, this essential thesis that a 'unified group' of castles were under construction simultaneously in the

Viennois, as they would later be in north Wales, is accurate. Historian Marc Morris agrees, suggesting that King Edward saw the 'unified group' of castles built in Savoy and perhaps 'want[ed] a lovely new set of fabulous castles in the mountains, like his cousins'.[4] Morris goes on to suggest that there was 'only one man for the job', a man with the ability, as we've said earlier, to construct simultaneously a group of castles to a high and varied specification.

Having visited both Saint-Georges-d'Espéranche and Harlech, I can indeed confirm the accuracy of Taylor's assertions in relation to the latrine projections: they are a close match. Furthermore, the treatment of the window design at Chillon is closely replicated by that at Harlech. Irritatingly, the Swiss restored the Chillon windows in the nineteenth century; however, the apertures closely, within centimetres, match the exact shape and design of those that grace the great gatehouse at Harlech. Taylor's assertions in regard of architectural evidence are still borne out by the built environment, but there's more. Putlog holes (literally 'put' 'log' in 'hole') are the cavities left in walls of the timber supports for the scaffolding used to construct those walls. Normally, they are horizontal, since the scaffolding was also horizontal.[5] Savoyard engineers, however, used helicoidal,[6] or slowly spiralling scaffolding in their construction. The putlog holes found at Harlech and Conwy are, unusually for the British Isles, helicoidal; in the Valais we find them at Saxon and Saillon. The garderobes[7] at Harlech, unique in Britain, are exactly the unusual design, inverted semi-conical set on corbels, also employed at La Bâtiaz in the Valais.[8] We have therefore numerous examples within the fabric of the castles built in Wales to link them with Savoy: we have windows, toilets and scaffolding holes. However, they are no proof in and of themselves of Maître Jacques' identity, they are merely confirmation of Savoyard builders having worked in both regions. Still, the case for a common identity does not rest upon the architectural evidence alone; we must take it together with the historical evidence cited earlier. The historical context of the Anglo-Savoyard relationship, the lack of a continuing archival reference to him in Savoy after 1275, his naming, once in England, Saint-George, and when these are added to the architectural evidence then we have, I suggest, evidence of common identity beyond reasonable doubt. Finally, Coldstream agreed, writing, 'his identification of James of St George's origins and the Savoyard elements in the castles in Wales are not in doubt and will certainly not be challenged here.'[9]

As autumn turned into the winter of 1278–9, Maître Jacques no longer appears in the court records – he was now based at Rhuddlan. Building in the Middle Ages was something that occupied the warmer months, the so-called building season of spring through to autumn – and this was especially true of the more northerly climes of north Wales. In Wales the main problem in winter was the shorter day, when candlelight was the only thing that illuminated the darkness for work. In Savoy the main blight of the winter months was snow, lots of it, so much of it that the great mountain passes, the Grand Saint-Bernard and Petit Saint-Bernard were impossible for travellers. Gloomy and damp though north Wales may have been, it was at least devoid of the heaps of snow he would have been used to, and oddly though he was now much farther north, the temperature would have been eased by the warming effects of the Gulf Stream – so in many ways winter would have passed more comfortably.

The surviving accounts roll for the building seasons of 1279 and 1280 together[10] cover a period from 5 March 1279 through to 3 November 1280. The work was concentrated on Rhuddlan rather than Flint; indeed by the end of 1280 the castle at Rhuddlan was more or less a finished structure. At Rhuddlan £5,611 had been expended in those two years – nearly £4 million at 2017 prices, no small sum. Of this the largest measure, nearly half, had been for the master masons and their wages, taking £2,083. The remainder had been diggers' wages of £204, carpenters of £124, transport charges of £1,531 and purchase of materials just £182. The bill for transportation sticks out quite markedly and reflects the need to bring much of the stone to site. It was preferable to use locally sourced stone to mitigate this cost; however, at Rhuddlan and to a lesser extent Flint this was not possible. The accounts prepared by William de Perton were certified 'under the supervision of the Master of James of St George, and the witness thereof'. [11]

Whereas £5,611 had been spent at Rhuddlan in 1279 and 1280 combined, the bills for Flint are far more modest. For 1279, 9 April until 29 October, a mere £61 was spent on the masons' wages there – nearly half that, £29.3s, on one feature alone, the revetment wall of the castle. Work at Flint appears to have been suspended at the end of the 1279 building season and not recommenced until August of 1280; the last operation, paid at task,[12] was the clearance of the lime kiln there.[13] Once the site had been reopened, the balance of the work that season seems to have been restricted to quarrying stone and construction of buildings to store lime and repair the lime kiln – in other words, largely work in preparation for a greater effort from 1281. The picture of 1279/80 in north Wales is then of concentrated work on the more important and larger Rhuddlan Castle with little work at the lesser Flint Castle. Maître Jacques therefore will have been largely overseeing the canalization of the River Clwyd and construction of the great castle at Rhuddlan before, and only then, turning his attentions to Flint.

The late appearance of Maître Jacques on the accounts at Flint, from November 1280, were a key argument used by Perfect against his involvement in its conception.[14] However, both Edwards and Taylor were certain that the cause was a pause in work at Flint and the concentration of activity at Rhuddlan.[15] Given the comparison of expenditures apparent in the archives, one is bound to support Taylor's view. The castle at Rhuddlan was intended to be a grand affair, the focus of the king's power in the four *cantrefi*. Flint was a much simpler construction, a staging point on the road from Chester to Rhuddlan and eventually the Conwy. It is only natural that a king should ask a master mason expensively imported from Savoy to concentrate on Rhuddlan before turning to complete Flint – strategy and common sense would seem to indicate so.

Work began in earnest at Flint with the arrival of Maître Jacques from November 1280. Lately, from May 1280, Jacques had been involved in assessing land and burgages in the new town at Rhuddlan as Bonel had proven unsatisfactory.[16] At Flint, masons' wages increased from £61 for the 1279 building season, April to October, to £650 for the slightly longer period from October 1280 until August 1281 – notwithstanding the slighter longer period being compared, a tenfold increase. Taylor was certain that 1281 represented a step change, writing, 'There can thus be little doubt that the year 1281 saw the biggest single advance of any in the progress of the Flint works.'[17] Detailed reading of Pipe roll TNA E101/674/23 allows us a fascinating insight into the sheer volume of effort required to complete even so modest a castle as Flint. Masons were paid for some 30,515 stones, each having to be hewn from the living rock and transported to site before being dressed and assembled. We are given names of the men who realized this difficult and back-breaking process: Master John of Chester, Walter of Lincoln, William of Southwell, William of Craven, Henry of Kirby, Elias of Moston, Michael le Normand, Robert of London, Robert of Ocle, John of Saint Faiths, William Seysil, Geoffrey Francis, Richard of Carlngton, William of Burton and Matthew Jardine – all recorded as contributing stones at between a penny and a penny and a half per stone. Recorded also are Peter Morel for work relating to the Great Tower and Thomas de Hardingesham for doorways of the Great Tower.[18] The Savoyard, William Seysil, as William Seysel will go on to work, as we shall see later, at Conwy. Other Savoyards noted at Flint include William Senin, likely to have begun life in the small hamlet of Senin near Parmilieu by the River Isère and Jean Pycard, almost certainly a rendering of the Vaudois family name Picard.[19] Flint would have been familiar to them as it was after all a *Carré Savoyard*, that is a square castle, towers at each corner, but one tower detached and of greater height and circumference serving as the keep and place of last refuge. We know that at least one of the curtain walls was now advanced enough to receive embrasures from the payments of fifty-one shillings made for same to John of Clifford, Richard of Wellingborough and John Page.

Further material that is itemized in the accounts for Flint is lime, costing £112.9s.6d (circa £80,000 today)[20] coming in four penny rings (or £12 bags today). The lime would provide mortar that would hold together the very fabric of the castle. Given the accounts we can estimate 87,000 bags of lime going to Flint alone – one must pause at this moment and imagine the movement of 87,000 bags of lime by cart to Flintshire in the thirteenth century, the building of Flint and Rhuddlan are then given perspective. The Pipe roll accounts for 17,000 bags having been provided between November 1281 and March 1282 alone – '*anno regni Regis Edwardi x° ante guerram*'. We also learn that parchment for accounts, joists for the tower floors and thatch for temporary roofs came to the site.[21] This was a task fit to have been set for Hercules himself. But if Maître Jacques was overseeing this monumental effort, we must also pause to reflect on the work of those named earlier, and in doing so we gain a new respect for our ancestors.

The first constable at Flint was a Savoyard knight long in the king's service, Sir Gerard de Saint Laurent, a household knight since at least 1274. He had accompanied Edward on crusade, which gives us a possible source for the resemblance of the Great Tower at Flint with the Tour Constance from Aigues-Mortes. Both the castle's patron, Edward, and its first constable, Gerard, had first-hand knowledge of the French crusader castle. We will never know the true origin of the Great Tower, but it has a number of potential fathers.

We can be clear from the archived accounts for the king's works in Wales that the sequence of jobs was broadly the following: firstly, a digging of ditches and palisade works at both Flint and Rhuddlan in 1277, oversight and continuation of same in 1278, concentration of work at Rhuddlan including canalization of the River Clwyd in 1279–81, and lastly concentration of work at Flint in 1281–2. Flint Castle remained unfinished, although defensible in 1282, whereas Rhuddlan was largely completed by this time.

Meanwhile, back in Savoy, Philippe was still having problems with the Bishop of Sion in the Valais. Accordingly, Philippe authorized construction of a new castle, more of a tower than a castle really, to be built at Saxon, on the southern slopes of the Rhône Valley, around six miles (ten kilometres) east of Martigny and on the opposite side of the wide valley from Saillon (Figure 2.1). With his erstwhile master mason now employed by his grand-nephew Edward in Wales, Philippe had to turn to seemingly the next masons off the family production line. As we have suggested, this production line had begun with a Maître Jean in the employ of Pierre, then Maître Jacques working for both Pierre and Philipe. Now at Saxon the Count of Savoy turned to Tassin and Giles de Saint-George whom we have earlier identified as potentially the sons of Jacques.[22]

The Savoyard archive allows us to date the circular tower[23] constructed there to 1279/80, exactly the same years in which work at Rhuddlan was coming to a conclusion. Payment of fifty *livres* was ascribed to '*Tassinum et Giletum fratrum ... pro dicta turre facienda*'[24] or the 'brothers Tassin and Giles ... for making that tower..[25] A man styled '*Beynardus*', whom we shall meet later in our story in Wales, also merits a mention at this point. The same helicoidal scaffolding technique that would be later employed in north Wales is evident, curling around the tower at Saxon. Beynardus, who was involved in digging the tower's foundation, gloried in the description '*celui qui dirige les brouettes*', which translates as 'the one who runs the wheelbarrows'.[26] One can imagine Beynardus running his wheelbarrows around the circular scaffolding of the growing tower at Saxon under the direction of the Saint-Georges brothers, a relationship with a family that will eventually lead him to Harlech around six years later. The tower became, with Saillon and La Bâtiaz, part of a network communicating by beacon any advance from the Bishop of Sion.[27] Unlike the castles constructed in the Viennois by their father, Saxon has survived the vagaries of time to provide a perfect example of the little castles constructed in Savoy that provided so much of the template for the castles yet to be built in north Wales.

In Britain, the political picture of north Wales from the standpoint of 1280 would require no more castles, as those built at Aberystwyth, Builth, Rhuddlan and Flint would provide Edward with the means to constrain Gwynedd. There is even the possibility that, had history unfolded differently, then Jacques might have found himself following his father and building a cathedral. Edward, with the support of Bishop Anian, had planned to relocate the existing cathedral at St Asaph to Rhuddlan. This suggestion, which survives in letters from both to the Pope, would have meant Rhuddlan becoming a city, thus the 1280 intention for it to become the spiritual and administrative centre for Edward in north Wales. Thus, it affirms that at this point Edward probably had little thought for a conquest of the whole of Gwynedd.[28]

The castles underway at Builth and Aberystwyth were far from finished. A report from the new Justiciar of West Wales, Bogo de Knovill, has survived from January 1280. Bogo de Knovill or Bewes de Knovill had been a loyal supporter of the royal cause during the Second Baronial War and throughout the First Welsh War. He had been sheriff of the counties of Shropshire and Staffordshire and keeper of the castles at Bridgenorth on the Severn and at the important border centre of Shrewsbury. Before being appointed Justiciar he had been the keeper of Dolforwyn Castle, or what was left of it following the siege of 1277. He wrote a report painting a sorry picture of the works he found at Aberystwyth, speaking of a castle without food and munitions, and worse one without 'locks' and 'bars'.[29] Bogo de Knovill went on to specifically suggest the intervention of the Master of the Works at Rhuddlan.[30]

We have evidence that at least some work was thus put in hand, but not by the Master of the Works at Rhuddlan, as instead, William de Canvil was ordered to receive two 250 marks from the Bishop of Saint Davids 'for the works of the castle of Lampadermaure … and to do the said works therewith'.[31] The Master of the Works at Rhuddlan was of course Maître Jacques, but since Knovill eventually employed Master Thomas from Bristol and others, then it seems Rhuddlan was more than occupying Maître Jacques at this time. The report points to the lack of any English preparedness or expectation of what was to come in 1282 but is also a reminder that Edward took some interest in the material state of his castles.[32]

Meanwhile, Edward was much involved in the negotiated return of Plantagenet lands in France, which culminated in the Peace of Amiens in 1279, aided by Savoyards Othon de Grandson and Jean de Grailly. This considerable diplomatic activity, including that recorded in the Calendar of Patent Rolls of 1280,[33] which attaches a word to Grandson that best describes his relationship with Edward personally and the English Crown professionally. On 26 July 1280, at Northampton, is issued a mandate to the usual source of finance, the Riccardi di Lucca, of a loan to Grandson. He's described as a member of the 'King's Household' but also the King's '*Secretarius*', which the translators of the CPR have helpfully rendered as 'king's secretary'.[34] But what did the word mean in the thirteenth century, and in an English context? Certainly not one, as in the modern sense, to undertake correspondence and administrative tasks, but rather, as the OED explains for the Middle Ages, a 'person entrusted with a secret' and more directly 'a confidential officer' of the king – in short what we might now call an envoy, and a senior one at that.[35]

The royal castles at Flint and Rhuddlan were not, however, the only castles building in north Wales at the close of the decade. Llywelyn's brother Dafydd had rebelled against his brothers' rule, then sought refuge in England and in the First Welsh War had sided with Edward against his brother. Accordingly, when the Treaty of Aberconwy was drawn up in the autumn of 1277, it sought not only to return the relationship between Crown and Llywelyn to that prior to the Treaty of Montgomery, it also sought to compensate Dafydd ap Gruffydd for his support of Edward. When the four *cantrefi* had been taken into royal hands, two of them, Rhufoniog and Dyffryn Clwyd, along with the Lordship of Hope, had been granted to Dafydd. The two *cantrefi* granted were not the reward Dafydd had anticipated, as they were of less importance and certainly not what Dafydd felt was his due for supporting Edward. Rhos and Tegeingl had been retained by the Crown and had become the site for the royal castles under construction at Flint (Tegeingl) and Rhuddlan (Rhos). In Edward's mind these new castles simply reinstated the control lost when Llywelyn had destroyed those at Dyserth and Deganwy, and of course, we should remember that Rhuddlan had been specified in his appanage.

The Lordship of Hope carried permission for a castle with it. Mentioned in the Domesday Book, the area was then the property of Gilbert de Venables. The castle would sit on a sandstone hill by the River Alyn, in the hills above the all-important coastal route into north Wales and with a good vantage of England. That building was underway at Hope, of Caergwrle Castle, can be seen from a gift of money made by Edward dated 12 November 1278: 'Dafydd ap Gruffydd, for the construction of his castle at Caergwrle. Sixty-six pounds. Thirteen shillings. Four pence [one hundred marks].'[36] Taylor suggests that the payment may imply that the granted castle might have been previously damaged by Llywelyn, but also that the payment was retrospective and therefore covered the 1278 building season – that Dafydd put the works in place immediately he took possession. There is some debate whether Dafydd's castle was a new construction or merely a repaired earlier work. John Manley found 'no hint from the excavation results [1988–90] of an earlier thirteenth century castle',[37] so the castle is more likely to have been built as new by Dafydd. Taylor goes on to suggest that, given the geographic proximity to Rhuddlan and Flint and Maître Jacques' role for Edward, the mason may have undertaken some work at Caergwrle, but there is no evidence to support or deny this idea.[38] If the building date is accepted, then work at Caergwrle was underway simultaneously with those for the king at Flint and Rhuddlan. What the payment does suggest is that Dafydd was still the king's man in 1278, that any dissatisfaction he had with his allotment of 1277 didn't extend to him not accepting the king's gift for the build or rehabilitation of his allotted castle.

Elsewhere, however, the facade of peace and harmony that had surrounded the relationship between Llywelyn and Edward at Worcester Cathedral in 1278 began to fray at the edges. Perhaps the first fly in the ointment was the Welsh *cantref* of Arwystli, which lay on the south-eastern border of Gwynedd, in mid-Wales, and had long been a disputed territory with Powys. Back in 1263, Llywelyn had ceded the *cantref* to rival Gruffydd ap Gwenwynwyn of Powys, before reversing his decision and reclaiming it in 1274. Following the Treaty of Aberconwy in 1277, the dispute arose again and was referred to Edward for conciliation. Llywelyn maintained that, as Arwystli was Welsh territory, then the Welsh law ought to apply, whereas Gruffydd ap Gwenwynwyn argued that as he was a Marcher lord, the law of the March, which was English common law, ought to apply. Edward decided not to decide and prevaricated upon resolving the matter. It has been suggested that Edward deliberately provoked Llywelyn in not deciding in his favour and not immediately treating his renewed vassal by Welsh law. Certainly, the matter belittled the Welsh prince, but I'm not so sure it was by design. The English naturally preferred their own law to what they saw as barbaric Welsh law, and this naturally equally alienated the Welsh.[39]

Morris suggests, something which I think governed Edward's motivations in pretty much everything that he did, that his main concern was not to repeat the mistakes of his father's reign. Edward had learned the very hard way, at an early age, where perceived weakness got you as a thirteenth-century monarch. There was also a casual racism in terms of the English treatment of the Welsh in the immediate years following the First Welsh War: the English viewed the Welsh as being fierce in battle, but fickle and not to be trusted in their bargains and relationships, casual sexually, less than civilized and generally of a lower order – in short barbaric. The Welsh had begun to be poorly treated by the English newcomers, but it was an ill treatment born more of attitude than by design. One who was also to lay his claim to English justice was a certain Madog ap Llywelyn,[40] who'd been exiled in England, received royal financial reward and now claimed what he saw as his right to Meirionnydd. His reward later of land in Anglesey would not be seen by Madog as fair recompense and be the kernel of a grievance that would return to haunt Edward.

In addition, Archbishop John Peckham records a list of several other Welsh legal complaints of English rule.[41] Dafydd would later summarize this Welsh feeling of being ill used by the English and their laws: 'though it was provided in the peace agreement that the Welsh should be tried in their causes according to Welsh laws, this was not observed with respect to Dafydd and his men.'[42]

However, perhaps the poor state of the new defences at Aberystwyth suggest a general feeling of relaxed overlordship of a defeated enemy who would accept subjugation and being put firmly in their place. That the Crown hadn't the least idea of what was to come is perhaps suggested by its willingness to allow key knights to leave the country, as evidenced by Pierre de Champvent being allowed leave to 'travel beyond seas' in the summer of 1281.[43] He wouldn't return, most likely from Savoy, until September 1282,[44] coming back to a very different country. This was of course the complacency of occupiers of foreign lands, in ignoring building resentment, which would come firmly back to bite them, the cause of surprise at many an uprising. As the new decade of the 1280s opened, unbeknownst to the English for a long while, tensions began to rise again in Wales.

Chapter Eight

During the night of 21 March 1282, a group of soldiers climbed the steep Norman motte of Hawarden Castle, near the border with England. The castle was new: Llywelyn had destroyed the original Norman motte-and-bailey castle back in 1265, but this was border country, and it had been rapidly reconstructed. The men moved quietly into position; it was Saturday, but not just any Saturday, this was the eve of Palm Sunday. There had been peace in Wales and the Marches since the autumn of 1277. That peace was about to be broken by the determined Welshmen that fell into the quiet of an English Easter. The small garrison at Hawarden slept, no doubt, after an evening eating and drinking. Inside the castle it was warm, and the men rested by the glow of comforting fires. Outside the castle it was cold and dark, the ground most likely wet as the invaders steeled themselves for the attack. As the men climbed the castle walls and reached the battlements, the alarm would have been given.

The defenders were not expecting to be attacked as they slumbered that Easter: the garrison was put to the sword. The holder of the castle, Marcher lord Roger de Clifford, was very badly wounded in the assault but survived to be taken prisoner by the assailant, Dafydd ap Gruffydd – he was a valuable prize. Clifford had fought with Edward at Evesham and accompanied him on crusade, being with him at Acre. On his return, as part of Edward's retinue that had traversed Italy and the Alps to Savoy in 1273, he had married whilst in Saint-Georges-d'Espéranche. Clifford had been rebuilding the castle at Hawarden, just six short miles (ten kilometres) from Dafydd's Caergwrle Castle.

The chronicler of Lanercost was one that wrote with monkish outrage that Dafydd, once allied to the king, had chosen Easter as a time to rebel.[1] It had long been the perceived custom amongst the men of Christendom that Easter was a time set aside from their bouts of periodic violence. This was a time of religious certainty; we should not overlook the sense of genuine horror that an attack at this time might provoke. If ever there was something that would reinforce amongst the English and French a sense of Welsh barbarism and somehow being on the extremity of Christendom, this was it. The capture of Hawarden that eve of Palm Sunday in March 1282 appeared to be the signal for a wider revolt, and almost at once the Welsh flew into rebellion, launching themselves upon the English. Thus began the Second Welsh War.

The causes of one war, especially those described as the 'Second' are often to be found in an earlier 'First' war. Most recently, in the last century, the seeds of the Second World War are to be found decisively in the First World War, the peace made at the end of the first war being in some way unsatisfactory to one party or incomplete. And so it was with the Second Welsh War: if we are to consider the reasons for the renewed conflagration, we must see the First Welsh War as the principal cause. Definitive historian of the Welsh wars John E. Morris wrote: 'No special cause for the rising need be sought beyond the natural wish for liberty and revenge.'[2] Quite so, the Welsh had been humiliated by the conclusion of the first war: Llywelyn ap Gruffydd had been once more reduced to being ruler of Snowdonia alone, and his brother Dafydd who'd expected much reward for his assistance of Edward had felt ill-used in receiving just his two *cantrefi*. Wales had once more been subjugated by the English, as they had been prior to the ascendancy of Llywelyn.

But still it was a tremendously risky and daring undertaking. The Gruffydd brothers had come to feel the full strength of Edward's determination in 1277–8 and must have known that his response would again be overwhelming. From the distance of many centuries, the rising looks to have had extraordinarily little chance of success and to have been the last throw of the dice by the princes of Wales, one that would ultimately lead not to their subjugation but to their total destruction. But perhaps it did not seem that way to the rebels who took so quickly to arms in 1282; perhaps they did indeed think there was some chance of success. In revolt the Welsh nurtured an outrage at English occupation and interference in their affairs, an outrage that had repelled lesser kings than Edward. But the 'Leopard'[3] was cut of a different cloth than his father, and with hindsight we can see clearly that his response would be total.

The rebellion appears to have been coordinated[4] and premeditated. The very next day the Marcher town of Oswestry was savagely attacked from Powys Fadog and elsewhere. Two days after Hawarden, the Welsh gained the castle at Aberystwyth by subterfuge though at least the doors and gates had been locked this time. Gruffydd ap Maredudd and Rhys Fychan ap Rhys ap Maelgwn invited the castle's constable to dinner no less, and there took him captive, whilst their men took the castle.[5] Initially no damage was done; however, within a day or two 'they burned the town and the castle and destroyed the rampart that was around the castle and the town'.[6] As Bogo de Knovill had feared, the castle at Aberystwyth had proven unequal to the task of restraining a Welsh rebellion. For the Welsh it was a hit-and-run attack, since they did not hold Aberystwyth. Within weeks, by mid-May, Edward dispatched Maître Jacques to 'construct' at 'the King's castle',[7] which implies much battle damage had been sustained. On 25 May, following an assessment of the work needed to make good the castle, requests were sent to Gloucester and Somerset for fifteen masons to be dispatched via Bristol. The name of one of those chosen by Maître Jacques was Maître Giles de Saint Georges. We have one wardrobe payment, from September 1282, in connection with Aberystwyth, to thank for identifying in full the man we think to be the son of Maître Jacques.[8]

Archaeological excavations, in 1975 and 1988, at Aberystwyth, confirm that work undertaken on the castle was indeed in two phases: the first from 1277 to 1282 in the aftermath of the First Welsh War, and phase two from 1282 to 1284 after the second war and under the auspices of Maître Jacques.[9] Giles had been previously employed, until at least 1280, by Count Philippe de Savoie, along with his likely brother, Tassin de Saint-Georges, in constructing his tower at Saxon in the Valais – now Giles too was in Wales. Whilst Tassin de Saint-Georges would remain in Savoy,[10] Taylor was convinced that *'Magistro Egidio de Sancto Georgio'* in the English wardrobe payment and *'Giletus de Sancto Georgio lathomus'* in the Savoyard archive were and are one and the same man – I think in the context of what we know it would be hard to argue otherwise. Between the Savoyard entry of 1280 and the English entry of 1282, he has acquired the *'Magistro'*. What is remarkable is that the English entry survived at all, since the scribe made a clerical error and attempted to strike out his entry, not sufficiently it seems. We have Taylor, the eagle-eyed former RAF intelligence officer, to thank for alerting us to both entries – one in London, the other Turin – of a man who 700 and more years ago found himself moving from the tower at Saxon and the Rhône Valley to mid Wales and the damaged castle at Aberystwyth. The common family name in both Savoyard and English records, the common profession, the common patrons, the likely ages for Jacques de Saint Georges and Giles de Saint Georges, led Taylor to suggest that Giles de Saint Georges was the son of Maître Jacques. Taylor made his case, most plausibly, for the family tree with 'controlled conjecture'.[11] His conclusion is hedged by his assertion that the link is 'not impossible' and therefore I think any challenge of hyperbole here would be unfair. We have no birth, death or marriage certificates – this is the thirteenth century – but his case does go, I think, beyond 'reasonable doubt'; certainly we have no evidence to the contrary.

Meanwhile, the castles at Flint and Rhuddlan apparently fared better than Aberystwyth; they were attacked on Palm Sunday, 22 March,[12] the day after the night attack on Hawarden. There are some accounts of them having fallen, but it is almost certain they withheld the onslaught and that reports of destruction refer to the associated towns growing around them rather than to the castles themselves. That neither castle appears to have fallen is perhaps fortunate, since neither had been completed at this point. Morris writes that both castles were 'in connection with Chester by water' which, if accurate, bears out Edward's wisdom in siting the castles as he had.[13] Siege engines were put to use in the assault on Rhuddlan, as evidenced by the Welsh use of stolen lead from Northop that had been intended for construction at Flint.[14] At Flint the first constable, Gerard de Saint Laurent, appears to have fallen at this point, as he no longer appears in the records following 1282. Sadly, we have no account of his death. On 25 March, writing to Roger de Mortimer, Edward, noting casualties at Flint, observed that certain of his men had been slain.[15] There is perhaps another allusion to his death in that his *'valettus'*,[16] or manservant, Sengin, was taken into the king's pay at this time.[17] His replacement at Flint would be William de Perton, the clerk who'd worked alongside Maître

Jacques at Rhuddlan. St Laurent was one of the first Savoyard casualties of the Welsh wars – he would not be the last.

The extent of Llywelyn's prior knowledge of the rebellion is the subject of much debate; he himself later denied any prior involvement. Either way, his brothers' attack on Hawarden and the subsequent widespread revolt left him with no option other than to join a full and irrevocable rebellion against Edward. Welsh historian Davies recalls: 'he had little option but to join the revolt and to assume its leadership, indeed he had probably every inclination to do so.'[18] Prestwich is condemnatory of Edward in driving Dafydd into common cause with his brother Llywelyn, calling his policy toward them following the First Welsh War 'remarkably inept'.[19] Some have seen Llywelyn's remaining in north Wales, whilst Dafydd immediately went south to encourage rebellion there, as evidence of the former's reluctance to join the revolt – I think this is unlikely. Having condemned Edward, Prestwich had earlier found it 'hard to imagine' that Llywelyn had been drawn into rebellion at the last moment.[20] The chronicler of Guisborough was in no doubt, waxing lyrically, likening Llywelyn and Dafydd to Herod and Pilate who had been similarly agreed in insurrection.[21] The chronicler of Chester was also in no doubt that the brothers had been acting in concert.[22] Perhaps these English monks are partial witnesses, but they should not be disregarded lightly.

Dafydd would later assign much of the blame for his insurrection to Reginald de Grey.[23] On 14 November 1281, Grey had been appointed Justiciar of Chester; he was granted the county of Cheshire, the king's demesne lands in north Wales, described as 'Engelfield [Tegeingl] and Ros', together with the 'castles of Chester and Flint' but not 'the castle of Rothelan'. There was also a mandate to the Savoyard constable of Flint, 'Gerard de Sancto Laurencio to deliver to him the castle of Flint'.[24] Gerard de Saint Laurent was to give up the castle by Michaelmas of 1281; the extent to which this actually happened on the ground is uncertain – as mentioned earlier the Savoyard perished in the rebellion of 1282 and possibly never left the castle.

It would be the arrival of Grey, to which Dafydd later pointed to as the beginning of the downward spiral in relations between himself and the Crown. Beverley Smith calls Grey's rule 'harsh and capricious';[25] if this is so, then it took little time to incite Dafydd to armed revolt: November 1281 to March 1282 is little time to reign as a tyrant. Nonetheless, despite Grey's testimony not having survived, an impartial reading of Dafydd's later complaints would conclude that he most likely had a case to answer. We will never know for certain if Dafydd's complaints of Grey were of an overly sensitive Welshman or an overly insensitive Englishman, but we can be certain of the subsequent rebellion. The Hagnaby chronicler tells us that a meeting had been arranged to reconcile Dafydd with Grey and Clifford, but that Dafydd intended to kidnap both Grey and Clifford. Clifford, on getting wind of the plot, retired to the supposed sanctuary of Hawarden Castle which was then subsequently attacked by Dafydd.[26] Whether the infringements of Dafydd's dignity which he reported warranted armed rebellion remains open to question, or whether the Hagnaby chronicler's tale holds water, we cannot tell – what is beyond doubt is the attack lit the fire of rebellion.

Edward heard of the rebellion almost immediately; on 25 March 1282 he issued writs carried by Bogo de Knovill for three commanders of English forces to suppress the rebellion: Roger de Mortimer in the Marches, Reginald de Grey at Chester and Robert de Tibetot, another who'd accompanied Edward on crusade, in west Wales. If Edward had thought ill of Llywelyn as a vassal who had refused to pay him due homage and had threatened his royal *majesté*, then one can only imagine how he might have responded to outright armed rebellion – and worse, outright armed rebellion of a man who'd treated with him at Aberconwy. That the attack initially came from his one-time ally Dafydd ap Gruffydd would have filled him with feelings of betrayal and treachery. Had not his father been betrayed and deceived many times, but not responded ruthlessly? News of Hawarden would have played into every prejudice the king held of the faithless and devious Welsh. In making his proclamation he declared that he would 'repress the rebellion and malice of the Welsh'. A little of the sense of English outrage at perceived Welsh duplicity is conveyed by the Chester chronicler, writing of Llywelyn, as being of a '*Stirps mendax, causa malorum*', a 'lying race, the cause of evil'.[27] The use of the word '*mendax*' is striking; it can be literally translated as 'lying' but also as 'deceptive' – it is the root of 'mendacious' and 'mendacity' in modern English. If Edward had learned one thing from his father's reign, it was that rebellion, betrayal and treachery had to be met with the full force a king's might.

A council was summoned to meet, at Devizes on 5 April, where Tibetot was replaced as the southern army commander by the Earl of Gloucester. The former Justiciar of Ireland, and brother to Jean de Joinville, French chronicler of Saint Louis, Geoffrey de Joinville, worked as an assistant to the Marshal of England. A general recall to arms brought Othon de Grandson back to England from Savoy, and by 7 May he was commanding seventeen lances[28] at Montgomery.[29] Roger de Mortimer had a further eighteen and the Earl of Lincoln '100 horse and 600 foot' and that 'within a month of David's capture of Hawarden over 200, within two months over 300, lances of the household and paid squadrons were in arms'.[30]

Household knights, fifteen to be exact, along with nearly 100 troopers, proceeded north to Chester under the command of Amédée de Savoie. The Savoyard was the second son of the late Thomas II de Savoie, Count of Flanders, elder brother to Pierre and Philippe, and the man whose request for payment from Henry III had done so much to damage the king's relationship with Simon de Montfort. Amédée had been born in 1249 and, along with his younger brother Louis, had been long in Edward's service. He was another that had been at Saint-Georges-d'Espéranche that summer of 1273 and had served in the First Welsh War in 1277 with the king – the King's Wardrobe expenses for 1278 note some £230 paid to Amédée in wages and expenses.[31]

Once at Chester, a relief expedition was mounted to come to the assistance of the beleaguered defenders of Flint and Rhuddlan. The Chester annalist suggests the castles had come under siege, '*eodem die*',[32] on the same day, as the attack on Hawarden, 21–22 March, and as mentioned earlier there is talk of lead for siege engines at Rhuddlan. Prestwich suggests that 'Llywelyn ap Gruffydd himself … took part in attacks on Flint and Rhuddlan.'[33] We may never know for sure, but nevertheless, after a siege of a month, on or about 21 April 1282, we know that Amédée de Savoie led his column along the road to Flint and Rhuddlan, a Savoyard-led English invasion of Wales. The evidence for the king having entrusted the relief of his castles to the future Count of Savoy comes from a letter dated 9 May: '*fu ozd nos a lever le sieche du Rodelan*,' that is 'for our lift of the siege of Rhuddlan.'[34]

The Welsh sieges of Flint and Rhuddlan now lifted, attention turned to the castles which had been damaged, as evidenced by the work in subsequent years to make good the attempts of the Welsh insurgents to bring them down. The relief operation was relatively short, Amédée being able to return to Chester within four days – on or about 25 April. The future Count of Savoy is recorded as '*domino … Capitaneo*' of the English relief army.[35]

Once back in Chester, news reached him of the death of his elder brother and heir apparent as Count of Savoy, Thomas III de Piedmont.[36] Amédée would be needed to help maintain order in Savoy.[37] Within three years Philippe himself would be dead without an heir, leaving Edward a role in the Savoyard succession. Philippe's will arranged for his niece Queen Alianor de Provence and her son King Edward I of England the solemn duty of awarding the Savoyard inheritance. So, it was in 1285 that Edward decided between two knights formerly in his service, Amédée and Louis. Edward's judgement was to make Amédée the Count of Savoy, whilst creating a new Barony of Vaud for his younger brother Louis. Amédée went on to be a successful Count of Savoy, gaining the epithet *grand* – becoming Amédée le Grand de Savoie. That the King of England should decide the Savoyard succession and indeed that the future Count of Savoy should lead the relief of Flint and Rhuddlan castles in 1282 speaks volumes of the intimacy of the relationship between the Kingdom of England and the County of Savoy in the late thirteenth century – despite Matthew Paris's protestations, the seeds sewn by Henry and Alianor were continuing to bear fruit.

If Llywelyn had had any doubts as to the wisdom of joining Dafydd's rebellion, those doubts must have surely ended in June. His wife, Eleanor de Montfort, had been with child at the moment the revolt erupted, in June she gave birth to a daughter for Llywelyn; she would be christened Gwenllian. However, childbirth in the thirteenth century was not an easy passage, and sadly Eleanor died on 19 June at Abergwyngregyn, and with her passed any hope Llywelyn had of a male heir. The body of this niece of Henry III, the daughter of Simon de Montfort, this cousin of Edward I and lately Princess of Wales, was taken to the Monastery of Fagan the Little or Llanfaes. On 12 July, members of Eleanor's personal household were given safe conduct whilst traveling back into England, leaving Llywelyn to face his moment of destiny alone.[38] It has been speculated that in despair and losing all hope he joined his brothers' fight.[39] We will never know for certain if this romantic lost cause led Llywelyn into battle, or if, as the Chester chronicler relates, that he was with Dafydd in rebellion from the beginning.[40] Following the war, little Gwenllian would be taken by Edward into the custody of a nunnery at Sempringham in Lincolnshire, there to live out her days in lonely contemplation of a life denied her, the last Princess of Wales.[41]

War was then, as now, an expensive business. Shortly after the attack on Hawarden the king was already resorting to the money houses of Italy to finance a campaign that he knew would be decisive in the struggle between King and Prince. The Calendar of Welsh Rolls records, on 14 April, 1,000 marks were immediately made available in London 'by the Riccardi[42] and further multiple supplies of 1,000 marks from Siena, Piacenza, Florence and others to total 11,300 marks,[43] and further advances of 1,000-mark portions for a similar sum from the same Italian wells on 10 June.[44] An order was sent to the Savoyard seneschal of Gascony, Jean de Grailly, for 'forty good crossbowmen on foot and twelve crossbowmen on horseback'.[45] At least half the cost of these Gascon crossbowmen would be met from Riccardi money.[46] The Gascons, along with their 70,000 bolts, including baneret Guillaume de Monte Ravelli, 'fought and swaggered, as befitted the forebears of d'Artagnan'. But the enormous financial demands of the Second Welsh War began to show the first cracks in the 'Riccardi system' as the merchants added the following ominous warning in a letter to Edward: 'thanks to God [the orders] have been paid up to the present and will continue to be paid if in our power.'[47] Requests were dispatched to all corners of the kings realm, both in England and overseas for the resources, food and materials of war that would furnish one of the greatest armies ever to be put into the field by a medieval King of England.

By 16 June Edward was in Chester once more, 'pitching his tent at Newton', today a suburb north-east of the city.[48] By 31 July, his brother Edmund, along with his wife Blanche d'Artois, had arrived in Chester.[49] There were to be two thrusts into north Wales this time. In addition to the coastal march from Chester to the Conwy by way of the forest road and Flint and Rhuddlan castles, there was to be a left flank to the English assault. Dafydd ap Gruffydd had been granted the two inland of the four *cantrefi* and his fiefdom would imperil the king's flank if not taken care of. Dafydd's territory encompassed Dyffryn Clwyd and Rhufoniog along with the castle at Caergwrle, but also Denbigh and Hawarden. Reginald de Grey was assigned the role of clearing the king's left flank, along with the traitorous Dafydd, from his lands. Edward moved along the coast road to Flint, where he'd arrived and encamped by 6 July,[50] and by the next Thursday he was once more at his castle of Rhuddlan. It's possible to assume the formerly besieged castle had not fallen or was defensible, as he'd taken Leonor with him[51] – quite something for a queen to travel into what was still to all intents and purposes a war zone.

Meanwhile, the English had also moved up the River Dee, Dafydd conceding Caergwrle without a fight, but not before slighting the castle he'd so recently reconstructed at the king's expense. By 16 June 1282, Grey had moved to take possession of what remained of the castle sitting high atop its hill. Manley's report of extensive excavations between 1988 and 1990 indicate that, within the castle, the English would have found little more than a 'building site'.[52] Master Richard of Chester, who had begun the work at Flint in 1277–8, assembled some 340 carpenters and directed seventeen workgroups of twenty men to repair the castle. By early July the workforce had risen to include over 600 diggers and up to thirty-five masons – as in 1277 the English progress would be slow but relentless. Following his sojourn down in Aberystwyth, Jacques had moved back to north-east Wales, where on 4 July 1282, he is recorded once more, this time at Caergwrle.[53]

Edward had visited Caergwrle or Hope, riding the short distance from Chester, following the capture of the castle, and had given instructions to Maître Jacques for its repair.[54] The work was not easy: workmen fell from the tower a number of days later, receiving compensation, hence our knowledge of the daily rigours of working with stone in high places.[55] The workmen were drawn from the northern and midland counties of England, and in addition to removing the tower left unsafe by Dafydd, they engaged in the vital work of clearing wells and ensuring the water supply of the new garrison.[56] A reminder that a master mason's work involved far more than building castles, it also involved their repair. Apparently the making good of the castle and its water supply was celebrated by the dispatch to the King of two barrels of newly recovered water, an interesting thought and a reminder of the importance to a castle of a good supply of drinking water, something Llywelyn had overlooked at Dolforwyn back in 1277.

Grey appointed Hugh de Pulford as constable of the castle and gave him a force of thirty crossbows and no less than 2,600 archers as protection for Maître Jacques, Master Richard and the men repairing the slighted castle.[57] Clearly, the English were expecting to be challenged, but Dafydd had withdrawn, not wishing to be caught in a besieged castle, fluidity of movement being the Welsh *modus operandi*. Grey took the castle of Ewloe overlooking the Dee estuary, uncontested as it had been back in 1277. As the English were protecting their flank for further progress, another castle was yielded without a fight by Dafydd, the seizure of which, earlier that year, had precipitated the whole revolt and subsequent war – Dafydd abandoned Hawarden Castle. Grey moved next into the two *cantrefi* granted to Dafydd for life by Edward, back in 1277, at the Treaty of Aberconwy: firstly, Dyffryn Clwyd and Ruthun, where a new castle had been begun in 1277, contemporaneously with those at Flint and Rhuddlan. A July or August 1277 payment relating to works there is our best evidence of castle building, that 'construction was going on at Ruthun castle'.[58] Its possible preliminary work had begun prior to the decision to grant Dyffryn Clwyd and Rhufoniog to Dafydd made on 10 October 1277. Dafydd would have assumed responsibility for castle work at Ruthun from this point, but sadly we have no record of his progress in the years between 1277 and 1282.

But by August 1282, the English had once more taken possession of whatever there was in terms of a castle at Ruthun. An English army came inland from Rhuddlan, following the River Clwyd by way of Llandyrnog to meet up with Grey at Ruthun by 28 August. We know that Edward himself was present at Ruthun between 31 August and 8 September and this visit is most likely in connection with a decision to resume work on the castle. In October we have evidence that Maître Jacques, like his patron Edward, had moved on from Caergwrle[59] to Ruthun and was being paid for 'clays'.[60] 'Clays' were the wicker screens used in thirteenth-century scaffolding. That autumn the king dismembered the lands of Dafydd ap Gruffydd, Rhufoniog and Dyffryn Clwyd, and of Powys Fadog, amongst his loyal lieutenants. The grants of land give us some idea of the king's movements, but also that of his household knights, including Othon de Grandson, who bore witness to each of the three charters.

On 23 October at Denbigh, the Justiciar, Reginald de Grey, was granted the castle at Ruthun and *cantref* of Dyffryn Clwyd for himself.[61] Dafydd's former overlordship was most certainly at an end, Edward installing men he could trust in Dyffryn Clwyd. Thereafter, responsibility for Ruthun and the castle being constructed there fell to Grey and falls from the Royal Archive.

Earlier, on 7 October at Rhuddlan, Edward had granted Castell Dinas Brân, which occupied a prominent hilltop site above the River Dee in Powys Fadog, to Jean de Warenne, Earl of Surrey.[62] The castle had probably been built in the 1260s, before his death in 1269, by the Lord of Dinas Brân, Gruffydd ap Madog, Prince of Powys Fadog, on the site of several earlier structures.

The king had made the grant of Ruthun from Denbigh, the centre of the second *cantref* he'd granted to Dafydd in 1277 – Rhufoniog. We are uncertain as to whether a castle had been begun at Denbigh by Dafydd; perhaps there is evidence of works in that Denbigh only fell to the English following a month-long siege that autumn of 1282.[63] The site of the present castle was granted to another loyal lieutenant, the man who'd been at the siege of Dolforwyn back in 1277 – Henri de Lacy, Earl of Lincoln. He was granted Denbigh, Ros and Rhufoniog at Rhuddlan, on 16 October 1282.[64] The dismemberment of Dafydd's one-time land as spoils of war to men who could be trusted by Edward was now complete. Rhos and Tegeingl would remain crown land in the possession of Edward himself, Dyffryn Clwyd had gone to Grey, much of Powys Fadog to Warenne and now Rhufoniog to Lacy. Again, as with Ruthun, that the castle works now fell into private hands meant they also fell from the Royal Archive. L. A . S. Butler suggests that with Henri de Lacy at Denbigh in October 1282 was not only the king himself, but also Maître Jacques. He suggests that the king had a 'close involvement in the siting of the castle and the plan adopted for it'.[65] If this is so, then it means that Denbigh evolved in a way as a mirror opposite of its nearby neighbours at Rhuddlan and Flint. Maître Jacques was involved at the earlier castles after initial work had been carried out, and then took over operations, but at Denbigh the opposite: he undertook initial work with the king before handing over to others. What we can see here would be Edward and Jacques operating in tandem: patron and master mason. Precisely how much design each of the partners was responsible for, has been, and will forever be, the subject of much debate, rather like which verse did Lennon write and which McCartney. What is certain is that they would become a formidable team.

The king's left flank had now been secured, the two *cantrefi* granted to the treacherous Dafydd retaken and placed in loyal hands, and order was being restored to the lands east of the Conwy. Ahead of Edward now lay the forbidding mountain fastness of Snowdonia, the very heart of Gwynedd. When he'd had just cause to take Gwynedd, Edward's father Henry III had twice sheathed his sword in the 1240s. Edward too had foregone an invasion across the Conwy, deciding to leave Gwynedd in the hands of Llywelyn in 1277, despite having taken the breadbasket of Anglesey. But now there would have to be a final reckoning with the House of Gwynedd, this was not 1241, nor 1247 or even 1277, it was 1282, Edward would now make an end of the perennial Gwynedd problem.

But also that summer Edward had learned of a disaster that had befallen an English army in south Wales, which had given him reason to pause. Edward's plan had been to strike into Wales with three armies: himself in the north, Marcher Lord Mortimer in mid Wales and Red Gilbert, the Earl of Gloucester, in the south. Edward had initially decided that his trusty fellow crusader, Robert de Tibetot, ought to lead the southern army but the Earl of Gloucester, perhaps living up to his fiery name, had insisted on control. Gloucester was to lead his army from Carmarthen and Dinefwr in the south toward Aberystwyth in mid Wales, thus cutting Llywelyn off from any hope of retreat southward from Gwynedd and restoring order to the south which had joined the rebellion.

On 17 June 1282, the army had sacked the Welsh castle of Carreg Cennen, whence they returned to Dinefwr Castle with the spoils. Traditionally, English columns travelling in Wales had been beset by hit-and-run guerrilla tactics, the Welsh taking advantage of their intimate knowledge of the land. Edward had been meticulously circumspect in his progress in north Wales, both in 1277, by use of the forest road and castles at Flint and Rhuddlan, but also in 1282, by his careful protection of his left flank in taking Caergwrle, Ruthun and Denbigh before progressing to the Conwy. But the impetuous Red Gilbert was not Edward; he had been travelling through south Wales with all the lack of care taken by earlier defeated English armies. As historian Morris confirms: 'carelessly without scouts'[66] they wandered into an ambush. Sure, enough at Llandeilo Fawr the Welsh descended like furies upon Gloucester's 100 knights and some 1,000 foot soldiers and destroyed them almost to a man. The result was a temporary stalling of Edward's three-pronged assault on Llywelyn. Edward replaced Gilbert de Clare with his own half-uncle Guillaume de Valence.

In the middle march, the king's commander and loyal servant, Roger de Mortimer, died on 26 October 1282, being replaced by Roger L'Estrange. What happened next would be pivotal in Anglo-Welsh history. No doubt Llywelyn felt the weakness of the English in the south, the potential weakness in mid Wales following the death of Mortimer, the strong English army led by the king across the Conwy to his immediate front – all of these things pulled Llywelyn south from Gwynedd toward a date with destiny.

But before Llywelyn moved south, and as Edward paused at the Conwy, the Archbishop of Canterbury, John Peckham,[67] intervened to prevent further bloodshed. Perhaps also on the mind of the archbishop was the damage the war was doing to his church: the recent burning of the cathedral at Saint Asaph in the Perfeddwlad would have displeased him greatly –ecclesiastical concern not overly welcomed by the king, who felt he had the troublesome Prince of Wales cornered. Edward's terms for Llywelyn had hardened since those offered and accepted at Aberconwy in 1277; the latest revolt had angered him to the point of losing all patience with the Welsh prince. Exile and land in England to the value of £1,000 for Llywelyn and banishment on crusade for Dafydd were the best and only terms Edward would offer. They were perhaps not meant to be accepted, and accepted they weren't. The intercession by the archbishop gives us an opportunity, not only to see the specific reasons the Welsh gave at the time for rebellion, but also the sentiment behind it, a sentiment that would echo down the centuries, as perhaps it was meant to.

Archbishop Peckham was an unlikely peacemaker between England and Wales, holding a traditional conservative worldview that saw the people of Wales as decidedly barbarian in their ways. Long before the war and his intercession, he had described Wales to Edward as *'vostre terre sauvage de Gale'*.[68] Nonetheless, intervene he did, and his exchanges with both Llywelyn and Dafydd survive in Peckham's *Registrum epistolarum*.

Dated, 11 November 1282, at Garthcelyn, we have recorded Llywelyn's response.[69] With a simultaneous appeal to myth and legend, in the Welsh prince's descent from the original founders of Britain, the descendants of the Trojan Brutus,[70] but also the status agreed by the Treaty of Montgomery, signed by the king and his father, as agreed by Ottobuono and sealed at Rhyd Chwima, we see Llywelyn holding firm. But one has the distinct feeling that the Welsh prince was writing for posterity rather than as part of any ongoing negotiation likely to bear fruit. The correspondence with Peckham clearly coveys that any negotiation the archbishop might have thought possible was manifestly futile; the Gruffydd brothers and King Edward were bent upon a path that would decide the fate of Wales for generations to come.

Dated as they were, 11 November, we can see that the communication with Peckham was undertaken from a position where events had already taken England and Gwynedd beyond the point of no return: further hostilities had already recommenced. These events perhaps explain more than any other the hardening of the line taken by Llywelyn and Dafyddtheir replies of 31 October and 11 November. Edward had a plan to complete the conquest and whereas in 1277 he had been content to merely punish the Welsh prince, now he intended to destroy him, and that required an assault on Snowdonia itself. His mood that November is expressed in a letter that survives in the Calendar of Welsh Rolls, in which he describes 'putting down the malice of the Welsh'.[71]

It seems it had been his plan all along; he'd intended to occupy Anglesey, as in 1277, thus depriving Llywelyn of his larder. Edward had brought up the Cinque Ports fleet to Chester once more, firstly to assist in the supply of his army relieving Flint and Rhuddlan. But then the king had a new and remarkably audacious plan: he would build a bridge across the Menai Strait from Anglesey to the mainland, a bridge of pontoon boats. The Menai Strait is some sixteen miles (twenty-five kilometres) in length, but only 13,000 feet (4,000 metres) wide at the narrowest point; the flow of water is tidal. On 24 May, he ordered Stephen of Penchester, the warden of the Cinque Ports, to choose up to twelve carpenters who might build boats and barges for the purpose, and they should be ready for work not later than 23 June. Accordingly, some 200 men from the Cinque Ports assembled on the Wirral shore of the River Dee. Sandwich, in the county of Kent, supplied twenty carpenters, and following abortive attempts to build in Kent, they found themselves journeying to the Wirral.

That summer, between 30 July and 9 August, the King's Wardrobe records payments made to Robert FitzJohn for poles from Chester in order to make punts and pontoons for the bridge. Master Richard began with a small construction camp near Llanfaes. The incredible structure soon took shape once the army under Luke de Tany, seneschal of Gascony before Savoyard Jean de Grailly, had occupied Anglesey. Striding across the Menai floated a bridge of interlinked boats bearing upon them a flat section of sufficient width to allow the army to make a crossing. Final construction had seen sixty carpenters cross to the island under Master Richard and a further 100 under Master Henry of Oxford. It was a colossal undertaking, most likely from a work camp near the site of the future castle at Beaumaris.[72] Master Bertram appears to have supervised the undertaking, with Master Richard being his deputy on this occasion.[73] Their reward was a tun of wine each, along with wine for the workforce.[74] Guisborough suggests the bridge was wide enough for sixty men to proceed abreast, which is most unlikely; the Hagnaby chronicler has a more plausible fifteen. The perils of reading medieval sources are evident when we consider that the 'lx' in the Guisborough chronicle may well be a scribal copy error from an original 'ix' – nine men being a whole lot more plausible than sixty.[75]

Five days prior to the intervention of Archbishop Peckham, some of the English took events into their own hands in search of glory. On 6 November 1282, Luke de Tany led a number of knights, including Othon de Grandson, who'd earlier been at Montgomery and Rhuddlan, and around 300 men-at-arms across the bridge. They passed beneath the lower slopes of the mountains opposite Anglesey, while behind them the tide reached its full height and cut off any route back. They were dangerously exposed to the classic Welsh tactic of ambush. The chronicler Walter of Guisborough, although he was not there and wrote from some years distance, gave a full account of what would become known as the Battle of Moel-y-Don,[76] as originally translated by Morris:

> ... the Welsh came down upon them from the mountains. Our men, panic stricken at the sight of their numbers, preferred to face the water rather than the enemy. They plunged into the sea, burdened as they were with their armour, and were all drowned in a moment.[77]

A Welsh chronicler wrote:

> And they desired to gain possession of Arfon. And then was made a bridge over the Menai; but the bridge broke under an excessive load, and countless numbers of the English were drowned, and others were slain.[78]

Their leader Luke de Tany paid for his impetuosity and lust for glory with his life; others, including the son of Llywelyn's prisoner Roger de Clifford, and Lord Chancellor Robert Burnell's sons Philip and William – in total sixteen knights – perished.[79] The Hagnaby chronicler, alone, suggests that Clifford, not Luke de Tany, led the charge, anxious to avenge his father's capture at Hawarden, which does, as Prestwich says, have a ring of 'plausibility' about it.[80] Remarkably, Othon de Grandson survived the battle and his horse carried him to the safety of Anglesey, but this would not be the first remarkable brush with death the Savoyard would have in his ninety-year-long life.[81] The Chester chronicler recalled that 'with much difficulty Lord Othon de Grandson escaped'.[82] The Lanercost chronicler took his account from Grandson whilst the Savoyard was with the King's army years later in the Scottish borderlands.[83]

The effect of the disaster was to strengthen the king's resolve; one can only imagine Edward's response on first hearing of Luke de Tany's pre-emptive assault on Snowdonia. The chronicler Thomas Wykes saw in the attack an attempt to pre-empt peace negotiations, and although negotiations continued, no peace or truce came into effect.[84] The defeat risked Edward's carefully laid plans, as had the earlier defeat at Llandeilo Fawr. It seemed that the king's servants were doing their best, in their eagerness to please the king, to handicap his subjugation of Gwynedd. Taylor suggests that the Welsh didn't destroy the bridge following their 'hit and run' victory, recording new materials being sent to Anglesey for bridgework between 23 November and 28 December.

Archbishop Peckham fired one last rhetorical salvo at Llywelyn and left for England. The archbishop was, like Pontius Pilate, washing his hands of the Welshman who claimed descent from Brutus – that these men of Troy, Peckham said, came by the island of Britain not without the tricks of the devil and idolatry.[85] In short, there was an adherence to prophecy and pagan ways that only the cleansing purification of Edward's army could now give remedy. With that, his patience exhausted, Archbishop John left Wales for Herefordshire, and Snowdonia to the cleansing he was sure would come. Although we have no surviving record, many scholars believe that the archbishop now pronounced a sentence of excommunication on Llywelyn.[86] In one last intervention, after the war, in June 1284, the archbishop reminded Edward, indeed he'd promised in 1282 in writing to the Princes of Gwynedd,[87] of the suffering of religious houses during the conflict. Peckham was as good as his word, and Edward duly compensated 107 religious houses, including those at Valle Crucis and Bangor. Edward, meanwhile, stood by the Conwy and would soon resume his assault, summoning more footmen to his ranks.[88] Edward's father had held back from a conquest of Gwynedd in 1247, when he would have been more than within his rights to go ahead, Edward himself had held back in 1277 when he left Llywelyn Uwch Gwynedd. This time there would be no leniency toward what Edward saw as the 'malice' that continued to emanate from the wilds of Snowdonia. This time would be the reckoning for the House of Gwynedd. Despite the disaster on the Menai, he would go on, and news from mid Wales would soon bring the king better news.

Llywelyn ap Gruffydd has become known in Wales by another name: *Llywelyn Ein Llyw Olaf* literally Llywelyn our Last Leader, or more usually Llywelyn the Last. This latterly fastened epithet carries with it all the baggage of romanticized history, of longing for a lost leader and a lost country. But we must be careful in writing history not to take visions and ideas from our own times and transpose them on to historical figures. The fragments of the past are left behind, like islands, by the receding tide of time and can make a trap for the romantically inclined.

In early December 1282, Llywelyn was at Abergwyngregyn, his familial seat in Snowdonia, not very far from the newly supposed battle-site of Moel-y-Don, the scene of his recent victory over the English. But as Edward licked his wounds across the Conwy and no doubt ruminated on the rash actions of Luke de Tany, Llywelyn led his army southward, perhaps equally rashly. The Welsh princes were, as ever, not defending land so much as defending freedom and independence of action. It had long been their tactic to trade land for the ability to keep an army intact and able to fight the invader. So, it's not surprising perhaps, that Llywelyn left Dafydd in charge of the defence of Snowdonia, sought to open a new front to the south.

Accounts of what happened from this point are confused and contradictory, but it is possible to piece together a likely story, even if we cannot arrive at a definitive narrative. Llywelyn made for the Marches of mid Wales, the land of the Mortimers, and there met his end. The circumstances surrounding his death are confused: there are reports of treachery, that Llywelyn was separated from his army by the ruse of a meeting with the Mortimers to broker either a truce or a promise of homage to the prince on the part of the Marchers. For some reason Llywelyn parted from his army and made for Aberedw, by the River Irfon, just to the south-east of Builth.[89] The Guisborough chronicler gives the name of the assailant as '*Stephano de Franketone*', or Stephen de Frankton.[90] Some chroniclers recorded that a knight had taken the life of the Welsh prince, but Morris was able to track down Stephen de Frankton with some degree of accuracy, writing, 'A Stephen de Frankton reappears in 1287 as a cenetar of Shropshire infantry in command of a company from Ellesmere.'[91] The Hagnaby chronicler suggests that Llywelyn was chased into a wood, put up a stout resistance, but died calling out his name, and that it was upon this recognition that he was decapitated.[92] Either way, the head of the fallen prince was then washed and despatched to Edward at Rhuddlan.

The head would be displayed in London, on a spike, adorned with a crown of ivy, mocking the prophecy that a Briton would eventually be crowned in London. In this spirit, Stephen of Saint George, writing from Orvieto a little later, described Llywelyn in terms that probably speak of the joy of many Englishmen after years of conflict with Gwynedd. He denounces the former prince as 'the old serpent … father of treachery, child of rebellion, son of iniquity, author of sedition, patron of ingratitude, convict of perjury and head of all evil'.[93] Once more with feeling one might observe.

In addition to the stone monument at Cwm-Hir there is another at the village of Cilmeri, inscribed '*Llywelyn Ein Llyw Olaf*' or 'Llywelyn, Our Last Leader', marking the spot where Llywelyn, the last native Prince of Wales fell. Almost certainly erroneously since Aberedw may be a more likely place. Thus passes Llywelyn ap Gruffydd from our tale, but his passing did not mark the end of the Second Welsh War, or indeed Anglo-Welsh wars. There is much written of his passing marking the end of an independent Wales. But in return for the title 'Prince of Wales' at the Treaty of Montgomery in 1267, he had accepted the King of England as his lord. Such romantic sentiments misunderstand the nature of homage, vassals and indeed feudality. True enough Llywelyn sought to test those bounds as far as he could, but in the end a king of England was always going to ensure what he saw as the natural order of things was maintained.

However, the war was not over with the passing of Llywelyn: his brother Dafydd remained at large. Edward, that December, sat by the Clwyd at Rhuddlan. His army weakened in Anglesey by the disaster of Moel-y-Don, he needed reinforcement in order to pursue his cause to ultimate victory. He had, not long after the beginning of the Welsh rising, in April, sent to Jean de Grailly in Gascony for military assistance. There had been difficulty in responding to this request: the king of France, as overlord of Gascony, forbad any participation of Gascon forces in Wales, as Edward remained his vassal for Gascony.

Nonetheless, ignoring Philippe, the Gascons began to appear. As Christmas 1282 passed into January of 1283, the great families of Edward's French lands arrived in Wales, as Morris lists: 'There came in person the Counts of Armagnac and of Bigorre, the lord of Bergerac, Roger de Mauleon, Arnald de Gaveston, Pierre de Greilly, Pierre Amanieu, Captal de Buch, the Viscount de Tarcazin and Guichard de Bourg, ex-mayor of Bordeaux.'[94] The nobles brought with them over

200 mounted crossbowmen and over 1,300 regular crossbowmen. Jean de Vesci had been to Gascony on Edward's behalf, and with the Gascons he had returned. He was sent to join Othon de Grandson, who'd narrowly survived Moel-y-Don, to join the Anglesey army. The loyal Savoyard would now lead the newly rebuilt army in Anglesey, first making good the bridge of boats to the mainland. If the army did not have a French tinge to it before, it certainly did now – packed full of, and led by men, from Savoy and Gascony.

Following the death of his brother, and having begun the revolt, Dafydd chose to fight on what became known from this point as 'Dafydd's War'. With 1283 but three weeks old, Edward was ready to make his next move: the army marched out from Rhuddlan and crossed the Clwyd, bound for the Conwy. But the wide estuary by his father's old castle at Deganwy would not be his goal: Edward had other ideas. Ever the master strategist, he moved inland and eschewed a direct assault upon the Welsh. The army moved upstream along the Conwy to Betws-y-Coed, before arriving at the tower castle of Dolywyddelan.[95] The single tower, standing on a rocky outcrop on the slopes of Moel Siabod overlooking the Lledr Valley, guarded the passage across north Wales at the head of waters that ran northward to Conwy and south-westward toward Harlech and Criccieth. The medieval road that progressed from the Conwy Valley into Meirionnydd passed close by the western side of the castle, not down in the valley as does the modern road.[96]

The lonely castle was built by, and once thought to be the birthplace of Llywelyn Fawr, the late departed Llywelyn ap Gruffydd's grandfather. It's now thought that Llywelyn Fawr was born at Tomen Castell, a small tower that had previously stood on a nearby hill. In besieging this outpost, Edward fully knew that he was no longer containing the House of Gwynedd but destroying it. After a short siege, on Monday 18 January 1283,[97] Dolywyddelan Castle fell to Edward and his army. Two days earlier, the Keeper of the Wardrobe had already called for eleven masons to be sent there.[98] In mid-winter, the king now rested his army once more; he could strike the mountain fastness of Snowdonia now from the south and from the east. Othon de Grandson controlled the sea to the west and could strike from the north – Dafydd and Gwynedd were now caught in a suffocatingly deadly embrace.

Wherever King Edward went at this time, so too it seems, did Maître Jacques. Building work at Dolywyddelan began immediately it was in English hands. By 1 February Maître Jacques was ordering and being supplied with steel from Chester for use at the newly taken castle.[99] Steel was a valuable commodity in the thirteenth century, as it could only be made in limited quantity. Smiths would be able to produce it in a complex process of heating and cooling the metal until they'd made steel that was both hard on the surface to be useful, but malleable internally enough not to be brittle and or shatter. The blacksmith was an artisan of some note, almost magical in his ways of making good steel, thus his product might be of such value as to be brought to site by a master mason, as here and accounted for, to the sum of four shillings, over twenty days' pay for a skilled tradesman. The steel seems to have been sourced in Chester and involved Master

Bertram in its shipment to Dolywyddelan.[100] It may have been for sharpening the mason's tools and or in the construction of a second 'camera'. This was added to the castle to increase accommodation available there and known as the West Tower.[101] It appears to have been the work of Maître Jacques and his eleven masons. The stone used was not local, but similar to that used in construction later at Conwy and sourced in and around Chester.[102] Of note is the request to Robert, the king's tailor, to supply eighty yards of white Irish linen, fifty-seven pairs of white stockings, one hundred pairs of shoes, one hundred pairs of gloves along with ten yards of canvas wrapping, all this to be dispatched from Chester to Dolywyddelan. Edward, it seems, was taking the modern expedient of equipping his garrison for winter conditions so prevalent in Snowdonia.

As time progressed the work progressed. In May, 'clays', the wicker screens used in thirteenth-century scaffolding, were shipped to Dolywyddelan and its rising *camera*. The clays were taken up the Conwy to Llanrwst by the vessel *Holy Cross* of Hythe, John Hampton commanding. Hythe was one of the Cinque Ports from which ships and their masters had earlier been summoned by the king. Later, work commenced on a new bridge and water mill, Dolywyddelan was being prepared for a new role as an outpost of the king on the lonely way from Conwy to Meirionnydd.[103]

Time, back in February, had passed for Edward back at Rhuddlan, with the consolidation of his armies at Dolywyddelan and at Bangor by the Menai Strait; his quarry Dafydd, it seems, was holed up at Castell y Bere to the south not far from Tywyn and the Dovey estuary. Simultaneously, the four English armies closed in for the kill. Edward moved once more, this time across the Conwy to the Abbey of Aberconewey, there to establish a headquarters from 14 March.[104] The second army, headed by Othon de Grandson[105] and Jean de Vesci, moved in a south-western direction from Bangor, firstly by way of Caernarfon then Criccieth on the Llyn Peninsula.[106] By 14 March, the Welsh castle of Criccieth was also in English hands; one by one the strongholds of Gwynedd were falling. Two other English armies, that of the king's uncle Guillaume de Valence from Aberystwyth and Llywelyn's nemesis Roger L'Estrange from Montgomery, came up from mid Wales to threaten Castell y Bere, with the army was Bogo de Knovill, who had been earlier at Aberystwyth.

Castell y Bere was another constructed by Llywelyn Fawr and sat atop a rocky outcrop on the eastern side of the Dysynni Valley, protecting an old route from Tywyn to Dolgellau, the southerly approaches to Gwynedd. The route to Meirionnydd, then as now, by way of the coast, was difficult and presented one with the wide estuary of the Afon Mawddach before reaching deeper into Meirionnydd. Far better to take the valley of the Afon Dysynni and the bridging point at Llaneltyd near Dolgellau and maybe the hospitality of nearby Cymer Abbey. Taylor, probably very rightly, suggests that Bere was the castle that Llywelyn Fawr had 'began to build for himself' in 1221, as recorded in the *Red Book* version of the Brut Tywysogion.[107] On its northern and western approaches the castle was protected by mother nature's precipitate faces; on the southern and eastern sides rock-cut ditches served as a moat defensive. The castle itself was a long, slender affair, following the contours of the land: at its northern and southern extremity it featured D-shaped apsidal towers that was a feature of many native Welsh castles, the slender rear tail of the tower providing additional castle accommodation. The south tower was built apart from the curtain wall in isolation, the southernmost part of the curtain being protected by the square middle tower and the round tower. All of the towers ran to two storeys, the middle square tower originally forming the function of central keep. Castell y Bere was much the largest of the castles built by Llywelyn Fawr, and a worthy prize.[108]

At Castell y Bere, on his last assignment for Edward, was that master siege-engine builder of Benauges and Dolforwyn: Master Bertram the Engineer.[109] It would seem Dafydd had fled Castell y Bere shortly beforehand, or more improbably during the ensuing siege. He headed north to Dolbadarn Castle in Snowdonia – the noose was tightening. The inference from the archive is that no less than three English armies converged on and besieged Castell y Bere. The custodian of Castell y Bere, Cynfrig ap Madog, surrendered the stronghold to English forces, amounting to 3,000 men, on 25 April.[110] Immediately, as at Dolywyddelan, steps were taken for repairs, in the allotment to Master Bertram, and his assistant Simon Le Counte, of five masons and five carpenters for new works.[111]

Within a few short months, Dafydd had lost Dolywyddelan, Criccieth and Castell y Bere, along with the abbey at Aberconwy. The Abbot of Vale Royal was at the abbey from 6 April, perhaps to begin negotiations for the movement of the abbey to make way for what Edward saw as an ideal site to replace the former castle across the Conwy at Deganwy, latterly destroyed by Llywelyn. Indeed, the relocation of the abbey at Aberconwy and its replacement by a castle became another consciously vindictive act on Edward's part to rid himself forever of the House of Gwynedd, since the abbey had been the burial ground of the princes.

At some point between 22 and 25 April, Othon de Grandson was detached, along with 560 men, from the forces surrounding Castell y Bere and sent northward the thirty-five miles (fifty-six kilometres) toward Harlech.[112] The record is the earliest mention, in this context, of *Hardelach* or Harlech we have. By April 1283, the future sites of Conwy, Caernarfon and Harlech castles were in Edward's hands, and it does not seem to have taken the king long to decide these three would be the home of the castles that would complete and hold his conquest of Gwynedd. Othon de Grandson and Jean de Vesci would join the king amongst his newly erected tents by the Cistercian monastery at Aberconwy as spring moved toward summer.

Before meeting the king at Aberconwy, Grandson and Vesci had led the Anglesey army to the siege of Castell y Bere, but we are certain of only a few of its movements. A bridgehead from the island to the mainland, most likely involving a rebuilding of the bridge of boats, is suggested for Bangor in late December 1282. Supplies for the army dispatched from Chester and Rhuddlan to Bangor are dated to the period 28 December–3 January 1283[113] and more thereafter. From Bangor we know it had passed Caernarfon,[114] where once the Roman fort of Segontium had stood. Whatever remained of Roman Caernarfon, there were dwellings and most likely there still stood the Norman motte, and perhaps the bailey too, erected by Hugh d'Avranches in the late eleventh century.[115] The fall of Criccieth is recorded but not to which army, the Anglesey army or that with the king at Dolywyddelan.[116] Criccieth was in English hands by 14 March, since Henry of Greenford received pay from this date as its constable,[117] but there is no record of a siege or battle, other than the colourful Langtoft account.[118] However, the archive is then precise in saying that Othon was at the siege of Castell y Bere.[119] This would suggest a deployment of his army (or elements thereof) from Bangor by way of Caernarfon and Criccieth to Castell y Bere before returning north to Harlech, then continuing to the king at Aberconwy. The movement of this army would most likely have been overland, but they also had naval support, which may have been used to ferry some troops along the coast.

If we are to consider a birthplace for the iron ring of castles, then it is most likely to have been amongst the tents of Aberconwy that spring of 1283. We can be almost certain that Othon de Grandson and Jean de Vesci had been at the future sites of Caernarfon and Harlech. Edward had not as yet, therefore his loyal lieutenants had been his eyes as to the castle sites.[120] Although Prestwich cautions us against suggesting Grandson had too important a role in planning these castles, his importance as a man with first sight of these sites and who could be trusted by Edward to see them, as if with his own eyes, should not be lightly discounted.[121] Perhaps in a tent in May 1283, we have, together, the king's most trusted knights, the king himself, and the man he'd sent to ordain his works in Wales.[122] Given his presence at Dolywyddelan, its very likely that Maître Jacques had been with the king's army. I do not believe it takes a large leap of the imagination to conclude that such a meeting was a possibility – we will never know for sure – but it remains a distinct possibility. If it happened, sadly no records have been passed down to us, but then in the thirteenth century no records were ever kept of the process by which kings reached their decisions, or the counsel they sought and were given.[123] It does seem that the parentage of Caernarfon and Harlech lay with those old friends of the king's, these 'band of brothers' who'd accompanied him on crusade, dined with him in Savoy and recently returned from Gascon service to command his Anglesey army. The parentage of the Edwardian castles in Wales fell to a great-grandson of a Count of Savoy, a knight himself from Savoy, a knight formerly married to a Savoyard, and a master mason from Savoy – it is no wonder they would have Savoyard characteristics.

That May, the last stronghold of Gwynedd fell to the English: Dolbadarn Castle, located at the base of the Llanberis Pass, deep in Snowdonia. There Dafydd dispatched messages as a 'Prince of Wales' to Ceredigion, but it was to a land now in English hands.[124] Dolbadarn was unusual amongst the castles of its builder, Llywelyn Fawr, in boasting a round tower keep of two floors above a basement, that evoked the English tower at Pembroke. Again, like Dolywyddelan, the keep had been surrounded by a curtain wall, of unmortared grit and slate stone. Within the courtyard, at the opposite end from the tower, sat the hall from which Dafydd gave his last orders as Prince of Wales. Some 3,000 to 4,000 English troops were still on the payroll and began searching the mountain passes for Dafydd. Morris writes that 'The Welsh evidently offered to surrender of their own accord ... That the surrenders were made in abandonment of David.'[125] Welshmen in pursuit of royal pardon joined the hunt for their erstwhile prince. There was nowhere left for Dafydd to take refuge; he fled into the mountains, there to await his fate like a wounded animal his final realm being the Bera Mountain, above the home of the Princes of Gwynedd at Abergwyngregyn. In June 1283, he attempted to evade capture in the mists of Snowdonia, just over a year since he had begun the rebellion, at Easter 1282, by descending upon the castle at Hawarden.

It would be said that Enian (or Anion), Bishop of Bangor, betrayed his last hiding place of Nanhysglain to the English. Dafydd was there with his wife, Elizabeth Ferrers, his two sons, Owain and Llywelyn, hiding in a small dwelling in the desolate Carneddau wilderness, the last native Prince of Wales. On the night of 21–22 June, men-at-arms climbed into the Welsh night to track down the fugitive. Medieval sources do not record the operation or the precise location of Nanhysglain, but we can imagine the commotion of their capture, and we do know a struggle ensued, since Dafydd, was apparently wounded in capture (*graviter vulneratus*): the last stand of the House of Gwynedd. That same night he was escorted to Rhuddlan by sixty archers to meet, no doubt, a jubilant Edward. From there he was taken to Chester, not far from the castle at Hawarden he had attacked the previous Easter, thence to Shrewsbury.

As Edward wrote, on 28 June 1283 to Gilbert de Clare from Rhuddlan:

> The tongue of man can scarcely recount the evil deeds committed by the Welsh upon the King's progenitors and him by invasions of the realm from time within memory ... but God, wishing as it seems, to put an end to these evil proceedings has, after the prince had been slain, destined David, as the last survivor of the family of traitors aforesaid, to the king's prison after he had been captured by men of his own race.[126]

Dafydd was nursed back to health. Edward was determined that the Welsh prince whom he'd sheltered from his brother, whom he'd fought alongside in 1277 and 1278, whom he'd rewarded with lands in the four *cantrefi*, that an example be made of him. He called a Parliament to be held in the border county of Shropshire, and notably omitted to call the clergy, who would have no blood on their hands.[127]

Walter of Guisborough described how Dafydd, having 'hid in the marshes for almost a year ... was taken prisoner' and 'like a deceiver and traitor' had been 'hanged drawn and quartered and its four members sent into four parts of England'. And so it was that Dafydd ap Gruffydd met his end in Shrewsbury.[128] The trial result was a foregone conclusion, the punishment meted out to the unfortunate Welshman was not new, but its use for a nobleman was. To be hung, drawn and quartered was a particularly barbaric means of execution, and reserved for those who kings saw as traitors. To be hung, drawn and quartered meant being dragged along the ground through the town by horses to the place of execution, there to be hanged until nearly dead, then to be cut down and literally cut into pieces whilst still alive. The chronicler of Lanercost wrote this verse:

> David of Wales, a thief and traitor,
> Slayer of men, of Church a hater,
> A fourfold criminal in life,
> Now dies by horse, fire, rope and knife.
> The ruffian thus deprived of breath
> Most meetly dies by fourfold death.[129]

The fourfold punishment, in the medieval mind, reflected the multiplicity of Dafydd's crimes: he was to be drawn behind a horse since he was a traitor, he was to be hanged since he had committed homicide, and lastly the most gruesome of all, he was to be quartered since he had plotted the death of the king. For Dafydd one more torture was added, his bowels were to be removed at the point of his quartering and burned in front of him – this as punishment for having carried out his original attack on Hawarden during the Easter festivities, or as the Dunstable annalist wrote: 'because it was done at the time of the Lord's Passion.'[130] In an age of religious certainty such a despicable act met with particular disapprobation.

Dafydd was the first of Edward's enemies from the Celtic fringe to be executed, but he would not be the last. Some have seen this as a cruel retribution meted upon his enemies, but this would be to take the executions out of context and to misunderstand the king's motives, in short to be guilty of presentism. Katherine Royer in her paper on medieval justice says that 'Edward I inscribed on the scaffold his feudal fury rather than a strategy to bring Wales and Scotland to heel with displays of ceremonialized justice.'[131] Dafydd, like William Wallace to come, met his end because he was seen by Edward as a vassal who had rebelled against his suzerain. This 'feudal fury' explains entirely Edward's actions toward the slain Llywelyn ap Gruffydd in fighting the Welsh wars and his subsequent execution of Dafydd. We should remember that Dafydd was one who'd fought alongside Edward in the First Welsh War, and that following that war, he had left his brother Llywelyn in possession of both his title and Gwynedd. Previously Edward had shown clemency to the rebel Jean de Vesci, now a key commander in the Welsh wars – Edward was more than capable of clemency, but woe betide a man who might spurn this clemency. To be hung, drawn and quartered was a dishonourable death, an announced death, not the honourable death of an enemy in war. Dafydd was shown and seen to be as a man without honour in an age when this was fundamental to how the nobility self-identified.

The chronicler of Lanercost had it that his body parts were displayed:

the right arm with a ring on the finger in York; the left arm in Bristol; the right and hip in Northampton; the left [leg] at Hereford. But the villain's head was bound in iron, lest it should fall to pieces from putrefaction and set conspicuously upon a long spear shaft for the mockery of London.[132]

As the Dunstable annalist put it, 'his head is extremely high on a stake over the Tower of London.'[133] There followed a most unseemly quarrelling over the body parts, as rival regions of the realm fought over the corpse of the departed Dafydd.[134] That trans-Pennine rivalry, in the form of a dispute over Dafydd's shoulder, and that Lincoln was fined for not joyfully receiving their body part are the tragicomic conclusion to a macabre execution and to the Second Welsh War. From the distance of over 700 years, it seems perhaps inevitable that it should have ended this way, both brothers' heads displayed together in London on pikes at the Tower. The ap Gruffydd brothers had attempted rebellion against Edward and a reversal of the results of the First Welsh War; these hopes would, in the end, prove to be futile. But the Welsh had always been able to hold the English at arm's length militarily and then politically in the past, letting the mountains and mists of Wales swallow invading armies before reducing them with hit-and-run tactics – what Clausewitz would later call the strategy of 'wearing out of the enemy'.[135]

English kings had always made efforts to subdue the Welsh before but had become dismayed and moved on to other things. Llywelyn and Dafydd had no reason to believe the late thirteenth century would be any different, but the Welsh hadn't bargained with their nemesis, Edward Plantagenet. It is a truism that wars are often caused by one side of a political quarrel misunderstanding the other, or a mutual misunderstanding, and in the case of Llywelyn and Edward, it was what Prestwich called a lack of 'any sympathy for, or understanding of, each other's position'.[136]

In the end the attempt to extend the polity of Gwynedd to encompass a nation of Welsh-speakers failed. It failed because of an inability to reconcile the competing interests of Welsh princes and Marcher lords. It proved impossible to form a united polity in the face of a neighbouring kingdom, England, keen to assert its own hegemony over the island of Britain. Whilst attempting to create an extended polity of Gwynedd, to more closely match the realm of Welsh-speakers, Llywelyn had never attempted to overturn the King of England's overlordship of Wales. But he had consistently failed to reach an accommodation with an English king, his acknowledged overlord – something for which, in the end, he paid for with his life.

With the decapitation of the princely class of Welsh society and or its conversion to a land-owning aristocracy in the English sense, we can see the emergence of the latter as a new nobility in Wales, the *uwchelwr*. Indeed, Carpenter suggests that this Welsh aristocracy were 'the real beneficiaries of the English conquest',[137] being no longer subject to the ambitions of Gwynedd to create a nation state centred upon north-west Wales. It is tempting to think of Gwynedd as representing a proto-Welsh 'state', but in thirteenth-century Wales, the perspective of Gruffydd ap Gwenwynwyn ought to be as valid as that of Llywelyn ap Gruffydd. Wales was more than Gwynedd: it was the Marcher lands, it was Powys and Deheubarth too.[138] Nevertheless, it was Gwynedd that fought longest and hardest for the greatest degree of autonomy, if not independence, from London.

The Chester chronicler relates how the passing of Llywelyn and his House of Gwynedd was viewed differently either side of Offa's Dyke, a hero to one side, a villain to the other, and perhaps these polarized views are inevitable. He tells us that two 'religiosi', clerics, one Welsh, one English, wrote epitaphs for Llywelyn, almost certainly apocryphal:[139]

The Welshmen as follows:

> Here lies the tormentor of the English.
> Here lies of Englishmen The tormentor,
> the guardian of the Welsh,
> The prince of the Welsh,
> Llewelyn the example of manners,
> The jewel of his contemporaries,
> The flower of the kings of the past,
> The model of those of the future,
> The leader, the glory, the law, the light of the people.[140]

The Englishman thus replied:

> Here lies the prince of deceptions
> And the plunderer of men,
> The betrayer of the English,
> A livid torch, a school of the wicked,
> For the Welsh a deity,
> A cruel leader, a murderer of the pious,
> [Sprung from] the dregs of the Trojans,
> From a lying race, a cause of evils.

In the end your view of Llywelyn or Dafydd will tend toward your being Welsh or English, or indeed Savoyard; history can simply record them as the last of the native Princes of Wales.

There are, today, three peaks of Snowdonia, Carnedd Gwenllian, named for Llywelyn's surviving daughter and the mountains Carnedd Llywelyn and Carnedd Dafydd, that look down at a Gwynedd now a part of a United Kingdom of England and Wales. They look down forever upon the iron ring of castles that would very soon rise to surround these lofty peaks.

Chapter Nine

At Easter 1278, the bodies of King Arthur and Queen Guinevere had been exhumed at Glastonbury Abbey amidst great ceremony. Edward was conscious of the hold on the Welsh soul of myth and legend. The *Flores Historiarum* records that in the summer of 1283: 'In Caernarfon, the body of Prince Maximi, his father the noble Constantine, was found, and the King was honourably enshrined in the Church.'[1]

Here again we have myth and legend marching purposefully into our story, harnessed almost certainly by Edward, deliberately to co-opt Welsh and British legend as his own, in order to legitimize his actions and extirpate any notion of any kingly authority other than his own. So, who were *'Maximi principis'* and his noble father *'Constantini'*?

The answer is part history and part powerful legend. Firstly, the history: Magnus Maximus, born circa 335 and living until 388, was a commander of the Roman legions in the province of Britannia. In 383 he usurped the imperial throne of Gratian and was declared emperor of the provinces of Britannia and Gaul, Valentinian II holding Rome. In 387 his imperial ambitions led him to an invasion of Italy which met with defeat and his death in 388. His father was not the, or indeed any, Constantine.[2] It is at this point, given the nature of late Roman history, especially in Britain, that history departs from known facts and begins to enter the lands of fantasy. It is very possible that the withdrawal of the Roman legions from Britannia, bemoaned by the Britons in 410, began or was largely effected in support of the imperial ambitions of Maximus.[3]

So much for the history; then comes the legend and mythology. The Pillar of Eliseg, near Llangollen, erected in the early ninth century illustrates the enduring hold Maximus had on the Welsh imagination – on it the Princes of Powys claimed descent from *Maximi*.[4] The Welsh began to tell tales orally, as part of the great saga *Mabinogion*, of the *'Breuddwyd Macsen Wledig'* or the 'Dream of Maximus'. The earliest written texts are later than the time of Edward, but linguists agree that the stories come from a very old Welsh oral tradition and stem from the time of Maximus, the historical figure, or shortly thereafter.

The tale relates a dream that Maximus had of a lovely lady in a faraway land, of how he travelled from Rome in search of her across mountains 'as high as the sky', following a 'mighty' river to the sea, of crossing the sea to a magical island, 'the fairest island in the whole world', to the far north-west of the island, 'the furthest shore', to a fortified city by the mouth of a river, 'where he beheld a castle, the fairest that man ever saw', the very stuff to set medieval hearts racing.[5]

Reading or hearing the poetry, as Edward must surely have done, it's not difficult to imagine why the apparent 'discovery' of the body of Maximus would be so important. Given the mythical Welsh regard for Caernarfon, as the one-time seat of Maximus, it's easy to see why Edward might choose it as the centre of his conquest. Maître Jacques had built for his great-uncle Philip a palace-castle in the Viennois, and now the idea for something far surpassing Saint-Georges-d'Espéranche filled the minds of Edward, Jacques and Othon. Edward would make a reality of the castle, 'fairest castle that man ever saw'. It would be he, not the Princes of Gwynedd, who would inherit the legacy of Maximus.

But Caernarfon was not the only mythical castle site, Harlech too had been the setting for the Branwen saga of the *Mabinogion*, *Branwen ferch Llŷr*. This tale told of the magical 'rock of Harddlech', a cauldron of life, of severed talking heads and of the 'Birds of Rhiannon' – heady stuff for the modern mind let alone the medieval mind.[6] There are many sound military reasons for Edward to have chosen to build the castles at Conwy, Caernarfon, and Harlech where he did. It is also very likely that Othon de Grandson and Jean de Vesci had provided him a reliable reconnaissance of the sites. However, in demolishing the abbey at Aberconwy where the Princes of Gwynedd were buried, in building at Caernarfon a castle to realize the dream of Macsen Wledig and finally that rock at Harlech with its singing birds bringing the dead back to life, sites immortalized in Welsh myth, in so doing Edward was knowingly and deliberately attempting to establish his dominance of Welsh identity, over the Welsh soul itself.

Edward moved from Conwy to Dolywyddelan in mid-May, along with his entourage; they were not present at the reinterment at Caernarfon. So, at either Conwy or Dolywyddelan the decisions were made that would result in the great castles at Conwy, Caernarfon and Harlech.[7] The ability in Jacques, that Edward had seen in the Viennois, would now show itself in north Wales: an ability to build multiple castles simultaneously. Maître Jacques would, however, now be working with a patron of considerably greater power and wealth than the Count of Savoy. In June 1283, construction began at more or less the same time for the three great castles that would come to dominate Wales. Just as in the Viennois, one would be a grand palace-castle, whilst the other two military bastions festooned with round towers. Unlike the Viennois, however, the new castles would be on a scale never imagined before, the greatest ever constructed in Europe by that time, and amongst the most powerful ever built at any time.

Earlier, on 17 March 1283, in anticipation of the forthcoming castle-building, some 200 woodcutters and a further 100 diggers had been summoned from Chester to Conwy, a sure sign of works to begin. Edward was moving quickly, having only arrived in Conwy on 14 March.[8] A writ issued by Edward to his Wardrobe at Chester sheds light on the earliest summons for the great castles to begin construction. He asked William de Perton and Master Richard to summon 'masons and quarry-breakers to Conwy'.[9] William de Perton was Keeper of the King's Wardrobe at Chester, in effect the keeper of the king's purse, and had prepared the accounts earlier at Rhuddlan to be certified by Maître Jacques. The Royal Wardrobe, part of the Royal Household, was responsible not just for the cloth, clothing and accoutrements worn by the monarchy in their official business and for adorning royal buildings and furnishings, but also for their expenditure and financial accounts. The King's Wardrobe or *garderoba* carried out much of the function of the Exchequer in thirteenth-century England. The Wardrobe had the ability to quickly finance the king's projects, as we can see with Edward's writ from Conwy. They also made payments to the king's favourites, as payments of Maître Jacques' wages on his arrival in England, and again later with the increase in payments for his services illustrates. In the late thirteenth century, we might imagine that William de Perton was carrying out a similar function for Edward, as might a Chancellor of the Exchequer today.

Master Richard had previously worked at Flint under the auspices of both Master Bertram and later Maître Jacques himself. Jacques, together with Richard and Bertram, alongside Perton, had built the castles in the four *cantrefi*, they were now being called upon to begin yet greater works. A further writ, also issued on 30 March 1283, called upon the bailiffs of Newcastle-under-Lyme to provide 'smiths and workmen'. Edward would rely in no small degree upon the iron-making smiths of Staffordshire, under the bailiffs of his brother Edmund.[10]

Taylor described Master Richard as 'deputy chief architect'[11] and it's quite possible to infer such a title from these writs. They involve the dispatch of Richard to Chester and the Midlands, on matters of great importance to the coming project. This suggests that Richard held some reasonable degree of seniority in the panoply of king's masons. However, that he might be spared to carry out such errands also implies that he be a 'deputy' rather than a 'chief architect', as the chief architect was required on site in north Wales. Turner agrees, describing Richard as Jacques' 'second-in-command',[12] having reflected that it had been 'the fate of many worthy men to be remembered, as the faithful lieutenant of someone more famous in history'.[13] This is not, whatsoever, to denigrate Master Richard in any way. He was, his entire life, a good and faithful servant to the Crown.

Meanwhile, the writs were continuing to fly from Edward. Whilst at Rhuddlan he issued a writ for timbers, originally intended for the enclosure of the town of Rhuddlan, to be forwarded to Caernarfon where they might be used. The writ, dated 20 June 1283, is in and of itself the first primary source we have for building works beginning at '*Carnarum*', what would become the castle of Caernarfon.[14] Payment was accordingly recorded for nine shiploads of timber to make their way along the north Welsh coast to allow work to begin.[15]

Back at Rhuddlan, it is very likely that another who had been with Jacques in Savoy was now leaving his mark upon the fabric of the castles in north Wales. Stephen the Painter, brushes and paints in hand, was decorating the king's chamber at Rhuddlan.[16] Taylor suggested that it was 'difficult to doubt' that Stephen was not one and the same man who'd painted chambers for Count Philippe at Saint-Laurent-du-Pont as organized by Jacques, in 1274–5.[17] It is unsurprising that

Jacques would bring to England a painter whom he trusted and worked alongside before. In this way numerous Savoyard artisans would make their way to England to stand alongside the many household knights and members of the comital family already there.

We imagine castles as the dark, cold and damp ruins we see them as today, but the buildings Jacques and Stephen created were of an entirely different character, especially the living quarters mentioned at Rhuddlan. We should think of plastered and painted walls, rich in multicoloured fabrics, tapestries and so on. Both Edward, and before him Philippe, would have wanted to show off their wealth and status through the interior of Rhuddlan and Saint-Laurent-du-Pont. The walls would have first been rendered with lime-wash to present a clean appearance. Paint came from pigments ground down from earths and stone, intense bright colours most prized in the time before electric lighting. Stephen had been painting a chapel and garderobe in the Chartreuse before going on to paint the king's chamber in north Wales.

Taylor went on to plausibly suggest that the '*Stephano pictori*' of Rhuddlan in 1283 and the '*Stephanum pictorem*' of Saint-Laurent-du-Pont of 1274–5, are indeed the same man, but also the same as a '*Stephano pictore Regis*' who had earlier worked at Westminster Hall in 1273. It is impossible to be certain, but the possibility is nonetheless intriguing. It lays open the prospect that Stephen may have been English. Furthermore, before all the aforesaid work, he may also have been responsible for work at Chillon.[18] If this be so, then the movement of artisans between the service of the Count of Savoy and the King of England might well not have been solely in one direction. Given that nothing remains of his work at Rhuddlan or Saint-Laurent-du-Pont, that he may have been responsible for the Saint Georges Chapel at Chillon renders its survival as our only way of experiencing the beauty of his work. There may well survive, in a corner of Switzerland, the work of an English artist whose work is otherwise lost to us.

As the dust settled on the Second Welsh War, there would be yet further drama for Edward and Leonor in Wales, but this time it wasn't the work of the House of Gwynedd. In February 1283, Edward had given the castle at Caergwrle, lately the fief of Dafydd, to his wife, Leonor. Although Jacques had now moved on to the other work sites underway in Wales, the repairs to Caergwrle had yet to be completed. On 25 June, Leonor was granted permission to hold a weekly market at what was hoped would become a new town, in the way of nearby Flint. Within the castle, there were a number of wooden buildings, including a chapel, a bakehouse and various site offices, a typical construction site even today. On 27 August 1283, Edward and Leonor were staying at Caergwrle, when the thing that people of the Middle Ages dreaded most broke out – fire. The royal couple, who'd escaped the clutches of the grim reaper a decade before with the attack of an assassin at Acre, managed their escape and survived.

News would soon come too, meanwhile, of the passing of the well-travelled artisan, Master Bertram the Engineer, on 29 February 1284. The date of his death is suggested from the precise date of the ending of his pay. It would seem he died at Caernarfon, where we have seen works had just begun. The constable there was responsible for his burial: 'To the chamberlain of *Karnarvon* ... Thirty-Six shillings and sixpence ... for the burial of Master Bertram the Engineer.'[19]

Maître Jacques' one-time companion at Rhuddlan, and his mentor Sir Jean de Mézos' companion at Benauges in Gascony, had gone. Bertram had travelled far from his homeland of Gascony in the service of Henry and then Edward. Having been born almost certainly before 1225, he had made over sixty years, straddling the greater part of the thirteenth century. Born perhaps as early as King John's reign, he'd seen the reign of his son Henry and into that of his grandson Edward.[20] But in our story he was the third part of a unique triangle of engineers and masons that encompassed Sir Jean de Mézos in Gascony and Savoy, himself in Gascony and England and lastly Maître Jacques in Savoy and England. That Bertram had worked alongside the man who would be in effect a mentor to Maître Jacques, before in turn working with him himself, is an often-overlooked element to the origins of both the castles in Savoy and of those in Wales. Master Bertram died at Caernarfon, as he had lived, in the service of the King of England, building and constructing: Master Bertram the Engineer.

As work was underway on his castles, in March 1284, the king and his royal household returned to Wales to arrange the political and legal settlement of affairs in north Wales, a settlement that would bring the Welsh ever closer, and thus far, permanently into the English realm. On 3 March, from the newly constructed castle at Rhuddlan, was issued the Statute of Wales the *Statutum Walliae*, which according to legal textbooks saw 'Wales annexed to Crown of England'.[21] Ivor Bowen's collected translation published in 1908 records Edward's words, in which he addressed 'his Subjects of his Land of Snowdon'. He justified his actions, as God's anointed king, by invoking 'Divine Providence' which had 'transferred' the 'Land of Wales' under his 'proper dominion.'. The king set out the model for the governance of Gwynedd and north Wales, to follow the English shire county form. There would be new counties of Anglesey, Merionethshire and Caernarfonshire, with sheriffs, bailiffs and coroners.[22]

Of the four *cantrefi*, *Tegeingl*, including the new castles of Flint and Rhuddlan,[23] would be placed into a new county, Flintshire. This county of Flintshire would be under the King's Justiciar in Chester, Reginald de Grey. In this Edward was returning to the settlement of the 1240s and not beginning anew. These lands had always been disputed between the English and the Welsh – the Welsh name for them *Y Berfeddwlad* literally meant 'the Middle Country' or 'Lands Between'. Of the remaining four *cantrefi*, Rhufoniog and Rhos (excepting Rhuddlan) were granted to Henri de Lacy, 3rd Earl of Lincoln, as the newly created Marcher Lordship of Denbigh, centred upon the new castle at Denbigh. Dyffryn Clwyd went to Reginald de Grey, again as a new Marcher lordship. Thus far then, the settlement was a mix of new royal lands, and Marcher lordships to reward loyal friends.

But the lands that formerly made up Gwynedd west of the Conwy would be taken entirely into royal hands, divided into the new counties of Caernarfonshire,

Merioneth and Anglesey. The new counties would be under the auspices of sheriffs,[24] Roger de Pulesdon on Anglesey, Richard de Pulesdon at Caernarfon and lastly Robert de Staundon at Merioneth, all of them salaried at £40 per annum. Overseeing these sheriffs would be a new Justiciar for North Wales. Edward appointed his loyal Savoyard friend and knight, Othon de Grandson, with John de Havering as his deputy.[25] An Exchequer would be created in Caernarfon for these three new counties, under a Chamberlain who reported directly to the Exchequer in Westminster. These new counties would then, for the time being, not be assimilated into the English governmental structure, but run as a royal fief.

As Justiciar for North Wales, Othon de Grandson had risen far from the the small castle by the banks of Lac de Neuchâtel. In medieval England a justiciar was analogous to what we might term a prime minister.[26] The English title Justiciar originated with the Latin *justiciarius* or *justitiarius*, meaning 'man of justice' or simply 'judge'. Davies uses the appellation of 'king's governor general',[27] being given 'wide ranging military, governmental, and judicial powers..[28] The Lord of Grandson had in the words of the Statue of Rhuddlan responsibility for 'Custody and Government of the Peace of Us the King in Snowdon'. Recognizing Grandson's contribution to the new castle construction, Davies goes on to conclude that 'much of his [Othon de Grandson's] attention … in these early years was devoted to … supervising the building of castles'.[29] Grandson was paid handsomely for 'keeping Wales', £1,000 per annum as justiciar and a further £100 for the castle at Caernarfon – in sum £1,100 which translates today to over £750,000![30] Rewards that would allow him to transform the modest Château de Grandson into something with more than the hint of Conwy about it.

Edward would go further in extending the Savoyard influence amongst his new realm and rising castles: he appointed Jean de Bonvillars as the Constable for Harlech and Guillaume de Cicon as first Constable for Conwy. Sitting astride the new stone monuments to Plantagenet power in Wales were knights from the Pays de Vaud and Jura, their birthplaces closer than the castles they now commanded. Prestwich remarks on the unique nature of the Savoyard stewardship: 'but it is striking that the Savoyards did not attempt to establish themselves as a new aristocracy in Wales, being content with official positions rather than grants of lands.'[31]

One is bound to ask why. During Henry III's reign the award of castles, land, positions and influence to foreigners had proven deeply controversial and had, in part, contributed to the Second Baronial War. Between the 1240s and the 1260s there had been a veritable migration from Savoy to England, led by the comital family, chiefly the uncles of the Queen: Guillaume, Pierre and Boniface. But these new Savoyard servants of the Crown were for the most part not of the comital family, and so not Edward's kin. But as with the comital family, the Grandsons, the Bonvillars, the Champvents, Joinville, the Estavayers and the Monts were bound, not by a loyalty that we might understand, that to a nation state: their loyalty was personally to Edward. Wisely perhaps they were content with carving out careers for themselves, and serving the king, rather than beginning a new Welsh aristocracy, lining their own pockets and that of their descendants. Christopher Tyerman rightly observed of the constables that Edward placed a premium on 'service by those dependent upon the king alone, independent of existing national factions' and of the Savoyard influence in England more widely that 'their main attraction' to the Crown 'was the presumption of loyalty'.[32] It's remarkable that the Savoyard influence which had attracted so much criticism during Henry's reign, and since by historians influenced by Matthew Paris, contrasts with the significant contributions from Savoy made during Edward's reign which had and has passed almost unnoticed. Perhaps the answer lay in these positions not carrying bequests of land, though they brought wealth and influence to those from Savoy. Far from making for the English Channel laden with golden money bags, those that came on the behest of Pierre de Savoie went on to be, perhaps, the most loyal of the loyal in serving the Plantagenet crown. We may ponder whether a King of England ever had such a reliable native-born coterie of followers. Pierre de Savoie had left a legacy in England, and it was now building and running the castles of north Wales.

Edward was replicating the governmental models, used hitherto by the Plantagenet monarchs in France, the Channel Islands and Ireland. It is no stretch to suggest that he was establishing in effect an English colony in north Wales and indeed that north Wales might serve as a model to later colonial governance. It has been said that Ireland was England's first colony; if that is so then north Wales was not far behind. Indeed, unlike Ireland, Wales remains an integral part of the United Kingdom, the Statute of Rhuddlan only being repealed as lately as 1887.[33] The counties of Merioneth and Caernarfonshire lasted until local government reorganization in 1974, merging into a new county of Gwynedd – Anglesey is still a unitary county to this day. The new towns of 'Flynt', 'Rothelan', 'Aberconewey' and 'Karnarvan' received their charters on 8 September 1284 at Flint.[34]

A legend began to be cited in the sixteenth century, the earliest written evidence of which is 1584, that Edward had promised the Welsh a new prince, who would be born in Wales and speak no English.[35] The tale told of Queen Leonor giving birth to a son whilst in Caernarfon and Edward offering that son to the Welsh as the Prince of Wales, thereby setting the precedent whereby the eldest son of the King of England and heir to the throne would evermore be the Prince of Wales. Except that the legend is almost certainly without any foundation at all, being the product of a latter-day legitimization of the then status quo.

Following the proclamation of the Statute of Wales at Rhuddlan in March, Edward moved forward to the castle-building site at Caernarfon to inspect the works there, bringing a heavily pregnant Leonor along with him. On the feast day of Saint Mark the Evangelist, 25 April 1284,[36] she was delivered of a son, whom the couple named Edward after the father.[37]

Young Edward was not the eldest son of the King of England at his birth, but the second son: he had an older brother, by ten years – Alphonso. It is quite possible that, given the imperial connections of Caernarfon, and the legend of Macsen Wledig, that the place of birth was a happy circumstance for Edward.

Indeed, it might be said that it would have been wiser to leave Leonor to give birth in the completed castle at Rhuddlan, rather than hazard a journey west to the building site that was Caernarfon. Nonetheless, Caernarfon was chosen, most likely by Leonor herself, as the place to give birth. A garden within the site had been laid for the nursing mother, and the actual birth may have taken place in the first storeys of what would become known as the Eagle Tower. An interesting suggestion by Leonor's biographer Sara Cockerill is that it is quite possible that the young Edward had been conceived in Caernarfon the previous summer, but we will of course never know.[38] Edward would soon be elevated to the position of heir to his father's lands and titles, as Alphonso died at Westminster in the August of 1284 whilst the royal couple was still away. But at his birth he was the 'spare' to Alphonso's 'heir', and so the eldest son as Prince of Wales legend has no basis.

Before hearing of their son's death, the royal couple undertook what amounted to a summer holiday in the newly conquered territory of north Wales. Firstly, in June, the royal entourage moved a little south from Caernarfon to the dark and brooding lake at Llyn Cwm Dulyn,[39] the Black Lake. The lake on the edge of the Carneddau range in Snowdonia is perhaps as remote and wild a place as they could have chosen to spend Edward's forty-fifth birthday. It was again, almost certainly, chosen for its place in Welsh mythology, the supposed burial place of Mabon ab Madron, a hero from the *Mabinogion* and the site where another hero, Lleu, was reputed to have transformed himself into an eagle. Given the mythological connections for the nearby future castles at Caernarfon and Harlech, it is noticeable how the *Mabinogion* looms large in Edward's thinking that summer of 1284. Cockerill suggests that the interest in Welsh mythology appears to have been Leonor's; if so, then the opportunity presented to co-opt Welsh culture to that of England may have been irresistible to Edward.[40]

After approaching a month in a tented idyll in the mountains, they moved on to Nefyn, on the Llyn Peninsula, there to hold a round table tournament, something Edward would have relished. Again, they could have chosen any site for the tournament, but in choosing Nefyn, a former princely residence, Edward was making a point.[41] Edward seemed to lose no occasion to remind the Welsh that he was now in charge. Nefyn was also the place from where Llywelyn and Eleanor de Montfort had written their last letters in 1282. The tournament, one team captained by Henri de Lacy, Earl of Lincoln, and the other by Richard de Burgh, Earl of Ulster,[42] rounded off what had been, since the birth of young Edward, essentially a royal holiday in north Wales – but a holiday with the added purpose of appropriating for himself Welsh mythology and reminding the conquered that they were conquered. By late September, the royal progress reached Overton, close to the original Anglo-Welsh border. They were joined by 1,000 Welsh minstrels, no less, to celebrate the fall of independent Wales. As the festivities ended Edward returned to Wales, visiting his loyal knights, who began the implementation of the Statute of Rhuddlan, and his architect Maître Jacques, who was raising three enormous castles in the conquered land. Edward visited each in turn, Conwy, Caernarfon and Harlech.

Othon de Grandson, accompanied by Jean de Vesci and Robert Burnell,[43] then travelled with the king on a north-to-south tour of Wales, taking in Harlech where the king saw his new castle rising, then Bere, one of the last of Dafydd's holdouts. The royal party continued to Llanbadarn [Aberystwyth] where the king saw the castle for the first time. Then south-westward visiting the cathedral at St David's where Antony Bek, Bishop of Durham's brother Thomas Bek, Bishop of St David's, gave the service on 26 November. Finally, the Welsh progress was completed in south Wales ending in Cardiff, Caldecott and Chepstow. That Christmas of 1284 the king spent in Bristol, his conquest of Wales complete.

The Jewels Roll for 1284 carries a sad footnote to the story of the House of Gwynedd:

> former seals of Prince of Wales Llywelyn and his brother Dafydd and Eleanor former Princess of Wales of 35 shillings and 10 pence weight of silver ... From them was made a new chalice ... which the King conferred on the new Abbey of Vale Royal.[44]

The very seals used by Llywelyn, his wife Eleanor and his brother Dafydd had been literally tossed into the melting pot and remade into a chalice that now adorned Edward's new abbey at Vale Royal in Cheshire.

But in the conquered land there would be one last calamity, within twelve days of Christmas 1284 the great abbey of Strata Florida was struck by lightning and save for the presbytery was burned to the ground. The abbey in mid Wales, inland from Aberystwyth, was known in Welsh as *Ystrad Fflur*, the Valley of Flowers. The house was an important primary historical source for early Welsh history: the *Brut y Tywysogion* was compiled within its learned walls. The Chester annalist sadly recalled that 'In general everything was burned by the fire including choral books and the bells.'[45] As 1284 came to a close, Gwynedd mourned the loss of its princely family and its autonomy, even as Wales mourned the burning of the very fabric of its cultural memory. It must have seemed, to some, that even the very heavens had been angry with Wales and that the Lord himself had turned his back.

But perhaps there is something to add to the story of the chalice, which might mean the Welsh clung to a vestige of the regalia of Gwynedd and their lost prince. Taylor makes a compelling argument, which Beverley Smith took up,[46] that the chalice placed at the abbey of Vale Royal may have been a silver chalice, but not the one made from the seals of Gwynedd. He suggests that a chalice found, along with an accompanying paten,[47] in 1890, by two workmen at Dolgellau in north Wales, may well have been the actual chalice.[48] Taylor hypothesizes that the chalice was hidden in the mountains of Meirionnydd for centuries before resurfacing; it's certainly a romantic notion and a more positive note upon which to dwell rather than the destruction of Strata Florida.[49] That the chalice may have found a final resting place in the National Museum of Wales, remains only a possibility, but nonetheless, a romantically pleasing one.

Chapter Ten

Work continued in north Wales, to realize Edward's plan for the establishment of royal control of Gwynedd, and in particular of castle construction at Conwy, Caernarfon and Harlech. The Calendar of Welsh Rolls records the military garrisons allocated for their defence: of note is the very few men required to garrison the castles. The defence of Caernarfon called for just forty men, including fifteen crossbowmen. To support the 'fencible men' would be a chaplain, a carpenter, a mason, a smith, janitors and watchmen.[1] Likewise, provision was made for Bere and Conwy, but at Harlech just ten crossbowmen were specified.[2] That so few are to be in their garrison is a token of the advanced design that will be used in their construction. The castles themselves will 'fight' alongside the defenders in withstanding any siege; they will not be simple passive shelters but weapons of war.

We have considered thus far the likely influence of the Savoyard Justiciar of north Wales, Othon de Grandson, on the work of castle-building now underway in Gwynedd. But there is another Savoyard knight we must also consider: Grandson's brother-in-law, Jean de Bonvillars.[3] On 3 December 1283, Bonvillars was paid expenses for supervising work in Wales. The exchequer clerk is quite clear, writing *'ad supervidendum'*, to supervise. If for Grandson we can only hypothesize, for Bonvillars the primary sources are unequivocal.[4] Bonvillars was another Savoyard knight in Edward's retinue, married to Agnès de Bonvillars whom we think likely to have been Othon de Grandson's sister. He'd been in the king's service for some time; we met him earlier bringing a letter to Grandson from Edward during the siege of Dolforwyn at the outset of the First Welsh War in 1277. He appears in the English archives of 1277, before next being recorded back in Savoy at Evian in March 1279[5] – probably betokening his accompanying Grandson's mission for the king to Gascony from January 1278.[6] The close relationship between Grandson and Bonvillars is illustrated by the appointment, in December 1278, of a relative, Othon de Bonvillars, as a justice on the Channel Islands, where Grandson was an absentee governor.[7] Jean would later be described, in 1284, as Othon's 'Knight Companion' – *'commiliti domini Ottonis de Grandisono'*.[8] He would also be a deputy to Grandson as justiciar, whilst additionally being the constable of the castle at Harlech. In 1285, his brother *'Henry de Bono Villar'*, Henri de Bonvillars, would become Prior of Wenlock, moving from its daughter house of Bermondsey.[9] The priory at Wenlock was a Cluniac re-foundation of an earlier seventh-century monastery and had been visited by, amongst others, Henry III. Henri de Bonvillars would be frequently employed on public business during the thirty-five years that he governed the priory of Wenlock.

In 1294, during the renewed unpleasantness with France, Guillaume de Grandson was forced to quickly step in and confirm that Henri was 'not in the power of the French King'. As earlier, in Henry's reign, the Savoyard would remain vulnerable to bouts of xenophobia.

As for his brother Jean, his role recorded in the archive of 1283 is of interest since it points to a role in the early construction of the castles in north Wales. Coldstream has suggested that evidence of his 'advice on castle design is neutral', having earlier acknowledged a supervisory role.[10] However, it is difficult to reconcile a supervisory role with a neutral influence on design. The key word here again is *supervidendum*, the same word used by the Savoyard scribe for 'household knight' Jean de Mézos earlier at Saillon, who Coldstream acknowledged had been 'closely involved ... with design'.[11] In assessing the role of another 'household knight', Bonvillars, we must try to determine, in the usual absence of job descriptions for the thirteenth century, what was meant by *supervidendum*. A direct translation would be 'overlook' or 'oversee' – dictionaries today describe that as to 'supervise, especially in an official capacity'. Our English word 'supervise' comes from the Latin *supervidere*,[12] which would imply a role for Bonvillars of something more than neutral, a role similar to that held by Mézos, a household knight supervising building, with an influence on design.

We also have clear primary-source evidence that Bonvillars worked alongside Maître Jacques, and indeed in a supervisory role. The accounts for Conwy survive in some detail for the period covering November 1285 to September 1286. For example, a payment recorded at Conwy, and dated 29 September 1286, records details of orders jointly made by Bonvillars and Maître Jacques.[13] That the task was assigned by both Bonvillars and Maître Jacques to Henry supports the understanding of *supervidendum* and his role of being more than 'neutral'. The same account goes on to record more detail of an active role for Bonvillars alongside Jacques: the primary sources are quite clear that both Savoyards are involved at Conwy.[14]

So, we can add to the paternity of the forthcoming castles in north Wales not only the king himself, of Maître Jacques de Saint Georges, his chief architect, of Othon de Grandson, his lifelong friend, but also of Jean de Bonvillars, the Savoyard household knight and kinsman[15] of Grandson. The great castles of north Wales take into their fibre yet more Vaudois DNA. Furthermore, when we come to think of the design specifics of the castles, we should remember that Edward and Othon, and likely Jean, had been on crusade to the Holy Land and would have been as familiar as most with the look and features of the castles of Outremer, and southern France from where they had originally sailed. The description *militi*, a knight, points to the likely input that Bonvillars might have into the castles. Like the king and his brother-in-law Grandson, he was a man of military expertise, having fought to gain and defend castles himself. Maître Jacques was a mason, an architect in modern parlance, and whilst he had constructed castles for the Counts of Savoy, he was not a fighting man. Who better to add the necessary military experience than a household knight trusted by both Edward and Othon, a fellow brother in arms? It has been suggested that the paternity ascribed to Maître Jacques for the north Welsh castles might be in question given the relative lack of sophistication of his Savoyard castles when compared with those in Wales. Whilst one answer would obviously be that in Wales he would be working with far greater resources, that of a King of England, not a Count of Savoy. We should not discount, as a source of some of the complexity, the unmeasurable paternity of the crusading knights, Grandson and Jean de Bonvillars – as well of course as to King Edward I himself. As observed earlier, I think it more than likely that the great castles of Gwynedd had many fathers, not just one – although it would be chiefly to one man that responsibility to realize them would lie: Maître Jacques de Saint Georges. The Savoyard trio would go on to do more than many in establishing Plantagenet rule in Wales, Grandson as Justiciar, Jean de Bonvillars as Deputy Justiciar[16] and Constable of the castle at Harlech and of course the master mason, Jacques de Saint Georges.

Taylor suggested that Jean de Bonvillars may well have played a key role in the foundation of Edwardian castle-building in Wales, evidencing it by Bonvillars being paid for, and therefore present throughout the period during which 'the crucial management appointments' were made.[17] On 20 November 1284, Bonvillars was paid twenty shillings whist with the king at Bere, but as Taylor noted, most of the payments made in the same paragraph pertain to October 1284, when the king was at Caernarfon. There, he had nominated his constables and made the further crucial appointment – that of Maître Jacques de Saint Georges, a grant for life, as 'Master of the Kings Works in Wales'.[18] The Calendar of Patent Rolls has the following entries, made in Caernarfon, for 20 October 1284:

> Grant, for life, to Master James de Sancto Georgio, king's sergeant, of 3s a day from the wardrobe, and at his death of 1s. 6d.a day to his wife Ambrosia if she survives him.

> Grant, for life. To Master Richard the engineer (Ingeniator), king's sergeant, of 12d a day from the Exchequer of Chester.[19]

Sadly, Taylor's hypothesis for Bonvillars being at Caernarfon at this fateful time can neither be proved nor disproved. The scribe making payment to Bonvillars does not confirm the period for which the payment was made. However, given all we know of the relationship between Edward and Othon de Grandson, and remembering that Jean de Bonvillars was both a kinsman of Othon's and his knight companion, it is not unreasonable to suggest that the Savoyard played a key role in the establishment of personnel required to bring Edward's castle-building ideas to fruition.

Edward made a further grant to Jacques of eight marks yearly, for summer and winter clothing, described as *'pro bono e laudabili servicio'*.[20] This and the wages grant to Maître Jacques, in and of itself, tells us much of what we need to know about the paternity of the Welsh castles. Looking for paternity in the roles of Jacques and Richard, the two 'king's sergeants', we have the salaries of three shillings per day and twelve pence per day, for context, into today's money, and adjusted for inflation by the UK National Archives calculation, Maître Jacques was being paid £104.11 per day and Master Richard nearly £35 – annualized these would be just over £38,000 for Maître Jacques and £12,775 for Master Richard.[21] By way of comparison a knight also earned three shillings per day.[22] We should also recognize that Maître Jacques was now to be paid from the King's Wardrobe accounts. Master Richard, as a lesser-paid craftsman, though recognized and named, would be paid from the Exchequer at Chester. These few lines confirm once more the relationship within the hierarchy of Jacques and Richard, the latter being important enough to mention by name, but not drawing anything like the salary awarded to Jacques, nor to be paid from the same source. A reasonable deduction of manager and deputy manager, in today's parlance, could easily be made. We have considered a number of times the revisiting of Maître Jacques' responsibilities in the castles of north Wales, discussing in detail the archive entries still extant and the reasonable translations we might make of the Latin texts; perhaps in the end we should simply 'follow the money' and just consider the entry from the Calendar of Patent Rolls for 20 October 1284 made at Caernarfon.

And so it was, from late 1284, that Guillaume de Cicon was first constable at Conwy and Jean de Bonvillars constable at Harlech. For the two men it might have seemed appropriate, as their homes in the Jura, Cicon and Rue, were as similarly distant as Conwy and Harlech. Constable was analogous to the French role of 'chatelaine' (or 'castellan'), denoting the man in charge of the castle on behalf of its owner, in this case, of course, Edward. Constable came from the Latin 'stabuli', meaning 'one who was an attendant of the stables'. 'Constabuli' then meant literally Count of the Stables; therefore, originally the role would have been the keeping of the king's horses – as always titles evolved.[23] Cicon had been the first constable at Rhuddlan, and that he was now entrusted with Conwy speaks volumes for his standing with Edward.[24] The primary role of the constable was to maintain the garrison of the castle, a task that Guillaume de Cicon would retain at Conwy, until his death sometime during 1310–11. Knighted at this time by the king was Guillaume de Cicon's brother, Stephen de Rognon,[25] yet another Savoyard knight who'd found preferment in England, fighting in Edward's army. Unlike Cicon, Rognon would return to Savoy.[26] As Constable of Harlech Castle, Jean de Bonvillars was awarded an annual fee of £149.0s.10d, adjusted to today's money a little over £100,000.[27] The gatehouse at Harlech would be the residence for Jean and Agnès, a long way indeed from the shores of Lac de Neuchâtel.

If we accept Taylor's suggestion that Jean de Bonvillars was, as Othon de Grandson's knight companion and one of Edward's household knights, at Saint-Georges-d'Espéranche in 1273, then it is also very likely that he too had seen the Castello di San Giorio di Susa as they climbed the Val Di Susa to the Mont Cenis together, en route to Count Philippe's castle.[28] At least three men, then, had seen the merlons decoratively topped by three finials at Susa, that would find their way to the battlements of the castle at Conwy (Figure 2.2) – Edward, Grandson and now also Jean de Bonvillars. This is interesting, because Bonvillars is the one of the three for which we have primary-source evidence of having been involved in the actual works at Conwy, '*supervidendum castra*' or 'supervise the castles'. However, we should also add, that unbeknownst to Taylor, Jacques may well have visited San Giorio, since Jean Bertrand de Canusco who died at Saint-Georges on 8 December 1277 '*in domus Magistri Jacobi Lathomi*' was of the clan that held Susa for the Savoyards. It is not a great stretch of the imagination then to suggest, that given the implied friendship, Jacques had visited the home of a man dying in his house.[29] As we have oft said, attaching the paternity of the Welsh castles is not an easy task. However, I would suggest that it is at the least possible Jean de Bonvillars was responsible for at least one of the decorative features of Edward's castles. Especially so, given there is some evidence of these finials having been also present at Harlech, where he was also constable.

Further evidence of Bonvillars' senior role in the direction of castle construction was highlighted by Swiss historian, Chapuisat, of a payment made in 1285 by the Riccardi di Lucca to Richard of Abingdon of 1,000 marks, financing the works underway in Wales. The writ was issued in Paris, dated 12 June 1286, and was executed 'under the supervision of Jean de Bonvillars'.[30] The Riccardi of Lucca were the source of much of Edward's finance for his castle-building, so for the payment to be under the supervision of Jean de Bonvillars confirms his key role in overseeing construction works.

Meanwhile, as the castle-building in north Wales started, events elsewhere in Europe began to occupy Edward's attention. The Welsh rebellion of 1282 was not the only uprising that Easter: the Mediterranean island of Sicily also saw a revolt against what was seen as foreign overlordship, except the result was much more successful for the rebels than in Wales. Whilst Edward was occupied with the problem of the Welsh, word had reached him of what became known as the Sicilian Vespers.[31] The Italian rioting against their Angevin-Capetian masters threatened to bring in France on one side and Aragon on the other, as well as involving the papacy. As in later centuries a local conflict had the distinct potential for developing into a wider European conflagration with the distinct possibility that it might suck in England. After all, Edward, in addition to being King of England, held Gascony as a fief of the King of France, and as such might be obliged to offer him military support in that capacity in any war with Aragon. On the other hand, Edward, on behalf of Gascony, had through years of diplomacy sought good relations with his neighbours across the Pyrenees, something his marriage to Leonor of Castile had successfully achieved. However, events subsequently concluded in a less-than-usual way – that is all combatants dying of natural causes.[32] The death of Charles d'Anjou would also mark the passing of the last of the kings married by the famous four daughters of Provence, that began our story – Louis, Charles, Henry and Richard were now all gone, leaving behind just Alianor in England and Marguerite in France to grieve their husbands.

Edward would have to ensure that the successors, Pope Honorius IV, King Philippe IV of France and King Alfonso III of Aragon, also wanted peace. Philippe IV of France was crowned at Reims Cathedral on 6 January 1286, the necessity of Edward paying him homage for Gascony presented the opportunity for a trip to France. Therefore, on 13 May 1286, Edward sailed from Dover to Wissant and thence, with no small baggage train, he travelled firstly to Amiens, where he duly paid homage to Philippe.[33] The avoidance of a European conflagration, begun by the Sicilian Vespers, then took Edward south to Gascony, far from what he now supposed to be a pacified Wales.

But Wales had not been pacified, and whilst Edward busied himself with high-level and complex European affairs, there had been another revolt by the Welsh. This time, it was not the now-decapitated House of Gwynedd that had flown to arms, it was the erstwhile loyal Rhys ap Maredudd of the house of Deheubarth in south-west Wales. Rhys was the son of Maredudd ap Rhys Gryg, who'd been imprisoned for want of loyalty by Llywelyn ap Gruffydd, a man, despite his previous grievances, as espoused by Llywelyn himself in 1282, who had remained loyal to the king: in short, a Welshman one might have thought unlikely to rebel. His fief was Castell Newydd Emlyn, or Newcastle Emlyn, strategically located on a steep-sided promontory overlooking the River Teifi, built around 1240. More recently Rhys had based himself at Dryslwyn Castle, increasing the strength of its fortifications; it had been built around 1220, possibly by Rhys Gryg his grandfather, as a home to the princes of Deheubarth.

Edward had left his realm in the hands of the Second Earl of Cornwall, Edmund, the son of his uncle Richard of Cornwall and his aunt Sanchia de Provence. Edmund was a man Edward had trusted before, taking care of England whilst the king had been away on campaign in Wales. Rhys, as '*Dominus de Estratewy*' or Lord of Tywi, had come to resent the imposition of the English county system following the Second Welsh War and begrudged the rule and authority of Robert de Tibetot as Justiciar of South Wales. But most of all, Rhys had wanted Dinefwr Castle, which he was denied and in short felt ill-rewarded for his loyalty to the Crown in the recent wars.

Resort to arms was made by Rhys from 8 June 1287, seizing the castles at Dinefwr and Llandovery, slaughtering the garrisons, before plundering his way to the gates of Carmarthen.[34] John Giffard was expelled from Carreg Cennen and the commote of Is Cennen (Carmarthenshire south of the Afon Cennen). The flames of rebellion may have reached or threatened Brecon.

Edmund responded with all the forces he could command: this revolt in Edward's absence was not going to be allowed to undo all the work the king had undertaken in the recent wars. Accordingly, some 10,000 to 11,000 soldiers began to make their way to south-west Wales. Edmund summoned the barons to Gloucester on 21 July, armies were assembled at Chester under Reginald de Grey, at Montgomery under

Roger L'Estrange and the main force under Edmund himself. Amongst Grey's Chester army were men from north Wales under John de Havering, men that is who could be spared from the works underway there – including, it seems, Jean de Bonvillars, Constable of Harlech castle.

Rhys was at Dryslwyn Castle, so the combined royal forces merged at Carmarthen and made for Dryslwyn, there to besiege the rebellious Rhys. Morris breaks down the components of the English armies as follows:

Reginald de Grey	English of Chester	700
	Welsh of Snowdon and Cantrefi	2,600
Roger L'Estrange	English of Shropshire	1,000
	Welsh of the Marches	1,940
Edmund of Cornwall	English of South Shropshire, Derbyshire & Herefordshire	2,010
	Welsh of Monmouth	360
Robert de Tibetot	Welsh of N. Pembroke & Cardigan	920
	Welsh of Carmarthenshire	1,000
	Crossbowmen	105
	Total	10,635[35]

What is worth noting from these numbers is that over half of the royal contingent was Welsh; therefore, we should see them as royal armies as much as English armies.

Edmund of Cornwall moved upstream of Carmarthen, up the Tywi Valley to Dryslwyn where, by 12 August, a siege was laid. Jean de Bonvillars, Tibbetot and Grey arrived on 15 August.[36] Unbeknownst to the army, Rhys was not about to be surrounded in a castle and had already made for the hills. The castle sits upon a rocky outcrop high above the flat floodplain of the Tywi. Rhys had only recently enlarged and improved the castle with the rewards of his loyalty to the Crown in the Welsh wars – making it 'one of the largest masonry castles ever raised by native Welsh lords'.[37]

Morris relates that Havering's north Welsh contingent was employed in building great siege engines, trebuchets to hurl big rocks at the castle. Recent archaeological research has found evidence of their work.[38] Turner attributes the building of the trebuchet 'probably' to Master Richard, who'd travelled down to Dryslwyn from his home at Chester with Grey. Many craftsmen drawn from Edward's domains in the north worked on the trebuchet, costing £17.9s.3d.[39] and being made up of timber, ox hides, horse hides, ropes, pulleys, nails, steel, iron, lead and even an anchor from Carmarthen.[40] A Master Adam is recorded as working in the quarry for two weeks with nineteen other men fashioning stone balls for the newly built siege machine.[41] The strength of the English army speaks of the nervousness, in the king's absence, on the part of the regent, Edmund, in allowing a revolt to take hold as had Dafydd's revolt of 1282. The trebuchet was, of course, again funded by the Riccardi di Lucca, Francesco and Salomon of their number escorting the bags of silver pennies to Dryslwyn.[42]

However, we must now relate what appears to have been a major setback for the besieging army, and one that was to take the life of a knight far from his home in Savoy. Mining was the medieval art of digging tunnels underneath castle walls in order to bring them down, and such mining operations had been attempted at Dryslwyn. Responsibility for the mine appears to have been with Master Richard.[43] We have a likely eyewitness account from Outremer of the successful undermining of a castle:

> He immediately ordered the rock on which the castle was situated to be undermined and props to be placed along the tunnel to support the works above. Then he had wood carried in and fire introduced. When the props had burned, the excavation suddenly fell in, and the tower which was nearest to the fire collapsed with a loud noise.[44]

Richard's work might not have been effective, the mine collapsing upon itself whilst several English knights had been inspecting the work – one of these knights was, apparently, Jean de Bonvillars.

The English chroniclers do not mention Bonvillars, but it would appear the Welsh do:

> And from the king's host from Wales, and from England, came against Dryslwyn. And then John Pennardd, leader of the men of Gwynedd, was drowned. And at last, by a long siege, they took the castle, and drove Rhys ap Moredudd into outlawry.[45]

In the light of writs for forces issued at Gloucester and Hereford in July 1287, Taylor identifies Pennardd as a Welsh chronicler's best approximation of Bevillard or Bonvillars. The works killed not only Jean de Bonvillars, but also took the life of the Earl of Stafford and Sir William de Montchesney, Gerard de Insulis and Nicholas Caro, such were the perils of medieval warfare. Given payment dates, a date for the collapse can be suggested as 'before 30 August'.[46] It was a sad, if very sudden end, to the *militi* Jean de Bonvillars, brother-in-law to Othon de Grandson, Deputy Justiciar[47] of north Wales, Constable of Harlech castle and a man, at Dryslwyn, a long way from Vaud. The castle fell on 5 September, with great damage to the castle; the royal forces captured Rhys's wife and son. Rhys made for the castle at Newcastle Emlyn, held by Roger de Mortimer, and took it, slaughtering its garrison.[48] In December, the English army hauled their siege engines from Dryslwyn to Cardigan, with the help of forty oxen, and then continued up the Teifi valley to Newcastle Emlyn, now needing sixty oxen to haul them.

The castle was besieged, and after a very short struggle fell in January 1288, but not before Rhys again fled. Morris suggests that 'as not a single man was missing out of the paid portion of the army, it would seem that the surrender was peaceable'. He goes on to suggest that perhaps it was the great trebuchet of Richard the Engineer that persuaded the rebels to concede so quickly. There was nothing like a large pile of big stones next to a siege engine to persuade a garrison whose lord had fled to submit.[49] Men had indeed been spared to scour the beaches near Cardigan for suitable stones, from where they'd been conveyed to Newcastle Emlyn.

Rhys now went on the run, a fugitive, as had been his fellow countryman Dafydd ap Gruffydd just six years earlier. The hunt for Rhys would be a long one, some say he fled to Ireland, but the manhunt would continue. Morris estimated that the rebellion had cost some £10,606, of which Kaeuper confirms £8,288 had been supplied by the Riccardi.[50] The 'Riccardi system' had once more shown itself invaluable to the Crown, crushing the rebellion with overwhelming force, despite the king and his household being away in Gascony.

Having accompanied her husband, Agnès de Bonvillars returned to Harlech[51] and their children,[52] who learned of the death of their father in south Wales and for the next few years Agnès carried on the role as Constable of Harlech castle alone. Indeed, Agnès de Bonvillars would remain as the Constable of Harlech Castle[53] until 1290,[54] when the executors of her late husband's will were pardoned expenses and a gift of forty marks from Edward was made.[55] And so was rendered Edward's recognition of the loyal and faithful service rendered to the Crown by Savoyard Jean de Bonvillars. At the same session at Westminster the possessions of the now-fled Rhys ap Maerdudd were taken care of, with Robert de Tibetot gaining the lands of the 'king's rebel in Wales, which are now in the king's hands by his forfeiture'.[56] And so ended the 1287 revolt of Rhys ap Maerdudd.

All this time, whilst the Welsh revolt was being suppressed and the[57] Sicilian business was being resolved, Edward was in Gascony. It is now that we have a not entirely explained or easily understandable interlude in the life of Maître Jacques de Saint Georges – he was summoned from Wales to Gascony during this period. At some point between 1287 and 1289 the Savoyard architect was called south by his master. But why? Edward didn't carry out any building works of note in Gascony at this time and it might be imagined the delivery of his castles in north Wales was still the overarching task. The journey from Wales to Gascony is not an easy one in the twenty first century, in the thirteenth it was an incredibly difficult one. A round trip of nearly 1,200 miles (1,900 kilometres) would be enough to severely tax most people and must surely have been undertaken for some significant reason. Taylor suggests that the journey south was made 'in or about November 1287'[58] in the company of John de Havering who'd been Justiciar of north Wales in Othon de Grandson's Gascon absence, which would further mean that travel was undertaken in wintertime. There were two ways to travel from Wales to Gascony in 1287: firstly, by horse to Dover, thence by ship to Calais, thence by horse the length of France; secondly, by horse to Bristol followed by a sea passage by way of the Bay of Biscay and Bordeaux. The overland journey through France took the same three weeks as that to Savoy; by sea it was a quicker fortnight.[59] Neither would be easy, the Channel in the thirteenth century was a quick route to an uneasy passage, beset by a rolling ship and bouts of nausea, along with freezing gale-force winds. The evidence for the Gascon trip is not extensive. Taylor found that payment was made to Jacques for 'going to the king in Gascony'[60] and Morris adds that the lack of archival material for Jacques in Wales between late 1287 and 1289 strengthens the certainty of the case, much in the same way as the absence of material in Savoy after his arrival in Wales points to the identification of the Savoyard Jacques as the same Marc Morris as the English Jacques.[61]

Morris presents the possibility that Jacques' visit to Gascony is related to the beginning of construction, by Edward, of a castle at Sauveterre-la-Lémance on the border between the Agenais and France. Sauveterre is unlike the castles in Wales: it is built upon high ground, dominating the confluence of the Lémance and Sendroux rivers. The castle, in terms of situation, concept and design, is more like those Jacques built for the Count of Savoy at Châtel Argent in the Val d'Aosta and Voiron in the Viennois. Morris 'tentatively' suggests that Jacques may have been responsible for the early design work, which would be later realized by Guillaume de Cosinges.[62] There is no primary-source evidence for Jacques' involvement, but it is as Morris suggests 'plausible'.[63] The author, having seen the limited remains of all the Savoyard works of Maître Jacques, can say this: 'it certainly looks like a Maître Jacques castle.' It's certainly possible that Jacques was involved in the conception of Sauveterre-la-Lémance but is the building of a small castle in the Agenais reason enough to bring the king's master builder all the way from north Wales to Gascony? One is bound to say that at the least it's unlikely. But then this is the thirteenth century, and the primary-source evidence for the likely trip is less than one hundred percent solid and the primary-source evidence for building work entirely lacking – so tentative and plausible are probably as far as we will be able to travel.

So, in 1288 until Edward's return north in 1289 we can say that it's almost certain Maître Jacques was called to Gascony, and that once there he may well have assisted in the founding of at least one castle. On 13 June 1289, Edward, his retinue, including Othon de Grandson and Maître Jacques de Saint Georges, returned north to England, their Gascon diversion at an end. Edward and Leonor spent time in Abbeville in their county of Ponthieu on the homeward journey, staying at the monastery of La Gard. Finally, on 12 August, a boat from Wissant to Dover saw them return to their kingdom after spending so much time in their faraway southern Duchy.

Sadly, we should note the passing at this time of Edward's faithful servant and Othon de Grandson's comrade in arms, Jean de Vesci. Although not a Savoyard himself, he'd married into the family so to speak through his first wife, Agnès de Saluzzo, a relative of both Alianor de Provence and Pierre de Savoie. He passed away at Montpellier in February 1289 and Leonor travelled to Oloron-Saint-Marie to collect his body. She arranged for it to be sent back to England, where he was buried at Alnwick Abbey in Northumberland.[64] So passed a man, who along with Grandson, commanded the army that had crossed the Menai Strait from Anglesey and been the first to see the site of the future castles at Caernarfon and then Harlech. The once-rebellious Vesci had fought alongside Montfort at Evesham and rebelled once more soon afterward, and yet Edward had offered clemency, which Vesci had rewarded with a life of service. Edward, Leonor, Vesci and Grandson had been close friends, and had had many adventures together, but these were now beginning to draw to a close. His old friend and comrade of many battles, Grandson, was an executor of his will.[65]

The end came years later for Rhys ap Maredudd, he had been on the run since January 1288 but was not found and captured until 1291, like with Dafydd there is talk of him being betrayed by Welshmen.[66] Robert de Tibetot sent Rhys in chains to Edward early in 1292. Rhys ap Maredudd was found guilty of murder, arson, theft and not least destruction of royal castles, he was executed for treason at York on 2nd June, his lifeless body hanging for three days before being cut down. As the Lanercost chronicler recorded "… et ad Eborum deductus, ibidem judicatus est, tractus, et suspensus" – "and conducted to York, there is sentenced, drawn and hung."[67] Rhys was left hanging from the gallows at Knaresmire, a low lying marsh south west of the city walls, it would become the permanent site of the gallows in York, and witness the hanging of the highwayman Dick Turpin in 1739.

Chapter Eleven

Whilst the affairs of the Sicilian Vespers, the fall of Tripoli, renewed threats to Acre and Outremer, and closer to home the Rhys ap Maredudd revolt were attracting the attentions of Edward and his retinue, the construction of his iron ring of castles at Caernarfon, Conwy and Harlech was underway.

Let us begin now a journey of the imagination, from the king's castle at Rhuddlan to the castle under construction at Caernarfon, in the time just before Maître Jacques was called away to Gascony in 1287. Our tour will take us along the coast road to Conwy, over the mountains to Harlech, before reaching the banks of the Menai at Caernarfon.

Travelling along the coast to the western extremity of the four *cantrefi*, we would come to the wide estuary of the River Conwy that bisects north Wales longitudinally from the Irish Sea deep into the Snowdonia Mountain range. The Afon Conwy is wide as it approaches the sea, but has gathered all that water unto itself in just twenty-seven miles (forty-three kilometres) from its source in the mountains. The name itself describes the river's nature, originally coming from the Welsh '*cyn*' for chief and '*gwy*' for water – therefore chief water. As you come to the Conwy you are at a long-standing political and geographical divide: behind you the Clywdian hills rise to no more than 1,893 feet (577 metres), ahead of you the Snowdonia range rears up to 3,560 feet (1,085 metres). The four *cantrefi* had been disputed lands between the English and the Welsh since before the arrival of the Normans. Snowdonia however was the mountain fastness that held the lands of the Princes of Gwynedd. As you gaze across the estuary, over your right shoulder would be the former castle built by Henry III at Deganwy, a frontier castle. Edward envisaged something entirely different. Across the river lay the abbey of Aberconwy, in which Llywelyn Fawr was buried, where Othon de Grandson had helped negotiate a peace following the First Welsh War. Edward would move the abbey and build a castle upon its site, at the foot of the mountain fastness; he would command Gwynedd now, he would build upon its frontier looking offensively outward, not as his father had done on its frontier, looking defensively inward.[1]

The castle would be sited upon a ridge of extremely rugged rock,[2] and would dominate and not be subject in any way to the threat of undermining. The outcrop ridge sits at the confluence of the minor Afon Gyfin and the Conwy, meaning that a castle built upon it would not only be perched upon impregnable rock, it would be surrounded on three sides by water, a natural defensive moat. It was upon this formidable rock that Maître Jacques and the king chose to site their castle. Its design would be largely constrained by the size and shape of the rock upon which it stood. Conwy Castle would take the form of a long rectangle divided into two between the main part of the castle and the royal apartments – essentially two castles added together side on.

The eastern and westward extremities of the stronghold, river and landward side would be protected by barbicans – the East and West Barbicans. The main rectangle of the castle, surrounding the outer ward, would be slightly bowed on one side and protected by no less than six towers, going clockwise from top left: the North-west, the Kitchen, the Stockhouse, the Bakehouse, the Prison and lastly the South-west. The royal apartments abutting the Stockhouse and Bakehouse towers and their joining curtain wall would be essentially an added *Carré Savoyard*: a square with four corner towers surrounding the inner ward, the aforesaid Stockhouse and Bakehouse, plus the Chapel Tower and King's Tower. The rectangle and the square sitting together would form the castle but could, if needs be, have been defended separately. The four towers enclosing the royal apartments and forming the *Carré Savoyard* were each topped by turrets, perhaps as a nod to Queen Leonor's Castilian heritage, or even perhaps at her suggestion. It is these turrets that may have had their origins in the Château de Lucens in the Pays de Vaud.

The main entrance to the castle was by means of an outer gate, reached from a bridge from the town, a town which would develop alongside the castle, to the West Barbican. The outer gate itself encompassed two turrets from which guard could be kept, secured by a portcullis. Once through the gate a visitor to the castle would be presented with a left-hand ninety-degree turn before being presented with another inner gate, above which he would find a wall complete with the then-novel, for British, feature of stone machicolations. The north-west and south-west towers would be able to provide flanking fire. This approach of bridge, gate, portcullis, barbican, left-hand turn, gate topped by machicolation and flanked by towers would present some challenge for any potential assailant.

Even as construction was concluding, what would be the sounds and smells our traveller might encounter? The building of a castle in the thirteenth century was a colossal undertaking. Within and around the castle there would have been hundreds of workers, in something that would have already looked like a small town. There would have been an extraordinary amount of noise, the smoke and sparks coming from the blacksmiths, the buzz and rasp of carpenters' saws, the masons cutting, carving and polishing the stone filling the air with a choking dust. This air would also have been filled with the sounds of many languages, English, but also much French in all its forms: Anglo-Norman, Langue d'Oil, Langue d'Oc and of course even Latin. The sound was deafening. The smells of the medieval town, of manure, of woodsmoke, of men working without washing so frequently. Conwy would have been an assault on the senses.

Once through the gate passage, a visitor to the castle would find a kitchen, bakehouse and brewhouse and their attendant aromas to his left, to his right the

Great Hall and a chapel. At the farthest end of the Outer Ward there was a well, ninety-one feet (27 metres) deep, and a middle gate protecting the entrance to the royal apartments (Figure 2.3). This middle gate, set in a middle curtain wall was protected by a drawbridge and again approached in an oblique way as with the outer/inner gate combination. Once into the Inner Ward and the *Carré Savoyard* of the royal apartments, one would be faced with cellars and a kitchen on the ground floor and the King's and Queen's chambers on the first floor. These King's chambers could well have been the *camera regis*, referred to in the previous chapter, for which Maître Jacques was paid.[3] Beyond the royal apartments stood the East Barbican which protected the water entrance to the castle. The castle would have been lime-washed to have presented a brilliant white external appearance. The castle was rendered a white colour by means of a lime whitewash, '*lait de chaux*', literally milk of lime, so would have presented an almost alien imposition in rural Wales. It's not an overstatement of the case to imagine that the completed castle at Conwy might be considered analogous to the effect the first Roman buildings had upon the native population, a thousand or more years earlier.

The gate protected by the western barbican at Conwy is most likely the first in the British Isles protected by stone machicolations.[4] As such it represents a new variation upon a defensive theme in the king's castles. In principle, machicolations are a means by which defenders can assail attackers who would otherwise be out of reach beneath them, attackers who have reached the base of the wall upon which the defenders stand. Originally this was achieved by hoards or hoarding, a temporary wooden shed-like construction that was placed on the exterior of the ramparts of a castle during a siege to allow the defenders to improve their field of fire. Machicolations were a more permanent affair, made from stone, created by stone corbels supporting an extension of the wall outward, whilst creating a gap through which to fire upon attackers. The English word 'machicolation' derives, as nearly all castle-related vocabulary derives, from Old French, with '*machecol*' rendered in Medieval Latin as '*machecollum*', which had derived from the Old French '*machier*' meaning 'to crush' or 'wound' and '*col*' meaning 'neck' – quite literally then 'neck crusher'. Stone machicolations had begun to emerge in the twelfth century, an early example being at Krak des Chevaliers in Outremer circa 1170.[5] But they had thus far not been employed in the British islands, and therefore their use by Maître Jacques at Conwy does represent an innovation.

The source of the innovation leads us once more into speculation, in the absence of hard evidence. We can say that his original castle at Yverdon sported hoardings, not machicolations, and that there is no evidence for stone machicolation at any of his works in Savoy. However, both Edward and much of his retinue, such as Othon de Grandson and Jean de Bonvillars, would have been familiar with them from their time in the Holy Land. Machicolation had been used in the Anglo-Norman realm from Château Gaillard in 1197, a product of King Richard's time in the Levant – it's unlikely that anyone involved at Conwy had, however, seen

Château Gaillard, as it was now decidedly in French hands and a long way from Savoy or England.

Perhaps the answer lies in genuine innovation and evolution. John Harris, writing in the *Castle Studies Group Journal*, says: 'One can more easily imagine a stone wall equipped with timber hoards (as Maître Jacques built at Yverdon) developing into the best-known, fully developed form of machicolation when reconstructed in stone (as at Conwy).'[6] In other words, perhaps the Conwy machicolations are the Savoyard hoards rendered in stone, in light of advice given by knights who'd seen the castles of Outremer. Harris goes on to suggest that wooden hoards indicated a reduced budget, and we know that Maître Jacques certainly had more funds to work with when building castles for King Edward than he had for the Counts of Savoy. There is evidence at Conwy for the use of hoards on walls and towers, putlog holes left in the fabric of the castle. So perhaps we have a combination of hoards, familiar to Jacques, and continuous machicolation across the gateway as a development of wooden hoards given the greater availability of funds and the greater threat to the castles in Wales than was the case in Savoy. Certainly, we will see from a tour of the castles built by the Savoyard that great care was taken with protecting the entrances to the castles, and each would in turn have unique solutions for making the weak point of the castle become its strong point.

The machicolation provided the gateway with two planes of defence, vertical and horizontal. Romantic imagination has conjured up boiling oil being distributed below, but more likely were simply arrows, crossbow bolts, hot sand and in case of a fire threatening the wooden gate below – simply water to put the fire out. It's not difficult to imagine the pain of hot sand getting into the joints of an armoured knight.

Before the western approach to the castle, beside the town walls and beneath what is now the Cadw carpark are the remains of what we think to be the offices from which the Master of the King's Works in Wales directed his operations.[7] The offices of the master of the works and his master masons would have been called the tracing house, a covered place where plans for particular elements of design might be drawn up.[8] At York Minster the tracing office of the master mason who built and designed the cathedral has survived. The drawing board at York was the floor and inscribed on it to this day are the patterns for individual pieces of stone. The floor surface was made up of plaster, re-laid again and again over time as new designs were required – at York the feet of the men, or perhaps children, whose feet flattened the plaster can still be seen. Drawings would be translated into wooden templates from which workers at the 'coalface' might render into stone. Architectural plans do not survive for the Edwardian castles, and it is quite possible they never existed in any detail.

The tracing house or houses would have been, in all probability, the venue for something we might all recognize from our modern working lives – the weekly meeting. A weekly site meeting at which all the heads of crafts (masons, carpenters etc.) might report progress and have work targets assigned was a key element in Maître Jacques' ability to deliver the simultaneous construction of three gigantic castles on budget and on time for Edward. Experimental archaeology is an instructive way of learning the past, and the thirteenth-century castle under construction at Guédelon in France has shed light upon the ways in which the master mason transmitted design to construction through such meetings.[9]

It should be remembered that Edward had first been introduced to Maître Jacques whilst the Savoyard was in the middle of building castles at Voiron, La Côte-Saint-André, Saint-Laurent-du-Pont, and the palace-castle of Saint-Georges-d'Espéranche for Count Philippe. The ability to manage one castle site, to act as the conductor of an orchestra for one assemblage of stone into a castle is an achievement, but the ability to do this for multiple sites a day's ride from each other is quite simply why Maître Jacques de Saint Georges is reputed to be one of the world's greatest castle builders. This ability has led some to dub him a 'project manager', but this is to assign the role of 'pilot' to Apollo astronaut Neil Armstrong. What we see in Maître Jacques is a master mason with knowledge of sophisticated geometry and mathematics, no doubt gleaned from his mason father Jean Cotereel, the builder of cathedrals. He had manipulated circles, squares and triangles to build in what he saw as proportionally correct shapes. The use of the root 2, the relationship between diagonal and square had been fundamental to Cotereel's work. As we shall see later at Caernarfon, in what Morris called 'a designer playing with geometrical shapes for effect',[10] the use of sophisticated geometry in north Wales is yet further evidence of Jacques being the son of Jean Cotereel and the likely grandson of the earlier phase mason at Lausanne, where mathematical pattern was inherent and fundamental in the symbolic use of design.[11] Building from drawings to templates to elaborate traverses of windows that survive at the cathedral in Lausanne – what we see is the emergence of the role of architect.[12] Not yet an architect as we understand the role, but nonetheless the genesis of the architect. It is instructive that the builders at Guédelon treat 'master-of-works' and 'architect' as synonyms, but we should stress again, not 'architect' as we understand the term.[13] We might simply observe once more that Maître Jacques is ascribed the title *'Magistro operacionum Regis in Wallia'* or 'Master of the King's works in Wales' to make our point.[14]

We will return to the differences between medieval master masons, masters of works and modern architects and how they might relate to patrons in subsequent chapters. Suffice to say at this point that the thirteenth century was not the twenty-first, and we must be careful not to ascribe to the medieval world more recent notions of the role of an architect. In the thirteenth century the role of the patron in a building's design was much more important than it might be today. For royal projects such as the castles of north Wales a leading role would be taken by the king himself, supported by key members of his retinue. As we have seen thus far important contributions might be made by men such as Othon de Grandson and Jean de Bonvillars. This is not to downgrade the role of a master of works, such as Jacques, but to say that his key role was to realize in stone the grand visions of others, not necessarily to innovate, as we might expect of an architect today. To oversimplify it, the master of works supplied the buildings the patron requested. Nevertheless, it would be from the tracing house or houses, now beneath the Cadw carparks at Conwy, that the simultaneous construction of the most impressive castles of the medieval world would be plotted – something to ponder when next parking your car at Conwy.

It's been suggested that travel between the head of operations and the works in progress at Caernarfon and at Harlech would most likely have been by boat, especially given the mountainous nature of the land between Conwy, the upper Conwy Valley and Harlech. However, I'm not so sure that would always be the case: we must remember that the Savoyard had been used to riding pack horses from the Count of Savoy's works at Châtel Argent in the Val d'Aosta to Saint-Georges-d'Espéranche in the Viennois by way of the 7,178 feet (2,188 metres) Petit Saint-Bernard Pass.

Taylor laid out the building records for Conwy to give us some insight into the materials used in construction for the year 1286, along with volumes and cost. Although it's been reproduced before, it is worth taking another look.[15]

Commodity	Source of Supply	Quantity	Cost
Charcoal		19 tons 2 qtrs 6 bush	£10.0s.4d
Sea-coal	Whelston in Bagillt	524 tons	£13.11s.6$^{1/2}$d
Lead	Flint	140 carrats	£182.11s.0d
Iron	Newcastle-under- Lyme or Chester	90 summe, 70 pieces	£44.17s.6d
Steel	Newcastle-under- Lyme	3 barrels	£10.6s.0d
Tin	Chester and Boston	500lb	£3.11s.4d
Nails	Newcastle-under- Lyme	125,000	£10.11s.8d
Ropes	Chester	Unspecified	£12.2s.10d
Timber		13,500 Shingles 11,644 Boards	£12.18s.8$^{1/2}$d
Scaffolding		2,000 Poles 1,180 Clayes	£9.8s.8d
Other items			£6.10s.11d

Firstly, let's look at those quantities of materials. The charcoal and sea-coal supplied are measured in tons. The ton has a long history and has acquired several meanings and uses over the years. The word comes into English as a way of describing a cask or barrel, 'tunne' in Old English, 'tonne' in Old French and 'tunna' in Latin. Since at this time a ton was principally a measure of liquid, but also since the liquid was carried in a barrel, it came to mean a size of barrel. Subdivisions of the ton for dry mass, such as charcoal, were quarters and bushels, the bushel being a dry measure of eight gallons or four pecks. The carrat would be a measure of precious metals that we now reserve for gold and diamonds as the carat. The barrels of steel would be, almost certainly, the barrel as a subdivision of a ton rather than an actual barrel. Amongst the timber are wood shingles or thin, tapered pieces of wood primarily used to cover roofs and walls of buildings to protect them from the weather. Historically shingles were split from straight-grained, knot-free bolts of wood. Lastly, for the scaffolding, poles would be self-evident, but clayes would be wattles, or hurdles, made with stakes interwoven with osiers.

For equivalence in terms of metric units, we can say that by the time of Queen Elizabeth I (300-plus years into the future from a 1286 standpoint) weights and measures in English use were:

- One pound (1lb.) equalled 0.45359237kg
- One quarter (1qtr.) equalled 12.7kg
- One Ton (1t.) equalled 1,016kg

Much of this charcoal, sea-coal, lead, iron, steel and tin would be bound for the blacksmiths of the construction site at Conwy. In feudal society, the blacksmith was amongst that rare breed of labourers, a free man, so specialized, prized and skilled was he. The blacksmith has often been likened to a magician, in being able to transform base materials into things of great beauty and necessity. Smiths skilfully used the colour of worked metal to indicate temperature: scarlet (270°C/520°F), cherry red (750°C/1,380°F) pale yellow to white (1,200°C/2,190°F), the latter would being when it could be shaped. As it was with the village blacksmith, so it was with the blacksmiths of a castle construction site.

The forge would have been the scene of much noise and colour, as the blacksmith used his smelter to win iron from ore, or as more likely in this case to collect it from iron for re-use. The anvil and the hearth would be used to beat the metals into the stuff of things to construct the castle. The key role of the blacksmiths at Conwy was to supply the teams of masons with the tools used in fashioning stone into castle. Experience at Guédelon has shown that perhaps the most important and ongoing work of the smiths would have been repairing and reworking the worn-out tools of the stonemasons – all that hitting stone with punches, chisels and lump hammers meant that in France one set of tools a day required attention – Conwy would have been no different.[16] The workers at Guédelon found it helpful for stonecutters to have a number of sets of tools, so that whilst a set was being serviced by the blacksmiths they could continue working – such is the value of experiential archaeology.

As we saw earlier, in 1283, the king had sent Master Richard the Engineer to Newcastle-under-Lyme to procure blacksmiths and materials for Conwy.[17] The supply of nails to Conwy would suggest that blacksmiths or nailors back in Staffordshire had taken care of the industrial-scale requirement for 125,000 nails. Newcastle-under-Lyme had a history of ironworking and ore extraction going back to Roman times. Chartered in 1251, in the thirteenth century, its population of around 800 people represented a centre for regional ironworking. The 'New' castle by the Lyme Brook had belonged to Simon de Montfort, but had been granted to Edward's brother, Edmund, in 1267. The supply from Staffordshire, as opposed to local sourcing, is indicative of Edward's ability to mobilize all the resources of his realm in building his castles. At Guédelon some 670 eight-inch nails were required for their roadway alone, so it's not difficult to see how the much larger Conwy could have consumed 125,000 nails in just one year. Later in the construction the iron and steel supplied would have been required for the many hinges and grilles embedded into the stonework, using up that other very costly supply listed: lead. Molten lead was used not only to make the finished castle as watertight as possible (very important in Wales), but in the form of molten lead as anchor within the masonry to attach metal fixtures. The attachment of hinges and grilles was not an easy labour, requiring the lead to be heated into its molten state in the blacksmith's hearth before being transported to the point in the castle required for fixing the metalwork – no doubt there was much cursing when things went wrong.

Returning to Taylor's summary of commodities consumed in the 1286 building season for Conwy, we come to the unspecified quantity of ropes that was supplied from Chester. As with the nails, unlike Guédelon where they are made on site, the supply of rope from Chester implies the industrial-scale production in England before shipment to each castle site in Wales. The advantages of economy of scale production at one point obviously outweighed the cost of carriage to site. Ropemaking was an activity particularly concentrated by rivers and at ports, in view of the need for ropes in shipping and by fishermen – Chester was an important medieval port on a major river, the Dee. Rope production from tree bark or hemp fibre required a long (often open-air) rope walk, a long space at which the fibres could be twisted together to make rope.

Timber for the construction site at Conwy was required in vast quantities, as we can see from the 1286 records. Oak was the preferred choice of wood for building the many roof timbers and doors required in the castle; other wood such as ash might be used for the many tool handles needed. Not only straight sections of wood were in demand: the beauty of oak is that it also supplied the curved sections for roofing, lending inbuilt strength to the finished structure by not having been cut against the grain. The poles and clayes for scaffolding and putlogs would have been from inferior wood. Not mentioned in the supply for 1286 would have been hazel, sweet chestnut and willow that might be woven into baskets for transporting mortar – their absence from the list might imply they'd already been supplied or were sourced locally. Guédelon experience has shown the value of cleft wood rather than sawn wood, cleft being split timber, as it's said to not cut across the grain and so be more resistant to water and less likely to warp.[18] Initial construction required oak and ash to be brought along the coast by sea from Cheshire and Lancashire, before felling of trees began in the Conwy Valley. The Calendar of Welsh Rolls cites military tree felling as having taken place at Conwy, Caernarfon and at Harlech but does not record the scale; however, both oak and ash are known to have been the principal tree species available in north Wales and in plentiful supply. Working beneath Maître Jacques at Conwy was Master Richard the Engineer, a 'carpenter by training and not primarily a mason',[19] whose expertise was invaluable when it came to the timberwork at Conwy. Amongst the names of the carpenters at work in 1286 at Conwy we find some very francophone family names, that most likely indicate a Savoyard origin. We find Michel de la Verdenoye, Bertoto Cokel and a Brodulpho[20] amongst those working upon the hall of Othon de Grandson, including new passagework underway.[21]

The key material for construction not listed in Taylor's summary of materials used for 1286 is stone. Guédelon, much smaller in scope than Conwy, is estimated to have required 30,000 tonnes of stone to completion.[22] Graham Lott reported work carried out for Cadw contained in British Geological Survey Reports, of the stone used to build Conwy. The rock upon which the castle sits is made up of deeply imbedded sandstone and limestone – precisely the two rocks preferable for castle construction. This means the stone was immediately on hand for masons, did not need to be brought to site and was available in readily formed blocks.[23] Such blocks required minimal work on the part of the quarry masons to prepare into the *pif*, *paf* and *pouf* required by the builder masons – in short Conwy was a site for a castle almost heaven sent. The eight towers incorporated into the castle design featured the largest and strongest stones of the *pif* category, the curtain walls smaller *pif* stones and finally the infill rubble between the walls, the *paf*. Masons gauged the sandstone by strength (*pif, paf, pouf*) by colour, that is by its iron content, the darker the stone the higher the iron content the stronger the stone. In constructing the walls, the masons would have inserted *boutice* or header stones at intervals, laid at right angles to the regular stones, protruding into the infill to strengthen the wall against projectiles that might be hurled by a trebuchet. Further strength could be added by laying the facing or ashlar stones horizontally, but laying the infill vertically, thus creating a cross-weave. The mortar is where the limestone comes in, as lime-mortar is the key ingredient that adheres the stones together. It was made by heating limestone to 900°C and then mixing it with water to create slaked lime. The slaked lime was then mixed with sand and water to make the mortar, most often by a secret recipe known only to the mortar makers and passed down, father to son. The mortar was laid in a rough, uneven fashion to allow it to adhere better to the stones set within it, to be better absorbed into the stone itself, again for added strength. Materials were hoisted using a treadmill winch, a two-man treadmill being able to lift up to half a tonne upward to the required works. Two men, rather like hamsters in a wheel, would walk in one direction to raise the stone before stopping and carefully, and under direction, walking the other way to lower into position – a skilled procedure.

So how did the masons measure what they were doing, given that no technical drawings were utilized as we might today. The answer lies in the yardstick,[24] the *pige* or rod, a measuring stick in the possession of the master mason responsible for a construction site. The *pige*, which still gives rise to a French idiom today, was

Fig 1.0 The statue of Beatrice de Savoie (c. 1198–c. 1267) in Les Échelles, Savoie. The daughter of Count Thomas I de Savoie and Marguerite de Genève, her marriage to Ramon Berenguer IV, Count of Provence, was to have a fundamental impact on the history of England and Wales, and to begin our story. Matthew Paris likened her to Niobe before writing, 'among the female sex throughout the world, no other mother could boast of such illustrious fruit of the womb as could she in her daughters.'

Fig 1.1 The sole surviving tower of the Château de Saint-Prex in the Canton de Vaud, Switzerland. The fortified *burgh* and castle were ordered by the Chapter of the Cathédrale de Lausanne and granted to their *Magister* Jean Cotereel. His potential attribution as the father of Master James of Saint Georges would make this the Savoyard master mason's childhood home.

Fig 1.2 Welsh castle builders, Savoyard style. Town walls, upper: at Saillon in the Valais Canton of Switzerland; below: at Conwy in north Wales. It was this likeness that first awakened the curiosity of the late Arnold Taylor when travelling through Switzerland by train en route to England from Italy.

Fig 1.3 The foot of the sole surviving tower of the Château de Saint-Georges d'Espéranche in the Viennois region of France. Much of the castle survived until as recently as 1794 but perished in the subsequent years, along with its building records, in the French Revolution. It was here that Count Philippe I de Savoie introduced his great-nephew, Edward I of England, to his master mason, Mâitre Jacques in June 1273. The castle shares much in common with Caernarfon, its polygonal towers built largely for display as a palace-castle.

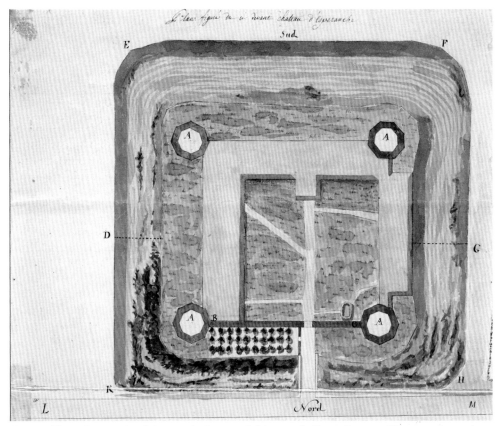

Fig 1.4 The colour-wash of the mostly destroyed Château de Saint-Georges d'Espéranche made in 1794 by Monsieur Chabord and held in the Archives d'Isère at Grenoble. The octagonal towers do not align with the sole remaining tower but the general arrangement of the castle is clearly shown.

Fig 1.5 Welsh castle builders, Savoyard style. Latrine shafts, from left: Château de Yverdon-les-Bains in the Canton de Vaud, Switzerland, Château de Saint-Georges d'Espéranche in the Viennois, France, and Harlech Castle in north Wales.

Fig 1.6 Windows and door openings, with their shallow segmented head, lacking a keystone, were also something of a Savoyard speciality. Top left: within the cellar of the Château de Saint-Prex; top right: Saint-Georges d'Espéranche; bottom right: Harlech Castle; and bottom left: Château de Chillon.

Fig 1.7 Château de Lucens in the Canton de Vaud in Switzerland. The castle belonged to the Bishop of Lausanne. When Guillaume de Champvent came to the see, he built the round tower seen here. Dendrochronology has shown that the roof was a later addition; within its eaves we find a masonry cylindrical projection much akin to the watch turrets that would be built at Conwy and Harlech in north Wales.

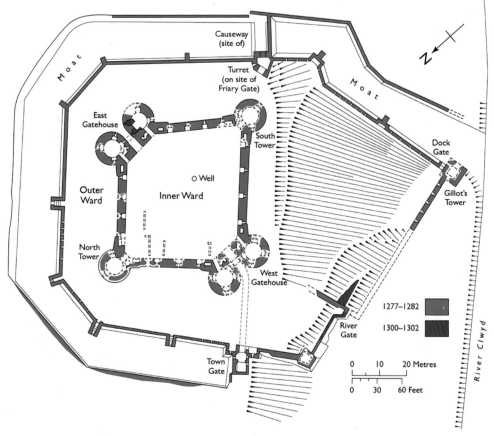

Fig 1.8 Rhuddlan Castle plan. (© *Crown copyright. Cadw, Welsh Government*)

Fig 1.9 Flint Castle. The great circular *donjon* foremost to the right.

Fig 2.0 Flint Castle plan. (© *Crown copyright.*
Cadw, Welsh Government)

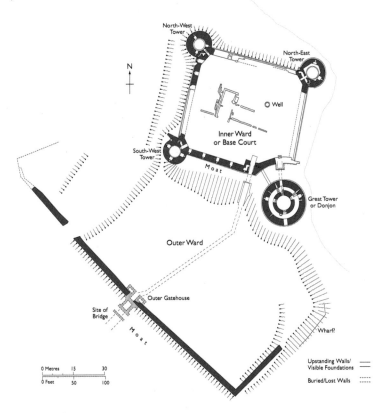

North-West Tower

North-East Tower

N

Well

Inner Ward or Base Court

South-West Tower

Moat

Great Tower or Donjon

Outer Ward

Outer Gatehouse

Site of Bridge

Moat

Wharf?

Upstanding Walls/ Visible Foundations
Buried/Lost Walls

0 Metres 15 30
0 Feet 50 100

Fig 2.1 Tour de Saxon, in the Canton de Valais, Switzerland, built by Giles and Tassin de Saint Georges for Count Philippe I de Savoie, along with Adam Boynard. The tower is noted for the use of helicoidal putlog holes found at Harlech, Conwy and Beaumaris castles in north Wales.

Fig 2.2 Welsh castles, Savoyard style. Three pinnacled merlons: upper at Conwy Castle in north Wales, lower at the Castello di San Giorio di Susa in Italy. Primary source evidence published in Italy has for the first time established a direct link between Maître Jacques de Saint Georges and the Castello di San Giorio di Susa.

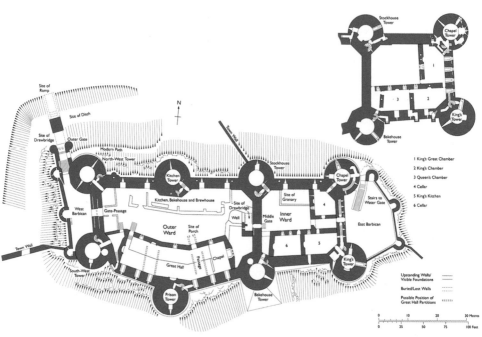

Fig 2.3 Conwy Castle plan. (© *Crown copyright. Cadw, Welsh Government*)

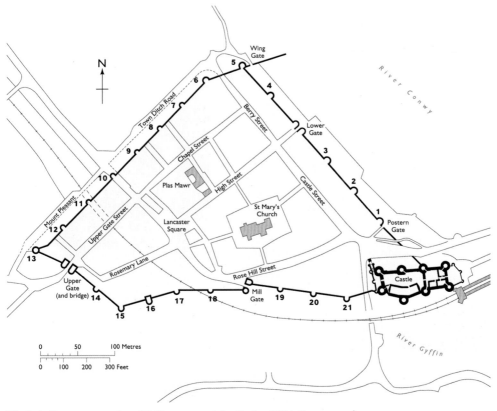

Fig 2.4 Conwy town plan. (© *Crown copyright. Cadw, Welsh Government*)

Fig 2.5 The Mill Gate in the town walls of Conwy in north Wales. The gate is documented as the work of masons headed by Savoyard Jean Francis or '*Franciscus Cementarius*' who had previously worked for Pierre de Savoie at Saillon and Chillon in what is now Switzerland.

Right: **Fig 2.6** Welsh castle builders, Savoyard style. Three Lancet windows with oculi tracery. The now partially obscured original circa 1275 window of the western face of the Cathédrale de Lausanne in the Canton de Vaud, Switzerland. Taken from a recreation of the original cathedral by the Lausanne History Museum.

Below: **Fig 2.6a** The development of what Christopher Wilson described as a 'Canterbury motif', the oculi. Top left: the North rose window of Canterbury Cathedral, from circa 1170; top right: the South rose window of the Cathédrale de Lausanne attributed by Marcel Grandjean to the father of Jean Cotereel, from circa 1205; bottom left: the three lancet with oculi window of the western face of the Cathédrale de Lausanne attributed by Marcel Grandjean as from circa 1275; bottom right: the recreation by Sidney Toy of the east window from the Great Hall at Conwy Castle in north Wales from 1283–6.

Fig 2.7 Harlech Castle. From left: the North-west Tower (*Le Chapel Tour*), the South-west Tower (*Le Wedercok Tour*), the Great Gatehouse and South-east Tower.

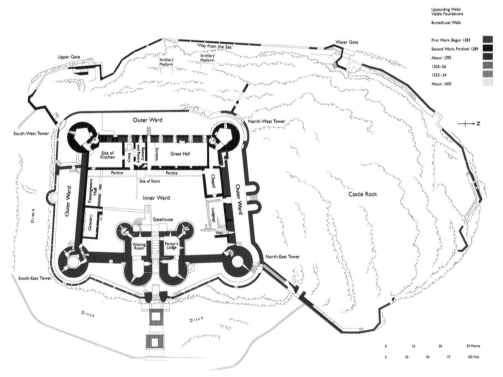

Fig 2.8 Harlech Castle plan. (© *Crown copyright. Cadw, Welsh Government*)

Fig 2.9 Welsh castles, Savoyard style. Top left: Harlech Castle window from the inner face of the Main Gatehouse; top right: Château de Chillon window from the inner courtyard; bottom left: Harlech Castle, corbelled latrine above the southern rock-cut ditch; bottom right: Château Le Bâtiaz, corbelled latrine from the northern curtain.

Fig 3.0 Caernarfon Castle. The southern curtain taken from across the River Seiont. From left: Eagle Tower, the Queen's Tower, the Chamberlain Tower and Queen's Gate.

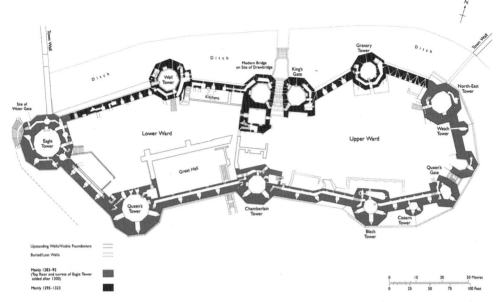

Fig 3.1 Caernarfon Castle plan. (© *Crown copyright. Cadw, Welsh Government*)

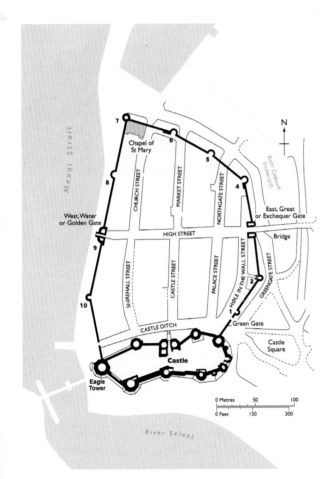

Fig 3.2 Caernarfon town plan.
(© *Crown copyright. Cadw, Welsh Government*)

Fig 3.3 Welsh castle builders, Savoyard style. A comparison of, upper: the Château de Champvent, a typical *Carré Savoyard* rebuilt by Pierre de Champvent, former Steward to Henry III and Chamberlain to Edward I; lower: Harlech Castle in north Wales, an adapted form of the *Carré Savoyard*.

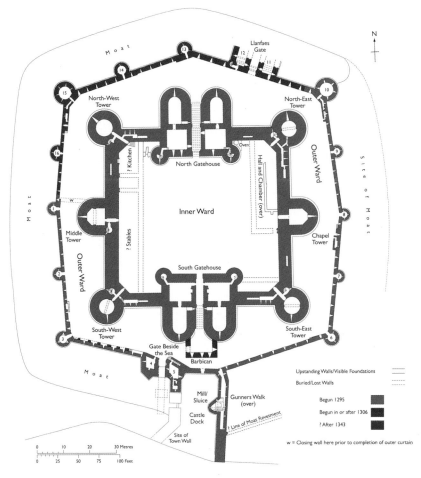

Labels in the plan (Fig 3.4):

Moat

Llanfaes Gate

13

12 11

14

N

15 North-West Tower

? Kitchen

10

North-East Tower

9

Oven

North Gatehouse

Hall and Chamber (over)

Outer Ward

16

Site of Moat

Inner Ward

Middle Tower

w

? Stables

Chapel Tower

9

9

Outer Ward

South Gatehouse

7

South-West Tower

South-East Tower

6

Gate Beside the Sea

3

Barbican

Moat

Mill/ Sluice

Gunners Walk (over)

4

5

Castle Dock

? Line of Moat Revetment

Site of Town Wall

Upstanding Walls/Visible Foundations

Buried/Lost Walls

Begun 1295

Begun in or after 1306

? After 1343

w = Closing wall here prior to completion of outer curtain

0 10 20 30 Metres
0 25 50 75 100 Feet

Fig 3.4 Beaumaris Castle plan. (© *Crown copyright. Cadw, Welsh Government*)

Fig 3.5 Beaumaris Castle. The Gate Beside the Sea.

Fig 3.6 The Welsh career of the Savoyards can mostly be found in the UK National Archive in Kew. Here highlighted are the names of Master James of St Georges and Sir Othon de Grandson. The text reads, '*Et Magistro Jacobo de Sancto Gregorio cementario facienti cementariam aule et camerarum Regis et Regine in castro de Conewey ad tascham. CCC.xx.li. sicut continetur ibidem.*' Which we can translate as, 'And to Master James of St George the mason, who was making a masonry of the hall and chambers of the King and Queen in the castle of Conwy paid by task. £320. as it is contained in the same place.'

Fig 3.7 Sir Othon de Grandson, Justiciar of North Wales, lifelong friend and envoy of King Edward I of England. Detail from an altar cloth that is thought to have been made in Cyprus for the Cathédrale de Lausanne, Switzerland, but now rests in the care of the Berne Historical Museum.

used in an age before standardized of weights and measures to ensure that at least on site a standard measure was used. So, if a yard was the measure along one's arm to the tip of your hand, the question arose, whose arm? The standard measure was said to be the king's arm,[25] but Edward could hardly be called upon at each site, so the master mason's arm was invariably used. And so, with the *pied* or foot also: if a mason was required to build ten feet of wall, then the *pied* would ensure that his ten feet equalled the mason's ten feet. Maître Jacques may never have encountered yards before, the French moving up from the foot or *pied* to the cubit or *coudée*, but the *coudée* was relatively easy to transform into yards as it measured the elbow to the outstretched fingertips, thus two *coudée*s pretty much made up a yard. When it came to smaller measurements, the *pouce* that Jacques would have known, literally the French word for thumb, equalled the English inch. Even in the thirteenth century workers from overseas arriving in England had to cope with new measurements.

To summarize, the French and English systems known to Maître Jacques would have been:[26]

Le pouce	The inch	The width of the thumb	2.5cm	1 inch
La paume	The hand	The width of the hand	7.5cm	3 inches
La palme		The space between 1st & 4th finger	12.5cm	5 inches
L'empan	The span	The space between thumb & 4th finger	20cm	8 inches
Le pied	The foot	The length from heel to farthest toe	30cm	1 foot
La coudée	The cubit	The length from elbow to farthest finger	45cm	1 cubit
	The yard	The length from torso to farthest finger	91.5cm	1 yard
La toise		The length across two outstretched arms	180cm	6 feet

Limestone was often preferred for decorative work; as it's softer and easier to work, it is the *pouf.* At Conwy imported coloured sandstones were used for arrow loops, windows, door jambs, and chimneypieces.[27] Local sandstones were used initially, from across the River Conwy, over on the Creuddyn Peninsula, but the finer work required later saw the masons resort to Helsby sandstone found in the Wirral and Cheshire areas – a boats haul along the coast.

The helicoidal Savoyard putlog holes evident in the towers illustrate the skills of the imported artisan stonemasons in easing their work. It's easier to move materials up and around a tower under construction by an inclined plain than it is to constantly have to use ladders on traditional horizontal scaffolding – such were the specialist skills that Edward had imported to England from Savoy. The scaffolding would have been constructed in such a way as to leave a small gap between the wood and emerging towers, and this gap would have allowed for the use of a plumb line to ensure the wall was rising vertically. Within the towers the staircases curling around, drew upon the jewel in the masons' craft, that of geometry. Construction of round towers was an art: laying out the circle on the ground, before building upward, possibly with the aid of a revolving mast, with plumb lines dangling from an attached horizontal pole.[28] In the tracing lodge the master mason produced a wooden template for the stone segments that would make up the staircase. Tracing out the pattern on to wood before the multiple segments were then produced by the banker masons to be in turn laid by the builder masons. Masons used a variety of tools in their work, with double-headed stone axes, pointed punches, flat chisels and set squares being amongst the most common.

So, if we had walked into the mason's lodge some time in 1285 or 1286, who was there? We know the names of the masons from the accounts left to us and kept in the UK National Archive, and some of the work they were paid to carry out:[29]

Philip de Darley	Alan de Bucknall
William de Thornton	Thomas de la Roche
John Flauner	Jean Francis
John de Bedford	Robert Fleming
William de la Launde	Guillaume Seysel
Roger de Cockersand	Pierre de Bononia (Boulogne)
Giles de Chalons	John of Sherwood
Robert de Frankby	John Bargas
Walter de Reading	William de Macclesfield
Simon de Gedling	Robert de Wirral
Richard de Kingston	Thomas Picard

Several of the masons illustrate the Anglo-Savoyard nature of the workforce: Jean Francis and working with him Roger de Cockersand, Guillaume Seysel, Pierre de Bononia, Giles de Chalons, John de Sherwood and Robert de Frankby. Jean Francis was believed by Taylor to be the *'Johannes Franciscus'* who worked at Chillon in 1266.[30] Also the *'Franciscus cementarius'*, or Francis the mason, who had built *'turris'* or turrets for Pierre de Savoie at Conthey in 1258, and Saillon, before building two chambers at Chillon in 1260–1.[31] Taylor's belief that the two were one and the same rests upon the remarkable likeness of the work in the Valais and at Conwy. At Saillon Jean Francis was working under Master of Works Sir Jean de Mézos; at Conwy he would be working under the direction of Maître Jacques. [32] Once more we have a reminder of the Anglo-Savoyard-Gascon triangle of masons involved in the works in Wales. Giles or Gillot de Chalons's origin may well have been the Chalon-sur-Saône in the Franche-Comté, or less likely Chalons in Champagne, but when we note that the Chalon in the Viennois was until recently Châlons then it's more than likely he was someone who'd worked alongside Maître Jacques at Saint-Georges-d'Espéranche.[33] Before joining the Francis work team at Conwy he would most likely have worked at Rhuddlan, where an account for 1304 relates a *'turris vocata Gillot'*.[34] Gillot de Chalons would live out his days in the town whose walls he'd laboured hard to build. He acquired three and a quarter burgages and spent his days by the Conwy, never returning to the Viennois. William Seysel is another Savoyard, from Seyssel, which now sits astride both the Haute-Savoie and Ain departments of France. He'd been previously employed at the works in Flint, so had been in Wales for as long as Maître Jacques, making it very likely he'd travelled from Savoy with him, and had worked for him previously.[35] Picard is another Savoyard family name, supplying many to the castle-building trade: there'd been a Vincent Picard at Yverdon,[36] a Jacques Picard at Saxon in the Valais,[37] a Jean Pycard at the building of Flint Castle,[38] now we find a *Thome* (Thomas) Picard being amongst those paid for adding four perche (twenty-two yards)[39] of stone to the wall by the Upper Gate at Conwy.[40] The name was and remains common within the Suisse Romande, including the aeronautical Piccard family, who lent their name to the *Star Trek* character Jean-Luc Picard. That Maître Jacques would bring with him men he trusted and had worked alongside in Savoy for over twenty years is unsurprising.[41]

Amongst the English at Conwy, Jean Francis was given charge of several masons listed earlier, one of which, Robert de Frankby,[42] is named perhaps amongst the dead of a later Madog-inspired Welsh rising of 1294, whilst living at Flint.[43] Another was Roger de Cockersand, Cockersand Abbey being a Premonstratensian house that had been founded in the previous century. The abbey (of which only the chapter house survives) was a short distance from Lancaster in the county of Lancashire, just across the water from Conwy to the north-east. It stood on a bleak, windswept neck of land which projects into the sea 'on the sands of Cocker', on the Lancashire coast to the south of what is now called Morecambe Bay, spreading over an acre of land. That Roger, a mason, hailed from a tiny locale dominated by a grand medieval abbey is also unsurprising – whether that was his origin or where he'd recently worked is lost to us, but it's almost certain he had honed his mason skills with the White Canons of Cockersand. Jean Francis, Roger de Cockersand and their fellow masons, from February 1286 to September 1287 (two building seasons) were employed in building the town walls, curtains and open-backed towers to a common pattern. The cost is recorded as £389.13s.8d for the main body of work.

These materials for the castle works at Conwy include those for the town walls, as they were built concurrently and formed an integral part of the overall defences – as they had for Jacques' likely father Jean's defences at Saint-Prex. As with the Savoyard fortified burgh, the overall scheme of Conwy is almost triangular; at Saint-Prex it was in fact exactly triangular. The walls at Conwy are of grey sandstone and limestone, sourced locally again at Conwy.

In building the castles and establishing a garrison for defence, it was natural that a town might grow around them. This had been the case at Flint and Rhuddlan and would be the case at Conwy and Caernarfon and to a much lesser extent at the more remote Harlech. English settlers, colonists, were encouraged to come to the new towns being established in Gwynedd to help service the new castles. But, notwithstanding the relocation of the monks of Aberconwy and the absence of the former land-owning members' ruling house, Llywelyn and Dafydd, there is no evidence of a wholescale eviction of Welshmen from their lands. To quote economic historian of Gwynedd, James Given, 'the demographic impact of borough creation seems to have been small.' Given goes on to calculate that the new towns under construction would take at most 5,000 acres.[44] Free Welshmen were seldom removed from their land and later, when new towns were created such as Pwllheli, care was taken to use the former demesne lands of Llywelyn and Dafydd. In Conwy the few Welshmen dispossessed for the building of the castle were relocated to the nearby commote of Creuddyn and Anglesey.[45]

For Nantconwy we know the names of former rebels who lost land: Dokyn Crach lost twenty acres; others losing unspecified land were: Madog ap Iorwerth, Einion ap Hywel, Ednyfed ap Einion and Owain ap Madog.[46] Further east in Flintshire, it has been suggested that newcomers from nearby England took more land, exchanging with the native Welsh by what they saw as fair exchange, but which left the Welsh with poorer upland plots, nursing resentment.[47] But this demographic change is probably driven more by geographic proximity to Chester than deliberate royal policy. Given claims, with researched sources, that 'Edward I deliberately pursued a policy of clemency towards those that had resisted him.'[48] This is in marked contrast to his latter-day image as an 'empire building tyrant', but one which chimes closely with the clemency shown toward Jean de Vesci following his rebellion after the late baronial war. However, if our visitor to Conwy had happened to venture out from the growing town into the surrounding villages, he may well have found the beginnings of dissent at the newly imposed burden of taxation the newcomers brought with them. Whereas Llywelyn had only begun to tax the population, the English state was more advanced in its financial acumen, something the Welsh population would increasingly resent as the years passed.

Looking northward, the almost triangular-shaped town of Conwy sits with its castle at the bottom right (Figure 2.4), the River Conwy on the right hand and the River Gyffin on its bottom side. This water protection on two of the three sides echoes the two flanks at Saint-Prex being protected by the Léman. If we begin walking from the castle, with the river to our right, we see three towers, before we meet the Lower Gate facing the Conwy. Moving along the wall, we reach a fourth and a fifth tower, where we take a sharp left turn to continue on the left-hand side of our almost triangle. The wall continues practically straight, protected by another seven towers. At the thirteenth, it turns sharply once more to encounter the second main gate, the Upper Gate. There, we might pause to consider the remarkable likeness of the gate below with the town gate still to be found at Saint-Prex. From the Upper Gate, we continue downhill past another five towers to the Mill Gate, having encountered three main gates in total, before ending our walk at the castle after the twenty-first and last tower. The bottom of the triangle isn't perfect: it contains a change of alignment at the fifteenth tower.

The Mill Gate (Figure 2.5) was constructed by Jean Francis and his team, for £118.7s. It is quite remarkable that the gate through which so many tourists enter Conwy is almost certainly the work of the man who had built the walls and tower of Saillon, over twenty years before, in the distant Upper Rhône Valley of what is now Switzerland. This is why the walls of Saillon reminded Taylor so much of Conwy when viewed from his train returning from Italy. The five 'common form' towers, two to the west and three to the east of the Mill Gate, are also the work of Francis and his team, at a cost of £126.11s, and the twelve latrines that were added to the town wall were constructed for just £15. The Mill Gate is also notable in that it did a whole lot more than merely provide access to the town: its gatehouse included the King's Wardrobe.[49]

The King's Wardrobe or *warderobe* in Norman French had originally just been the place that kept the king's clothes, *warderobe* being the Norman French variation of *garderobe*. By the thirteenth century and Edward's reign, the wardrobe had grown into a veritable civil service, being responsible for keeping the royal army, and in particular the Conwy garrison, supplied with all its needs. This building might be said to be the Royal Corps of Logistics of its time, and indeed the beating heart of the new English presence in Conwy. The Mill Gate, in its entirety of stonework, was completed for £125 but we have further detail of the carpentry required to make the timber-framed chamber that occupied the first floor. Master Laurence of Canterbury completed this for £15.10s in 1285/6. Therefore, with stone, lead, carpentry and so on, the Mill Gate came to some £150.[50] The National Archive records the Keeper of the Wardrobe's miscellaneous expenses for the period 1283–4, a wonderful insight into the beginning of the work at Conwy.[51]

The road pattern within the town was principally of two roads emanating from the Upper Gate before splitting into three to avoid what is now St Mary's Church. These three roads, including High Street, then terminated in one crossroad running parallel to the river. In scope, this is essentially three roads from one point of the triangle (Upper Gate) fanning out toward one road meeting them all as they finish by the river. The same pattern can be observed at Saint-Prex where the triangular burgh, jutting out into the lake, has three roads beginning at the lakeside point and ending at one parallel road running alongside what was the moated side. I am not suggesting that Conwy is a replica of Saint-Prex, as the topography of the land is quite different, but I am suggesting that the overall concept is remarkably similar: what is essentially a triangle with castle at one point, water defences to two sides and lastly a basically three-road system topped by a single road. Was Maître Jacques replicating his likely childhood hometown? We may never know, because if he did, he left no record. It's tempting to see patterns, and to conjecture, but the similarity is not imagined: aerial photography quickly reveals the suggestion.

If Maître Jacques was replicating in some way at Conwy his hometown of Saint-Prex then the fenestration within the castle in Wales may hold another piece of evidence linking him with the Cathedral of Lausanne and so with Jean Cotereel. The three-lancet window of the hall at Conwy, topped by a semi-circular arch, has been likened to the now mostly hidden western window at Lausanne Cathedral, itself of three lancets beneath a more angular Gothic arch (Figure 2.6).[52] Taylor pointed to the similarity, Hislop also, and to stylistic parallels in the great rose

143

window at Lausanne.[53] The building date attributed to the Lausanne window of 'around 1275' raises the intriguing possibility that this may be the work of Maître Jacques developing the style of his grandfather's rose window. Perhaps we see in the eastern great hall window of Conwy a familial development of Lausanne, itself a development of Canterbury (Figure 2.6a). That we might discern a link between Canterbury and Conwy by way of Lausanne might be described as remarkable. Whilst such architectural evidence can be misleading, as can similitude in town plans, taken together the evidence that the father of Maître Jacques was Jean Cotereel grows ever more suggestive. That the grandson was replicating the work of his grandfather. That the boy born by the *Via Jacobus* was indeed *Magistro Jacobo*.

Chapter Twelve

The day's horse ride from Conwy to Harlech might have seemed onerous for many, but for Maître Jacques, who'd trekked between Châtel Argent in the Val d'Aosta and the Viennois, up and over the 7,000 and some feet of the Petit Saint-Bernard Pass, the passage wouldn't not have been unduly taxing. The Savoyard was a man of the mountains and Snowdonia would have been a little of home.

The ride would have taken him due south of Conwy into the heart of Snowdonia, by the ever-narrowing River Conwy. Just ten miles (sixteen kilometres) upstream, on the right-hand bank, he would have come to the construction of the new Cistercian abbey at Maenan near Llanrwst, the abbey of Saint Mary and All Saints being built there for the monks of Aberconwy who were being displaced by the construction underway at Conwy. Jacques had passed this way back in September 1283 when he had been sent to receive the estate for construction from the bailiff of the Earl of Lincoln, Henri de Lacy.[1] Payment of £40 was made to the abbot for the site of his abbey at Aberconwy, the instruction coming just two days after Jacques was at Maenan, from the Keeper of the Wardrobe to William de Perton.[2] The abbey was dissolved, along with most of the other monasteries in Britain, during the reign of Henry VIII and destroyed. However, walls, some six feet thick, thought to belong to the cloister which Jacques may well have walked, if in need of a meeting with the abbot, were uncovered in 2011 during work for the hotel that now occupies the site.

A further twelve miles (nineteen kilometres) upstream, crossing the Conwy at Betus (Betws-y-Coed), and then leaving the Conwy to follow its tributary, the Lledr, to climb into the hills, Jacques would have come to the castle at Dolwyddelan and its welcoming English garrison. The reputed birthplace of Llywelyn Fawr had been taken by Edward back in January 1283 and Jacques had been involved in the repairs necessary after its capture. Dolwyddelan might well have required a call by the Master of Works for some time following 1283, since work to strengthen the defences there continued until at least 1286. Certainly, military protection for those travelling from Conwy down to Harlech would have been the responsibility of the garrison at Dolwyddelan as Jacques passed the high country in the shadow of Mount Snowdon. The road today takes the Crimea Pass, but this turnpike dates from the 1850s, so it is more likely that Jacques would have followed an earlier road, the Roman *Sarn Helen* that headed south from Dolwyddelan along a hidden valley before steeply climbing. The road which gets progressively wilder as it climbs is named after Saint Elen of Caernarfon, a Celtic saint, whose story is told in The Dream of Macsen Wledig, part of the *Mabinogion*. She is said to have ordered the construction of roads in Wales during the late fourth century. The road then fell toward the valley of the River Dwyryd, where Jacques would have left the old Roman road to follow the river to the sea. As he turned from the road, he would have seen the remains of Tomen-y-Mur, a Roman fortress and later Norman motte, evidence of earlier attempts to bring Gwynedd under occupation. At Maentwrog he would be able to smell the sea, as here the Dwyryd becomes tidal. Keeping south of the river, he would pass what is now the sand dune area of the Morfa Harlech, much less extensive in his day than today, since the sea has retreated some way. Ahead now he would begin to see the castle works atop the dome like rock of mythology which had probably been sited by Othon de Grandson (Figure 2.7).

Othon de Grandson had been the first of the king's retinue to set eyes upon the future castle site at Harlech, back in April 1283, when he had arrived at the head of the army moving forward from Castell-y-Bere. As discussed earlier, to whom the credit belongs for the siting of the castle on the large dome of rock that sat beside the Irish Sea is lost to history. Edward and Leonor may have been aware of the *Mabinogion* tales relating to the site, Grandson may have confirmed its suitability for a castle or had the original idea himself, given that the rock is the perfect site to locate a castle. Either way the site was soon chosen by Edward. Following his visit there in August 1283, he had entrusted the future castle site to five squires: Jean Cosyn, Ebal de Mont, John of Gayton, Jean de Scaccario and Peter of Cornhill.[3]

The first two named are of Savoyard origin. Firstly there was Jean Cosyn, or Jean Cosyn de Grandson, who would go on to be a lawyer in the service of his relatives Gérard de Vuippens and Othon de Grandson; he was mentioned at Mancetter in 1304.[4] The second named was none other than Ebal IV de Mont, the son of Windsor Castle constable Ebal II de Mont, and nephew of Ebal III de Mont, the owner of the Mézos-built castle at Rolle by the Léman. We know of squires from Geoffrey Chaucer's *Canterbury Tales*. They would usually be the son of a knight, in their early twenties, with experience of war; they could ride well and were possessed of the knightly virtues, in essence a knight in waiting.[5] The squires had custody of the site until the appointment of Hugh de Wlonkeslowe as first constable in October 1284.[6] Wlonkeslowe's tenure would be a short one, being replaced by the Savoyard kin of Othon de Grandson, Jean de Bonvillars, within a year on 5 October 1285.[7] Works began in 1283 and through 1284 as evidenced by monies in 1283 of £160 and of wages paid to Hugh of Leominster as Clerk of Works, both at Caernarfon and Harlech.[8] What Ebal thought of the dome of rock at Harlech, having been brought up in the gentile surroundings of Windsor Castle but being the grandson of the Ebal de Mont, whose perch sat amongst the trees overlooking the Léman and the distant Alps, is sadly lost to us.

Morris thought Harlech an 'old Welsh fortress',[9] an idea more recently espoused by Paul Martin Remfry.[10] Those supporting the idea of a Welsh 'fortress' at Harlech have offered several suggestions. One concerns the aforesaid squires:

the proposition is ventured that the squires were left in garrison of an existing fortification. Indeed, the archival record does say '*municione*' or fortification as their billet, but we should remember from Flint and elsewhere that it was normal practice to first erect a wooden palisade or fortification around an intended worksite for protection and it is therefore more likely that this is the '*municione*' mentioned by the scribe. It's perhaps more likely that Edward left squires in charge of a fortified worksite than a Welsh castle for which knights, not squires, might have been in order.

Proponents also point to the visit mentioned earlier of Edward to Harlech in August 1283. Surely, they say, Edward, the King of England, wouldn't have been safe visiting an unfortified worksite. However, Conwy and Caernarfon were both but worksites, and yet received royal visits. But going further in critique of the Welsh castle theory, Jeremy Ashbee writing the latest edition (2017) of the Cadw guidebook confirms that absolutely no archaeological evidence has been found to validate the claim.[11] Ashbee ably presented the problems associated with pre-existing occupation at Harlech as:

> To begin with no known document makes any mention of any Welsh castle or *llys* at Harlech. In fact, records show that the princes governed the commote (administrative district) of Ardudwy from a *llys*[12] located just a few miles away – at Ystumgwern near Dyffryn Ardudwy. Moreover, considering the earliest surviving fabric within the existing building, it is clear that it represents something very different from those castles built by the princes. The plan was larger and more regular than most, incorporating architectural features without native Welsh parallels, such as projecting round corner towers. In sum it is most likely that the castle on this [Harlech] site was established by the English in 1283.[13]

Evidence of some kind of administrative occupation at Harlech may be further diminished by Llywelyn's biographer, Beverley Smith. He confirms of the commote in which Harlech stands, that:

> Ardudwy was centred on Ystumgwern, and letters bearing either of these names can be assumed to have been written at the court [*llys*], located in close proximity to the *maerdref*, whose hall[14] was subsequently removed and reconstructed within the walls of the castle at Harlech.[15]

We should add that some Welsh sources[16] split Ardudwy into *Ardudwy Is Artro* and *Ardudwy Uwch Artro*, the importance of which is that Harlech is *Uwch Artro* and Ystumgwern is *Is Artro*[17] – but whether this distinction, within Ardudwy, applied in the thirteenth century is unclear, as is the reason for the *llys* of one commote being dismantled and taken to a castle in another. That the court located at Ystumgwern would be relocated to Harlech does imply, as Ashbee suggests, that no such court pre-existed at Harlech.[18]

Before we entirely dismiss Remfry's notion of a pre–Edwardian Harlech and accept fully Ashbee's critique thereof, we need to say that the native Welsh castles were not always built as administrative centres or at the commotal *llys*[19] – often they were built simply as a show of strength. Remfry recalls the journey made through Meirionnydd and Gwynedd in the late twelfth century by Gerald of Wales, where the writer describes two castles now lost to us.[20] But a clear problem with identifying either of Gerald's castles, specifically Deutrait or Deudraeth with the Harlech site is that Deutrait or Deudraeth is identified as being in the commote of Eifionydd and the Harlech site is in Ardudwy. Remfry counters by suggesting the borders were fluid, but nonetheless Gerald does seem clear as to its location. The other problem is that we think we know the precise location of Deutrait or Deudraeth, also known as Castell Aber Iâ. It is a now-demolished castle built at the south-western tip of a short rocky ridge in woodland known as Y Gwyllt to the west of Portmeirion village which was, as Gerald suggested, in twelfth-century Eifionydd. Castell Aber Iâ or Deudraeth was a motte built up over a natural rocky outcrop with a stone tower atop it, one of the earliest Welsh stone castles. The other castle described by Gerald at Carn Fadryn (or Carn Madryn) lay on the westernmost mountain of the Llyn within a prehistoric hill fort; only a little unmortared stonework remains.[21] But perhaps most tellingly we should also remember, at this point, the words of the garrisoning order made by Edward for the site of Harlech on 21 October at Caernarfon. For the sites at Harlech, Caernarfon and Conwy the words 'in garrison there' are used to describe the location, whereas at Castell y Bere 'there in garrison at the castle' is used in its place.[22] The specific mention of an existing castle at Castell y Bere may not be an oversight on the part of the scribe, he may well have been consciously describing the garrison of an existing castle rather than a castle worksite. Therefore, the evidence for a pre-existing castle at Harlech remains to be convincingly given.

The Harlech Dome is a geological dome in southern Snowdonia. It extends approximately from Blaenau Ffestiniog in the north to Tywyn in the south, and includes Harlech, the Rhinogydd, Barmouth and Cadair Idris – but the rock upon which the castle was being built is a natural place to fortify. The 200 feet (61 metre) perch for the castle itself is composed of hard sandstone and mudstone, thus not only providing a ready supply of building material but also making it next to impossible to undermine the castle.[23]

Workmen had cut through the rock to create a ditch around the castle works in the summer building season of 1285.[24] A payment of £186.14s.11½d was made to quarriers and hodmen to clear the stone, along with smiths for their tools, a further payment of £18.6s.6d being paid for the iron and steel required for these tools. Visitors to Harlech today, as then, would appreciate the sheer hard labour required in creating the castle ditch from the rocky outcrop upon which the castle sits. The digging of the rock-cut ditch at Harlech is more evidence that points away from a Welsh castle being there before 1283, certainly one built by Llywelyn Fawr. His castles of Dolywyddelan and Castell y Bere both featured the provision of 'rock-cut ditches' as additional defence.[25] That Harlech's was dug out in 1285 not before, invites the question, if there was a castle before 1283, why did it not have the more usual rock-cut ditch?

Our arrival in the summer of 1286 would have found a castle taking shape at Harlech, as an evolution of the latest in thirteenth-century castle design, and unlike anything tried thus far in north Wales. If Conwy was a multifaceted new town complete with castle, and Caernarfon would be a palace-castle in the mould of Saint-Georges-d'Espéranche then Harlech would be something new. Taking shape above Cardigan Bay and the Morfa Harlech was a castle entirely military in nature, a mailed Plantagenet fist deep into the heart of Gwynedd.

Firstly, this would be layered defence, a concentric system of walls beginning with an outer wall protecting an outer ward within which sat the main square body of the castle. At each of the four corners of the castle, much like a *Carré Savoyard*, sat a great circular tower – but unlike the Savoyard castles none of the towers would form the *donjon* (Figure 2.8). No, the design at Harlech would represent the latest evolution in castle design, to turn the weakest part of the castle into its strongest, the gateway. The hole pierced into the curtain wall to provide entrance to the castle would be protected not by a simple gateway as at Rhuddlan, the gatehouse would be enlarged to such an extent that it formed the *donjon*, the main living space of the castle, and the quarters for the new constable, Sir Jean de Bonvillars and his wife, the Lady Agnès, sister of Othon de Grandson. In concept the gatehouse at Harlech could be best described as almost a castle within a castle, as if a square Norman *donjon* had been relocated from the centre and deposited directly over the gateway. The gatehouse, the dominating feature of Harlech, is essentially square. On the outward side it presents two very large towers that don't quite meet, on the inward side two smaller towers (in terms of circumference not height) separated by the living space, denoted by three large evenly spaced windows. These windows themselves betray the builders of the castle, as they are entirely of the same dimensions and design as those found at Chillon by the Léman. Indeed, the two outer towers of this gatehouse *donjon* also betray the origins of their builders, they carry the evidence of helicoidal putlog holes, the sloping scaffolding used in their construction as they'd also been used for example in the tower at Saxon in the Valais.

The origin of this design is much debated, since it was new to north Wales, and had not been employed by Maître Jacques before. Earlier examples of the design are to be found at Caerffili in south Wales and at Tonbridge in Kent, and perhaps to some extent in St Thomas's Tower at the Tower of London. Coldstream sees in this evidence that Maître Jacques was tutored in castle design by Master Robert of Beverley who is documented as having been responsible for Edward's works at the Tower. She went on to write: 'it is well within the accepted limits of methodology to suggest that he could have been Robert of Beverley.'[26] This is speculation, based upon Robert being responsible for St Thomas's tower at the Tower of London, and she acknowledges she has no primary-source evidence for this assertion. Indeed, we have no record of Robert working in north Wales, nor do we have any evidence of his working at either Caerffili or Tonbridge, and what is more, his death in 1285 presents a problem. Goodall agrees with her suggestion that Robert of Beverley might be the designer of Tonbridge and possibly Caerffili. But when she suggests Robert as a possible 'tutor' for Jacques,[27] he then defends Taylor, confirming Taylor had gone 'to great lengths to prove how the details of the Welsh castles spoke of the continental training of Master James of St George, and in most points, he was absolutely right'.[28] Goodall then goes on to highlight the 'English architectural tradition' and suggests 'archive drawings in the King's Works' as an influence. But, I would contend, whilst this may be so, it is at least equally likely that this English heritage was passed by way of Jean Cotereel and Jean de Mézos, the former having built a cathedral in the English style and the latter having worked himself for King Henry III

Therefore, the idea of Robert of Beverley acting as 'tutor' for Maître Jacques at Harlech, or indeed as Coldstream implied more generally, seems unlikely: it both lacks primary-source evidence and ignores the primary-source evidence pointing in the direction of his 'continental training'.[29] But this training did not include a Harlech-style gatehouse, so if not Robert of Beverley, then who? Perhaps the most convincing theory put forward as to the way in which the ideas of the gatehouses at Tonbridge and Caerffili may have been transmitted to Harlech and Jacques is by way of Aberystwyth. As very plausibly argued by Hislop, Aberystwyth may well have been the intermediate model; we certainly know from the primary sources that Jacques had only recently (in 1282) been to the castle there. Hislop wrote: 'It may therefore be stated with a reasonable degree of confidence that the main gatehouse of Aberystwyth was based on the Inner East Gatehouse of Caerphilly.' He went on to perhaps seal the deal by writing, 'The affinities with Caerphilly suggest that ... Master Jacques borrowed the concept for replication at Harlech.'[30]

The parentage, then, of the gatehouse at Harlech is most likely to have been Tonbridge and Caerffili, but which came first? David and Barbara Martin wrote an excellent paper on the gatehouse at Tonbridge, in which they explored the age of the structure there, for which there are no written records of building. They discussed the wide variety of dates that have come in and out of vogue for Tonbridge, ranging from 1216 to 1300, before citing D. F. Renn from *Tonbridge and Some Other Gatehouses* (1981): 'It is historically difficult to see Tonbridge (gatehouse) [constructed] after 1271, and Caerffili (gatehouse) [constructed] before 1272.'[31] This would then firmly place Tonbridge as earlier than Caerffili, both of which were built for the Clare family, something surely of no coincidence. Historic England dates Tonbridge as having been completed by 1260; such an early dating would make it the work of Richard de Clare, who died in 1262, and Caerffili the work of his son Gilbert de Clare, Red Gilbert, whom we have met earlier. It is interesting to add at this point would be that Edward, on his return to England in 1274, had stayed at Tonbridge en route to London, and as we have seen with the pinnacled merlons of Susa, it would not be the first time that he had been impressed by a castle and made mental note to himself for future use. Renn writing in the Cadw guidebook for Caerffili avoids giving an exact date for the gatehouse there, other than the '1270s' – but he does say that the designs are 'almost identical'. Something a cursory examination of the two gatehouses confirms they appear to be the work of one (unnamed) designer.[32] Coldstream, citing Renn, agrees, saying, 'they are almost certainly the work of the same designer.'[33]

We can perhaps progress by describing the *donjon* gatehouse at Harlech with appropriate comparison to Caerffili (and thereby also Tonbridge). The gatehouse is formed of three storeys, as is Caerffili, the ground floor divided by the gateway passage, the first and second floors running across the whole breadth. Two D-shaped towers are presented to the exterior; at Harlech they are more prominent than the shallower towers at Caerffili. The twin towers on their outward projection have a greater separation at Caerffili, while at Harlech the distance between them is more than halved. Further, the twin D-shaped towers project from the outline of the square *donjon* at Caerffili, whereas at Harlech they run flush to the curtain wall to form a neater, more purposeful outline. It is perhaps problematic to compare the crenels and merlons since the gatehouse at Caerffili is in a reconstructed (1931–3) form. What we can see of them today, if they represent the originals, they are cruder than at Harlech. Turning to the inner side of the gatehouse, both castles present towers of a slenderer nature, given that they would primarily serve as access stairways to all floors rather than outright defensive positions. However, the inner towers at Harlech stand prouder of the main structure than at Caerffili – given their height, it might be argued they present a clearer firing position than at Caerffili.

The internal plans are less easy to compare given the reconstruction at Caerffili. However, we can say that in concept they almost certainly shared the idea of guardhouses sitting either side of the main gate passage, with accommodations on the higher floors for the Constable and his family. The first floor at Harlech comprised a great chamber, a lesser chamber, both facing inward, and within the giant D-shaped towers two bedchambers. At Harlech the narrow space between the two towers was filled by a chapel, complete with a narrow window. It has been suggested that this might have been a deterrence to assailants firing on the gatehouse, as in an age of religious certainty they might believe they were firing at God. The uppermost floor is believed, with little certainty, to have provided accommodation for visiting dignitaries.

It is in the decoration of the gatehouse that Harlech once more varies from Caerffili. The first floor at Caerffili is graced by three very small and narrow windows, the one above the inner passage elevated. Tonbridge differs slightly in that the three windows are straightly placed. The second floor at Caerffili and Tonbridge is illuminated by two much larger windows. Harlech features, on both floors, three large windows that are pretty much an exact match for those at Chillon in Savoy.[34]

St Thomas's Tower, at the Tower of London, built between 1275 and 1279 is certainly, by primary sources, the work of Robert of Beverley. It is similar in concept to Caerffili, Tonbridge and Harlech, but quite different in execution. The London gate is a riverside gatehouse; there are no D-shaped towers flanking the gateway, just slender, slight towers at each corner with no inner towers, except for one corner which carries the small square tower of an adjacent gateway. St Thomas's has but two floors, with five small narrow windows to the fore. Entrance was by way of a wide watergate from the river. The inner wall presents a wider watergate topped by a much later three-windowed face, and the tower has a single upper floor. Of the gatehouses being considered as having paternity of Harlech, it is the least similar by comparison.

The central entrance passage, common to all three gatehouses, can be compared in terms of the complexity of their defence. Tonbridge, almost certainly the first built, featured a large portcullis protecting a pair of doors, thereafter three murder holes, followed by a further sequence of murder holes, doors and portcullis.[35] Harlech, the last built, working from the outside, benefitted from doors, followed by a portcullis, arrow loops from the flanking guardrooms, thence a second portcullis, a further set of doors, a third portcullis, and finally a third set of doors to the inner courtyard.[36] Not dissimilar, but perhaps Harlech with its extra portcullis was an enhancement.

In summary we can see a clear links between Caerffili, Tonbridge and Harlech. However, whereas the Clare castles are very similar in execution, Harlech appears to be a clear evolution of the design, not a copy. Therefore, by which ever means Maître Jacques came by the design, be it relaid to him by Edward or Gilbert de Clare, or as Hislop suggests by way of Aberystwyth, Maître Jacques created a significantly advanced form of the design concept – not from any tutoring given by the deceased Robert of Beverley, but rather from an ability, learned at his father's knee, developed by Jean de Mézos, to create in stone, in this case to adapt and evolve a pre-existing, but relatively new building form. Paddy Griffith, writing of the great French fortress designer Vauban said, 'He was much better at popularizing than innovating.'[37] Maître Jacques and Vauban suggest that it is not necessary to be an innovator to become a great mason, as has been suggested colourfully: 'the architect's genius was not to go fishing for new forms in the void.'[38] We must be careful not to ascribe to masons of the thirteenth century the attributes of twenty-first century architects.

At Harlech we would have met a man named Adam Boynard in the English records. The year 1286 is unusual for Harlech, in that the detailed accounts from which the overall records shown in the Pipe Rolls are available. The accounts which have survived for the period December 1285 to September 1286 list Boynard a number of times, involved in the movement of material:[39]

Date	Cost of	Commodity	From / To	Amount £ s d
10 February	Hire of 6 horses	Iron	Caernarfon to Harlech	2 shillings
3 March	Hire of 27 horses	Stone for the kiln, in the castle, iron, steel and nails	Caernarfon and free quarry to Harlech	6 shillings and 9 pence
24 March	Hire of 11 horses	Iron	Caernarfon to Harlech	3 shillings and 8 pence
21 April	Hire of 1 horse	Tools	Harlech to Criccieth	3 pence
2 June	Hire of 46 horses	Lime	The quarry to Harlech	9 pounds
25 August	Hire of 65 horses	Lime and sand	The sea to Harlech	10 pounds 3 shillings and one and a half pence
15 September	Hire of 84 horses	Lime, sand and earth	The sea to Harlech	14 pounds

So who was this Adam Boynard? Taylor suggested he was the 'Beynardus' we last met constructing the tower for Count Philippe at Saxon.[40] Boynard and Beynardus might be similar names but why would Taylor be so confident in thinking the man with the 'wheelbarrows' a thousand miles away in the Valais might be the man named in the Harlech records of 1286. The fireplace hoods that can be seen in the gatehouse at Harlech, where Jean and Agnès de Bonvillars most likely warmed their hands on chill days in north Wales, can also be found at the tower that 'Beynardus' constructed for Count Philippe de Savoie at Saxon.[41]

'Beynardus' is more fully styled as 'Beynardus rex ribaldorum' in the Savoyard records for Saxon – Beynardus, King of the Ribalds. In the twelfth-century French court, an official named King of the Ribalds investigated all crimes committed within the precincts of the court, and controlled vagrants, prostitutes, brothels and gambling houses. The Ribalds appears in the military of the twelfth century – organized into units with their own flags and kings, they were the first to attack and scale the enemy walls. A thirteenth-century Ribald flag is described as 'white, with the ribalds painted looting and gambling'. Dressed and armed lightly, if at all, they erected catapults and scaled them. 'Nude like a ribald' was a contemporary term. In military campaigns, Ribalds may have acted as pimps, with most armies having plenty of 'whores, boys, and Ribalds'. Certainly, the King of the Ribalds punished prostitutes as well as his own. So on a construction site at Saxon for Count Philippe our 'Beynardus' may have either procured or controlled prostitutes. The household roll for Count Amédée V de Savoie of a gift made at Cambai in 1296 of 100 shillings to 'Regi dicto Adam' or 'the king called Adam' gave

Taylor the confirmation that Adam Boynard had acquired the epithet '*rex* as *rex ribaldorum*' at Saxon before moving to Harlech and Wales.[42] The one-time 'King of the Ribalds' would become a burgess of Harlech and acted as bailiff in 1291–2[43] – some advancement for a man of wheelbarrows and prostitutes in the Valais just ten years earlier.

The detailed accounts for 1286 perhaps show another Savoyard working alongside Adam Boynard at Harlech – whom we last met at Aberystwyth in 1282, and before that at Saxon in the Valais in 1280 – being none other than Giles de Saint Georges. Enigmatically, the counter roll of Adam of Wettenhall lists alongside Adam Boynard a man variously described as '*Gilet*' (once), '*Gillet*' (twice), and '*Gylet*' (thrice). Taylor maintained that '*Gilet*' was Giles de Saint Georges as '*Gilet*' closely follows the '*Giletus*' of the Savoyard records as applied to '*Giletus de Sancto Georgio*'. He further suggested that the uncommon lack of a surname in the Harlech record might be the result of the son of Maître Jacques being so well known to scribes that they didn't feel the need to attach a family name. This is perhaps reaching a little, given the frequent appellation '*de Sancto Georgio*' attached to Maître Jacques himself. Perhaps telling in relation to both the '*Beynardus*' and '*Giletus de Sancto Georgio*' of the Savoyard accounts for Saxon in 1280 is the absence of them in Savoy from the time of their potential appearance in Wales. Taylor's assertion of the origins of Boynard and Giles de Saint Georges, and that they were working at Harlech in 1286, is, most likely as can be ascertained, accurate. Going back to the gatehouse link with Aberystwyth, and before that to Caerffili, the presence of Giles de Saint Georges at both Aberystwyth and Harlech would only add fuel to Hislop's suggestion outlined earlier.

Another Savoyard that our traveller of 1286 would have met at Harlech would be Albert de Menz. He was paid for building a chimney in the chamber used by the Constable, Jean de Bonvillars. After all a roaring fire would have been a necessity in the cold of the Irish Sea winds.[44] Menz was also paid for a number of freestone details,[45] and his origin is most likely to have been Le Mintset formerly Menze near Martigny-Combe in Valais, not far from La Bâtiaz. He would later, in 1289, be paid for window mullions in the main castle hall. Another Savoyard at Harlech could well be Perrotus whose horses were hauling stone, sand and lime to the castle in 1286 – he was another of the Saxon contingent, having worked there in 1280 along with Boynard and under Giles de Saint Georges.[46]

The work of Maître Jacques at Harlech, and by extension of men like Boynard, Perrotus and Menz, has been questioned, given the absence of references directly related to Jacques, as are found in the archives related to Conwy. For Taylor, the helicoidal putlog holes on the gatehouse outer towers and the corbelled latrine, whose twins are to be found at La Bâtiaz, are convincing enough evidence (Figure 2.9). However, others have pointed out that we have no evidence for Maître Jacques working at La Bâtiaz[47] and that both features are evidence of Savoyard masons at work, such as Adam Boynard, Albert de Menz and Giles, but not necessarily

Maître Jacques himself. We can place at least Boynard and Giles in the Valais at this time and so likely sources of the features mentioned thus far.

But there was one more piece of architectural evidence that cannot be so easily dismissed. Running down the side of *le Chapel Tour* (North-west Tower) at Harlech is a latrine shaft. There is an identical latrine shaft by the sole surviving tower at Saint-Georges-d'Espéranche in the Viennois. The South-west Tower at Yverdon bears the scars of exactly the same style of latrine shaft, having once adorned the castle. We have therefore a simple architectural strand that binds Yverdon of 1260 with Saint-Georges-d'Espéranche of 1273 and Harlech of 1286 (Figure 1.5).[48] The three castles bear little in common with one another: they were built in different decades and regions for three different patrons, Pierre de Savoie, Count Philippe I de Savoie and King Edward I of England. The major influences on castle design are geography: the lie of the land; the patron: the preferences of the paymaster; and lastly the budget: the resources available to build the castle. In the chief influences on the design of these castles are major differences, which have given us three very different castles. Pierre with a limited budget on flat terrain gave us Yverdon, Philippe with a bigger budget, also on flat terrain, but specifying a palace-castle, gave us Saint-Georges-d'Espéranche, whilst Edward with the biggest budget by far of all and building a military stronghold high upon a rock gave us Harlech. But if the castles are so different, it is in perhaps the small details that the common authorship is revealed – the simple humble latrine shaft. Neither Pierre, nor Philippe, nor especially Edward would care for the design of latrine shafts – suffice for them that there were latrines. But the Master Mason? The latrine shafts at these three castles reveal the style of handwriting employed by the author in fulfilling three very different briefs. It is in these latrine shafts that we see, in architectural evidence, something to go alongside the primary-source material, to confirm that at Yverdon, Saint-Georges-d'Espéranche and at Harlech, that *Magistro Jacobo Lathomo*, Maître Jacques de Saint Georges, was most definitely a designing hand.

If Harlech can be considered a modified *Carré Savoyard* castle, then the *Carré* is not quite *Carré*, it is not quite square. Slightly narrower in length on the seaward side, possibly to encompass the great gatehouse on the landward side or perhaps the lie of the land. Today the four towers are described as the South-east, South-west, North-west and North-east towers running clockwise from the gatehouse. However fourteenth-century documents give their original names: in 1321 '*Lu Tour de la Chapel*' and '*La Tour de Prisoun*' and in 1343 '*le chapeltour*', '*le gemeltour*', '*le Wedercok Tour*' and '*le prison tour*'.[49] The delightful Frenglish is a mix of English and French words but with the English grammatical word order – such was the Anglo-French melange that was the Anglo-Norman state. If there was a weathercock high above the South-west Tower, then the prevailing winds from the Irish Sea would have constantly sent it spinning dizzily. Within the inner ward or bailey there would have been a number of structures leaning against the curtain wall. Looking from a Chillon-type window in the gatehouse, and looking clockwise, we would have seen the granary, then a gap to be filled in 1307 by another building – the significance of which we'll come to later – the kitchen, the hall and the chapel. Outside of the main curtain wall and entirely encompassing it was a second wall: Harlech presented a concentric defence. Outside of that to the seaward side there was a platform for defensive engines (trebuchets etc.). The southern and eastern sides were protected by a moat, the western and northern sides by the precipitate fallaway of the colossal dome upon which the castle stands. As with all of Edward's Welsh castles, resupply by sea was a key element in their situation. At Harlech a narrow, wall-protected pathway extended from close by the South-west Tower via the Upper Gate, then down steeply toward the sea, where the 'Gate Next the Sea' provided access.

The worksite we would have found at Harlech on our journey of 1286 would have been alive to the chiselling of stone, the cries of workmen, the smell of woodsmoke, the shaping of wood, all set against the backdrop of the Welsh mountains and Irish Sea. The workforce amounted to some 277 masons, 115 quarriers, 30 smiths, 20 carpenters and another 546 general labourers.[50] As with Conwy, iron and steel were being brought to the site from Chester by sea, originating from Edmund Crouchback's forges at Newcastle-under-Lyme in Staffordshire. Again the mass production of the many iron and steel fittings required for the castle, such as nails and door hangings, was more effectively produced in one place and shipped than by seeking to produce them all on site – an early case of industrial production. We saw earlier the provision of 125,000 nails for Conwy in the 1286 building season; the number supplied by Ralf and John FitzThomas for Harlech was another 130,000, plus some 9,000 board nails supplied by Adam, all from the busy forges of Newcastle-under-Lyme.[51] Limestone for the mortar and limewash was coming from Anglesey and Caernarfon. Much of the stone not coming from the Harlech dome itself was being shipped by sea, along the coast, from a quarry above Ceunant Egryn, seven miles to the south. The quarry produced a sandstone freestone known later as Egryn Stone. Architectural historians have overlooked the significance of Egryn Stone as a type, but it is well known to the local people of the area as a distinct type. It is a medium to coarse sandstone, dominated by quartz grains, containing some lithic shards (fragments of older rocks). Egryn Stone had previously been used at the Cistercian Cymer Abbey and was particularly useful where masons needed a sandstone capable of fine decorative working. Edward had used the abbey in the recent war and made a donation for recompense, so it's not a leap of imagination to suggest that the abbey pointed the way for the builders of Harlech as to where they might source a finer stone than available up at Harlech. The precise route of the stone from the quarry to the sea is now lost to us, as is the collapsed quarry face, and the seaside wharfs for transshipment, but attempts have been made to plausibly retrace the journey made down to the sea.[52] No doubt the Savoyard carving the Welsh stone would have thought it akin to the Molasse stone they knew from the Pays de Vaud.

The castle appears to have been built in stages, that is not a continuous construction.[53] Structural breaks in the curtain walls seem to show that around eight-feet-high walls were constructed quickly, to be finished to their full height in a later stage – this would seem to be indicative of the need to quickly have some defence of the site at an early stage in what was still a hostile environment, hence the early wooden fortifications indicated by sawyers on site and squires for protection.[54] For the first two years of construction we are lacking many of the detailed accounts that survive for Conwy, which may be a result of the later rebellion at Caernarfon in 1294 destroying records kept in the exchequer there.[55] Nonetheless, it is not, as has been suggested, that very little money was expended at Harlech, another of the ideas put forward by those proposing a pre-existing castle. Fortunately, we have confirmation, at least, of the overall expenditure for north Wales in these early years: £9,414 made by William of Louth[56] from the Wardrobe account – a good proportion of which was intended for Harlech's workforce and resulted in the aforesaid eight-feet walls constructed in the first stage of operations. What Taylor called this 'omnibus' payment of £9,414.4s.11d was issued to cover the period from March 1282 to the end of 1284.[57] Following the earlier (1283–4) work, of establishing at least that eight-foot-high curtain, the work of 1285 seems to have been the aforementioned castle ditch or moat to the eastward and southern side of the castle. The westernmost towers (le Chapel Tour and le Wedercok Tour) would not have been apparent to us in 1286; they would be constructed last in 1288–9. A Master William of Drogheda is recorded as having built these towers and their associated turrets.[58]

The 1286 building season, for which the detailed records survive, included work on the other towers, internal buildings, chapel and gatehouse. It would be the 1287 season, the year that Maître Jacques left for Gascony, that would see the most intensive work carried out. Some have seen this as evidence that Maître Jacques' influence at Harlech is less than hitherto suggested. In particular, the latrine shaft by le Chapel Tour so suggestive of the work of Maître Jacques stood beside a tower constructed in 1288–9, during his absence. How could this latrine shaft have been built whilst he was over a thousand miles away? Perhaps the answer lies in the work of Wilson[59] and Goodall[60] whereby the Master of the King's Works would leave patterns for basic elements, such as latrines, in the tracing room of the Harlech site. It then becomes very possible that he left the work in the capable hands of artisans such as Adam Boynard and left to do the king's bidding in Gascony. Conclusive evidence for this suggestion is lacking in the non-survival of any such written plans – but that is not to say they did not exist, and there one-time existence would answer contemporary critics of Maître Jacques.

The Welsh castles were not far away from Edward's thoughts whilst he was away in south-west France. It was common in the Middle Ages for castles to be decorated in a manner to overtly show off their owners. Whilst Edward, Grandson and Jacques were away in Gascony, an order was placed from Bordeaux for 200 shields bearing the royal arms to be made in Bordeaux and dispatched to Wales, and no doubt Harlech was amongst the castles to be so adorned.[61]

We skipped the building on the South Range, beside the granary, because it tells us much of the way in which Edward, and those after him, sought to finally bring Wales to his will, and through his eyes, become the rightful ruler of Britain. Next to the granary would stand the Ystumgwern Hall, a building that had literally been disassembled in situ and brought to stand within the castle at Harlech. But why? The hall had been at Ystumgwern, some five miles south of Harlech, and was part of a *llys* complex there – in 1307 it was removed to Harlech. A *llys* was a Welsh royal court, a place where law was administered. Edward had by the *Statutem Walliae* of 1284 replaced the preexisting legal system with a new anglicized county system based on the new justiciar Othon de Grandson at Caernarfon. Harlech sat within the new county of Merionethshire, Edward had no need of the *llys* at Ystumgwern. The removal of the hall from the *llys* complex at Ystumgwern meant that the site was forever lost to coming generations who may have used the hall as a rallying point at which to meet and plan an uprising against their new English rulers. But what is remarkable, and telling, is that Edward did not have the hall destroyed: he had it removed and placed within his castle. Once more within this story we are struck by the thorough ruthless efficiency of Edward: he was assimilating Welsh culture, eating the territory and making it his own – the local population would come to him now if it had need of law – he was the law.

When Edward returned from Gascony, he found the now largely complete castle at Harlech in the hands of the Lady Agnès de Bonvillars, she having held the post of constable in the years since the death of her husband Jean de Bonvillars and former constable at Dryslwyn. Maître Jacques still held the post of Master of the King's Works in Wales when he was appointed the new constable at Harlech in July 1290.[62] If we accept that Jacques was the son of Jean Cotereel, Constable of the castle at Saint-Prex, then Jacques had finally attained the rank of his father, both master mason and constable of a castle. From this Welsh Roll we can also bring up to date the remarkable (for the thirteenth century) record we have of his career in terms of wages. It is fiendishly difficult to calculate annual pay or wages for the thirteenth century, since we are only given weekly (for Savoy) and daily (for England) numbers to work with, and we do not know how these might be precisely annualized. Did the daily rates apply to every day?[63] Was the pay just for the building season or throughout the year? Nevertheless, we can use the numbers to give us a broad idea of the progression in pay and how it might relate to others.

So, having acknowledged the health warning in handling these figures, we can see that Jacques arrived in the known records at Yverdon in 1260 being paid 'ten *sol* and six *denier* every week',[64] that would annualize at just under twenty-seven *livres* (27l). When moving to Wales in 1278, his initial salary was one shilling per day whilst at court, and two shillings per day otherwise. Since he was almost entirely away from court, we should use the latter number and assuming as Taylor showed pay for a seven-day week, this would represent an annual salary of just over £36.

Upon being made Master of the King's Works in 1284, his salary rose to three shillings per day,[65] an annualized payment of just over £53. We can thus see the progression from 27 *Livres* in 1260 to £36 to £53 – a remarkable level of detail for the thirteenth century.

Contextualizing medieval money is also fiendishly difficult, especially the *livres* used in Savoy. The Savoyard archive does not tell us whether the pay was *livres Lausanneois* or *livres Viennois*. The value of *Livres* in francophone Europe depended upon location, and eventually the highest value, the *livre Tournois*, would be accepted as standard – but this had not happened in 1260, and in any case, Savoy not part of the Kingdom of France. Things become a little easier when we come to the English record, because we are dealing with a regularized centralized currency.

But for what it is worth, Prestwich reminds us that the usual ratio between English pound and French *livre Tournois* until the 1290s was 1 to 4.[66] If we assume parity of equivalence between the 27 *livres* paid to Maître Jacques in Yverdon and the £36 pounds in Wales, then some significant increase, perhaps fourfold might be seen. However, if we assume something like the ratio for *livres Tournois* suggested by Prestwich, then we have a tenfold increase.

So far, we've attempted to establish a progression in pay between 1260 and 1290, but what does that represent in modern terms? Once more meaningful calculation is difficult across nearly 800 years. However, using the UK National Archive online converter, we can try: they convert the £36 1278 salary as equivalent to over £26,000 at 2017 values, adding that with it one might have bought 47 horses or 102 cows and that it represented 3,600 days of a skilled tradesmen's pay. The 100 marks salary from 1290 is equivalent to over £48,000 at 2017 values, enabling Jacques to acquire 77 horses or a herd of 146 cows.

Year	Location	Daily Pay	Annualized Pay	Eqv Eng d[67]
1260	Yverdon	10s 6d[68]	£27.6s.0d	1638d
1278	Flint & Rhuddlan	2s	£36.10s.0d	8760d
1284	Conwy etc.	3s	£54.15s.0d	13,140d
1290	Harlech		£66.0s.0d	15,840d

By contrast Richard the Engineer had been granted a little over £18 per year for life in 1284. Valued and skilful as Richard was, Jacques had now been given nearly four times that number. For further context the master mason at Builth in 1277 was being paid 4s 4½d per week[69] or just over £11 per annum – Jacques was being paid three times that rate in 1278, rising to five times in 1284. Tellingly the salary represents 6,600 days or over 18 years a skilled tradesman's pay – Jacques was now being paid a considerable sum indeed, but he was no mere tradesman.[70]

As we have seen, and will see, there has been a contemporary critique of the role of Maître Jacques in Wales in the late thirteenth century. One is bound to say at this point, the near doubling of an already considerable salary from 1278 in 1290 speaks volumes. I think we can safely say that King Edward I of England, no spendthrift, was sufficiently enamored of his influence upon a project he saw of national importance to reward Jacques handsomely. As they say perhaps, we should 'follow the money' in assessing importance to the king.

In the words of Welsh historian Davies: 'Here – and particularly at Harlech and Beaumaris – the idea of the keepless castle, whose strength lay in its twin set of curtain walls and in massively imposing gatehouses, was taken to its logical conclusion.' In what Davies calls the 'formative role of Master Jacques of Saint Georges and his fellow workers in their construction' we most definitely find what Pevsner described as architecture.[71] In 1260, with his father, Maître Jacques has begun work on his first 'keepless castle'. What our traveller would have found at Harlech in 1286 was indeed the logical conclusion of its development, Jacques was taking on board all he'd learned and absorbed over the intervening twenty and more years.

Chapter Thirteen

The third castle under construction in 1286 and in the care of the Master of the King's Works Jacques de Saint Georges would have been Caernarfon, one-time Roman *Segontium*, by the western entrance to the straits of Menai and in the shadow of Yns Mon or Anglesey. The journey from Harlech to Caernarfon would most likely have been by sea, or at least partly by sea, as the wide bays formed as the rivers Dwyryd and Glaslyn emptied the rains of Snowdonia into the Irish Sea made a land journey long and circuitous. Across the bay from Harlech our traveller would probably have headed first for the castle he could see along the coast at Criccieth. The landward route from Harlech to Criccieth is, even today with the bridges in place, some fifteen miles (twenty-four kilometres) but by sea this reduces to just five miles (eight kilometres).

Upon crossing the bay, courtesy of the boatman, we would land in Eifionydd beneath a towering promontory of volcanic rock and a castle. The castle at Criccieth had been first mentioned in 1239 and was most likely the work of Llywelyn Fawr; it had subsequently been held by Llywelyn ap Gruffydd until his late demise in the war of 1282. The name Criccieth may well come from the imprisonment there of Gruffydd ap Llywelyn, who later fell to his death at the Tower of London, in 1244. *Crug Caeth*: *'caeth'* may mean 'prisoner' and thus the name could mean 'prisoner's rock'. Llywelyn ap Gruffydd had been using it as a seat of power, evidenced by a letter to Edward of 1274, which was sent from Criccieth.[1] Sadly, we have no record of the fall of Criccieth to the English in January 1283, but as we saw earlier, it was perhaps the Anglesey army under Othon de Grandson and Jean de Vesci moving south from Caernarfon that was responsible.

Criccieth Castle then was not the work of Edward but would be heavily strengthened by him. It sits high upon a headland separating two beaches that sit before the modern town, thus giving it a view south and west across Cardigan Bay. Edward had himself visited his new acquisition in 1283 and 1284 before bestowing the status of English borough upon Criccieth in November 1284. The English constables would be Henry of Greenford then Sir William Leyburn, whom our traveller would meet along with his garrison of thirty men. Unlike most other Welsh fortresses, the inner ward at Criccieth was shielded by a gatehouse flanked by two large D-shaped towers and protected by a gate and portcullis, with murder holes in the passage, and arrow loops in each tower. The gatehouse was and still is the major feature of the castle. This unusual Welsh design may well have been copied from English works on the Marches at Beeston Castle, Cheshire or Montgomery Castle, Powys. The castle had an irregular shape, determined by the rock on which it stood. The Outer Ward was roughly triangular in shape, the South-west and Northern towers at two points, but with the South-east tower at a midpoint adjacent to the Inner Ward, which was as we saw above guarded and dominated by the inner gatehouse.

Upon coming ashore at Criccieth we may well have found the gatehouse towers recently extended in height, and it is possible that this was the work of Maître Jacques. Criccieth had been included in the omnibus payment for all the Welsh castle works of 1283 and 1284. We have problems dating the works at Criccieth since the accounts that might confirm this are no longer with us. Most likely too a timber Great Hall had been added, Taylor estimated the total cost of the works to be no more than £500.[2] Richard Avent concurred and suggested that additional rebuilding work was partly reparation of damage caused by the taking of the castle and partly the raising of structures to an extra storey, specifically the south-west and south-east towers. Possibly the northern tower was then made to serve as an engine tower – in the absence of detailed records it's impossible to be certain.[3]

Criccieth on to Caernarfon would be another seventeen miles (twenty-seven kilometres) and this time it is by land that the shortest distance is to be had, heading north, bisecting the Llyn peninsula and skirting to the west of the Snowdonia mountains – a journey that might reasonably easily have been accomplished by horse within a day. The route would have taken that used by the old road from Roman Segontium and the main road today. We would have first crossed the Afon Dwyfor where there had been until recently a Norman motte-and-bailey castle at Dolbenmaen. Llywelyn Fawr had moved the local centre of authority down to the newly constructed Criccieth in the 1230s. Then on past Mynydd Cennin, Bwlch Mawr to our left and Snowdonia to our right – indeed Bwlch Mawr means 'Big Pass'. Our traveller would be passing the battle site of Bryn Derwin, where thirty years earlier the sons of Gruffydd ap Llywelyn had fought over the inheritance of *Uwch Gwynedd*: just the wind now from the Irish Sea to mark where a vanquished land had been contested. The exposed nature of the land to be traversed is best described by Ptolemy who called it *Ganganorum Promontorium*, which referred to it having long been explored by Celtic explorers from across the Irish Sea, the *Gangani*. Indeed, it is thought that the very name *Llyn* is of Irish origin. Travelling north we would most likely also have been beset by a bitter westerly wind bearing rain of the horizontal variety. We may have encountered pilgrims along the way heading to the most westerly point of the Llyn peninsula, Bardsey Island, otherwise known as the island of 20,000 saints. Saint Cadfan's monastery there was a major thirteenth-century tourist attraction in a time when religious pilgrimage was the primary reason you might leave your own locality.

Our destination would be in the Welsh language Yr Gaer yn Arfon, or the fort in Arfon, a reference to the former Roman fort of Segontium. The Arfon itself a reference to the proximity across the Menai Strait of Yns Mon or Anglesey. Descending toward Caernarfon and the sea we may well have been reminded once more of the legend of Macsen Wledig: 'at the mouth of the river he saw a great castle, the fairest that anyone had seen.' The castle seen from even afar would have been unlike anything else seen thus far, nothing like Harlech or Conwy – an enormous castle of imperial Roman proportions rising by the Menai (Figure 3.0). Count Philippe had asked Maître Jacques to build him a palace-castle in the Viennois. Edward had grander visions in mind for Caernarfon: his palace-castle would surpass anything yet built in imperial splendour – Edward was to build perhaps the greatest castle of the medieval age, and Maître Jacques was the man he employed to build it for him.

Taylor suggested that the castle had pretensions of Constantinople, the Theodosian walls no less. Prestwich found that this linkage had 'been convincingly demonstrated' by Taylor. Going further, he firmly stated that 'the style of the castle is very clearly derived from the walls of the imperial city of Constantinople.'[4] However, Abigail Wheatley doubted this thesis[5] and pointed to Roman inspirations closer to home. Others have suggested the castle was the legend of Macsen Wledig rendered in stone, still others that it was Camelot realized by a new Arthur, while others could find echoes of Queen Leonor's Castile in the vision rising by the Menai. What is certain is that Welsh people of the time understood the imperial allusions, as the castles built in Arfon were built in the 'old city of the Emperor Constantine'.[6] What is also certain is that Edward wanted to elicit the reaction of all that saw it, that is still given centuries later: 'Wow!'

Construction had begun shortly after the English army from Anglesey under Othon de Grandson and Jean de Vesci had passed this way in early 1283. Household knight Sir Eustace de Hache with clerk John of Dunster had been so tasked on 24 June 1283.[7] Early works included, in July 1284, the demolition of previous dwellings to make way for the castle.[8] These works referenced the beginnings of a townward moat protecting the castle under construction. The reference to '*mote*' as a moat rather than the use of '*fosse*' will become important shortly. As we have seen at previous sites, such as at Flint, one of the earlier tasks was to create a protective palisade around the works. William de Perton was ordered to dispatch all the necessary timber from Chester on 23 July 1283.[9] The new castle began to consume enormous amounts of timber. Twenty shiploads left Liverpool in June, even before that order to Perton. Further cargoes left Rhuddlan and Conwy, and now the war was won the bridge of boats traversed recently by the army was dismantled and the wood sent to Caernarfon to aid 'the construction of the castle' and the 'town then began'.[10]

Taylor likened the walls of Caernarfon to the Theodosian walls of Constantinople, writing that Caernarfon was 'reflecting in its symbolism its own Roman origins and using the likeness of the Theodosian walls of Constantinople to invoke the imperial theme'.[11] He drew attention to the fact that the original name for the West or Water Gate of the town walls at Caernarfon was the 'Golden Gate', a name also used at Constantinople.[12] Comparison has been made to Denbigh, but Taylor noted the lack of Roman-style colouring to the walls at Henri de Lacy's castle. I have only been able to confirm the presence of one man that Edward or Maître Jacques might have known, who may plausibly have seen Constantinople. That man would be Savoyard Guillaume de Cicon, whose family came from the Franche-Comté just miles north-west of Grandson, Yverdon and Savoy. As mentioned earlier, an ancestor of Cicon's had been with the crusade that had sacked Constantinople in 1204, one Othon de Cicon. He had accompanied his uncle Othon de La Roche[13] on the Fourth Crusade, and became Lord of Karystos[14] from 1250 (at least) to his death around 1266.[15] Taylor noted that Guillaume de Cicon's first arrival in the English record of 13 November 1276 follows closely the recapture of Karystos by the Byzantines under Licario also in 1276.[16] Was it possible that Guillaume de Cicon, who had become the first constable at Conwy, had returned from the fallen family fief of Karystos? If so, was it further possible that Guillaume had visited Constantinople? There is one thing to add to the puzzle: the Castello Rosso built by the Byzantines in 1030, rebuilt by the crusaders after its capture by them between 1209 and 1216 has a remarkable feature – an octagonal tower exactly as would find its way into the design of Caernarfon. Taylor thought a link more than possible, but although an intriguing possibility, it remains conjecture until we can firmly place Guillaume de Cicon in the family fief of Karystos before coming to Wales.

Wheatley suggested that the Theodosian walls are not primarily polygonal (they're mostly square) and the Roman decoration of the walls is equally suggestive of many Roman sites in England.[17] Richard Morris helpfully adds that Constantinople and Caernarfon differ in the material of construction – the Theodosian walls are stone and tile whereas Caernarfon achieves its banding with differing colours of sandstone.[18] But these are details of architectural design, something I think that would concern Edward less than the overall imperial impression. Certainly, the Roman lacing design of coloured walls was a deliberate act to 'invoke the imperial theme' and a theme reflecting, most likely, Constantinople. It is very possible to see in Caernarfon an echo of Constantinople, but an echo also reflected via Karystos. Taylor, rightly, says that Caernarfon was designed to be much more than a military fortification as at Harlech, or even a centre of administration as at Conwy – it was designed from the beginning to be a 'palace-castle'.

Whilst acknowledging the imperial (both Roman and Arthurian – Wheatley and Morris correctly remind us that Roman and Arthurian were often conflated in the medieval mind)[19] connections of Caernarfon for decoration, and likeness in many ways to Conwy in terms of conceptual form, one doesn't have to look too far for the origins of Edward's idea for a palace-castle itself. If we go back to the summer of 1273 and Edward's return from crusade, alongside his retinue, including Othon de Grandson and Jean de Bonvillars, we can imagine his arrival at another, earlier, palace-castle designed and built by Maître Jacques: Saint-Georges-d'Espéranche in the Viennois. Caernarfon is Saint-Georges-d'Espéranche writ large, built by a patron with a much larger purse, who had imperial pretensions of a Roman or Arthurian, or both, nature – built furthermore with the military and architectural experience that Jacques had gleaned in the intervening decade of continuous castle building.

Saint-Georges-d'Espéranche had been built by Count Philippe de Savoie as a palace-castle too, when he had succeeded his brother, and left cold and damp Chillon up in the Alps for the balmier climate of the Viennois that he knew, having for so long held the see of Lyon. Sadly, as we related in earlier chapters, not much is left of Philippe's palace-castle, but from what is left and surviving drawings we can reasonably discern a *Carré Savoyard*, but with four polygonal towers, not round towers as employed elsewhere in Savoy. Prestwich agreed with Taylor, suggesting that the octagonal towers anticipated Caernarfon.[20] The plan made by Chabord in 1794,[21] held in the archive at Grenoble (Figure 1.4), clearly shows four eight-sided polygonal towers.[22] This is the castle that formed the basis, in his imagination, of what Edward wanted Jacques to build for him in north Wales; the genesis of the conception of Caernarfon as a palace-castle is in the Viennois – Taylor was right to make this functional connection plain.[23] He necessarily qualifies his conjecture with a 'maybe' but I think we can be more certain, by reading that as 'almost certainly'. Saint-Georges-d'Espéranche lacks the Roman lacing style of mural decoration afforded to Caernarfon, but nevertheless it is clear that in 1283 Edward took as his base ingredient for Caernarfon the castle he'd seen in the Viennois a decade earlier, and added more than a dash of Constantinople by way of Cicon Karystos.

The debate as to whether the main stylistic influence, those banded walls et al., alludes to Constantine, Macsen Wledig or Arthur is a long one. Was Edward the King to appropriate Welsh myth and legend? The siting of Caernarfon and Harlech suggests so. Was Edward the King to appropriate the myth of Arthur? The exhumation at Glastonbury and the holding of a round table at Nefyn suggests so. We will never be certain precisely what was in Edward's mind, but we can agree that it was primarily in Edward's mind that the allusions were made. Perhaps he had heard an oral version of the *Mabinogion*, perhaps he had Arthurian aspirations – perhaps both are true. That Caernarfon is meant to appropriate Welsh myth, to appeal to an imperial past and an Arthurian past all at once. Morris argued convincingly that Caernarfon was an 'Arthurian castle in all but name'.[24] For Edward the imperial association, including the use of stone from Segontium, allied to his enthusiasm for all things Arthurian, pointed in but one direction.

But there is one more suggestion that has yet to be made fully: perhaps the allusion to Constantinople by way of Karystos and Guillaume de Cicon was meant to refer to New Rome, not to Rome. When Constantine had moved the Roman capital from Italy to the little Greek colony by the Bosporus it had been given the name of *Nova Roma*.[25] Perhaps we can add to the imperial and Arthurian evocation one more – that Caernarfon was to be a *Nova Roma*, a new seat of imperial power to encompass but eclipse the past. Wheatley found some evidence for this in the reuse of stone from nearby Segontium.[26] The symbolism of Caernarfon continues to intrigue us.

So, in terms of much of its basics, Caernarfon was essentially a Saint-Georges-d'Espéranche built to a bigger budget, with a form akin to Conwy, and built to account for the lie of the land and the need to encompass the pre-existing Norman motte and bailey on the site.

Upon arrival in 1286, our traveller would have come across a busy worksite, the growing castle bounded on two sides by water, as at Conwy, this time the Menai Strait and the Afon Seiont. The castle and adjoining town site occupied what was in effect a peninsula, almost an island, surrounded by the Seiont to the south, the Menai Strait to the north and the estuarine Afon Cadnant to the east. The nature of this island has been lost to us, since the Cadnant has subsequently been culverted. Once more, as had his father at Saint-Prex, and he at Yverdon and Conwy, Maître Jacques would make much of available natural water defences at Caernarfon.

The castle itself is a long, narrow structure, essentially two castles joined together, another double castle as at Conwy (and Grandson). The two castles can be described as the Upper Ward, which encompassed the motte of the original, and the Lower Ward which held the more important structures. The Norman motte survived until the late nineteenth century, as evidenced by photographs taken in 1870 and accounts for the higher level of the Upper Ward.[27] Caernarfon containing within its walls the original Norman motte of Hugh d'Avranches, perhaps shows Edward reasserting a lost right not establishing a new one after all, thus emphasising the difficulty in precisely attributing his motives.[28] However, the new castle, in fact, swung the castle around 180 degrees to be due west of the original motte, the original castle having its bailey due east of the motte. The geometry of the polygonal towers and castle itself was indicative to Morris of 'a designer playing with geometrical shapes for effect'[29] and so we need to look a little closer at these walls and towers. The Upper Ward curtain is essentially a hexagon, the Lower Ward a pentagon.

Beginning at what would many centuries later be known as the Queen's Gate,[30] where we may have arrived from the direction of Harlech, our visitor may have inspected the works (Figure 3.1). Below that impressive gate there may have been, in 1286, evidence of the original Norman bailey that occupied this land. Moving along the Seiont, we would first come to the Cistern tower, which held a stone-lined tank for collecting rainwater, before coming to the Black Tower (*Blaketour*),[31] then the Chamberlain tower which marked the limit of the Upper Ward. Continuing along the outer side of the lower ward we would come to the Queen's Tower (*Bele Estre*[32] or *Tour de Baner*[33]), the fabled decagonal Eagle Tower ('Great Tower')[34] of which much more later, before heading back toward our start point. The footings of the octagonal Well Tower (*Le Welle Tour*)[35] would have been next, then the beginnings of what would become the imposing complexity of the King's Gate, a two-octagonal-towered gatehouse with bent entrance, which would return us following, the Upper Ward, to the footings of the octagonal Granary Tower, the more fully completed octagonal North-east Tower before arrival back at the Queen's Gate.

It is possible that the Queen's Gate or perhaps the King's Gate at Caernarfon influenced work being carried out at Denbigh by Henri de Lacy. Denbigh had been granted to the Earl of Lincoln by Edward at the end of the recent war, and both Edward and Maître Jacques had been present at the planning stage. The second phase of building at Denbigh featured a tremendous three-polygonal-towered gatehouse arranged with two towers facing outward, and one inward. Furthermore, the Denbigh gatehouse would feature a statue above the entrance, thought to be of Edward I, but now sadly missing. The King's Gate at Caernarfon would also be adorned with a statue – rare in England – this time of Edward of Caernarfon, Edward's son King Edward II. However, this still-existing statue at Caernarfon was added much later than construction and maybe an echo of Denbigh.[36] It is also possible that the Queen's Gate, of two polygonal towers, may have been originally intended to mirror the gate at Denbigh with a third tower to the inward[37] – this is however speculative as we have no primary source or archaeology to support the theory. Butler noted the similar administrational function may have informed style.[38] There is a stylistic link between Denbigh and Caernarfon without doubt; however, the extent to which one sequentially followed the other and whether plans were ever fully realized are sadly lost to us.

Returning to the fabled Eagle Tower: this was the centre of royal government, the home for Othon de Grandson as Edward's viceroy in north Wales. The decagonal tower would comprise a basement and three floors, topped off by three turrets. The castle and tower could be entered from the outside by means of the water gate, which continued the theme throughout the castles of having resupply access by sea. Each of the successive floors from the basement upward measure between thirty to thirty-five feet across (nine to just over ten metres). So, if we imagine four floors, the basement, the ground, the first and the second, then the first floor was originally the principal apartment of the castle, the living space. The enormously thick walls of the tower accommodated space, for amongst other things octagonal chapels on the ground and first floors as evidenced by surviving *piscina* or well for holy water. Originally, as we shall see, the first floor marked the extent of the tower, the second floor and turrets being added later. The battlements atop the tower and its turrets were decorated by, amongst other things, the eagles from which the tower gets its name. It has been suggested, not least in a 2006 exhibition within the tower itself, that the eagles may have been put there as an allusion to the Grandson heraldry. However, this may have been a misunderstanding of the Grandson heraldry itself. The *famille de Grandson* did not use the eagle, but three coquilles St Jacques on a red bend, as we can see from the tomb of Othon de Grandson and the Château de Grandson to this day. The coquilles were not, as thought by some, a reference to Grandson's crusade in 1270 along with Edward,[39] but predate that by some years, and reference an earlier Grandson who died in Jerusalem.[40] The eagle that appears on the English branch of the family, the Grandisons, appears with Guillaume de Grandson, Othon's brother. That the tower would bear the heraldry of the deputy justiciar, not the justiciar, is not impossible but is rather unlikely.

Unlike the castles we've visited at Conwy, then at Harlech, Caernarfon has not passed to us the wealth of building and construction primary-source material. In short, we know far less about its construction than we would like. Which is a pity because as Caernarfon, unlike Conwy and Harlech, was not built with locally sourced stone, we cannot be certain as to the actual source of the stone used. What we can say is that it was the usual combination of limestone and sandstone. Lott describes the primary stone, as a pale grey limestone very hard in nature, and available in regular blocks that needed the minimum of dressing by the masons.[41] Such limestone is available on nearby Anglesey and farther along the north Welsh coast by the Great Orme – such sources necessitated the movement of stone by sea to the site at Caernarfon,[42] the banded coloured stone, added to create Roman stylistic echoes, was of sandstone. Lott identified two sites especially: the area between Penmon and Benllech, on the eastern side of Anglesey, the other at Vaynol, on the southern mainland bank of the Menai Strait, not far from where Telford and Stephenson would later bridge the narrow waterway. Both sites afforded easy access to the sea and a short passage to Caernarfon.[43]

We should pause now to consider the enormous activity underway in Gwynedd from 1283. Lott was under no misapprehension as to the driving force behind the multiplicity of simultaneous works, suggesting that Maître Jacques had acquired a 'unique' understanding of the resources needed to assemble the multiple castles then in construction, something he'd learned well in the Viennois.[44] Not just the quarrying and shipping of stone, but the felling and shipping of enormous quantities of timber, the forging of countless metalwork items in England for shipment to Wales – this was an undertaking without precedent on the island of Britain since the days of the Emperor Hadrian. Once more we must consider that to describe Maître Jacques as a mere 'project manager' is to entirely understate the achievement of the building of Conwy, Harlech and Caernarfon, let alone ignore his career we've described thus far as a master mason, architect and builder extraordinaire.

In 1286, our traveller would have been met with a partially constructed castle, the curtain walls facing the Seiont and the Menai Strait growing to completion, the southern wall by the Queen's Gate likewise. The least complete, though protected at least by a great ditch, was the northern or town-side wall. The reason would be that this elevation was protected by the pretty much extant town walls and so provided a large defensible *enceinte* of castle and town. In charge of the ditch digging at Caernarfon we would have found Master Manasser de Vaucouleurs, who hailed from Geoffrey de Geneville's county of Champagne in eastern France, Vaucouleurs being some thirty miles (fifty kilometres) east of Joinville, and later a temporary home for Jeanne d'Arc. It's possible that Manasser had been known to Maître Jacques in Savoy, but it's more likely the link was Geoffrey de Geneville, as the Lordship of Vaucouleurs was a vassal of the Lordship of Joinville. Maître Jacques had earlier employed him at Caergwrle, where he'd been involved in digging the well and paid six pence for his trouble. He'd been paid for seven *toise*, a *toise* being a unit of measurement in use in France and Savoy as the length across two outstretched arms. We can be certain that *la toise* was in common use in Savoy from the construction of the tower at Saxon in the Valais by Master Giles de St

George, along with Adam Boynard, as it's recorded that payment at Saxon was 'For the Tower of Saxon at task made of ten *toise* height.'[45] The Savoyard were bringing their measurements to Wales along with their building methods; the castles of north Wales would be measured by the outstretched arms of the Savoyard artisans. Master Manasser was employed as master and director of the diggers at Caernarfon, where he later became a burgess and where, before his death, he held office as one of the town bailiffs.[46] He'd died by 28 May 1293, when his wife Mary was described in the Calendar of Welsh Rolls as 'late the wife of Manasser Le Fosseur of Carnarvon ... Kings Bailiff in Karnarvan'.[47]

An example of the often-clever techniques used by the builders to ensure alignment of towers with walls is shown by the projecting stone on the north-west face of the North-east Tower which gave a siting point to the alignment of the town wall. This projecting stone tells us that the tower to that height preceded the town walls in construction, and the height the tower had reached by October 1284.[48]

Whilst we lack detailed accounts for the building at Caernarfon, we do have yearly expenditure totals, from which we can see a slackening pace of construction: for 1284/5 it was £3040, 1286 it was £1773, for 1287 £1379, just £156 in 1288, £170 in 1289, £50 in 1290 and lastly a meagre £42 in 1292.[49] Payments for 1289/90 appear to have been overseen by Deputy Justiciar Guillaume de Grandson.[50] The building phases for Caernarfon has been the subject of some conjecture over the past century, and introduced the original idea that attributed the building of the castle not to Maître Jacques but to a Master Walter of Hereford. Master Walter was a significant master mason, and indeed directed the construction of the Cistercian house at Vale Royal in Cheshire in 1277. Vale Royal was no small undertaking, being a high Gothic church of Westminster proportions employing nearly a hundred masons at its inception and still just over fifty by 1280. Working for Master Walter at Vale Royal was Philippe Le Charpentier, from 1278 until 1280, thereafter he worked at Flint in 1286 and at Caernarfon in 1295, 1305 and 1320. Philippe has been identified as the Philippe de Saint-Georges worked for Count Philippe de Savoie in 1274–5 in the Viennois – not an impossible identification given the movement of others from Saint-Georges like Gillot de Chalons.[51] Our traveller to Caernarfon of 1286 would be unable to find Master Walter, as he would have to journey back to Vale Royal to meet that appointment. Master Walter was Master of the Works at Vale Royal until 1290.[52] The confusion arose as a decade later Master Walter would be appointed as master mason for Caernarfon Castle. Taylor was able to show that the castle was 'a single design conceived as a unity at the time construction was begun on it in 1283–4.'[53] Coldstream acknowledged that Walter was not responsible for the southern curtain at Caernarfon. How could he have been? It was constructed before he was there. But she cites architectural historian John Harvey, who had said that Walter and Master Richard of Chester 'shared responsibility' for the 'design of the castles'.[54] There are two deep flaws for Caernarfon in this assertion: firstly Walter's late arrival in 1295,[55] secondly Richard being primarily a carpenter not a mason.[56] For Master Walter, in particular at

Caernarfon, his role was in finishing the castle, not in conceiving it or beginning it. His skill was as an ecclesiastical mason, with a talent for decoration,[57] rather than a military mason. Hislop points to an interesting facet of the King's Gate at Caernarfon, largely built after Maître Jacques had left for Beaumaris. The portcullis grooves in both the King's Gate are semi-circular in profile, a characteristic of royal works in England since the early thirteenth century, but those of the other castles built in north Wales have square profile grooves – something Hislop identifies as a Maître Jacques' signature.[58] Indeed, we can see in the grooves of these gates, the hand of the ecclesiastical mason, Master Walter of Hereford, but noting an ecclesiastical mason also employing an experienced Savoyard carpenter.

The lack of detailed primary sources for Caernarfon has allowed much conjecture to fill the vacuum. Another case in point are the domical vaults[59] which echo those built at Acton Burnell in Shropshire, taken as showing the influence of Edward's Lord Chancellor, Robert Burnell.[60] However, it has been pointed out that since Burnell was such a close friend and colleague of Othon de Grandson, and that he would have been equally familiar with Acton Burnell, then the comparison may equally be his influence – such are the perils of making purely stylistic comparisons without the corroboration of building records.

Given the lack of detailed building records for Caernarfon, the extent to which the castle was constructed by 1286 and indeed in the first building phase (Figure 3.1) rests upon a description we have of the castle at the time of Master Walter's arrival, a memorandum attached as a postscript of a letter sent by Master Walter himself on 25 February 1296:

> You should note that there are on the unfinished wall about the moat/ditch of the castle of Caernarfon, there are 4 unfinished towers that are contained in the lengthwise wall of 18 perche[61] [99 yards]; of which wall there are 8 perches [44 yards] contained in height-wise 12 feet, and 10 perche [55 yards] is contained in height-wise 24 feet; and these walls contained in thickness 15 feet.[62]

Now what exactly was being described at Caernarfon in late February of 1296? Peers originally translated '*motam*' as 'motte',[63] as certainly there had been a Norman motte within the castle curtain wall, from its construction until removal in the twentieth century. Except in England the Anglo-Normans had begun to shift the meaning of the word '*motte*' or '*motam*' from the mound upon which a castle was built to the ditch surrounding the mound – the origin of our word 'moat'. As confirmation of this shift the following later appears in the archive for Beaumaris: '*motam ubi castrum Bello Marisco*' – since there was never a '*motte*' at Beaumaris we can be certain the '*motam*' being referred to at Caernarfon, as at Beaumaris, was indeed a moat or ditch.[64] We should also remember that the archive for the very beginning of castle construction in 1283 has already referred to the castle ditch or moat as a '*mote*' not a '*fosse*'.[65]

The description also gives us the details of four '*inchoate turres*' or 'unfinished towers'. If we look at Caernarfon we can see that between the extant North-east Tower and extant Eagle Tower there were, and are, indeed four towers –

the Granary Tower, the two towers that would flank the King's Gate and the Well Tower. Indeed, this northern stretch of wall was flanked on its outer town side by a moat or ditch. Taylor measured the walls and towers of this section and discovered that, omitting the towers, the wall today 'tallies closely enough' with the memorandum of 1296[66] – we are therefore reading a description, from February 1296, of the northern wall at Caernarfon between the Eagle Tower and North-east Tower. The memorandum gives the heights for the wall as varying between twelve feet and twenty-four feet to a thickness of fifteen feet – certainly '*inchoate*' or 'unfinished' but also certainly begun to some reasonable degree.

So how much of this construction can be attributed to the time before Master Walter was appointed to his role at Caernarfon? Well, the answer is probably most of it since, in the time from his arrival at the beginning of the 1295 building season, we know that the period up to 10 September had been taken by repairs to the castle, leaving just a very short and insufficient time window of just a couple of months for the northern wall to be raised to the reported height. Extant then would be the southern curtain wall, the great wall that impresses visitors so much today as they park their cars by the Seiont. This is important in revealing the genius of Maître Jacques and showing him to be far more than the 'project manager' described by some. The southern curtain is tunnelled through in order to provide a gallery for archers; an attacker might find himself faced with the withering fire from triple banks of arrow loops –defences hailed by Liddiard as 'highly sophisticated' and 'some of the most up-to-date military engineering of its day'.[67] In suggesting that mouldings show Master Walter as being 'able to influence details of design if not the whole scheme', Coldstream is perhaps overstating the influence of a no doubt hugely talented ecclesiastical mason.[68] We may find 'moulding' attributable to Master Walter, but we cannot attribute to him the shape and form and tower placement of the walls and therefore their design, and crucially the ingenuity of the southern curtain wall and its arrow-loop defence – that would be his predecessor Maître Jacques de Saint Georges. As Taylor said, Caernarfon was fundamentally a single design from the outset, that had largely been completed in the first four building seasons under Maître Jacques, save for the northern side which Master Walter finished.[69] Analysis, and a more accurate translation, of the written record allow us then to clear away the fog of speculation and firmly suggest that our traveller of 1286 would have seen an incomplete castle, but been able to identify the design, shape and form we are able to behold and marvel at today.

The town walls at Caernarfon, as at Conwy, encircled what would become a new town, a *ville neuve*, to be the centre of the new county of Caernarfonshire. Construction had begun 9 October 1284 and involved a total expenditure for that year of £1,818, equal to that allocated to the castle itself at that time.[70] Following along the coast from the Eagle Tower, the walls ran due north to the then outflow of the Afon Cadnant, returning to the castle by way of the riverbank (Figure 3.2). Along the quayside, earth and timber at this stage, ran two stretches of wall interrupted at their centre point by the West Gate, or Water Gate or Golden Gate with its echo of Constantinople . This twin-towered and portcullis-protected gate could only be approached by water in the thirteenth century. Each of the two Menai-facing town-wall sections was further guarded at midpoint by D-shaped wall towers. Turning to follow the Cadnant, the town walls then carried a further three D-shaped wall towers before meeting the main entrance to the town – the twin-towered drawbridge protected East Gate or Exchequer Gate. Later, in 1301, a fine medieval bridge was constructed to cross the Cadnant from the gate to the mainland. From the East Gate a further section of wall continued to the North-east Tower, interceded by a further two towers. Within these walls and guarded by the castle, the new town had a grid street pattern that is retained to this day. Running across the town from East Gate to West Gate was High Street. At right angles from it left three roads to the north: Northgate Street, Market Street and Church Street – and at right angles to the south: Palace Street, Castle Street and Shirehall Street. In total, the still-extant town walls of eight towers and two gateways are 800 yards (734 metres) in length. Archaeological exploration at Caernarfon in 2020 has found evidence of the daily lives of the builders. Saintonge-ware in the form of a green wine jug handle was found: evidently the builders had the pleasure of Gascon wine. Othon de Grandson, along with Robert Burnell, had negotiated the return of the Saintonge region north of the Gironde to Edward in 1278[71] – perhaps Grandson himself was quaffing the fruits of his labours as construction of the walls began. Indeed, as a reward for services rendered in the Second Welsh War, Grandson had been rewarded with twenty casks of wine, and a further twenty-six casks for Jean de Vesci; conquest it seems was thirsty work.[72]

The reorientation of the castle, swung about the axis of the original motte by 180 degrees, created a very different defensive structure. Edward, through Maître Jacques, did not just recreate the castle of Hugh d'Avranches, he created an entirely more comprehensive centre of settlement and government. The castle would be the cornerstone, quite literally, of the new town of Caernarfon, the castle as part of a defensive whole which also encompassed the town walls themselves. So rather than a motte and bailey, we have an entire medieval town, surrounded by walls, water defences on three sides, the rivers Seiont, Cadnant and the Menai Strait. This is the same concept employed by Maître Jacques at Conwy, and indeed the very same concept that he'd known as an apprentice to his father Master Jean at Yverdon back in Savoy and that he'd known as a boy, by the Léman, at Saint-Prex, each time growing ever more complex.

The East Gate or Exchequer Gate held rooms that served the purpose of containing the Exchequer, created by the Statute of Rhuddlan in 1284. The Exchequer would be the home of the Chamberlain of North Wales himself. The chamberlain held responsibility for Edward's revenues from the newly created counties of Anglesey, Caernarfonshire and Merionethshire – accounting for them directly to the Exchequer in London.[73] The chamberlain at the time of our traveller's visit would have been '*Magistro Roberto de Belvero*' or Robert of Belvoir, who we find regulating the expenditure by Maître Jacques and others on the rising castles of north Wales. Alongside him we would, most likely find Hugh of Leominster, Clerk of Works for Harlech and Caernarfon[74] and one-time clerk to Alianor de Provence,[75] who will later succeed Belvoir as Chamberlain. We have a record from January 1284 of the purchase of cloth for the exchequer 'over the gate of Caernarfon'.[76] And so, the conquered territory was under the Justiciar based in the Eagle Tower, and the Chamberlain based in the Exchequer Gate – the very centre of Edward's new realm.

It is at this point we must take a careful note of the men wielding power in north Wales, because it can be a little confusing at first sight. As we have seen, the Justiciar was Sir Othon de Grandson, but as we have also seen he was soon with the king in Gascony (and then hostage in Castile) and would be then mostly away from Britain on various errands for Edward. Therefore, he may have been dispensing justice from the Eagle Tower only in the few years up and until 1287. The position of his deputy does seem to have been less than clear. Written in 1291–2 we have confirmation of Othon de Grandson's role as 'Justiciarii Regis Northwall', but secondly that at various times, officially or unofficially, John de Havering, Jean de Bonvillars and Guillaume de Grandson held the post of 'locum' or deputy.[77] Havering had become the official deputy to Grandson back in 1284,[78] but this document appears to show that Grandson's brother-in-law Jean de Bonvillars and brother Guillaume de Grandson acted as much as an unofficial, or as Taylor puts it, 'personal deputy'.[79] That a change from Jean de Bonvillars to Guillaume de Grandson would have followed the former's demise at the siege of Dryslwyn in August 1287, is at least supported by a primary source.[80]

Our traveller of 1286 would have found three tremendous undertakings underway in north Wales that summer, and Caernarfon is perhaps the most interesting given its intended role as a palatial castle and attendant allusions to mythology. Much of the ultimate decoration, the three turrets above the Eagle Tower, the eagles upon them, the King's Gate and its statue and what would become known as the Queen's Gate, much of this would be yet to come to pass.

But even as the castles of north Wales came into being, Edward seemingly taking a hold of his new lands, events soon began to multiply that threatened to derail his reign. He had hoped the coming years would allow him to return to *outremer*, to crusade once more, and indeed Othon de Grandson did carry out a reconnaissance for him in 1291, only to find himself amidst the fall of Acre. A Scottish succession crisis would portend the troubles that would plague Edward north of the border, before Philippe IV of France would reignite the Capetian-Plantagenet wars by taking Gascony by subterfuge. But just before these national events, the winter of 1290 and summer of 1291 would bring more personal woes and see Edward losing both his wife and mother. The end came for Leonor on Saint Andrew's Eve, 28 November 1290, in the evening, the archives sadly record her passing, '*Decessus Regine*'.[81] They had been married for thirty-six years; we can begin to gauge Edward's grief, in that no government business (writs) were issued for three days – Edward's world as he'd known it was gone. Leonor's embalmed body was borne in great state from Harby to Westminster Abbey, its resting places en route would later be marked by beautiful memorial crosses. Queen Alianor de Provence had died on 24 June 1291. It had been a remarkable journey for the beautiful young girl from Provence, the woman whose marriage to Henry III of England had begun the deepening of the Anglo-Savoyard relationship for a century to come, A recent assessment of Alianor and Leonor comes from Lisa Hilton, who wrote: 'Eleanor of Castille is the better remembered of the two. Yet it is the first of the southern princesses [Alianor] who was the greater English Queen.'[82]

So troubles suddenly came to Edward in droves, the passing of his mother, his wife, a succession crisis in Scotland and his old enemies in Gwynedd and France stirring again. War with France forced Edward into calling up men from Wales. A tax had been levied to pay for the war, of which the final installment was due on 30 September 1294, and a muster called for the same day at Shrewsbury.[83] Wales was a tinderbox waiting to catch fire once more. An unguarded tinderbox too, its royal garrison's being denuded of men for the war effort – newly built Harlech being reduced to just nineteen men.[84]

Chapter Fourteen

What happened next is not easy to piece together. Reports are fragmentary or non-existent, but what we can say for certain is that they were a complete and total surprise to Edward. Firstly, reports began to filter to him that Geoffrey Clement, his deputy justiciar in south Wales, had been murdered. Clement had only recently been sent into Cardiganshire to recruit for the war in Gascony. Then came the terrible news that his new town and castle at Caernarfon had been overrun and set afire, and that the sheriff of Anglesey, Roger de Pulesdon had also been murdered, reputedly hanged from the eaves of his own house;[1] some said it was more a savage lynching.[2] The *Annales* of Nicholas Trevet tell us that 'that both town and castle are burned', he also goes on to say that 'a great multitude of the English' who 'without suspicion had come to the market and were slain within'.[3] The town walls of Caernarfon had been breached, the East Gate overrun, together with its exchequer that ran the three new counties that once made up Gwynedd. Amidst the shouting and cascading rolls of parchment and paper went the accounts, including most likely the building records for Caernarfon, but also Harlech, that are now lost to us. If we have difficulty piecing together the story of Maître Jacques and the Savoyards in Wales, then the Welsh Revolt of 1294 and French Revolution of 1789 are the biggest single culprits – a reminder that, whatever the merits, civil commotion destroys history. The very centre of royal administration in Caernarfon was destroyed, the exchequer seen by our traveller in 1286 was looted and burned, a later record from 1306 recounted, 'the rolls of the said exchequer … were burnt in the said castle of Carnervan during the war in Wales.'[4]

On Anglesey the large and prosperous town and trading port of Llanfaes was burned. It was the *maerdref* of the commote of Dindaethwy,[5] and had once been the very centre of Gwynedd, having thrived under Llywelyn Fawr and Llywelyn ap Gruffydd. It was the Monastery of Fagan the Little at Llanfaes that held the bones of Eleanor de Montfort, the late wife of Llywelyn ap Gruffydd. At besieged Flint the constable, Leye, had to burn the associated town himself, to deny it to the rebels surrounding the castle.[6] This was a common enough tactic in the period, to deny the besieging army shelter and material. The rebels were attempting to remove entirely the imposition on Gwynedd of Edward's direct rule. The royal castles at Flint, Rhuddlan, Conwy, Harlech, Criccieth and Castell y Bere were all under siege, as were the baronial castles of Builth, Ruthun, Denbigh, Mold and Hawarden. As at Caernarfon, where construction was not yet complete, so at Denbigh where the unfinished castle works of Henri de Lacy fell to Welsh rebels.

Ruthun, Mold and Hawarden soon fell too, but Harlech atop its rock and the strong walls of Flint, Rhuddlan and Conwy held firm. Flint and Rhuddlan held with garrisons of twenty-four horse, twenty-four crossbow and one hundred and twenty archers at one, and four horse, twelve crossbows and twenty-four archers at the other – Morris doesn't say at which but one assumes Rhuddlan had the greater number. There was also Master Richard brought in quickly from Chester to strengthen the walls and repair the artillery.[7] It was at Conwy, most likely, that Maître Jacques found shelter that autumn, as that was the base of his operations; his survival means he was unlikely to have been at the stricken Caernarfon. For the Savoyards a long way from home it was going to be a long winter. At Criccieth, Sir William Leyburn was holding out with a garrison of twenty-nine men plus another forty-one souls who were sheltering within the castle.[8] John Griffiths gave the number as a garrison of twenty men plus seven men from the town and three from Harlech joined by thirteen women and nineteen children.[9]

It was much the same picture along the coast at Harlech, where amongst those sheltering in the castle that winter would be Adam Boynard. Harlech had just a garrison of twenty men, just two-thirds of the original garrison,[10] under the command of the son of Robert de Staundon, Vivian de Staundon,[11] alongside them another eighteen men like Boynard, who had taken shelter within the stout walls, accompanied by nineteen women and twenty-six children.[12] Griffiths gave the number slightly higher as three small boys and four infants of the castle plus twenty-one children of the town, totalling twenty-eight children.[13] We have the names of those within the castle that winter, Adam Boynard is the first listed, but three Welsh names are also listed, so the 'Men of Harlech' of 1294/5, and the women and children too, were Savoyard, English and Welsh.[14] The Savoyards were now on the edge of the world and menaced by something a good deal more threatening than the Bishop of Sion.

In mid Wales, Aberystwyth Castle, where Clement's widow had fled since her husband's murder, was once more besieged. But unlike the Second Welsh War it was, this time, holding its own. Besieged for six weeks, at Builth Castle the defences held, its garrison of 'three heavy and three light horse, twenty crossbows and forty archers' proving resilient in defence.[15] John Giffard, one-time Montfortian and constable at Builth, who had been at Orewin Bridge and the denouement of Llywelyn ap Gruffydd, made no less than five attempts to fight his way to Builth to relieve the castle there, finally succeeding around 12 November with a force of ten knights, forty light cavalry and twenty foot soldiers.[16] On 23 November, from Worcester, Edward granted the power to Giffard 'to receive to the King's peace and will Welshmen of the land of Buelt and of adjoining parts wishing to come to the King's peace'.[17]

In the south, the castle at Kenfig near Bridgend, one of the earliest castles in Wales, was besieged and fell. Morlais fell, Caerffili and Llantrisant came under siege; there were reports that more than half of the town at Caerffili had been set to the torch. Morlais had been another unfinished and in a remote location, the Taff Gorge, and so defence proved impossible. At Caerffili, however, the sophisticated strong defences of Gilbert de Clare held firm. What Edward was hearing was a confused picture of a rapidly spreading forest fire, this or that castle under siege or having fallen, that this was not a locally based rebellion as that of Rhys ap Maredudd: this was a national rebellion. His patiently recovered or conquered Wales was on fire.

Edward had been in Worcester in the late summer, leaving Portsmouth on 21 August in search of funds and spiritual aid for his impending struggle with Philippe; he'd gone to Worcester seeking the aid of Wulfstan, the long-dead former Bishop of Worcester. His search for funds had been helped by at least the find of some £32,000 of crusade funds and the promise that the English Church was richer than he'd imagined. On 21 September, he met with the leading churchmen and, in the teeth of much opposition and after recourse to threatening them with being declared outlaws, he won a tax that amounted to half their money. The Riccardi system having now collapsed amid what amounted to a thirteenth century credit crunch, Edward was finding raising funds less than easy. As he'd said to the Church, was he not a wronged servant of the Church thwarted in his attempt to go to the aid of the Holy Land by a deceitful French king. As Edward turned his thoughts to how to extract funds from his barons, the first news of trouble to the west in Wales arrived at court. The money raised for the recovery of Gascony from Philippe would now be diverted to put up the Welsh fire.

On 15 October, writs went out to the magnates of the land to join the king at Worcester. The order went out to the 'sheriffs and bailiffs and subjects' of 'Nottingham, Derby, Lancaster, Westmorland, Cumberland and York' to join with Edward as 'the king is shortly setting forth to repress the malice and rebellion of certain Welshmen who have committed homicides, burnings, robberies and other enormities against his peace'.[18] Just over a week later, the order, on 22 October to the counties of Shropshire and Staffordshire, and on 22 November to the men of Gloucestershire, demonstrated that this was a widespread mobilization.[19] The scribe in Westminster was issuing so many safe-conduct passes to those joining the king's colours that he didn't record even half of those taking part, Henri de Lacy, Earl of Lincoln, for example, heading for his castle at Denbigh so fast he wasn't recorded. But amongst those actually recorded were Jean de Warenne, Earl of Surrey, Walter de Huntercombe having returned from the Isle of Man, Roger Bigod, Earl of Norfolk, Humphrey de Bohun, Earl of Hereford, Guillaume de Valence, Earl of Pembroke and John de Havering.[20] On 20 October, the order had gone out to divert supplies from the Gascon campaign for use in Wales; Gascony and Philippe IV would have to wait – one war at a time.[21] On 12 November, Parliament stung by the rebellion granted Edward a tenth of all movables.[22]

In early November Henri de Lacy, Earl of Lincoln, was indeed in much haste to rush to Denbigh and his castle, still under construction, there. He didn't wait for a supporting royal army as Trevet tells us:[23] 'When in the day of Saint Martin [11

November], near the town of Denbigh, the Welsh met the Earl of Lincoln with great power, and when they had joined battle, they thrust him away.'[24]

The unfinished works at Denbigh had, indeed, fallen, whilst the eastern curtain and towers were still under construction, something of a defensible structure had been raised in the southern and western defences, supported by the town walls, but this had not proven strong enough yet to withhold Madog's assault.[25] Though defeated, the chastened Henri de Lacy lived to fight another day, and would return to Wales, but with the main royal army. Meanwhile, the plight of the besieged Castell y Bere in mid Wales was directly addressed by Edward on 18 October: the Earl of Arundel, Richard FitzAlan, was to organize a relief expedition 'to supply such help and work as he can ... that the King's castle of Bere shall be furnished with victuals ... and so that the King's men therein shall be aided and saved by all means that are possible'.[26] On 27 October, he was further ordered to join the castle's constable, Robert FitzWalter, who'd been at Portsmouth preparing to sail for Gascony, at Shrewsbury 'on the morrow of Martlemas [Martinmas]', 12 November.

Edward had instructed FitzWalter 'by word of mouth' to mount the expedition 'to succour and furnish the King's castle of Bere, the safe-guarding of which ... the King desires with all his heart'.[27] Enjoined in this enterprise were also Bogo de Knovill and Roger LeStrange, the latter to make the expedition an Anglo-Welsh undertaking by addition of men from Powys. The long-standing loyalty of men from Powys to the Crown is suggested, as holding to some extent, by the order given to Roger LeStrange on 28 October 'to receive into the King's peace all Welshmen of the land of Powys wishing to come into the King's peace'.[28]

Robert FitzWalter was the only son of Sir Walter FitzRobert of Woodham Walter in Essex, a descendant of William Longespée, 3rd Earl of Salisbury, illegitimate son of Henry II. FitzWalter was new to the job, having only recently, on 28 June 1292,[29] taken over from Joan de Turberville, widow of Hugh de Turberville[30] who'd held the post since the departure of Huntercombe and had fought alongside Jean de Bonvillars at the siege of Dryslwyn in 1287. What became of FitzWalter's relief expedition is unknown, but we do know he survived and is noted in later service with the king.

One can imagine the plight of the 'King's men' at Bere as they looked out over the remote Dysynni Valley at the foot of Cader Idris that October as they were besieged, praying for help to come. Morris thought the subsequent silence betokened the defenders of Bere being saved.[31] Taylor[32] and others since were less sure. It is more than likely that help did not come, and if FitzWalter ever arrived it was likely too late, and Castell y Bere was almost certainly taken – certainly the settlement close by was burned but what became of its beleaguered defenders is not known. The 1952 excavation of the site found late-thirteenth-century pottery associated with charred timbers, thought to be the roof of the well house.[33] W. W. E. Wynne, when writing up the first excavations of the site in 1861, said that 'this castle was destroyed, probably (if one may judge from the great quantity of charcoal found in the ruins) by fire'.[34] Buildings in the castle courtyard had been destroyed, together with the well house, also in the castle courtyard. It's difficult to reconcile this burning and destruction with the castle's survival.[35] What is certain is that 1294 marked the end for the Castell y Bere: it was never thereafter reoccupied, falling into the dramatic ruins that remain.

As a footnote to the concluded story of Castell Y Bere, we should pause for thought at the plight of one-time constable Walter de Huntercombe, listed earlier joining the king's army. Before taking possession of the Isle of Man for Edward, Huntercombe had had built for himself a new chamber at Bere, and been recompensed by the exchequer £31 for it, over £21,000 in today's money. However, Huntercombe complained that he was still owed a further twenty-five marks, again around £21,000 in today's money. The problem was that his request for reimbursement had, it seems, been burned during the Welsh attack on the exchequer at Caernarfon and we find Huntercombe still in 1306 seeking repayment for his loss.[36]

Meanwhile, also on 15 October, a summons was sent to Edmund Crouchback to also join the counsel at Worcester and then that his 'men with horses, armour and other necessaries shall be ready the Sunday following at Chester'.[37] Edmund, along with Henri de Lacy, Earl of Lincoln, had been under orders to lead the main English army to Gascony. Similarly summoned that day, amongst others, were Guillaume de Valence, Roger Bigod and Humphrey de Bohun, except that their men should report to Brecon.[38] Listed amongst those travelling from Westminster on 24 October is Othon de Grandson's cousin, Pierre de Champvent: since at least 1290 in Edward's household as a steward, and erstwhile steward to Edward's father Henry,[39] he had, the previous year, been promoted to one of the key English offices of state, that of King's Chamberlain.[40] Despite Grandson's absence on his long travels in the Holy Land, Armenia and Italy, there would be a key *famille de Grandson* presence in the English army setting out to quell the rebellion.[41] That the coastal castles were besieged is likely evidenced by an order to provide them with fresh victuals by sea given to John de Havering on 25 October.[42]

According to the chronicler Guisborough: 'sedition was excited by "two names" Madog and Morgan.'[43] So who were Madog and Morgan? Like Rhys ap Maerdudd, the lately executed rebel of 1287, Madog was an unlikely rebel who, if perhaps better handled by the Crown, might not have been a rebel at all. He was the son of Llywelyn ap Maerdudd, the last Lord of Meirionnydd, who had been forced into exile in England by Llywelyn ap Gruffydd after the Battle of Derwin Bridge of June 1255. It is possible even that young Madog had been born in England, making him an English-Welsh rebel. In exile, Madog's father had received financial support from Henry III in his efforts to recover his patrimony in Meirionnydd from the rising star of the Prince of Wales. It appears then that Llywelyn ap Maredudd had made his peace with the prince when he fell in battle in 1263, given the warmth of the Welsh chroniclers description of his denouement and that payments from the royal exchequer had ceased in 1262.[44] But the patrimony of Meirionnydd remained unrecovered, which is why, during the First Welsh War, Madog ap Llywelyn had sided with the king against Gwynedd. Indeed Edward does seem to have suggested that any postwar settlement might include the return of Meirionnydd to the man described in the English archives as the Lord of Meirionnydd.[45] However, as we saw earlier, the Treaty of Aberconewey left Gwynedd, including Meirionnydd, in the hands of Llywelyn ap Gruffydd, still styled Prince of Wales. So Welsh dissatisfaction with the postwar settlement would not be restricted to Dafydd ap Gruffydd but extended to Madog ap Llywelyn too. In 1278, Madog had indeed appeared before the king's justices to seek recovery of Meirionnydd from Llywelyn.[46] Following the Second Welsh War, with Meirionnydd now incorporated into the new county of Merionethshire, Madog was compensated with lands on the isle of Anglesey, at Lledwigan Llan near Llangefni.[47] Madog's rebellion began in Anglesey, probably with the sacking of Llanfaes and its church, potentially confirmed by the annalist in Chester, who wrote: 'Madog ap Maredudd began war in Anglesey.'[48] That the annalist mistakenly attributes Madog's father as Maredudd and not Llywelyn (Maredudd was actually Madog's grandfather), shouldn't necessarily obscure the thought that Madog's rebellion began on Anglesey. That would accord with Madog's having been granted land there and the early, and apparently unexpected, calamity that befell nearby Caernarfon. Indeed, the two murderers of Roger de Pulesdon, Grono of Twrcelyn and Trahern ap Bleddyn of Talybolion, were both men of Anglesey.[49]

Morgan ap Maerdudd was the son of Maerdudd ap Gruffydd, the Lord of Caerleon, of Machen and of Maud until he had been, twenty years earlier, dispossessed by Red Gilbert, Gilbert de Clare, 7th Earl of Gloucester and ruler of Glamorgan and much of south Wales. Caerleon had been a Roman legionary base of antiquity and indeed its stone had been surrendered for use in the castle built earlier in the century by William Marshal. Castel Machen or Maerdudd had been built by Maeredydd Gethin, Lord of Gwynllwg, before about 1201. The castle had been used as a retreat by Morgan ap Hywell, also Lord of Gwynllwg, after he had lost his main stronghold of Caerleon. It then passed temporarily to Gilbert Marshal, Earl of Pembroke, in 1236, when he captured the castle and held it for a while. In 1248 the castle passed to Morgan ap Hywell's grandson Maredudd, father of Morgan ap Maredudd, before being taken by Red Gilbert de Clare. Such was the complicated taking and retaking of patrimony common to the Welsh Marches, at one time belonging to the Lords of Gwynllwg, then the Marshals, then the Clares and back again. Morgan had sought to recover his patrimony by legal means, first from Llywelyn ap Gruffydd and then from the Crown, in both instances unsuccessfully. During the Second Welsh War he'd sided with Dafydd ap Gruffydd but always maintained his issue was with Gilbert de Clare not with the Crown. It's not surprising that Morgan might resort to warfare when legal means had been denied him.

Responding to the wildfire engulfing Wales, Edward organized his available forces into three, not unlike the First and Second Welsh wars: a northern army to strike once more toward Gwynedd to relieve his newly built but besieged castles, a midland army to strike into mid Wales and lastly a southern army to move into south Wales. The order to assemble the northern Army had, as we saw, gone out from Westminster on 15 October and resulted in Sir Hugh de Cressingham[50] amassing the following numbers awaiting the king at Chester on 1 December.[51]

	Constables	Foot Soldiers
Derbyshire	11	2,474
Cumberland	19	1,900
West Riding of Yorkshire	13	1,300
Yorkshire	37	3,700
City of York	8	800
Nottinghamshire	3	2,340
Lancashire	25	2,540
Westmorland	8	855

For a total of 124 constables and 15,909 men, no doubt Chester, with armed rebellion at its doors, was glad of the influx of men. In addition there were the garrisons holding Flint and Rhuddlan, mostly centred on the latter much larger castle, which from payroll records Edwards described as 'considerable'.[52] The midlands force, down at Montgomery, drawn from Shropshire and Staffordshire, had now grown to some 112 constables and 11,460 foot soldiers.[53] In charge of the Montgomery force was William de Beauchamp, 9th Earl of Warwick[54] and High Sheriff of Worcestershire, a close friend of Edward's and a veteran of the First Welsh War. He was the son of William III de Beauchamp, who'd acquired Warwick through marriage to heiress Isabel de Maudit. The Beauchamp family had acquired their seat of Elmsley Castle in the twelfth century, the name meaning 'beautiful field' in French. The family crossed to England from Normandy with the conqueror in 1066 and are not to be confused with families of the same name but different Norman origins in Bedfordshire and Somerset. Beauchamp would soon fight the critical battle of the Madog rebellion.

A smaller force, originally summonsed to Cardiff[55], but later mustering at Carmarthen[56] to operate in south Wales, under Edward's half-uncle, Guillaume de Valence, Earl of Pembroke and Roger Bigod, 5th Earl of Norfolk, was made up as follows:[57]

	Constables	Foot Soldiers
Wiltshire	5	500
Somerset	5	500
Herefordshire	14	1,400
Gloucestershire & Forest of Dean	16	1,600

So, with three royal armies, a not-insignificant 31,369 men, a large army by English medieval standards, Edward was taking the rebellion very seriously. But it was not until 5 December 1294 that Edward reached Chester, arriving with cavalry, some 350 lances, to join the mustered infantry.[58] The next day Edward heard Mass at the church of Saint Werburg, now the cathedral.[59]

The Chester chronicler gives us the date of Edward's move into Wales, and his route. It wasn't the usual coastal route by way of Flint; no, this time the king 'on the morrow he set out for Wrexham'.[60] The army split, Edward taking around 5,000 men, the remaining 10,000 making directly for Rhuddlan, such is apparent from claims for payment of the soldiers from wardrobe accounts.[61] Wrexham lay some fifteen miles (twenty-four kilometres) to the south-west of Chester in the newly created Lordship of Bromfield and Yale, Jean de Warenne, the Earl of Surrey's land, but formerly (until as recently as 1282) the Welsh *cantref* of Maelor in what was the lands of Madog ap Gruffydd in Powys Fadog. Less than ten miles (sixteen kilometres) south of Wrexham lay the king's manor of Overton by the River Dee, established by royal charter as recently as 1292 and with some fifty-six taxpayers living there. Overton, visited by Edward in the aftermath of the Second Welsh War, had its origins in a mention in the Domesday Book as a manor and had acquired a castle by the mid-twelfth century when it had been the fief of Madog ap Maerdudd, the last prince of a unified Powys. However, it had been an early target for Madog's rebellion (on 3 January, Edward would issue a pardon to a Madog Goch and his brother Nynnyaw for 'lately burning the King's manor at Overton'.)[62] In 1286, Edward had granted Overton to his late wife, Leonor, so its 'burning' would be personal. Perhaps seeing what was left of Overton was one of Edward's reasons for routing by way of Wrexham, but the primary reason was the route it opened to Clwyd, and the rebels at Ruthun and Denbigh. So, having left Chester on 7 December, Edward had camped in the environs of Wrexham and Overton from 11 December.[63]

Meanwhile in Gwynedd, Madog was now styling himself Prince of Wales, the title last held by the brothers, Llywelyn and Dafydd ap Gruffydd. In a later minor land grant issued in December 1294 Madog uses the title 'Prince of Wales, Lord of Snowdonia'.[64] For Edward it may have seemed that the many-headed Hydra of Gwynedd had grown yet another head to strike at him.

Breaking camp on 15 December from Wrexham, the army turned and headed west further into Wales, following the old drover's road through the Llandegla Forest and by way of the village of Llandegla, crossing the River Alyn before entering the Vale of Clwyd. The small village took its name from the Welsh Saint Tecla, the small church there attached to the abbey at Valle Crucis which would lend its window design to the church at Moudon in the Pays de Vaud. An odd tradition, in a land of odd traditions, was connected with St Tecla's Well, a spring in a field close to the church. Sufferers of what was known as *Clwyf Tecla*, or St Tecla's disease, washed themselves in the well after sunset and walked round it three times, leaving an offering of four pence, afterwards spending the night in the church – it's not recorded if any of the passing army of Englishmen availed themselves of the opportunity. By 18 December, the army was into the valley of the River Clwyd and camped at Derwen-Llanerch just five miles (eight kilometres) short of Ruthun.

As Edward camped by the Clwyd, the first supplies organized by John de Havering were making landfall at besieged Harlech on 18 December. Along with some provisions, welcome reinforcements of seven extra men for the garrison were able to be landed, welcome since two of the defenders had already been killed.[65] It's not difficult to imagine the relief, weeks before Christmas, of Adam Boynard and the garrison at Harlech in seeing the white sails appearing on the horizon: deliverance was at hand. The besieged garrison at Criccieth would have to wait until January for their own supplies to be landed.[66] The resupply by sea of besieged Harlech and Criccieth are the fruits of a lesson learned well by Edward during the Montfortian wars with his father, and the way in which his great-uncle Pierre de Savoie's castle at Pevensey had similarly resisted a year long siege.

Meanwhile for Edward's army, once into the Vale of Clwyd, their goal was first Ruthun, in Dyffryn Clwyd, and its castle, followed by Denbigh, in Rhufoniog, and its castle, the scene, nearly a month earlier, of Henri de Lacy's rebuff at the hands of the Welsh rebels. The burned timbers at Denbigh surrounding the unfinished castle, no doubt a reminder that the castles of north Wales could only provide shelter when brought to completion. The Welshman from nearby Llannerch was perhaps right when, before and conceivably with knowledge of the rebellion, he'd cursed in court and threatened, 'By the body of Christ … before the middle of the month the constable and other English will hear such rumours that they will not wish to come again to Wales.'[67] Henri de Lacy would have to renew his efforts at Denbigh, to first repair and then construct the remainder of the castle. The destruction at Denbigh is perhaps evidenced that the army camped a few miles to the south at Llech in Kinmersh, the latter being an anglicization of Cinmerch now styled Nghinmeirch. The army was passing through a land of ancient wells; here they passed Saint Dyfog's well. As Edward and his army marched by Denbigh thoughts must have turned to what they'd find at Caernarfon. It took Edward two weeks to subdue Dyffryn Clwyd and Rhufoniog, but by around 23 December he'd marched on past Henilan and the cathedral at Saint Asaph and reached Rhuddlan and the sea, his forces reunited, his flank again protected. Indeed, Reginald de Grey had sent some elements of his force upstream from Rhuddlan to meet the king's army heading downstream.[68] We have been able to fairly precisely follow Edward's army from Chester to Rhuddlan by following the place and dates of patents issued in his name and preserved in the Calendar of Patent Rolls.[69]

Leaving Henri de Lacy behind at Rhuddlan, Edward quickly moved on to Conwy for the feast of Christmas where he, no doubt, found Guillaume de Cicon, his garrison and Maître Jacques sheltering within the strong walls of Conwy. Trevet recounted that 'the King of England held the feast of the Nativity of our Lord at Aberconewey'.[70] The *Perfeddwlad* would have appeared to have been considered reasonably pacified once more, since the new Archbishop of Canterbury travelled to Conwy to meet Edward. Robert Winchelsey had been the Chancellor of Oxford University when the previous incumbent, John Peckham, had died in 1292 – he'd been elected bishop without input from either Edward or the pope, who one imagines had plenty on their plates. Winchelsey travelled to Rome for his consecration, which Celestine V performed on 12 September 1294. During his return journey up the *Via Francigena*, he learned of the many events since he'd left England.

The Hagnaby chronicler, at this point, suggests something that is not recorded elsewhere: he writes that 1,000 Welshmen now surrender themselves to Edward just before Christmas of 1294, and were offered pardon provided they agreed to provide military service in Gascony. This, the chronicler maintains, they agreed to do, but when they returned to Madog, to whom they'd agreed to capture for Edward, he responded with such an impassioned speech that they once more returned to his cause.[71] The speech is missing from the chronicle, but the response of the thousands of Welshmen was '*se malentes mori in terra sua quam alibi*', that they preferred to die in their own country rather than elsewhere.[72] Coming from the chronicles of an English monk in Lincolnshire, this has a ring of plausibility about it. If it was your lot to die in battle, men, then as now, would choose to die defending their home villages rather than the lands of some far-off liege lord, and in this regard, they were no different than the reluctant Englishman called to fight in Gascony from Cambridgeshire.

Following Christmas and New Year festivities at Conwy Castle,[73] hosted by the constable Guillaume de Cicon, Edward set out for the west on, most likely, 7 January 1295 and is recorded at Bangor[74] on the same date.[75] The Wardrobe *Book of Prests*[76] suggests that the army reached as far west as Nefyn[77] on the Llyn peninsula by 13 January, where Edward had once held an Arthurian tournament. But this time there would be no fun and games. He was now deep in what we might now call 'enemy territory' and more vulnerable than he knew. Without governmental records we must fall back on the incomplete accounts of the chroniclers. Trevet tells us that Edward lost his baggage train to Welsh attack, and had to fall back on Conwy where, for a while, he was besieged and had to resort to drinking '*aquam melle*', water with honey.[78] Sure enough the *Book of Prests* records him back at Conwy on 21 January.[79] Guisborough also gives us the water-with-honey story, adding bread to the diet, which lends it credibility, but also adds that winter floods were adding to Edward's mobility issues.[80] But the chronicler also adds the anecdote that Edward was offered the last barrel of wine for himself, but declined it, offering to share it, declaring, 'All necessary should be shared in common' because 'I am the origin and cause of this.' If the anecdote is true, and it has the ring of truth about it, that would indicate that the ill-fated move to Bangor and Nefyn had indeed been Edward's idea.[81] Morris dated the loss of what he called Edward's 'commissariat train', to either 9 or 10 January, before paraphrasing Guisborough's 'enduring a Welsh siege' by adding that Edward had to 'submit to the indignity of a siege.'[82] The siege seems to have been a combination of Madog's forces occupying much of Gwynedd to the south and west of Conwy, and the winter storms and flooding that prevented resupply from across the river and by sea, the very route that the castle had been sited to exploit. So, there was Edward, and the Savoyards, the constable of Conwy, the by-now-knighted Sir Guillaume de Cicon,[83] and the by-now-also-knighted Sir Pierre de Champvent,[84] and possibly Maître Jacques, holed up in their new castle by the Conwy, in the teeth of a Welsh winter and surrounded by a hostile population. We can make too much, perhaps, of his plight: there wasn't much chance of being overwhelmed by Madog's forces. The Dunstable chronicler was sure the Welsh had had the worst of the fighting,[85] but nonetheless it was a galling experience, since Edward no doubt ruminated that he'd expected to be recovering Gascony by now, not shivering in north Wales. He was drinking water with honey rather than Saint Émilion.

Suffering alongside Edward that winter was his Savoyard chamberlain, Pierre de Champvent, who learned well the advantages of stout castle walls. Following the siege he would later return to the Pays de Vaud and undertake, with his brother Guillaume, extensive works at the Château de Champvent. That the Vaudois castle overlooking Grandson and Bonvillars bears Welsh hallmarks (Figure 3.3) comes as little surprise. It seems that the architectural cross-fertilization betwixt Savoy and the British Isles began to flow in both directions.[86]

But next, both Trevet and Guisborough possibly mislead us, and countless historians, including the otherwise excellent Morris, by next telling us that, once the waters subside, Conwy is relieved by the Earl of Warwick, but without giving us many details. Morris took this to mean that the decisive engagement of the Welsh wars, the final battle, took place in the Conwy Valley. Has the Earl of Warwick ridden all the way up from mid Wales to relieve Conwy? No. Thankfully for historians the chronicler at Worcester gives us the name of the battlefield: 'Meismeidoc'. Edwards, writing in 1924, was able to pinpoint the correct location, Maes Madog, now identified more accurately as Maes Moydog. He pointed to *Meis* as a rendering of the Welsh word for field, Maes, and Moydog as the parish of Moydog, still today the site of farms Moydog Fawr, Moydog Fach and Moydog Uchaf. The name stretches back to the thirteenth century in the form of M'dok, Moydok and Moydauk.[87] If Trevet helped misguide us to the location, his description of the battlefield as '*in quondam planate inter duo nemora*', that is on a 'plain between two woods' does seem to fit with Maes Moydog even today.

The Worcester annalist wrote:

5 March, Guillaume de Beauchamp, Earl of Warwick fought a war with the Welshmen in the place which is called in their tongue Meismeidoc; and they were laid low, of seven hundred noble men, in addition to the men who were drowned and fatally wounded. However, their Prince,[88] Madog ap Llywelyn, dishonourably, barely escaped.[89]

Morris also misidentified the date of the battle as 'a day or two before 24 January',[90] but the Worcester chronicler clearly sets the date of the last battle of the Welsh wars as 5 March 1295.

Madog, like Llywelyn before him, had been drawn to mid Wales, and like the former prince it would be his downfall. The Earl of Warwick had been at Montgomery since December – it seems that he got wind of Madog's move south-westward from Gwynedd in February, and accordingly moved his army to Oswestry. On 4 March, Warwick received very specific intelligence of Madog's movements and moved back to Montgomery and thence to Maes Moydog to meet the Welsh advance. Warwick's army had dwindled in size since December, and now counted 119 mounted bannerets, knights and cavalry, some 26 constables and just 2,689 foot soldiers plus a small number of crossbowmen and archers. Madog's number is unknown but thought to be smaller. Amongst the number of Warwick's army was Robert FitzWalter, and now was the time for him to take his revenge for the fall of Castell y Bere. Richard FitzAlan, Earl of Arundel, husband to the Savoyard Alésia Di Saluzzo, was another at Maes Moydog seeking retribution for Bere. Also with Warwick was William de Pole, son of Gruffydd ap Gwenwynwyn, Powys as ever ranged against Gwynedd. The Mortimers were represented by William de Mortimer, the brother of Edmund, 2nd Baron Mortimer.[91] The foot soldiers were mostly men of Shropshire defending what they would have seen as an impending invasion of their county by men bent on pillage. Morris saw in the battle the genesis of English tactics of archery against tightly packed formations, in this case spearmen[92] – but this is now thought less likely.[93]

What is certain is that Madog was on the receiving end of a crushing defeat; if we take the Worcester chronicler at his word and compare with the known reductions in Warwick's payroll after the battle, we can see that the Welsh dead outnumbered the English by between seven and ten to one. That many of Madog's men were drowned, according to the Worcester chronicler, suggests that the battle ended in a rout and chaotic flight pursued by Warwick's forces. The River Vyrnwy and its tributary the Banwy to the north of the battle site, swollen by the known weather of that winter, is where many found their end. The Hagnaby chronicler, likely drawing from an eyewitness wrote: 'the Welshmen held their ground well, and they were the best and bravest Welsh that anyone has seen.'[94] Warwick's tactics were crucial in the overwhelming nature of the defeat, most likely by the encirclement of his enemy coupled with use of elite crossbowmen and some archery.

To the west, the sieges of Harlech and Conwy were concluding. On 22 January, at Conwy, Robert de Staundon had received by hand £100 for provisions and arms to be sent to beleaguered Harlech.[95] In this regard, Richard de Havering was sent across to Ireland to organize supplies,[96] and as a result four Irish ships delivered much needed provisions and arms to Harlech and Criccieth. On 31 March and 6 April to Harlech and 3, 6 and 11 April to Criccieth. The *Godyer* of Rosponte, County Wexford, was one such ship, the crews from Waterford and Wexford protected by no less than eighteen crossbowmen and three archers – they weren't taking any chances. Corn, herring, salt fish, sea coal, canvas, cloth, wax and tallow, along with crossbow quarrels, bows, arrows, utensils and footwear came across the sea from Ireland,[97] followed by wheat and oats from Lancashire[98] For Adam Boynard the long winter of fear within the walls of Harlech was over; the castle he'd helped to build had stood firm.[99]

On 6 March, the day after Maes Moydog, as Edward remained at Conwy building up supplies for his next move, an English army under Reginald de Grey, a column made up of cavalry and infantry, set out from Rhuddlan in the direction of Penllyn,[100] midway between Criccieth and Harlech castles. It is not recorded but it is almost certainly Grey and his army that Adam Boynard and the beleaguered shelterers within Harlech would have first seen coming down along the coast from the north – salvation. In addition to relieving both Criccieth and Harlech, it's most likely that Grey was hunting down Madog ap Llywelyn. An undated letter attributed to him, and likely to have been for Edward, gives some detail of the manhunt underway in Ardudwy to the south and east of Harlech.[101] Acting on intelligence, he thought he'd located Madog in a wood *'en le plus fort de tut Ardodewey'* or 'in the strongest place in Ardudwy'. But Madog evaded capture; he would eventually surrender himself to John de Havering in July and spend the rest of his days in the Tower of London.

Edward left Conwy on 9 April, but it was not at first to travel back to England, or indeed to south Wales where the submission of Morgan ap Maredudd lay, but westward once more to the island of Anglesey, as the Chester annalist recalled, 'the Lord King, Edward, took Anglesey and subjected it to himself.'[102] He had another castle in mind, and this would be the crowning glory of his reign, and indeed the apogee of medieval castle design.

Chapter Fifteen

etween 21 and 25 November 1294, Edward had gathered his nobles for a
council of war at Worcester, and it's most likely that it was then a decision
was taken to build a new castle on Anglesey. We don't know whether
Maître Jacques was at Worcester with the king: his presence was unlikely and not
recorded. Carpenters and ditch diggers needed for preparatory work had already
been brought to Chester, receiving pay on 6 December.[1] On 7 December, Sir
Henry Latham[2] was ordered to sail for Anglesey with a force of 500 men to be
carried in twelve ships. It's possible to conclude that, along with taking the Welsh
breadbasket of Anglesey, that Edward was making safe the future castle site and
preparing to build.[3]

The last reference to Maître Jacques had been his time as Constable at Harlech
castle, which had ended on 28 December 1293. Assuming his handover of the
castle in the first weeks of 1294, he disappears from the records for the turbulent
year of 1294, so we cannot be certain of his whereabouts during the outbreak of the
Madog rebellion. He next appears in the written record on 7 February 1295, when
given money to arrange for the purchase of material for scaffolding and pontoons
on the Wirral peninsula, to build another bridge across the Menai. The *Book of
Prests* describes the payment of £8 as 'by their own hands at Conwy 7 February', so
he was at Conwy, at least on that day, and therefore possible he'd spent Christmas
with the king and endured the siege.[4] It's possible that the genesis of the castle to
come may well have transmitted itself from Edward to Jacques during the long
hours of the siege. It also means that the king had the ability to send Jacques to
the Wirral and Chester by sea (probably) or by land across the river, on or around
7 February, and so the waters must have receded enough by this point to enable
communication.

Not quite a month later, on 4 March, Edward is giving Maître Jacques a 'hurry
up' as a 'clerk of the chancery' is dispatched 'hastily' to the Wirral, asking Jacques
to bring pontoons to Conwy with all speed – kings, and certainly not this king,
were never the most patient of men.[5] The scale of the requirement for wood was
later shown by a subsequent inquisition, showing that Masters Jacques and Richard
had together ordered the felling of no less than 2,300 trees belonging to the abbot
of Saint Werburgh's at Chester and others at Huntingdon, Cheveley, Eccleston,
Mollington and Saughall.[6] The felling of over 2,000 trees, and subsequent
shipment from Chester to Conwy, was no small undertaking.

Then, a few days later, on 11 March, a further payment is recorded to Maître
Jacques for the purchase of timber to build a bridge – there will indeed be another

bridge of boats to stride across the Menai, helping to facilitate the construction of the new castle on Anglesey.[7] At this point we have payments of wages to Maître Jacques that may reveal the name and origin of his clerk. On 31 March he received £5 and two marks 'by hand' from a man identified as *'Colinhij'* or Colin. There is no family name given, and later he is identified further as *'Colino clerico'*[8] or Colin the Clerk. Taylor, by extraordinary attention to archival detail, identified that there had been a *'Colini'* in the service of Philippe de Savoie back in 1271–2 in Savoy.[9] Joining the dots, he drew attention to *'Collard clericus'* in the accounts a decade earlier for the castle at Harlech in the company of *'Giletus'*, Giles de Saint Georges, and Adam Boynard. Quite plausibly, in the light of all we know of Jacques bringing a coterie of Savoyards to Wales with him, it is not an unreasonable suggestion, though ultimately unprovable without a family name, that the clerk of Jacques de Saint Georges was a Savoyard called Colin, previously with him in Savoy.[10]

Another week passes until another payment to Maître Jacques, on 8 April, this time for stonemasons' tools, iron and boards to go along the coast to Bangor, on the far bank across from Anglesey. Activity was growing, a new castle was in the offing.[11] On 10–11 April, Edward and Maître Jacques crossed the Menai to Anglesey, and tents were pitched at Llanfaes where the recent rebellion had begun.[12] We can trace the genesis of the castle in the *Book of Prests*, for just over a week later, on 17 April, the castle is first referred to, but is as yet unnamed – it's described as the *'novo castro … apud Lannuais'*.[13] Maître Jacques has apparently now crossed to Anglesey and has begun castle-building operations at Llanfaes.

The very next day, 18 April, the new castle has a name, *'Beau Mareis'*. It will be the castle of the beautiful marshes.[14] There has been a trend in recent times to diminish the role of Maître Jacques in the creation of the castles of north Wales, some of which we have dealt with earlier in this book. At Flint the input of Master Richard is touted, at Rhuddlan there was almost certainly a contribution from Master Bertram, at Conwy a definite role for Jean de Bonvillars, at Harlech the unlikely idea, yet unproven, that there was an earlier castle on the rock there, and at Caernarfon the work of Master Walter of Hereford has been championed. It seems ironic that British writers, of late, have appeared to bend over backwards in seeking to lessen the role of the Savoyard mason, whereas at the Château de Grandson and elsewhere in what was Savoy, French and Italians are keen to find a role for him in building their castles despite a lack of primary sources – nativism does indeed seem to be in vogue. But whatever the dubious merits of some of these theories, the castle at Beaumaris is very well documented from the beginning, as the work of *'Magistro Jacobo de Sancto Georgio'* – and it will be the apogee of thirteenth-century castle design.

Walter of Winchester was appointed as Clerk of the Works, and again we see the relationship, that Naef had misunderstood at Yverdon, between Pierre Mainier and Maître Jean, that between the *'clerico'* and the *'Maître d'ouvre'*. As we noted earlier Knoop and Jones had spelt out the relationship: 'Normally on important works ... a master mason and a treasury official ... were associated.'[15] In the case of Beaumaris it would be *'Magistro Jacobo de Sancto Georgio'* and *'Waltero de Winton' clerico'*.[16]

To hold Anglesey was to hold Gwynedd, as the low-lying and fertile island was the breadbasket of the principality. Successive English kings had sought to take possession of the island to bend recalcitrant princess of Gwynedd to their will. Beaumaris wouldn't be the first castle attempted on the island: Hugh d'Avranches and his Normans had built Castell Aberlleiniog some two miles distant, but it had succumbed to siege in 1094 and its defenders put to the sword. Edward had learned well from the year-long siege of Pevensey in his youth: castles by the sea could be resupplied. This lesson had been brought home to him personally by the events of the recent rebellion: the new castle on Anglesey would be built by the sea. This meant an entirely flat site on the 'beautiful marshes', difficult ground with no advantage offered by natural defences like the rock at Harlech. But for Maître Jacques this would be a return to the problems encountered during the building of his first castle, on marshy wet flat ground at Yverdon by the Lac de Neuchâtel.[17] If Yverdon was his Alpha then Beaumaris would be his Omega: he'd learned much about building castles in the thirty-five years since he'd laboured with his father at Yverdon. Maître Jacques would pour all those years of castle-building into Beaumaris; it would be his last major project and a fitting epitaph to a long career. It was now time for the Savoyard 'ugly duckling' to build a 'swan' by the Menai.[18]

In the coming six months Master Walter would receive the unprecedented sum of £6,736[19] for the works at Beaumaris, nearly £5 million in today's money. The primary reason for the considerable cost of the new castle was the paucity of resources on the island with which to build a castle, particularly the want of an adequate supply of stone. The shipment costs for Beaumaris were higher than Conwy, Harlech and Caernarfon had been throughout their construction a decade earlier. This would have to be shipped across to the island at great expense and labour. The first task was, as always, to make the site safe, which required the digging of ditches and earthworks around the future castle.[20] These last works alone required 1,800 *fossatores* or ditch diggers and cost £1,468.12s – just over an incredible £1 million.

Edward stayed on Anglesey until 6 May, and from there he made a royal progress through the once-more-pacified Wales: firstly Bangor, then Llanrug, as nearby Caernarfon was not yet safe. By 11 May he'd reached Dolgellau, thence onward by way of Talybont and Towyn [Tywyn] into south-west Wales and Cardigan and Newcastle Emlyn.[21] There is no record of his having stayed at Harlech, but this would have been on his line of march, and a visit may be alluded to in payment for subsequent work at Harlech to strengthen its defences, which would in turn point to Edward's continuing interest in his castles. Following the Madog rebellion siege, it was decided to complete the outer walling at Harlech, to wall in the northern base of the castle rock. The constable, Robert de Staundon appears to have carried out this work, a 1305 payment pertaining to which may indicate Edward's ordering of construction during his progress south (Figure 2.8).[22]

Once into Glamorgan, he was at Merthyr Tydfil on 14 and 15 June, and took the submission of Morgan ap Maredudd – Morgan had been at pains to say his quarrel had been with Gilbert de Clare and not the Crown.[23] The rebellion was over. Wales could now be considered pacified once more, and so he began to head back to Beaumaris. 17 June found him at his appanage castle of Builth, the 22nd at Welshpool, near the site of the late battle at Maes Moydog, before arriving back at Conwy by 30 June. On 7 July, Edward made his first stay at Caernarfon since the rebellion and sacking of the town, repairs by now advancing to such an extent as the castle being able again to accommodate the king. It would be on 10 July 1295 that Edward would cross the Menai again to Beaumaris to meet with Maître Jacques once more and survey the works now underway.[24]

The records of the time are normally the stuff of the accountant not the poet. We have, for example, the record that Beaumaris in this time consumed 2,428 tons of sea coal to help with the production of lime mortar, 640 quarters of charcoal, 3,277 boards, cords ropes and chains, 8 loads of lead, 160 pounds of tin, 314 bends of iron and of course a colossal weight of nails – 105,000 of them.[25] But Edward's visit that July has thrown up a more poetic image, and not one normally associated with the Edward Longshanks of popular imagination. Edward stayed at Beaumaris this time, rather than Llanfaes, since thatched wooden buildings for accommodation had now been constructed on site. The land allotted to what would become the inner ward of the castle was some three-quarters of an acre, and it would have been thronged with tents, wood smoke and the noise of the upward of 2,000 men toiling to begin work on the castle. But amidst all this clanging of tools and many tongues, the archives record that a minstrel was hired to play for the visit of the king on those long July evenings. We might imagine him listening to the lyre and pondering his recent troubles: with Madog, with Philippe IV, the passing of his late beloved queen, Leonor, and perhaps too with the no doubt attendant Maître Jacques.

Ade [Adam] de Cliderhou [Clitheroe], harpist, for playing the cythara[26] [lyre] before the King at Beaumaris for two nights, given by his own hand at Beaumaris, 12 July [1295], ten shillings.[27]

What was planned for Beaumaris was a concentric[28] castle without equal;[29] the earlier castles had, to some extent been concentric, but had been limited by the topography – now the entirely flat site by the Menai offered the chance to create something of perfection. Much ink has been spilled, as discussed earlier, in the Byzantine inspiration for the castle at Caernarfon: its polygonal towers and banded stonework do have imperial pretentious. But far less has been written of the debt owed to the Theodosian walls of Constantinople in the building of the castle at Beaumaris. This is likely because the debt is not to the style of the architecture so much as the principle of defence. In simple terms the Theodosian walls[30] offered a triple-lock defence, beginning with an outer water obstacle, followed by twin walls of increasing height, the first lower than the second, both protected by flanking towers. The outer wall protected the inner wall from siege engines, whilst the inner wall protected the outer through crossbow fire from the flanking towers. The three barriers, should an attacker be strong enough to penetrate one or two lines, created 'kill zones' between them, especially the space between the inner and outer walls. Concentric defence had grown popular in the west following the adoption of eastern styles in Outremer, most notably at Belvoir and Krak des Chevaliers.[31] In Britain Caerffili and the Tower of London had adopted forms of concentric defence, but like Rhuddlan and Harlech, topography or other concerns limited the masons' plans. This was a well-known principle of defence in depth – it was expensive to be sure, but offered incredible security to the defenders and is why Constantinople remained unconquered for so long. But whereas the Theodosian walls had circled a city, in north Wales they'd circle a castle. If we are looking for the inspiration for Beaumaris, then yes to Outremer, yes to Caerffili and to the Tower of London,[32] but the primary source was those Theodosian walls, and as at Caernarfon we know of only one man in Edward's entourage who'd seen them: the Savoyard constable of Conwy Castle, Sir Guillaume de Cicon.

Beaumaris would be perfectly symmetrical, the inner walls a square, one might say a *Carré Savoyard*, but this time two Harlech/Caerffili/Tonbridge-style gatehouses would be employed, one built into the northern elevation, the second opposite, into the southern elevation. At each corner of the square would be a round tower, at midpoint in the eastern and western walls a supporting D-shaped tower. So that we would have, running clockwise from the south-west tower first the middle tower, then the north-west tower, the northern gatehouse, the north-east tower, the chapel tower, the south-east tower and the southern gatehouse before returning to our start point – a perfectly symmetrical square (Figure 3.4). For a man, whose likely father and grandfather had built the cathedral at Lausanne, there may have been particular satisfaction in the beautiful vaulted chapel built into the tower of the hallway along the east-facing wall. The first-floor chapel was to have been a chapel royal, for the private use of the king, but like the castle, the tower above the chapel was never completed.

The gatehouses, as at Harlech, provided the function of the *donjon* or keep, and would house the residences of the castle. This inner curtain wall would be over fifteen and a half feet thick (nearly five metres) and thirty-six feet high (eleven metres). The lower outer wall, set an average of sixty feet (eighteen metres) away from the inner curtain, would feature five towers on its western side, the fifth at the corner in front of the north-west tower would be of greater size, then two towers on the northern elevation before a gateway, the Llanfaes gate, then the eastern side of five towers would be a mirror of the western side, again the corner tower in front of the north-east tower being of increased size. The southern wall would feature no towers as this would contain the complex of gateways to the castle.

The outer walls bowed slightly to their midpoint to create a perfectly symmetrical octagon. Surrounding these concentric walls would be the wide water-filled moat first dug by the *fossatores* at great expense in 1295. The curtain walls and towers of Beaumaris bear silent witness to the Savoyards amongst the builders who raised them, the inclined and helicoidal putlog holes for the scaffolding a signature that had travelled far from Saillon and Saxon to the Menai.

As at Caernarfon the inner curtain walls contain, at first floor level, long covered passageways that offered protected communication between all parts of the castle, and especially between the protective towers. But at Beaumaris they also contained a new feature unique to the castle, the rather ingenious incorporation of indoor latrines, or '*petite mesones*' as they were called, sixteen of them accessible from these wall passages, and a further sixteen from the wall walks, which do not empty by means of projections out of the walls but by way of '*les issues*' or ducts into pits which were scoured by '*gutterers*' or drains and channels into the moat. Perhaps the ingenious system asked too much of the English defenders once built, as a later (1306) report on the castle suggested they were in need of '*fer' netto de ordure*' or cleaning of rubbish from their drains.

A recent innovation, first employed in Britain for Jean de Warenne at Sandal, then for Gilbert de Clare at Caerffili and the Tower of London, would be the bent or right-angle approach to the castle on the southern side (Figure 3.5). That is that the gateway in the outer wall did not align with the southern gatehouse. This meant that attackers having overcome the outer wall had to turn right then immediately left before attempting to assault the southern gatehouse – difficult for infantry, almost impossible for siege engines. Similarly on the northern, landward side, the Llanfaes Gate was offset from the northern gatehouse. Edward, Warenne and Clare were all most familiar with the bent-approach protection for castle defence.

The sophistication of the defences afforded the castle can be gauged from a journey into the castle by way of the Gate next the Sea, the southern entrance from the Menai shore. Firstly, an assailant would have encountered a drawbridge, before reaching the gatehouse itself set into the outer wall. The heavy wooden doors were protected by machicolations above, and once inside two parallel 'murder slots' protected the gate passage. Then the ninety-degree right- and left-hand turns mentioned before encountering the main gatehouse of the inner wall. This gatehouse was subsequently afforded further protection in the form of a barbican, which had a shooting platform on the three sides of its wall head. The southern gatehouse itself was a colossal Harlech affair – an attacker was now faced with no less than ten barriers to entry. Firstly, outward-opening double doors, followed by a portcullis, then five parallel murder slots overhead, arrow loops from the guard rooms on either side of the passageway, a second portcullis, inward-opening doors, another row of murder slots above the passageway, a third pair of double doors, a third portcullis protected by another murder slot – this way into the castle would by virtually unassailable.

The moat that surrounded the twin walls of the castle provided yet another layer of defence, a wide water obstacle in and of itself, but also a defence against mining. Maître Jacques had used hard rock at Harlech and Conwy on which to build his castles, very difficult to impossible to dig through and undermine, but Beaumaris was a flat, waterlogged site. The moat was fed by water from the sea dock and the Menai, which meant any undermining work was liable to find itself flooded by sea water very quickly.[33]

There was to be an associated town at Beaumaris too, as there had been at Caernarfon, Rhuddlan and Flint. It should come as no surprise to us that the plan for Beaumaris has been found to mirror that at Conwy which, as we saw earlier, we can relate to Yverdon, which could in turn be related to Saint-Prex – the common denominator? – *Magistro Jacobo de Sancto Georgio*. Lilley wrote of 'suspicions that there was a common hand behind them', that is betwixt Beaumaris and Conwy, going on to conclude, 'The similarities in their plans are therefore very close.'[34] Between the work of Taylor and Lilley we can make a strong case for the laying out of the towns of Beaumaris and Conwy being of the same author,[35] and before that Yverdon, and before that Saint-Prex.[36] The towns of north Wales are clearly the work of Maître Jacques de Saint Georges, Yverdon the work of Maître Jean and his son Maître Jacques, Saint-Prex the work of Jean Cotereel. The evidence linking them is ultimately unprovable but compelling and adds to the impression that Taylor asserted, of a dynasty of stonemasons at work in England, then Savoy, then Wales. If it were so, then they represent perhaps the most significant family of mason architects known to us from the Middle Ages. Sadly, the evidence is only merely strongly suggestive. For all the work on the new town, it came at the cost of the Welsh inhabitants of Llanfaes, who were evicted, finding a *villeneuve* on the western most side of Anglesey, across the Menai from Caernarfon at Newborough.[37]

In the summer of 1295 Maître Jacques was given what in effect was a colossal pay rise. In July Edward granted him the manor at Mostyn in Flintshire at a rent, payable to the exchequer in Caernarfon of three shillings a year. The manor was in fact worth some £25.16s.7d annually - if we use the UK National Archive to approximate present day values we see that an annual rent of just over £110 was being paid for a manor worth £18,996! We are used in the twenty-first century to assets, such as company cars and the like being added to salary packages, here in 1295 we find the equivalent. No doubt a servant of the crown today would welcome such a reward for years of service.[38]

We saw earlier that at Caernarfon, Master Walter of Hereford had by the summer of 1295 taken over the work there. This involved both the repairs to the damaged castle, and the raising to their full height the existing walls there. The town walls, at least, had been restored by 10 September 1295.[39] We also saw that from February 1296 we have a full account of the progress of the castle, up and until the Madog rebellion, written by Master Walter upon his commencement of works. The reply at Caernarfon was in response to a query from Edward requesting an update that was also sent to Maître Jacques at Beaumaris, the writ of privy seal of the initial request dated 29 September 1295.[40] We can see from this request that Edward intended both Caernarfon and Beaumaris to be 'defensible' by 11 November 1295, clearly with the concern that a further rebellion might occur. The replies have not survived, but a further request was on 13 February, for which the replies do survive.[41]

The reply from Walter of Hereford at Caernarfon of 25 February, complaining of lack of funds but giving an accurate report of the work carried out before his time, we have already seen.[42] But the reply written from Conwy jointly by Maître Jacques and Walter of Winchester for Beaumaris is the only occasion we get to hear the voice of the Savoyard master mason, Master of the King's Works in Wales.

> To their very dear lordships, the treasurer and barons of the exchequer of our Lord the king, James of St George and Walter of Winchester send greeting and due reverence.
>
> Sirs,
> As our lord the king has commanded us by letters of the exchequer to let you have a clear picture of all aspects of the state of works at Beaumaris, so that you may be able to lay down the level of work for this coming season as may seem best to you, we write to inform you that the work we are doing is very costly and we need a great deal of money.
> You should know:
>
> (i) That we have kept on masons, stone cutters, quarrymen and minor workmen all through the winter, and are still employing them, for making mortar and breaking up stone for lime, we have had carts bringing this stone to the site and bringing timber for erecting the buildings in which we are all now living inside the castle, we also have 1,000 carpenters, smiths, plasterers and navvies, quite apart from a mounted garrison of ten men accounting for 70s a week, 20 crossbowmen who add another 47s. 10d, and 100 infantry who take a further £6.2s.6d.
>
> (ii) That when this letter was written we were short of £500 for both workmen and garrison. The men's pay has been and still is very much in arrears, and we have the greatest difficulty in keeping them because they simply have nothing to live on.
>
> (iii) That if our lord the king wants the work to be finished as quickly as it should be on the scale on which it has commenced, we could not make do with less than £250 a week throughout the season with it, this season could see the work advanced. If, however, you feel that we cannot have so much money, let us know, and we will put the workmen at your disposal according to whatever you think will be the best profit of our lord the king.

As for the progress of the work, we have sent a previous report to the king. We can tell you that some of it already stands about 28 feet high and even where it is lowest it is 20 feet. We have begun 10 of the outer and four of the inner towers, that is the two for each of the two gatehouse passages. Four gates have been hung and are shut and locked every night, and each gateway is to have three portcullises. You should also know that at high tide a 40 ton vessel will be able to come fully laden right up to the castle gateway so much have we been able to do in spite of all the Welshmen.

In case you wonder where so much money could go in a week, we would have you know that we have needed – and shall continue to need – 400 masons, both cutters and layers, together with 2,000 minor workmen, 100 carts, 60 wagons and 30 boats bringing stone and sea-coal, 200 quarrymen, 30 smiths and carpenters for putting the joists and floorboards and other necessary jobs. All this takes no account of the garrison mentioned above, nor any purchases of materials, of which, there will have to be a great quantity.

As to how things are in the land of Wales, we still cannot be any too sure. But, as you well know, Welshmen are Welshmen, and you need to understand them properly if, which God forbid, there is a war with France and Scotland, we shall need to watch them all the more closely.

You may be assured, dear sirs, that we shall make it our business to give satisfaction in everything.

May God protect your dearest lordships.

PS – And, Sirs, for God's sake be quick with the money for the works, as much as ever our lord the king wills, otherwise everything done up till now will have been of no avail.

Aberconwy, 27 February 1296.[43]

We can see from the letter that the inner walls already stood to, between twenty and twenty-eight feet (six and eight and a half metres) of their eventual thirty-six feet (eleven metres) in height – an incredible achievement in almost one building season. It had also once been thought that the building of the inner and outer walls had been undertaken at different times, but we can quite clearly see Maître Jacques is referring to *tours dehors* and *dedenz* or outside and inside towers. This clearly indicates the concentric pattern that we see today was intended from the very beginning in conception and not an afterthought. We can also see that provision for supply from the seaward side of the castle was there from the very beginning and fundamental to its concept, as it had been at Harlech, Caernarfon and Conwy – and earlier still at Flint and Rhuddlan. Edward had learned well from the holdout of the 'nest of Savoyards' at Pevensey.[44]

Money was immediately dispatched from London to Beaumaris,[45] and a further £1,000 was sent in early April,[46] but 1296 would not see the £250 every week requested by Maître Jacques; in fact they received less than half that, £100, because as Wales had distracted Edward from Gascony, so Scotland would now distract him from Wales. At the beginning of the decade he'd sent Othon de Grandson on what was very likely to have been a reconnaissance preparatory to an expedition to secure Outremer, then Philippe IV had intervened and taken Gascony by deception, then Madog ap Llywelyn had taken advantage of Anglo French preparations for war to launch his rebellion, now John Balliol in Scotland took advantage of events to conclude an alliance with Philippe – as we said earlier, crusade was to be forever the next-but-one thing on Edward's to-do list, with foes closer to home continually destabilizing his plans.

In October 1295, a Scottish embassy to Philippe IV of France agreed to the Treaty of Paris, an alliance, the *auld alliance* between Scotland and France.[47] Like Llywelyn ap Gruffydd before him, Jean Balliol had violated the 'glue' that held medieval society together, he'd gone against his act of fealty. On 16 December 1295, Edward summoned his nobles to meet with him at Newcastle on 1 March 1296. On 23 January the nobles of the exchequer were asked to finance 1,000 men-at-arms and 60,000 infantry for war with Scotland; this army would need £5,000 a week to operate. Events were going to overtake castle-building in Wales.[48] How much Edward was the author of his own problems has caused much ink to be spilled over the centuries since he himself was conscious of his role as vassal to Philippe IV for Gascony, but does not seem to have brought this consciousness to bear in his relationship with Balliol: he was ever conscious of *his* rights in both relationships, to the detriment of both.

In the meantime, the work at Beaumaris continued, albeit at a slackened pace. Some 16,200 freestones were conveyed to the site, along with 32,583 tons of stone ferried across the Menai. The financial resources now committed was a trickle when compared to the torrent of 1296: £330 for the 1297 building season when compared to over £4,000 in 1296. In June 1297, far from the £250 per week that Jacques and Walter had requested, the total allotment for works at Beaumaris was down to just a tenth of that, £25 per week.[49] One of the contractors for the work that summer of 1296 was the Savoyard Jean Francis who we last met constructing the town walls at Conwy; at Beaumaris he helped move over 14,000 freestones to site.[50] It had been a long road for '*Johannes Franciscus*', one that began at Saillon in the Valais, constricting the precipitate walls and towers that so reminded Taylor of Conwy (Figure 1.3), to Chillon and on to Conwy, a road that would reach its end by the Menai and the beautiful marshes of Anglesey.

On 1 March 1296, Edward arrived in Newcastle, and joining him there was Robert VI de Brus, now the 6th Lord of Annandale, his father, the man passed over in favour of Jean Balliol, being Robert V de Brus, who died on 31 March 1295.[51] Whilst the army waited, the Scots attacked and unsuccessfully besieged Carlisle Castle where Brus had once been the constable. The Scots had been emboldened by the February confirmation of their alliance with France, and with it offers of French support which never came.[52] But it was the date of the attack that would again, as it had earlier with Dafydd ap Gruffydd at Hawarden, shock contemporaries: the attack was made on Easter Sunday 1296. Edward moved his army to Berwick-upon-Tweed, the first of the towns he'd demanded the previous October, and offered terms to the burgesses of the town and the Scottish garrison at the castle, to both surrender.[53] They did not, and what's more offered the king the disrespect of their naked backsides. There was now going to be only one outcome, the rules of medieval warfare offered no hope of clemency for defenders of a town who refused to open their gates in times of siege and subsequently lost – the town was taken by Edward amidst great bloodshed.[54] Jean Balliol now formally renounced his fealty and homage to Edward,[55] as Edward had indeed done himself when threatened by Philippe IV. Balliol's claim that the original fealty had been 'extorted by force' has been subsequently refuted by Scottish historian Duncan as 'manifestly false'.[56]

It was only after receipt of this revocation on 5 April that Jean de Warenne moved up the coast to Dunbar Castle, and an invasion of the Scottish kingdom began.[57] An attempt by the Scottish army to break the siege there resulted, on 27 April 1296, in the Battle of Dunbar, and a wholesale and total defeat for the Scots. A short siege and capture by Edward of Edinburgh followed, then the capture of Stirling Castle, before Jean Balliol sought terms. On 7 July, he revoked the French treaty, that had so infuriated Edward, and on 8 July at Montrose made his submission.[58] Edward, as overlord, revoked the four-year-old kingship of Jean Balliol, who by now must have been wishing he'd remained an English noble. The throne of Scotland was now vacant and would remain so for some time as Edward had no plans to reopen the Great Cause, to the disappointment of Robert VI de Brus.[59] The Welsh rebellion had been suppressed, and war with Scotland won, so now surely Edward could turn his reigns once more toward France and attempt the recovery of his appanage in France, his ancestral lands of Gascony from the duplicitous scheming Philippe IV.

After an illness in the autumn of 1295, Edward's brother, Edmund, Earl of Lancaster, had finally been able to sail for Gascony accompanied by Henri de Lacy, Earl of Lincoln. Just before Edmund had left, they had received news of the passing of another tower of the age, Gilbert de Clare, 7th Earl of Gloucester. Red Gilbert died at Gloucester on 7 December 1295.[60] He'd been married to Edward's daughter, Joan, for just five years, and though a Montfortian at Lewes, he'd played a role in Edward's escape from captivity and joined him at Montfort's denouement at Evesham. But perhaps posterity would most remember him from the great castle he'd built at Caerffili, a masterclass of concentric design, including the gatehouse, following that at the family's Tonbridge Castle, that would form the model for Beaumaris and Harlech.

The army sent to Gascony was a much-reduced force than had been planned before the Welsh and Scottish rebellions: the treasury was now bare. The idea was for Edmund and Edward to catch Philippe IV in a twin attack: Edmund in Gascony, Edward and his Flemish and Savoyard allies from Flanders. But first Edmund had to retake Gascony, and that wasn't going to be easy. By now Philippe had been in possession of Edward's lands for two years and was well entrenched. Upon arrival they tried and failed to retake Bordeaux, then fell back upon Bayonne, where the expedition foundered upon the rock of poverty, and the army dispersed for want of funds. It was a disaster. There, on 5 June 1296, Edmund Crouchback, younger son of Henry III of England and Alianor de Provence, nephew of the House of Savoy, crusader knight, one-time King of Sicily, 1st Earl of Lancaster since the demise of Simon de Montfort, departed this life of, so it was said, a broken heart. His body was firstly taken to Bordeaux, thence to England for burial. For Edward, it was another body blow – within a few short years he'd lost his mother, his wife and now his loyal brother.[61] It would be with Edmund in mind that Edward called a Parliament in the autumn of 1296 at the town which bore the name of the saint for which Edmund had been named, Bury St Edmunds, and at a time to coincide with his feast day.

Edward had been continuously in need of access to cash since his break with the Riccardi di Lucca. He would in the end come to terms with another Italian house, the Frescobaldi, but in the meantime, enemies pressed and cash was short. In November 1296, the laity granted him a tax. It is against the background of the impending financial crisis of 1297 that we will take leave of our story, because it sets the context by which the great castle-building epoch of Wales comes to an end.

Building work at Caernarfon and Beaumaris will continue a while, but at an increasingly slower pace, which ultimately will lead to both castles never being truly finished. As for the Savoyards in north Wales, Maître Jacques continued to work for Edward, but would soon be taken from the Welsh works to follow the King to renewed war with Scotland. On 30 August 1298 responsibility for his three shillings a day pay would transfer to the more generalized care of the Keeper of the King's Wardrobe, no longer associated specifically with Beaumaris.[62] He would be involved in building work in Scotland, but no longer build any new castles. His last major project for Edward was to build him a machine to knock castles down, not to build them – the great trebuchet *War Wolf*, his *Loup de Guerre*. When disassembled, the siege engine would fill all of thirty wagons in an IKEA-like multiplicity of parts. It apparently took five master carpenters and forty-nine other labourers at least three months to complete.[63]

Edward was so proud of his *Loup de Guerre* that when assembled outside of Stirling Castle in 1304, the garrison offered to surrender; he refused to accept the surrender until he'd battered the walls awhile with his new creation. It's a supreme irony that the last involvement of *Magistro Jacobo de Sancto Georgio* in history, arguably one of the greatest castle builders of the European Middle Ages was to build a machine to destroy castles not to build them. But his legacy is not *War Wolf*, it is Beaumaris, the perfectly conceived castle by the Menai, that, even in its unfinished state, stands a silent witness to the man who built stunning medieval monuments of north Wales. We will discuss his legacy and the afterlife, so to speak, of his castles in the last chapter of this book, but before that we must turn to the other castle builders that had travelled so far from the distant Alps to Snowdonia to work alongside Maître Jacques as they would have known him.

So, what had Edward's Welsh castles cost his realm? Taylor gave us neat totals: of the first wave, Flint £6,224.7s.3d, Rhuddlan £9,292.11$^{1/2}$d, Builth £1,666.9s.3$^{1/2}$d, and Aberystwyth £3,885,17s.11$^{1/2}$d. Of the second wave: Harlech £8,190.2s.4$^{1/2}$d, Conwy £13,761.9s.10$^{1/2}$d, Caernarfon £12,308,3s.9$^{1/2}$d and Beaumaris £11,389.0s.9d, and alterations to native Welsh castles: Criccieth £318,17s.4$^{1/2}$d and Castell y Bere £265.5s.10$^{1/2}$d. There had been two unallocated 'omnibus' payments of £1,551.0s.11d and £9,414.4s.11d bringing the total outlay up to 1304 to £78,267.11s.6d.[64]

For Edward, with England's traditional twin enemies of Scotland and France, 'the Auld alliance', continuing to plague him, the end came as renewed hostilities in Scotland commenced in 1307. He was on his way north to Scotland, when on 7 July 1307 at Burgh by Sands near Carlisle on the Solway Firth, the grandson of Béatrice de Savoie, the great-grandson of Count Thomas I de Savoie, departed this life. It was fitting perhaps that this builder of so many castles should die on his way to another campaign, sword in hand so to speak. His attempts to reconcile being, at once a vassal of the King of France for his great-grandmother's lands in Aquitaine, whilst being suzerain to the Prince of Wales and King of Scotland proved to be in vain. Yet this much misunderstood, and of late vilified, King of England, left his kingdom wider than he had found it – certainly with more castles – and perhaps, like his father, that is a fitting epitaph that his grandfather, John, lacked. Edward the first of that name left Wales a firm part of his realm. A union, for good or ill, that has endured to this day.

Chapter Sixteen

So, as the era of castle-building in north Wales was drawing to a close, what had happened to the Savoyards who'd come to England and Wales? As we saw, Maître Jacques would follow Edward to Scotland but would not build more castles of note. Edward's loyal friend and envoy, Othon de Grandson, would return to England and Scotland, giving the chronicler at Lanercost an eyewitness account of the fall of Acre. He returned to diplomatic service for the Crown, and along with his relative Gerard de Vuippens, was instrumental in an eventual peace with Philippe IV of France, that saw the return of Gascony.[1] Eventually Grandson would return to Savoy, but only after the death in 1307 of his lifelong friend, Edward. He worked on completing the building work at the Château de Grandson, employing Savoyards returning from Wales and possibly Welsh craftsmen. The wall-walk that would grace his castle, before it was enclosed much later, was of a particularly Anglo-Norman style – he'd learned well, during his time in England, how to build castles.[2]

But for Edward and Othon the road had run its course; they had been together since they were boys. They fought the battles of Lewes and Evesham together in 1264 and 1265 against the Montfortian rebels. They took the cross together, the Ninth Crusade in 1271, Othon reputedly sucking poison from Edward when the latter was attacked by an assassin. In 1277 and 1278 they fought the First Welsh War against the House of Gwynedd, Othon doing much to negotiate the Treaty of Aberconwy in 1278 that ended hostilities. When war broke out again in 1282, they fought the Second Welsh War together, Othon leading Edward's army across the Bridge of Boats from Anglesey, barely surviving the Battle of Moel-y-Don, before being the first to sight the future sites of castles at Caernarfon and Harlech. Othon was at the sieges of Dolforwyn and Castell y Bere, that did so much to win the wars for Edward. Edward made his friend the first Justiciar of North Wales, Othon's office being in the Eagle Tower at Caernarfon. When Edward and Othon went to Gascony in 1287 the latter stayed in Burgos, Castile, as a hostage for Edward's good intentions between Gascony and Castile. Later in 1291, when Acre was threatened by the Mamluks, Edward sent Othon as head of the English delegation of knights. When Acre finally fell to the Mamluks, bringing the crusades to a close, who was the last knight onto the boats? Othon de Grandson, helping his old friend Jean de Grailly, wounded, onto the boat. Upon the death of his wife, Leonor de Castile, a tomb was built in the abbey at Westminster that bears the image of a knight – it is none other than Othon de Grandson.[3]

Whatever you may think of the Welsh wars, the Montfortian rebellion or the crusades, the friendship of these two extraordinary men who met when they were two little boys endured a lifetime – and they had all the adventures you could have in the medieval world. There would be a story, told later by Jean d'Ypres:

There was formerly in Savoy a certain Lord of Grandson to whom a son was born. The astrologers summoned to examine, calculate, and cast his nativity, said that the new-born child, if he lived, would be great, powerful, and victorious. There was a man present, perhaps superstitious, perhaps gifted with second sight, who, taking a log from the fire, said that the boy would survive so long as the log lasted; he then closed that log up in the wall so that it should last longer. The boy lived, grew, reached old age, and then extreme old age, always increasing in honour, until when he was very old and wearied by the tedium of living, he had the aforesaid log brought out from the wall and thrown upon the fire, and soon after it was completely consumed, the knight swiftly died.[4]

Sir Othon de Grandson departed this life in April 1328, living a life of some ninety years. He died at Aigle, having given his last will and testament there on 4 April and probably died the following day, 5 April 1328. His body was then transported back along the lake, past Chillon and the vineyards of Lavaux to his last resting place of Lausanne.[5] His will requested burial at the Cathédrale de Lausanne, so much of which had been built by the likely father of Maître Jacques, Jean Cotereel. The funeral probably took place on 12 April, as described in his last will:

I elect burial in the Cathedral Church of the Blessed Mary of Lausanne. Likewise, I will and order that my body be carried to the grave by two men at arms, with my arms, preceded by my banner, mounted on two horses, the price of £100, one with a blanket to my arms, the other shod and with harness; these two horses, armed and covered, will be donated to the church of Lausanne in remission of my sins.[6]

He closed by bequeathing gifts to the cathedral, save for the 'small gold cross and a statue of the Virgin Mary, of silver,[7] which I usually carry with me'. These last words give us an insight into the man behind the legend, the pious crusader knight to the end.[8] His tomb is there to this day, to the left of the chancel, paying silent witness to the seven centuries that have passed, one-time Justiciar of north Wales and the Eagle Tower of Caernarfon.

His brother, Guillaume de Grandson, former Deputy Justiciar of North Wales and lifelong knight and friend of Edmund Crouchback, stayed on in England. He was with Edmund when he died in Gascony, and it is said is commemorated on his tomb – if so then both the Grandson brothers are memorialized in Westminster Abbey. He went on to serve Edward in Scotland, notably at Falkirk in 1298, alongside his kinsman Pierre de Champvent. Becoming the first Baron de Grandison, he like his brother would live to old age, but unlike his brother he would found a dynasty in England, married to Sybil Tregoz: the Grandisons. Sybil was of the Anglo-Norman Tregoz family of Herefordshire, the see of late Savoyard Bishop, Pierre d'Aigueblanche in Henry's time. Having lived at Ashperton,[9] to the west of Ledbury, for many years, Guillaume died in 1335, and was buried along with Sybil, who'd died the year before, at Dore Abbey in Herefordshire. Reputedly Guillaume had gifted the abbey a piece of the true cross which Othon de Grandson had acquired during the fall of Acre in 1291. Their son John Grandison would become the Bishop of Exeter; several works of art associated with him survive in the British Library, the British Museum in London and the Louvre in Paris. John Grandison donated the tenor bell to his cathedral, which still sounds to this day adorned with the family name, Grandson, from the Lac de Neuchâtel.[10] When founding a church at Ottery St Mary in Devon, John Grandison perhaps spoke well of his father and uncle when he wrote that it was his desire

> for insuring the never ending remembrance of the deeds of valour and charity wrought by his family and friends, noble and gentle, who together with their willing followers and loyal comrades, whether in England, in France, in Scotland or the Holy Land, helped to fashion the realm and win the nation's place in the world's history which we now gratefully inherit.[11]

Of the other knights who'd come to Wales as constables, Gerard de St Laurent had died in the Second Welsh War at Flint, Jean de Bonvillars had died during the Rhys ap Maredudd revolt at Dryslwyn, but Guillaume de Cicon was still there at Conwy, and would remain in post until his death by May 1311.[12] In the aftermath of the Madog rebellion, a somewhat chastened Edward had employed Jean de Havering, along with Cicon, to undertake an investigation into the Welsh complaints that had led to the uprising.[13] In November 1296, he had been asked to be additionally Keeper of the commotes of Arllechwedd Uchaff and Arllechwedd Issa. Together the commotes formed the *cantref* of Arllechwedd, a key territory within the old principality of Gwynedd, encompassing the entire west bank of the Conwy, upon which his castle sat.[14] Guillaume de Cicon, then, remained a key officer of the Crown in north Wales until the end. We know that he'd been married during his forty-plus years in Wales as he left a son, Jean de Cicon, who was still in Wales in 1317, but thereafter records of his life end, meaning potentially he'd returned to the Franche-Comté.[15] Almost at the end of his life, in 1309, Edward's son, now Edward II, had rewarded Cicon, for his long service to his late father, £30 per annum, or over £18,000 in today's money, which looks to have been by way of a pension.[16] The last resting place of Guillaume de Cicon is unknown; perhaps he remains at Conwy still, but his life had been a long one, beginning on the Greek island of Euboea, before moving to Wales and long service to the Crown – another knight brought to England under the auspices of Othon de Grandson who had proven a loyal and trusted Savoyard servant to Edward.

Ebal IV de Mont would also follow Edward to Scotland, becoming Constable at Stirling and Edinburgh. He had been close to Leonor de Castile, and upon her death was granted the manor at Shirling near Sandwich in Kent; he further benefitted from the gain of Templar lands in Lincolnshire upon the suppression of the order. By 1318 Ebal IV de Mont, son of Ebal II de Mont, had died and was buried at the Cluniac abbey of Bermondsey. His father had begun life high above Lac Léman at the small castle of Mont Le Grand and ended it at Windsor Castle; he himself had been a squire entrusted with the defence of castle works at Harlech before going on to a lifetimes service with the Crown – the lives of the father and son encapsulate the Savoyard story in England and stretched out over a century of service.[17]

Pierre de Champvent would return to Savoy, but not before fighting alongside Edward and Guillaume de Grandson at the Battle of Falkirk, despite being 60 sixty years of age at the time.[18] In his retirement he would begin works on his own castle that would reflect his time in England. Pierre de Champvent died in 1303, after a lifetime's service to both Henry III and Edward I; sadly the Champvent line would be extinguished by 1326 when the Château de Champvent and its land passed to the Count of Savoy. His son Jean de Champvent had been in Edward's service since at least 1285 when a squire; he would be knighted in 1297 and serve the Crown during the war with Philippe IV in Flanders, and by 1299 he had risen to the rank of banneret. After serving Edward during the Scottish wars, like Grandson he doesn't go on to serve during the reign of Edward II.[19]

Amédée V de Savoie would be the Count of Savoy until his death in 1323, and would be so highly regarded that he was later styled *Le Grand*. He was succeeded by his son, Edward. One of the more overlooked legacies of the service given by Amédée to England, is that an Edward would become Count of Savoy.

There is a story of Amédée that speaks much of the family loyalty that existed between the English crown and the ruling house of Savoy that merits a telling and dates from 1292, during the problems surrounding the Scottish succession. Having been invited by Scottish nobles to adjudicate the Scottish succession much in the same way as he'd previously adjudicated the succession of Amédée in Savoy, Edward called upon Amédée to travel all the way from Lac Bourget to Berwick upon Tweed to give evidence in his support. Thanks to Hugh de Voiron, Amédée's clerk we have details of the journey, one trodden so often by the Savoyards in our story and the knighting by Edward of Savoyard squires in Darlington of all places.

In far away Savoy, Amédeé V de Savoie made ready for a journey too, the Count of Savoy was going to visit his illustrious relative the King of England. The journey and its expenses as recorded by Amédeé's clerk, Hugh de Voiron (later a canon of St Martins le Grand in London),it gives us an insight into the details of the many journeys undertaken by Savoyard travellers over the decades of this story from the Alps to England.

The journey began at Amédeé's castle of Le Bourget, sometimes called the Château de Thomas II, it had been built on land by Lac Bourget owned by the monks of Hautecombe Abbey. Thomas, Count of Flanders, Amédeé's father had wanted somewhere to stay on his visits back to Savoy that accorded with his status and the palace castle at Le Bourget was the result. It lay across Lac Bourget on the underdeveloped bank opposite Aix, construction had begun back in 1248 and was complete by 1253. Le Bourget was then the childhood home of Amédeé, preferring it to the Chillon that had been the preference of Pierre and Saint-Georges d'Espéranche of Philippe his predecessors. At some point in March they sat out for England, reaching Lyon by at least 25th March, not listed but a journey that would most likely have taken them by the newly constructed Master James castles of Saint-Laurent-du-Pont, Voiron and La Côte Saint-Andre. There Hugh de Voiron records a payment to a certain Armandus, a saddler, for five saddles and bridles for the palefrei or palfreys of the count and his three knights "quando ivit in Angliam" or "when he went to England." A reminder that Counts travelled in less splendour than kings and that provisions for horses were a major part of any thirteenth century journey. A palfrey was a type of light horse that was highly valued as a riding horse in the medieval period. It was a smooth gaited horse that could amble, suitable for riding over long distances, easier on the rear upholstery of the weary thirteenth century traveller.

Some thirty miles (fifty kilometres) north east of Lyon they reached the fortified monastery at Ambronay, founded many centuries earlier in the time of Charlemagne. There we learn that a new riding horse was bought by Amédeé for an militi de Anglia, an English knight accompanying the party. From there the party rode, mostly by the old Roman road northwards, the Via Agrippa, by way of the crossing of the Saône tributary, the Veyle, at Pont-de-Veyle and its castle, crossing the Saône at the cathedral city of Châlon-sur-Saône, Bussy-le-Grand and its castle, on to the County of Champagne and Troyes on the Seine, and Provins until they reached Paris. A thirteenth century journey across France was mostly a route from castle to monastery to castle by way of an old Roman road.

On arrival in Paris a pause from the open road, a chance to forward messengers to England heralding their impending arrival, and back to Savoy with messages of safe arrival, even for a count travel in the thirteenth century could be a hazardous business. The big city, then, as now, afforded the party the chance to go shopping. Henri, the count's jester was provided with a furred tunic, Amédeé had a ring altered and acquired a new saddle, perhaps both ring and saddle had been irritating him on the long ride up from Savoy. Stephen Audri, a burgess of Paris, is noted as supplying cloth and leather and making two suits for the count, it was always a good idea, even then to arrive in London adorned in Parisian garments. After a stay of just a few days in Paris they continued north across the Somme and Picardie to Saint Omer before reaching the channel at the small port of Wimereux just five kilometres north of Boulogne. The crossing to England just a short twenty-four miles (40 kilometres) to the port of Dover beneath its towering castle and the road to London. We are told that Livres Tournois had been used for payments in

France, the record now makes clear in England, then, as now, it was the Pound Sterling.

Once in London they joined with Edward for his journey north to deliberate upon the Great Cause of Scotland. They travelled by way of Bury St Edmunds (27th-30th April), Darlington (25th–26th May to which we shall return shortly), Durham (27th May) before finally arriving at Berwick upon Tweed where they arrived on 1st June. This was a journey of over a thousand miles (over 1,600 kilometres) and had taken some three months in the saddle. We know from Hugh de Voiron's accounts that Othon de Grandson was not the only Savoyard to have dealings with the Riccardi di Luca, the mention of "Pino de Luca" in London suggests that Amédeé too had an account with the Italians.

Back at Darlington, on Whit Sunday and Monday, 25th and 26th May 1292, Edward (most likely) had knighted four Savoyard squires who'd been with Amédée's party at Saint Cuthbert's church in Darlington. We have Hugh de Voiron's accounting for the ceremonial bathing, provided by the king's barber for twenty-three shillings:

> "Recorded at Darlington, for the King's barber, for four baths, in these are dubbed new knights, including three shillings for covering them in said bath – twenty-three. Shillings."[20]

The word "addobatorum" being a latinised rendering of the Old French "adober" meaning to dress with armour or adorn, the act of dubbing also been known by its Old French origin of "adoubement". The ceremony itself later gave rise to the English word "Accolade" which gives us a graphic picture of the ceremony from its Occitan origin "acolada", literally "to the neck" which in Occitan meant "embrace". It had been thought for a time by some historians that thirteenth century English knighting ceremonies did not include the ritual bathing, the archive in Turin confirms that it very much did. This tale speaks volumes for the loyalty the ruling family of Savoy owed the Plantagenets of England, and the lengths quite literally they were prepared to travel to offer that support.

We know of the passing of the knights, the nobility, for it is recorded well in both England and Switzerland, but what of the artisans who followed them to Wales? Sadly, we do not know what ultimately became of Jean Francis or Adam Boynard beyond the last references where we have them at Beaumaris and Harlech in 1295–6. Given that Jean Francis had been active at Saillon and Brignon in at least 1260, then by the mid-1290s he must have been of advancing years and it cannot have been long before death caught up with him. We may not know of his passing, or even the place of his passing, but he left us a legacy at Saillon, Chillon, Conwy and Beaumaris that has stood the test of seven centuries. He was never a master mason, always a *cementario*, a builder, and perhaps it is not too fanciful to imagine him as Ken Follett's fictional character Tom Builder in his novel *Pillars of the Earth* to fashion a picture of him in the mind's eye.

For Adam Boynard we know equally less, after the 1294–5 siege of Harlech. As a burgess of Harlech he is unlikely to have returned to Savoy; it's likely he had a family in Wales. Which leaves us the possibility that today's people living in north Wales are, in small part, descended, not just from the people of Llywelyn's principality of Gwynedd and the English settlers who came to north Wales, but also from the Savoyards too, who came so far to build castles. It is very possible that the descendants of the *'King of the Ribalds'* are to this day walking the roads of Snowdonia. Marc Morris, in writing his history of the Norman Conquest, suggested it was 'high time' we stopped seeing in the Battle of Hastings, a struggle between us (the Saxons) and them (the Normans), and realize that they are both now us. To some extent this is equally true of the thirteenth-century struggles between the King of England and Gwynedd, and those taking part, Welsh, English, Savoyard are, now, us. Some of the Savoyard artisans returned home, we find English styles in churches and castles throughout the region. Notably the windows of the former priory at Grandson, the battlements of the castle at Grandson, the windows of the church St. Etienne of Moudon that copy those at the abbey of Valle Crucis in Wales, and the windows at the former priory at Contamines-sur-Arve that echo those at Harlech Castle.

So what of Maître Jacques himself? If the passing of Othon de Grandson is well documented, and I was able to hold his last will and testament in my own hand, then alas the fate of the Master of the King's Works in Wales is not recorded. Like Jean Francis and Adam Boynard, he was not, in the end, of the nobility, he was a master mason, but to the end also a *cementario*. In the context of the suggestion that he was some form of 'project manager' rather than a builder of castles, a record from 11 July 1306 gives eloquent riposte, as he is referred to as *'Magistro Jacobo de Sancto Georgio Cementario Regis'*. On 30 September 1307, we have his last appearance in the archive, at Beaumaris, perhaps his greatest creation, still unfinished, receiving wages of £8 'until the new King [Edward II] or his council should decide or ordain otherwise'. A year later, by 7 December 1308, the greatest castle builder of the medieval period was no more. A writ issued on that date regarding his manor at Mostyn noted his passing.[21] If he had a tomb or tombstone, which he lacks, then perhaps these are the words he would have liked: *'Cementario Regis'*, the 'King's builder', for that is who he was. But then he is in no need of a tombstone, because millions of visitors every year walk around, and gaze upon, with awe, the monuments he created. In 2019 I brought a party of Swiss historians and castle custodians to visit the castles of north Wales. *'C'est énorme'* of Conwy, and 'Wow' of Caernarfon need no translation – I think this is the reaction, even so many centuries later, that both Edward, Othon and Jacques would be happy with.

Ultimately, the key to understanding the influence of the Savoyard knights and builders who came to England to build and garrison the castles of north Wales is to understand where the County of Savoy fitted within the wider francophone world, and in particular the triangle that can be drawn between England, Gascony and Savoy. This triangular relationship is a function of the familial links between

England and Savoy that follow the marriage of Henry III to Alianor de Provence, but also the resulting political links between Savoy and the wider Plantagenet world that included both England and Gascony, the latter being the last vestiges of the Angevin Empire. When we add to the mix the long-standing pilgrimage links that put Savoy on the mainline between England and Rome, then we can understand the context of what follows.

King Edward I of England was brought up in a court deliberately surrounded by Savoyards, as Pierre de Savoie sought to protect the familial investment in the heir to the English throne by way of protecting their niece, the Queen of England. The Savoyard influence on the English court filtered to the entire realm, both in England and in Gascony. It is within this context that we see Gascon mason Master Bertram travelling to England, and Jean de Mézos travelling from Gascony to Savoy – they were in effect working for the 'same firm'. If we are to look for the genesis of the castles in north Wales, then it is in 1254, when following the siege of Benauges, Bertram and Mézos move on to work for Henry III and Pierre de Savoie.

It is in the County of Savoy that Mézos will work alongside some of the men who will be most influential in north Wales, Maître Jacques and Jean Francis. Meanwhile in England, the influence of Pierre de Savoie has brought the sons of Savoyard noblemen to the English court, where they will be brought up under the watchful eye of Alianor and Pierre. The boys – Othon de Grandson, his brother Guillaume and Jean de Bonvillars – will become lifelong friends and allies of Edward when he becomes king. They will join Pierre de Champvent, who was already in London, and later be joined by Guillaume de Cicon, a Savoyard but from the Byzantine east. In time all these ingredients will come together in the stone castles of north Wales; some will build them, some will advise on their construction and some will be put in charge of them – but all of them working to one end, to support King Edward I of England, a descendant of the Counts of Savoy.

In recent years the ground-breaking work of Arnold Taylor, building on the earlier work by Sir John Goronwy Edwards, has been questioned by Nicola Coldstream in a number of papers and articles. It is only right that subsequent generations of historians re-examine the work of those that have gone before, as a check and balance, but also to move forward our understanding. It is in this spirit that we will turn to Coldstream's own work and open it up to evaluation. In her critique of Taylor, Coldstream rightly draws attention to the purely stylistic nature of the Savoyard influences of the Welsh castles: the helicoidal putlog holes, the three-pinnacled merlons, the Chillon-style windows, the latrine shafts, etc. She further suggests, rightly, that the fundamentals of the castle's architecture drew from the Anglo-French milieu. However when she suggests that this was 'a milieu that was familiar to Edward I but not to James of St George',[22] she had erred, ignoring entirely the part played in the formative career of Maître Jacques by the Gascon *magistri ingeniatorum* of Henry III, a native of the aforesaid Anglo-French milieu, Jean de Mézos. Maître Jacques de Saint Georges would have been most familiar with the Anglo-French building styles and techniques, both through his mentor Jean de Mézos and his patron, Pierre de Savoie. Indeed when she searches for an English tutor, suggesting Robert of Beverley,[23] although acknowledging this was 'undocumented', we should look no further than Jean de Mézos, who was indeed recorded as having worked on numerous occasions, over many years between 1266 and 1275,[24] with Maître Jacques in Savoy, and documented, as we saw earlier, in a senior role.[25] A documented period of at least ten years working alongside a Gascon mason, knighted for his work for Henry III, should provide as much evidence as we need for a source of exposure to Anglo-French building styles and indeed a mentor. It has been said of the castles, as of their 'being more English in inspiration'.[26] But the Blanquefort gatehouse in Gascony that may reappear in Rhuddlan, the Gascon round towers that appear in Savoy tell a more nuanced story of a triangular relationship between Gascony, Savoy and England. The geometrical patterns expressed in the fabric of both the Notre-Dame de Lausanne and Caernarfon Castle, and the windows in Lausanne Cathedral that continue the themes of Canterbury and foreshadow those later used at Conwy Castle, tell of a complex relationship between England and Savoy that flowed to and fro.

In this Anglo-Savoyard-Gascon triangle, the Savoyard Jean de Grailly, who'd arrived in Gascony with Pierre de Savoie and Henry III, who'd been appointed seneschal but was then dismissed, was wounded at Acre, but saved by Othon de Grandson, died in around 1301. However, posterity would know the name of the family from the Pays de Gex once again in the form of his grandson, Jean III de Grailly who would be a founding knight of Edward III's chivalric Order of the Garter, a key knight fighting for the Plantagenets in the Hundred Years' War and capturing the French King Jean II at the Battle of Poitiers in 1356 – the grandson of Jean de Grailly was, according to French chronicler Jean Froissart, the very model of chivalry.

Meanwhile, turning to the castles once more, Coldstream compared the sophisticated nature of the architecture in Wales with the primitive work found in Savoy – adapting Pevsner's comparison between 'architecture' and 'building'[27] and likening the castles of north Wales to a 'swan' when compared to the 'ugly duckling' of Savoy.[28] These comments do point to an obvious truth which needs an answer. Fundamentally, that answer lies in two parts. Firstly, the Savoyard castles and Welsh castles fulfil differing functions: in Wales they are to dominate the region, providing both a military but also an administrative function in what amounted to a conquest, whereas in Savoy they were mostly mountain sentinels or gate posts. Secondly, the Welsh castles were built for a patron whose annual income of £30 million in today's money far outweighed that of the patron in Savoy of just £3 million. Architects, then as today, can only create according to the required function prescribed by the patron, and to the budget available to the patron. Therefore, any comparison of the quality and scope of the castles in north Wales and Savoy is rendered meaningless.

Coldstream goes on to query the contribution of the Savoyard master mason in the design of the Welsh castles, drawing attention to the less than ideal arrangement of the twin-towered gatehouses at Rhuddlan, describing them as 'an amateurish first attempt by Master James'.[29] She goes on to support her claim for his having 'received help' in design, by suggesting 'Master Bertram has a good claim to have inaugurated the gatehouses at Rhuddlan'.[30] Indeed he has, and perhaps we should refer to Taylor's earlier 1989 paper, where he had indeed speculated at length that they were, in design, the work of the Gascon mason, Master Bertram, suggesting that their possible design origin was the ducal castle works in Gascony at Blanquefort.[31]

There is much discussion as to who held the most sway in terms of their fraction of input into the design of the castles of north Wales and, given their iconic status, rightly so. The patron would be the most important voice, and the voice of a patron such as King Edward I of England would be a strong one. Nothing has survived to give us the extent of his involvement in the written record, save for one recorded endenture of work carried out for him by Maître Jacques later in Scotland at Linlithgow. The record is the only one that records the direct relationship between Edward and Jacques, and is the primary source for believing Edward to be an active and ever-present patron in terms of the earlier Welsh castles. The level of micromanagement that the endenture reveals is considerable, Edward was no hands-off patron; there is first an instruction to build 'une porte de piere e deus Tours', a twin-towered stone gatehouse, and 'deus tours de pyere', two stone towers, then 'ad chaunge son propos' or a change of mind: to save money the work is to be of timber not stone, then plans for the church and its tower followed by the associated financial arrangements.[32] A number of themes are apparent from the document; firstly, the aforementioned direct relationship between Edward and Jacques; secondly, the detail to which it extends, suggesting that to the end Jacques was an active master mason – 'Mestre Jakes de seint Jorge le Machoun' – involved in the design of works not just their administration; and thirdly, the impact of Edwards straightened financial circumstances. It has become fashionable, with some large degree of anachronism, to call Maître Jacques a 'project manager' or an 'administrator', but the primary sources are quite clear on this: they introduce his role into England with the word 'ordinandum' and disregard Pevsner's advice of this term at our peril.[33] Following his period working for his father, he is described at Yverdon in July 1267 as a 'cementarii'; thereafter, in Savoy, from 1269 until 1275, he is nearly always called a 'lathomo/lathomi'; when he first arrives in England in 1278, he is called (as had Bertram and Mézos before him) an 'ingeniatori' before acquiring his name 'de Sancto Georgio'. But in these last entries in Scotland, we see Edward using 'Le machoun' before one final record for 1306 when he is described as 'Cementario Regis' – in the thirty-nine years since he began as a cementarii at Yverdon, Magistro Jacobo has now acquired the addition of 'Regis' to his job title, the same Maître Jacques de Saint Georges, Maître Jacques, the old man we began our story with, by May 1309.[34] He received no epitaph – he began and ended his career, as had his father, and would his sons, a stonemason.

In concluding that 'Construction of the castles depended upon Maître Jacques' organizing skills, but their design did not', Coldstream, as Simpson before her, goes too far.[35] But whilst the 'project manager' and 'administrator' tags are inappropriate for a lifelong stonemason, they do point to the unique ability that attracted his royal patron. As the builders at Guédelon will no doubt testify, building one castle is a daunting task, but to build three or four simultaneously is what makes Maître Jacques stand out amongst his contemporaries. But this unique talent should not lessen his talent as a stonemason; indeed it magnifies it, because the role of Master of Works, in the late thirteenth century has no modern equivalence. It encompassed project manager, purchasing manager, administrator, builder and, yes, architect too – but not the role of architect as we understand it today. In his recent architectural appraisal of the work in Wales of Maître Jacques, Malcolm Hislop began the rebalancing of Coldstream's analysis in writing, 'but the downplaying of his creative role goes too far, and is less easy to take seriously'.[36] Whilst Edward had no plans for the Welsh castles when he likely met Maître Jacques in 1273, it would be this unique ability that marked him out in the king's memory when the relationship with Gwynedd deteriorated, and a memory that was, I think, jogged by the advice of his loyal lieutenant Othon de Grandson. The confluence of Edward's memory, with the requirement to build multiple castles simultaneously in Wales, when passed through the added medium of Othon de Grandson having most likely employed Maître Jacques himself at Lucens and Grandson, these were the stars that had to align to create what became the castles of north Wales.

The search for the single guiding light of castle designer is, however, a fruitless one. Perhaps it's helpful to imagine that tent in the spring of 1283, set up within the monastery precinct at Aberconwy. Within that tent, around a table, would be Edward the King, and around him would be his loyal lieutenants: Othon de Grandson, Jean de Bonvillars, Guillaume de Cicon, Jean de Vesci, Gilbert de Clare and, yes, Maître Jacques de Saint Georges too.[37] If it is true that Edward saw the fortifications of Outremer and Saint-Georges-d'Espéranche, then so too did Othon de Grandson and Jean de Bonvillars, but they saw the rebuilt Chillon and the new castle of Yverdon too. Indeed, Grandson is the very conduit by which Maître Jacques comes to England, Taylor thought so, evidenced by the Dolforwyn letter discussed earlier, and it is a suggestion that Prestwich endorsed:

> It is very likely that Otto's influence was important in the choice that Edward made of the Savoyard Master James of St George to play a leading role in the castle-building programme in Wales.[38]

Taylor and Prestwich are right: in order to understand the castles of north Wales, it is necessary to understand first the relationship between Edward and Othon – if all roads lead to Rome, then for us all roads lead through Grandson. There are no minutes of the meetings that resulted in the castles, but we can reasonably imagine that the leading role was played by Edward himself, but whilst taking care not to overestimate them we should take equal care not to underestimate them either. The evidence for their input is not 'neutral': the written record establishes a supervisory role for Jean de Bonvillars;[39] an understanding of the route taken by the Anglesey army in 1283 shows that Othon de Grandson and Jean de Vesci saw the castle sites before anyone else, and at the head of an army too,[40] and lastly, as we've seen, we should not overlook the presence of Guillaume de Cicon in Latin occupied Byzantine Greece before the came to England.[41]

Exactly what element of which castle was the result of the influence of who, is, as we've said, an ultimately fruitless task – the castles of north Wales are the product of all of the aforementioned men, and of Maître Jacques too, because his task was to turn their vision into stone. In the end, to borrow a phrase from Hollywood, we should 'follow the money', that those involved, to quote Hislop, 'in the belittling of Master James' architectural reputation' need to explain away the primary sources that point to his extensive involvement in castle-building for over forty years which resulted in a salary significantly above and beyond those of his contemporaries. Whatever the niceties of architectural critique, the primary sources are quite clear – a long and significant career across Europe in building castles coupled with a salary in England beyond comparison. As we suggested earlier, we can 'second guess' Edward with any amount of spilled ink, but we can be sure, he was not by reputation a king to pay a salary to someone who did not earn it.

This is not to say that the castles were an entirely Savoyard creation; they were not – Master Richard the Engineer and Masters Walter and Henry of Hereford made notable contributions. But we must not let, as has been the case of late, a genuine interest in native British sources cloud the reality that the castles were born of a unique blend of influences that drew from the whole of the Plantagenet familial triangle of England, Gascony and the County of Savoy. Several contemporary Savoyards, their history and culture long subsumed with that of France, have visited the castles with little or no idea of their connection to them, and that is not right. I hope it is not too sentimental to remember the words of Swiss historian Jean-Pierre Chapuisat, who came to England many years ago to find something of his own past:

> the visit of all these places where the memory of Savoy remains present today, seven centuries apart, communicated to me the emotion of the pilgrim and strongly encouraged me to persevere.[42]

Hislop's reanalysis, like Coldstream's, is based fundamentally upon the evidence of architecture, the built environment, but Taylor's original analysis stood upon twin pillars – architectural and written primary sources – and whilst architectural style may be contested, the written testimony we have seen in London, Turin and elsewhere is difficult to repute. As a historian I stand with Taylor's understanding of the primary sources,[43] which point to an extraordinary career that took a man of undoubted talent all the way from the Alps to Snowdonia building castles – and these castles at Yverdon in Switzerland and the UNESCO-listed castles of north Wales stand in testimony to his work nearly eight centuries after his passing.

Lastly, there is the thesis puts forward that Maître Jacques was the son of Jean Cotereel, and that he in turn was the son of an English architect, that Maître Jacques himself had castle-building sons, Giles and Tassin. If we join up the theses of Wilson, Grandjean and Taylor, add that to the silent witness of the architecture in Vaud and north Wales, and think that it would have been quite natural for Jean Cotereel to name his son born by the *Via Jacobus*, Jacques – then it is possible that we have four generations of a family with English origins working within Savoy and then England: perhaps these are the true 'English influences' in the castles of north Wales.[44] This joined-together thesis will always remain unprovable, but nonetheless, it has equal merit at the very least with the other unprovable theses suggested for the origins of English design in the castles of north Wales built by a Savoyard.

Professor Robert Bartlett said: 'In the medieval world, all politics, were family politics'[45] and Henry and later Edward began to rely upon the support of the wider family of Alianor de Provence, her maternal family, the House of Savoy. As Alianor herself wrote to Edward of Philippe I de Savoie *'Et par ce, beau dos fis, que nous ne poüms ne ne devons faillir à li, kar il ne failli mie à nos en nostre besong,'* that is, 'And because, good, sweet son, we can not and should not fail him, for he has never failed us in our need.'[46] They stood by the English Crown through the Montfortian and Welsh wars because they were their family. Matthew Paris and many others may have doubted Henry's wisdom in bringing across to England his wife's family, but the Savoyard history of the castles in Wales continues to bear witness to the fruits of the relationship. I hope we have been able to reawaken 'the memory of Savoy in these places'.

Appendix

Key Primary Sources

22 November 1253
Bazas, Gascony
Pro Johanne de Mesoz et Bertramo ingeniatore – Mandatum est P. Chacepork' quod, si Johannes de Mesoz, Bertramus Le Engynnur, Geraldus de Winton, Wilhelmis de Nantuyl, Willelmus Le Gelus et Nicholas Anglicus, magistri ingeniorum, nondum habuerint robas suas quas dominus rex eis dedit quando Castrum de Benaug.[1]
For Jean de Mézos and Bertram the Engineer – Command of P. Chacepork' that, if Jean de Mézos, Bertram the Engineer, Gerald to Winton, Guillaume de Nantuyl, Guillaume Le Gelus and Nicolas Anglicus, master engineers, have not yet robes that the king gave them at the Castle of Benauges.

25 September 1254
Bordeaux, Gascony
Pro Johanne de Maysoz – Mandatum est eisdem quod Johanni de Maysoz, qui a rege suscepturus est arma militaria apud Burdegalam, sine dilacione habere faciant ea que ad miliciam suam pertinent, sicut alles novis militibus consueverunt invenire. Teste apud supra (apud Burdegallam xxv die Septembris).[2]
For Jean de Mézos – Commanded that the same Jean de Mézos, that had taken up arms with us at Bordeaux, shall without delay have made those things that belong to the knighted, just as knights are accustomed to find, according to the above (at Bordeaux, 15th day of September).

December 1257–December 1258
Aigle, Valais
Idem libravit Francisco cementario pro tascheria nove camere iuxta turrim et Conteis.
Also considered, Francis the builder, for the task of a new room, next to the tower at Conthey.[3]

1260–2
Chillon
The following records for 1260 to 1262 are all from the *Compotus de Valeisio et Chablasio de Anno LXI.* That is, the accounts of the Valais and Chablais of the year 61. That is the twelve months from 3 February 1260 until 3 February 1261 prepared for the Castellan of Chillon. However, collected with them are accounts for the Custodian or Guardian of fortifications, Pierre Mainier, from the period 1 May 1261 until 4 March 1262 and Pierre de Sassons, Castellan of Saillon for the period 24 June 1261 until 2 February 1262.

1260–1

Chillon

In expensis domini Iohannis de Masot euntis apud Sallon ad turrim de Sallon devisandam .vi. sol. .viii. den. preter illos quos expendit apud Sallon.

The expenses of Jean de Mézos when he was at Saillon for the tower of Saillon. Six *sol* eight *den.* Those whom he considers at Saillon.[4]

March 1261–May 1262

Account of Pierre Mainier, Chillon

De quibus libravit Francisco cementario de taschia .viii.xx. et .x.librarum et duabus robis de quadraginta sol. pro turre de Sallon facienda de sexaginta et decem pedibus altitudinis tam in grosso muro quam in avante pedibus et in merlis, de duodecim pedibus pissitudinis usque ad primam travaturam et decem pedibus a secunda travatura superius. x. lib.[5]

Item in liberatione magistri Iohannis cementarii a die qua recessit a domo sua veniendo versus Yverdunum, videlicet prima die maii hoc anno [1 May 1261] usque ad secundam dominicam quadragisime, videlicet quintam diem intrante marcio [5 March 1262], per quadraginta et quatuor septimanas, qui cepit duodecim solidos qualibet septimana, xxvj. lib. ij.sol. In liberatione magistri Iacobi filii sui per idem tempus, capientis singulis septimanis decem solidos et sex denarios, xxiij.lib. ij.sol. In vadiis suis et calciatura sua et pannis lineis, capientis quinque solidos per mensem, per dictum tempus .lv.sol. In medicinis ipsius magistri Jacobi tempore egritudinis sue .xxv.sol. In liberatione magistri Petri Mainier custodis operum domini per idem tempus pro se duobus equis et uno valeto suo capientis ut predictus magister Iohannes. Xxvj.lib. viij.sol.

For the discharge of Master John the mason from the day when he came from his home to Yverdon, assuredly the first day of May of this year [1 May 1261] until the second Sunday of Lent [5 March 1262] for forty-four weeks who received twelve *sol* per week. Twenty-six *livres* and eight *sol.* For the discharge of his son Maître Jacques for same period receiving ten *sol* and six denier every week. Twenty-three *livres* and two *sol.* For his wages and shoes and his linen bandages receiving five *sol* per month. Fifty-five *sol.* For Maître Jacques himself, medicine for the time of his illness. Twenty-five *sol.* For the discharge of Master Pierre Mainier Custodian of the Lord's works for the same period two horses for himself and one for his servant as Master John aforesaid. Twenty-six *Livres* and eight *sol.*[6]

1261–2

Account of Pierre de Sassons, Saillon

In expensis domini Iohannis de Masot ad supervidendum ibi situm turris per tres dies. Vj.s.vj.d.

The expenses of Jean de Mézos to oversee the siting of the tower for three days Six *sol* six *den.*[7]

Idem libravit Francisco de summa centum sexaginta et decem librarum et duarum robarum de quadraginta solidis quam debet habere pro turre de Sallon, septuaginta

pedum altitudinis duodecim pedum pissitudinis et duodecim pedum de vacuo interius,
preter decem libras liberatas eidem per magistrum Petrum Mainier, de quibus computavit
in compoto suo. .L.lib. x. den.[8]

Also considered Francis, the sum a total of one hundred and seventy *Livres* and
two robes of forty *solidis*, which he must have for the tower of Saillon, seventy feet
in height, twelve feet thick and twelve feet deep inside, apart from the ten pounds
delivered to it by Maître Pierre Mainier, of whom he counted in his own account.
Fifty *Livres* Ten *den*.

1265–7

*In expensis **domini Iohannis de Masoz** apud Yverdunum infirmantis per xxviii dies, de*
*mandato domini, vi lib xii den. . .in acquietancia **Magistri Jacobi Cementarii** hoc anno*
et de anno preterito. . . qui Jacobus percipit Yverdunum de domino in feudo, decem libras
viannensium singulis annis. xv. lib.

The expenses of Jean de Mézos at Yverdon whilst sick for twenty-eight days, by
command of his Lord, six *livres* 12 *den* … in the acquittance (discharge of a debt)
of Maître Jacques the mason for this year and the year before that … he Jacques
has the fee of Yverdon, ten *livres* Vienne every year. xv. *Livres*.[9]

1267–8

*In expensis **Magistri Jacobi Lathomi** euntis apud Salinas pro operibus putei per xj*
*dies, capientis quolibet die iij.s. pro expensis, xxxiij.s. Idem libravit **domino Johanni de***
***Masouz** moranti apud Salin' pro dictando opera putei Salino xxix.lib. xix.s. vj.d.*

'The expenses of Maître Jacques the stonemason going to Salins-Les-Thermes for
the works of the well for eleven days, taking per day three *sol* for expenses, thirty-
three *sol*. Also considered Lord Jean de Mézos detained at Salins-Les-Thermes for
dictating the well works at Salins-Les-Thermes twenty-nine *Livres*, nineteen *sol*,
six *den*.[10]

1 April 1269–15 August 1269

Magistro Jacobo Lathomo, x Lib.
Maître Jacques the mason, ten *livres*.[11]

23 August 1271

(at Chambéry) Montmélian

*Die dominica in vigilia beati Bartholomei. **Magistro Jacobo lathomo** de mandato*
*domini. xii. sol. Item in expensis eiusdem et **Guigonis de Vercors** quando fuerunt apud*
Montem Melianum. ii. sol.

On Sunday, the eve of St Bartholomew. By command of Maître Jacques the mason.
twelve *sol*. Also the expenses of Guy de Vercors when they were at Montmélian,
two *sol*.[12]

21 September 1273

(at Chambéry) The Viennois[13]

Magistro Jacobo lathomo misso in Viennensem, xiiij.s.

Maître Jacques the mason having been sent to the Viennois, fourteen *sol.*[14]

22 November 1273

(at Saint-Georges d'Espéranche) Saint-Laurent-du-Pont

Magistro Jacobo lathomo et magistro Johanni de Gray missis ad Desertum, x.s.'

Maître Jacques the mason having been sent to the wilderness, ten *sol.*[15]

26 November 1273

(at Saint-Georges d'Espéranche) probably Saint-Laurent-du-Pont

Magistro Jacobo lathomo et magistro Johanni de Gray missis ad Desertum, x.s.

Maître Jacques the mason and Master John de Gray having been sent to the wilderness, ten *sol.*[16]

27 February 1274

(at Evian) Monthey, Valais, near Saint-Maurice-d'Agaune

Item domino Iohanni de Maso et Magistro Jacobo missis ad Montez, viij.s.

The same for Sir John de Mézos and Maître Jacques having been sent to Monthey, eight *sol.*[17]

15 March 1274

(at Evian) Gümmenen,[18], between Morat and Berne

In expensis domini Iohannis de Massout, Hugneti de Chillon,19 Magistri Jacobi, Rolleti de Cletis, qui fuerunt ad Contaminam per octo dies, iiij.lib,xvij.s.vij.d.

For the expenses of Lord John de Massout, Hugneti de Chillon, Maître Jacques, Rolleti de Cletis, who were in Gümmenen for eight days. Four *livres*, seventeen *sol* and seven *denier.*[20]

18 March 1274

(at Evian) Saint-Georges d'Espéranche

Magistro Jacobo lathomo pro expensis suis redeundo ad Sanctum Georgium, x.s.

Maître Jacques the mason for his expenses on his way home to Saint-Georges d'Espéranche-d'Espéranche, ten *sol.*[21]

6 May 1274

(at Chillon) Gümmenen, between Morat and Berne

Hugneto et Magistro Jacobo lathomo et magistro de Romanis, missus ad Contaminam .xxx.s.

For Hugnetus and Maître Jacques the mason and Master de Romanis, having been sent to Gümmenen, thirty *sol.*[22]

14 May 1274

(at Chillon) Côte-San-André and Voiron

Magistri Jacobo lathomo misso ad Costam et ad Voyron .iiij.s.

Maître Jacques the mason having been sent to Côte-San-Andre and Voiron, four *sol*.[23]

16 May 1274

(at Chillon) Gümmenen, between Morat and Berne

Magistro Iacobo lathomo misso Contamine .xv.s.

Maître Jacques the mason having been sent to Gümmenen, Fifteen *sol*.[24]

19 May 1274

(at Chillon) Probably Saint-Laurent-du-Pont and Chillon

Magistro Jacobo lathomo pro expensis suis et Magistri de Romanis Veniencium de Deserto ad dominum apud Chillon .xxviij.s.

For Maître Jacques the mason for his expenses and the expenses of Master de Romanis coming from the wilderness to their Lord at Chillon, twenty-eight *sol*.[25]

5 June 1274

(Cossonay) The Viennois

Magistro Jacobo lathomo pro xxx diebus fuit in operibus domini in Vien' .lx.s.

For Maître Jacques the mason for thirty days where he was working for the Lord in the Viennois, sixty *sol*.[26, 27]

28 June 1274

(at Voiron) The Viennois

Magistro Jacobo, de quatuor lib, que dantur sibi per annum pro roncino suo tenendo, xl.s. Item eidem misso Vienn pro expensis suis xx.s.

For Maître Jacques, concerning four *livres*, which are given to him per annum for keeping his packhorse, forty *sol*. To the same person having been sent to the Viennois for his expenses, twenty *sol*.[28]

21 August 1274

(at Voiron) Côte-Saint-André

Domino Petro de Langis et Magistro Jacobo missis ad Costam, xxv.s.

Lord Peter de Langis and Maître Jacques the mason having been sent to Côte-Saint-Andre, twenty-five *sol*.[29]

28 August 1274

(at Voiron) Unknown

Magistro Jacobo, de iiij lib, que dantur sibi per annum pro roncino suo tenedo, xl.s.

Maître Jacques about four pounds, which are given to him per year for taking a packhorse, forty *sol*.[30]

29 August 1274

(at Voiron) Bresse

*Domino Petro de Langis et **Magistro Jacobo** missis in Brissiam, lx.s.*

Lord Peter de Langis and Maître Jacques having been sent to Bresse, sixty *sol*.[31]

15 September 1274

(at Voiron) Bourg-en-Bresse

*In expensis domini Petri de Langis et **Magistri Jacobi** quando fuerant apud Burgum In Brissia, preter sexaginta sol. tune sibi traditos, xiiij.s.*

For the expenses of Lord Peter de Langis and Maître Jacques when they had been at Bourg-en-Bresse, in addition to sixty *sol* paid to them, fourteen *sol*.[32]

23 September 1274

Côte-Saint-André and Saint-Laurent-du-Pont

*In expensis **Magistri Jacobi** per quinque des ad Costam et ad Sanctum Laurencium.*

For the expenses of Maître Jacques the mason for five days at Côte-Saint-André and St-Laurent-du-Pont.[33]

16 October 1274

(at Saint-Georges-d'Espéranche) Bourg-en-Bresse and Châtillon-sur-Chalaronne in Bresse

*In expensis domini Petri de Langis, **domini Iohannis de Massout, Magistri Jacobi** et aliorum apud Burgum in Brixiam et apud Castillionem, preter centum solidos tunc eis traditos, Cv.s.*

For the expenses of Lord Peter de Lang, Sir John de Mézos, Maître Jacques and other people at Bourg en Bresse and at Châtillon-sur-Chalaronne, in addition to one hundred *sol* given to them, one hundred and five *sol*.[34]

23 October 1274

(at Saint-Georges-d'Espéranche) Romans-sur-Isère

*item **Magistro Jacobo** misso ad Romans, v.s.*

also Maître Jacques having been sent to Romans, five *sol*.[35]

5 November 1274

(at Saint-Georges-d'Espéranche) Saint-Laurent-du-Pont

*In expensis **Magistri Jacobi** lathomi per duas vices ad Sanctum Laurencium de Deserto, xiiij.s.*

For the Expenses of Maître Jacques the mason for two turns at Saint-Laurent-du-Pont, Fourteen *sol*.[36]

19 December 1274

(at Saint-Georges-d'Espéranche) Saint-Laurent-du-Pont

In expensis Magistri Jacobi lathomi quando fuit apud Sanctum Laurencium per septem dies, xiiij.s.

For the expenses of Maître Jacques the mason when he was at Saint-Laurent-du-Pont for seven days, fourteen *sol.*[37]

28 January 1275

(at Saint-Georges-d'Espéranche) Côte-Saint-André, Voiron and Saint-Laurent-du-Pont

In expensis domini Bosonis et Magistri Jacobi lathomi euncium apud Costam, Voyron et Sanctum Laurencium, xxxviij.s.

For the expenses of Master Bosonis and Maître Jacques the mason going to Cote-Saint-André, Voiron and Saint-Laurent-du-Pont, thirty-eight *sol.*[38]

25 March 1275

Romont, Côte-Saint-André and Saint-Laurent-du-Pont

Magistro Jacobo Lathomo misso ad Romont, xxx.s.In expensis ipsius Magistri Jacobi quando fuit ad Costam et ad Sanctum Laurencium per septem dies, xiiij.s.

Maître Jacques the mason having been sent to Romont, thirty *sol*. For the expenses of Maître Jacques himself when he was at Cote-Saint-Andre and at Saint-Laurent-du-Pont for seven days, fourteen *sol.*[39]

26 April 1275

(at Saint-Georges-d'Espéranche) Saint-Georges-d'Espéranche- and Bourg-en-Bresse

Domini Petro de Langis, domino Johanni de Massout, Magistro Jacobo missis apud Burgum In Bressia, vj.lib.

Lord Peter de Langis, Sir Jean de Mézos and Maître Jacques having been sent to Bourg-en-Bresse, six *livres.*[40]

4 May 1275

Bourg-en-Bresse

In expensis domini P.de Langis, domini Jo. de Massout et Magistri Jacobi apud Burgum per octo dies, preter sex lib. Tunc sibi traditis, lv.s.

For the expenses of Lord Peter de Langis, Sir Jean de Mézos and Maître Jacques at Bourg-en-Bresse for eight days, in addition to Six *livres* given to them then, fifty-five *sol.*[41]

6 May 1275

(at Saint-Georges-d'Espéranche) Côte-Saint-André and Voiron

Domino Johanni de Massout recedenti, xxx.s. Magistro Jacobo lathomo misso ad Costam et ad Voyron, xxx.s.

For Sir Jean de Mézos leaving, thirty *sol*. Maître Jacques the mason having been sent to Cote-Saint-Andre and Voiron, thirty *sol*.[42]

17 June 1275
(at Saint-Georges-d'Espéranche) Bourg-en-Bresse
Magistro Iacobo misso ad Burgun in Bressia, xxv.s.
Maître Jacques having been sent to Bourg-en-Bresse, twenty-five *sol*.[43]

5 July 1275
(at Saint-Georges-d'Espéranche) Bourg-en-Bresse
Magistro Iacobo misso ad Burgum In Bressia, x.s.
Maître Jacques having been sent to Bourg-en-Bresse, ten *sol*.[44]

27 July 1275
(at Voiron) Côte-Saint-Andre
*In expensis domini Petri de Langis et **Magistri Jacobi** et domini Iohannis de castellario quando fuerunt apud Costam, xxij.s.*
For the expenses of Lord Peter de Langis and Maître Jacques and Lord John de Castellario when they were at Cote-Saint-Andre, twenty-two *sol*.[45]

9 August 1275
The Valdigne[46] and Aosta, both in the Aosta Valley, Italy
Magistro Iacobo lathomo misso In Vaudam et Augustam, L.s.Item eidem quando fuit in Vaudino per xxv dies quia non habitat nisi triginta sol. xlv.s.
Maître Jacques the mason, having been to Valdigne and Aosta,[47] fifty *sol*. For the same person when he was in Valdigne for twenty-five days because he only got thirty *sol*, forty-five *sol*.[48]

23 September 1275
(at La Rochette)[49] The Viennois
*Magistro Jacobo lathomo misso In Vienn' x.s.fort; Johanni Hel'misso **domino Eadmundo de Anglia**, ij.s.vj.d. **Magistro Jacobo lathomo** pro emenda roncini sui asallati, C.s. Eidem pro convencione facta con ipso de roncino suo tenere per annum, iiij.lib.*
Maître Jacques the mason, having been sent to the Viennois, ten *sol*. John Hel having been sent to Lord Edmund of England, two *sol* six denier. To Maître Jacques the mason for buying his packhorse in Aosta,[50] one hundred *sol*. To the same for an agreement made with him for keeping his packhorse per annum, four *livres*.[51]

1274–5
(at Bourg-en-Bresse)
*In domo domus fori facta, in taschiam datam per dominum P. de Langes militem, **dominum Johannem de Masoz militem et Magistrum Jacobum lathomum** Guidoni et Martino de Molend per litteras ipsorum quas reddunt.*

In my market-place, by task given by knight Lord P. de Langes, knight Lord Jean de Mézos and Maître Jacques the mason, Guy and Martin de Molend answered in writing, which they render there.[52]

Undated entry
(at Saint-Laurent-du-Pont)
*In stipendii operacionum ... In fossato de legreta et cindencium nemus in alveo dicte aque, et tunc fuit datam in tascham dictum opus Magistro P. de Falaverio per **Magistrum Jacobum**, xij.lib. x.s.v.d.*
The campaign works are ... On the road from the legreta cindencium woods and a stream of said channel, And then it was given in the task by Master P. de Falaverio by Maître Jacques. Twelve *livres*, ten *sol* and five *deniers*.[53]

Undated entry
*Idem libravit Magistro Garnerio terriliatori pro domo tegularie faciendo ... per composicionem factam cum eo per dominum Petrum de Langes, **dominum Johannes de Masout**, Hugonem Boterie et **Magistrum Jacobum** ... xxv. Lbr.vienn.*
He gave the same to Master Garnerio making tiles for the home ... by means of the agreement have been made with it according to the Lord Peter de Langes, Lord Jean de Mézos, Hugh Boterie and Maître Jacques ... Twenty-five Livres Viennois.[54]

Undated entry
(at Bourg-en-Bresse) travelling from Bourg to Saint-Georges
In expensis lathomi missi apud Sanctum Georgium et aysiamentis suis portandis, xxv.s.vj.d.
For expenses of the mason travelling back with his baggage from Bourg-en-Bresse to Saint-Georges-d'Espéranche, twenty-five *sol* six *Denier*.[55]

21 March 1277
Down Ampney, Gloucestershire
March 21, Down Ampney. To R. [Robert Burnell] Bishop of Bath and Wells, the chancellor, and to **Othon de Grandisono**. The king commends the care and solicitude exhibited by them in his affairs in the court of France ... especially as the king has no one about him whom he believes could know the premises and do his will in the premises better and more advantageously than them, not even if he himself were to attend to the matters there in person.[56]

31 March 1277
Dolforwyn
Au Roy de Englterre. Al sun tres cher seignur saluz. Sachez sire ke nous asegames le Chastel de Doluereyn le mekreydy en la simeine de Paskes ... Sachez sire ke quant le chastel sera en vostre mein, il auera mester de grant amendement; por quoi nous auerrums

mester de eukun homme ke de tels choses se feust entremettre e ke leument vosist empleer
vos deners, kar nous y mettoms Mestre Bertram je dout ke il ne devisast trop de choses e
par aventure vos deners ne serreint assez bien emplee com serreit, e por ce sire mandez
nous de ceste chose vostre volonte. Sachez sire ke la lettre ke vus nous avez envoye par mon
sire Joh de Bevilar nous vint a graund socour, kar sachez sire ke nostre ost semble bien ost
de graunt seignur, e ce ne poet on mine fere sans deners. Sire a Deu ke vous gard, mandez
nous votre estat e vostre volonte. Ceste lettre feu fete a Dolverein le Samedy apres Paskes.
The sender reports that they laid siege to the castle of Dolvoreyn [sic] on the
Wednesday in Easter Week [31 March 1277] … Informs the king that when the
castle comes into his hands – *il auera mester de grant amendement* – it will need much
repair. Wherefore there will be need of some man who will take these matters in
hand, and will loyally employ the king's money. For if the sender employs Master
Bertram for the work, he fears that Master Bertram will devise too many things,
and perhaps the king's money will not be so well employed as it needs to be. Asks
the king's will in this matter. Thanks the king for the letter sent by the hand of
John de Bevilar, which was of great assistance, for the sender's force looks like the
force of a great lord and this cannot be done without money.[57]

10 August 1277
Flint
Vincencio clerico pro duobus solidis quos dedit diversis hominibus precepto O. de
Grandisono pro maremio leuando apud Flind, ijs.
Vincent gave to the clerk for the two *sol* [shillings] that he gave to various men by
order of Othon de Grandson for having carted timber in Flint, two shillings[58]

8 December 1277
Saint-Georges-d'Espéranche
Actum apud sanctum georgium de esperenchis in domo magistri iacobi lathomi.
Enacted at Saint-Georges-d'Espéranche in the house of Master James the Mason.

7 April 1278
Edington, Somerset
Jacobo Ingeniatori a die Martis in perpacationem vadiorum suorum . Xvij.Dierum
usque ad presentem diem. Xvijs. Eidem Jacobo eunti in partibus Wallie ad ordinandum
opera castrorum Ibidem pro vadiis suis et expenses suis a die presenti usque ad diem
Dominicam proximam post festum sancti Johannis aute Portam Latinam Per .xxix. Dies
.lviij.s.
Given to Jacques the Engineer, a day in March, for payment, in arrears, of his
wages for 17 days until the present day. Seventeen shillings. To the same Jacques
going to parts in Wales for ordering the works of castles, the same for his wages and
his expenses, from the present day until next Day of the Lord after the Festival of
Saint Jacques Before the Latin Door for twenty-nine days. Fifty-Eight Shillings.[59]

21 May 1278

Westminster

Magistro Jacobo Ingeniatori pro vadis suis per .vij. Dies post diem dominicam Proximam post festum sancti Johannis ante Portam Latinam ipsa die Dominica computata per quos fuit extra curiam .xiiij.s. Eidem pro vadiis Suis per tres menses subsequentes per quos erit extra curiam ad Visitandum castra de flint et Rothelan .viij.li.viij.s. ; et sic in toto .ix. li.x.s.

Given to Maître Jacques Engineer for his wages for seven days, after the Day of the Lord after the Festival of Saint John Before the Latin Gate, The very Day of the Lord having been counted, for during which days he was away from court. Fourteen shillings. To the same the following days, during which he stayed at court, Eight shillings. To the same for his wages for the three following months, during which he will be out of court, in order to visit the castles of Flint and Rhuddlan. Eight pounds and eight shillings and so in total Nine pounds ten shillings.[60]

18 June 1278

*Garcioni **Magistri Jacobi le Mazun** revertenti ad dominum suum usque Rothelan ad expensas suas .xij.d.*

Given to the servant of Maître Jacques the mason, coming back to his Lord until Rhuddlan for his expenses. Seven pence.[61]

19 September 1278

Magistro Jacobo Ingeniatori pro vadiis suis a die Assumpcionis beata Virginis Ipso computato usque ad diem Omnium Sanctorum per .lxxviij. Dies, ipso percipiente extra curiam per diem .ij.s., viij.li.li.xvj.s.

Given to Maître Jacques Engineer for his wages from the Holy Day of the Virgin's Assumption, this day having been counted, until the day of All Saints for seventy-eight days, himself being out of court for the day. Two shillings, Seven pounds sixteen shillings.

April 1283

Harlech

*pacatum domino **Othon de Grandisono** ad sustentacionem D et lx peditum secum euncium de Castro de Bere usque Hardelach xx.li per talliam.*

Given for pacifying, to Lord Othon de Grandson, for the support of five hundred and sixty of men going with him from Castel-y-Bere to Harlech, Twenty pounds by tally.[62]

21 October 1283

Caernarfon

The king has committed in like manner to **William de Cycun** [Guillaume de Cicon], the castle of Aberconewey [Conwy], with the armour, etc., and has granted to him 190 *livres* yearly for the custody thereof, to be received as above, on condition

that he shall have continuously have in garrison, in addition to himself and his
household, at his cost thirty fencible men, of whom fifteen shall be crossbowmen
one chaplain, one artiller, a carpenter, a mason and a smith, and of the others shall
be made janitors, watchmen and other ministers of the castle. Order is given to all
bailiffs etc. (as above).[63]

3 December 1283

*Johanni de Byveillard militi eunti in Walliam ad supervidendum castra domini Regis
ibidem precepto Regis, pro suis expensis eundo, morando et revertendo.*
To the knight Jean de Bonvillars, going to Wales to supervise the castles of the
Lord King by Order of the King, for his expenses whilst going there, staying there
and coming back.[64]

20 October 1284

Caernarfon
Grant, for life, to **Maître Jacques de Sancto Georgio**, king's sergeant, of 3s a day
from the wardrobe, and at his death of 1s. 6d.a day to his wife Ambrosia if she
survives him.[65]

12 February to 13 December 1285

Caernarfon
Magistro Jacobo de Sancto Georgio, Magistro operacionum Regis in Wallia.
Maître Jacques de Saint Georges, Master of the King's Works in Wales.[66]

1286

Conwy
*eidem Henrico pro fractura graduum camere Regis in castro predicto et pro oriolo in
medio castro facts ad tascham predicto Henrico traditam per dominum J. de Bonouillar'
et Magistrum Jacobum.*
To the same Henry for breaking of steps in the King's chamber in the castle
aforesaid and the oriole made in the castle for the task given to the aforesaid Henry
by Lord Jean de Bonvillars and Maître Jacques.[67]

5 September 1286

Conwy
*Die Dominica 8 die Septembris eisdem R.et S. pro 500 bayardis ab eisdem emptis per
dominum Johannem de Bonovillario, precio 100 3s, et missis apud Carnarvan pro
operibus ibidem, 15s. Eodem die eisdem R. et S pro 16 bayardis ab eisdem emptis per
Magistrum Jacobum 5s 4d.*
On Sunday the 8th day of September the same R. and S. for 500 barrows from the
same bought by Lord Jean de Bonvillars, price 5 pounds 3 shillings, and deposing
forth for their works at Caernarfon. On the same day the same R. and S. for 16
barrows from the same bought by Maître Jacques 5 shillings and 4 pence.

29 September 1286

Conwy

*Tasch' cyment'. Die Dominico 29 die Septembris **Johanni Franceys, Willelmo Seysel, Roger de Cokersond, Petro de Bononia, Gillotto de Chalons** ... tascatoribus diversorum operum.*

Masons tasks. Sunday 29th Day of September [1286] Jean Francis, Guillaume Seysel, Roger de Cockersand, Pierre de Boulogne, Giles de Chalons ... various works by task.[68]

3 July 1290

Havering

July 3, Havering. To all to whom, etc. Notification that the king has committed to **Maître Jacques de Sancto Georgio** his castle of Hardelagh during pleasure, so that he shall receive yearly 100 marks at the exchequer of Kaernarvan for so long as he shall be constable of the said castle, reckoning in that sum the wages that the king previously granted to him yearly. To Agnès, late the wife of **John Beuillard**. Order to deliver to the said Jacques by indenture the said castle, and other stock there.[69]

1291–2

*Rex mandat Baronibus quod allocati faciant Magistro Roberto de Belvero. xx. li. quas per preceptum **Johannis de Bonovillar** defuncti super tenentis locum **Ottonis de Grandisono** tunc Justiciarii Regis Northwall liberavit Johanni de Haueringg nuper constabulario castri Regis de Kaernernan pro custodia eiusdem castri a festo sancti Michelis anno regni nostri xiij usque ad festum Natalitatis Domini proximum sequentem, silcut per **Willelmum de Grandisono** postmodum tenentum locum predicti **Ottonis** ibidem coram Rege est testificatum.*

The King mandates barons Twenty Pounds which were allocated to Master Robert of Belvoir. Which we note was by the command of the deceased Jean de Bonvillars, who formerly held the place of deputy to, Othon de Grandson, then King's Justiciar of North Wales, absolved by John de Havering, not long ago Constable of the King's castle of Caernarfon, for custody of the castle from the feast of Saint Michael in the Thirteenth Year of Our Reign [Michaelmas (October) 1285} to immediately following the Feast of the Nativity of our Lord [1288], as by Guillaume de Grandson, afterwards the sitting deputy of the aforesaid Othon, in that very place in the presence of and witness of the King.[70]

17 April 1295

Llanfaes

Magistro Jacobo de Sancto Georgio de prestito super diversis necessariis providendis pro nova castro per manus proprias 17 die Aprilis apud Lannuais. 60s.

Maître Jacques de Saint Georges the prest of diverse necessities for the provision of the new castle given by hand on 17 April at Llanfaes, Sixty shillings.[71]

25 February 1296

Conwy

Scriptum apud Conewey 25 die Februarii. Memorandum quod in muro inchoato circa motam castri de Carnaruan sunt iiij turres inchoate qui quidem murus continet in longitudine xviij perticatas; et de istis perticatis viij perticate continent in altitudine xij pedes, et x perticate continent in altitudine xxiiij pedes; et iste murus continet in spissitudine xv pedes.

You should note that there are on the unfinished wall about the moat / ditch of the castle of Caernarfon, there are 4 unfinished towers that are contained in the lengthwise wall of 18 perche[72] (99 yards); of which wall there are 8 perches (44 yards) contained in height-wise 12 feet, and 10 perche (55 yards) is contained in height-wise 24 feet; and these walls contained in thickness 15 feet.[73]

27 February 1296

Conwy

A lour treschiers seigneurs le tresurier e as barons del escheker nostre seignur le roy Jakes de Seint George e Wauter de Wyncestre saluz e duwes reverences. Pur ce sires que nostre seignur le roy nous ad comande par ses lettres del eschekier que entotes choses suer lestat des oueraygnes de Biaumarreys apertement vous certifiens, issi que vous peussez ordiner lestat de meisme loevre pur ceste seeson qui est a venir selonc ce que vous verrez que mieutz soit a faire, vous fesoms saver que loevre qui nous fesoms est de grant coust dont il nous avoye molt.

Sachez sites que nous avons tenu tot cest iver e uncore tenoms macheons tailleurs de piries, quarreurs, menutz overiers fesantz mortier e debrisantz pirres pur chautz, carettes amenantz pirres pur chautz e merrym a edifier en chastel la ou nous sumes touz demorrantz ore, e si avoms 1,000 charpentiers, feivres, daubours e fosseurs, sanz la garenson a chivaux covertz dont ylyont to qui prenont 70s. la symeyne, e si avons 20 arblastiers qui premont 47s. 10d. e 100 hommes de pie qui prenont £6. 2s. 6d. la symeyne. E sachez sires quant ces lettres furent faites nous deuions quei as ouerours quei a la garneson plus de cink centz livres dont eux ont eu molt grante defaute e uncore ont, e si avons molt grant peine de les retentir pur ce quil nont dont vivre. E sachez chiers sires que si nostre seignur le roy voet que loevre se perfate vistement ausi come mestier serreit e sicome ele est commence nous ne venoms que nous peusseoms eschaper meyns desorenavant tant come le seeson dure que de £250 la symeyne, e ensi porroit loevre estre bien avance ceste seeson. E si par aventure vous sentez que nous ne peusseoms tantz deners avoir, le nous mandez e nous mettoms overcools a vostre volunte selonc ce que vous verrez que mieutz soit pur le profit nostre seignur le roy.

Endroit de lestat de loueraygne autrefoiz lavons mande a nostre seignur le roy, si vous fesoms savoir que loevre est daucinme pret de 28 piez haut e la ou ele est plus basse ele est de 20 piez haute, e si sont comence 10 tours dehors e quatre dedenz, a chescune porte deus pur les alees, e si sont quatre portes perdues qui sont closes de lok chescuine noit, e a chescune porte serront trois portes colisces. E sachez sires que un vesseal de poys de 40 toniaux porta venir a la pleine mer chargee a la porte du chastel maugre touz les Galeys tut avons nous fait.

E que vous ne esmervaillez ou tantz deners soient despenduz la symeyne, vous fesons saver quilyad convenu e couendra quatre centz macheons quei tailleurs quei couchours, 2,000 menus oueriers e 100 charettes e 60 carres e 30 bateaux portanz pirres e charbon de mer, e deus centz quarreours e 30 fevres e charpentiers de mettre les gistes e les planches du chastel e autres oueres necessaries; sanz la garneson avant nomee, e ostre les achatz dont yly couendra molt. Endroit sires de lestat de la terre de Gales, nous nensavons uncore si bien nony, mais vous savez bien que Galeys sont Galeys e vous les devez bien conustre et font a duter detant le plus si les gerres de France et Descose veysent avant peynse de bien faire en touz pointz.

A Dieu treschiers seignurs qui vous gard.
Escrites a Aberconewey le 27 iour de Fevrier.

E pur Dieu sires hastes les deners pur loueraigne tant come nostre seignur le roy le voet, car tant ilyad fait uncore poy vaut si plus mysoit fait.'

To their very dear lordships, the treasurer and barons of the exchequer of our Lord the king, James of St George and Walter of Winchester send greeting and due reverence.

Sirs,

As our lord the king has commanded us by letters of the exchequer to let you have a clear picture of all aspects of the state of works at Beaumaris, so that you may be able to lay down the level of work for this coming season as may seem best to you, we write to inform you that the work we are doing is very costly and we need a great deal of money.
You should know:

- That we have kept on masons, stone cutters, quarrymen and minor workmen all through the winter, and are still employing them, for making mortar and breaking up stone for lime, we have had carts bringing this stone to the site and bringing timber for erecting the buildings in which we are all now living inside the castle, we also have 1,000 carpenters, smiths, plasterers and navvies, quite apart from a mounted garrison of ten men accounting for 70s a week, 20 crossbowmen who add another 47s. 10d, and 100 infantry who take a further £6. 2s. 6d.
- That when this letter was written we were short of £500 for both workmen and garrison. The men's pay has been and still is very much in arrears, and we have the greatest difficulty in keeping them because they simply have nothing to live on.
- That if our lord the king wasn't s the work to be finished as quickly as it should be on the scale on which it has commenced, we could not make do with less than £250 a week throughout the season with it, this season could see the work advanced. If, however, you feel that we cannot have so much money, let us know, and we will put the workmen at your disposal according to whatever you think will be the best profit of our lord the king.

As for the progress of the work, we have sent a previous report to the king. We can tell you that some of it already stands about 28 feet high and even where it is lowest it is 20 feet. We have begun 10 of the outer and four of the inner towers, that is the two for each of the two gatehouse passages. Four gates have been hung and are shut and locked every night, and each gateway is to have three portcullises. You should also know that at high tide a 40-ton vessel will be able to come fully laden right up to the castle gateway so much have we been able to do in spite of all the Welshmen.

In case you wonder where so much money could go in a week, we would have you know that we have needed – and shall continue to need – 400 masons, both cutters and layers, together with 2,000 minor workmen, 100 carts, 60 wagons and 30 boats bringing stone and sea-coal, 200 quarrymen, 30 smiths and carpenters for putting the joists and floorboards and other necessary jobs. All this takes no account of the garrison mentioned above, nor any purchases of materials, of which, there will have to be a great quantity.

As to how things are in the land of Wales, we still cannot be any too sure. But, as you well know, Welshmen are Welshmen, and you need to understand them properly if, which God forbid, there is a war with France and Scotland, we shall need to watch them all the more closely.

You may be assured, dear sirs, that we shall make it our business to give satisfaction in everything.

May God protect your dearest lordships.
Aberconwy, 27 February 1296

P.S. And, Sirs, for God's sake be quick with the money for the works, as much as ever our lord the king wills, otherwise everything done up till now will have been of no avail.

Notes

Chapter One

1. Sapaudia first appears in Ammianus Marcellinus, who described it as the southern district of *Provincia Maxima Sequanorum*, the land of the *Sequani* enlarged by the Diocletian Reforms. It originally covered the area around *Lac Neuchâtel*, the land of the ancient *Allobroges*. Its prefect appeared in the late Roman List of Offices. During the 5th century, the Burgundians settled in the area, forming the Kingdom of the Burgundians, the capital of which was *Lugdunum Segusianorum* (Lyon). For centuries thereafter, the names Burgundy and Sapaudia/Savoy became intricately linked. In the mid-9th century, Sapaudia was ruled by the Bosonid duke Humbert as part of the realm of Upper Burgundy. In 933, it was incorporated into Rudolph II's Kingdom of Arles, the Arelat or Second Kingdom of Burgundy.
2. During the time of the failing Kingdom of Arles or Burgundy the Great Saint-Bernard Pass had been held for a time by Saracens based in Province, a Christian leader, Bernard de Menthon, forced them off what was then still given the Roman name of Mons Jovis around 972, he founded a hospice on the pass after whom the mountain – and much later the rescue dogs who were trained there – were then named.
3. Peter H. Wilson. *The Holy Roman Empire*. Second ed. (London: Penguin, 2017). 362.
4. Of course, Voltaire was describing the Empire of his time saying, '*Ce corps qui s'appelait et qui s'appelle encore le saint empire romain n'était en aucune manière ni saint, ni romain, ni empire*' but the Empire of the thirteenth century could have merited the same epithet. Quoted from *Essai sur l'histoire générale et sur les mœurs et l'esprit des nations*, Chapter 70 (1756).
5. Peter H. Wilson. *The Holy Roman Empire*. Second ed. (London: Penguin, 2017). 196–7.
6. Ibid. 37.
7. There is a charter dated 21 January 1042 describing Humbert as '*Hubertus Comes*' in Carutti (1888), *Documenti del libro primi*, XXVII, 196.
8. Humbert had supported Konrad in his campaigns against Odo II, Count of Blois, and the Archbishop of Milan. Konrad had inherited Burgundy, when Rudolf III, the last King of Burgundy, had died on 6 September 1032, sending his crown and insignia to Konrad. On 2 February 1033, Konrad had himself elected and crowned King of Burgundy, thus he now held the three kingdoms, Germany, Italy and now Burgundy.
9. Provence named as the first Roman province in Gaul. The county was largely agrarian in nature and sparsely populated, its principal towns being those on the Rhône, Avignon and Arles. The latter giving its name to the entire, now only titular, Kingdom of Arles, which also comprised Savoy and Burgundy.
10. The young Ramon Berenguer was the son of Alfonso II, Count of Provence, the name rightly implying the Catalan origins of the family, the House of Barcelona. When his father had died in 1209, Ramon had been away living in the Templar castle at Monzón in the Kingdom of Aragon.
11. Margaret Howell. *Eleanor of Provence* (Oxford: Blackwell Publishers Ltd, 1998). 2.
12. Ibid. 1.
13. Alison Weir. *Queens of the Crusades: Eleanor of Aquitaine and Her Successors* (London: Penguin Random House UK. 2020). 453.
14. *La Divina Commedia, Paradiso, Canto* VI. '*Quattro figlie ebbe, e ciascuna reina, Raimondo Berlinghieri, a cin le fece Romeo, persona umile e peregrina.*'
15. Eugene L. Cox. *The Eagles of Savoy: The House of Savoy in Thirteenth Century Europe* (Princeton: Princeton University Press, 1974). 22. Writes that 'The 'Romeo' of whom Dante speaks was Romeo de Villeneuve, grand baile of Provence at the time the marriages were negotiated.
16. Wurstemberger, vol 1. 83. "*Durch seine ausge zeichnet schöne Beatrix erwarb sich Graf Thomas Stellen in den Stammbäumen der meisten, und zwar der erlauchtesten europäischen Herrschergeschlechter.*" Or "Because of his exceptionally beautiful Beatrix, Count Thomas earned places in the family trees of most, and indeed the most illustrious, European dynasties."
17. Chron. Majora Eng Vol 3. 105. Chron. Majora Lat. Vol 5. 477. "*Fuerat autem mater ejus præsens, comitissa vero dicta Provinciae, nomine Beatrix, quæ pignora sua, quasi altera Niobe, glorianda poterat intueri. Nec erat in sexu muliebri mater in mundo, quæ de tali fructu ventris ac tanto, videlicet filiabus, poterat gloriando gratulari.*"

18. Alianor de Provence did indeed have many uncles, the Count of Savoy Amédée IV, and his many younger brothers, mostly vying for careers within the church, but not at the same time forsaking temporal and military power, Guillaume, Pierre, Boniface and Philippe being amongst the most notable, but also Thomas who had married into the County of Flanders, so important to the English textile interest. Most important in the context of English affairs will be Guillaume then Pierre who will hold the Honour of Richmond and Boniface who will become Archbishop of Canterbury.

19. Fœdera, 217. '*Littera Regis comiti Subaudiæ, de matrimonio cum Alianora filiâ Raymundi comitis Provincia , nepte ejus , contrahendo … Eodem modo scribitor W. Valens ecclesiae electo,*' Or 'Letters of the King, to the Count of Savoy, contracting of the marriage to Alianor, daughter of Count Ramon of Provence, his niece … Written in the same way to Guillaume, Bishop Elect of Valence.'

20. Fœdera, 217. "*An. 19 Hen. ill. HENRICUS, DEI gratia, Rex Angliæ, &c. amico suo karissimo nobili viro, A. Subaudiæ, & marchioni Italiæ, salutem. Gratan nimis & acceptam habentes voluntatem, quæ nos inducit ad foedus amicitiæ inter nos & vos ineundum, sicut inter prædecessores nostros & vestros mutuus semper extitit dilectionis affectus, sinceritatem vestram inde co- piosâ prosequimur gratiarum actione; cupientes, quantum in nobis est, quòd contracta dudum inter progenitores nostros amicitia nostris non deficiat temporibus, set potius suscipiat incrementum.*" Or "in the 19th Year of our reign. Henry III. Henry, by the grace of God, King of England, &c. to his dear friend, a noble, A[médée]. of Savoy, and Marquess of Italy, greeting. Grateful, having an exceedingly well-accepted will, which induces us to enter into a league of friendship between us and you, just as there has always been a mutual affection between our predecessors and yours, we will pursue your sincerity with pious thanksgiving; desiring, as much as is in us, that a friendship long ago contracted between our ancestors would not fail in our time, but would rather accept an increase." Henry is clearly referencing the contracted marriage between his father, John and Alais of Savoy.

21. Alain Marchandisse. 1997. 'Guillaume de Savoie un Monstrum Spiirituelle et Belua Multorum Capitum sur le Trône de Saint Lambert?' Bulletin de la Société Royale le Vieux-Liège XIII: 666. '*En fait, les perspectives de cette union étaient véritablement alléchantes, tant pour l'époux que pour son futur oncle par alliance. Le souverain anglais y voyait le moyen de récupérer les biens perdus par les Plantagenêts sous le règne du roi de France Philippe II Auguste, de jouer à nouveau un rôle de premier plan sur le continent et de faire pièce à la politique matrimoniale menée par les Capétiens, notamment en Provence.*' Or 'In fact, the prospects for this union were truly attractive, both for the husband and for his future uncle by marriage. The English sovereign saw it as a means of recovering the property lost by the Plantagenets under the reign of King of France Philippe II Auguste of playing again a leading role on the continent and of making room for the matrimonial policy carried out by the Capetians, especially in Provence.'

22. Margaret Howell. *Eleanor of Provence* (Oxford: Blackwell Publishers Ltd, 1998). 16.

23. Chron. Majora Eng. Vol 1. 7. "'There were assembled at the king's nuptial festivities such a host of nobles of both sexes, such numbers of religious men, such crowds of the populace, and such a variety of actors, that London, with its capacious bosom could scarcely contain them. The whole city was ornamented with flags and banners, chaplets and hangings, candles and lamps and with wonderful devices and extraordinary representations, and all the roads were cleansed of mud, and dirt, sticks and everything offensive. The citizens too, went out to meet the King and Queen, dressed out in their ornaments … … they proceeded thither dressed in silk garments, with mantles worked in gold and with costly changes in raiment, mounted on valuable horses, glittering with new bits and saddles and riding in troops arranged in order. They carried with them three hundred and sixty gold and silver cups, preceded by the kings' trumpeters and with horns sounding, so that such a wonderful novelty struck all who beheld it astonishment. The Archbishop of Canterbury, by the right especially belonging to him, performed the duty of crowning, with the usual solemnities, the Bishop of London, attending him as dean … The ceremony was splendid with the gay dresses of the clergy and knights who were present … … Why should I describe all those persons who reverently ministered in the church as was their duty? Why describe the abundance of meats and dishes on the table? The quantities of venison, the variety of fish, the joyous sounds of the gleemen and the gaiety of the waiters? Whatever the world could offer in pleasure and magnificence was there brought together from every quarter.'" The Archbishop of Canterbury officiating the coronation was Edmund of Abingdon who had been appointed just recently in 1233 and would hold the post until his death in 1240, he was canoniseized in 1246. He rests to this day at the Abbey of Portigny in Burgundy, France. The Bishop of London officiating the coronation was Roger Niger, following his death in 1241 he too was canoniseized.

24. David Carpenter. *Henry III: The Rise to Power and Personal Rule 1207–1258* (New Haven: Yale University Press, 2020). 179. 'Christ conquers, Christ reigns, Christ Rules. To the Queen of the English, health and life.'

25. Chron. Majora Eng. Vol 1. 182. "'On the night of the 16th of June [1239], a son was born at Westminster to the king by his wife Eleanor. At this event all the nobles of the kingdom offered

their congratulations, and especially the citizens of London; and they assembled bands of dancers, with drums and tambourines, and at night illuminated the streets with large lanterns. The Bishop of Carlisle initiated the infant, and the legate baptiseized him, although he was not a priest, but Edmund Archbishop of Canterbury, confirmed him, and at the wish of the king the name of EDWARD was given to him."' However, Paris incorrectly recorded the date. See E. B. Fryde, D. E. Greenway, S. Porter & I. Roy. 1986. *Handbook of British Chronology*. Third ed. London: Offices of the Royal Historical Society. 34. And Michael Prestwich. *Edward I* (Yale: Yale University Press, 1997). 4. "'Edward was born at Westminster on the night of 17 June 1239.'"

26. Stephen Church. *Henry III: A Simple and God-Fearing King* (London: Penguin Random House, 2017). 3.
27. Guillaume de Savoie, from 1220 he'd been the Dean of the Cathedral of Vienne, and from 1225 the Bishop Elect of Valence. The year before his death he'd been elected as Prince Bishop of Liege. He died in mysterious circumstances in Viterbo in 1239.
28. Our view of Guillaume de Savoie, and indeed his brothers, will be coloured forever by one chronicler, Matthew Paris, who for example, described Guillaume de Savoie as a '*monstrum spirituale et belua multorum capitum*'. Or a 'many-headed spiritual monster'. This view of the will colour the traditional historiographical view of the Savoyards in England and Wales, the subject of this book, for many centuries, and we would do well to remember it is the view of one chronicler. For balance, Jean-Pierre Chapuisat. 'A Propos des Relations entre la Savoie et l'Angleterre au XIII Siècle'. *Bulletin Philologique et Historique* 1 (1960): 430–1. Felt that this may well have been a Benedictine prejudice against the House of Savoy with its Franciscan connections.
29. Alain Marchandisse. 1997. 'Guillaume de Savoie un Monstrum Spiiirituelle et Belua Multorum Capitum sur le Trône de Saint Lambert?' Bulletin de la Société Royale le Vieux-Liège XIII: 690.
30. Before coming to England, Pierre de Savoie had been involved in a long struggle with the House of Geneva in the Pays de Vaud and fighting the Battle of Lausanne, to be installed as Bishop thereof.
31. Chron. Majora Eng. Vol 1. 320. "'About the same time [1240]. Peter of Savoy, the queen's uncle, on whom the king had bestowed the earldom of Richmond, came to England, as he perceived that it was such a profitable country. The king went to meet him on his arrival and received him the inexpressible joy, entrusted himself and his possessions to his counsel, and also enlarged his lands by the gift of several more.'" Chron. Majora Lat. Vol 4. "*Circa eosdem dies, Petrus de Sabaudia, avunculus reginæ, cui rex comitatum de Richemundia contulerat, venit in Angliam, quam sibi senserat fructuosam. Quem rex adventantem occurrens cum gaudio suscepit incomparabili, se suaque consiliis ejus exponendo, et ipsius terras cum donativis plurimis ampliando.*"
32. *The Honour of Richmond* (or English feudal barony of Richmond) in north-west Yorkshire was granted to Count Alan Rufus by King William the Conqueror in 1071. The honour comprised 60 knight's fees and was one of the most important fiefdoms in Norman England.
33. CChR Henry III vol 1 1229–1257, 252. 'Gift to Peter of Sabaudia, and his heirs, the honour of Richemund, with its liberties and free customs, to hold by the service due therefrom' dates the gift as 20 April 1240 at Westminster.
34. John Goodall. *Richmond Castle and Easby Abbey* (London: English Heritage, 2016). 22.
35. Hugh M. Thomas, 'Subinfeudation and Alienation of Land, Economic Development, and the Wealth of Nobles on the Honor of Richmond, 1066 to c. 1300,' *Albion: A Quarterly Journal Concerned with British Studies* 26 (1994): 399.
36. Ibid. 401, Table 1 gives a 1280 summary of income for the Honour of Richmond by county, twenty-first century equivalents in brackets: Yorkshire £701 (£486,542), Nottinghamshire £1 (£694), Lincolnshire £693 (£480,990), Hertfordshire £81 (£56,219), Cambridgeshire £85 (£58,995), Norfolk £189 (£131,179), Sussex £61 (£42,338) for a total of £1,811 (£1,256,959).
37. David Carpenter. *Henry III: The Rise to Power and Personal Rule 1207–1258* (New Haven: Yale University Press, 2020). 212.
38. Hugh M. Thomas, 'Subinfeudation and Alienation of Land, Economic Development, and the Wealth of Nobles on the Honor of Richmond, 1066 to c. 1300,' *Albion: A Quarterly Journal Concerned with British Studies* 26 (1994): 408.
39. Eugene L. Cox. *The Eagles of Savoy: The House of Savoy in Thirteenth Century Europe* (Princeton: Princeton University Press, 1974). 194.
40. '*construire dans le territoire des Noires-Joux, maisons, villages, bourgs et châteaux, sans autre réserve que celle de suzeraineté immédiate de l'empire*'. However, the family title to the lands, predated this document and acquisition of the region by the empire itself. Lambert I de Grandson is mentioned in 994 AD alongside the Archbishop of Lyon and Rudolf III of the Kingdom of Burgundy – so it looks almost certain that the family association with Lac Neuchâtel dates from the dying days of Arelat. Indeed, there is a strong possibility it dates from 981–3 AD and his predecessor, Adalbert I de Grandson – in so doing this would place the Grandson line as beginning contemporaneously with that of the House of Savoy and a cause of the collapsing state of the Second Kingdom of Burgundy.

See Girart Dorens. 1909. Sir Otho de Grandison 1238?–1328. Transactions of the Royal Historical Society 3: 127. n2.

41. The fourth, Aymon became the Bishop of Geneva, the fifth, Hugues a monk at Romainmôtier, the others likewise a church career.

42. Maxime Reymond, *'Le Chevalier Othon I de Grandson,' Revue historique vaudoise* 28 (1920): 162. *'est l'ami de Pierre de Savoie, le chargé d'affaires.'*

43. Pierre I de Grandson himself had English links before Pierre de Savoie took his son there, having been in receipt of a pension from King Henry III. It's not thought, however, that he ever went to England. Maxime Reymond was of the impression he had, but there is no evidence either way. Maxime Reymond. 'Le Chevalier Othon I de Grandson' Revue historique vaudoise 28 (1920): 162.

44. Michael Prestwich. *'Othon de Grandson et la Cour d'Edouard I'* in *Othon I de Grandson (vers 1240–1328)* (Lausanne: Cahiers Lausannois d'Histoire Médiévale, 2020). 3. Published in French *'C'était donc assurément par le frère de Béatrice [de Savoie], Pierre, qui vint en Angleterre en 1240, que les contacts d'Othon de Grandson avec l'Angleterre furent établis.'* Or 'It was therefore assuredly through Béatrice's [of Savoy], Pierre's brother, who came to England in 1240, that Otho de Grandson's contacts with England were established.'

45. Aug. Burnand, *'La date de la naissance d'Othon 1er, Sire de Grandson,' Revue historique vaudoise* 19 no 5 (1911): 130. *'Il faut fixer 1238 comme la date de la naissance d'Othon.'* We can translate to 'we must fix 1238 as the date of the birth of Othon.' Later Maxime Reymond. 'Le Chevalier Othon I de Grandson' *Revue historique vaudoise* 28 (1920): 163. Suggested *'date de naissance d'Othon vers 1240.'*

46. More recently Swiss historiography has cautiously settled on *'vers 1240'* or 'around 1240'. See Bernard Andenmatten. *Othon I de Grandson (vers 1240–1328)* (Lausanne: Cahiers Lausannois d'Histoire Médiévale, 2020). v–vi.

47. In the law of the Middle Ages, and especially within the Holy Roman Empire, an allod (Old Low Franconian allōd or fully owned estate', from all 'full, entire' and ōd 'estate', in Medieval Latin allodium), also allodial land or allodium, is an estate in land over which the allodial landowner (allodiary) had full ownership and right of alienation, and is not therefore a vassal to no one, other than the emperor.

48. Wurstemberger, vol 1. 242. *"sieht man mächtige Grafen, freie Barone, kleinen Adel, Städteburger, gleichsam um die Wette, ihm zueilen, um ihm ihre freien Herrschaften und Güter zu ver kaufen, zu schenken, oder wie sich die Urkunden ausdrücken, zu Lehn aufzugeben, und sich, bisweilen sogar nur ihre Söhne, wieder damit belehnen zu lassen, und ihm dafür die Huldigung zu leisten."* Or "one sees mighty counts, free barons, citizens of towns, as it were in a race, to rush to him to sell or give him their free dominions and goods, or as the documents put it, to give up fiefdom and themselves, sometimes even only their sons to have it enfeoffed again, and pay homage to him in return."

49. Bernard Andenmatten. *La noblesse vaudoise face à la Maison de Savoie au XIII siècle. La Maison de Savoie et le Pays de Vaud* (SHSR, 2005)). 35. *'les problèmes d'une petite aristocratie en mal de numéraire.'*

50. Eugene L. Cox. *The Eagles of Savoy: The House of Savoy in Thirteenth Century Europe* (Princeton: Princeton University Press, 1974). 166-7.

51. The 300 number, given its source, and the way it was gathered, I'm inclined to agree with, and comes from Jean-Pierre Chapuisat, *'A Propos des Relations entre la Savoie et d'Angleterre au XIII Siècle,' Bulletin Philologique et Historique* 1 (1960): 432. Lower estimates include the 170 of David Carpenter. *Henry III: The Rise to Power and Personal Rule 1207–1258* (New Haven: Yale University Press, 2020). 217.

52. The castle had been high above Lac Léman since at least 996 AD in the dying years of the old Kingdom of Burgundy, a very early example of a castle in the region.

53. Ebal II de Mont was the second son of Ebal I de Mont and Béatrice. Their eldest son, inheriting their lands in Vaud, was Henri de Mont, and their third son was Rudolph de Mont, who followed a career in the church as a Canon of Lausanne before becoming a Dean of Avenches. The youngest child was a daughter, Alice, who married Raymond de Montricher.

54. E. B. Fryde, D. E. Greenway, S. Porter & I. Roy. *Handbook of British Chronology*. Third ed. (London: Offices of the Royal Historical Society, 1986). 75.

55. Esther Rowland Clifford. *A Knight of Great Renown: The Life and Times of Othon de Grandson* (Chicago: The University of Chicago Press, 1961). 12. Clifford's flourishing biographical style has been more recently criticized by Swiss historian Bernard Andenmatten in his forward to 2020. Othon I de Grandson (vers 1240-1328). Lausanne: Cahiers Lausannois d'Histoire Médiévale.vi. Nonetheless her work remains the only full biography of his life published in English.

56. Michael Prestwich. *'Othon de Grandson et la Cour d'Edouard I'* in *Othon I de Grandson (vers 1240–1328)* (Lausanne: Cahiers Lausannois d'Histoire Médiévale, 2020). 4.

57. Eugene L. Cox. *The Eagles of Savoy: The House of Savoy in Thirteenth Century Europe* (Princeton: Princeton University Press, 1974). 200. Cox 'At the same time [1251] a widening net of vassalage embraced the lords of Grandson, Belmont, La Sarraz and Cossonay.' Citing Wurstemberger, vol

1. 135. *'Schade, dass die Urkunden nicht mehrere der jenigen Personen nennen, die seine Angelegenheiten so an hänglich und so erfolgreich besorgten: bekannt sind vor nehmlich Wilhelm von Chanvent, Peter von Granson, Wilhelm von Greisy, Humbert von Ferney.'* Or "It is a pity that the documents do not name several of the people who took care of his affairs so devotedly and so successfully: Guillaume de Chanvent, Pierre de Granson, Guillaume de Greisy, Humbert de Ferney are the most well-known." And Ibid. 264. n22 *"Von Petern von Granson findet sich zwar keine Belehnungs urkunde aber er selbst kömmt so häufig im Gefolge Peters von Savoyen vor, dass sich an seinem Lehensverhältniss"* Or "There is no enfeoffment document from Pierre de Grandson," but he appears so often in the entourage of Peter von Savoy that his feudal relationship can be inferred." More recently Daniel de Raemy is a lot less sure writing in 2020. *Le Château Résidence d'Othon de Grandson'* in Othon I de Grandson (vers 1240–1328). Lausanne: Cahiers Lausannois d'Histoire Médiévale. 174 *'La seigneurie de Grandson est probablement l'une des dernières terres allodiales du pays de Vaud; son Maître, Othon, n'est pas vassal des Savoie.'* Or 'The seigneury of Grandson is probably one of the last allodial lands in the Pays de Vaud; its Master, Otho, is not a vassal of the Savoyards.' A reading of Wurstemberger does not quite support Cox in full, there being confirmation only of the vassalage of Belmont, La Sarraz and Cossonay. But given this vassalage by members of the *famille de Grandson* nor does it entirely support de Raemy's unequivocal suggestion that no homage on the part of Pierre de Grandson was made. There is simply no firm evidence to support either notion. Whatever the precise feudatory relationship between the Lords of Grandson and Counts of Savoy, ally of the Count or vassal of the Count, to the English it is certain that Othon de Grandson was regarded as a Savoyard and that Pierre de Savoie placed him in the household of the Lord Edward to help protect the Savoyard investment in the future King of England. So in the end the matter remains a detail of purely Vaudois interest.
58. Wurstemberger, vol 1. 318. n29. *'Actum, presentibus et vocatis … Henrico domino de Chavenz, Petro domino de Granzun.'*
59. CCR Henry III vol 7 1251-1253, 109. *'Pro Petro Gransun et magistro Willelmo de Wytsand. Mandatum est J. Maunsell' quod una cum W. de Haverhull'. thesaurario regis, et camerariis suis provident quod Petrus dominus Gransun sine dilacione habeat super annuum feodum suum xx. libras, qualitercumque perquirantur, mutuo aut alio modo; et quod similiter magister Willelmus de Wytsand' habeat x. libras, de dono regis. Et hoc nullatenus omittant. Teste ut supra. Per regem.'* Appears above *'De damis datis. Mandatum est custodi foreste de Wauberge quod in eadem foresta faciat habere Ebuloni de Montibus duos damos, de dono regis. Teste rege apud Rading' xviij. die Junii. Per R. Waler'.'* Both of which appear below *'Pro Petro de Sabaud'.- Mandatum est vicecomiti Cantebr 'quod, inspecta carta quam Petrus de Sabaud 'a rege habet de honore de Richemund', omnes libertates et quietancias in ea contentas firmiter teneri faciat, etiam si eisdem minus plene usus sit. Teste ut supra. Per regem.'* All of which looks like Henry taking care of Pierre de Savoie's business.
60. CPR. Edward I vol 1 1272–1281, 188.
61. Maxime Reymond, *'Le Chevalier Othon I de Grandson,'* Revue historique vaudoise 28 (1920): 162. *'Il était majeur en 1263, c'est-à-dire qu'il avait alors plus de quinze ans.'* Translates as 'He was of legal age in 1263, that is to say he was over fifteen years of age at the time.' So, if we work from a date of birth as 1240 then a legal age would be 1255, and accord with 'since our early childhood and his own'. This August 1263 document is Minutes of Evidence Taken Before the Committee for Privileges … to Determine the Abeyance of the Barony of Grandison. 1854. House of Lords: London. 169 *'Nos Agnes, domina de Grandisono, tutrix legitima liberorum nostrorum Petri et Willelini, Girardus, Jaquetus et Henricus, pro se et fratre suo Otonino, filii predicte domine'* which by listing Othon in this way does suggest his absence by 1263 at least. But also, as Reymond suggests that's he's attained an age of at least 15 years.
62. Sara Cockerill. *Eleanor of Castile: The Shadow Queen.* Second Edition ed. (Stroud: Amberley Publishing, 2014). 69.
63. Maxime Reymond, *'Le Chevalier Othon I de Grandson,'* Revue historique vaudoise 28 (1920): 163.
64. Michael Prestwich. *Knight: The Medieval Warrior's (Unofficial) Guide* (London: Thames & Hudson, 2010). 22.
65. Jean-Pierre Chapuisat, *'Au service de deux rois d'Angleterre au XIIIe siècle : Pierre de Champvent,'* Revue historique vaudoise 72 (1964): 157–75. Citing TNA C62/28 m 7 … *'Precipimus tibi quod facias habere Petro de Chavent vadletto nostro quinque marcas ad unum runcinum emendum de dono nostro.'*
66. TNA C60/59,46 Fine Roll Henry III (1261–1262), m8.
67. Michael Ray, 'The Savoyard Cousins: A Comparison of the Careers and Relative Success of the Grandson (Grandison) and Champvent (Chavent) Families in England,' *The Antiquaries Journal* 86 (2006): 151.
68. E. B. Fryde, D. E. Greenway, S. Porter & I. Roy. 1986. *Handbook of British Chronology.* Third ed. London: Offices of the Royal Historical Society. 74. Ebal would be a royal steward from 1256 until 1263, alongside his compatriot, see note below, Imbert Pugeys.

69. Imbert Pugeys or Imbert de Savoie, a valet in the king's chamber would become constable at Hadleigh Castle in 1244 and Oxford Castle in 1253. Advancing further, from 1257, the Savoyard became a steward of the royal household and castellan of the Tower of London before eventually passing away in 1263. Imbert married one Joan de Aguillon, their son gave the family name to what would become Stoke Poges in Buckinghamshire. Stoke Poges would later be the setting for Thomas Gray's poem 'Elegy Written in a Country Churchyard' written between 1745 and 1750. For tenure as Steward of the Royal Household see E. B. Fryde, D. E. Greenway, S. Porter & I. Roy. 1986. *Handbook of British Chronology*. Third ed. London: Offices of the Royal Historical Society. 74.

70. Jean-Pierre Chapuisat, '*Au service de deux rois d'Angleterre au XIIIe siècle: Pierre de Champvent,*' *Revue historique vaudoise* 72 (1964) : 162. Citing CChR Henry III. vol 2 1226–1257, 35. and TNA C 53/51. Imbert de Montferrand from Bugey, not far to the north-west of Boniface de Savoie's see of Belley.

71. Sara Cockerill. 2014. *Eleanor of Castile: The Shadow Queen*. Second Edition ed. Stroud: Amberley Publishing. 69.

72. Huw Ridgeway. 'The Lord Edward and the Provisions of Oxford (1258): a study in faction' In *Thirteenth Century England: Proceedings of the Newcastle-upon-Tyne Conference, 1985* (Woodbridge: The Boydell Press, 1986). 89–99.

73. John Robert Maddicott. 'Edward I and the Lessons of Baronial Reform: local government, 1258–1260'. *Thirteenth Century England: Proceedings of the Newcastle-upon-Tyne Conference, 1985* (Woodbridge: The Boydell Press, 1986). 19.

74. CChR Henry III vol 1 1229–1257, 386.

75. Eugene L. Cox. *The Eagles of Savoy: The House of Savoy in Thirteenth Century Europe* (Princeton: Princeton University Press, 1974). 241. 'the Savoyard seems to have become for a time a kind of regent for his great-nephew.'

76. TNA C47/9/1.

77. David Carpenter. *Henry III: The Rise to Power and Personal Rule 1207–1258* (New Haven: Yale University Press, 2020). 496. 'The heir to the throne was the rock on which Savoyard fortunes were founded.'. And Ibid. 181. Carpenter gives details of other Savoyard influences around the Lord Edward as a boy, amongst them, 'Willhelma' Alianor's chief lady-in-waiting, and Constable of Windsor Castle. And Ibid. 217. Bernard de Savoie. 'thus, giving the Savoyards control of the castle housing the heir to the throne.'

78. Jean-Pierre Chapuisat, '*Au service de deux rois d'Angleterre au XIIIe siècle: Pierre de Champvent,*' *Revue historique vaudoise* 72 (1964): 163–4. We know of there not being in England from a document, dated January 1264, in the Vaudois Cantonal Archive that excludes being written in England and to which their seals are attached. ACV C XV 2/2.

Chapter Two

1. Wurstemberger, vol 4. No 526. Pierre de Savoie obtained a royal grant for 'the place commonly called Contamina' between Morat and Bern, now German-speaking and called Gummenen. This naturally defensible position close to Bern and atop bluffs dominating the crossing of Saane marked the high watermark of Savoyard expansion towards the lands of the German-speakers. He would build there a key castle and walls to defend the frontier, neither of which there remains a trace of today.

2. Eugene L. Cox. *The Eagles of Savoy: The House of Savoy in Thirteenth Century Europe* (Princeton: Princeton University Press, 1974). 297.

3. *La Finanza Sabauda*, vol. 1, 16. 'domino Enrico de Bono Vilair castellano de Rota'.

4. Bernard Andenmatten, *La maison de Savoie et la noblesse vaudoise (XIIIe–XIVe s.) (Société d'histoire de la Suisse romande*, 2005).

5. P.M.L de Charrière, *Les Dynastes de Grandson jusqu' au XIIIe Siècle* (Lausanne, 1866), 109, 111, 116–7 and 119; *Cartulaire de Roumainmôtier* (XIIe siècle), ed. A. Pahud, (Cahiers Lausannois d'Histoire Médiévale, xxi Lausanne, 1998), nos. 73 and 75.

6. *La Finanza Sabauda*. vol. 1, 63. '*Compotus de Valeisio et Chablasio de anno LXI*, '*Item in liberatione magistri Iohannis cementarii a die qua recessit a domo sua veniendo versus Yverdunum, videlicet prima die maii hoc anno* [1 May 1261] *usque ad secundam dominicam quadragisime, videlicet quintam diem intrante marcio* [5 March 1262], *per quadraginta et quatuor septimanas, qui cepit duodecim solidos qualibet septimana, xxvj. lib. ij.sol. In liberatione magistri Iacobi filii sui per idem tempus, capientis singulis septimanis decem solidos et sex denarios, xxiij.lib. ij.sol. In vadiis suis et calciatura sua et pannis lineis, capientis quinque solidos per mensem, per dictum tempus .lv.sol. In medicinis ipsius magistri Jacobi tempore egritudinis sue .xxv.sol. In liberatione magistri Petri Mainier custodis operum domini per idem tempus pro se duobus equis et uno valeto suo capientis ut predictus magister Iohannes. Xxvj.lib. viij.sol.*' Or 'Account of the Valais and Chablais of the year 61. For the discharge of Master John the mason from the day when he came from his home to Yverdon, assuredly the first day of May of this year [1 May 1261] until the second Sunday of Lent [5 March 1262] for forty-four weeks who received twelve *sol* per week. Twenty-six *livres* and eight *sol*.

For the discharge of his son Maître Jacques for same period receiving ten *sol* and six denier every week. Twenty-three *livres* and two *sol*. For his wages and shoes and his linen bandages receiving five *sol* per month. Fifty-five *sol*. For Maître Jacques himself, medicine for the time of his illness. Twenty-five *sol*. For the discharge of Master Pierre Mainier Custodian of the Lord's works for the same period two horses for himself and one for his servant as Master John aforesaid. Twenty-six *Livres* and eight *sol*.'

7. *La Finanza Sabauda*. vol. 1, 118. '*In acquietancia magistri Jacobi cementarii hoc anno preterito ... qui Jacobus percipit [sc apud] Yverdunum de domino in feudo decem libras viannensium singulis annis.xv.lib.*' Or 'in the acquittance (discharge of a debt) of Maître Jacques the mason for this year and the year before that ... he, Jacques, has the fee of Yverdon, ten *livres Viennois* every year. Fifteen *livres*.'

8. *La Finanza Sabauda*. vol. 1, 73. '*Magistro Jacobo lathomo, .x.lib.*'

9. ACV A a 194 1–44. His surname was not mentioned contemporaneously with his life but later as '*totum tenementum quod fuit quondam magistri Johannis dicti Cotereel*'. Or 'That which was once the master of the whole holding of John called Cotereel' Marcel Grandjean found 19 references to Master Jean Cotereel between 1210 and posthumously in 1318 For the full list and texts see Marcel Grandjean. 1963. *A Propos de la Construction de la Cathédrale de Lausanne (XII–XIIIe Siecle)*. Genava XI: 276.

10. ACV C V a 24. '*Iohanni, magistro operis Lausannensis*' Or 'John, Master of the Works of Lausanne'. Marcel Grandjean. 1963. *A Propos de la Construction de la Cathédrale de Lausanne (XII–XIIIe Siècle)*. Genava XI: 278 '*La seule chose à peu près certaine, c'est que Jean Cotereel est le maître d'œuvre des deux dernières étapes de la cathédrale*.' Or 278 'The only thing that is more or less certain is that Jean Cotereel is the master builder of the last two stages of the cathedral'.

11. ACV C V a 24. Transcribed in Charles Roth. 1948. Cartulaire du Chapitre de Notre-Dame de Lausanne. Lausanne: Librairie Payot. 294. No 331. as '*Capitulum Lausanne ... nos dedit in feodum Iohanni , magistro operis Lausannensis . . . posas terre apud Sanctum Prothasium , nec debent esse de meliori terra arabili nec de peiori , et ipse fecit hominium ligium in manu c ., prepositi Lausannensis , ad opus capituli , et promisit quod ipse faceret mansionem apud Sanctum Prothasium , in municione quam ibi capitulum de novo faciebat , et heres eius primogenitus ibidem post eum faceret mansionem , et illud feodum post eum non divideretur inter heredes suos , sed solus primogenitus illud haberet qui mansionem • apud Sanctum Prothasium faceret . Debet etiam inde reddere annua tim capitulo X. solidos in vigilia sancti Prothasii ? , qui debent in festo sancti Prothasii a distribui in matutinis presentibus canonicis , quod festum tunc fuit receptum in capitulo ut fieret .IX . leccionum . Actum in carentena, anno ab incarnatione Domini. MCC XXX IIII. , in crastina beate Marie Magdalene. Interfuerunt dominus B. episcopus, C. prepositus, Vu. thesaurarius, Io. cantor, Vu ., prior sancti Marii, G. sacrista , C. de Fonz , N. de Cha ., A. de No. Cas. , Io. succentor, Ia. de Gral. , P. de Vi ., Ame ., P. de Fru ., R. de Ro ., R. de Vul ., U. Da ., G. de Bor ., Ia . de Bor. celerarius, Hen. de Fru ., R. de Monz , Ot . de Gran ., Vu . de Gumuens .* Roth noted before the transcript '*Concession par le chapitre de Lausanne à Iohannes, Maître de la fabrique de Lausanne de trente poses de terre sises à St-Prex, à charge pour lui, et d'y résider et d'y faire résider son fils aîné après lui.*' Or 'Concession by the Lausanne chapter to Iohannes, master of the Lausanne works, of thirty poses [in the Canton de Vaud the 'Pose' was an area of land that a ploughman could work in a single day, and so could vary] of land located in St-Prex, dependent on him, and to reside there and make his eldest son reside there after him.' Marcel Grandjean. 1969. La 'carentena' du Chapitre de Notre-Dame de Lausanne dans le cloître de la cathédrale. Revue historique vaudoise 77: 'en 1234, le 23 juillet, le Chapitre inféode au Maître d'œuvre de la cathédrale une terre ä Saint-Prex' Or 'in 1234, on July 23, the Chapter enfiefed to the master of works of the cathedral [Jean Cotereel a land in Saint-Prex.'. Of note is a witness to the enfeoffment, Othon de Grandson, the uncle of the knight, Sir Othon de Grandson of English fame.

12. Charles Roth. Cartulaire du Chapitre de Notre-Dame de Lausanne. (Lausanne: Librairie Payot, 1948). 290–3. No 330. And 295. No 333. '*Iohannes, magister operis Lausannensis, tunc castellanus Sancti Prothasii.*' Or 'Jean, Master of the Works of Lausanne, then castellan of Saint-Prex.'

13. Ibid. 437. No. 504. '*et dedit Iohanni, filio magistri operis* [Lausanne]' Ibid. 459. No. 537. '*Capitulum dedit Johanni filio magistri, domum que fuit Richardi Provain.*' Ibid. 488. No. 582. '*quod cum capitulum Lausannenses concessisset Iohanni clerico, filio magistri operis, domum que fuerat Richardi Provain.*' Ibid. 153. No. 137. '*Iohannes, filius magistri operis.*' These four entries from the Lausanne Cartulary are dated 1210, circa 1210, 1216 and 1217. They clearly identify Jean Cotereel as being the son of the Master of Works of the preceding phase of building at Lausanne to that carried out by Cotereel himself.

14. Jean Bony (1957) 'The Resistance to Chartres in Early Thirteenth-Century Architecture', *Journal of the British Archaeological Association*, 20:1, 47, 'The similarities between the choir of Lausanne and the Trinity Chapel at Canterbury are even most remarkable. The pattern of the elevation and the proportion are the same, a number of details are identical, and the two buildings could almost be the work of the same architect. I do not mean to say that William the Englishman left England in 1184 to take up the direction of the workshop of Lausanne Cathedral — although this cannot be ruled out. But at least the two masters belonged to the same group, and I think it can be proved that the

architect of Lausanne had been to England and had even worked at Canterbury — let us say, under William the Englishman.' Then Marcel Grandjean, '*A Propos de la Construction de la Cathédrale de Lausanne (XII–XIIIe Siècle)*,' Genava XI (1963): 284–5 and most recently by Christopher Wilson writing in. 2004. *Die Kathedrale von Lausanne und ihr Marienportal im Kontext der europäischen Gotik.* Freiburg: der Universität Freiburg. 90 'In his article of 1957, Jean Bony demonstrated beyond all reasonable doubt that the main internal elevations of the choir and transepts of Lausanne were heavily influenced by by the most easterly and latest part of the Early Gothic work at Canterbury.' Wilson then identified a further twelve links, Ibid. 94–8. Of which we should particularly note 'The tracery of the south transept rose window. This is both a translation into masonry and an elaboration of the pattern used in the iron armatures within the oculi of the eastern transept of Canterbury.' Ibid. 97. The relevance of this feature will become clear when we discuss the castle at Conwy later. Before writing '. . . in the western parts of Lausanne the use of Canterbury motifs continued alongside a new creative impulse, namely the exploitation of contemporary English sources.' Ibid. 112. And regarding the origin of Jean Cotereel 'The possibility that Johannes or Jean Cotereel ... was of English descent has been proposed by Marcel Grandjean and the hypothesis has much to recommend it, Ibid. 122. Bony, Grandjean and Wilson have identified as the English nature of the work, and Cotereel's family name, we can attribute an English origin for Jean Cotereel and his anonymous Master of Works at Lausanne father.

15. Arnold Taylor. *Studies in Castles and Castle-Building* (London: The Hambledon Press, 1985). 24. 'When we give to the position of Master John, which is implicit in the 1261 statement, the evaluation it evidently deserves, the possibility – to put it no higher – that he is the same John as the *magister operis Lausanensis* can hardly be excluded.'

16. Marcel Grandjean, '*A Propos de la Construction de la Cathédrale de Lausanne (XII–XIIIe Siecle)*,' Genava XI (1963): 278. '*Cotereel est un nom étranger au Pays de Vaud et aux régions avoisinantes.*' Or 'Cotereel is a foreign name in the Pays de Vaud and neighbouring regions.'

17. In England today the common form would be Cotterill. The surname is derived from an occupation, 'the cotterel' or 'Coterelle' who was an inferior tenant, probably holding an absolute villenage. In Mark Anthony Lowe, Patronymica Britannica, A Dictionary of Family Names of the United Kingdom. London: John Russel Smith, 1860. 'In feudal times, ‹the coterellus held in absolute villenage and had his person and goods disposed at the pleasure of the Lord.› Kennet›s Paroch. Antiq. He was probably so called, like the Cotmanni, or Cottarii of Domesd. from residing in a cottage. Another origin may be from the cotarelli, costeraux, cotemux, mercenary soldiers and freebooters whose trade was war and pillage, (Conf. Brabazon) and who were so called from the coterel, a large knife they carried. Cotgrave defines cotereaux as 'a certaine crue of peasantly outlawes who in old time did much mischiefe unto the nobilitie and clergie.'

18. Jean Bony (1957) The Resistance to Chartres in Early Thirteenth-Century Architecture, Journal of the British Archaeological Association, 20:1, 47, Marcel Grandjean, '*A Propos de la Construction de la Cathédrale de Lausanne (XII–XIIIe Siècle)*,' Genava XI (1963): 284–5. Christopher Wilson writing in '*Die Kathedrale von Lausanne und ihr Marienportal im Kontext der europäischen Gotik*' (Freiburg: der Universität Freiburg, 2004). 123–4. '[Cotereel drew] heavily on contemporary English sources and thereby ... set himself apart from all of his fellow exponents of the French gothic tradition.' And Earlier Wilson had agreed with the basic English origins of the Cotereel family, writing 'Cotereel was the son of the architect who began the walls of the choir [at Lausanne] and that the latter was of English origin.'

19. '*Magistri Iohannis cementarii*' at Yverdon and '*Iohanni, magistro operis Lausannensis.*' at Saint-Prex.

20. *La Finanza Sabauda*, vol. 1, 63 '*magistri Iohannis cementarii a die qua recessit a domo sua veniendo versus Yverdunum.*' And Ibid. 69. '*Iohanne Cotelerii de Sallon*'.

21. ACV C V a 24. '*et heres eius primogenitus*' Or 'his eldest son and heir'.

22. Arnold Taylor. *Studies in Castles and Castle-Building* (London: The Hambledon Press, 1985). 24. 'while the ground-plans of the two towns [Yverdon and Saint-Prex are far from duplicates – they occupy very different sites and are twenty-five years apart in date – nevertheless they have certain basic characteristics in common; each has a layout based on three streets radiating from a point near the south-eastern extremity of the site; both are fully provided with water defences, Saint-Prex mainly natural and partly man-made, Yverdon's mainly man-made and partly natural; the parallelism of their orientation is striking.' Keith D. Lilley. '"The Landscape of Edward's New Towns: Their Planning and Design"' in *The Impact of the Edwardian Castles in Wales* (Oxford: Oxbow Books, 2010). 106–7. '"The GIS plan of Beaumaris was reversed to create a mirror-image and reproduced at the same scale as the town plan of Conwy. When the two plans are placed beside each other, the reversed GIS plan of Beaumaris shows a remarkable coincidence of features. The castles sit in the same relative position, as do the churches and quaysides. The orientation of the T-shaped street patterns also matches. Moreover, the street dimensions of Conwy match perfectly those of Beaumaris, both

sharing a slight widening on their approach towards the castle entrances. The similarities in their plans are therefore very close."'

23. Arnold Taylor, 'Some notes on the Savoyards in North Wales, 1277–1300. With special reference to the Savoyard element in the construction of Harlech Castle,' *Genava XI* (1963): 291. Citing A. Naef, 1908. *Chillon: la Camera Domini*, 33, Victor Van Berchem, 1913. *La Ville Neuve d'Yverdon*, 220, Louis Blondel, 1935. *L'architecture militaire*, Genava, 1935. 288-89, Ibid. 1949. *Le Château de Brignon*, Vallesia. 30, Ibid. 1954. *Les Châteaux et le bourg de Conthey*, 155, and Roger Deglon, 1949. *Yverdon au moyen âge*, 25. '*le véritable architecte et ingénieur militaire de Pierre II*' and '*le Maître d'ouvre général du comte.*'

24. Ibid. 291. n9. 'The present writer, fully aware of exposing himself to a charge of heresy, feels obliged o challenge this long-accepted interpretation of Mainier's status and functions, with its ascription, explicit or implied, of the chief architectural authorship of all Peter of Savoy's military works. He does so, (a) on the negative ground that, in his view, there is no real documentary evidence in the various relevant accounts to support it, and (b) on the positive ground that precisely analogous and near-contemporary accounts for royal building works in England make it almost certain that Mainier's duties, far from being of an architectural and constructional character, were on the contrary wholly administrative and financial. In regard to (a), the accounts name him explicitly as '*clericus domini*' (CHIAUDANO F. S., i, p.11) and '*custos operum dominum*' (Ibid. 58, 63), but never as '*magister operum domini*' (i.e. *Maître d'ouvre*). There is no reason to suppose that when the title 'magister' is applied to him in 1261-2 (Ibid. 63) it is used any differently from the sense in which it is applied to other senior household clerks, such for example as Master Arnold. When it is stated (Ibid. 25) that the castellan of Conthey and Saillon paid 30 pounds for the work of building the new donjon of Conthey '*per consilium Petri Manerii*', this need mean no more than that Mainier assigned the 'task' (presumably to *Franciscus cementarius*), negotiated the price and the conditions, and authorized the payment. With regard to (b), an exact analogy to the position and functions of Mainier in the works service of Count Peter is provided by that of Giles of Oudenarde, king's clerk, in that of King Edward I: the accounts for Edward's works at the Tower of London between 1275 and 1285 were presented throughout by Giles in his capacity as '*custos operacionum domini Regis*'; they were certified 'by the view and testimony' of the master mason, Master Robert of Beverley, who alone of the two is styled '*magister operacionum*' and who in modern terms would be regarded who was '*custos operacionum*' for the castle works at Flint and Rhuddlan, occupied precisely the same position vis-à-vis the '*magister operacionum*', Master James of St George, who again would be regarded as the architect. as the architect. William de Perton, a senior wardrobe clerk who was '*custos operacionum*' for the castle works at Flint and Rhuddlan, occupied precisely the same position vis-à-vis the '*magister operacionum*', Master James of St George, who again would be regarded as the architect.'

25. *OED*, March 2019, Oxford University Press. ORIGIN [Custody late Middle English : from Latin *custodia*, from *custos* '*guardian*'.

26. *OED*, March 2019. Oxford University Press. ORIGIN [Clerk] Old English cleric, *clerc* (in the sense 'ordained minister, literate person'), from ecclesiastical Latin *clericus* 'clergyman' (see cleric); reinforced by Old French *clerc*, from the same source.

27. *OED*, March 2019. Oxford University Press. ORIGIN [Master] Old English *mæg(i)ster* (later reinforced by Old French *Maître*), from Latin *magister*; probably related to *magis* 'more'.

28. *La Finanza Sabauda*. vol. 1, 11. '*Idem libravit Petro Manerii clerico domini ad operationes ipsius domini faciendas . . .*'

29. Ibid. 58. '*Petri Mainier custodis operum domini*'.

30. Ibid. 63. '*magistri Petri Mainier custodis operum domini*'.

31. For '*Custodis Operum Domini*' see La Finanza Sabauda. vol. 1, 58 and 63.

32. M. Walraet, *Les Chartes-lois de Prisches (1158) et de Beaumont-en-Argonne (1182). [Contribution à l'étude de l'affranchissement des classes rurales au XIIe siècle].* (1944). 145.

33. Louis Blondel, '*L'architecture militaire au temps de Pierre II de Savoie: Les donjons circulaires*,' Genava XIII (1935): 289. '*Il est alors qualifié de custos operum domini.*' And '*Il dirige la construction de tout le château d'Yverdon.*'

34. N. Pevsner, 'Terms of Architectural Planning in the Middle Ages,' *Journal of the Warburg and Courtauld Institutes* 5 (1942): 233. n4.

35. J. G. Edwards, 'Edward I's Castle-Building in Wales,' *The Proceedings of the British Academy XXXII (1944)*: 20 . n2. Citing Chancellor's Roll 84, m. I 'Compotus Magistri Willelmi de Luda, custodis de garderoba regis'.

36. *La Finanza Sabauda*. vol. 1, 58. '*Francisco cementario*'.

37. Ibid. 63. '*magistrii Iohannis cementarii*'.

38. Arnold Taylor. *Studies in Castles and Castle-Building* (London: The Hambledon Press, 1985). 141. '*Rex dilectis sibi Magistro Jacobo de Sancto Georgio et Walter de Wynton clerico custodibus operacionum*

castri nostra de Bello Marisco, salutem.' And *'Rex scribit eodem modo et sub eisdem verbis Magistro Waltero de Hereford et Hugoni de Leyministr' clerico, custodibus castri Regis et ville de Kaernaruan.'*

39. Douglas Knoop & G. P. Jones. *The Mediaeval Mason: An Economic History of English Stone Building in the Later Middle Ages and Early Modern Times* (Manchester: Manchester University Press, 1933). 18. 'The king's master mason had authority mainly, no doubt, over the workmen and actual building work while his colleague was chiefly concerned with finance, but it may be noted that the master mason had a share in the responsibility for the accounts: Robert of Beverley figured at least once as an auditor of accounts.' Knoop and Jones thus allowing for a Master of Works also having a hand in financial matters, as we shall see with Maître Jacques.

40. Arnold Taylor. *Studies in Castles and Castle-Building* (London: The Hambledon Press, 1985). 23-24 'we may note that the account does not by implication downgrade John by saying that he gets the same pay as Master Pierre Mainier the *custos operum domini*, but rather the reverse – Pierre Mainier is to get the same pay as Master John. And yet it is this Pierre Mainier whom Swiss archaeologists and art historians have from Albert Naef onwards have again and again insisted, as I believe quite wrongly on calling '*le véritable architecte et ingénieur militaire de Pierre II*', 'the chief architect and designer and builder of his castles.'

41. Louis Blondel, *'L'architecture militaire au temps de Pierre II de Savoie: Les donjons circulaires,'* *Genava* XIII (1935): 291. Skipping by 'Jacques' a 'stonemason' unremarked *'Les travaux de maçonnerie étaient exécutés par Jacques, tailleur de pierres (lathomus).'* And misattributing the works at Caernarfon and Conwy as *'comme Carnavon, construit en 1284 par le Maître maçon Walter of Hereford avec Henry of Ellerton submagister, et Conway édifié la même année aussi par Ellerton.'* 280.

42. Louis Blondel, *'Le Château de Saxon: Note Complémentaire,'* *Vallesia* IX (1955): 87. n1. *Mr. A. J. Taylor a publié une série d'études remarquables sur les châteaux anglais, plus particulièrement sur ceux du Pays de Galles dont il est l'inspecteur ; il a montré les rapports entre leur architecture et celle des châteaux construits par la Maison de Savoie. Le 'maître de St-Georges', architecte qui avait déjà travaillé à Yverdon, puis à St-Georges d'Espéranche, devint le maître d'œuvre principal du roi pour ses forteresses du Pays de Galles.'* Or 'Mr. A. J. Taylor has published a series of remarkable studies on English castles, more particularly those in Wales of which he is the inspector; he showed the relationship between their architecture and that of the castles built by the House of Savoy. The 'master of St-Georges', an architect who had already worked in Yverdon, then in St-Georges d'Espéranche, became the king's main contractor for his fortresses in Wales.'

43. Daniel de Raemy. *Châteaux, donjons et grandes tours dans les Etats de Savoie (1230–1330)* (Lausanne: Cahiers d'archéologie romande 98 et 99, 2004). 285. *'On l'a déjà dit, ce personnage que certaines études du siècle passé ont qualifé abusivement d'architecte, de Maître d'œuvre ou même d'ingénieur, n'est pas un homme de l'art. Il s'agit bien d'un clerc, originaire de Chambéry, chargé de représenter le maître de l'ouvrage, soit Pierre de Savoie.'* Or 'It has already been said that this character, which some studies of the past century have described as an architect, architect, or even engineer, he is not a man of art. He is indeed a clerk, originally from Chambéry, responsible for representing the owner of the work, Pierre de Savoie.'

44. *La Finanza Sabauda.* vol. 1, 63.

45. TNA currency converter.

46. Arnold Taylor. *Studies in Castles and Castle-Building* (London: The Hambledon Press, 1985). 24.

47. Louis Blondel, *'L'architecture militaire au temps de Pierre II de Savoie: Les donjons circulaires,'* *Genava* XIII (1935): 289. *'Maître Jean cementarius qui vient d'Yverdon.'* Compare with *'magistri Iohannis cementarii a die qua recessit a domo sua veniendo versus Yverdunum.'*

48. Arnold Taylor. *Studies in Castles and Castle-Building* (London: The Hambledon Press, 1985). 24. 'When we give to the position of Master John, which is implicit in the 1261 statement, the evaluation it evidently deserves, the possibility – to put it no higher – that he is the same John as the *magister operis Lausanensis* can hardly be excluded.' And Daniel de Raemy. *Châteaux, donjons et grandes tours dans les Etats de Savoie (1230-1330).* Lausanne: Cahiers d'archéologie romande 98 et 99, 2004). 334. writes *'La défense horizontale basse par les courtines, idée anglo-saxonne, pourrait avoir également pénétré plus directement chez nous par le nord, (Saint-Gobain, Domfront, etc.). Maître Jean, ainsi que son fils Jacques, en auraient la paternité en terres savoyardes. C'est eux d'ailleurs qui imposent un type d'archère, certes à embrasure oblique dans la tradition philippienne, mais dotés tout de même d'une ébauche de niche. Ces niches sont couvertes d'une voûte en mitre, particularité présente exclusivement outre-Manche. Jean et Jacques seraient donc bien anglais et connaîtraient le nord de la France (Normandie, Champagne, Île de France). Ont-ils également emprunté la commodité de l'échafaudage hélicoïdal – dispositif somme toute assez rare – à la tour Maîtresse du château de Coucy ou, plus près de chez nous, à celle, royale par Philippe Auguste, de Villeneuve-sur-Yonne vers 1220 ? S'il n'y a aucune preuve formelle que le Maître Jean puisse être identifié à Jean Cotereel, dernier architecte de la cathédrale Notre-Dame de Lausanne, ce que nous venons de mettre en évidence dans cette étude contribuerait à rendre plus plausible cette identification.'*

Which we can translate as 'The low horizontal defence by curtain walls, Anglo-Saxon idea, could have also penetrated more directly to us by the north, (Saint-Gobain, Domfront, etc.). Master Jean, as well as his son Jacques, would have paternity in Savoyard lands. It is they who also impose a type of arrow loop, even though with an oblique embrasure in the Philippine tradition, still has a draft niche. These niches are covered with a mitre vault, a feature uniquely found across the English Channel. Jean and Jacques might well be English and would know the north of France (Normandy, Champagne, Ile de France). Have they also borrowed the convenience of helicoidal scaffolding – a rather rare feature – at the main tower of the Château de Coucy or, closer to home, at the royal tower by Philippe Auguste, from Villeneuve-sur-Yonne to 1220? If there is no formal evidence that Jean can be identified with Jean Cotereel, the last architect of the Notre-Dame cathedral in Lausanne, what we have just highlighted in this study would contribute to making this identification more plausible.'

49. Arnold Taylor. *Studies in Castles and Castle-Building* (London: The Hambledon Press, 1985). 22. 'We may thus here be in the presence not of two but of three generations of master masons, Master John (d. after 1261 and before 1268), Master James (d.1309), and Master James's sons Master Tassin and Master Giles.'
50. Ibid. 21.
51. We can be certain of the name of his wife, Ambrosia, as this is confirmed by later English records see CPR Edward I vol 2 1281–1292. 137. 'his wife Ambrosia'. Taylor reminded us that Ambrosia is the feminine form Saint Ambrose. Ambrose was serving as the Roman governor of Aemilia-Liguria in Milan when he was unexpectedly made Bishop of Milan in 374 by popular acclamation. That a Savoyard might choose the name for a daughter to honour a Milanese Saint might be considered normal. But this suggestion might be taken a step further when we think of the children, Tassin and Giles. Louis Blondel wrote '*Ce nom de Tassin est du Nord d'Italie ou de la Lombardie en partie dans les états de Savoie . . . Tasse est avec St Victor un des Saints de Milan*' Or This name of *Tassin* is from northern Italy or Lombardy partly in the states of Savoy . . .*Tasse* is with St Victor one of the Saints of Milan.' That a mother, herself named for a Milanese Saint, might name her son for another Milanese Saint begins to establish a trail. But we need confirmation of a link between Tassin and Giles and between them and Saint-Georges and their father. Such links were thankfully found by Taylor in Chambéry Arnold Taylor. *Studies in Castles and Castle-Building* (London: The Hambledon Press, 1985). 17. n1. Citing the Archives de la Savoie, Chambéry, Inv. 135, fo. 17, pacquet 14, pièce 7. The contract is between Tassin and Boso, Chaplain to the Count of Savoy, regarding a castle built at Falavier. The name survives '*Taxinus de Sancto Georgio lathomus*' or 'Tassin de Saint Georges the stonemason' For the link to Saint-Georges and hence the parental link for Giles see Louis Blondel. '*Le Château de Saxon: Note Complémentaire*' Vallesia IX (1955): 87–8. '*Probablement du chantier de St-Georges d'Espéranche.*' Or 'probably from the St-Georges d'Espéranche site.' For *Giletus* and *Tassinum* being brothers we have firm primary source evidence from the Comptes du châtelain de Chillon Guy de Bonard, 12781279, Copies, pp. 329–31; idem, de Guy de Bonard, 1279–1280, Copies, pp. 339–55. Quoted in Louis Blondel. '*Le Château de Saxon*' Vallesia IX (1954): 169. '*Primo litteram de conventionibus turris Sayssonis faciende per Tassinum et Giletum fratrum suum in taschiam. Item litteram de quinquaginta libr. maur. solutis per Guidonem Bonardi, Tassino et Gileto fratribus pro dicta turre facienda*' Thus we have good evidence that Jacques and Ambrosia de Saint Georges and their children Tassin and Giles were indeed a family.
52. Vitruvius. *The Complete Works of Vitruvius* (Hastings: Delphi Publishing Ltd, 2019). Book 1, Chap 5, 990. Taken from Vitruvius. 1914. The Ten Books on Architecture, trans. M. H. Morgan. London. '*Turres itaque rutundae aut polgoneae sunt facindae; quadratas enim machinae celerius dissipant, quod angulos arietes tundendo frangunt, in rotundationibus autem, uticuneus, ad centrum adigendo, laedere non possunt.*' Or 'The towers must be round or polygonal. Square towers are sooner shattered by military engine, for the battering ram pounds their angles to pieces; but in the case of the round towers, they do no harm, being engaged, as it were, in driving wedges to their centre.'
53. The Philippine castle design is today being recreated at Guédelon in France.
54. Hugh Kennedy. *Crusader Castles* (Cambridge: Cambridge University Press, 1994). 186–9. 'It would be natural to assume that changes [such as round towers] and developments in the architecture of castles in the Crusader east would be reflected in Western Europe ... In fact the evidence is at best ambiguous.' And 'As Fossier recognized, the Crusaders brought back from the east new methods of attacking castles, not new theories of military architecture. In both east and west, architects and builders tried and adapted, coming up with solutions which were sometimes the same and sometimes different; experiment and experience, rather than architectural influences from the other end of the Mediterranean, were the deciding factors.' For a partly contrary view A. W. Lawrence. 1983. A Skeletal History of Byzantine Fortification. The Annual of the British School of Athens. vol 78. 'It may still be argued that this [Byzantine influence on Frankish architecture] is coincidence and

that the crusading Franks evolved their new fortifications without outside help, or possibly with the help of Classical texts rather than Byzantine models. This is a matter of opinion, but in the light of the examples discussed above the writer finds it difficult to believe in the hypothesis of independent evolution.'

55. Nicola Coldstream, 'Architects, Advisers and Design at Edward I's Castles in Wales,' *Architectural History: Journal of the Society of Architectural Historians of Great Britain* 46 (2003). 24. 'In Savoy, however twin towered gatehouses did not exist.' The paper was reproduced in an article for *Late Medieval Castles* (Woodbridge : The Boydell Press. (2016). 41–60. Hereinafter only the original paper is cited.

56. Daniel de Raemy cites no evidence either way for a barbican but does confirm a door flanked by the guard tower, ditch spanned by a drawbridge and outer and inner curtain walls, quoting Jean-Fred Boekholt see Daniel de Raemy. *Châteaux, donjons et grandes tours dans les Etats de Savoie* (1230–1330) (Lausanne: Cahiers d'archéologie romande 98 et 99, 2004). 60. Regarding the existence of a barbican Mottaz says 'the construction of one is indicated in the accounts of the chatelaine of Chillon, unfortunately Diebold Schilling's drawing is incomplete on this point and can not be used to fix the shape of this fortification. This detail has only a very minor importance, and in the drawing, I gave this barbican the rectangular shape that most often find in our country [Switzerland].'

57. Eugene Mottaz, '*Note sur la construction du château d'Yverdon,*' *Revue historique vaudoise* 8 (1900): 363.

58. Ibid. 365. 'The construction of the walls and towers of the castle presented a difficulty ... The foundations of this considerable work fell below the level of neighbouring rivers and even of Lake Neuchâtel.'

59. Eugene L. Cox. *The Eagles of Savoy: The House of Savoy in Thirteenth Century Europe* (Princeton: Princeton University Press, 1974). 298.

60. Eugene L. Cox. *The Eagles of Savoy: The House of Savoy in Thirteenth Century Europe* (Princeton: Princeton University Press, 1974). 298. n69.

61. In 1854 Sir Henry Paston Bedlingfield was laying claim as co-heir to the abeyant Grandison Barony. The documents produced to substantiate aforesaid claim included the deed of 1263.

62. Minutes of Evidence Taken Before the Committee for Privileges ... to Determine the Abeyance of the Barony of Grandison. 1854. House of Lords: London. 169 '*Nos Agnes, domina de Grandisono, tutrix legitima liberorum nostrorum Petri et Willelini, Girardus, Jaquetus et Henricus, pro se et fratre suo Otonino, filii predicte domine.*' Or 'We Agnès, Lady of Grandson, Guardian of our legitimate children Peter and William, Girard, Jacques and Henry, for them and their brother Othon, the sons said Lady.'

63. Louis Blondel, '*Le château et le bourg de Conthey,*'. *Vallesia* IX (1954): 149–64.

64. Louis Blondel, '*Le château de Brignon,*' *Vallesia* IV (1949): 19–34.

65. Louis Blondel, '*Le bourg et le château de Saillon,*' *Unsere Kunstdenkmäler* 1 (1950): 8–9.

66. André Donnet & Louis Blondel. *Château du Valais* (Olten: Editions Walter, 1963). 121.

67. *La Finanza Sabauda*. vol. 1, 26. '*Idem libravit Francisco cementario pro tascheria nove camere iuxta turrim et Conteis.*' And 58-9 '*De quibus libravit Francisco cementario de taschia .viii.xx. et .x.librarum et duabus robis de quadraginta sol. pro turre de Sallon facienda de sexaginta et decem pedibus altitudinis tam in grosso muro quam in avante pedibus et in merlis, de duodecim pedibus pissitudinis usque ad primam travaturam et decem pedibus a secunda travatura superius. x. lib.*' And duplicated in the account of Ibid. 68. '*Francisco ... pro turre de Sallon.*'

68. Louis Blondel, '*L'architecture militaire au temps de Pierre II de Savoie: Les donjons circulaires,*' *Genava* XIII (1935): 290. Blondel gave Mézos in Gascony as the possible origin for Jean de Mézos. Subsequently accepted by Taylor. *Master Bertram, Ingeniator Regis*. Studies in Medieval History presented to R. Allen Brown (Woodbridge: The Boydell Press, 1989). 292 n.21. Mézos lay on the Via Campino to Santiago de Compostela around midway between Bordeaux and Bayonne. Jean de Mézos is variously recorded in the Gascon and Savoyard records as Mesoz, Maysoz, Masoz, Masot, Masouz, Maso and Massout. Hereinafter for simplicity's sake we will use the modern form Mézos.

69. Arnold Taylor. *Studies in Castles and Castle-Building* (London: The Hambledon Press, 1985). 12.

70. Louis Blondel, '*L'architecture militaire au temps de Pierre II de Savoie: Les donjons circulaires,*' *Genava* XIII (1935): .290. '*ad turrim de Sallon devisandam*' and '*ad supervidendum ibi situm turris.*'

71. RG i, no 2828; Close Rolls 1253-54, 194. '*Pro Johanne de Mesoz et Bertramo ingeniatore – Mandatum est P. Chacepork' quod, si Johannes de Mesoz, Bertramus Le Engynnur, Geraldus de Winton, Wilhelmis de Nantuyl, Willelmus Le Gelus et Nicholas Anglicus, magistri ingeniorum, nondum habuerint robas suas quas dominus rex eis dedit quando Castrum de Benaug.*'

72. Louis Blondel, '*L'architecture militaire au temps de Pierre II de Savoie: Les donjons circulaires,*' *Genava* XIII (1935): 290..

73. Today the ruins of Benauges lie by the French commune of Arbis in the Gironde department, Nouvelle Aquifer region.

74. RG i, no 2689; Close Rolls 1253–4, 173. '*Teste Rege in castris apud Lupiac.*'

75. RG i, no 3462; Close Rolls 1253–4, 275 '*Pro Johanne de Maysoz – Mandatum est eisdem quod Johanni de Maysoz, qui a rege suscepturus est arma militaria apud Burdegalam, sine dilacione habere faciant ea que ad miliciam suam pertinent, sicut alles novis militibus consueverunt invenire. Teste apud supra (apud Burdegallam xxv die Septembris).*'

76. CCR Henry III vol 6 1247–1251, 82. '*Liberate etiam Magistro Bertrando de Saltu, Ingeniator, x liberas.*'

77. Sault-de-Navailles appears in 1273 as Sanctus-Nicolaus de Saltu in the Bordeaux Registers. The village is some twenty plus miles north-west of Pau and fifty odd miles inland, in the shadow of the Pyrenees.

78. Jean Pierre Chapuisat, '*De Mont-sur-Rolle à Windsor, de la Dullive à Dumfries ... La Maison de Savoie et le Pays de Vaud,*' *Bibliothèque historique vaudoise* 97 (1989): 120.

79. Ibid.

80. Louis Blondel, '*L'architecture militaire au temps de Pierre II de Savoie: Les donjons circulaires,*' *Genava* XIII (1935): 283.

81. Daniel de Raemy. *Châteaux, donjons et grandes tours dans les Etats de Savoie (1230-1330)* (Lausanne: Cahiers d'archéologie romande 98 et 99, 2004). 282–3.

82. Louis Blondel, '*L'architecture militaire au temps de Pierre II de Savoie: Les donjons circulaires,*' *Genava* XIII (1935): 290. '*cum stipendii magistorum venentium de ultra Jurim.*'

83. *La Finanza Sabauda*, vol. 1, 41. '*In expensis domini Iohannis de Masot euntis apud Sallon ad turrim de Sallon devisandam .vi. sol. .viii. den. preter illos quos expendit apud Sallon.*' Or 'The expenses of Jean de Mézos when he was at Saillon for the tower of Saillon. Six *sol* eight den. Those whom he considers at Saillon.' And Ibid. 68. '*In expensis domini Iohannis de Masot ad supervidendum ibi situm turris per tres dies. Vj.s.vj.d.*'. Or 'The expenses of Jean de Mézos to oversee the siting of the tower for three days Six *sol* six den.'

84. Ibid. 118. '*In expensis domini Iohannis de Masoz apud Yverdunum infirmantis per xxviii dies, de mandato domini, vi lib xii den . . .in acquietancia Magistri Jacobi Cementarii hoc anno et de anno preterito ... qui Jacobus percipit Yverdunum de domino in feudo, decem libras viannensium singulis annis. xv. lib.*' Or 'The expenses of Jean de Mézos at Yverdon whilst sick for twenty-eight days, by command of his Lord, six *livres* 12 *den* . . .in the acquittance (discharge of a debt) of Maître Jacques the mason for this year and the year before that ... he Jacques has the fee of Yverdon, ten *livres* Vienne every year. xv. Lib'

85. Martigny-Region. 'The Bayart Tower'. *Martigny Region*. www.martigny-region.ch/tourism/bayart-tower-366.html retrieved 3 September 2021. 'This keep, 19 metres high and almost 10 metres wide, was built around 1260 by the architect Pierre Meinier.'

86. Étienne-Louis Borrel. 1884. *Les monuments anciens de la Tarentaise (Savoie)*. Paris: Ducher. 150–3. And Bernard Demotz. 1987. *L'État et le château au Moyen Âge : l'exemple savoyard. Journal des savants*: 27–64.

87. ADS SA 9312.Jean de Mézos is described as '*moranti apud Salinas pro dictando opere putei de Salinas*' whilst Maître Jacques is '*euntis apud Salinas pro operibus putei per xj. dies, capientis quolibet die 3s. Pro expensis suis.*' N. Pevsner, 'Terms of Architectural Planning in the Middle Ages,' *Journal of the Warburg and Courtauld Institutes* 5 (1942): 236. Pevsner is quite clear on the term applied in Savoy of Jean de Mézos, '*dictando*'. 'should a house collapse which had been built by a mason (a '*magister Comacinus*') for a patron who commissioned him '*ad opera dictandi.*' In this context '*dictare*' can only mean to dictate how the house is to be built'

88. Martigny has a long past, *Gaulish Octodurus* had first been conquered by the 5 Legion of the Roman Republic back in 57BC becoming Roman Forum *Claudii Augusti*, later renamed 'to *Forum Claudii Vallensium* — it remained an obvious place too for fortifications.

89. In 1240 Pierre de Savoie sent a castellan to Romont to build a castle and found a village. The Peace of Evian in 1244, had confirmed the Savoyard rights to Romont.

90. Eugene L. Cox. *The Eagles of Savoy: The House of Savoy in Thirteenth Century Europe* (Princeton: Princeton University Press, 1974). 302–3.

91. Arnold Taylor, 'Some notes on the Savoyards in North Wales, 1277–1300. With special reference to the Savoyard element in the construction of Harlech Castle,' *Genava* XI (1963): 292.

92. See below page 133.

93. Arnold Taylor, 'Some notes on the Savoyards in North Wales, 1277–1300. With special reference to the Savoyard element in the construction of Harlech Castle,' *Genava* XI (1963): 292. '*Idem libravit Petro Uldrici carpentario et eius socio euntibus apud Rotundum Montem pro operibus domini, pro expensis ipsorum cum uno runcino qui portabat aysiamentum ipsorum ... xxv.s.*' Or 'The same considered to Peter Uldrici the carpenter and his companions who went to Romont for the works of the Lord, for the expenses of their own, with one packhorse who was carrying for ease ... Twenty-five *sol*.'

94. Nicola Coldstream, 'Architects, Advisers and Design at Edward I's Castles in Wales,' *Architectural History: Journal of the Society of Architectural Historians of Great Britain* 46 (2003): The context being gatehouse design.

95. We will come later to the specifics of the role of 'tutor' played by Jean de Mézos in the career of Maître Jacques de Saint Georges. But for Jean de Mézos as directing the works of Maître Jacques in Savoy see Arnold Taylor. 1989. Master Bertram, Ingeniator Regis. Studies in Medieval History presented to R. Allen Brown. Woodbridge: The Boydell Press. 294. n31. Reproduced from Arnold Taylor. *Studies in Castles and Castle-Building.* (London: The Hambledon Press. 1985). 93 citing Chambéry Archive, ADS SA 9312. *'In expensis Magistri Jacobi Lathomi euntis apud Salinas pro operibus putei per xj dies, capientis quolibet die iij.s. pro expensis, xxxiij.s. Idem libravit domino Johanni de Masouz moranti apud Salin' pro dictando opera putei Salino xxix.lib. xix.s. vj.d.'* Or 'The expenses of Maître Jacques the stonemason going to Salins-Les-Thermes for the works of the well for eleven days, taking per day three *sol* for expenses, thirty-three *sol*. Also considered Lord Jean de Mézos detained at Salins-Les-Thermes for dictating the well works at Salins-Les-Thermes twenty-nine *Livre*, nineteen *sol*, six den.' This attribution of '*dictando*' to Jean de Mézos at a site also carrying primary source evidence of Maître Jacques, is the closest we will come in primary sources to a 'tutor'.
96. La Finanza Sabauda, vol. 1, 63. *'magistri Arnaundi fossatoris circa opus fossati de Chillon'.*
97. Louis Blondel, *'L'architecture militaire au temps de Pierre II de Savoie: Les donjons circulaires,'* Genava XIII (1935): 289.
98. The tomb beneath which he lies bears the inscription that he made peace between King Henry III of England and King Louis IV of France, whilst this is true this is perhaps one of the most understated epitaphs in history, even the addition of *'Vir illustris ac srenuissimus'*, 'the illustrious man, and of great energy' don't go far enough.
99. Christopher Tyerman, 'The House of Savoy: Thirteenth Century England and the Medieval Community – The Savoia at the Court of Henry III of England (1216–1272)' Seventh Annual Savoy History Lecture (American Delegation of Savoy Orders, New York, 27 October 2009).
100. Jean Pierre Chapuisat, *'De Mont-sur-Rolle à Windsor, de la Dullive à Dumfries … La Maison de Savoie et le Pays de Vaud,' Bibliothèque historique vaudoise* (1989). 120.

Chapter Three
1. The English archives gives us some of the detail of his expenses at this time, all handled by the wardrobe and the good offices of the Riccardi of Lucca: merchants at Acre some 880 *livres* and a further 1,333 *livres* 6 *sol* and 8 den.
2. Prestwich suggests the Annalist of Dunstable, who is our source in this regard, may have meant Orlandino da Pogio who was a leading member of the Riccardi of Lucca. See Michael Prestwich. *Edward I* (Yale: Yale University Press, 1997). 100. n39.
3. Richard W. Kaeuper. *Bankers to the Crown: The Riccardi of Lucca and Edward I* (Princeton: Princeton University Press, 1973). 81.
4. TNA E101/261/1.
5. TNA E372/143 m 35d.
6. Richard W. Kaeuper. *Bankers to the Crown: The Riccardi of Lucca and Edward I* (Princeton: Princeton University Press, 1973). 2–4.
7. Thomas W. Blomquist, 'Commercial Association in Thirteenth-Century Lucca,' *The Business History Review* 45 (1971): 159.
8. Ibid. 160.
9. CCR *Edward I* vol 1 1272–1279. 413.
10. Richard W. Kaeuper. *Bankers to the Crown: The Riccardi of Lucca and Edward I* (Princeton: Princeton University Press, 1973). 5.
11. Ibid. 27.
12. Michael Prestwich. *Edward I* (Yale: Yale University Press, 1997). 81. Philip de Berizon of Genoa another 666 *livres* 13 *sol* and 4 den, to the Templars in Paris some 4,000 *livres*, the carriage of a chest with silks and carpets 18 *sol*, furs acquired in Bruges for the upcoming coronation another 100 *livres*, in total 7,687 *livres* paid to Robert Burnell in London on his behalf by the merchants of Lucca. Loans from the Riccardi, to cover the period from his arrival at Trapani until his arrival in England totalled another £22,364, being a king on crusade and his travels was proving a costly business, but one the merchants of Lucca were happy to finance. See CPR Edward I vol 1 1272–1281, 131–2. An example of both the influence of Othon de Grandson and the Riccardi at this point concerns the Italian involvement in the profitable wool trade. The Riccardi undertook to buy 120 sacks of wool from the abbot of the Cistercian house of Meaux in Holderness, Yorkshire at the Boston fair. The abbot subsequently reneged on delivery of the wool, the Riccardi wrote seeking redress to, amongst others, their friend and customer, Grandson. See Richard W. Kaeuper. *Bankers to the Crown: The Riccardi of Lucca and Edward I* (Princeton: Princeton University Press, 1973). 37.
13. TNA E159 / m 63 31d. His brother, Henri de Grandson, the Bishop of Verdun from 1278, is known to have received loans from the Riccardi in the 1290s, another who received loans was the Prior of

Wenlock, Henri de Bonvillars, brother of Jean de Bonvillars, who would owe some one hundred marks in 1290.

14. Richard W. Kaeuper. *Bankers to the Crown: The Riccardi of Lucca and Edward I* (Princeton: Princeton University Press, 1973). 28–30.

15. E. B. Fryde, D. E. Greenway, S. Porter & I. Roy. 1986. *Handbook of British Chronology*. Third ed. London: Offices of the Royal Historical Society. 35. Burnell had been one of the Regents ruling England in Edward's absence on Crusade, along with Walter Giffard, Archbishop of York and Roger de Mortimer. Anthony Bek, Joseph de Chauncy, Othon de Grandson and Jean de Vesci had been with Edward in the Holy Land.

16. Richard W. Kaeuper. *Bankers to the Crown: The Riccardi of Lucca and Edward I* (Princeton: Princeton University Press, 1973). 85.

17. CPR Henry III vol 4 1247–1258. 237–8. And Ibid. 288.

18. Chron. Thomas Wykes, 197–8.

19. CPR Henry III vol 3 1232–1247. 469.

20. CPR Henry III Vol 3 1232–1247. 469. Latin text Wurstemberger vol 4. No 191."*Amedeus IV Comes recognoscit in feudum a rege Angliæ castra de Aviliana, de Bardo, et villas Secusiæ et S. Mauritii in Chablasio, pro qua recognitione accipit Comes a rege Mille libras Sterlingorum. 1246. Januarii 16. ap. Westmonasterium. Tria diplomata Heorici Regis, pro Amedeo, Comite Sabaudiæ et Marchione Italiæ. Rex concedit Amedeo, Com. Sab, et March, in Italia, pro homagio quod fecit pro Castro Auyllan et villa Secucie, cum Pallacio et castro de Bardo et villa S. Mauritii in Chablasio, tenendis de Rege et heredibus suis sibi et heredibus suis in feodo imperpetuum, M. libras bonorum Sterlingorum de thesauro suo, percipiendas London. ad Scaccarium Regis de dono suo. De quibus M. libris Rex solvit ei, pro manibus, D. marcas, et ei solvere tenetur D. marcas ad festum Pasche anno regni suo tricesimo; et residua D. marcarum ad festum S. Michaelis anno eodem, preter feodnm suum quod percipere debet ad eundem terminum.*"

21. Michael Prestwich. *Edward I* (Yale: Yale University Press, 1997). 84. Citing AST Inv. Sav. 51. Fo. 257. Mazzo I, no 8. Eugene L. Cox. *The Eagles of Savoy: The House of Savoy in Thirteenth Century Europe* (Princeton: Princeton University Press, 1974). 411.

22. At Conwy Castle.

23. Those in Edward's party are detailed in Arnold Taylor. *Studies in Castles and Castle-Building* (London: The Hambledon Press, 1985). 29 and 35.

24. Chron. Thomas Wykes, 255. '*die Mercurii proxima post festum Sanctæ Trinitatis descendit de monte Cenisii, et in quindena Sanctæ Trinitatis venit apud Sanctum Georgium prope Lugdunum.*' Or 'from the Wednesday next after the feast of the Holy Trinity they descended from Mont Cenis and arrived at Saint-Georges near Lyon.'

25. Ibid. Dates added in the margin by the translator. See also Henry Gough. Itinerary of King Edward the First throughout his reign, A.D. 1272–1307, exhibiting his movements so far as they are recorded. vol 1. (Paisley: Alexander Gardner, 1900). 24.

26. Chron. Thomas Wykes, 255. Dates added in the margin by the translator. See also Henry Gough. Itinerary of King Edward the First throughout his reign, A.D. 1272–1307, exhibiting his movements so far as they are recorded. vol 1 (Paisley: Alexander Gardner, 1900j. 24.

27. CPR Henry III vol 4 (1247–1258). 270. 'Charter granting to Edward, eldest son and heir of the king, all the land of Ireland, except the cities of Dublin and Limerick, with their counties, and the city of Athlone (de Dalon), which the king keep, and except 500l. of land which the king is bound to evaluate to his brother, Geoffroy de Lezingnan, in the Irish desert, and 40l of similar land promised to Robert Waleraund; all of the county of Chester with its castles and towns, with the conquest of Wales by the king within these limits, namely Rothelan, Dissard and Gannoc [Deganwy] and the other land of Pervethelat [Perfeddwlad]; the whole city of Bristol with the castle (castello); the Three Castles, namely, Grosmund, Skenefrith and White Castle, 'with honour; the castles of Mungomery, Karmerdyn [Carmarthen] and Cardigan; the castle of Buelt [Builth]; the Château du Pic in the spotlight; Stamford and Graham with honor; all the late country of the Earl of Eu in England; Gernereye and Geresy and the rest of the sea islands; the mansion of Freemantle (Frigido Mantello) saving the king all the lands of crozier (crociis) and the guards of the empty churches in all the lands above where the king should have the guard of right. To stand with him and his heirs, on condition that they are never separated from the crown of England and that no one, because of this concession, can at any time claim a right over it, but that 'they remain entirely with the kings of England forever. Renewal to him also of the gift of the land of Gascony and the island of Oléron, on the condition that they remain in the lordship of the crown of England. Witnesses: Peter, Bishop of Hereford, J. de Plessetis, Earl of Warwick, Geoffrey of Lezingnan and William of Valencia, the King's brothers, Peter of Sabaudia, John Maunsell, Provost of Beverley, J. Prior of Newburgh, King's Chaplain , William de Gray, William de Chaeny, Nicholas de Sancto Mauro, William Gernun and others. 14 February 1254, Bazas, Gascony, France.

28. *La Finanza Sabauda*. vol. 2, 122. *'Die Lune in festo beati Laurencii apud Sanctum Georgium de Sperenchi.'*
29. Ibid. 76. *'Die mercurii apud Costam Sancti Andrée.'*
30. Ibid. *'Die Jovis apud Voyronem.'*
31. The Chartreuse region had been the birthplace of the Carthusian order, which took its name from these mountains, a great monastery was nearby having been founded as a hermitage back in 1084. The Carthusians lived in individual cells rather than dormitories, their log cabins opening towards a gallery that allowed them access to the communal areas, the church, refectory, and chapter room. A resilient bunch too, an avalanche, the constant plague of the mountains, had wiped out their monastery in 1132, but they had rebuilt.
32. *La Finanza Sabauda*. vol. 2, 78. *'Die Martis apud Sanctum Laurencium in deserto.'*
33. Ibid. 78. *'Die mercuri apud Chamberiacum.'*
34. Ibid. 79. *'presentibus domino Humberto de Seysello.'*
35. Ibid. 85. *'Die Dominica ante navitatem beate Marie apud Montemmelianum.'* And Ibid. 88. *'Die Dominica post navitatem beate Marie apud Mosterium Tarentaysia.'*
36. Ibid. 91. *'Die June in festo beati Mathei apostoli apud Castrum Argenti.'* And Ibid 92. *'Die Martis in festo beati Mauricii apud Augustam.'*
37. *La Finanza Sabauda*. vol. 2, 107. *'Die Martis, apud burgum Montis Jovis.'*
38. Ibid. 109. *'Die June apud grungias de Martiura'* And Ibid. 110. *'Die Martis apud Seyllon'*. And Ibid. *'Die mercurii apud Conteys.'*
39. Ibid. 112. *'Die Martis in vigilia Beati Martini apud Chillonem.'*
40. Ibid. 114. *'presentibus episcopis de Lausanna, de Gebennis ... comite Gruerie.'*
41. Arnold Taylor. *Studies in Castles and Castle-Building* (London: The Hambledon Press, 1985). 11. 'sounds uncommonly like James of St George.' Citing AST Inv. Sav. 69. fo.5, mazzo 1, no 4. *'Idem liberavit Jaquetto de sancto Jorio per litteras domini xv. Li.'* In Ibid. n4. Taylor suggests 'we may have here the only reference so far discovered in Savoy records to Master James the mason as being 'of St George'. See n218.
42. For example, 19 May 1274 in Household roll of Count Phillip of Savoy, Archivio di Stato di Torino, Inv, Savoia 38, fo. 46, nos 3 and 4. *'Magistro Jacobo lathomo pro expensis suis et Magistri de Romanis Veniencium de Deserto ad dominum apud Chillon, xxviij.s.'*
43. AST Inv. Sav. 69. fo. 5, mazzo I, nos 3, 4. *'Johannes Franciscus'*.
44. Ibid. no 4 *'Idem liberavit Jacquetto de Sancto Jorio per litteras domini xv. Li.'* *'Jacquetto de Sancto Jorio'* Taylor ascribes to Maître Jacques. But this attribution by toponym is not well supported by the context of history, Maître Jacques has almost certainly not yet worked at the Saint-Georges in the Viennois that is the likely source of his name in England, what's more at no point is the toponym applied to him in Savoy, only in England. It's far more likely that this 'Jacquetto de Sancto Jorio' hails from Saint-Jeoire in Faucigny, which is attested as being referenced as Sancto Jorio in the thirteenth century. Maître Jacques is not described as de Sancto Georgio until 3 November 1280, and only in England, never in Savoy. Furthermore, we should remember that the earliest building records for Saint-Georges-d'Espéranche are no earlier than 1270, and therefore it is most unlikely that 1266 records in Savoy would associate Jacques with an as yet not yet started castle. *La Finanza Sabauda*. vol. 1, xiv and xvi. '[For] 1270 à 1272 Deux comptes de *Thomas de Becunet châtelain de St George de Livrées par lui faittes à divers ouvriers pour la fabrique et des livrées à l'occasion du reçu des droits de la Châtelainie de St George.'*
45. *La Finanza Sabauda*. vol. 1, 118. *'Magistro Jacobi cementarii ... apud Yverdunum.'*
46. Both the sees of Sion and Lausanne retained temporal as well as spiritual authority over much of their lands, Sion being a part of the Archdiocese of the Tarentaise centred on Moutiers and Lausanne on the Archdiocese of Besançon.
47. *La Finanza Sabauda*. vol. 2, 280. *'presentibus domino Guillelmo de Chanens, domino Jacobo de Granzon.'* And Ibid. 281. *'presentibus domino Willelmo de Chavenz, domino Jacobo de Grancon.'* And Ibid *'presentibus Guillelmo de Chavenz et domino Jacobo de Granconz.'*
48. *La Finanza Sabauda*. vol. 2, 278. *'Die Jovis ibidem apud Yverdon.'* And Ibid. 282. *'Die mercurii apud Cletas.'*
49. Eugene L. Cox. *The Eagles of Savoy: The House of Savoy in Thirteenth Century Europe* (Princeton: Princeton University Press, 1974). 411–12.
50. Writing in Arnold Taylor. *Studies in Castles and Castle-Building* (London: The Hambledon Press, 1985). 34 Taylor suggest that 'work on the castle probably began in about 1268 or 1269; that by the beginning of 1271 some part of it was already in use ... building went on for a further three years or so.'
51. *La Finanza Sabauda*. vol. 1, xiv and xvi. '[For] 1270 à 1272 Deux comptes de *Thomas de Becunet châtelain de St George de Livrées par lui faittes à divers ouvriers pour la fabrique et des livrées à l'occasion du reçu des droits de la Châtelainie de St George.'*

52. Arnold Taylor. *Studies in Castles and Castle-Building.* (London: The Hambledon Press. 1985). 33. *'Sentence prononcée par Edmond, fils du roi d'Angleterre ... Attum apud Sanctum Georgium de Speranchia.'* Citing Rég. Dauph ii, no. 10980. And *La Finanza Sabauda.* vol. 2, 123 *'Die June in festo beati Laurencii [10 August 1271] apud Sanctum Georgium de Sperenchi ... [Pro] Camera domini mundanda.'.*

53. M. Chabord was Engineer of the Bridges and Roads of the Isère Department in 20 Fructidor of the Second Year of the French Republic one and indivisible – 11 September 1794.

54. Malcolm Hislop. *James of St George and the Castles of North Wales* (Barnsley: Pen & Sword Books Ltd, 2020). 12. 'The choice of polygonal towers ... was probably due to aesthetics ... because they had no special merit from a defensive perspective.'

55. ADI Serie L, no. 198, pacquet 1. The letters in the following report by Chabord relate to the accompanying colour-wash plan (Figure 1.4) *'Le cydevant Château d 'Espéranche est flanque de quatre tours A, octogones (voir le plan cyjoint figure), dont les murs ont cinq pieds d'épaisseur. Vers le sommet de ces tours, il existe quelques embrasures. Les murs extérieurs de cedit bâtiment, ainsi que le mur BC servant de clôture à la grande cour du côté du nord, ont aussi semblable épaisseur. Des fossés, comme le plan l'indique, regment tour au tour de ce vaste bâtiment, et ont de largeur depuis trente a cinquente pieds, sur dix a dix-huit pieds de hauteur.'* Or 'The side of the Château d' Espéranche is flanked by four towers (A), octagons (see the plan attached figure), the walls of which are five feet thick. Towards the top of these towers there are a few embrasures. The exterior walls of this building, as well as the wall (B to C) serving as an enclosure for the great courtyard on the north side, are also of similar thickness. Ditches as the plan indicates, surround this vast building, and are thirty to fifty feet wide, and ten to eighteen feet high.' We thus have the best description we can now have of the Château d'Espéranche. The surviving elements of the castle in 1794 being the four towers (A), one face of the curtain wall (B–C) and the surrounding moat, which was then drained to a marsh on its northern face. But enough had survived until 1794 to identify a Carré Savoyard, but with octagonal not round towers.

56. Building accounts for Saint-Georges d'Espéranche-d'Espéranche for the years 1270-72 had survived until 1793.

57. Arnold Taylor. *Studies in Castles and Castle-Building* (London: The Hambledon Press, 1985) Plate 23.

58. Ibid. Plates 22 & 23.

59. Ibid. 39.

60. Ibid. 36.

61. Daniel de Raemy. *Châteaux, donjons et grandes tours dans les Etats de Savoie* (1230-1330) (Lausanne: Cahiers d'archéologie romande 98 et 99, 2004). 200. *'la premiere ouvre entièrement conçue par le maçon-architecte Jacques de St-Georges'.*

62. Louis Blondel of February 1952, Cited in Arnold Taylor. *Studies in Castles and Castle-Building* (London: The Hambledon Press, 1985). 12. 'As I could very often notice the master mason are named after the last great construction where they worked. Now it is beyond any doubt that the castle of St Georges constructed between 1270 and 1272 was the most important at that time.'

63. RUE Maître JACQUES Bâttiseur du Château XIIIe Siècle.

64. Fœdera, 504. *'UNIVERSIS presentes literas inspecturis, Philippus comes Sabaudia, salutem in Domino. Noverit universitas vestra quod nos fatemur recepisse serenissimo principe, domino Edwardo, DEI gratiâ, ilustrissimo Rege Angliæ, in feodum, castrum Avillan', villam secus, cum palatio & castro de Bardo, & villam sancti Mauritii in Chablay, qua & quas sub eo modo retinemus & retinebimus, sicut ea tenuit à, recolende memorie, domino H, patre dicti domini Regis, quondam dominus Amedeus comes Sabaud• frater noster; Et, pro predicts feodo & terris, fatemur nos magium, in manibus predicti domini Regis. fecisse presentialiter ho– In cujus rei testimonium presentes literas fieri fecimus patentes, nostro sigillo munitas, apud Sanctum Georgium de Sperench', xxv. die Junii, anno Domini MCCLXXIII.'*

65. Arnold Taylor. *Studies in Castles and Castle-Building* (London: The Hambledon Press, 1985). 41.

66. Ibid. 42.

67. Fœdera, 504. *'en la presence le noble baron mon sire Phelip counte de Sauvoye e de Burgoyne. Mon sire Johan de Vescy. Mon sire Roger de Clyfford. Sire Simon de Genevile. Sire Otes de Grantson.'*

68. The *Fœdera* is a collection of of 'all the leagues, treaties, alliances, capitulations, and confederacies, which have at any time been made between the Crown of England and any other kingdoms, princes and states.' It was published by Thomas Rymer, volume 1, referenced for this book published in 1816.

69. Fœdera, 504. *'quoddam castrum apud Abrunol prope castrum de Monte Gomery de novo engere ... Vobis mandamus districte inhibentes, ne castrum illud construere.'* Or 'a new castle at Abrunol near to the castle of Montgomery ... we order strictly prohibiting the construction of a castle'.

70. Henry Gough. *Itinerary of King Edward the First throughout his reign, A.D. 1272–1307, exhibiting his movements so far as they are recorded* vol.1 (Paisley: Alexander Gardner, 1900). 25.

71. Edward interestingly uses the same words in paying homage to Philippe as his father Henry had earlier used with Louis following the Treaty of Paris in 1259. Edward swearing that he was Philippe's man for 'all the lands I ought to hold from you'. Opinion is divided as to whether we

should read anything into the 'ought' in terms of lost Plantagenet lands in France, but since it would have been expressed in French as *devrait* which can be translated as either should or ought and thus implied criticism of Capetian holding of Plantagenet lands. Furthermore, the language can be read as confirming that Aquitaine had been an allodial fief before 1259 and had not subsequently lost that status by the terms of the treaty of Paris, because the homage depended, upon complete fulfilment of the terms of the 1259 treaty. Since the lost lands had not been restored as agreed, then Aquitaine, so the argument goes, reverted to being an allod, and was not the subject of French suzerainty. It was argued that the homage performed by Henry III applied only to those lands given him by Louis IX in exchange for Henry's renunciation of Normandy, Poitou, Maine, Touraine, and Anjou. Thus, when Edward performed his homage in 1273, he swore fealty for those lands which he 'ought to hold' from the king of France by implication, Edward neither recognized, nor owed, any feudal obligations for Aquitaine because the kings of France had failed to relinquish the lands promised in the treaty of Paris, and so were, essentially, in breach of contract. These legal niceties would become crucial twenty years later when Philippe IV attempted to seize Gascony from Edward.

72. St Martin Le Grand was a college of secular canons of ancient origin, with a collegiate church to dedicated to St Martin of Tours. The church was especially interesting since it was responsible for the sounding of the curfew bell in the evenings, which announced the closing of the city's gates. The college church of St Martin Le Grand was not very far from the house granted to Othon de Grandson following the late baronial war. Following Savoyards Guillaume de Champvent and Louis de Vaud as Deacons of St Martin would be William of Louth, Keeper of the Wardrobe.

73. Jean-Pierre Chapuisat, 'Au service de deux rois d'Angleterre au XIIIe siècle: Pierre de Champvent,' *Revue historique vaudoise* 72 (1964): 163. n2.

74. Ibid. The charter bears the usual Savoyard witness list: Imbert Pugeys, Ebal II de Mont, Pierre de Champvent, Imbert de Montferrand and Guillaume de Champvent.

75. CPR Edward I vol 1 1272–1281, 49.

76. Ibid. 119.

77. Jean-Daniel Morerod. *La Cathédrale Notre-Dame de Lausanne: Monument européen, temple vaudois.* (Lausanne: *La Bibliothèque des Arts*, 2012). 22.

78. Esther Rowland Clifford. *A Knight of Great Renown: The Life and Times of Othon de Grandson* (Chicago: The University of Chicago Press, 1961). 46.

79. Sara Cockerill. *Eleanor of Castile: The Shadow Queen.* Second Edition ed. (Stroud: Amberley Publishing, 2014). 267.

80. Girart Dorens, 'Sir Otho de Grandison 1238?–1328,' Transactions of the Royal Historical Society 3 (1909): 125-195.

81. CPR Edward I vol 1 1272–1281. 143.

82. Girart Dorens, 'Sir Otho de Grandison 1238?–1328,' Transactions of the Royal Historical Society 3 (1909): 128.

83. CFR Edward I 1272–1307. 65.

84. The lands of the Rhône south and west of its exit from Lac Léman at Geneva are widespread and varied, firstly the lands east of the river were not France, France began at the Rhône, the lands to the east of the river were the Holy Roman Empire. These lands were divided between the Count of Savoy, the Count of Provence and the Count of Albon. This last county had since the days of its Count Guiges IV been known as the Dauphiné and its Count the Dauphin of Viennois. It would be a later deal between its rulers and France by which the French obtained the Dauphiné that French heirs to the throne be known as the Dauphin. The Dauphin's of the Viennois were long standing rivals of the Counts of Savoy – and Philippe especially so since he'd chosen to reside in the lands adjoining the Dauphine. Pierre and latterly Philippe had acquired much land in the Viennois, that is the fertile land to the east of Vienne and the Rhône, acquired more using their purse than their sword. So much land that an enclave of Savoy existed to the west of Dauphine attached only to the Savoy proper by the road to Chambéry. The Savoyards had acquired this territory to extend their suzerainty of the Mont Cenis from Italy all the way to the boundary with France, the Rhône.

85. Bruno Galland, '*Un Savoyard sur le siège de Lyon au XIIIe siècle : Philippe de Savoie,' Bibliothèque de l'école des chartes* tome 146 livraison 1 (1988): 54.

86. The see of Vienne had become an Archdiocese in the 5th century, George an Archbishop circa 699 AD.

87. The veracity of the authenticity of the name to this particular Saint Georges is added to by the year of his canonization, 1251, almost certainly a train set in motion by the papal stay in Lyon and Philippe de Savoie.

88. Of the castles under construction for Philippe de Savoie, the most important of these was at Voiron, built atop a commanding perch overlooking the road from Vienne and Lyon to Grenoble, where a route diverges toward Chambéry. We know that Voiron had been a pre-existing castle rather than a new-build as it had been granted to Philippe in 1255 (along with Tolvon and Bocsozel). So, work at

Voiron amounted to adding to the fortifications there rather than building a new castle. Control of Voiron, itself in the narrow neck of territory that connected the enclave to Savoy would give Philippe control of both exits from the Mont Cenis: by way of both Grenoble and Chambéry. Behind Voiron lay the Massif de la Chartreuse, a large limestone mass which sits as the prelude to the Alps and was seen as the historic boundary between the Dauphine and Savoy. Looking east, the road from Voiron to Grenoble takes the right-hand valley, and the road to Chambéry the left via the Vallee des Echelles, where another road diverges from the Chambéry road to the Carthusian Monastery of Grande Chartreuse. There Philippe built another castle – St Laurent du Pont, guarding access to the monastery and the Chambéry road. Cote-San-André guarded a nearby town, recently granted a market, the castle being built on a rocky spur overlooking the town and the plain of Bievre. These castles would underpin Savoyard dominion of their lands by the Rhône in the face of the Dauphins.

89. Arnold Taylor. *Studies in Castles and Castle-Building* (London: The Hambledon Press, 1985). 93–6.
90. *La Finanza Sabauda.* vol. 1, xiv and xvi. '[For] 1270 à 1272 *Deux comptes de Thomas de Becunet châtelain de St George de Livrées par lui faittes à divers ouvriers pour la fabrique et des livrées à l'occasion du reçu des droits de la Châtelainie de St George.*'
91. This would fit both the context of the archives and the lack of pre-existing development in the valley toward Les Echelles in the thirteenth century.
92. *La Finanza Sabauda.* vol. 1, 118. '*In expensis domini Iohannis de Masoz apud Yverdunum infirmantis per xxviii dies, de mandato domini, vi lib xii den … in acquietancia Magistri Jacobi Cementarii hoc anno et de anno preterito … qui Jacobus percipit Yverdunum de domino in feudo, decem libras viannensium singulis annis. xv. lib.*'
93. Arnold Taylor. Master Bertram, Ingeniator Regis. Studies in Medieval History presented to R. Allen Brown (Woodbridge: The Boydell Press, 1989). 294. n31. Reproduced from Arnold Taylor. *Studies in Castles and Castle-Building* (London: The Hambledon Press, 1985). 93 citing Chambéry Archive. Jean de Mézos is described as '*moranti apud Salinas pro dictando opere putei de Salinas' whilst Maître Jacques is 'euntis apud Salinas pro operibus putei per xj. dies, capientis quolibet die 3s. Pro expensis suis.*'
94. RG i, no 3382: Close Rolls 1253–54, 263. '*Johanni de Meysat, Ingeniatori*'.
95. Ibid. 275. '*Mandatum est eisdem quod Johanni de Maysoz, qui a rege suscepturus est arma militaria apud Burdegalam, sire dilacione habere faciant ea que ad miliciam suam pertinent, sicut allis novis militibus consueverunt invenire. Teste ut supra (apud Burdegallam xxv. die Septembris.*'
96. Arnold Taylor. *Studies in Medieval History Presented to R. Allen Brown* (Woodbridge: The Boydell Press, 1989). 294.
97. Nicola Coldstream, 'Architects, Advisers and Design at Edward I's Castles in Wales,' *Architectural History: Journal of the Society of Architectural Historians of Great Britain* 46 (2003): 29. 'Another administrator was Sir John Masot, a household knight' and 'Masot frequently worked in association with James of St George' Oddly, given she acknowledges his role 'with design', in discussing Mézos, she makes no mention whatsoever of his Gascon and hence Anglo-French origin. Which is curious given her assertion that the Welsh castles are 'not Savoyard but Anglo-French'. Coldstream suggests Mézos is 'first recorded at Saillon in 1261.' Whereas Taylor had pointed to Bazas in Gascony on 22 November 1253 as our first record, along with Master Bertram.
98. Eugene L. Cox. *The Eagles of Savoy: The House of Savoy in Thirteenth Century Europe* (Princeton: Princeton University Press, 1974). 290–1.
99. Bâgé itself is variously rendered as Baugé, Baugie, Baujiu, Baugia, Biaujua comes from a Gallo-Roman villa belonging to a certain Balgiasius.
100. S. Provana de Collegno. *Notizie e documenti d'alcune certose del Piemonte*, II (Torino: Paravia, 1900). 208. Doc 38.
101. Aug. Burnand, '*Vaudois en Angleterre au XIIIe siècle, avec Othon Ier de Grandson: (d'après M.C.-L. Kingsford),' Revue historique vaudoise* 19 no 7 (1911): 213.

Chapter Four
1. Nicholas Trivet, *Annales sex regum Angliae qui a comitibus Andegavensibus originem traxerunt.*
2. The name *Curtana* or *Curtein* (from the Latin *Curtus*, meaning short.)
3. Michael Prestwich. *Edward I* (Yale: Yale University Press, 1997). 90.
4. Edward would not be seated on the well-known 'King Edward's Chair' used most recently at Elizabeth II's coronation in 1953, since Edward had the chair made in 1296, some twenty-two years after his own coronation.
5. The Laudes Regiæ had its origins in ancient Rome, when emperors had entered the Eternal City after triumph in a great battle, they were met by the chants of the people.
6. CCR Edward I vol 1 1272–1279. 68 'To the Sheriff of Gloucester. Order to provide 60 oxen and cows, 60 swine, 2 fat boars, 60 live sheep, 3,000 capons and hens and 40 bacon-pigs against the king's coronation feast at the octaves of Easter … Like orders for various quantities of provisions to

the sheriffs of the following counties: Buckingham and Before, Oxford, Kent, Surrey and Sussex, Warwick and Leicester, Somerset and Dorset and Essex.' There are further copious orders of food to be provided 'for the king's use' dated 28 February on the subsequent pages of the CCR.

7. Robert Kilwardby would be an archbishop with but a walk on part in the life of Edward, he'd been appointed by Pope Gregory X in 1272 whilst Edward was returning from the Holy Land and would leave Canterbury and England for an Italian cardinal's hat in 1278. He died in Italy in 1279 and was buried in the Dominican convent in Viterbo, Italy.

8. CPR Henry III vol 4 1247–1258. 270, 'Charter granting to Edward, eldest son and heir of the king … all of the county of Chester with its castles and towns, with the conquest of Wales by the king within these limits, namely Rothelan, Dissard and Gannoc [Deganwy] and the other land of Pervethelat [Perfeddwlad]; … the castle of Buelt [Builth] 14 February 1254, Bazas, Gascony, France.' We should note also that two of the witnesses of Edward's appanage were the Savoyards Pierre de Savoie and Pierre d'Aigueblanche.

9. Fœdera, 505. '*Litteræ L. principis Walliæ, de invitatione suâ ad festum coronationis Regis Angliæ*' or 'Letter to Llywelyn, Prince of Wales, on his invitation to the feast of the coronation of the King of England.'

10. E. B. Fryde, D. E. Greenway, S. Porter & I. Roy. *Handbook of British Chronology*. Third ed. (London: Offices of the Royal Historical Society, 1986). 85.

11. Robert Burnell had been born in 1239 at the village which carried his family name, Acton Burnell in Shropshire. He'd worked as a clerk in Henry's royal chancery, the office that wrote all of the royal documents before, by 1257, moving into Edward's personal household.

12. CChR Edward I 1257–1300, 187. The Witness list to this charter is not recorded in the CChR but is listed in The Royal Charter Witness Lists of Edward I (1272–1307) from The Charter Rolls in the Public Record Office transcribed and edited with an introduction by Richard Huscroft, List and Index Society, no. 279 (1999), 2. Then Huscroft, Witnesses)

13. Michael Prestwich. '*Othon de Grandson et la Cour d'Edouard I*' in *Othon I de Grandson (vers 1240–1328)* (Lausanne: Cahiers Lausannois d'Histoire Médiévale, 2020). 14.

14. CCR Edward I vol 1 1272–1279. 136. 3 November 1274, Northampton. To Llwelyn, son of Griffin, Prince of Wales. Order to come to the king at Shrewsbury on Sunday after St Andrew and the other things he ought to do to him.'

15. Llywelyn Fawr or Llywelyn the Great was Llywelyn ap Iorwerth. He succeeded as Prince of Gwynedd in 1200 and during the reign of King John sought to turn the English king's troubles to his advantage by growing Gwynedd into an overlordship of all Welsh rulers.

16. Dr. Adam Chapman. 'Bryn Derwin 1255' *The Inventory of Historic Battlefields in Wales*. Last modified Jan 2017. http://battlefields.rcahmw.gov.uk/wp-content/uploads/2017/02/Bryn-Derwin-1255-Chapman-2013.pdf.

17. J. Beverley Smith. *Llywellyn ap Gruffudd: Prince of Wales*. Ebook. ed. (Cardiff: The University of Wales Press, 2014). 82. Suggests his mother to have either been a Senana (more likely) or a Rhunalt (less likely.)

18. *Princeps Walliae*, Prince of Wales was a new term in 1245, one Dafydd ap Llywelyn Fawr had begun styling himself thus in 1244, before the Norman conquest Welsh leaders had sometimes styled themselves 'Reges or Kings of the Britons'

19. Dafydd ap Llywelyn had signed the Treaty of Gwerneigron in 1241. Clause 12 said 'In these and all other matters Dafydd will be at the wish and command of the king and obey the law in all things in his court.' TNA C66/49. Following a rebellion and the death of Dafydd, Llywelyn ap Gruffydd his nephew had signed the Treaty of Woodstock in 1247. Clause 1 said 'Owain and Llywelyn will likewise give their homages to the king and his heirs.' And Clause 2 'Owain and Llywelyn grant and quitclaim for ever the Four Cantrefi'. TNA E36 /274. Henceforth the four cantrefi were given to the then Lord Edward as his appanage. Subsequently Llywelyn ap Gruffydd had taken advantage of royal weakness in following the Second Baronial War to recover the cantrefi and the title Prince of Wales at the 1267 Treaty of Montgomery. TNA C53/56.

20. David Carpenter. *Henry III: The Rise to Power and Personal Rule 1207–1258* (New Haven: Yale University Press, 2020). 74-7.

21. Montgomery Castle had first been built from 1071 by Roger de Montgomery who had come to Britain with William the Conqueror, the family fief lay in Normandy, including Saint-Germain-de-Montgomery and Sainte-Foy-de-Montgomery.

22. CCR Edward I vol 1 1272–1279. 51.

23. Fitz being 'son' [of] from the Old French filz, the origin of the modern French fils.

24. *The famille de Clare* had its origins like most of the Anglo-Norman nobility, in Normandy itself: Gilbert was descended from Richard de Clare, the eldest son of Gilbert de Brionne, a fief midway between Lisieux and Evreux and south of Rouen. Richard (and his brother Baldwin) had crossed the

channel with William in 1066, and were rewarded with much land, including Tonbridge (of which more later) and the fief of Clare in Suffolk, hence the family name.

25. J. Beverley Smith. *Llywellyn ap Gruffudd: Prince of Wales*. Ebook. ed. (Cardiff: The University of Wales Press, 2014). Apple.

26. Derek Renn. *Caerffili Castle*. Revised ed. (Cardiff: Cadw, 1989). 10.

27. Ibid. 3.

28. R. R. Davies. *The Age of Conquest: Wales 1063–1415* (Oxford: Oxford University Press, 1987). 322.

29. J. Beverley Smith. *Llywellyn ap Gruffudd: Prince of Wales*. Ebook. ed. (Cardiff: The University of Wales Press, 2014). Apple.

30. Ibid.

31. John E. Morris. *The Welsh Wars of Edward I* (Oxford: Clarendon Press,1901). 111. 'It was rather a truce than a peace, for obviously there was not yet a final settlement.'

32. Beverley Smith calculates those payments were made in full and promptly between 1267 and 1269, That the 1270 payment was only partially made in part payments, thereafter payments continue in sporadic fashion until they dry up completely.

33. The Close Rolls are a record created by the Chancery to preserve a central record of closed letters issued by said chancery in the name of the Crown.

34. CCR Edward I vol 1 1272–1279. 2. '2 December 1272, Westminster 'To Llwelyn, son of Griffin, Prince of Wales. Whereas according to the form of peace concluded between the late king and Llewelyn, the latter is bound to the king in 3,000 marks to be paid at Christmas next … This Llwelyn is to neglect in no wise, as he loves the king and his honour, and as the king specially trusts him.'

35. J. Beverley Smith. *Llywellyn ap Gruffudd: Prince of Wales*. Ebook. ed. (Cardiff: The University of Wales Press, 2014). Apple.

36. Michael Prestwich. *Edward I* (Yale: Yale University Press, 1997). 172. 'One means frequently employed by Llywelyn to retain allegiance of Welsh rulers is evidence of their reluctance to accept his lordship. In 1261 he demanded that Maredudd ap Rhys should hand over twenty-four hostages, and in 1274 Gruffydd ap Gwenwynwyn gave his son Owain to him as a hostage. The same technique was used on a wide scale in 1271, when Llywelyn was reinforcing his authority in mid Wales.'

37. CCR Edward I vol 1 1272–1279. 2. '29 November 1272, The New Temple [London]. Order to L[lywelyn], son of Griffin, Prince of Wales. Order to come to the ford of Montgomery in person, so that he be there in the octaves of St Hilary next, to make oath of fealty to the king before the kings envoys whom the king shall send there specially to receive the fealty, as they shall cause him to know on the king's behalf, as the government has come to the king by his father's death, and he has caused his peace to be proclaimed, and the prelates, earls, barons and other proceres of the realm have promptly and without omission made oath of fealty and have done the other things that they could do or make to the king in his absence by reason of his crown and royal dignity, and L[lywelyn] is bound, to do the like, as he knows.'

38. The Calendar of Close Rolls or Chancery Close Rolls are a collection from 1204 until 1903 of letters close. A Latin transcript of the close rolls for the reign of Henry III, letters close from 1227 to 1272 was published as Close Rolls of the Reign of Henry III (14 vols, HMSO, 1902-38). An English calendar of the close rolls from 1272 to 1509, including the reign of Edward I was published as Calendar of the Close Rolls (47 vols, HMSO, 1900–63). The originals are kept by the UK National Archive at Kew under reference C54, and are here referred to as CCR followed by the King and volume. Letters close, which were usually of an executive nature conveying orders and instructions, and, therefore of a private and personal nature, were issued folded and 'closed' by the application of the great seal. They were enrolled on the close rolls. Unlike the complex process involved in making up (engrossing) letters patent, a much simpler process existed for letters close, their nature being more private and personal, and therefore less solemn and formal. The letter was made out either by the chancellor or keeper of the great seal at the request of the sovereign, and in his name. The letter had to be attested before sealing with the great seal.

39. CCR Edward I vol 1 1272–1279. 2.

40. Derek Wilson. Medieval Kings and Queens (Bristol: Immediate Media Co, 2017). 43.

41. CCR Edward I vol 1 1272–1279. 241. '24 June 1275, Westminster. To Llwelyn, son of Griffin, Prince of Wales. Order to do before the king at Chester in the octaves of the Assumption next to do homage and take the oath of fealty and to do the other things that he, like other nobles and liegemen (*fideles*) of the king, is bound to do the king by reason of the crown and royal dignity.'

42. Ann. Cestrienses, 102-3. '*Idem Rex apud Cestriam venit ut tractaret cum principe Wallie Lewelino et cito pro contemptu dicti principis recessit*.' Or 'Also the king came to Chester, that he might treat with the prince of Wales, Llywelyn, and soon left in cause of the contempt from that prince.'

43. Henry Gough. Itinerary of King Edward the First throughout his reign, A.D. 1272–1307, exhibiting his movements so far as they are recorded vol 1. (Paisley: Alexander Gardner, 1900). 50–1.

44. CPR Edward I vol 1 1272–1281, 104. '10 September, Chester. Mandate to Llewellin, son of Griffith, Prince of Wales. whom the king has several times commanded to be at Chester to do his homage and fealty to be at Westminster three weeks after Michaelmas [October] next to do so.'

45. Michael Prestwich. *Edward I* (Yale: Yale University Press, 1997). 174. 'However, he [Llywelyn] claimed in proclamations to his own people that peace had been made, and raised tax, on the pretext that he needed the money to pay Edward what was due to him. This alarmed some of the Welsh, and it must be suspected that Llywelyn was in fact collecting funds with a view to war.'

46. Eleanor de Montfort and Llywelyn ap Gruffydd were married as originally her uncle Henry and aunt Alianor had once married, '*per nuncios per verba de presenti*' canon law endorsed a marital bond that was made in this way, with the full consent of both individuals, before witnesses.

47. OED, March 2019, Oxford University Press. ORIGIN of fealty. Middle English : from Old French *feau(l)te*, fealte, from Latin *fidelitas* (see fidelity). Fidelity. ORIGIN of fidelity. late Middle English: from Old French *fidelite* or Latin *fidelitas*, from fidelis 'faithful', from fides 'faith'. Compare with fealty. Therefore in Old French, and so the word as understood by Edward and his contemporaries, Fealty had a common root in the Latin word for faithful.

48. Chron. Guisborough, 5. '*Leulinus, princeps Walliæ ... sibi in uxorem quondam domini Symonis de Monteforti*'.

49. CCR Edward I vol 1 1272–1279, 325. '23 January 1276, Winchester 'To Llwelyn, son of Griffin, Prince of Wales …. the king again re-summons him to be before him fifteen days from Easter.'

50. Gregory X died 10 January, Innocent V died 22 June, Adrian V died 18 August, the next Pope was John XXI who began his reign 8 September.

51. CCR Edward I vol 1 1272–1279, 278. 'To Ralph de Sandwyco, the king's steward, Order to cause Master Bertram, the king's engineer, to have six oaks in the park of Odyham or in the foreign wood there, to make therewith the king's engines, as Bertram shall cause him to know on the king's behalf.'

52. TNA C47/ 35/7. A no 24. 'To the Sheriff of Oxon' *Precipimus tibi quod meremium illud quod magister Bertramus Ingeniator noster, tibi liberabit sive fuerit infra ballivam tuam sive extra cariari usque London' ad ingenia nostra ibidem inde facienda prout idem Bertramus tibi dicet ex parte nostra. Teste me ipso apud Langele xxvij die Aprilis anno regni nostri quarto.'* And is endorsed '*Ad cariandam meremium domini regis de boscho qui vocatur Bocholte extra Kyngesclere in comitatu Suhamptes usque ad aquam apud Kaversham. Et ad cariandum meremium de boscho de Burhfildebur in comitatu Berks' ad eundem locum, xiiij.libr. xj.s.*'

53. Arnold Taylor. *Master Bertram, Ingeniator Regis. Studies in Medieval History presented to R. Allen Brown*. (Woodbridge: The Boydell Press, 1989). 295.

54. CCR Edward I vol 1 1272–1279, 359–61. November 17, Westminster. The king after his coronation, in the second year of his reign, ordered Llywelyn (Lewelino) son of Griffin, prince of Wales, to come to do the homage and fealty due to him for the land of Wales; and Llywelyn did not come for this purpose within a year of the coronation, so the king caused him to be summoned at Chester in the quinzaine of the Assumption in the third year of his reign to do the said homage and fealty, and he offered him safe and secure conduct in coming, staying, returning etc, although the king was not bound to do so. And Llywelyn did not come at that day, but sent certain frivolous excuses by his envoys and by letter to the king, so that it was decided he should be summoned again to be At Westminster for the aforesaid purposes in three weeks from the following Michaelmas. At which day he did not come, but sent unreasonable excuses as before, so that it was decided that he should be again summoned to come to Westminster in the octaves of St Hillary following for the aforesaid purpose. And Llywelyn did not come at that day, but excused his absence by letters and envoys insufficiently, as above, so that the king, of his grace, caused him to be summoned a third time to come to Westminster in three weeks from the following Easter to do his homage and fealty. On which day Llywelyn did not come, but pretended insufficient excuses by his letter and envoys, as before so that R. Archbishop of Canterbury and certain bishops and other prelates, earls and barons strongly besought the king that they by themselves and their envoys might ask inform and induce Llywelyn to do his homage and fealty, and that the king would supersede for the time further extension of the said matter. To which prayers the king acceded, so that they frequently sent the archdeacon of Canterbury as their envoy to Llywelyn to treat upon this matter, which could not be consummated, although the archdeacon laboured much to this end with due expedition … Afterwards, in fifteen days from Michaelmas, in the fourth year of the reign, at Westminster Llywelyn signified to the king by his letter that he would come to Montgomery or Oswestry (Album Monasterium Johannis filii Alani) to do his homage to the king … And hereupon … it is agreed by common council of all the aforesaid prelates, earls, barons and others that the king shall not hear the aforesaid petition of Llywelyn, and shall not admit his excuses noted above, but that he shall go against Llywelyn as his rebel and disturber of his peace.'

55. Maredudd ap Rhys Gryg (died 1271), was the son of Rhys Gryg, a Welsh prince of Deheubarth. he swore allegiance to Llywelyn in 1258, he later that year sided with the king. Consequently, on 28 May 1259, Maredydd was put on trial for treason, the first trial of its kind in Wales. He was found guilty by a council of native lords and imprisoned in Criccieth Castle. In 1261, Maredudd was granted reconciliation with Llywelyn under severe terms

56. Michael Prestwich. *Edward I* (Yale: Yale University Press, 1997). 170. 'but it was Llywelyn's attitude, not Edward's, that explains why war broke out in 1276. The survival of Llywelyn's rule depended on his achieving notable success against the English : Edward, in contrast, did not need to bolster his prestige by means of a struggle with the Welsh.'

Chapter Five

1. CCR Edward I vol 1 1272–1279, 358.
2. TNA C 47/2/2 no 5. '*E fet a sauer ke ceaus ke vent a Montgomery dirront ke mester Bertram, les charpentiers e les alebasters ke vindrint de Lundres, les mineors e le deaus monceors Henry de Greenford e Robert de Vilers receuerunt leur gages par les mains sire Richard de Boys et Lyone le fiuz Lyone, e par la vueue sire Otes de Grauntson, des deners le queues le Roy fitliuerer as auaundiz Richard d Leone pur fere une partie de ses besoines.*
3. CPR Edward I vol 1 1272–1281, 184.
4. John E. Morris. *The Welsh Wars of Edward I* (Oxford: Clarendon Press, 1901). 12.
5. OED, March 2019, Oxford University Press. ORIGIN *Destrier.* Middle English : from Old French, based on Latin *dextera* 'the right hand', from dexter 'on the right' (because the squire led the knight's horse with his right hand)..
6. CPR Edward I vol 1 1272–1281, 184.
7. A banneret was a knight who commanded his own troops in battle under his own banner. His banner was square or rectangular rather than a long pennon. The rank was entirely military rather than the socio military rank of knight.
8. Also known as Alésia di Saluzzo.
9. Jean de Bonvillars is variously recorded in English archives; Bevillard, Beylard, Bevilar, Beuillar, Beuillard Byvelard, Beillar, Bomlard, Bonovillario, Byveillard and Bonouillar We will continue to use the form in use today – Bonvillars.
10. Aug. Burnand, '*Vaudois en Angleterre au XIIIe siècle, avec Othon Ier de Grandson : (d'après M.C.-L. Kingsford),' Revue historique vaudoise 19 no 7 (1911):* 212. *We can discern his relationship from the description of his son, also Jean de Bonvillars as 'neveu d'Othon de Grandson'.*
11. Arnold Taylor, 'Master James of St George,' *The English Historical Review* 65 (1950): 442.n7. Citing TNA C62/68. '*Liberate … dilecto nobis in Christo fratri Henrico Priori de Wenlok centum marcas ad unam filiarum Johannis de Bevillard defuncti fratris eiusdem Prioris inde maritandam de dono nostro.*'
12. CPR Edward I vol 2 1281–1292, 481. Fellow Vaudois, Jacques de Cossonay would follow Henri de Bonvillars at Wenlock from 1291.
13. Jean Pierre Chapuisat, '*De Mont-sur-Rolle à Windsor, de la Dullive à Dumfries … La Maison de Savoie et le Pays de Vaud,' Bibliothèque historique vaudoise* 97 (1989): 119.
14. Guillaume de Cicon appears in the English archives variously as; Cykun, Cycons, Chycun, Sicoms, Sicun, Sycun and even Dygoin.
15. Arnold Taylor, 'Some notes on the Savoyards in North Wales, 1277–1300. With special reference to the Savoyard element in the construction of Harlech Castle,' Genava XI (1963): 290. A n6 citing TNA C 62/52. '*Willelmi Cykun nuper venientis ad nos in nuncium a portibus transmarinis ad partes Angl' ex parte Ottonis supradicti.*' Or 'Guillaume de Cicon recently came to us with news from overseas to parties English on the side of the above named Othon.'
16. Fœdera, 588. '*De homagio Othonis com' Palatini Burgundia. A. D. 1281 . Nos Otho comes palatinus Burgondiæ, & dominus Salinen' notum facimus universis præsentas litteras inspecturis, quod nos tenemus, in feodo & in homagio, ab excellentissimo viro, domino Edwardo, divina gratia, Rege Angliæ, Duce Aquitaniæ, & principe Dirlande, pontarliam, & castellaniam, & pediagium ejusdem loci, & totum illud quod habemus en Veras, cum apenditiis eorumdem. Item Culumontem, & Joygne, & la Chandarlle, cum suis pertinentiis universis, prout tenet a nobis Johannes de Cabilone, avunculus noster. Item castrum de Jou, cum suis appenditiis, prout dictus Johannes de Cabilone, avunculus noster, tenet a nobilis ariere feodum. Et prædicta omnia confitemur, & recognoscimus nos tenere a dicto domino Rege in feodo & homagio, secundum quod est expressum; salva fidelitate nostrorum dominorum. In quorum testimonium damus & concedimus dicto domino Regi præsentes litteras, nostro sigillo sigillatas. Dat' Lugd' anno Domini MCCLXXXI. Mense Januarii.*'
17. TNA C 62/69 m 5 bis.
18. Arnold Taylor, 'Some notes on the Savoyards in North Wales, 1277–1300. With special reference to the Savoyard element in the construction of Harlech Castle,' *Genava* XI (1963): 290–1.

19. Letter 29.9.99. CR 1251-3, 465. For the St Laurents in the mid-thirteenth century, *Cartulaire du Chapitre de Notre Dame de Lausanne, première partie*, ed. C. Roth (Lausanne, 1948), n339.

20. J. Beverley Smith. *Llywellyn ap Gruffudd: Prince of Wales*. Ebook. ed. (Cardiff: The University of Wales Press, 2014). Apple.

21. Michael Prestwich. *Edward I* (Yale: Yale University Press, 1997). 177. 'In what was in many ways a civil war in Wales, it must have been obvious to the English king that it was to his advantage to give full encouragement to Prince Dafydd, Gruffydd ap Gwenwynwyn and those Welsh rulers who were ready to throw off their allegiance to Llywelyn.'

22. Adam Chapman. 'Welshmen in the Armies of Edward I'. in *The Impact of the Edwardian Castles in Wales* (Oxford: Oxbow Books, 2010). 175. 'The final conflict between Gwynedd and the English Crown was as much a conflict between Welshmen as it was between Welsh and English.'

23. C. J. Spurgeon, 'Builth Castle,' *Brycheiniog* 18 (1978/9): 54.

24. Robert J. Dean. *Castles in Distant Lands: The Life and Times of Othon of Grandson* (Willingdon: Lawden Haynes Publishing, 2009). 19.

25. Ibid .iii.

26. Lawrence Butler & Jeremy K. Knight. Dolforwyn. *Montgomery Castle* (Cardiff: Cadw, 2004). 27.

27. Arnold Taylor, 'Some notes on the Savoyards in North Wales, 1277–1300. With special reference to the Savoyard element in the construction of Harlech Castle,' *Genava* XI: 298. 'In a letter to King Edward, written at Dolforwyn during the siege, and dated 3 April 1277, Othon de Grandson said that when the castle surrendered it would need much repair, and expressed his fears that if he assigned the work to Master Bertram the latter would 'devise too many things and perhaps waste the king's money, and therefore some other man would be needed who would take the matter in hand' (Cal. Ancient Correspondence concerning Wales, p.31).'

28. Frédéric Joseph Tanquerey. *Recueil de Lettres Anglo-Françaises, 1265–1399*. (Paris: Librairie Ancienne Honoré Champion, 1916) .5–6. Incorrectly dated as '*Avant 1272*' or 'Before 1272' and misidentified as a letter from '*Roger de Mortimer à Henri III*' but reproduced otherwise correctly as 'Au Roy de Englterre. *Al sun tres cher seignur saluz. Sachez sire ke nous asegames le Chastel de Doluereyn le mekreydy en la simeine de Paskes ... Sachez sire ke quant le chastel sera en vostre mein, il auera mester de grant amendement; por quoi nous auerrums mester de eukun homme ke de tels choses se feust entremettre e ke leument vosist empleer vos deners, kar nous y mettoms Mestre Bertram je dout ke il ne devisast trop de choses e par aventure vos deners ne serreint assez bien emplee com serreit, e por ce sire mandez nous de ceste chose vostre volonte. Sachez sire ke la lettre ke vus nous avez envoye par mon sire Joh de Bevilar nous vint a graund socour, kar sachez sire ke nostre ost semble bien ost de graunt seignur, e ce ne poet on mine fere sans deners. Sire a Deu ke vous gard, mandez nous votre estat e vostre volonte. Ceste lettre feu fete a Dolverein le Samedy apres Paskes.*' Or 'To my dear Lord Salut! Be aware that we besieged the castle at Dolforwyn on the Wednesday in Easter Week [31 March 1277] ... Please know sir that when the castle will be in your hands it will be in need of great reworking; for what we have to tell you about a man, such things must be mediated, and that you save your money. Master Bertram, I doubt he does not estimate too much of things and by adventure your money. By this sir, tell of this your will. Know sir that the letter we have sent by my Lord Jean de Bonvillars has come to us in great earnestness. By the knowledge of our Lord that our host seems to be great and of a great Lord, and that this is not creation without money. Sir, God keep you, let us know how you are and what your will is. It is the letter at Dolforwyn, the Saturday after Easter [3 April 1277].'

29. John Goronwy Edwards, ed. 1935. Calendar of ancient correspondence concerning Wales (Cardiff: Cardiff University Press Board, 1935). 30–1. Edward spent the Easter of 1277, not with his army, but on pilgrimage to Walsingham. Henry Gough. Itinerary of King Edward the First throughout his reign, A.D. 1272–1307, exhibiting his movements so far as they are recorded. vol. 1 (Paisley: Alexander Gardner. 1900). 69.

30. Ibid. index.

31. The historiography of this is long, in 1916, Frédéric Joseph Tanquerey. *Recueil de Lettres Anglo-Françaises, 1265–1399* (Paris: Librairie Ancienne Honoré Champion, 1916). 5-6. Misidentified the author as Roger de Mortimer. Then John Goronwy Edwards, ed. Calendar of ancient correspondence concerning Wales (Cardiff: Cardiff University Press Board, 1935). 30-31. Identified as 'probable' that the author was Henri de Lacy, but ambiguously perhaps, qualified his identification by listing in his index 'Sir Otto de Grandison' as a potential author, marked with a '?' Taylor, writing in 1976 in his paper '*John Pennard, Leader of Gwynedd*' added to the debate 'the possibility must not be overlooked that the king's correspondent was de Grandson rather than de Lacy.' Taylor had then muddied the water by suggesting another author, Amédée de Savoie, Arnold Taylor. *Studies in Castles and Castle-Building* (London: The Hambledon Press,1985). 5. n2. 'It is not unlikely that he [Amédée] was the writer of the letter' also collected in this publication was the earlier paper' *John Pennard, Leader of the Men of Gwynedd*' 212. n1. Nicola Coldstream, 'Architects, Advisers and Design at Edward I's Castles in Wales,' *Architectural History: Journal of the Society of Architectural Historians of Great*

Britain 46 (2003). 26. 'was probably Amadeus of Savoy' but this was taken from Taylor's aforesaid 1985 note. However, Taylor, having identified two possible authors, finally in 1989 came down on the side of Grandson, not Amédée (or indeed Henri de Lacy), as the author. Arnold Taylor. *Master Bertram, Ingeniator Regis*. Studies in Medieval History Presented to R. Allen Brown (Woodbridge: The Boydell Press, 1989). 296. n41. 'For a number of reasons, however, the author of this present paper believes them [the Dolforwyn letters] to have been sent by Sir Otto de Grandison.' The Cadw guidebook of 2004, for Dolforwyn, written h Lawrence Butler and Jeremy K. Knight, says 'the Earl of Lincoln [Henri de Lacy] reported to the king' such are the perils of an unsigned letter.

32. John E. Morris. *The Welsh Wars of Edward I* (Oxford: Clarendon Press, 1901). 121. Otto de Grandison had no feudal obligation, but the others were all tenants-in-chief and men of position.'

33. CCR. Edward I vol 1 1272–1279. 493. 'March 21, Down Ampney. To R.[Robert Burnell] Bishop of Bath and Wells, the chancellor, and to Othon de Grandisono. The king commends the care and solicitude exhibited by them in his affairs in the court of France ... especially as the king has no one about him whom he believes could know the premises and do his will in the premises better and more advantageously than them, not even if he himself were to attend to the matters there in person.'

34. Arnold Taylor. Studies in Medieval History Presented to R. Allen Brown (Woodbridge: The Boydell Press, 1989). 296.

35. TNA C47/2/2 no 5.

36. Michael Prestwich. 'Edward I in Wales' *in The Impact of the Edwardian Castles in Wales* (Oxford: Oxbow Books, 2010). 4. 'A letter of April 1277, which Taylor plausibly argued was from Otto de Grandson ... It is very likely that Otto's influence was important in the choice that Edward made of the Savoyard Master James of St George to play a leading role in the castle-building programme in Wales.'

37. A muster was the assembly of troops in preparation for battle. The word comes from the Old French *'moustrer'* which itself came from the Latin *'monstrare'*, meaning 'to show'. Military service for most of the medieval period was based on land ownership. This feudal system determined that all holders of a certain amount of land were obliged to accept knighthood and do military service for their feudal overlord, either in person or by raising forces.

38. Geoffrey de Joinville, brother of French chronicler of Saint Louis, Jean de Joinville, had been Justiciar of Ireland from 1273 until 1276.

39. *Song of Caerlaverock* from 1300 cited in Michael Prestwich. Knight: The Medieval Warrior's (Unofficial) Guide (London: Thames & Hudson, 2010). 169. 'On the appointed day the whole host was ready, and the good King with his household, then set forward against the Scots, not in coats and surcoats, but on powerful and costly chargers; and that they may might not be taken by surprise, well and securely armed. There were many rich caparisons embroidered on silks and satins; many a beautiful pennon fixed to a lance, and many a banner displayed. And afar off was the noise heard of neighing horses: mountains and valleys were everywhere covered with sumpter horses and wagons with provisions, and sacks of tents and pavilions.'

40. R. R. Davies. *The Age of Conquest: Wales 1063–1415* (Oxford: Oxford University Press, 1987). 335.

41. Richard W. Kaeuper. *Bankers to the Crown: The Riccardi of Lucca and Edward I* (Princeton: Princeton University Press, 1973). 178.

42. Sir Maurice Powicke. *The Thirteenth Century 1216–1307* (Oxford: Oxford University Press, 1953). 543.

43. Gerald of Wales. *The Journey Through Wales and The Description of Wales* (London: Penguin Books Ltd, 1978). 209. 'It was there [the forest of Coleshill] in our own time that Henry II, King of the English, was badly mauled when he made his first assault on Wales. In his youthful ardour and rash enthusiasm he was unwise enough to push on through this densely wooded pass, to the great detriment of his men, quite a few if whom were killed.' The battle of Coleshill also known as the Battle of Ewloe, was fought in July 1157. The description of Henry's struggles in the densely wooded pass no doubt influenced Edward in cutting through the forest his road.

44. CPR Edward I vol 1 1272 1281, 213 4.

45. Chron. Thomas Wykes, 272. *'silva tantæ densitatis et amplitudinis'* or 'the dense forest of great size'.

46. John E. Morris. *The Welsh Wars of Edward I* (Oxford: Clarendon Press, 1901). 130.

47. Fœdera, 544. *'in castris apud le Flynt prope Basingwerk'*.

48. The Calendar of Welsh Rolls are 7 rolls held by the UK National Archive in Kew, Ref C77, they were calendared and published in 1912. They comprise Enrolments of letters patent, letters close and charters issued under the Great Seal and other documents relating to Welsh affairs, Welsh rulers and to Edward I's conquest of Wales. They cover the period from 1276 until 1294 and are here abbreviated in reference as CWR.

49. CWR 1277-1326, 160. 'both at Le Chaylou and Rothelan'.

50. Ibid. 164. 'viewer of the king's works in those parts both at Le Cayllou and Rothelan'.

51. TNA E101/3/15. '*Vincencio clerico pro duobus solidis quos dedit diversis hominibus precepto O. de Grandisono pro maremio leuando apud Flind, ijs.*' Or 'Vincent gave to the clerk for the two *sol*[shillings] that he gave to various men by order of Othon de Grandson for having carted timber in Flint, two shillings' The horse-drawn cart was the most common way of transporting material.

52. Ibid.

53. J. G. Edwards, 'Edward I's Castle-Building in Wales,' *The Proceedings of the British Academy XXXII* (1944): 18–19. 'in the Middle Ages building operations in British were concentrated into what was called 'the season' – the period of the year extending from about April to about November ... this fact is reflected very clearly in the accounts' we need to remember that the 'building season' at Flint in 1277 did not being until the last week of July, with the arrival of the English army, at the earliest and was thus clearly not a full building season. Edward's confirms the term 'season' as being contemporary to the thirteenth century in north Wales by citing '*seisonam*'and '*la seeson*' and '*ceste seeson*' in references in his footnote Ibid. 19. n1.

54. J. G. Edwards. 1951. The Building of Flint. *The Flintshire Historical Society* XII: 11.

55. John E. Morris. 1901. *The Welsh Wars of Edward I.* Oxford: Clarendon Press. 130. 'A strong post was thus made, though the works were but temporary, and of wood, for there was no time to prepare stone.' This was a view with which Edwards disagreed. J. G. Edwards. 1944. Edward I's Castle-Building in Wales. *The Proceedings of the British Academy* XXXII: 33 'the mistaken idea that Flint castle was at first only a wooden structure ... first propounded by the late Dr. J. E. Morris.' But this rather depends upon what we mean by 'at first'. Morris was clearly referring to the summer and autumn of 1277. In his paper J. G. Edwards. 1951. The Building of Flint. *The Flintshire Historical Society* XII: 14. Edwards modified his view somewhat, writing 'At Flint during the first five weeks building in stone would be less important' he evidenced this by a ratio of '3 masons to 1 carpenter' at Flint compared to '13 masons to 1 carpenter' later at Beaumaris. More recently Vicky Perfect. 2012. *Flint Castle: The story of Edward I's first Welsh castle.* Mold: Alyn Books Ltd. has suggested that as building work commenced in 1277, and Maître Jacques was not yet in Wales, then he was not involved in its planning or scope – that an entire summer building season had been undertaken before his arrival. Her argument rests and falls on the extent of the 1277 works in stone. Edwards had clearly set out that for the first five weeks this was negligible, so what of the period thereafter until the end of November? Well, Edwards again confirmed that for the period until 10 October, the ratio remained '1 mason to 3 carpenters', only for the six weeks to 21 November does the ratio of masons improve, and then only to '33 masons to 57 carpenters to 100 diggers' – at no time, unlike later at Beaumaris, is the number of masons in relation to the number of carpenters even close to what we might expect for castle building to be underway in a substantial way. Edwards seems to have rested his suggestion of stone works at Flint in 1277 on a 1278 account '*Et in stipendiis cuiusdam plumbarii cooperientis turres* [sic in full] *in castro predicto per predictum tempus.*' The lead roofing attached to *turres* or towers at Flint in 1278. He surmised, correctly, that one would only add lead to the roof of a finished tower. This would suggest that at least two of the towers at Flint were extant in 1278, and given that work paused in 1278, were built largely in 1277. However, Arnold Taylor. *The Welsh Castles of King Edward I* (London: The Hambledon Press, 1986). 20 n1. observed, rightly, that we cannot be thinking of one of the completed towers as the *donjon* tower, since that was only completed in 1286, leaving three towers to consider. Furthermore, he noted 'it should not be forgotten that there was a fifth – the outer gate tower shown in the plan of Flint inset in Speed's map of Flintshire (1610). When the Pipe Roll records the purchase of lead '*ad turres cooperiend*' in *eodem castro*' and the wages of a plumber ... the reference might be this tower and only one of the others.' Going on to add that early completion of the Gate Tower is evidenced by the Grant of Burgages of 1281. In short that it may well have been only one of the four castle towers completed in 1277. This suggestion would, in effect, square with the thinking of Morris, Edwards and Taylor – and render Perfect's suggestion unlikely.

56. John E. Morris. *The Welsh Wars of Edward I.* (Oxford: Clarendon Press, 1901). 130.

57. Ibid.

58. Arnold Taylor. *The Welsh Castles of King Edward I* (London: The Hambledon Press, 1986). 17. 'For the first few weeks each labour category was treated as a military unit and placed under a knight who shared with the clerk who had directed its recruitment responsibility for the issue of its wages.'

59. Brut, 267.

60. J. Beverley Smith. *Llywellyn ap Gruffudd: Prince of Wales.* Ebook. ed. (Cardiff: The University of Wales Press, 2014). Apple.

61. Ibid.
62. C. J. Spurgeon, 'Builth Castle', *Brycheiniog* 18 (1978/9): 54.
63. Christopher Rothero. *The Scottish and Welsh Wars 1250–1400*. 20 ed. (Botley: Osprey Publishing Ltd, 1984). 3. 'They were migrant tribesmen, half warriors, half farmers, often living out meagre lives (when they were not raiding and feuding) by keeping cattle and sheep, as they had done so for thousands of years. Not content with their own lands, the men of the tribe left the bards and concealed homes above the valleys each spring to raid and pillage in the lands around their principality. Such was their reputation that pious Englishmen regarded two pilgrimages to St Davids as being equal to the hardship and dangers of one to Jerusalem.'
64. Gerald of Wales. *The Journey Through Wales and The Description of Wales* (London: Penguin Books Ltd, 1978). 297–8.
65. Lodowyk van Velthem, 1725. (Ed. Le Long). Spiegel Historiaal, Book IV, c. 5. 'Edward, King of England, came to Flanders. He brought with him many soldiers from the land of Wales. In the very depth of winter, they were running about bare-legged. They wore a red robe. They could not have been warm. The money they received from the King was spent in milk and butter. They would eat and drink anywhere. I never saw them wearing armour. I studied them very closely and walked among them to find out what defensive armour they carried when going into battle. Their weapons were bows, arrows and swords. They also had javelins.'
66. Winston S. Churchill. *A History of the English-Speaking Peoples* (New York: Rosetta Books, 2013). 240.
67. Ibid. 241.
68. R. R. Davies. *The Age of Conquest: Wales 1063–1415* (Oxford: Oxford University Press, 1987). 76.
69. Brut, 383. cited in J. Goronwy Edwards. 'Edward I's Castle-Building in Wales' *The Proceedings of the British Academy XXXII* (1944): 30. 'on St James's day [25 July] Edmund the King's brother, accompanied by an army, came to Llanbadarn, and began the building of Aberystwyth castle.'
70. Aberystwyth Castle is generally referred to in medieval records as Lampader or Lampadarn as noted, or Lampadervaur from the local Welsh place name Llanbadarn Fawr, and should not be confused with Lampeter or Llanbedr some twenty miles distant to the south.
71. J. Goronwy Edwards. 'Edward I's Castle-Building in Wales' *The Proceedings of the British Academy XXXII* (1944): 30. 'Henrico de Hereford cementario eunti apud Kaermerdyn pro castro de Lampader firmando, ad suas expensas, Xs.' Or 'Mason, Henry of Hereford, moving to Kaermerdyn [Carmarthen] for the strengthening of the castle of Lampader [Aberystwyth], at their own expense, 10 shillings.'
72. Malcolm Hislop. *James of St George and the Castles of North Wales* (Barnsley: Pen & Sword Books Ltd, 2020). 70.
73. TNA SC 1/23/53 '*Richard le Enginour le Rey, un Burgeys de Cestr*'.
74. TNA E101/485/19.
75. Arnold Taylor. *Master Bertram, Ingeniator Regis. Studies in Medieval History presented to R. Allen Brown*. (Woodbridge: The Boydell Press, 1989). 298. n49.
76. Rick Turner. 'The Life and Career of Richard the Engineer' in *The Impact of the Edwardian Castles in Wales* (Oxford: Oxbow Books, 2010). 46–58.
77. Ibid. 46. 'Richard was put in charge of 1,850 men mustered at Flint to begin work on the castle there and at Rhuddlan … but how much [design] was left to Master Richard [at Flint] and Master Bertram [at Rhuddlan] is a matter of speculation. Once Master James took overall charge of work at Flint and Rhuddlan in April 1278, Richard may have moved on to other works for he disappears temporarily from the records.'
78. Marc Morris. *A Great and Terrible King* (London: Windmill Books, 2009). 154. This colourful picture comes from the Annals of Thomas Wykes. Chron. Wykes, 272–3. '*et quia inter Cestriam et terram Lewelini interjacet quaedam silva tantae densitatis et amplitudinis, quod exercitus regis eam nullatenus poterat sine discrimine pertransire; prostrata sen secata ipsius silvæ portione non modica, progrediendi in terram principis sibi et complicibus suis latissimum patfecit ingressum et terram ipsum violentis ausibus occupatam triumphaliter introivit.*' Or 'Between Chester and Llywelyn's country lay a forest of such denseness and extent that the royal army could by now means penetrate through without danger. A large part of this forest being cut down, the king opened out for himself a very broad road for an advance into the prince's land, and having occupied it by strong attacks he entered through it in triumph.'
79. The motte of Robert of Rhuddlan's castle still remains, the line of its Bailey traceable in nearby fields, a little downstream of the Edwardian castle at Twthill. It was reputedly built upon the site of Gruffydd ap Llywelyn's hall.
80. Arnold Taylor. *Rhuddlan Castle* (Cardiff, Cadw, 2008). 1.
81. Arnold Taylor. *The Welsh Castles of King Edward I* (London: The Hambledon Press, 1986). 27.n6. 'Edward was at Rhuddlan intermittently from 19 August and continuously from 27 September to 18

or 19 November ... For part if not all of his stay he was accommodated by the Rhuddlan Dominicans, who were paid for their hospitality and given a donation towards the glazing of their new church.' TNA E101/350/23.
82. CChW 1244–1326, 4.
83. Arnold Taylor. *The Welsh Castles of King Edward I* (London: The Hambledon Press, 1986). 27.
84. Michael Prestwich. *Edward I* (Yale: Yale University Press, 1997). 180.
85. Gerald of Wales. *The Journey Through Wales and The Description of Wales* (London: Penguin Books Ltd, 1978). 199. 'This island produces far more grain than any other part of Wales. In the Welsh language it has always been called 'Mon mâm Cymru' which means 'Mona the mother of Wales'.
86. J. Beverley Smith. *Llywellyn ap Gruffudd: Prince of Wales*. Ebook. ed. (Cardiff: The University of Wales Press, 2014). Apple.
87. Carl von Clausewitz. *Principles of War* (Mineola: Dover Publications Inc. 2003). 50–1.
88. "The king and prince have provided sufficient security to observe the articles agreed by the aforementioned representatives [Robert Tibetot and Anthony Bek for Edward, Tudor ab Ednyfed and Gornonwy ap Heilin for Llywelyn] of both sides: i.. Llywelyn places himself at the will and mercy of the king and will give him £50,000 for disobedience, damages and injuries by him and his men, seeking by this sum the king's grace and mercy. ii. Llywelyn quitclaims to the king the Four Cantrefi as fully as the late King Henry or his son, the king, ever held, as well as all lands which the king has seized except for Anglesey. If Llywelyn makes a claim to lands occupied by others than the king outside the Four Cantrefi, the king will give him justice according to the laws and customs of the districts in which those lands lie.? iii. Llywelyn will come to give fealty to the king at Rhuddlan and before coming he will be absolved [from excommunication] and the interdict on his land lifted...." Aberconwy 9th November 1277. TNA E36/274.
89. J. Beverley Smith. *Llywellyn ap Gruffudd: Prince of Wales*. (Cardiff: The University of Wales Press, 2014). Apple.
90. Richard W. Kaeuper. *Bankers to the Crown: The Riccardi of Lucca and Edward I* (Princeton: Princeton University Press, 1973). 179.
91. The Chronicler of Lanercost records '50,000 pounds of silver' Herbert Maxwell. 1913. *The Chronicle of Lanercost, 1272–1346*. 16.
92. The £50,000 fine was pardoned as early as 11 November 1277 and was most likely originally imposed in order to establish in the treaty Llwellyn's war guilt.
93. CPR Edward I vol 1 1272–1281. 253.
94. The location of the collapsed gateway was discovered during archaeological investigations in 1995-97, when a large stone platform was discovered in the moat, just west of Edward's outer curtain wall and about 98 feet (30 metres) from the Beauchamp Tower.
95. Tracy Borman. *The Story of the Tower of London* (London: Merrell Publishers Limited, 2015). 44.
96. Ibid. 52.
97. Ibid.
98. Robert of Beverley was master mason at the Tower of London from 1271 until 1284.
99. Although we should acknowledge that the conception of Henry's works at Westminster Abbey, were almost entirely, the work of Robert of Beverley's predecessors; Henry de Reyns and John of Gloucester – see David Carpenter. Henry III: The Rise to Power and Personal Rule 1207–1258 (New Haven: Yale University Press, 2020). 334-5. 'All historians agree that the main features of the design were settled (and a large part of the church built) in Master Henry's time.'
100. Michael Prestwich. *Medieval People* (London: Thames & Hudson, 2014). 306. 'The obvious choice for the work was Robert of Beverley, royal master mason of London and Westminster but he was still engaged on great building works at the Tower of London.'
101. Nicola Coldstream, 'Architects, Advisers and Design at Edward I's Castles in Wales,' *Architectural History: Journal of the Society of Architectural Historians of Great Britain* 46 (2003). 24. 'It is difficult to see how Edward I could possibly could have predicted that the ugly duckling at work in Savoy would turn into the swan of Wales.'
102. A description that Swiss historian de Raemy describes as 'rhétorique' Daniel de Raemy. 2004. *Châteaux, donjons et grandes tours dans les Etats de Savoie (1230–1330)*. Lausanne: Cahiers d'archéologie romande 98 et 99.769. Taylor had earlier, perhaps less rhetorically, described the relationship as being between 'the little Savoy castles and ... the much bigger and more elaborate North Wales castles.' Arnold Taylor. 1985. *Studies in Castles and Castle-Building*. London: The Hambledon Press. 18.
103. Hugh Kennedy. *Crusader Castles* (Cambridge: Cambridge University Press, 1994). 37.
104. Louis Blondel, 'L'architecture militaire au temps de Pierre II de Savoie: Les donjons circulaires,' *Genava* XIII (1935): 277.
105. Louis Blondel, 'L'architecture militaire au temps de Pierre II de Savoie: Les donjons circulaires,' *Genava* XIII (1935): 28. 'c'est par ce chemin, passant par les possessions de la couronne anglaise, que nous sont parvenues les nouvelles formes de l'art militaire.'

106. Nicola Coldstream, 'Architects, Advisers and Design at Edward I's Castles in Wales,' *Architectural History: Journal of the Society of Architectural Historians of Great Britain* 46 (2003): 24. 'To adapt Pevsner's famous comparison, if in Wales we have architecture, in Savoy we merely have building. Against this it could be argued that the conditions in Savoy did not allow Master James to display the talents that emerged when he came to Wales.' N. Pevsner. 1942. Terms of Architectural Planning in the Middle Ages. Journal of the Warburg and Courtauld Institutes 5: 233. 'In the highly specialized civilization of the Roman Empire the difference between planning in architecture and carrying out, between designing and actual building was clearly understood.' To attach the word 'building' to the 'architecture' of Saint-Georges-d'Espéranche in this context, given that Pevsner was illustrating his point in terms of Roman attitudes to building and architecture, and Saint-Georges is consciously built in Roman style, does seem more than unduly harsh.

Chapter Six

1. Daniel de Raemy. *'Le Château Résidence d'Othon de Grandson' in Othon I de Grandson (vers 1240–1328)* (Lausanne: Cahiers Lausannois d'Histoire Médiévale, 2020). 166.
2. Ibid. 179. *'L'exode de la main d'œuvre savoyarde a lieu précisément au moment où le chantier du château de Grandson débute, mais on peut imaginer que la conception générale de l'édifice a été proposée par Jacques avant son départ.'* Or 'The exodus of the Savoyard workforce takes place precisely when the work on the Château de Grandson begins, but one can imagine that the general design of the building was proposed by Jacques before his departure.'
3. Annick Voirol Reymond. Grandson Castle 1000 years of history (Grandson: Artgraphic Cahiers d'archéologie romande 98 et 99, 2013). 3.
4. Jean Pierre Chapuisat, *'De Mont-sur-Rolle à Windsor, de la Dullive à Dumfries ... La Maison de Savoie et le Pays de Vaud,'* Bibliothèque historique vaudoise 97 (1989): 118.
5. Monique Fontannaz & Brigitte Pradervand. *Les monuments d'art et d'histoire de la Suisse* (Bern: Société d'histoire de l'art en Suisse SHAS, 2015). 128. Guillaume de Champvent also rebuilt the fifteen miles distant Château de Bulle, which retains a similar great circular donjon tower to Lucens. However, we can be certain this was not the work of Jacques de Saint-Georges since dendrochronology of the tower's timbers date to 1291-3, by which time he'd long been in the service of Edward. Bulle therefore appears to be another's replication of what have been built over a decade earlier at Lucens. Daniel de Raemy. 2004. *Châteaux, donjons et grandes tours dans les Etats de Savoie (1230–1330). Lausanne: Cahiers d'archéologie romande* 98 et 99. 211.
6. Daniel de Raemy. *Châteaux, donjons et grandes tours dans les Etats de Savoie (1230–1330)* (Lausanne: Cahiers d'archéologie romande 98 et 99, 2004). 131.
7. Monique Fontannaz & Brigitte Pradervand. *Les monuments d'art et d'histoire de la Suisse.* (Bern: Société d'histoire de l'art en Suisse SHAS, 2015). 162. 'son parapet en léger encorbellement constitue le premier exemple régional de ce type, avant ... Grandson (1277–80) ... qui se trouvent en grand nombre au Pays de Galles.' Or 'its parapet is lightly encorbelled, constituting the first example of this type in the region ... before ... Grandson (1277–80) ... which are found in great number in Wales.'
8. Ibid. 141.
9. The better-preserved example at Falavier, the work of Jacques' son Tassin, is easier to see. The roof space was not enclosed as ar Lucens. The guette or lookout is essentially d shaped with its outer face flush with the tower below. It is reached today by a wooden staircase. The pattern for a guette would almost certainly have been left in Savoy by Jacques for use by Tassin from 1280.
10. Daniel de Raemy. *Châteaux, donjons et grandes tours dans les Etats de Savoie (1230–1330)* (Lausanne: Cahiers d'archéologie romande 98 et 99, 2004). 130–1. 'conservée en partie ... restes de la guette'.
11. Michael Prestwich. *Edward I* (Yale: Yale University Press, 1997). 215. 'their towers [Conwy] with watch turrets'. Toy had earlier been of the impression the turrets at Conwy were primarily watch turrets Sidney Toy. 1984. *Castles: Their Construction and History* (Mineola: Dover Publications Inc.) 269. 'and four of them [towers] have high turrets from which the approach or distant operations of an enemy could be observed.'
12. Bernard Andenmatten & Daniel de Raemy. *La Maison De Savoie En Pays De Vaud* (Lausanne: Editions Payot Lausanne, 1990). 164. 'certainement par une main-d'œuvre en relation étroite avec la Maison de Savoie' Or 'Certainly, by a workforce in close relation with the House of Savoy'.
13. Daniel de Raemy. *Châteaux, donjons et grandes tours dans les Etats de Savoie (1230–1330)* (Lausanne: Cahiers d'archéologie romande 98 et 99, 2004). 285. 'La grand tour du château d'Yverdon en 1275–1277, sans doute sous la direction du Maître Jacques de Saint-Georges.'
14. Household roll of Count Phillip of Savoy, AST Inv, Savoia 38, fo. 46, nos 3 and 4. *'Magistro Jacobo lathomo pro expensis suis et Magistri de Romanis Veniencium de Deserto ad dominum apud Chillon, xxviij.s.'*
15. AST Inv Savoia 38, fol. 46, nos. 2 and 4.

16. Nicola Coldstream, 'Architects, Advisers and Design at Edward I's Castles in Wales,' *Architectural History: Journal of the Society of Architectural Historians of Great Britain* 46 (2003): 24. 'his [Taylor] belief in Master James's abilities as a designer perhaps led him to discount the lower standard of construction in Savoy.' And 'it is difficult to see how Edward I could possibly have predicted that the ugly duckling at work in Savoy would turn into a swan in Wales.'

17. Subject to attribution.

18. Michael Prestwich describes these turrets at Conwy as 'watch turrets' in Michael Prestwich. *Edward I* (Yale: Yale University Press, 1997). 215.

19. Marcel Grandjean, 'A Propos de la Construction de la Cathédrale de Lausanne (XII-XIIIe Siècle),' Genava XI (1963): '*on peut penser qu'elle a été exécutée vers l'époque de la consécration solennelle (1275).*' Or 'we can think that it was executed around the time of the solemn consecration (1275).'

20. Arnold Taylor. *Studies in Castles and Castle-Building* (London: The Hambledon Press, 1985). Plate 19.

21. An excellent account of thirteenth century travel can be found in Ian Mortimer. *The Time Travellers Guide to Medieval England* (London: Vintage. 2008). 122–42.

22. Arnold Taylor, 'Some notes on the Savoyards in North Wales, 1277–1300. With special reference to the Savoyard element in the construction of Harlech Castle,' *Genava* XI (1963): 297.

23. The archival records for the English court, commonly known as pipe rolls, are a collection of financial records maintained by the English exchequer of payments and receipts of royal officials (Figure 3.6). The county-by-county record written on parchment and rolled for carriage and safe keeping exist from the mid twelfth century until the mid-nineteenth century and provide most of our primary sources for Maître Jacques in England. The accounts are divided into two; 'rotali de particulis' or 'Rolls of Particulars' and summarized rolls. Once the accounts had been audited, they were then summarized in a consolidated form. Sadly, for historians the detailed accounts have not survived so much as the summarized accounts, as we shall see later. In the meantime, the Royal Wardrobe accounts for 1278, available at the National Archives of the UK (TNA) (collected as Chancery Miscellanea) in Kew introduces Maître Jacques to English accounts. The National Archives, TNA, who hold these records describe the Royal Wardrobe as 'a department within the Royal Household, responsible not just for the cloth, clothing and accoutrements worn by the monarchy in their official business and used to adorn royal buildings and furnishings but also for their expenditure and financial accounts.'

24. TNA C 47/4/1. *'Jacobo Ingeniatori a die Martis in perpacationem vadiorum suorum . Xvij.Dierum usque ad presentem diem. Xvijs. Eidem Jacobo eunti in partibus Wallie ad ordinandum opera castrorum Ibidem pro vadiis suis et expenses suis a die presenti usque ad diem Dominicam proximam post festum sancti Johannis aute Portam Latinam Per .xxix. Dies .lviij.s.'* Or Edington (Somerset), 7 April 1278. Given to Jacques the Engineer, a day in March, for payment, in arrears, of his wages for 17 days until the present day. Seventeen shillings. To the same Jacques going to parts in Wales for ordering the works of castles, the same for his wages and his expenses, from the present day until next Day of the Lord after the Festival of Saint James Before the Latin Door for twenty-nine days. Fifty-Eight Shillings.'

25. TNA C 47/4/1. *'Magistro Jacobo Ingeniatori pro vadis suis per .vij. Dies post diem dominicam Proximam post festum sancti Johannis ante Portam Latinam ipsa die Dominica computata per quos fuit extra curiam .xiiij.s. Eidem pro vadiis Suis per tres menses subsequentes per quos erit extra curiam ad Visitandum castra de flint et Rothelan .viij.li.viij.s. ; et sic in toto .ix.li.x.s.'* Or 'Westminster, 21 May 1278. Given to Maître Jacques Engineer for his wages for seven days, after the Day of the Lord after the Festival of Saint John Before the Latin Gate, The very Day of the Lord having been counted, for during which days he was away from court. Fourteen shillings. To the same the following days, during which he stayed at court, Eight shillings. To the same for his wages for the three following months, during which he will be out of court, in order to visit the castles of Flint and Rhuddlan. Eight pounds and eight shillings and so in total Nine pounds ten shillings.' And Ibid. *'Garcioni Magistri Jacobi le Mazun revertenti ad dominum suum usque Rothelan ad expensas suas .xij.d.'* Or '18 June 1278. Given to the servant of Maître Jacques the mason, coming back to his Lord until Rhuddlan for his expenses. Seven pence.' And TNA C 47/4/1. *'Magistro Jacobo Ingeniatori pro vadiis suis a die Assumpcionis beata Virginis Ipso computato usque ad diem Omnium Sanctorum per .lxxviij. Dies, ipso percipiente extra curiam per diem .ij.s., viij.li.xvj.s.'* Or '19 Sept 1278. Given to Maître Jacques Engineer for his wages from the Holy Day of the Virgin's Assumption, this day having been counted, until the day of All Saints for seventy- eight days, himself being out of court for the day. Two shillings, Seven pounds sixteen shillings.'

26. The Vercors Massif is a range of rugged plateaux and mountains in Savoy in what's now the French Pre-Alps. It lies west of the Dauphiné Alps, from which it is separated by the rivers Drac and Isère. The cliffs at the massif's eastern limit face the city of Grenoble.

27. Arnold Taylor, 'Some notes on the Savoyards in North Wales, 1277–1300. With special reference to the Savoyard element in the construction of Harlech Castle,' *Genava* XI (1963): 297. *'Guiloto de*

Vergers ducenti sex fossatores de Kenington usque Rothelan ad suas expensas, xxvj. s. viij.d.' Or dated 14 July 1278 'Guy de Vergers, six hundred road and ditch builders of Kenington all the way to Rhuddlan to their expenses, twenty-six *sol* and eight pence.' the earlier likely Savoyard references held in Turin are *'Magistro Jacobo Lathomo de mandato domini, xij.sol, Item in expensis eiusdem et Guigonis de Vercors quando fuerent apud Montem Melianum. Ij.sol.'* And *'Item domino Guigoni de Vercors et Guidoni lathomo missis ad Sanctum Georgium, xx.s.'* See *La Finanza Sabauda*, vol. 2, 126.

28. Ibid. *'Gioto de Vergers eunti apud Rothelan ad morandum ibidem super operarios Regis pro vadiis et expensis suis.'* or dated 21 July 'Guy de Vergers moves to stay at Rhuddlan to be placed over the King's workers for wages and expenses.'
29. CCR Edward I vol 1 1272–1279, 449.
30. Arnold Taylor. *Studies in Castles and Castle-Building* (London: The Hambledon Press, 1985). 65.
31. W. Douglas Simpson, 'James de Sancto Georgio, Master of the Works to King Edward in Wales and Scotland,' *Transactions of the Anglesey Antiquarian and Field Society* (1928): 31–41. 'He [Master James] is never spoken of as a master mason' and 'an able, exact, conscientious and energetic administrator.' Simpson had not seen the evidence of the Savoyard archive, which clearly identifies a *'Magistro Jacobo Lathomo'*, Maître Jacques the stonemason. Such was the service given by Arnold Taylor in looking further than the English records.
32. Arnold Taylor. *Studies in Castles and Castle-Building* (London: The Hambledon Press, 1985). 64.
33. John R. Kenyon. 'Arnold Taylor's Contribution to the Study of the Edwardian Castles in Wales' in *The Impact of the Edwardian Castles in Wales* (Oxford: Oxbow Books, 2010). 152.
34. TNA C47/4/1 *'Eidem Jacobo eunti in partibus Wallie ad ordinandum opera castrorum'* And *'Visitandum castra de flint et Rothelan.'* Or 'To the same Jacques going to parts in Wales for ordering the works of castle.' And 'in order to visit the castles of Flint and Rhuddlan.'
35. N. Pevsner, 'Terms of Architectural Planning in the Middle Ages,' *Journal of the Warburg and Courtauld Institutes* 5 (1942): 236. 'The word *'ordeneur'* occurs also in connection with *'architecteur'* in one of the first literary documents of Italian Renaissance influence on France, Christine de Pisan's Life of Charles V of about 1400. Here, however, the context, *'vrai architecteur, deviseur certain, et prudent ordeneur'* indicates that *'ordeneur'* is meant rather to stress the administrative side of architecture, although no other passage is known to me in which *'ordinatio'* must be taken to refer to a patron or his representative merely supervising a building job. But the sequence of *'architecteur'*, *'deviseur'*, *'ordeneur'* sounds very much like a sequence of architect–designer–administrator.' And 'To sum up, it can be maintained that whenever the terms *'dispositio'*, *'ordinatio'*, *'disegnare'*, 'deviser' and their derivatives or translations into other languages are found, they may be said to allude to architectural designing and planning and not to purely clerical work.'
36. Arnold Taylor. *Studies in Castles and Castle-Building* (London: The Hambledon Press, 1985). 73 & 80.
37. *La Finanza Sabauda.* vol. 1, 11. *'Idem libravit Petro Manerii clerico domini ad operationes ipsius domini faciendas.'* And Ibid. 58. *'Petri Mainier custodis operum domini.'* And TNA E101/351/9 *'Hugoni de Leominstr' clerico'* And *'Walter de Wynton clerico custodibus'.*
38. Christopher Wilson. *The Gothic Cathedral* (London: Thames and Hobson Ltd, 1990). 140. 'scale drawings were probably not a new thing, that they helped raise the standing of their authors mainly through their affinity with the august discipline of geometry, and that the ability of architects to delegate the day-to-day running of sites was a consequence not just of the use of scale drawing but the virtual ending of technical innovation … Because the processes of building became more a matter of routine than previously, there were likely to be far fewer unforeseen problems requiring the personal attention of architects. Thus, architects of major projects were liberated from the need to be constantly present at a single site, and if their work was particularly in demand, they became able to commute between several sites.'
39. Michael Prestwich. *Medieval People* (London: Thames & Hudson, 2014). 306.
40. Ingeniatori being the dative of Ingeniator, that is to the object, the 1278 scribe in England using *'Ingeniatori'* in the sense of 'to Maître Jacques the Engineer' or 'Given to Maître Jacques the Engineer.'
41. Arnold Taylor. *Studies in Castles and Castle-Building* (London: The Hambledon Press, 1985). 65. 'a concise definition of *ingeniator* is less easy. 'Engineer', though convenient and therefore commonly used, is, in view of modern connotation, too narrow; moreover, it has a military flavour, and the functions exercised by *ingeniatores* in the twelfth and thirteenth centuries were by no means only military. For the word is commonly used, not only of the master of engines of war, but also in the wider sense of the 'contriver' or 'deviser' of all kinds of building works. It is not capable of concise translation into modern terminology, for it embodies something of all those functions which today are shared between the architect, the contractor and the resident superintendent of works.'
42. In the first century BC, found once again in the 14th century, Vitruvius uses the terms *'architectus' 'architecti' 'architectura' 'architectorum'* in Vitruvius. 1914. The Ten Books on Architecture, trans. M. H. Morgan. London.

43. N. Pevsner, 'The Term 'Architect' in the Middle Ages,' *Speculum* 17 (1942): 556. The terms *'architectus'* and *'architector'* were little used during the Middle Ages.

44. *OED*, March 2019, Oxford University Press. ORIGIN (Engineer) Middle English (denoting a designer and constructor of fortifications and weapons; formerly also as *ingineer*): in early use from Old French *engigneor*, from medieval Latin *ingeniator*, from *ingeniare* 'contrive, devise', from Latin *ingenium* (see engine); in later use from French *ingénieur* or Italian *ingegnere*, also based on Latin *ingenium*, with the ending influenced by -eer.

45. 2005. Oxford Latin Desk Dictionary. Oxford: Oxford University Press.

46. Vitruvius. *The Complete Works of Vitruvius* (Hastings: Delphi Publishing Ltd, 2019). Book 1, Chap 2, 959. Taken from Vitruvius. 1914. The Ten Books on Architecture, trans. M. H. Morgan. London. *'Architectura autem constat ex ordinatione'* Or 'Architecture depends on order'.

47. Ibid. Pliny the Younger had used 'ordinandum' in a similar vein to our scribe when writing: *'ad ordinandum statum liberarum civitatum'* or 'to be sent to regulate the state of the free cities' to his friend Maximus when he was sent to the province of Achaea. In Pliny the Younger cited in Alan K. Bowman, Peter Garnsey, Dominic Rathbone, The Cambridge Ancient History, Cambridge University Press, 117.

48. Nicola Coldstream, 'Architects, Advisers and Design at Edward I's Castles in Wales,' *Architectural History: Journal of the Society of Architectural Historians of Great Britain* 46 (2003): 25. 'Only once is there even a hint of a design process, when in summer 1278 he was sent 'ad ordinandum' the work on the castles. This term is interpreted to mean design, but it can also mean setting out.' The Pevsner citation is from N. Pevsner. 1942. Terms of Architectural Planning in the Middle Ages. Journal of the Warburg and Courtauld Institutes. 5. 232–7. Ibid. 2003, 23. And Ibid. 2016, 109. 'This term can cover matters of design.'

49. N. Pevsner, 'Terms of Architectural Planning in the Middle Ages,' *Journal of the Warburg and Courtauld Institutes* 5 (1942): 235. 'Thus, the Sacrist Rolls of Ely contain the entry under 1323–4: *'Datum cuidam de Londonia ad ordinandum novum opus ... 38. 4d.'* Mr. Chapman in his excellent edition of the rolls has shown that this passage very probably refers to the visit of a distinguished London carpenter (William de Hurle?) in connection with the design of the octagon tower.' And Ibid. 236. 'To sum up, it can be maintained that whenever the terms *'dispositio'*, *'ordinatio'*, *'disegnare'*, *'deviser'* and their derivatives or translations into other languages are found, they may be said to allude to architectural designing and planning and not to purely clerical work.'

50. RG i, no. 3646; Close Rolls 1253-4, 302. *'Mandatum est Rogero Scissori et Bonacio Lumbard quod habere faciat fratri Hugoni, templario, tunicam, superunciam, pallium et capam: et Magistro Bertramo unam robam, unum tabadum et unum lectum, scilicet unum chalonem, unum huceam et duo lyntheaminac et Johanni de Mesot unam robam et Petro Le Burguynun unam robam, de dono regis. Teste ut supra (Teste apud Millan' xxviij die Maii anno xxxviiij.)*

51. Arnold Taylor. Studies in Medieval History Presented to R. Allen Brown (Woodbridge: The Boydell Press, 1989). 293. 'Peroto le Burguilun pro uno roncino suo mortuo in servicio Regis.' Or 'Peter of Burgundy for a horse killed in the King's service.'

52. CPR Henry III vol 4 1247–1258, 270.

53. TNA E 101/486/22

54. The Perche was a medieval French measure of length or height equivalent to 5.5 yards. Old French *perche* from Latin *perticate* meaning measuring rod. In England the measurement was therefore referred to as a rod.

55. J. Goronwy Edwards, 'Edward I's Castle-Building in Wales,' *The Proceedings of the British Academy XXXII (1944)*: 23. n1. Citing 'item in quodam palicio magno facto circa ballium forinsecum ad tascheam pro 49 perticatis, pro perticata facienda* 6s. 8d, £16.6s.8d.'

56. Ibid. Brattice, from the French *bretèche*, originally referred to part of a castle. This was a small wooden structure, sometimes *temporary*, that projected out beyond the main part of a castle wall, so as to give flanking fire along that wall whilst still offering some degree of protection. Since it's unlikely the castle wall had by then been finished it's possible the brattice referred to was in fact the redundant palisade.

57. C. J. Spurgeon, 'Builth Castle,' *Brycheiniog* 18 (1978/9): 54.

58. Ibid.

59. J. Goronwy Edwards, 'Edward I's Castle-Building in Wales,' *The Proceedings of the British Academy XXXII (1944)*: 22 *'operaciones castri de nouo constructi apud Buelt per preceptum regis, videlicet ad operaciones magne turris in eodem castro, unius muri lapidei cum sex turriculis circumsingentibus castrum predictum, pontis turneicii cum duobus magnis turrellis, et unius muri lapidei prope eundem pontem icludentis intrinsecum ballium, unius fossati extra murum predictum, et unius muri lapidei incepti super idem fossatum ad includendum ballium forinsecum.'* Or 'Operations of the new castle constructed at Builth by order of the king, that is to say operations of a great tower in the said castle, one stone wall and six turrets

encompassing the aforementioned castle, drawbridge and two great towers, and one stone wall near the same bridge intrinsically including the bailey, one ditch outside the wall aforementioned, and one stone wall begun over the same ditch to the enclosed outer bailey.'

60. C. J. Spurgeon, 'Builth Castle,' *Brycheiniog* 18 (1978/9): 47–59.

61. J. Goronwy Edwards, ' Edward I's Castle-Building in Wales,' *The Proceedings of the British Academy* XXXII (1944): 66. Appendix 1.

62. C. J. Spurgeon, 'Builth Castle,' *Brycheiniog* 18 (1978/9): 54.

63. Michael Prestwich. *Edward I* (Yale: Yale University Press, 1997). 208. 'Much the most important were Flint and Rhuddlan.'

64. Maryline Martin & Florian Renucci. *Guédelon: A Castle in the Making* (Rennes: Editions Ouest-France, 2016). 44.

65. John Speed. 1611. The theatre of the empire of Great Britaine. John Sudbury & Georg Humble: London.

66. CWR 1277–1326, 165. 'Order to cause proclamation to be made that a market shall be held at Flint every week on Thursday and that a fair of nine days shall be held there yearly on the eve, the day and the morrow of Whitsunday and on the six following days, as the king wills that such market and fair shall be held there.'

67. TNA E101/485/19. '*Denariis subtractis de diversis operaiis propter defectum laboris.*' Or 'Pence having been subtracted from different works because of defective labour.'

68. Arnold Taylor. *The Welsh Castles of King Edward I* (London: The Hambledon Press, 1986). 19.

69. Robert de Rhuddlan had been a Norman adventurer at the time of the Conquest. As a lieutenant of Hugh de Avranches, then Earl of Chester. He'd built castles at Deganwy and Rhuddlan, often fighting the Welsh, they eventually caught up with him, displaying his severed head on the mast of one of their ships.

70. Arnold Taylor. *The Welsh Castles of King Edward I* (London: The Hambledon Press, 1986). 28. '*Pro duabus domibus emptis apud Rothelan ad ponendum in castro Rothel' per manus Magistri Bertrami Ingeniatoris. xxvj.s. viiij.d. Pro una alia domo ad item castrum. xij.s.*'

71. Arnold Taylor. *Rhuddlan Castle* (Cardiff, Cadw. 2008). 2.

72. CWR 1277–1326, 160. 'To all to whom, etc. Notification that the king has appointed Nicholas Bonel his receiver of all the money issuing from the issues of the king's two cantreds and of the parts adjoining during his pleasure, and that he has also appointed him his surveyor of his works in those parts, both at Le Chaylou and at Rothelan, as he has enjoined upon him by word of mouth and as Guncelin de Baddelmere [sic] has similarly enjoined upon him on the king's behalf.'

73. CWR 1277–1326, 164. 'To Guncelin de Badelesmere, justice of Chester, and Howel son of Griffin, the king's bailiffs of the cantreds, and Nicholas Bonel. Notification that the king has appointed them and given them power by the presents to assess his burgages at Rothelan and Flint and to grant and demise at a fixed rent all his lands in those parts. This order is during the king's pleasure.'

74. TNA E101/350/26 '*Garcioni Magistri Bertrami Machinatoris auxilianti carpentarios, pro vadiis suis v. dierum proximo preteritorum* [19-23 October 1277] *xx.d*' And '*Garcioni Magistri Bertrami pro stipendiis eiusdem dici Dominice et Lune et Martis sequent* [24-26 Oct] *ij.d.*'

75. TNA E101/467/7 '*Expense et empciones circa ingenia domini regis facte per providenciam Magistri Bertrami a die Pasce* [17 April 1278] *anno domini regis sexto, et stipendia carpentariorum circa ingenia.*'

76. That according to legend Arthur had fought on behalf of and with the Britons in their rear-guard defence of their island against the invading English was something that Edward chose to overlook. From a twenty-first century perspective, it's easy to be cynical and suspect Edward of a ploy to colonize the mythology of the Welsh.

77. Geoffrey of Monmouth. *The History of the Kings of Britain* (London: Penguin Books Ltd. 1966).

78. Gerald of Wales. *The Journey Through Wales and The Description of Wales*. (London: Penguin Books Ltd, 1978). 316.

79. '*Hic jacet sepultus inclitus rex Arturius in insula Avalonia.*'

80. Arnold Taylor, *Studies in Castles and Castle-Building*. (London: The Hambledon Press. 1985). 89..

81. TNA C 47/4/1. '*Magistro Jacobo Ingeniatori pro vadis suis per .vij. Dies post diem dominicam Proximam post festum sancti Johannis ante Portam Latinam ipsa die Dominica computata per quos fuit extra curiam .xiiij.s. Eidem pro vadiis Suis per tres menses subsequentes per quos erit extra curiam ad Visitandum castra de flint et Rothelan .viij.li.viij.s. ; et sic in toto .ix.li.x.s.*' Or 'Westminster, 21 May 1278. Given to Maître Jacques Engineer for his wages for seven days, after the Day of the Lord after the Festival of Saint John Before the Latin Gate, The very Day of the Lord having been counted, for during which days he was away from court. Fourteen shillings. To the same the following days, during which he stayed at court, Eight shillings. To the same for his wages for the three following months, during which he will be out of court, in order to visit the castles of Flint and Rhuddlan. Eight pounds and eight shillings and so in total Nine pounds ten shillings.'

82. Ibid. '*Garcioni Magistri Jacobi le Mazun revertenti ad dominum suum usque Rothelan ad expensas suas .xij.d.*' Or '18 June 1278. Given to the servant of Maître Jacques the mason, coming back to his Lord until Rhuddlan for his expenses. Seven pence.'

83. Ibid. 28.

84. Arnold Taylor. *The Welsh Castles of King Edward I* (London: The Hambledon Press, 1986). 28. '1278 witnessed a full and intensive building campaign, operations on the castle alone amounting to £2746 in the fifteen months from December 1277 and thereby exceeding by practically £1,000 the combined current expenditure at Flint (£890), Aberystwyth (£679) and Builth (£262). In addition 54 per cent of the Clwyd canal expenditure was also incurred in this period, bringing the total outlay between December 1277 and March 1279 to over £3160. There can thus be no question that the Rhuddlan works were regarded at this time as the principal single undertaking in Wales.'

85. TNA E372 / 122, rot28 d.

86. TNA E372 / 122, rot28 d. '*magnum fossatum in quo … est portus qui ducit a mari usque castrum*' or a great ditch in which the port leads from the sea until the castle.

87. TNA E32/131. rot26 d. '*operantium circa clausturam ville*' Or 'Works of the ditch around the tow'.

88. Arnold Taylor. *The Welsh Castles of King Edward I* (London: The Hambledon Press, 1986). 103. '*de partibus Hoylaund*'.

89. CWR 1277–1326, 241. The alteration to the course of the River Clwyd is confirmed by a 16 October 1282 reference '. . . and all the marsh that is within the new course of the river of Cloyt [Clwyd] and the old course of that river, which marsh used anciently to pertain to the town of Rothelan [Rhuddlan].'

90. For example, at Romont (1240) and Yverdon (1260)

91. This first gatehouse, at Dover Castle, would be damaged by Prince Louis in his abortive attempt at the crown of England before being rebuilt in its current form by Hubert de Burgh between 1221 and 1227.

92. Pevensey Castle faced a lengthy siege during the Second Barons' War from the rebel baron Simon de Montfort, following Henry's defeat in the Battle of Lewes. Defeated members of the royalist army fled to Pevensey, pursued by de Montford's forces, but the garrison refused an invitation to surrender and endured over a year of besiegement. It was described as a 'nest of Savoyards' by Henri Buathier. 1995. JEAN Ier DE GRAILLY un chevalier européen du XIIIe siècle. 35. Buathier no doubt got this expression from the earlier paper by Jean Pierre Chapuisat. 1978. *Quelques variations sur un thème connue : En relisant certains comptes de châtellenies du XIII siècle.* Which discussed in part the siege of Pevensey. '*Une autre conséquence de la guerre anglaise, dite des Barons, surgit dans les comptes de la châtellenie de Chillon. On y paie ce qui est dû à Nantelme de Cholay, soit Choulex, qui avait été en garnison à Pevensey, forteresse de la côte méridionale, en Sussex, restée aux mains de Pierre de Savoie pendant tout le temps du conflit anglais ; ce fut un nid de résistance et une excellente tête de pont.*' Or 'Another consequence of the English war, known as the Barons [War], arose in the accounts of the châtellenie de Chillon. We [the Savoyards] pay what is due to Nantelme de Cholay, that is to say Choulex, who had been stationed at Pevensey, a fortress on the south coast, in Sussex, which remained in the hands of Pierre de Savoie throughout the time of the English conflict; it was a nest of resistance and an excellent bridgehead. ' This gives us the name of at least one of the knights who held Pevensey, for he is paid upon his return to Savoy by Pierre de Savoie.

93. Christopher Gravett. *English Castles 1200–1300* (Botley: Osprey Publishing Ltd, 2009). 55–61.

94. Henry Gough. Itinerary of King Edward the First throughout his reign, A.D. 1272–1307, exhibiting his movements so far as they are recorded. vol. 1 (Paisley: Alexander Gardner, 1900). 38.

95. R. Allen Brown. *English Castles* (London: Chancellor Press, 1970). 99.

96. David Martin & Barbara Martin, 'A Reinterpretation of the Gatehouse at Tonbridge Castle,' *Archaelogia Cantiana* 133 (2013): 235–76.

97. There has been much debate as to the dating of the gatehouse at Tonbridge Castle. Dates have ranged between 1216 and 1300. The current guidebook gives a date no later than 1258. The consensus is that the building sequence was Tonbridge, Caerffili, Harlech then Beaumaris. See David Martin & Barbara Martin. 2013. A Reinterpretation of the Gatehouse at Tonbridge Castle. *Archaelogia Cantiana* 133: 271–5.

98. Arnold Taylor. *Rhuddlan Castle* (Cardiff, Cadw, 2008). 3–4.

99. Nicola Coldstream, 'Architects, Advisers and Design at Edward I's Castles in Wales,' *Architectural History: Journal of the Society of Architectural Historians of Great Britain* 46 (2003): 25.'They [the Rhuddlan gatehouses] seem to be a less advanced type than either the Clare or London gatehouses or those of the 1280s.' And 'The inconvenient arrangement may show that the gatehouses [at Rhuddlan] were never intended for residential use, but it could alternatively be seen as an amateurish first effort by Master James.' And Ibid. 26. and Ibid. 116. 'Master Bertram has a good claim to have inaugurated the gatehouses at Rhuddlan.'

100. Blanquefort, on the Gironde near Bordeaux. Likely to have been a castle site since the eleventh century, a square tower surrounded by a wooden palisade. Henry III then Edward I, Kings of

England and Dukes of Aquitaine, acquired the castle and the land through two purchases in 1254 and 1270 from Adélaïde de Blanquefort and her husband Bernard de Trancaléon. Castle works under Henry and later Edward have no primary sources and are dateable only to the 'late thirteenth century' and the donjon to the fourteenth.

101. Arnold Taylor. *Master Bertram, Ingeniator Regis. Studies in Medieval History presented to R. Allen Brown.* (Woodbridge: The Boydell Press, 1989). 303–4. Marc Morris writing in Marc Morris. 'Edward I's Building Works in Gascony' in *The Impact of the Edwardian Castles in Wales* (Oxford: Oxbow Books, 2010). 171 and Ibid. n18. was less sure of the Blanquefort connection for Master Bertram and critical of Taylor's suggestion. Morris dismissed Taylor's theory suggesting the works at Blanquefort belong to the fourteenth century and that what Taylor took to be a twin-towered gatehouse was 'clearly not' Morris cites Jacques Gardelles, Les Châteaux, 102–3. But as Renn pointed out of Gardelles' work and French castle dating in general, dating evidence is wanting. We can say stylistically the *donjon* is fourteenth century, but dating for the curtain wall and gateway are, at the least, open to question. So, whilst the *donjon* at Blanquefort is clearly fourteenth century, other works could well be earlier, and this could include a gateway once entered across a bridge and flanked by twin round towers – if we don't call this a twin-towered gatehouse then I struggle to find other words to describe it. Ultimately the lack of primary sources for dating evidence render any confirmation either way futile and purely the realm of theory and architectural historians. But, for this writer, Taylor's theory is not what Morris called 'spurious', it remains, to put in no higher, a possibility, and one that would explain much. Irrespective of Morris' critique of the Blanquefort theory, Master Bertram's Gascon origin and work alongside Mézos are there in the primary sources.

102. Nicola Coldstream, 'Architects, Advisers and Design at Edward I's Castles in Wales,' *Architectural History: Journal of the Society of Architectural Historians of Great Britain* 46 (2003). 23. 'Although Taylor cited the strengthened corner tower of Yverdon as a precedent for Flint the Yverdon example is not an isolated tower but a part of the curtain wall.'

103. Daniel de Raemy. *Châteaux, donjons et grandes tours dans les Etats de Savoie (1230–1330)* (Lausanne: Cahiers d'archéologie romande 98 et 99, 2004). 828.

104. R. Allen Brown. *Castles from the Air* (Cambridge: Cambridge University Press, 1989). 117. 'mostly under the direction of Master James of St George … The principal strength of the castle lies in the inner ward and the keep, built on the plan familiar in the thirteenth-century France, Savoy and elsewhere (Dourdan, Yverdon) of a rectangular enclosure with angle towers, one of which is greatly enlarged and here off-set (south-east), to be the donjon. In short Flint had a tower keep as its donjon.'

105. Vicky Perfect. *Flint Castle: The Story of Edward I's First Welsh Castle* (Mold: Alyn Books Ltd, 2012). 19. 'Most historians credit Master James of St George with the design of all the castles built in Wales by Edward I. However, in the case of Flint, this is a false claim.'

106. TNA C47/4/1 *'Eidem Jacobo eunti in partibus Wallie ad ordinandum opera castrorum'* And *'Visitandum castra de flint et Rothelan.'* Or 'To the same Jacques going to parts in Wales for ordering the works of castle.' And 'in order to visit the castles of Flint and Rhuddlan.'

107. Arnold Taylor, 'Master James of Saint Georges,' *The English Historical Review* 65 (1950): 438–9 Taylor drew the distinct conclusion regarding Flint and Rhuddlan 'The implication of the records is that he was chief master mason at Rhuddlan and Flint between 1278 and 1282 and that in that position he was directly responsible, under the King and his advisors, for the erection of those two castles.'

108. Rick Turner. 'The Life and Career of Richard the Engineer' in *The Impact of the Edwardian Castles in Wales* (Oxford: Oxbow Books, 2010). 53. 'He [Master Richard] was almost certainly a carpenter by training and not primarily a mason.'

109. Vicky Perfect. *Flint Castle: The story of Edward I's first Welsh castle.* (Mold: Alyn Books Ltd, 2012).

110. Malcolm Hislop. *James of St George and the Castles of North Wales* (Barnsley: Pen & Sword Books Ltd, 2020). 258–9.

111. Keith D. Lilley. 'The Landscape of Edward's New Towns: Their Planning and Design' in *The Impact of the Edwardian Castles in Wales* (Oxford: Oxbow Books, 2010). 109. 'the Tour de Constance offers a superficial resemble to Flint's great offset tower.'

112. Arnold Taylor. *Master Bertram, Ingeniator Regis, Studies in Medieval History presented to R. Allen Brown* (Woodbridge: The Boydell Press, 1989). 302.

113. Nicola Coldstream, 'Architects, Advisers and Design at Edward I's Castles in Wales,' *Architectural History: Journal of the Society of Architectural Historians of Great Britain* 46 (2003): 33. 'James of St George was a consummate organizer … In Savoy Master James had supervised over a vast area and difficult terrain a large number of building programmes that were in progress simultaneously.'

Chapter Seven
1. *La Finanza Sabauda.* vol. 1, 63.
2. TNA C 47/4/1.

3. Arnold Taylor, 'The Castle of St Georges D'Espéranche,' *The Antiquaries Journal* 33 (1953): 40. Taylor wrote 'There is still, however, a gap to be bridged between the Master James who looks like having designed St Georges round about 1268 and the Master James of St George who was working in Wales in 1278; and it can now be accepted as fairly certain that, as indeed with the gap between Yverdon and St Georges, it will not be bridged by the surviving records alone. Is there, then, sufficient architectural evidence – in the form, for example, of similar features employed in the construction both of Savoy and of the North Wales castles – that will serve to supplement the deficiencies of the written record and speak with no less decisive voice? It is the claim of this paper that there is. It is not, of course, sufficient that the castles of Yverdon, St Georges, Flint, Rhuddlan, Aberystwyth, Conway, Harlech and Beaumaris should all have four sided wards with corner towers, for that basis ground plan is far too common in the later thirteenth century to be, by itself, significant for our purpose. When, however, we find that eight of the castles named, no fewer than five (i.e., Two in Savoy [St Georges and Yverdon] and three in Wales [Rhuddlan, Conway and Harlech]) either have or had latrine projections not merely placed in exactly the same positions, but designed on similar lines and to similar dimensions, we are perhaps on firmer ground. And when, further, from among these five, we compare the surviving projection at St Georges with the best preserved of the two that remain at Harlech, the resemblance seems to be sufficiently close to suggest a direct relationship. As previously noted, the St Georges projection measures 8ft. 2 in. by 2ft. 1 in. The corresponding dimensions of the projection of adjoining the north-west tower at Harlech are 8ft. 10 in and 2ft 2in. These two features, which are . . . marked by the closest similarity of treatment; the working-in of the stone capping is identical, and both examples are alike in being square-ended, whereas those at Rhuddlan and Conway are chamfered off to shade into the main face of the curtain. It would be odd indeed if the only definable and particular point of resemblance between the Savoy and North Wales castles were to be found in this lowly appendage, but of course this is not the case. It could, for example, be demonstrated that in their original form the great two light windows that adorned the keep-gatehouse at Harlech closely paralleled windows at Chillon, on Lake Geneva, which belong to alterations made to that castle by Pierre of Savoy in c. 1260 . . . We may, however, here briefly notice a detail of window construction that is of more general application. We have spoken earlier of the shallow segmental head, without keystone, which characterizes the principal windows at both Yverdon and St Georges. This type of head, besides being seen in perfection in the Harlech gatehouse windows, was employed in the embrasures and rear-arches of Flint, Rhuddlan, Denbigh, Conway and Harlech, while at Caernarvon it is the form of the embrasure head used almost exclusively in the southward parts of the castle (i.e., those built between 1283 and 1290). It is also worth remarking that the full-centred arch, which though something of a rarity at this date is found in the great hall at Conway, in embrasures in the eastern corner tower at Harlech, and in the barbican at Beaumaris, is matched by a blocked opening in the east wall at St Georges, as well as by the heads of the embrasures in the octagonal tower there. Finally there is another aspect of the matter that seems to deserve attention ... St Georges was not the only castle under construction in the Viennois in 1274, but that works were also in progress at Voiron, La Côte-Saint-André (Costa) and Saint-Laurent-du-Pont (Sanctus Laurentius de Deserto). On the general evidence of the records we should be justified in supposing that all were under the surveillance of Master James the mason, and that in all probability he was their architect. If this supposition is correct, we are also led to an interesting parallel. Though virtually nothing of these other buildings remains standing, we know from various sources that all of them were characterized by round towers, in contrast to the octagonal towers of St Georges. This seems to suggest a deliberate choice of the octagonal design for the building that was to serve ceremonial uses and rank as the count's summer palace, the round-tower plan being reserved for castles of a more ordinary nature. Whether polygonal towers were more costly to build and therefore regarded as more of a luxury, whether they were thought to present a more decorative appearance, or whether they merely allowed more conveniently planned rooms, are questions that cannot be entered into here. The point that is interesting to note, in the present context, is than in north Wales, as in Savoy, not only do we have a unified group of castles in which round towers are the rule and polygonal towers the exception, but, further, that the status of the principal Welsh exception, namely Caernarvon, has something in common with that of the Savoy exception, namely St Georges. For Caernarvon was essentially intended as a palace of the English principality of Wales, the formal, official seat of the prince's government, and it may be that in some way similar ideas underlie the distinctive treatment accorded to both buildings. In the case of St Georges, the destruction alike of buildings and of building accounts has robbed us of evidence that might have been conclusive. Nevertheless, in the fragments that remain [of St Georges] it looks as if we can descry a remnant of the early handiwork of the architect whose later achievement in North Wales was to win him lasting greatness.'

4. Marc Morris. *Castle* (London: Windmill Books, 2012). 126.

5. Today we still use the word putlog or putlock – Oxford English Definition 'a short horizontal beam that with others supports the floor planks of a scaffold.'

6. André Chatelain, 'Recherche sur les Châteaux de Philippe Auguste,' Archéologie Médiévale vol. 21 (1991): 115–61 wrote that the origins of helicoidal put-logs may well have been Villeneuve-Sur-Yonne around 1220.

7. OED, March 2019, Oxford University Press. ORIGIN late Middle English: French, from garder 'to keep' + robe 'robe, dress'; compare with wardrobe. The Garderobe meant 'small room' or 'cupboard', which is often where medieval toilets were located. The Norman habit of substituting W for G in speaking French gives us the English word 'Wardrobe.'

8. Christopher Gravett. The Castles of King Edward I in Wales 1277–1307 (Botley: Osprey Publishing Ltd, 2007). 36.

9. Nicola Coldstream, 'Architects, Advisers and Design at Edward I's Castles in Wales,' Architectural History: Journal of the Society of Architectural Historians of Great Britain 46 (2003): 20. 'his identification of James of St George's origins and the Savoyard elements in the castles in Wales are not in doubt and will certainly not be challenged here.'

10. TNA E372 124 rot 29.

11. Ibid. 'per visum ac testimonium Magistri Jacobi de Sancto Georgio.'

12. 'Ad tascham' or At task work, as opposed to weekly wages, was as the name implies payment for a specific task.

13. Arnold Taylor. The Welsh Castles of King Edward I (London: The Hambledon Press, 1986). 20. 'Et Ricardo de Franckevill et Waltero de Bridleton cementariis pro factum viij perticatar' et viij pedum muri fosse Castri ad tascham xxix.li iij.s. viz pro qualibet perticata lxx.s. et pro viij pedibus xxiij.s.'

14. Vicky Perfect. Flint Castle: The Story of Edward I's First Welsh Castle (Mold: Alyn Books Ltd, 2012). 19. 'It is documented that Master James did not enter the payroll of Flint Castle until 1 November 1280.'

15. J. G. Edwards, 'The Building of Flint,' The Flintshire Historical Society XII (1951): 9–10. Edwards defined three stages of work at Flint. '(i) In the first stage, the work was pressed forward at speed. The object presumably was to establish a strong defensive position without delay. (ii.) In the second stage, the pace of construction was considerably slackened. found in the fact that much more labour was at this stage being concentrated upon the building of Rhuddlan, presumably because its more forward geographical position gave it priority in military importance. (iii.) In the third stage, the main effort was transferred back to Flint, and the work there was much accelerated; at Rhuddlan, on the other hand, activity was markedly curtailed.' Edwards dated each stage: Firstly the abbreviated 1277 building season, secondly the 1278, 79 and 80 seasons, thirdly the 1281 season until completion. He based this analysis upon five of the six building accounts in the TNA in Kew that he saw. Taylor subsequently added a sixth account which only confirmed Edwards's analysis.

16. This had originally been the task of Nicholas Bonel see, CWR 1277–1326, 164. 'To Guncelin de Badelesmere, justice of Chester, and Howel son of Griffin, the king's bailiffs of the cantreds, and Nicholas Bonel. Notification that the king has appointed them and given them power by the presents to assess his burgages at Rothelan and Flint and to grant and demise at a fixed rent all his lands in those parts. This order is during the king's pleasure.' But CPR Edward I vol 1 (1272–1281), 370. suggests the task had, by the summer of 1280, passed to Maître Jacques 'Appointment of William de Perton, king's clerk and Maître Jacques, Keeper of the works at Rothelan, to execute the commission which certain persons were lately appointed to do, but have not done, to wit, to assess all land and places at Rothelan, and to deliver to them all persons willing to receive and hold them of the King at competent service, except the King's meadow, which is to be reserved in demesne.'

17. Arnold Taylor. The Welsh Castles of King Edward I (London: The Hambledon Press, 1986). 21.

18. TNA E101/674/23.

19. Arnold Taylor, 'Some notes on the Savoyards in North Wales, 1277 –1300. With special reference to the Savoyard element in the construction of Harlech Castle,' Genava XI (1963): 298. n31 & 32. And Arnold Taylor. The Welsh Castles of King Edward I (London: The Hambledon Press, 1986). 20. n10. 'There daily wages are … John Pycard, 5d.' Taylor noted there had been a Vincent Picard engaged on the construction of the castle at Yverdon. The Picard name became famous in recent years via the aeronautical exploits of the Piccard family, for which the Star Trek character Jean-Luc Picard was named.

20. TNA currency converter.

21. Ibid.

22. For the link to Saint-Georges see Louis Blondel. Le château de Saxon: note complémentaire. Vallesia X (1955): 87–8. 'probablement du chantier de St-Georges d'Espéranche.' Or 'probably from the St-Georges d'Espéranche site.' For Giletus and Tassinum being brothers Comptes du châtelain de Chillon Guy de Bonard, 12781279, Copies, pp. 329–31; idem, de Guy de Bonard, 1279-1280, Copies, pp. 339–55. Quoted in Louis Blondel. 1954. Le château de Saxon. Vallesia IX: 169. 'Primo litteram de

conventionibus turris Sayssonis faciende per Tassinum et Giletum fratrum suum in taschiam. Item litteram de quinquaginta libr. maur. solutis per Guidonem Bonardi, Tassino et Gileto fratribus pro dicta turre facienda'

23. The tower built at Saxon is more advanced than that built by Pierre II at Saillon in 1261, and had five floors, its entrance 10 metres above the ground. The second floor provides for archery defence, the third for a corbelled latrine, the fourth a chimney.

24. Louis Blondel, 'Le château de Saxon,' *Vallesia* IX (1954): 169 *'Primo litteram de conventionibus turris Sayssonis faciende per Tassinum et Giletum fratrum suum in taschiam. Item litteram de quinquaginta libr. maur. solutis per Guidonem Bonardi, Tassino et Gileto fratribus pro dicta turre facienda'*

25. Louis Blondel, 'Le château de Saxon: note complémentaire,' *Vallesia* X (1955): 87–8.

26. Louis Blondel, 'Le château de Saxon: note complémentaire,' *Vallesia* X (1955): 87–8.. *'Nous donnons ici un résumé succinct des dépenses faites. - Girard de Mûris, «terrailleur» (terrassier), et Beynard, régi ribaldorum, qui dirige les brouettes, reçoivent pour faire les fondations de la tour en tâche XVII livres V sous mauricie.'* Or 'We give here a brief summary of the expenses incurred. Girard de Mûris, 'terrailleur' (digger), and Beynard, *regi ribaldorum*, who directs the wheelbarrows, receive to make the foundations of the tower in task XVII books V under mauricie.' This account is mentioned in the inventory of Mr. Chiaudano, *La Finanza Sabauda* nel sec. XIII, vol. I (in Biblioteca Délia Società storica subalpina, t. 131), p. LXXVI, No 3, but has not been published; it corresponds to the inventory Savoia 69, fo 69, mazzo 1, No 1. It completes the account of Guy Bonard, lord of Chillon for the period of 13 October 1279 to 12 March 1280 of which we have given extracts in our cited article.

27. Louis Blondel, 'L'architecture militaire au temps de Pierre II de Savoie: Les donjons circulaires,' *Genava* XIII (1935): 292. Blondel noted that an account of 1354 by the Savoyard Bailiff of the Valais gave instructions for signal fires for the Valaisan fortifications of Conthey, Saillon, Saxon, La Bâtiaz.

28. Arnold Taylor, 'Rhuddlan cathedral: a 'might-have-been' of Flintshire history,' Journal of *the Flintshire Historical Society* 15 (1954-5): 44–5.

29. TNA C49/4/1. 'And know Lord, the castle all bare, without vittles and garrison and without crossbows and belts ... and either send to Montgomery for armour, crossbow bolts and vittles if God pleases. We do not desire to leave either the guard of the castle or of the town to the help of God ... Whatsoever he came there, it does not have locks nor bars to the mule gate of the city, they are all open during the day and the night, so that I have to put on locks and watches of the doors whatsoever responds at the doors of the day or the night if God pleases ... the gates of the town had either no locks nor bars and were left upon day and night.'

30. *'ke il maunde a Lampadarvaur le mestre del ouerayne Rothelan ou aukun autre meistre ke sotil oume seit de ouerayne.'*

31. CCR Edward I vol 2 1279–1288, 145. 'To Thomas, Bishop of St Davids Order to pay out of the money he owes the king, to William de Canvill 250 marks for the works of the castle of Lampadermaure. To the aforesaid William. Order to demand and receive the sum from the bishop, and to do the said works therewith by the view and testimony of Robert Tibbetot.'

32. Michael Prestwich. *Edward I* (Yale: Yale University Press, 1997). 208. 'The part played by the King himself in the planning.of the new castles is unfortunately far from clear. A letter from Bogo de Knovill about the poor situation at Aberystwyth in 1280 makes it clear that the problems were to be explained to the King himself, but the surviving records do not reveal in Edward's case the kind of detailed orders about architectural matters that survive from Henry III's reign.' Prestwich is not certain of the extent of Edward's involvement in his castles, given the lack of primary sources this is a reasonable position. The Bogo de Knovill letter does at least show that Edward was not 'out of the loop' as it were, but is not in and of itself evidence of involvement in design.

33. The Calendar of Patent Rolls or Chancery Patent Rolls are a collection from 1201 until 2012 of Letters patent were letters issued open or 'patent' expressing the sovereign's will on a variety of matters of public interest, sealed with the sovereign's great seal pendent. The patent rolls record the issue of letters patent from the reign of King John until the present day. An English calendar of the patent rolls from 1232 to 1582 was published as Calendar of the Patent Rolls (HMSO, 1906-). The originals are in the care of the National Archive in Kew under the reference C66, and are here referenced and abbreviated as CPR followed by the King and volume. A complex procedure culminated in the making up (engrossment) of a letter patent, bearing largely on activities in the Signet Office and Privy Seal Office, the administrators of the sovereign's lesser seals below the great seal.

34. CPR Edward I vol 1 1272–1281, 389.

35. OED, March 2019, Oxford University Press. ORIGIN [Secretary] late Middle English (originally in the sense 'person entrusted with a secret'): from late Latin *secretarius* 'confidential officer', from Latin *secretum* 'secret', neuter of *secretus*.

36. John Manley, 'Excavations at Caergwrle Castle, Clwyd, North Wales: 1988–1990,' *Medieval Archaeology* 38 (1994): 86. '*David fillio Griffini, ad construendum castrum suum de Kaierguill, de dono Regis. Lxvj. li. xiij.s.iiij.d.*'
37. Ibid.
38. Arnold Taylor. *Studies in Castles and Castle-Building* (London: The Hambledon Press, 1985). 177 8. 'it would not be surprising if those works [Caergwrle] were under James's overall direction also.'
39. Marc Morris. *A Great and Terrible King* (London: Windmill Books, 2009). 175.
40. Madog was the son of Llywelyn ap Maerdudd, the one-time Lord of Meirionnydd who'd fought against Llywelyn ap Gruffydd at the battle of Bryn Derwin in 1256 and had been accordingly deprived of his patrimony.
41. John Peckham. 1884. Registrum epistolarum fratris Johannis Peckham, Archiepiscopi Cantuariensis Volume 2. (Cambridge: Cambridge University Press) Lists the following; Complaint of Lord David (445–7), Complaints of the Men of Ros (447–51), Complaint of Rys the Little of Estrad Tywy (451–2), Complaint of Llewellyn and Howel, Sons of Rys (452–3), Complaint of the Sons of Maredud son of Oweyn (453–4), Complaint of the Men of Ystradaluy (454–5), Complaint of the Men of Penliti (455–8), Complaint of Goronou Son of Heylyn (458–60), Complaint of the Men of Tregeayl (460–3)
42. Huw Pryce. The Acts of Welsh Rulers: 1120 to 1283 (Cardiff: University of Wales Press, 2005). 652.
43. CPR Edward I vol 1 1272–1281, 454.
44. Jean-Pierre Chapuisat, '*Au service de deux rois d'Angleterre au XIIIe siècle: Pierre de Champvent*,' *Revue historique vaudoise* 72 (1964): 168.

Chapter Eight
1. *The Chronicle of Lanercost*, 33. 'the Welsh nation, unable to pass their lives in peace, broke over their borders on Palm Sunday, carrying fire and sword among the people engaged in procession, and even laid siege [to some places – probably referring to Flint and Rhuddlan; whose Prince Llywelyn, deceived (more's the pity) by the advice of his brother David, fiercely attacked his lord the King; as we read written about Christ, 'him whom I loved most hath set himself against me."
2. John E. Morris. *The Welsh Wars of Edward I* (Oxford: Clarendon Press, 1901). 149–150.
3. Edward had been compared to a Leopard in the 1264 Song of Lewes. 'Whereunto shall the noble Edward be compared? Perhaps he will be rightly called a leopard. If we divide the name it becomes lion and pard … A lion by pride and fierceness, he is by inconstancy and changeableness a pard, changing his word and promise, cloaking himself by pleasant speech.'
4. J. Beverley Smith. *Llywellyn ap Gruffudd: Prince of Wales*. Ebook. ed. (Cardiff: The University of Wales Press, 2014). Chap. 9. Apple. 'it would seem … [there was] a single purpose and a coordinated plan'
5. Ibid.
6. Brut, 383 cited in J. G. Edwards, 'Edward I's Castle-Building in Wales,' *The Proceedings of the British Academy* XXXII (1944): 30.
7. TNA E101/3/29. '*ad castrum Regis ibidem construendum*'
8. Arnold Taylor. *Studies in Castles and Castle-Building* (London: The Hambledon Press, 1985). 19 A n2. Citing TNA C47/2/4 m 3. '*Magistro Egidio de Sancto Georgio Cementario pro vadiis suis … Per xx dies … .xx.s.*' Or 'Master Egidio [Giles of Saint-George the mason for his wages … For twenty days … Twenty shillings.' Egidio being the Italian name derived from Latin Aegidus, Gilles being its Old French form and Giles its modern English form.
9. David M. Browne. 'Builth and Aberystwyth Castle 1277 –1307' in *The Impact of the Edwardian Castles in Wales* (Oxford: Oxbow Books, 2010). 70.
10. AST, Inv. 69, fo. 5, mazzo 1, no. 9. '*Tassinus lathomus*' is recorded at Chillon in 1286/7 and Geneva in 1288, and archives de la Côte d'Or, Dijon, B.7083. '*Magister Tassinus*' at Treffort in 1291-2.
11. Arnold Taylor. *Studies in Castles and Castle-Building* (London: The Hambledon Press, 1985). 21-22. 'Master James of St George may easily have lived to be well over 70. Let us therefore assume instead that he was at least 80 in 1309 and 32 or more in 1261. If he married at the age of 25 this would then have been no later than 1254, so that a further step into the realms of controlled conjecture would give 1255 as a likely date for the birth of his eldest child. Supposing that child to have been Tassin, and Giles to have been two years younger, they would have been 25 and 23 respectively at Saxon in 1280, and Giles would have been 25 at Aberystwyth in 1282, not too young an age to have been a 'master' if he serviced his apprenticeship from age 15 or thereabouts, particularly with so distinguished a father. Thus it is not impossible – at present we can put it no higher – that the Master James of St George and Master Giles of St George who appear briefly together at Aberystwyth in the records of 1282 were father and son, like Master John and Master James at Yverdon in 1261; if so, Giles would in all likelihood have been apprenticed to his father during the busy castle building period at St Georges-d'Espéranche and elsewhere in the Viennois during the early 1270s.'

12. Ann. Cestrienses, 108-9. '*et castrum de Rothelan eodem die obsedit.*' Or 'and laid siege to the castle of Rhuddlan on the same day.'
13. John E. Morris. *The Welsh Wars of Edward I* (Oxford: Clarendon Press, 1901). 154. 'but the castles of Flint and Rhuddlan held out and were in connection with Chester by water.'
14. Ibid. 31
15. CWR 1277-1326, 212. 'that certain Welsh malefactors went by night to the castle of Hawardyn, with horses and arms ... and in addition their aiders went feloniously to the king's castle at Flynt and burned certain houses their as far as possible (ut potuerant) and slew certain of the king's men there.'
16. Would translate literally as Valet but perhaps manservant is better, from Old French *vaslet*, from *vassellittus*, diminutive of Late Latin *vassallus* ('manservant, domestic, retainer'), from *vassus* ('servant').
17. Catalogue of Ancient Correspondence concerning Wales, 201.
18. R. R. Davies. *The Age of Conquest: Wales 1063–1415* (Oxford: Oxford University Press, 1987). 348–9.
19. Michael Prestwich. *Edward I* (Yale: Yale University Press, 1997). 232. 'It was after the first Welsh war that he [Edward] made political errors. To have driven two men who had been such bitter rivals as Llywelyn and Dafydd into the same camp was remarkably inept.'
20. Ibid. 183. 'He [Llywelyn], more than anyone else, was capable of organizing nationwide resistance to the English, and it is hard to imagine that he was merely drawn into the rebellion at the last minute.'
21. Chron. Guisborough, 9. '*et sic Herodis et Pilati inita concordia et facta conjuratione valida insurrexerunt*'
22. Ann. Cestrienses, 108-9. '*de consilio fratris sui Lewelini*' or 'with the counsel of his brother Llywelyn.'
23. Reginald de Grey had long experience in English law, he'd been Sheriff of Nottinghamshire, Derbyshire and the Royal Forests and a Constable of Chester Castle, a Constable of Nottingham Castle (1265/6) and Constable of Northampton Castle (1267–1268). He was Justice of Chester in 1270 and Sheriff of Chester (1270–4).
24. CPR. Edward I vol 1 1272–1281, 464
25. J. Beverley Smith. *Llywellyn ap Gruffudd: Prince of Wales*. Ebook. ed. (Cardiff: The University of Wales Press, 2014). Chap. 9. Apple.
26. Michael Prestwich, 'Document: Edward I's Wars in the Hagnaby Chronicle,' *Journal of Medieval Military History* X (2002): 199. and for full Latin text 206–7.
27. Ann. Cestrienses, 110. '*Stirps mendax, causa malorum.*' Or 'From a lying race, a cause of all evils.'
28. John E. Morris. *The Welsh Wars of Edward I* (Oxford: Clarendon Press, 1901). 156.
29. Arnold Taylor. *Studies in Castles and Castle-Building* (London: The Hambledon Press, 1985). 49.n4. '*Die Iovis vij Maii, Waltero de Bello Campo, eunti In municionem Montis Gomerii cum domino Otone de Grandisono capitaneo eiusdem municionis.*' Or 'Thursday, the seventh of May, Walter de Beauchamp, going to the fortification of Montgomery and Lord Othon de Grandson as the captain of the same fortification.'
30. John E. Morris. *The Welsh Wars of Edward I* (Oxford: Clarendon Press, 1901). 156.
31. Ibid. 45.
32. Ann. Cestrienses, 108. '*et castrum de Rothelan eodem die obsedit.*' Or 'and laid siege to the castle of Rhuddlan on the same day.'
33. Michael Prestwich. *Edward I* (Yale: Yale University Press, 1997). 182. 'Llywelyn ap Gruffydd himself was not slow to join in what was rapidly becoming a nationwide rebellion and took part in attacks on Flint and Rhuddlan.' Citing The Welsh Assize Roll, 1277–1284, ed. J. Conway Davies (Cardiff, 1940), 352.
34. Arnold Taylor. *The Welsh Castles of King Edward I* (London: The Hambledon Press, 1986). 31. n1. Citing TNA SC1/24/94. The letter quoted is from John Wyall of 9 May testifying to have served under Amédée de Savoie.
35. Arnold Taylor. *Studies in Castles and Castle-Building* (London: The Hambledon Press. 1985). 49. n4. '*Die mercurii viiij April, domino Amadeo de Sabaudia Capitaneo municionis Cestrie cum viij equis coopertis percipienti per diet ix.s. pro vadiis suis per idem tempus, x. Li.vij.s*' Or 'On Wednesday 8 April, the Lord Captain Amédée de Savoie at Chester and eight horses covered securing by day nine shillings, for the wages of men by the same time, Ten *livres*, seven shillings.'
36. Thomas III de Piedmont had felt aggrieved at being previously passed over as count in favour of his uncles, Pierre and then Philippe. Jean I, the Dauphin had died falling from a horse and as Humbert I the new Dauphin coming to power by marriage of Jean's sister Anne to Humbert, Baron of La Tour de Pin, had brought more land to the Dauphine then Thomas III had seen an opportunity to settle old scores with the Dauphine. He had been making war on the Dauphin for land in the Manche de Coligny when he died near La Côte-Saint-André. Thomas and Amédée's younger brother, Louis, had written to King Edward from Savoy begging leave for his brother to return. Count Philippe had previously delegated Piedmont to Thomas.
37. CPR Edward I vol 2 (1281–1292), 30. Amédée was granted two years protection to travel 'beyond seas' on 14 July at Rhuddlan. Arnold Taylor. *Studies in Castles and Castle-Building* (London: The Hambledon Press, 1985). 46-7.

38. CWR 1277–1326, 234.
39. J. Beverley Smith. *Llywellyn ap Gruffudd: Prince of Wales*. Ebook. ed. (Cardiff: The University of Wales Press, 2014). Apple.
40. Ann. Cestrienses, 108. '*David filius Griffini pacis perturbator efectus est, de consilio fratris Lewlini principis Wallie.*'
41. Following the deaths of Llywelyn and Dafydd the fate of their children was firstly that little Gwenllian, daughter of Llywelyn and Eleanor de Montfort, was placed in the Priory at Sempringham in Lincolnshire, where she remained until her death in 1337. As for the children of Dafydd, his daughter, Gwladys was also sent to a religious house in Lincolnshire, the convent at Sixhills, where she also spent the remainder of her life. Of the sons of Dafydd ap Gruffydd, Llywelyn ap Dafydd was arrested and taken to Rhuddlan to be imprisoned alongside his brother, Owain ap Dafydd. A force of cavalry and infantry were deployed to escort Llywelyn and Owain out of Gwynedd to Bristol before the end of July 1283. Llywelyn ap Dafydd died at Bristol Castle in 1287 and was buried in the nearby Dominican church (now known as Quakers Friars). His burial was paid for by Edward. His brother Owain would remain a prisoner until the end of his life, he was reportedly still alive in 1325, the last male heir of the House of Gwynedd.
42. The thousand marks being made available by 'Bonruncinus Walterii and his fellows, merchants of Lucca of the society of the Riccardi.' Prestwich writes that 'the Riccardi received little by way of financial reward' for their loans to Edward, given the churches prohibition on usury, which is in and of itself quite remarkable. The answer as to why, lays in the access crown patronage gave them to English markets. such as using the King's Exchequer Courts to pursue their debtors and special access to the English wool market. During the period where they were bankers to the English Crown, the Riccardi were involved in around half of all the forward contracts with English wool-producers. See Michael Prestwich. 1997. *Edward I* (Yale: Yale University Press). 241.
43. CWR 1277–1326, 215–6.
44. Ibid. 230–1.
45. Ibid. 217.
46. Michael Prestwich. *Edward I* (Yale: Yale University Press, 1997). 240..
47. Richard W. Kaeuper. *Bankers to the Crown: The Riccardi of Lucca and Edward I* (Princeton: Princeton University Press, 1973). 185, 187.
48. Ann. Cestrienses, 108. '*fixit tentoriam apud Neuton*' Or 'pitching his tent at Newton.'
49. Ibid. '*Vigilia Sancti Petri ad Vincula venit Eadmundus frater Regis cum uxore sua Regina Navere apud Cestriam versus regem.*'
50. Ibid. '*In octavis Apostolorum Petri et Pauli castra metatus est cum exercitu suo apud Flint et munivit Castellum.*'
51. Ibid. '*Die Jovis proxime post octavus apostolorum venerunt rex et regina cum exercitu suo apud Rothelan.*'
52. John Manley, 'Excavations at Caergwrle Castle, Clwyd, North Wales: 1988 – 1990,' *Medieval Archaeology* 38 (1994): 126.
53. Arnold Taylor. *The Welsh Castles of King Edward I* (London: The Hambledon Press, 1986). 39. n7. '*Heyn de Thoruy [sc cementario] prosternenti turrim de Hope ad tascham. Xij.d., Magistro Jacobo precipiente*' Or 'To Henry de Thoruy [namely a mason] for knocking down the tower of Hope, Seven pence, Maître Jacques ordering.'
54. John Manley, 'Excavations at Caergwrle Castle, Clwyd, North Wales: 1988–199,' *Medieval Archaeology* 38 (1994): 88.
55. Arnold Taylor. *The Welsh Castles of King Edward I* (London: The Hambledon Press, 1986). 39. '*cuidam operario qui cecidit de alta Turri de Hop' et fuit Iesus, ex dono Regis Xij.d., domino J de Monte Alto precipiente.*' Or 'certain workers who fell from the high tower at Hope' and it was of Jesus, the gift of the King twelve pence. The Lord Jean de Mahout ordering.'
56. Ibid. '*cuidam operario qui cecidit de alta Turri de Hop' et fuit Iesus, ex dono Regis Xij.d., domino J de Monte Alto precipiente.*' Or 'The account gives details of the many items provided for the works, such as 'clays' for scaffolds, lime for making mortar and two sieves for mixing it, a pair of scales, locks for the entrance gate and hinges for the little gate.'
57. John E. Morris. *The Welsh Wars of Edward I* (Oxford: Clarendon Press, 1901). 161.
58. TNA E101/3/16. '*eunti apud Ruffyn super constructione castri de Ruffin.*'
59. Arnold Taylor. 1986. *The Welsh Castles of King Edward I*. London: The Hambledon Press. 39. It's likely that James left ongoing works at Caergwrle in the care of Ralf of Nottingham, and a Savoyard who'd worked under a James at Flint, John Pycard. Ibid. n8. The first four weeks of Ralf's wages are authorized '*per preceptum Magistri Jacobi.*' By the order of Maître Jacques.
60. TNA E101/3/29. '*Et Magistro Jacobo Machinatori pro Clays' empt' apud Ruffyn, v.d.*' Or 'And Maître Jacques Engineer for clays at Ruthun, five pence.'
61. CWR 1277–1326, 243. 'The castle of Ruthin and the *cantref of Defferencloyt.*'
62. Ibid. 240. 'The castle of Dynasbran'

63. L. A. S. Butler. *Denbigh Castle* (Cardiff: Cadw, 2007) .6. 'Whatever the nature of the defences at Denbigh, they were strong enough to withstand a month's siege by the English in the autumn of 1282.'

64. CWR 1277–1326, 241. 'Notification that the king has granted by this charter to Henry de Lacy, Earl of Lincoln, the cantreds of Ros and Roewynnock [Rhufoniog and the commote of Dynmael [Denbigh].'

65. L. A. S. Butler. *Denbigh Castle* (Cardiff: Cadw, 2007). 7. 'The presence of the king's master mason and chief building organizer, James of St George may well indicate the king's close involvement in the siting of the castle and the plan adopted for it.'

66. John E. Morris. *The Welsh Wars of Edward I* (Oxford: Clarendon Press, 1901). 166.

67. Archbishop John Peckham had come the see of Canterbury on 25 January 1279. He was a native of Sussex who was educated at Lewes Priory, as a Franciscan he studied at the University of Paris under Bonaventure, where he would later teach theology. Whilst in Paris his Franciscan theology came up against, amongst others, the great theologian Thomas Aquinas. In around 1270, Peckham had returned to England, where he had taught at the University of Oxford.

68. J. Beverley Smith. *Llywellyn ap Gruffudd: Prince of Wales*. Ebook. ed. (Cardiff: The University of Wales Press, 2014). Chap. 10. Apple.

69. John Peckham. 1884. Registrum epistolarum fratris Johannis Peckham, Archiepiscopi Cantuariensis: Volume 2. Cambridge: Cambridge University Press.469. '*Responsiones Walensium. Primo, quod licet dominus rex de Quatuor Cantredis et aliis terris ab eo datis magnatibus suis ac de insula Engleseye, nullum voluerit habere tractatum, tamen consilium principis non permittit, si contingat aliquam pacem fieri quin tractetur de praemissis eo quod isti cantredi sunt de puro principis tenemento in quibus merum ius habuerunt principes et praedecessores sui a temporibus Kambri filii Bruti; tum quia sunt de principatu, cuius confirmationem princeps obtinet per bone memoriae Ottobonum sedis apostolice legatum in regno Anglie, consensu domini regis et sui patris ad hoc interveniente, sicut patet cartas eorum inspicienti; tum quia etiam equius est quod veri heredes teneant dictos cantredos de domino rege pro pecunia et serviitiis consuetis, quam eos dari extraneis et advenis , qui etsi fuerunt regis aliquando, tamen per vim et potentiam.*' Or 'Welsh Responses. First, although the king has not wished to the four cantrefi and the other lands given by him to his magnates, and the island of Anglesey, the prince's council does not permit any discussion of these should peace be made, since those cantrefi belong solely to the prince, and the princes predecessors from the time of Cymryw Camber, the son of Brutus have had the sole right to them because they belong to the principality whose confirmation the prince obtained from the papal legate Ottobuono with the consent of the king and his father, as their charters show, and because it is fairer that the true heirs hold the said cantrefi from the king for the accustomed money and services than for them to be given to strangers and newcomers; true, the lands were held for a time by the king, but only by force.' And '*Item, idem princeps non tenetur dimittere hereditatem suam et progenitorum suorum in Wallia a tempore Bruti, et etiam sibi confirmatam per Romane sedis legatum, ut dictum est, et terram in Anglia receptare, unde linguam, mores, leges ac consuetudines ignorat; ubi possent etiam sibi quaedam maliciouse imponi ex odio inveterato a vicinis Anglicis, quibus terra illa privaretur imperpetuum.*' Or 'Also, the prince is not obliged to abandon his inheritance and that of his ancestors in Wales since the time of Brutus, and confirmed to him by the papal legate, and receive land in England, where he is ignorant of the language, manners and laws and customs and where certain things could be maliciously imposed upon him by the inveterate hatred of the neighbouring English who would be deprived of that land forever.' '*Item, populus Snaudon' dicit quod licet princeps vellet dare regi seysinam eorundem, ipsi tamen nollent homagium faceri alicui extraneo, cujus linguam, mores, legesque penitus ignorant. Quia sic posset contingere eos imperpetuum captivari, ac crudeliter tractari, sicut alii cantredi circumquaque per ballivos regis ac alios regales alias tractati fuerunt, crudelius quan Saraceni, pront patet in rotulis quos vobis miserunt, sancte pater.*'Or 'Also, the people of Snowdonia say that, even if the prince wished to give possession of them to the King, they do not wish to do homage to a stranger, of whose language, manners and laws they are entirely ignorant, since they could be captured and treated cruelly, just as the other cantrefi everywhere were treated more cruelly than the Saracens by the king's bailiffs and other royal officers as it is clear from the rolls they have sent to the archbishop.'

70. Geoffrey of Monmouth. *The History of the Kings of Britain* (London: Penguin Books Ltd. 1966). 15 'from Brutus the first King of the Britons' And 40 'Brutus had ... three famous sons whose names were Locrin, Albanact and Kamber ... Kamber had that part which now lies beyond the River Severn, now called Wales.' See n646 for their references to Monmouth's legendary kings.

71. CWR 1277–1326, 275. 'to put an end finally to the matter that he has now commenced of putting down the malice of the Welsh, as Llywelyn son of Griffith and other Welshmen, his accomplices, have so many times disturbed the peace of the realm in the king's time and in the time of his progenitors, and they persist in their resumed rebellion.'

72. Ibid. 235. '18 August 1282, Rhuddlan. To the king's barons and the subjects of the Cinque Ports in his garrison in Anglesey. Writ of aid in favour of Luke de Tany whom the king is sending in garrison and defence of those parts and to provide and make a bridge there and order to cause him to have cords and anchors necessary for the construction of the bridge as he shall direct.'

73. Rick Turner. 'The Life and Career of Richard the Engineer' in *The Impact of the Edwardian Castles in Wales* (Oxford: Oxbow Books, 2010). 49. '*Master Bertram et R socio suo*' Or 'Master Bertram and Richard his companion.'

74. Ibid.

75. Michael Prestwich, 'Document: Edward I's Wars in the Hagnaby Chronicle,' *Journal of Medieval Military History* X (2002): 200. n13.

76. The encounter has become known as the Battle of Moel-y-Don, suggesting a site opposite Moel-y-Don, Anglesey. However, this site does not fit the description very well and originated in a ferry crossing, recent examination has suggested a site farther north nearer to Llanfaes, Edward's Anglesey work-camp. This would mean either a mainland site at Traeth Lafan or Abergwyngregyn.

77. John E. Morris. *The Welsh Wars of Edward I* (Oxford: Clarendon Press, 1901). 179-80. For an alternative translation J. Beverley Smith. *Llywellyn ap Gruffudd: Prince of Wales*. Ebook. ed. (Cardiff: The University of Wales Press, 2014). Chap. 10. Apple. 'When they had reached the foot of the mountain and, after a time, came to a place at some distance from the bridge, the tide came in with a great flow, so that they were unable to get back to the bridge for the debt of water. The Welsh came from the high mountains and attacked them, and in fear and trepidation, for the great number of the enemy, our men preferred to face the sea than the enemy. They went into the sea but, heavily laden with arms, they were instantly drowned.'

78. Brut, Peniarth MS20, Jones 120 & 228, cited *The Inventory of Historic Battlefields in Wales* at http://battlefields.rcahmw.gov.uk/collections/getrecord/404319 retrieved 6 November 2018. '*Ac a vanassant goresgin arvon ac ena y gwanaeth pwyd y bont ar venei ac y torres y bont o tra llwith ac y bodes aneirif or season ac ereill a las.*'

79. Ann. Cestrienses, 110–12. Has a full list of the knights who perished – Dominus Willelmus de Audethleye, Dominus Lucas de Taneiey, Dominus Ricardus de Wellis, Amari Burdet, Petrus de Lamare, Ph. Burnell, Willelmus Burnell, Henricus Tyeis, Howelus fil. Griffini, Roger de Clifford Junior, Willelmus de Lindeseye, Willelmus le Butiler, Thomas de Halton, Willelmus de Oudingishelys, Petrus de la Quarere and Walterus le Jaie.

80. Michael Prestwich. 'Document: Edward I's Wars in the Hagnaby Chronicle' *Journal of Medieval Military History* X (2002): 200.

81. Othon de Grandson would later command the English knights at Acre, surviving its siege and fall in 1291.

82. Ann. Cestrienses, 112. '*Cum magna difficultate evasit dominus Otto de Graunson.*' Or 'with much difficulty Lord Othon de Grandson escaped.'

83. *The Lanercost Chronicle*, 38. 'During that war in Wales a bridge of boats was made in the place called Menai, that is, between Snowdon and Anglesey, where Sir William de Audley, Lucas Tanay and Roger de Clifford and many others, old and young were drowned.

84. Chron. Thomas Wykes, 290.

85. John Peckham. 1884. Registrum epistolarum fratris Johannis Peckham, Archiepiscopi Cantuariensis: Volume 2. Cambridge: Cambridge University Press. 474. '*Qualiter demum Brutus, Dianæ praesagiis, non sine diaboli praestigiis per idoloatriam immolate cervæ venatitiæ obtentis, insulam Brittanicam pervaserit, per famosas historias declarator*' Or 'In what way did Brutus, after Dianæ's foretelling, and not without the tricks of the devil by the idolatrous sacrifice of a hunted doe, obtained entry to the British island, by the famous stories you proclaimed.'

86. J. Beverley Smith. *Llywellyn ap Gruffudd: Prince of Wales*. Ebook. ed. (Cardiff: The University of Wales Press, 2014). Apple. The chronicler Wykes certainly thought so, Chron, Wykes. 290. '*in Lewelinum ut puta prævaricatorem et perjurum et David fratrem ejus et omnes eorum complices et fau tores excommunicationis sententiam fulminavit.*' Or 'in Llewelyn, as, for instance, a transgressor and a perjurer, and his brother Dafydd, and all their accomplices and supporters, he [the archbishop] struck down the sentence of excommunication.'

87. 'In addition you strike against the king, saying that the royal churches and church people are cruelly ravaged and killed by tyranny, to which we reply that the lord king was attacked by evils not that he made then, certainly neither has he considered making them; conversely he has voluntarily offered to us, of which I will urge him on when opportune, he intends to repair the churches at his own cost, though he puts this off until he can forever calm this period of warfare, as if he did this earlier they might again be destroyed by brigands.'

88. CWR 1277-1326, 259. 'To all the king's bailiffs and faithful subjects of the counties of Nottingham and Derby to … choose 300 footmen and to bring them to the king … The like in co. Lancaster …

200 footmen … The like in co. Hereford … 200 men … The like in cos … Staffordshire and Salop … 1,000 footmen.'

89. Dr. Adam Chapman. 'Irfon Bridge 1282' *The Inventory of Historic Battlefields in Wales*. Last modified Jan 2017. http://battlefields.rcahmw.gov.uk/wp-content/uploads/2017/02/Irfon-Bridge-1282-Chapman-2013.pdf

90. Chron, Guisborough, 12-3. '*Cumque videretur a quodam ex nostris, Stephano scilicet de Franketone … Revertentibus ergo nostris obtenta victoria, praedictus Stephanus perrexit ut videret quinam essent illi duo quos percusserat, et visa facie Leulini et cognita, amputaverunt caput suum, et ad regem nostrum cum gaudio detulerunt.*' Or 'And when he was seen by one of our men, namely Stephen of Franketone … then, as our men were returning to battle, Stephen went to see who the two men were whom he had wounded, and when the face of Llywelyn had been seen and recognized, they cut off his head.'

91. John E. Morris. *The Welsh Wars of Edward I* (Oxford: Clarendon Press, 1901). 184.

92. Michael Prestwich, 'Document: Edward I's Wars in the Hagnaby Chronicle,' *Journal of Medieval Military History* X (2002): 200.

93. Arnold Taylor. *Studies in Castles and Castle-Building* (London: The Hambledon Press, 1985). 229-231 n2. Citing BNF MS. Lat . 8567, fo.3er '*ille serpens antiquus, prodiciionis pater, rebellionis alumpnus, iniquitatis filius, sedicionis inuentor, ingratitudinis fautor, periurij reus et caput omnis mailicie quondam Princeps Wallie Lewolinus.*' Or 'that the old serpent Llywelyn the one-time Prince of Wales, father of treachery, child of rebellion, son of iniquity, author of sedition, patron of ingratitude, convict of perjury and head of all evil.'

94. John E. Morris. *The Welsh Wars of Edward I* (Oxford: Clarendon Press, 1901). 188.

95. Henry Gough. Itinerary of King Edward the First throughout his reign, A.D. 1272–1307, exhibiting his movements so far as they are recorded. vol 1. (Paisley: Alexander Gardner, 1900). Edward and his army left Rhuddlan on 13 January, by the 14 they were at Llanrwst, following the siege of Dolywyddelan, Edward was back at Rhuddlan 27 January.

96. Richard Avent. *Dolywyddelan Castle Dolbadarn Castle Castell y Bere*. 2010 ed. (Cardiff: Cadw, 2004). 25.

97. TNA E101/351/9 para 38. '*die Lune*'.

98. Arnold Taylor. *The Welsh Castles of King Edward I* (London: The Hambledon Press, 1986). 44. n2.

99. TNA E101/351/9. '*Pro calibis empto per manus Magistri Jacobi Ingeniatoris ad municionem dicti Castri. iiij.s.*' (*sc. de Doluidaleyn*). Or 'The steel purchased by the hand of Maître Jacques the Engineer to fortify said castle. [of Dolwyddelan] Four shillings.'

100. TNA E101/351/9 m5. '*Et pro stipendiis v. hakeneirum deferentium calibem de Cestr' usque Rothelan pro municione dicti castri de Doluidaleyn per diem Martis ix. diem Februarii … Et Magistro Bertramo Ingeniatori pro stipendiis quorumdam hominum portantium meremium et palic' de castro Rothelan usque ad aquam carianda versus Angles' per ij. Dies. v. s.*'

101. Arnold Taylor. *The Welsh Castles of King Edward I* (London: The Hambledon Press, 1986). 44.

102. Richard Avent. *Dolywyddelan Castle Dolbadarn Castle Castell y Bere*. 2010 ed. (Cardiff: Cadw, 2004). 28.

103. Arnold Taylor. *The Welsh Castles of King Edward I* (London: The Hambledon Press, 1986). 44.

104. Henry Gough. *Itinerary of King Edward the First throughout his reign, A.D. 1272–1307, exhibiting his movements so far as they are recorded.* vol. 1 (Paisley: Alexander Gardner.1900). 140-1.

105. Marc Morris. 2009. *A Great and Terrible King.* London: Windmill Books. 188.

106. C. R. Peers. 'Harlech Castle.' *Transactions of the Honourable Society of Cymmrodorion* (1921–2): 64. 'Edward sent an army under Otto de Grandison and John de Vescy to match along the coast through Caernarvon to Harlech, keeping up communications by sea.'

107. Arnold Taylor. *The Welsh Castles of King Edward I* (London: The Hambledon Press, 1986). 75.

108. Richard Avent. *Dolywyddelan Castle Dolbadarn Castle Castell y Bere*. 2010 ed. (Cardiff: Cadw, 2004). 37–40.

109. TNA E101/351/9. '*Magistro Bertramo Ingeniatore apud castrum de Bere pro ingeniis ibidem faciendis*' Or 'In the same place, at Castell y Bere, for engines made by Master Bertram.'

110. Guillaume de Valence and Roger L'Estrange offered terms on 22 April 1282. £80 to be given for its surrender, TNA C47/2/4. records a payment so made of £53, 6s and 8d.

111. John E. Morris. *The Welsh Wars of Edward I* (Oxford: Clarendon Press, 1901). 193.

112. TNA C47/2/4. '*pacatum domino Othon de Grandisono ad sustentacionem D et lx peditum secum euncium de Castro de Bere usque Hardelach xx.li per talliam.*' Or 'Given for pacifying, to Lord Othon de Grandson, for the support of five hundred and sixty of men going with him from Castell y Bere to Harlech, Twenty pounds by tally.'

113. TNA E101/4/1.

114. John E. Morris. *The Welsh Wars of Edward I* (Oxford: Clarendon Press, 1901). 191. Caernarfon took its very name from the Roman settlement there, *Y gaer yn Afon* meaning the 'the stronghold in the land over against Mon', *Mon* being the Welsh word for Anglesey. The precise date of the taking

of Caernarfon is not possible, the closest we can get is on or before 1 April 1283. This date comes from TNA E101/4/1 where Hugh of Leominster is accounting for knights and squires being paid to '*municione de Kaernarvon*' for the period 1 April to 11 June 1283. The dates for Bangor and Criccieth may well imply a date between 3 January and 14 March.

115. Arnold Taylor. *The Welsh Castles of King Edward I* (London: The Hambledon Press, 1986). 80. By the middle of July the next year, 1284, houses were being demolished to make way for the new castle under construction. '*portantibus meremium de domibus prius factis de Carnarnan et prostratis pro fossat' ville ibidem faciend.*' Or 'carrying timber from the existing demolished houses at Caernarfon for making a ditch in the same place.'
116. Ibid. 73. Taylor held the view that Criccieth 'may' have been captured by a detachment from the King's army at Dolywyddelan.
117. Richard Avent. *Criccieth Castle.* Cardiff: Cadw (1989). 4. 'There are no surviving records relating to the capture of the castle [Criccieth], but it was in English hands by 14 March, from which date Henry of Greenford received wages as its constable.'
118. Chron. Langtoft, 180-1. '*Vynt Jon de Vescy … Of Pitayle saunz noumbre de Baskles e Gascons … En mores e mountaynes raumpent cum lyouns. S'en vount of les Engleys, ardent les mesouns, Abatent les chastels, tuent les felouns, Passez sunt le Marche, entrez en Snaudouns.*' Or 'Comes Jean de Vesci … with footmen without number of Basques and Gascons … In moors and mountains they clamber like lions. They go with the English, burn the houses, Throw down the castles, slay the wretches. They have passed the Marches and entered into Snowdon.' Langtoft writing of the 'Basques and Gascons' under Vesci and Grandson. Langtoft's use of the plural '*les chastels*' would seem to suggest the army was involved at both Criccieth and Castel y Bere thus confirming the route suggested by John E. Morris. *The Welsh Wars of Edward I* (Oxford: Clarendon Press, 1901). 191. 'Grandison and Vescy spread out their division westwards from Bangor to Carnarvon and soon penetrated to Harlech.'
119. TNA C47/2/4 see above note 680.
120. The key role of Othon de Grandson in building the Welsh castles had been highlighted by Maxime Reymond, '*Le Chevalier Othon I de Grandson,*' *Revue historique vaudoise* 28 (1920): 164. '*Le pays conquis, Othon fut chargé d'en administrer la partie nord et d'y construire des forteresses sûres: il avait appris de Pierre de Savoie, comme aussi pendant son séjour en Terre Sainte, la manière de les édifier.*' Or 'The country conquered, Othon was responsible for administering the northern part of it, and building there, secure fortresses: he had learned from Peter of Savoy, as also during his stay in the Holy Land, how to build them.'
121. Michael Prestwich. '*Othon de Grandson et la Cour d'Edouard I*' in *Othon I de Grandson* (vers 1240–1328) (Lausanne: Cahiers Lausannois d'Histoire Médiévale, 2020). 12. But we should remember Edward's earlier words of Grandson in a different context, but still relevant CCR. *Edward I* vol 1 1272–1279. 493. 'March 21, Down Ampney. To R.[Robert Burnell] Bishop of Bath and Wells, the chancellor, and to Othon de Grandisono. The king commends the care and solicitude exhibited by them in his affairs in the court of France … especially as the king has no one about him whom he believes could know the premises and do his will in the premises better and more advantageously than them, not even if he himself were to attend to the matters there in person.' Given the difficulty in the King visiting both Caernarfon and Harlech whilst the war was still ongoing, it is not difficult to imagine him assigning the task of 'scoping' the future castle sites to Grandson and Vesci.
122. Henry Gough. *Itinerary of King Edward the First throughout his reign, A.D. 1272–1307, exhibiting his movements so far as they are recorded.* vol. 1 (Paisley: Alexander Gardner. 1900). 140–1. Edward was at Aberconwy from 14 March until 10 May and from 4 June until 16 June. In the intervening period he had journeyed down the Conwy to Llanrwst and Dolywyddelan once more, and briefly on to Cymer Abbey
123. Malcolm Hislop. *James of St George and the Castles of North Wales* (Barnsley: Pen & Sword Books Ltd, 2020). 3. 'There were … numerous members of his [Edward's] noble entourage who had their personal experience of castles, including the military advantages and drawbacks of particular aspects; there would be no shortage of opinions and advice to draw upon.' The Savoyard design input into the Edwardian castles owed no small debt to Othon de Grandson, Jean de Bonvillars and Guillaume de Cicon.
124. *Littere Wallie.* J. G. Edwards. Ed. (Cardiff. University Press, 1940). 75–7. Dafydd held Dolbadarn until at least 2 May 1283 as evidenced by despatched he sent from there styled '*Princeps Wallie et dominus Snoudonie.*'
125. John E. Morris. *The Welsh Wars of Edward I* (Oxford: Clarendon Press, 1901). 194–5.
126. CWR 1277–1326, 281.
127. Ibid. 282.
128. It's recorded that the executioner of Dafydd ap Gruffydd, Geoffrey of Shrewsbury, was paid the grand sum of one pound for carrying out the sentence of death.

129. *The Lanercost Chronicle*, 35. '*David Walensis, epuos, ignis, funis, et ensis, Infelix, fatum tibi dant recis et cruciatum. Es nece – fur, proditor, ac homicida, Hostis et ecclesiae debes de jure perire.*'

130. Ann. Dunstable, 294. '*Quia illud fecit tempore Dominicæ Passionis*'

131. Katherine Royer, 'The Body in Parts: Reading the Execution Ritual in Late Medieval England,' *Historical Reflections/Réflexions Historiques* 29 (2003): 327.

132. *The Lanercost Chronicle*, 35.

133. Ann. Dunstable, 294. '*Caput autem ejus in Turri Londoniæ super palum altissimam est affixum.*'

134. Michael Prestwich. *Edward I* (Yale: Yale University Press, 1997) .203. 'the Londoners carried off the head in triumph, but the citizens of York and Manchester disputed possession of the right shoulder. The men of Lincoln refused to accept any part, and as a result incurred royal displeasure, only remitted once a substantial fine had been paid.'

135. Carl Von Clausewitz. *On War* (London: Penguin Books, 1968). 182.

136. Michael Prestwich. *Edward I* (Yale: Yale University Press, 1997). 231. 'Neither Edward, nor his greatest Welsh adversary, Llywelyn ap Gruffydd, displayed any sympathy for, or understanding of, each other's position.'

137. David Carpenter. *The Struggle for Mastery: Britain 1066–1284* (London: Penguin Books Ltd, 2004). 514.

138. For a reappraisal of Powys in the thirteenth century see Robert Stephenson, 'Re-thinking Thirteenth Century Powys.'

139. Ann. Cestrienses, 110–1. '*Walensis sic:- Hic jacet Anglorum Tortor, tutpr Wenidorum. Princeps Wallorum Lewelinus, regula morum Gemma tornorum, Flos regum preteritorum Forma futurorum Dux, lans, lex, lux populorum. Anglicus respondit sic:- Hic jacet errorum Princeps et pedo virorum Proditor Anglorum Fax livida, secta reorum, Numen Wallorum Crux dux homicida piorum Fex trojanorum Stirps mendax, causa malorum.*'

140. '*Tornorum*' is taken by the translator to be '*Coævorum*' – and so '*Gemma Tornorum*' becomes '*Gemma Coævorum*' – the jewel of all of his age, that is of his contemporaries.

Chapter Nine

1. *Flores Historiarum*, 59. '*Apud Kaernervan, corpus Maximi principis, patris imperatoris nobilis Constantini, erat inventum, et rege jubenete in ecclesia honorifice collocatum.*' Or 'In Caernarfon, the body of Prince Maximi, his father the noble Constantine, was found, and the King was honourably enshrined in the Church.'

2. Magnus Maximus was the son of a Roman general, Flavius Julius Eucherius.

3. The last dateable evidence we have of Roman occupation of Wales and Deva (Chester) is from 383, the year Maximus began his bid for power.

4. Charles Kightly. *Chieftains and Princes: A Power in the Land of Wales* (Cardiff: Cadw, 1994). 13.

5. *The Mabinogion*. (London: Penguin Books Ltd.1976). 127–9. 'The ruler Maxen Wledig was emperor of Rome, and he was handsomer and wiser and better suited to be emperor than any of his predecessors … In his sleep Maxen had a dream. He saw himself travelling to the end of the valley and reaching the highest mountain in the world – it seemed as high as the sky – and having crossed this mountain he saw himself journeying through the flattest and loveliest land anyone had ever seen. Great broad rivers flowed from the mountain to the sea, and he made along these rivers to their outlets, and though his journey was long he finally reached the mouth of the greatest river anyone had seen … and the ship set out across the sea until it came to the loveliest island in the world. When he had crossed this island from one sea to the other, to the very farthest reaches, he saw steep slopes and high crags and a harsh rough land the like he had never seen, and beyond it in an island in the sea … and at the mouth of the river stood a great fortress's the handsomest ever. The gate was open and he entered. Inside Maxen saw a fine hall: its roof seemed all of gold, its sides of luminous stones all equally precious, it's doors all of gold … This tale is called the Dream of the Ruler Maxen, and this is its end.'

6. Ibid. 67-84. 'Bran the Blessed son of Llŷr, was the crowned king of this island … One afternoon he was at a court of his at Harddlech in Ardudwy; he was sitting on the rock of Harddlech overlooking the sea … for I will give you a cauldron the property of which is this: take a man who has been slain today and throw him into it, and tomorrow he will fight as ever, only he will not be able to speak … Bran commanded them to cut off his head … you will spend seven years feasting at Harddlech, with the Birds of Rhiannon singing to you.'

7. Sara Cockerill. 2014. *Eleanor of Castile: The Shadow Queen*. Second Edition ed. Stroud: Amberley Publishing. 302–3.

8. Henry Gough. *Itinerary of King Edward the First throughout his reign, A.D. 1272-1307, exhibiting his movements so far as they are recorded*. vol. 1 (Paisley: Alexander Gardner.1900). 141.

9. Arnold Taylor. *Studies in Castles and Castle-Building* (London: The Hambledon Press, 1985). 116. Citing TNA SC/13/152. 'Edward, by the grace of God King of England, Lord of Ireland and Duke

of Aquitaine, to his beloved clerk William de Perton, greeting. We command you to cause to be bought diverse tools and other necessaries, as our beloved Richard the Engineer will tell you for making ditches at Aberconwy. You are also to cause to come to Conwy masons and quarry-breakers, as the same Richard will tell you. You are in no wise to omit these matters. Given under our privy seal at Aberconwy, the 30 day of March in the 11th year of our reign.'

10. Arnold Taylor. *Studies in Castles and Castle-Building* (London: The Hambledon Press, 1985). 116. Citing TNA SC/13/152. 'We command and firmly enjoin you to be intendent and helpful to our beloved Richard the Engineer, the bearer of these present letters, in providing us with smiths and other workmen as the same Richard will tell you on our behalf. We also command you to aid the same Richard with cartage for carrying materials and things needed for our works at Aberconwy, as the same Richard will tell you on our behalf. And, as you love us and our well-being, you are in no wise to overlook this.'

11. Ibid. 116.

12. Rick Turner. 'The Life and Career of Richard the Engineer' in *The Impact of the Edwardian Castles in Wales* (Oxford: Oxbow Books, 2010). 49. 'During the early years of the construction of Caernarfon Castle and town walls, beginning in the summer of 1283, Richard acted as Master James of St George's second-in-command.'

13. Ibid. 46.

14. TNA C47/35/11. '*Pro cariagio Pele et maeremii, que provisa fuerunt ad claudendum villam Rothelane, ut ea cariare possit usque Carnarum prout ei iniunximus.*' Or 'For carriage of stakes and scaffolding, that were planned for enclosing the town of Rhuddlan, so as to carry them to Caernarfon in case we need to attach them there.'

15. TNA E101/351/9.

16. Arnold Taylor, 'Some notes on the Savoyards in North Wales, 1277–1300. With special reference to the Savoyard element in the construction of Harlech Castle,' *Genava* XI (1963): 300. '*Stephano pictori depingenti cameram Regis, et pro coloribus emptis per ipsum et pro stipendiis suis, xiiiij.s.*' Or 'Stephen the painter decorating the King's chamber and for colours bought by him and his wages, fourteen shillings.'

17. Arnold Taylor, 'Some notes on the Savoyards in North Wales, 1277–1300. With special reference to the Savoyard element in the construction of Harlech Castle,' *Genava* XI (1963): 300. '*Pro camera domini pingenda ad precium factum per Stephanum pictorem per manum Magistri Jacobi, lx.s. Pro camera domini pingenda per dictum Stephanum per manum predicti Magistri Jacobi, lx.s. Pro capella et garderoba domini pingenda … factum per dictum Stephanum per manum ipsius Magistri Jacobi.l.s.*' Or 'The room for the price of painting made by Stephen painter by hand of Maître Jacques, sixty *sol*. The room for the price of painting made by Stephen painter by hand of the aforesaid Maître Jacques, sixty *sol*. For the painting of a chapel and wardrobes … It said of Stephen by the hand of Maître Jacques, fifty *sol*.'

18. Ibid. 301.

19. Arnold Taylor. Studies in Medieval History Presented to R. Allen Brown (Woodbridge: The Boydell Press, 1989). 314–15 n55 and 56.

20. Ibid. 289.

21. Ivor, Bowen. *The Statutes of Wales, collected, edited, and arranged by Ivor Bowen* (London: T. Fisher Unwin, 1908).

22. Ibid. 'Edward, by the Grace of God King of England, Lord of Ireland, and Duke of Aquitaine, to all his Subjects of his Land of Snowdon, and of other his Lands in Wales, Greeting in the Lord. The Divine Providence, which is unerring in its own Government, among other gifts of its Dispensation, wherewith it hath vouchsafed to distinguish Us and our Realm of England, hath now of its favour, wholly and entirely transferred under our proper dominion, the Land of Wales with its Inhabitants, heretofore subject unto us, in Feudal Right, all obstacles whatsoever ceasing ; and hath annexed and united the same unto the Crown of the aforesaid Realm, as a Member of the same Body. We have Provided and by our command ordained, That the Justices of Snowdon shall have the Custody and Government of the Peace of Us the King in Snowdon, and our Lands of Wales adjoining; and shall administer Justice to all Persons whatsoever, according to the original Writs of Us the King, and also the Laws and Customs underwritten. We likewise will and ordain that there be Sheriffs, Coroners, and Bailiffs of Commotes in Snowdon, and our Lands of those parts. A Sheriff of Anglesea, under whom shall be the whole Land of Anglesea, with its Cantrefi, Metes, and Bounds. A Sheriff of Caernarvan, under whom shall be the Cantref of Arvan, the Cantref of Arthlencoyth, the Commote of Ruthun, the Cantref of Thieen, and the Commote of Yvionith. A Sheriff of Meirioneth, under whom shall be the Cantref of Meirioneth, the Commote of Ardovey, and the Commote of Penthlin, and the Commote of Deyrinoin, with their Metes and Bounds. A Sheriff of Flint, under whom shall be the Cantref of Englefield (Tegeingl), the Land of Maillor Sexeneyth, and the Land of Hope, and of the Land adjoining to our Castle and Town of Rothelan unto the Town of Chester, shall from henceforth be obedient under Us to our Justice of Chester, and shall answer for the Issues of the same

Commote at our Exchequer of Chester. There shall be Coroners in the same Counties, to be chosen by the King's Writ, the tenor whereof is to be found among the original Writs of the Chancery. There shall likewise be Bailiffs of Commotes who shall faithfully do and discharge their Offices and diligently attend thereto, according to what shall be given them in charge by the Justices and Sheriffs. A Sheriff of Carmarthen, with its Cantrefi and Commotes and ancient Metes and Bounds. A Sheriff of Cardigan and Llanbadam (Aberystwyth, with its Cantrefi and Commotes, and Metes and Bounds. There shall be Coroners in these Counties, and Bailiffs of Commotes, as before.'

23. Much of Flintshire, including Rhuddlan, would in 1535 be spun off into the new county of Denbighshire.
24. Sheriff coming from a shortening of Shire Reeve.
25. John E. Morris. *The Welsh Wars of Edward I* (Oxford: Clarendon Press, 1901). 199. John de Havering a son of Richard de Havering , who was steward of the estates of Simon de Montfort, he had previously served as Sheriff of Hampshire.
26. J. H. Baker. *An Introduction to English Legal History* (4th ed.). (Oxford: OUP, 2007). 15.
27. R. R. Davies. *The Age of Conquest: Wales 1063–1415* (Oxford: Oxford University Press, 1987). 364.
28. Ibid.
29. Ibid. 365–6.
30. TNA 101/351/2.
31. Michael Prestwich. *Edward I* (Yale: Yale University Press, 1997). 207.
32. Christopher Tyerman, 'The House of Savoy: Thirteenth Century England and the Medieval Community – The Savoia at the Court of Henry III of England (1216-1272)' Seventh Annual Savoy History Lecture (American Delegation of Savoy Orders, New York,27 October 2009).
33. Ivor, Bowen. *The Statutes of Wales, collected, edited, and arranged by Ivor Bowen* (London: T. Fisher Unwin, 1908).
34. CWR 1277–1326, 289. 'To archbishops, etc. Notification that the king wills that his town of Flynt shall be henceforth a free borough. To the same. The like for the town of Rothelan. To the same. The like for the town of Aberconewey. To archbishops, etc. The like for the town of Karnarvan.'
35. The earliest written origin of this spurious claim is by David Powel who was a Welsh Anglican clergyman and historian who published the first printed history of Wales in 1584.
36. Ann. Cestrienses, 114. '*Eodem anno* [1284] *natus est Eadwardus filius Regis Edwardi in Wallia apud Caernarvon die Sancti Marci Evangeliste.*'
37. Christopher Given-Wilson. *Edward II: The Terrors of Kingship* (Milton Keynes: Penguin Books, 2016). 3.
38. Sara Cockerill. *Eleanor of Castile: The Shadow Queen*. Second Edition ed. (Stroud: Amberley Publishing, 2014). 304.
39. Marc Morris. *A Great and Terrible King* (London: Windmill Books, 2009). 192.
40. Sara Cockerill. *Eleanor of Castile: The Shadow Queen*. Second Edition ed. (Stroud: Amberley Publishing, 2014). 303.
41. R. R. Davies. *The Age of Conquest: Wales 1063–1415* (Oxford: Oxford University Press, 1987). 355.
42. Ann. Cestrienses, 114. '*Edwardus rex fecit tyrocinium fieri apud Nevin in Wallia ubi comes Lincolniensis Henricus de Lascy habuit unam partem et Ricardus de Burgo Comes de Ulvester alteram.*' Or 'King Edward caused a tournament to be held at Nefyn in Wales, where the earl of Lincoln, Henry de Lacy, was the leader of one side, and Richard de Burgh, earl of Ulster, on the other.'
43. Marc Morris. *A Great and Terrible King* (London: Windmill Books, 2009). 195.
44. TNA E101/331/14. '*sigilli Princ' Wallie quondam Leulini et David fratris eius et Alianor quondam Princ' Wallie, pond' xxxv.s. x.d ... from de quibus factus fuit unus novus calix ... quem Rex contulerat nove Abbatie de Valle Regali.*'
45. Ann. Cestrienses, 114. '*per ordinem universum vero quicquam combustum est Illo igne preter solam ecclesiam cum libris choralibus et campanis.*' Or 'In general everything was burned by the fire including choral books and the bells.'
46. J. Beverley Smith. *Llywellyn ap Gruffudd: Prince of Wales*. Ebook. ed. (Cardiff: The University of Wales Press, 2014). Apple.
47. A paten is a plate used for holding wafers during holy communion, and hence is usually found with a chalice used to hold the accompanying wine.
48. If the Dolgellau chalice is the Vale Royal chalice, then it currently forms a part of the Royal Collection and resides in the National Museum of Wales. It is described as a 'thirteenth-century, silver-gilt chalice with a plain, flattened hemispherical bowl, on a stem engraved with trefoil leaves, with a central knop divided into twelve lobes. The circular foot is embossed with two rows of twelve trefoil-shaped lobes, the upper row plain, the lower engraved with stiff leaves. The maker's name, which is signed under the foot, appears to be Nicholas of 'Herford', now the village of Hartford in Cheshire, where the family of Nicholas was based.' Its provenance is suggested as being 'among the largest and finest surviving English medieval chalices and may have been made for the monastic foundation of Cymer Abbey. This piece and the paten (RCIN 69049) were found on the mountainside of Cwm

Mynach, near Dolgellau, in 1890. They were purchased by Baron Schroder in 1892. They became the subject of a belated treasure trove inquest and were bequeathed to the Crown [King George V] on his death in 1910.' Allison Stiellau writes that the hidden location of the chalice and paten, found by the two workmen amidst vegetation is suggestive of their being hidden by monks from Cymer as opposed to thieves, and likely they were hidden to save them falling into the hands of Henry VIII's commissioners during the dissolution of the monasteries in the sixteenth century. She reasons that thieves would have quickly sold them on, whereas the monks may have been content to hide them and so protect them from the fate that befell much church plate at the time. But if the monks of Cymer were so keen to protect them, was it because of the origin of the chalice or merely that they were precious religious artefacts? Arnold Taylor and Jenkyn Beverley Smith certainly thought it might be because they knew them to hold the precious metal of the seals of the family of the last native princes of Wales. Taylor rightly confirms that the original melted chalice was assigned to the goldsmith 'Nigello' or Nigel, and yet the chalice carries the name Nicholas on its foot. He then suggests that it's possible that Nigel the goldsmith handed the princes seals to Nicholas and asked him to make the chalice 'on or about 8 December 1283' he concluded 'There does, however, seem to the writer to be a sufficiently strong thread . . . to support a suggestion that there may be more than ordinarily good reason why the Dolgellau chalice could hardly have found a more appropriate final resting place than the National Museum of Wales.' See Allison Stielau, 2014 'The Dolgellau Chalice and Paten,' Object narrative, in Conversations: An online journal for the Center for the Study of Material and Visual Cultures of Religion. And Arnold Taylor. *Studies in Castles and Castle-Building* (London: The Hambledon Press, 1985). 200.

49. Arnold Taylor. *Studies in Castles and Castle-Building* (London: The Hambledon Press, 1985). 199.

Chapter Ten
1. CWR 1277–1326, 291. '21 October 1283, Caernarfon, 'The king has committed to John de Havering' during pleasure his castle at Kaernarvon [Caernarvon], with the armour and all the things forming the munition of the castle, and has granted to him 200 marks yearly for the custody, to be received at the exchequer of Kaernarvan [Caernarfon] by the hands of the chamberlain, on condition that he shall have continuously have in garrison there, in addition to himself and his household, at his cost forty fencible men, of whom fifteen shall be crossbowmen, one chaplain, one artiller, a carpenter, a mason and a smith, and of the others shall be made janitors, watchmen and other ministers of the castle. Order is given to all bailiffs etc 'to be intendent on John as keeper of the castle in those things that pertain to the custody. The king has committed in like manner to Walter de Huntercomb the castle of Bere, and has granted to him 200 marks yearly for the custody, to be received as above, on condition that he shall have continuously there in garrison at the castle at his cost forty fencible men, of whom fifteen shall be crossbowmen, one chaplain, one artiller, a carpenter, a mason and a smith, and of the others shall be made janitors, watchmen and other ministers of the castle. Order is given to all bailiffs etc (as in preceding). The king has committed in like manner to Hugh de Wlonkeslowe the castle of Hardelawe [Harlech, with the armour, etc, and has granted to him 100 *livres* yearly for the custody, to be received as above, on condition that he shall have continuously in garrison there at his cost thirty fencible men, of whom ten shall be crossbowmen one chaplain, one artiller, a carpenter, a mason and a smith, and of the others shall be made janitors, watchmen and other ministers of the castle. Order is given to all bailiffs etc (as above). The king has committed in like manner to William de Cycun [Guillaume de Cicon], the castle of Aberconewey [Conwy], with the armour, etc, and has granted to him 190 *livres* yearly for the custody thereof, to be received as above, on condition that he shall have continuously have in garrison, in addition to himself and his household, at his cost thirty fencible men, of whom fifteen shall be crossbowmen one chaplain, one artiller, a carpenter, a mason and a smith, and of the others shall be made janitors, watchmen and other ministers of the castle. Order is given to all bailiffs etc (as above).
2. Ibid.
3. As noted earlier, Jean de Bonvillars was the son of Henri de Bonvillars, the first châtelain of Rue for Pierre de Savoie. The family is first named in 1110 as one 'Hugh de Binvillar.The small village of Bonvillars lies just a few short kilometres from Grandson. We met Jean earlier at the siege of Dolforwyn in 1277 as bearer of a message to kid kinsman Othon de Grandson.
4. TNA E101/351/12. '*Johanni de Byveillard militi eunti in Walliam ad supervidendum castra domini Regis ibidem precepto Regis, pro suis expensis eundo, morando et revertendo.*' Or 'Sadly, the amount of the payment has been torn away. But what survives translates as 'To the knight Jean de Bonvillars, going to Wales to supervise the castles of the Lord King by Order of the King, for his expenses whilst going there, staying there and coming back.', Michael Prestwich. '*Othon de Grandson et la Cour de Edouard I*' in. *Othon I de Grandson (vers 1240-1328)* (Lausanne: Cahiers Lausannois d'Histoire Médiévale, 2020). 12. '*Jean de Bonvillars supervisa les travaux de construction du château de Conwy.*' Or 'Jean de Bonvillars supervised the construction works of the Castle of Conwy.'

5. AST Baronnie de Vaud 27, Mézières 1. The feudal relationship between Jean de Bonvillars and Othon de Grandson is highlighted by a 1279 deed sealed at Evian in Savoy. It concerns the sale of the fief of Mézières between Rue and Moudon to '*Johannes de Bono Vilario Milites*', the knight Jean de Bonvillars. The deed mentions fealty to the Count of Savoy but also the Lord of Grandson. '*Salva fidelitate domini de Grandissono*' Or 'save fidelity to the Lord of Grandson'.

6. TNA E101/3/16. and TNA E101/308/3. and Archivo di Stato, Torino, Baronnie de Vaud 27, Mezieres 1.

7. CPR Edward I vol 1 1272–1281, 296.

8. TNA E101/4/8.

9. CPR Edward I vol 2 1281–1292, 192.

10. Nicola Coldstream, 'Architects, Advisers and Design at Edward I's Castles in Wales,' *Architectural History: Journal of the Society of Architectural Historians of Great Britain* 46 (2003). 29. 'Among several Savoyards given administrative duties in north Wales, Sir John de Bevillard [Jean de Bonvillars], who in 1295/6 supervised the works at Conwy and Caernarfon and, with James of St George, allocated the masons' tasks.' But in Nicola Coldstream. 'James of St George' in *The Impact of the Edwardian Castles in Wales* (Oxford: Oxbow Books, 2010). 42. 'Several Savoyards, notably John de Bevillard [Jean de Bonvillars] and William de Cicon, were appointed to senior duties in north Wales. Yet … evidence for their advice on castle design is neutral.'.

11. Ibid. 'Another administrator was Sir John Masot, a household knight who was … closely involved with design.' The 1283 record for Bonvillars is TNA E101/351/12. '*Johanni de Byveillard militi eunti in Walliam ad supervidendum castra domini Regis ibidem precepto Regis, pro suis expensis eundo, morando et revertendo.*' Or Sadly, the amount of the payment has been torn away. But what survives translates as 'To the knight Jean de Bonvillars, going to Wales to supervise the castles of the Lord King by Order of the King, for his expenses whilst going there, staying there and coming back.' By comparison that for Mézos in Savoy had been *La Finanza Sabauda*, vol. 1, 41. '*In expensis domini Iohannis de Masot euntis apud Sallon ad turrim de Sallon devisandam .vi. sol. .viii. den. preter illos quos expendit apud Sallon.*' Or 'The expenses of Jean de Mézos when he was at Saillon for the tower of Saillon. Six *sol* eight den. Those whom he considers at Saillon.' And Ibid. 68. '*In expensis domini Iohannis de Masot ad supervidendum ibi situm turris per tres dies. Vj.s.vj.d.*'. Or 'The expenses of Jean de Mézos to oversee the siting of the tower for three days Six *sol* six den.' The key word being then '*supervidendum.*' We should also note that both men, were in this context described as knights. TNA E101/351/12 '*Johanni de Byveillard militi*' and Arnold Taylor, 'Some notes on the Savoyards in North Wales, 1277–1300. With special reference to the Savoyard element in the construction of Harlech Castle,' *Genava* XI (1963): 302. '*Johannem de Masoz militem*'.

12. *OED*, March 2019, Oxford University Press. 'ORIGIN [Supervise] late 15th century (in the sense 'survey, peruse'): from medieval Latin *supervis-* 'surveyed, supervised', from *supervidere*, from *super-* 'over' + *videre* 'to see'.

13. TNA E101/485/28. '*eidem Henrico pro fractura graduum camere Regis in castro predicto et pro oriolo in medio castro facts ad tascham predicto Henrico traditam per dominum J. de Bonouillar' et Magistrum Jacobum.*' Or 'To the same Henry for breaking of steps in the King's chamber in the castle aforesaid and the oriole made in the castle for the task given to the aforesaid Henry by Lord Jean de Bonvillars and Maître Jacques.'

14. TNA E101/485/28. '*Die Dominica 8 die Septembris eisdem R.et S. pro 500 bayardis ab eisdem emptis per dominum Johannem de Bonovillario, precio 100 3s, et missis apud Carnarvan pro operibus ibidem, 15s. Eodem die eisdem R. et S pro 16 bayardis ab eisdem emptis per Magistrum Jacobum 5s 4d.*' Or 'On Sunday the 8 day of September the same R. and S. for 500 barrows from the same bought by Lord Jean de Bonvillars, price 5 pounds 3 shillings, and deposing forth for their works at Caernarfon. On the same day the same R. and S. for 16 barrows from the same bought by Maître Jacques 5 shillings and 4 pence'

15. Arnold Taylor, 'Some notes on the Savoyards in North Wales, 1277–1300. With special reference to the Savoyard element in the construction of Harlech Castle,' *Genava* XI (1963): 290. n5. Taylor suggests that it is vey likely Jean de Bonvillars was brother-in-law to Othon de Grandson. 'In a letter of 1292 or 1293 Otto speaks of Sir John's brother Henry de Bonvillars as he would if he were his own brother or brother-in- aw, '*mon /rere le prior de Wenloc*' ('L', SC 1, XXVI, 34).'

16. Whilst John de Havering served as official Deputy Justiciar, Jean de Bonvillars served as personal deputy to the Justiciar – for finer points of the distinction see Arnold Taylor. 1985. *Studies in Castles and Castle-Building*. London: The Hambledon Press. 215.

17. Arnold Taylor. *Studies in Castles and Castle-Building* (London: The Hambledon Press, 1985). 213-4. 'By October 1284 at latest John de Bevillard was back in Wales again, for an entry dated on Sunday 5 November, when the king was at Castell y Bere, records the payment to him of 20s, wages in respect of ten days spent in attendance with the court. The actual dates are tantalizingly not specified; however, fourteen of the nineteen entries in the paragraph concerned relate to wages accruing

during October, and if this applies also to the payment to de Bevillard it could well be significant. October 20 and 21 1284 are the enrolment dates, at Caernarfon, first of the provision made for life employment of the master of the works in Wales, James of St George, with a contingent widow's pension for his wife Ambrosia, and of Master Richard of Chester; and secondly, of the appointment of the constables of Caernarfon, Conwy, Harlech and Bere and of the arrangements made for the castles' garrisons. Taken together, these were the crucial 'management' appointments for Edward's whole castle building programme.'

18. TNA SC/8/106/5278 *'Mestre Jakes de Seint George, chef mestre des ouereignes le Roi en Gales.'* Or 'Maître Jacques de Saint Georges, Chief Master of the King's Works in Wales.' Amongst the first to recognize the significance of this title was Welsh Wars historian John E. Morris writing over a century ago. John E. Morris. *The Welsh Wars of Edward I* (Oxford: Clarendon Press, 1901). 145. 'we can hardly be wrong in inferring that the latter [Master James de St George] was the chief architect and designer of the great Edwardian fortresses' *as magister operacionem regis in Wallia.'* Arnold Taylor. *Studies in Castles and Castle-Building* (London: The Hambledon Press, 1985). 71. Taylor noted that the overall accounts of Richard of Abingdon, Chamberlain of Caernarfon, for the period 13 January 1283 until 7 January 1286 summarizing expenditure at Caernarfon (£3,036.19s.51/2d), Conwy £3313.1s.2d), Criccieth (£48.8s.91/2d) and Harlech (£205,1s.51/2d) when taken together with payment of wages on the same account to *'Magistro Jacobo de sancto Georgio, Magistro operacionum Regis in Wallia'* naturally inferred the latter was responsible for the former – not an unreasonable logical deduction. When one adds his successor's account, Robert de Belvoir of October 1285 to December 1290, and find James again referred to as 'Master of the king's works in Wales', then we have two accounts covering the key building work at Caernarfon, Conwy and Harlech. It is for those that revise the Savoyards role to find an explanation for these accounts, other than the obvious one that, variously the *'lathomo' 'cementario'* and *'Ingeniator'*, from Savoy was as responsible as any single man could be for the Edwardian castles.

19. CPR Edward I vol 2 1281-1292, 137.

20. Arnold Taylor. *Studies in Castles and Castle-Building* (London: The Hambledon Press, 1985). 68.

21. TNA currency converter.

22. Robert Bartlett. The Making of Europe: Conquest, Colonization and Cultural Change 950–1350 (London: Penguin Books Ltd, 1993). 114.

23. In France the word evolved in a different way to that in England, the Connétable de France was the commander in chief of the French army until 1627.

24. *Littere Wallie.* J. G. Edwards. Ed (Cardiff. University Press, 1940). 146. *'dominus Willelmus Chykoun constabularius dicti castri de Rothelano'*

25. Rognon lies around twenty-two miles (35 kilometres) north-east of Besançon in the Franche Comte de Bourgogne

26. TNA C47/3/21. *'Domino Stephano de Rouenyhoun germano domini Willelmi Sicoun redeunti versus patriam de dono Regis vj.li.xiij.s.iiij.d., quem Rex fecit militem.'* Or 'Lord Stephen de Rognon true brother of Sir Guillaume de Cicon returns to his homeland, as a gift of the King Six Pounds, Thirteen Shillings and Four Pence. Which the King gave to the knight.'

27. CWR 1277–1326, 302. 'To all bailiffs and subjects to whom, etc. Notification that the King has committed to John de Benelare [Jean de Bonvillars] during pleasure his castle of Herdelagh with the armour and all other things in the munition of the castle and granted to him £149.0s.10d yearly for the custody thereof … to wit for himself and his wife 4s. a day.' 4 shillings a day would equate to a salary element of the constable's fee being £73 per annum.

28. Arnold Taylor. *Studies in Castles and Castle-Building* (London: The Hambledon Press, 1985). 35. Taylor in another journal work went on to confirm this was hypothesis by confirming the first primary source evidence for Jean de Bonvillars in England is his message to Dolforwyn Castle in 1277 in Ibid. 211–2.

29. Enrico Lusso in 'A Warm Mind-Shake, Scritti in onore di Paolo Bertinetti.' Tra Savoia, Galles e Provenca, Magistri costruttori architteonici in castelli del Piemonte duocentesco Edited by a cura del Dipartimento di Lingue e Letterature Straniere e Culture Moderne dell'università degli Studi di Torino. (Turin: Edizioni Trauben, 2014), 305.

30. Jean-Pierre Chapuisat source CCR VI (1427–1516) Appendix 290. As sited in Arnold Taylor. *Studies in Castles and Castle-Building* (London: The Hambledon Press, 1985). 216. *'Per visum et testimonium dilecti et fidelis nostri Johannis de Bonouillar.'* Or 'and of the testimony of our faithful and beloved, under the supervision of Jean de Bonvillars.'

31. The Sicilian Vespers was an Easter 1282 revolt by the native population against its francophone rules, the King of Sicily, Charles d'Anjou, the brother of the late King Louis IX of France. The *Vespiri siciliani* broke out as a local response to the eastward expansionist policies of Charles d'Anjou, who was not content with being King of Sicily. He had sought far greater realms but expected the poor Sicilians to fund his empire building, something they were less than keen to do. The revolt led to

the intervention of Peter III of Aragon in Sicily and the overthrow of French rule, thus bringing the prospect of a Franco-Hispanic war over Sicily involving the papacy, the Italians and of course, as Duke of Aquitaine, the English king.

32. Firstly, on his way to campaign in Sicily, Charles d'Anjou King Charles I of Sicily (aka King of Naples and of Albania and of Jerusalem) passed away on 7 January 1285 at Foggia within his Kingdom of Naples. Then the Pope, Martin IV departing this life on 2 April 1285. Then King Philippe III of France died at Perpignan on 5 October 1285 whilst trying to bring the Aragonese to battle - making him the second French king in succession, after his father Louis IX, to die of illness amidst a failing army. Lastly King Peter III of Aragon was to die on 11 November 1285 at Vilafranca del Penedès.

33. *La Finanza Sabauda.* vol. 2, 291. An interesting name fleetingly appears once more at this point, Aigueblanche, in the form of a Jean d'Aigueblanche who accompanies Edward. The passing of Pierre d'Aigueblanche in 1268 had not seen the end of Savoyard influence in Hereford, for from 1278 Jean had been the Dean of the Chapter of Hereford Cathedral. Interestingly the accounts for Philippe de Savoie for 1272 describe him as *'archidiaconi'* and note a payment of eighteen *sol* and 6 *den* paid from Savoyard coffers, we are sadly not told for what service.

34. John E. Morris. *The Welsh Wars of Edward I* (Oxford: Clarendon Press, 1901). 209.

35. Ibid.

36. Chris Caple. *Excavations at Dryslwyn Castle* (Leeds: The Society for Medieval Archaeology. 2007). 187.

37. Sian E. Rees & Chris Caple. *Dinefwr Castle Dryslwyn Castle.* Revised ed. (Cardiff: Cadw, 1999). 12– 3. 'Rhys had been rewarded for his loyalty to the Crown in the war of 1282-83, and it was probably the wealth derived from his new lands which enabled him to invest in the extensive building programme at Dryslwyn ... All in all Rhys had made Dryslwyn one of the largest masonry castles ever raised by native Welsh lords, a structure impressive enough to rival any number of strongholds raised by Anglo-Norman and English lords of the March.'

38. John E. Morris. *The Welsh Wars of Edward I* (Oxford: Clarendon Press, 1901). 212.

39. Rick Turner. 'The Life and Career of Richard the Engineer' in *The Impact of the Edwardian Castles in Wales* (Oxford: Oxbow Books, 2010). 49. 'Materials had been obtained before his [Master Richard] arrival, and payments were made for large quantities of timber, hides, ropes, pulleys, nails and lead with a total recorded cost of £17.9s.3d.'

40. Chris Caple. *Excavations at Dryslwyn Castle.* (Leeds: The Society for Medieval Archaeology. 2007). 188. TNA E372/132 m1 'And for an anchor taken from Walter Goban by Master Richard the Engineer for the Kings' Engine outside Dryslwyn Castle 40s.'

41. Rick Turner. 'The Life and Career of Richard the Engineer' in *The Impact of the Edwardian Castles in Wales* (Oxford: Oxbow Books, 2010). 49. 'In addition, Master Adam and nineteen others spent a fortnight in a quarry making stone balls for the siege engine.'

42. Richard W. Kaeuper. *Bankers to the Crown: The Riccardi of Lucca and Edward I* (Princeton: Princeton University Press, 1973). 196.

43. TNA E372/132 m1 'Master Richard the Engineer to cut a trench and throw down the walls ... And for 5 axes and 2 pick-axes bought and delivered to Richard the Engineer to do the same.'

44. Hugh Kennedy. *Crusader Castles* (Cambridge: Cambridge University Press, 1994). 105 quoting a likely eyewitness account of mining by Fulcher of Chartres. 253–4.

45. Arnold Taylor. *Studies in Castles and Castle-Building* (London: The Hambledon Press, 1985). 209– 11. For the account in full see Thomas Jones (ed. and trans), Brenhinedd y Saesson (Cardiff, 1971), 260–1. '*Anno Domini Mil cc.lxxxix. y torres rnng y brenin a Rys ap Mredudd ap Owain ap Gruffydd ap yr Arglwydd Rys, yr hwnn oedd arglwydd y Dryslwyn. Ac yn hynny o amser y doeth llu y brenin o Gymry a Lloegr am benn kastell y Dryslwyn. Ac yna boddes John Penardd, tywysoc gwyr Gwynedd. Ac o'r diwedd drwy hir ymladd y kad y kastell, a gyrv Rys ap Mredudd ar herw.*' Or '1289 AD, there was a breach between the king and Rhys son of Maredudd son of Owain son of Gruffudd son of the Lord Rhys, who was lord of Dryslwyn. And during that time the king's host from Wales and England came against the castle of Dryslwyn. And then John Pennardd, leader of the men of Gwynedd, was drowned. And at last, after a long siege, the castle was taken, and Rhys ap Maredudd was driven into outlawry.'

46. Chris Caple. *Excavations at Dryslwyn Castle* (Leeds: The Society for Medieval Archaeology. 2007). 189. Caple cites Taylor as the origin for the date, after giving some detail of the mine. 'attempts were made to undermine the castle walls in order to bring them down. A troop of 26 specialist diggers arrived at Dryslwyn, and from Monday 25 to Thursday 28 August, they are recorded as being paid to bring down the wall of the chapel by removing stones and mortar. When a group of leading knights from the Anglo-Welsh army rashly entered the 'mine' to inspect the work, the props gave way and both the ground and wall above suddenly collapsed onto them, crushing them to death.' TNA E101/4/16 m3. '*Fossatores Item pacacio xxvi fossatoribus ad removendos lapides et morttirium ad capellam et ad prosternendum murum capelle pro diebus Lune, Martis, Mercurii et Jovis per iiii dies, xxvi s. iiii d. unde magister capit per diem iiii d. et quilibet de aliis iii d.*' Or '14 Diggers – also paid to 26

diggers to remove stones and mortar at the chapel and to throw down the wall of the chapel for the days Monday, Tuesday, Wednesday and Thursday for 4 days 26s 4d, of whom the master takes 4d a day and each of the others 3d.'

47. Whilst John de Havering served as official Deputy Justiciar, Jean de Bonvillars served as personal deputy to the Justiciar – for finer points of the distinction see Arnold Taylor. *Studies in Castles and Castle-Building* (London: The Hambledon Press, 1985). 215.

48. Arnold Taylor. *Studies in Castles and Castle-Building* (London: The Hambledon Press, 1985). 214.

49. John E. Morris. *The Welsh Wars of Edward I* (Oxford: Clarendon Press, 1901). 219. 'Payments to infantry and workmen £6,116, payments to feudal lords for cavalry £1,400, Cost of garrison of Dryslwyn after capture £1,936, Expenses of siege of Emlyn £534, Repairs and new works at Llanbadarn £320, Repairs and new works at Carmarthen £169, Garrison of Dynevor £111. Total £10,606.

50. Richard W. Kaeuper. *Bankers to the Crown: The Riccardi of Lucca and Edward I* (Princeton: Princeton University Press, 1973). 198.

51. Arnold Taylor. *Studies in Castles and Castle-Building* (London: The Hambledon Press, 1985). 219. Taylor took the following '*liberavit eidem Johanni et predicte Agneti … apud le Cadou*' to betoken her accompanying his journey to South Wales, he identified Le Cadou as Llangadog in Carmarthenshire.

52. We know of at least one child of Jean and Agnès de Bonvillars, a daughter. Henri de Bonvillars, Jean's brother, the Prior of Wenlock, acted as guardian of one of the orphaned daughters upon her marriage in 1292. TNA C62/68 '*Liberate … dilecto nobis in Christo fratri Henrico Priori de Wenlok centum marcas ad unam filiarum Johannis de Bevillard defuncti fratris eiusdem Prioris inde maritandam de dono nostro.*'

53. A woman as constable of a castle was very rare, but not unheard of, see Michael Prestwich, 'Isabella de Vescy and the Custody of Bamburgh Castle,' *BIHR* xliv (1971): 148–52.

54. CWR 1277–1326, 326.

55. Ibid. 326–7. 'July 10 at Westminster To whom, etc. Notification that the king has pardoned the executors of the will of John de Bonovillario, late constable of his castle of Hardelagh, in consideration of the good service rendered by him to the king in his lifetime, 80l. of the 100l. that the king caused to be paid to John for the munition of that castle, provided that the executors answer to the king for the remaining 20l.' In the same spirit Edward pardoned Agnès de Bonvillars the sum of 100s fine due from her for allowing a monk to escape her custody see CWR 1277–1326, 328. For the gift of 40 marks see Arnold Taylor. *Studies in Castles and Castle-Building* (London: The Hambledon Press, 1985). 74. n1.

56. CWR 1277-1326, 327. 'To all to whom, etc. Notification that the king has committed to Robert Tibetot the towns, the castles and all the lands that belonged to Rhys, son of Mereduc, the king's rebel in Wales, which are in the king's hands by his forfeiture.'

57. Chron. Guisborough, 17.

58. Arnold Taylor. *The King's Works in Wales 1277–1330* (London: Her Majesty's Stationery Office, 1974). 363.

59. Marc Morris. 'Edward I's Building Works in Gascony' in *The Impact of the Edwardian Castles in Wales* (Oxford: Oxbow Books, 2010). 167.

60. Arnold Taylor. *Studies in Castles and Castle-Building* (London: The Hambledon Press, 1985). 73. n3. *Citing Calendar of Ancient Correspondence Concerning Wales.* 120. 'To Maître Jacques and William Le Bescle going to Gascony to the king, for their expenses, 5s.'

61. Marc Morris. 'Edward I's Building Works in Gascony' in *The Impact of the Edwardian Castles in Wales* (Oxford: Oxbow Books, 2010) 174. n26.

62. Taylor was convinced this was Guillaume de Geneva, making the castles actual builder also a Savoyard.

63. Marc Morris. 'Edward I's Building Works in Gascony' in *The Impact of the Edwardian Castles in Wales* (Oxford: Oxbow Books, 2010). 173.

64. Alison Weir. *Queens of the Crusades: Eleanor of Aquitaine and her Succesors* (London: Penguin Random House UK, 2020). 644.

65. CPR Edward I vol 2 1281–1292, 356.

66. Brut, Peniarth MS. 20 (Cardiff 1941), sub anno 1290, suggests that Rhys ap Maredudd may have been betrayed by his own men in the woods of the commote of Malláen (North Carmarthenshire).

67. Chron. Lanercost , 89.

Chapter Eleven

1. *Flores Historiarum*, 58. '*Rex Edwardus apud Aberconewey ad pedes montis Snoudoniæ fecit erigi castrum forte.*' Or 'King Edward caused a castle to be erected at Aberconwy at the foot of Mount Snowdon.'

2. Graham Lott. 'The Building Stones of the Edwardian Castles' in *The Impact of the Edwardian Castles in Wales* (Oxford: Oxbow Books, 2010). 115 'The castle is sited … on a rugged coastal

    ridge formed by rocks of Ordovician Age (440–450 million years) from the Conwy Mudstone formation, which includes the Conwy Castle Grit Member on which the castle sits.'

3. TNA E101/485/28.
4. Robert Liddiard. 'A Research Agenda for the Edwardian Castles' in *The Impact of the Edwardian Castles in Wales* (Oxford: Oxbow Books, 2010). 196. 'Conwy exhibits one of, if not the first, example of stone machicolations in the British Isles.'
5. John Harris, 'Machicolation: History and Significance,' *The Castle Studies Group Journal* 23 (2009–10). 193.
6. Ibid. 196.
7. Dr Kate Roberts (Principal Inspector of Ancient Monuments, Cadw). John Marshall. In discussions with the author. 11 July 2019. Conwy Castle. This would align with the record '*Pro quodam muro sicco lapis' facto ad tascham inter castrum de Conewey et cameram Magistro Jacobi de Sancto Georgio.*' Or 'in front of a wall of dry stone built at task, between the castle of Conwy and the chamber of Maître Jacques de Saint Georges.' TNA E101/485/28.
8. Maryline Martin & Florian Renucci. *Guédelon: A Castle in the Making* (Rennes: Editions Ouest-France, 2016). 35.
9. Ibid. 37. 'The master mason's role is also to supply technical information and explanation about construction choices … He hands out any necessary architectural plans and explains the technical vocabulary. The meeting closes with the allocation of jobs for the coming week and a discussion about how to undertake these tasks. The weekly site meeting has permitted a collective approach rather than a top down organisation and is integral to the project's [Guédelon's] success.'
10. Richard K. Morris. '*The Architecture of Arthurian Enthusiasm: Castle Symbolism in the Reigns of Edward I and his Successors*' in *Late Medieval Castles* (Woodbridge: The Boydell Press, 2016). 361. 'Analysis of the plan of Caernarfon Castle reveals a designer playing with geometrical shapes for effect.'
11. For an excellent diagrammatic representation of the application of geometrical shapes in the design of Lausanne cathedral see. Henri Cevey. '*Ou l'Hermétique s'entrouvre*' in *Merveilleuse Notre-Dame de Lausanne, Cathédrale Bourguignonne* ed. Paul Chaudet (*Lausanne: Editions du Grand-Point*, 1975). 100–1.
12. Michael Prestwich. *Medieval People* (London: Thames & Hudson, 2014). 306.
13. Maryline Martin & Florian Renucci. *Guédelon: A Castle in the Making* (Rennes: Editions Ouest-France, 2016). 38. 'The Master-of-Works/Architect was an important figure in the 13th century.'
14. TNA E372/131/26. Maître Jacques is described in the accounts of 13 February 1283 through 7 January 1286 when being allocated pay for the period of 12 February 1285 until 13 December 1285 as '*Magistro Jacobo de Sancto Georgio, Magistro operacionum Regis in Wallia.*' Or 'Maître Jacques de Saint Georges, Master of the King's Works in Wales.' In the accounts of Richard of Abingdon, Chamberlain at Caernarfon.
15. Arnold Taylor. *The Welsh Castles of King Edward I* (London: The Hambledon Press, 1986). 57.
16. Maryline Martin & Florian Renucci. *Guédelon: A Castle in the Making* (Rennes: Editions Ouest-France, 2016). 52.
17. Arnold Taylor. *Studies in Castles and Castle-Building* (London: The Hambledon Press, 1985). 116. Citing TNA SC/13/152. 'We command and firmly enjoin you to be intendent and helpful to our beloved Richard the Engineer, the bearer of these present letters, in providing us with smiths and other workmen as the same Richard will tell you on our behalf. We also command you to aid the same Richard with cartage for carrying materials and things needed for our works at Aberconwy, as the same Richard will tell you on our behalf. And, as you love us and our well-being, you are in no wise to overlook this.'
18. Maryline Martin & Florian Renucci. *Guédelon: A Castle in the Making* (Rennes: Editions Ouest-France, 2016). 77.
19. Rick Turner. 'The Life and Career of Richard the Engineer' in *The Impact of the Edwardian Castles in Wales* (Oxford: Oxbow Books, 2010). 53. 'He [Master Richard] was almost certainly a carpenter by training and not primarily a mason.'
20. Arnold Taylor. *The Welsh Castles of King Edward I* (London: The Hambledon Press, 1986). 55. n6. Taylor speculated with some plausibility that *Brodulpho* may well be one and the same as *Magistro Rodulfo carpenatrius* that had appeared in the Savoyard Chillon accounts of 1257-58. *La Finanza Sabauda*, vol. 1, 11. '*Idem Libravit magistro Rodulfo carpentario.*'
21. TNA E101/485/28. '*Tasch' carpent' Eodem die Dominico Micheli de la Verdenoye, Bertoto Cokel et Brodulpho carpentario pro quibusdam novis aluris in aula domini Ottonis apud Conewey et pro allis operibus factis in eadem aula et reoarac ad tascham 70s.*' Or 'Carpentry tasks. Also, the same Sunday [29 September 1286] Michel de la Verdenoye, Bertoto Cokel and Brodulpho carpenters for some new passages in the hall of Sir Othon [de Grandson] at Conwy and for other works performed in the same hall and repairs by task 70 shillings.'

22. At the time of writing (2019) the structure is not yet complete.
23. Graham Lott. 'The Building Stones of the Edwardian Castles' in *The Impact of the Edwardian Castles in Wales* (Oxford: Oxbow Books, 2010). 115. 'They [the sandstone and limestone layers] exhibit a regular, closely spaced joint pattern, perpendicular to the bedding, which naturally breaks up the rocks into irregularly sized, tabular blocks, similar to those used to construct the castle walls.'
24. The yardstick is to this day idiomatic of an agreed set of parameters and 'To move the yardstick' entered the English language as an idiom for altering parameters of any situation.
25. Reputedly King Henry I (1068–1135) used his own arm as a standard for the yard.
26. Measurements are very approximate and given as a visualisation of equivalencies only.
27. Graham Lott. 'The Building Stones of the Edwardian Castles' in *The Impact of the Edwardian Castles in Wales* (Oxford: Oxbow Books, 2010). 115. 'other more colourful sandstones were brought in for decorative use for both internal and external features such as arrow loops, windows, door jambs and chimney-pieces.'
28. Charles Phillips. *The Medieval Castle* (Yeovil: Haynes Publishing, 2018). 41. Such a device has been used at Guédelon.
29. TNA E101/485/28. '*Die Dominico 7 die Julii Johanni de Bedeford*' and '*Die Dominium 29 die Septembris Johanni Franceys, Willelmo Seysel, Rogero de Cokersond, Petri de Bononia, Gillotto de Chalons, Johanni de Schirewode, Roberto de Fraunkeby*' and '*Eodem die Dominico Johanni Franceys, Willelmo Seysel*' and '*Roberto Flemming*' and '*Eodem die Dominico Johanni Flauner*' and '*Philippo de Derleye, Alano de Bokenhale, Willelmo de Thornton et Thome de la Roche … Eodem Johanni Bargas*' and '*Waltero de Roding, Willelmo de la Launde, Willelmo de Maclesfield, Simoni de Gedling et Roberto de Wirhale … Eodem die Riccardo de Kingeston et Thomas Picard.*'
30. AST Inv. Sav., 69, Fo. 5, Mazzo 1, No. 3 (c), dorso. '*Johannes Franciscus*' And *La Finanza Sabauda* vol. 1, 62. '*Idem (sc. P. Mainier, custos operum domini) solvit Francisco, et Stephano de Arborenges, de summa xliij librarum que debebantur eis pro duabus cameris faciendis in casali retro turrim de Alingio in taschiam, xliij lib., et sic soluti sunt de toto.*'
31. *La Finanza Sabauda*, vol. 1, 26. '*Idem libravit Francisco cementario pro tascheria nove camere iuxta turrim et Conteis.*' And 58-9 '*De quibus libravit Francisco cementario de taschia .viii.xx. et .x.librarum et duabus robis de quadraginta sol. pro turre de Sallon facienda de sexaginta et decem pedibus altitudinis tam in grosso muro quam in avante pedibus et in merlis, de duodecim pedibus pissitudinis usque ad primam travaturam et decem pedibus a secunda travatura superius. x. lib.*' And Ibid. 68. '*Francisco … pro turre de Sallon.*' And Ibid. 62. '*Francisco … pro duabus cameriis.*'
32. Arnold Taylor. *The Welsh Castles of King Edward I* (London: The Hambledon Press, 1986). 128.
33. Chalon-sur-Saône lies on the Rhône, a third of the way from Dijon to Lyon, within the Franche-Comté de Bourgogne. Whilst it is a possible origin, given especially that in the late there thirteenth century the Free County was attached to Savoy by way of the marriage of Count Philippe I to Alix, Countess of Burgundy, a more likely candidate is the small hamlet of Chalon in what's now the Isère Department. Chalon, Isère, was known until recently as Châlons, and lies just 18 miles (29 kilometres) to the south-west of Saint-Georges-d'Espéranche. Chalon, Isère has but a few dwellings and a mayor's office, but intriguingly one of the two roads there is named '*Chenin des Tours*' and down the road a very short way a château is named '*Les Tours*.'
34. TNA E101/486/15.
35. Arnold Taylor, 'Some notes on the Savoyards in North Wales, 1277–1300. With special reference to the Savoyard element in the construction of Harlech Castle,' *Genava* XI (1963): 298. n32. Taylor adds that there was also a '*Perronetus de Saysello*' working on the castle of Amédée V de Savoie at Le Bourget in 1291–2.
36. Arnold Taylor, 'Some notes on the Savoyards in North Wales, 1277–1300. With special reference to the Savoyard element in the construction of Harlech Castle,' *Genava* XI (1963): 298. n32.
37. Louis Blondel, '*Le château de Saxon: note complémentaire*,' *Vallesia* IX (1955): 87–8.
38. Arnold Taylor, 'Some notes on the Savoyards in North Wales, 1277–1300. With special reference to the Savoyard element in the construction of Harlech Castle,' *Genava* XI (1963): 298. n32.
39. The Perche was a medieval French measure of length or height equivalent to 5.5 yards. Old French *Perche* from Latin *Perticate* meaning measuring rod. In England the measurement was therefore referred to as a rod.
40. TNA E101/485/28. '*Eodem die Ricardo de Kingeston et Thome Picard pro 4 perticatis in fossato [muri … versus occident] ibidem at tascham, percipientibus pro perticata 37 shillings., £7.8s.*' Or 'Also Richard de Kingeston and Thomas Picard for 4 Perche in the ditch [wall] by task, percipiently 37 shillings per Perche, £7. 8 shillings.'
41. Nicola Coldstream, 'Architects, Advisers and Design at Edward I's Castles in Wales,' *Architectural History: Journal of the Society of Architectural Historians of Great Britain* 46 (2003): 28.
42. Frankby is a small village on the north-western tip of the Wirral Peninsula close to West Kirby.
43. Arnold Taylor, 'Scorched Earth at Flint in 1294,' *Journal of the Flintshire Historical Society* 30 (1984): 93.

44. Given cites numbers of 700 acres for Conwy, Caernarfon 1,464 acres and Beaumaris would be 1,486 acres, no number is supplied for the compact Harlech site, in James Given. 1989. The Economic Consequences of the English Conquest of Gwynedd. Speculum 64: 20. n40.

45. James Given, 'The Economic Consequences of the English Conquest of Gwynedd,' *Speculum* 64 (1989). 20.

46. Ibid. Table 1.

47. Helen Fulton. *The Outside Within: Medieval Chester and North Wales, in Mapping the Medieval City: Space, Place and Identity in Chester c. 1200–1600* (Cardiff: University of Wales Press, 2011). 153.

48. James Given, 'The Economic Consequences of the English Conquest of Gwynedd,' *Speculum* 64 (1989):, 22. n47. Given cites Great Britain, Record Commission, Registrum vulgariter nuncupatum 'The Record of Caernarvon,' ed. Henry Ellis (London, 1838), p. 137; Lewis, Mediaeval Boroughs, 178–9.

49. Jeremy A. Ashbee. *Conwy Castle and Town Walls* (Cardiff: Cadw, 2015). 63.

50. Arnold Taylor. *The Welsh Castles of King Edward I* (London: The Hambledon Press, 1986). 54.

51. TNA E 101/351/9.

52. Christopher Wilson writing in '*Die Kathedrale von Lausanne und ihr Marienportal im Kontext der europäischen Gotik*' (Freiburg: der Universität Freiburg, 2004).noted especially the debt owed by the south transept rose window at Lausanne to the eastern transept of Canterbury. The western window is a part of the cathedral of which Wilson says 'the use of Canterbury motifs continued ... alongside ... the exploitation of contemporary English sources.' That the 'preceding phase [before the post 1220 Cotereel phase] ... had incorporated more Canterbury borrowings than any other church on the European mainland.' Before endorsing the idea of Cotereel's English ancestry as having 'much to recommend it'.

53. Arnold Taylor. 1985. *Studies in Castles and Castle-Building*. London: The Hambledon Press. Plate 19, Malcolm Hislop. *James of St George and the Castles of North Wales* (Barnsley: Pen & Sword Books Ltd, 2020). 115–7. 'Parallels [with the Conwy window] are difficult to bring to mind, but it's originality suggests that it may represent a design peculiar to Master James. In this regard it is worth considering the early thirteenth century window in the south transept of Lausanne Cathedral as a possible model ... It only takes a short flight of the imagination to see the Lausanne rose as the progenitor of the Conwy window. That there should be two references to Lausanne at Conwy seems to confirm the window tracery was determined by Master James.'

Chapter Twelve
1. CWR 1277–1326, 275. '11 September 1283, Macclesfield, To Maître Jacques de Sancto Georgio. Order to go in person to the town of Maynan, and to take seisin thereof for the king's use by the delivery of the bailiff of Henry de Lacy, earl of Lincoln, of Ros.'

2. TNA E372/136/33.

3. Arnold Taylor. *The Welsh Castles of King Edward I* (London: The Hambledon Press, 1986), 66. n3. '*Scutiferi de hospicio regis morantes in municione apud Hardelegh.*' Or 'Squires of the king's household staying for some time at the fortifications at Harlech. Citing also TNA E101/4/1 and TNA E101/4/8 for wages.

4. Aug. Burnand, '*Vaudois en Angleterre au XIIIe siècle, avec Othon Ier de Grandson : (d'après M.C.-L. Kingsford),*' *Revue historique vaudoise* 19 no 7 (1911): 214.

5. Michael Prestwich. *Knight: The Medieval Warrior's (Unofficial) Guide* (London: Thames & Hudson, 2010). 33–4.

6. CWR 1277–1326, 291. 'The King has committed in like manner to Hugh de Wlonkeslowe the castle of Hardelawe.'

7. Ibid. 302. 'To all bailiffs and subjects to whom, etc. Notification that the King has committed to John de Benelare [Jean de Bonvillars] during pleasure his castle of Herdelagh ... Mandate to Hugh de Wlonkeslowe to deliver the castle and armour etc, to John by indenture.'

8. TNA E101/351/9 '*Hugoni de Leominstr' clerico in partem solucionis vadiorum suorum de tempore quo fuit ultra operarios apud Caernaruan et Herdelawe annis xj et xij, £15.0s.11/2d.*' Or 'Hugh of Leominster, clerk, in part payment of his men's wages from the time where there have been more workers ar Caernarfon and Harlech in the years 11 and 12 [Edward's Regnal Years and so 1283 and 1284].'

9. John E. Morris. *The Welsh Wars of Edward I* (Oxford: Clarendon Press, 1901). 198. 'Criccieth and Harlech, Dolywyddelan and Bere, were old Welsh fortresses, of which Harlech was largely rebuilt on the Edwardian model.'

10. Paul Martin Remfry. *Harlech Castle and Its True Origins* (Disgwylfa, Ceidio, Gwynedd: SCS Publishing, 2013).

11. Jeremy Ashbee. *Harlech Castle* (Cardiff: Cadw, 2017). 5–6.

12. We need at this point to understand a little of native Welsh administrative organisation. Welsh principalities were divided into *cantrefi* then commotes. A commote or *cymwd* was a basic unit of

land made up of one hundred *trefi* (small village). The *trefi* within a commote could be either free or bonded settlements. Each commote had a royal *maerdref* inhabited by bondmen within which were the buildings of the *Llys*. A *Llys* was a hall where the Welsh law would be dispensed, that is to say a royal court.

13. Jeremy Ashbee. *Harlech Castle* (Cardiff: Cadw, 2017). 5–6.
14. Measuring 18 feet (approx. 5.5 metres) by 37 feet (approx. 11 metres) see J. Beverley Smith. 2014. *Llywellyn ap Gruffudd: Prince of Wales*. Cardiff: The University of Wales Press. Chap 5. Apple.
15. J. Beverley Smith. *Llywellyn ap Gruffudd: Prince of Wales*. Ebook. ed. (Cardiff: The University of Wales Press, 2014). Chap 5. Apple.
16. The source for this is of nearly three centuries later, (*cymydau*) of Wales, as listed by Gruffudd Hiraethog (d.1564) in NLW Peniarth MS.147.
17. The *Afon Artro* or River Artro is a small (5 miles/7 kilometres) river, within Ardudwy, that flows into Cardigan Bay near Llanbedr.
18. Jeremy Ashbee. *Harlech Castle* (Cardiff: Cadw, 2017).38–9. 'the sheriff of Merionethshire was paid for 'taking down the lord prince [Edward]'s hall at Ystumgwen and re-erecting it inside Harlech castle, together with making windows and louvres, and for making a new pantry and buttery in the same hall.' C. R. Peers. 'Harlech Castle.' *Transactions of the Honourable Society of Cymmrodorion* (1921-2): 63–82. Appendix II. Survey of Harlech by William de, 8 August, 17 Edward III (1343). '*Item quod aula vocata Styngwernehalle cum penticio magne aule possunt reparari pro iij.li.*' Or 'Also that the hall called Styngwernehalle with the *penticium* of the great hall may be repaired for three pounds.'
19. Richard Avent. *Dolywyddelan Castle Dolbadarn Castle Castell y Bere*. 2010 ed. (Cardiff: Cadw, 2004). 5.
20. *Giraldus Cambrensis*, Cap.VI. 'where two stone castles had newly been sited, they were; one in Evianyth [Eifionydd] in the direction of the mountainous north, it was of Chanani [Cynan], which is named Deutrait [Deudraeth; the other, however, across the river in the direction of the sea at the head of the Lhein [Llyn]., it was of Oenei [Owain], which is named Karmadrun [Carn Fadryn] ' The Thorpe translation is 'We crossed the Traeth Mawr and Traeth Bychan. These are two arms of the sea, one big, one small. Two stone castles have been built there recently. The one called Deudraeth belongs to the sons of Cynan and is situated in the Eifionydd area, facing the northern mountains. The second which is called Carn Madryn, belongs to the sons of Owain: which is on the Llyn Peninsula, on the other side of the river and it faces the sea.' Gerald of Wales. 1978. *The Journey Through Wales and The Description of Wales*. London: Penguin Books Ltd. 195.
21. Richard Avent. Dolywyddelan Castle Dolbadarn Castle Castell y Bere. 2010 ed. (Cardiff: Cadw, 2004). 4. 'During his tour of Wales in 1188 with Archbishop Baldwin of Canterbury to gather recruits for the Third Crusade, Gerald of Wales (d. 1223) mentions two castles that had recently been erected in Gwynedd at Deudraeth and Carn Madryn. If the present-day identification [note qualification] of these castles is correct, they are striking by the complete contrast in their in their location and style of construction. Deudraeth has been identified as Castell Aber lâ, which now lies within Clough William Ellis' coastal Italianate village of Portmeirion and consisted of a motte built up over a natural rock outcrop originally surmounted by a stone tower. Carn Madryn is generally thought to be Carn Fadryn, the westernmost mountain on the Llyn Peninsula, which has a small enclosure of unmortared masonry on its summit within an earlier prehistoric hillfort.'
22. CWR 1277–1326, 291. October 1283, Caernarfon, 'The king has committed to John de Havering' during pleasure his castle at Kaernarvon [Caernarfon], with the armour and all the things forming the munition of the castle, and has granted to him 200 marks yearly for the custody, to be received at the exchequer of Kaernarvan [Caernarfon] by the hands of the chamberlain, on condition that he shall have continuously have in garrison there, in addition to himself and his household, at his cost forty fencible men, of whom fifteen shall be crossbowmen, one chaplain, one artiller, a carpenter, a mason and a smith, and of the others shall be made janitors, watchmen and other ministers of the castle. Order is given to all bailiffs etc 'to be intendent on John as keeper of the castle in those things that pertain to the custody. The king has committed in like manner to Walter de Huntercomb the castle of Bere, and has granted to him 200 marks yearly for the custody, to be received as above, on condition that he shall have continuously there in garrison at the castle at his cost forty fencible men, of whom fifteen shall be crossbowmen, one chaplain, one artiller, a carpenter, a mason and a smith, and of the others shall be made janitors, watchmen and other ministers of the castle. Order is given to all bailiffs etc (as in preceding). The king has committed in like manner to Hugh de Wlonkeslowe the castle of Hardelawe [Harlech, with the armour, etc, and has granted to him 100 livres yearly for the custody, to be received as above, on condition that he shall have continuously in garrison there at his cost thirty fencible men, of whom ten shall be crossbowmen one chaplain, one artiller, a carpenter, a mason and a smith, and of the others shall be made janitors, watchmen and other ministers of the castle. Order is given to all bailiffs etc (as above). The king has committed in like manner to William de Cycun [Guillaume de Cicon], the

castle of Aberconewey [Conwy], with the armour, etc, and has granted to him 190 livres yearly for the custody thereof, to be received as above, on condition that he shall have continuously have in garrison, in addition to himself and his household, at his cost thirty fencible men, of whom fifteen shall be cross-bowmen one chaplain, one artiller, a carpenter, a mason and a smith, and of the others shall be made janitors, watchmen and other ministers of the castle. Order is given to all bailiffs etc (as above).

23. Graham Lott. 'The Building Stones of the Edwardian Castles' in *The Impact of the Edwardian Castles in Wales* (Oxford: Oxbow Books, 2010). 116 'The castle is sited on a rugged, fault-bounded cliff line composed of the hard sandstones and mudstones of the Rhinog Formation of the Harlech Grits Group ((Cambrian 488–542 million years).'

24. TNA E372/131/26. '*ad operacionem fossati de rupe ante castrum de Hardelagh.*' Or 'for the digging of the ditch from a cliff in front of the castle of Harlech.'

25. Richard Avent. *Dolwyddelan Castle Dolbadarn Castle Castell y Bere*. 2010 ed. (Cardiff: Cadw, 2004).- See 'Bird's Eye' visualizations and ground plans for both Dolwyddelan and Castell y Bere.

26. Nicola Coldstream, 'Architects, Advisers and Design at Edward I's Castles in Wales,' *Architectural History: Journal of the Society of Architectural Historians of Great Britain* 46 (2003). 27. 'it is well within the accepted limits of methodology to suggest that he could have been Robert of Beverley.'

27. Ibid. 26. 'A more likely tutor to James of St George, however, although undocumented in this case, is Robert of Beverley.'

28. John. A. A. Goodall. 'The Baronial Castles of the Welsh Conquest' in *The Impact of the Edwardian Castles in Wales* (Oxford: Oxbow Books, 2010). 157–8. '*The History of the Kings Works* and Arnold Taylor in his other published works went to great lengths to prove how the details of the Welsh castles spoke of the Continental training of James of St George, and in most points he was absolutely right. What he omitted to notice was that whatever their detail, their bones and body reflected a variety of forms and sophistication that cannot be explained without reference to the English architectural tradition of King John and King Henry III.' This is entirely correct but can be explained by the influence of Jean de Mézos rather or as well as 'archive drawings' as suggested by Goodall.

29. For Jean de Mézos as directing the works of Maître Jacques in Savoy see Arnold Taylor. Master Bertram, Ingeniator Regis. Studies in Medieval History presented to R. Allen Brown (Woodbridge: The Boydell Press, 1989). 294. n31. Reproduced from Arnold Taylor. *Studies in Castles and Castle Building* (London: The Hambledon Press, 1985). 93 citing Chambéry Archive. '*In expensis Magistri Jacobi Lathomi euntis apud Salinas pro operibus putei per xj dies, capientis quolibet die iij.s. pro expensis, xxxiij.s. Idem libravit domino Johanni de Masouz moranti apud Salin' pro dictando opera putei Salino xxix. lib. xix.s. vj.d.*' Or 'The expenses of Maître Jacques the stonemason going to Salins-Les-Thermes for the works of the well for eleven days, taking per day three *sol* for expenses, thirty-three *sol*. Also considered Lord Jean de Mézos detained at Salins-Les-Thermes for dictating the well works at Salins-Les-Thermes twenty-nine Livre, nineteen *sol*, six den.' This attribution of 'dictando' to Jean de Mézos at a site also carrying primary source evidence of Maître Jacques, is the closest we will come in primary sources to a 'tutor'.

30. Malcolm Hislop. *James of St George and the Castles of North Wales* (Barnsley: Pen & Sword Books Ltd, 2020). 70. 'it is it's [Aberystwyth affinities with the Inner East Gatehouse of Caerphilly in particular that are striking … It may therefore be stated with a reasonable degree of confidence that the main gatehouse of Aberystwyth was based on the Inner East Gatehouse of Caerphilly.' And Ibid. 260. 'The affinities with Caerphilly suggest that … Master James borrowed the concept for replication at Harlech.'

31. David Martin & Barbara Martin, 'A Reinterpretation of the Gatehouse at Tonbridge Castle,' *Archaelogia Cantiana* 133 (2013): 273.

32. Derek Renn. *Caerffili Castle.* Revised ed. (Cardiff: Cadw, 1989). 36–7.

33. Nicola Coldstream, 'Architects, Advisers and Design at Edward I's Castles in Wales,' *Architectural History: Journal of the Society of Architectural Historians of Great Britain* 46 (2003): 26. 'The plans of the Clare gatehouses are so similar that they are almost certainly the work of the same designer.'

34. Arnold Taylor. *Studies in Castles and Castle-Building* (London: The Hambledon Press, 1985). 10. Taylor measured the windows at Harlech and compared them with measurements taken by Jean-Pierre Chapuisat at Chillon. By width Harlech was 1.52 metres and Chillon 1.53, by height Harlech was 3.88 and Chillon 3.86.

35. David Martin & Barbara Martin, 'A Reinterpretation of the Gatehouse at Tonbridge Castle,' *Archaelogia Cantiana* 133 (2013): 244.

36. Arnold Taylor. *Harlech Castle* (Cardiff: Cadw, 2015). 20.

37. Paddy Griffith. *The Vauban Fortifications of France* (Oxford: Osprey Publishing, 2006). 50.

38. Daniel de Raemy. *Châteaux, donjons et grandes tours dans les Etats de Savoie* (1230-1330). (Lausanne: Cahiers d'archéologie romande 98 et 99, 2004). 'the architect's genius was not to go fishing for new forms in the void, but to transcribe in the ground, with stone and wood, the very precise desires of his patron in order to answer their requirements in defensive, residential and prestigious matters.'

39. TNA E101/485/27. The packhorse and the horse-drawn cart were the most common way of transporting material.
40. See earlier page 128.
41. Jeremy A. Ashbee. *Harlech Castle* (Cardiff: Cadw, 2017). 20.
42. Arnold Taylor, 'Some notes on the Savoyards in North Wales, 1277–1300. With special reference to the Savoyard element in the construction of Harlech Castle,' Genava XI (1963): 308.
43. TNA 372/138/25.
44. TNA E101/485/26.
45. TNA E101/485/27.
46. Arnold Taylor, 'Some notes on the Savoyards in North Wales, 1277-1300. With special reference to the Savoyard element in the construction of Harlech Castle,' Genava XI (1963): 308.
47. Nicola Coldstream, 'Architects, Advisers and Design at Edward I's Castles in Wales,' *Architectural History: Journal of the Society of Architectural Historians of Great Britain* 46 (2003): 28–9. 'John Francis, who may have imported the corbelled latrines found at Harlech, which was built at La Bâtiaz only after 1280-1, when Master James was in Wales and could not have seen it.' Now this observation rests upon the dating of the corbelled latrines at La Bâtiaz. To recap the history, the castle there had been built before 1259 by the Bishop of Sion, it had then been besieged by Pierre de Savoie in 1259 and acquired by pledge in 1260. We know that in the next decade that Pierre de Savoie added the circular donjon tower, confirmed by dendrochronology, but that its top floor was added by the Bishop of Sion, Pierre d'Oron on his requisition in 1280–1. Taylor referred to this in Arnold Taylor. *Studies in Castles and Castle-Building* (London: The Hambledon Press, 1985). 14 'La Bâtiaz was afterwards recovered by the bishops, who undertook extensive repairs to its other buildings in 1280–1.' It is to this that Coldstream attached her suggestion that 'Master James was in Wales and could not have seen it.' Taylor got his history of La Bâtiaz from André Donnet & Louis Blondel. Château du Valais (Olten: Editions Walter, 1963). 121-4. But the Swiss authors were silent in terms what these repairs amounted to, other than an additional floor added to the tower, *Le quatrième étage, plus récent, a été construit sous l'évéque Pierre d'Oron, en 1281, par le châtelain Rodolphe; il est voûté sur croisées d'ogives, avec un couronnement en pyramide maintenant ruiné.* So in actuality we cannot definitively date the corbelled latrines, and therefore support a suggestion by Coldstream that James hadn't seen it or by Taylor that he had. In the absence of primary sources, we cannot know.
48. Arnold Taylor. *Studies in Castles and Castle-Building* (London: The Hambledon Press, 1985). 40. '[Yverdon, Saint-Georges, Rhuddlan, Conwy and Harlech] ... have or had latrine projections not merely placed in exactly similar relative positions, but designed on similar line, and to similar dimensions ... the Saint-Georges projection measures 8 ft. 2 in. by 2 ft. 1 in. The corresponding dimensions of the projection adjoining the north-west tower at Harlech are 8 ft. 10 in. and 2 ft. 2 in. 'Taylor noted that the design when applied to Rhuddlan and Conwy had not been square-ended but chamfered.
49. C. R. Peers. 'Harlech Castle.' *Transactions of the Honourable Society of Cymmrodorion* (1921–2): 63-82. Appendix II. The Survey of 1321 and Survey of Harlech by William de, 8 August, 17 Edward III (1343).
50. Arnold Taylor. *The Welsh Castles of King Edward I* London: The Hambledon Press, 1986). 67.
51. TNA E101/485/27
52. Tim Palmer. *Egryn Stone: a forgotten Welsh freestone* (Arch. Camb, 2007). 149–60.
53. Jeremy Ashbee. *Harlech Castle* (Cardiff: Cadw, 2017). 6.
54. Arnold Taylor. *The Welsh Castles of King Edward I* (London: The Hambledon Press, 1986), 66. n3. '*Scutiferi de hospicio regis morantes in municione apud Hardelegh.*' Or 'Squires of the king's household staying for some time at the fortifications at Harlech'. Citing also TNA E101/4/1 and TNA E101/4/8 for the squire's wages. For the sawyers under Richard of Mountsorrel see TNA E101/351/9. Paras 26, 27 and 31.
55. J. G. Edwards, 'Edward I's Castle-Building in Wales,' *The Proceedings of the British Academy* XXXII (1944): 21 n1. Reproduced many of the early payments that do survive for 1283–4.
56. William of Louth had been appointed cofferer of the Wardrobe on 18 October 1274, followed Savoyards Guillaume de Champvent and Louis de Vaud as Dean of St Martins-Le-Grand, and was later elected to the see of Ely on 12 May 1290 and consecrated on 1 October 1290. For a brief summary of his career see E. B. Fryde, D. E. Greenway, S. Porter & I. Roy. 1986. *Handbook of British Chronology*. Third ed. London: Offices of the Royal Historical Society. 78.
57. TNA E372/130. rot5 d. And Arnold Taylor. *The Welsh Castles of King Edward I.* (London: The Hambledon Press. 1986).49. n9. Having earlier been reproduced in J. G. Edwards. Edward I's Castle-Building in Wales. *The Proceedings of the British Academy* XXXII (1944): 20. n2. '*Compotus Magistri Willelmi de Luda, custodis de garderoba regis, de receptis et missis in expedicione eiusdem regis in partibus Wallie et in vadiis et stipendiis diversorum cementariorum, carpentariorum, fossatorum, coupiatorum, carbonariorum, vintenariorum et eorum magistorum per totum tempus predictum apud Cestriam, Hope,*

Rothelan, Conewey, Caernarvan, Crukyn, Hadel, West Wallia, et alia diversa loca in guerra predicta, £9414.4s.11d. sicut continentur in rotulo de particulis quem idem Magister Willelmus liberavit in thesauro a die dominica in ramis palmarum anno x usque festum sancti Edmundi regis anno xiii incipiente et quodam partie anni xiii.'. Or 'And in wages and the wages of different stonemasons, carpenters, ditch diggers, coopers, charcoal burners, vintners and their masters the entire time aforesaid at Chester, Hope, Rhuddlan, Conwy, Caernarvan, Crukyn, Harlech, West Wales, and the other different places in the said war, £ 9414. 4. 11d. which are contained in the of particulars of the same Master William [of Louth], considered in the Wardrobe account.'

58. Arnold Taylor. *The Welsh Castles of King Edward I* London: The Hambledon Press, 1986). 69. Citing TNA E101/501/23 no. 63. 'Master William Drygda N. tower towards the sea, 491/2 ft. high at 45s. per ft. £111.7s.6d. Turret on same, 19ft . at 12s. per foot £11.8s. S. Tower towards sea, 52 ft. high at 45s. per foot. £117. Turret on same, 19ft at 12s per foot. £11.8s.' Master William of Drogheda is later recorded as a burgess of Caernarfon.

59. Christopher Wilson. *The Gothic Cathedral* (London: Thames and Hobson Ltd, 1990). 140.

60. John. A. A. Goodall. 'The Baronial Castles of the Welsh Conquest' in *The Impact of the Edwardian Castles in Wales* (Oxford: Oxbow Books, 2010). 157–8.

61. Arnold Taylor. *The Welsh Castles of King Edward I* (London: The Hambledon Press, 1986). 72. *'pro CC targeis factis apud Burd' de armis Regis per preceptum Regis nunciante domino Othone de Grandissono ad mittend' in Walliam ad municionem castrorum Regis ibidem £31.1s.'* Or 'For two hundred targets (shields) made at *Burdigala* (Bordeaux) of the arms of the King by command of the King having been announced by Othon de Grandson to be sent to the Kings fortifications and castles the same £31.1s.' *Burdigala* was the archaic name for Bordeaux. In the thirteenth century much more of Roman *Burdigala* remained than today, the city wall, amphitheatre and aqueducts remained wholly or partly extant.

62. CWR 1277–1326, 326. 'July 3, Havering. To all to whom, etc. Notification that the king has committed to Master James de Sancto Georgio his castle of Hardelagh during pleasure, so that he shall receive yearly 100 marks at the exchequer of Kaernarvan for so long as he shall be constable of the said castle, reckoning in that sum the wages that the king previously granted to him yearly. To Agnès, late the wife of John Beuillard. Order to deliver to the said James by indenture the said castle, and other stock there.' And TNA C47/2/10 Memorandum of Instructions dated August 1290. *'Vne letre a Maistre Jakes de Sent George kil preigne le chastel de Hardelah e le garde sauvement a son peril ... Vne lettre a Maistre Robert de Beauver kil de taunt de tens cum il a este tresorer en Gales delivre a Maistre Jakes de Sent George son fee ke le Roy li a graunte a terme de Savoie vie.'* The appointment was not much in the way of a salary increase for James, since Edward reckoned his existing wages of just over £54 a year as included in his constable's fee of 100 marks, or £66. Edward not one noted for being overly generous.

63. Arnold Taylor. *The Welsh Castles of King Edward I* (London: The Hambledon Press, 1986). 20 n10. Taylor suggested that for Flint 'Master James is paid continuously, i.e., 7 days a week' whereas the others there were paid for a 6-day week. So, we will take Taylor's 7-day week as the basis for calculations.

64. *La Finanza Sabauda.* vol. 1, 63. *'Compotus de Valeisio et Chablasio de anno LXI, 'Item in liberatione magistri Iohannis cementarii a die qua recessit a domo sua veniendo versus Yverdunum, videlicet prima die maii hoc anno* [1 May 1261] *usque ad secundam dominicam quadragisime, videlicet quintam diem intrante marcio* [5 March 1262], *per quadraginta et quatuor septimanas, qui cepit duodecim solidos qualibet septimana, xxvj.lib. ij.sol. In liberatione magistri Iacobi filii sui per idem tempus, capientis singulis septimanis decem solidos et sex denarios, xxiij.lib. ij.sol. In vadiis suis et calciatura sua et pannis lineis, capientis quinque solidos per mensem, per dictum tempus .lv.sol. In medicinis ipsius magistri Jacobi tempore egritudinis sue .xxv.sol. In liberatione magistri Petri Mainier custodis operum domini per idem tempus pro se duobus equis et uno valeto suo capientis ut predictus magister Iohannes. Xxvj.lib. viij.sol.'* Or 'Account of the Valais and Chablais of the year 61. For the discharge of Master John, the mason from the day when he came from his home to Yverdon, assuredly the first day of May of this year [1 May 1261] until the second Sunday of Lent [5 March 1262] for forty-four weeks who received twelve *sol* per week. Twenty-six *livres* and eight *sol*. For the discharge of his son Maître Jacques for same period receiving ten *sol* and six denier every week. Twenty-three *livres* and two *sol*. For his wages and shoes and his linen bandages receiving five *sol* per month. Fifty-five *sol*. For Maître Jacques himself, medicine for the time of his illness. Twenty-five *sol*. For the discharge of Master Pierre Mainier Custodian of the Lord's works for the same period two horses for himself and one for his servant as Master John aforesaid. Twenty-six Livres and eight *sol*.'

65. CPR Edward I vol 2 1281–1292, 137. 'Oct. 20. Carnarvon. Grant, for life, to Maître Jacques de Sancto Georgio, king's sergeant, of 3s. a day from the wardrobe, and at his death of Is. 6d. a day to his wife Ambrosia if she survive him.'

66. Michael Prestwich. *Edward I* (Yale: Yale University Press, 1997). Notes on Money. 'until the great French debasements the 1290s, the usual ratio of the English currency to the *livre tournois* was about 1:4.'
67. Using ratio of 4 *Livres tournois* to £1 as above.
68. Yverdon weekly.
69. C. J. Spurgeon, 'Builth Castle,' *Brycheiniog* 18 (1978/79): 47–59.
70. TNA currency converter.
71. R. R. Davies. *The Age of Conquest: Wales 1063–1415* (Oxford: Oxford University Press, 1987). 359–60.

Chapter Thirteen

1. Richard Avent. *Criccieth Castle* (Cardiff: Cadw, 1989). 3.
2. Arnold Taylor. *The Welsh Castles of King Edward I* (London: The Hambledon Press, 1986). 74.
3. Richard Avent. *Criccieth Castle* (Cardiff: Cadw, 1989). 15.
4. Michael Prestwich. *Edward I* (Yale: Yale University Press, 1997). 211–4. 'The most intriguing origin of any of the architectural features adopted by Edward's masons is that of the remarkable multi-angular towers and dark stripes in the stonework at Caernarfon. This has been convincingly demonstrated by A. J. Taylor … The style of the castle is very clearly derived from the walls of the imperial city of Constantinople.'
5. Abigail Wheatley. 'Caernarfon Castle and its Mythology.' in *The Impact of the Edwardian Castles in Wales* (Oxford: Oxbow Books, 2010). 129–39.
6. *The History of Gruffydd ap Cynan; The Welsh Text*. Arthur Jones. Ed. (Manchester: University Press, 1910). 132–3. 'Earl Hugh [d'Avranches] came to his domain in great force and built castles and strong places after the manner of the French and was lord over the land. A castle he built in Anglesey, and another in Arvon in the old city of the Emperor Constantine, son of Constans the Great.' This anonymous eleventh century source is unequivocal.
7. TNA E101/351/9. 'Eustachio de Hachi, Militi, deputato custodi ultra opera et cariagia necessiaria ad constructionem castri et ville de Carnaruan' Or 'Eustace de Hache, knight, whose task is to keep the work and necessary carriage for the building of the castle and town of Caernarfon.' And: 'The digging and preparation the new most of Caernarfon.'
8. Arnold Taylor. *The Welsh Castles of King Edward I* (London: The Hambledon Press, 1986). 80. By the middle of July the next year, 1284, houses were being demolished to make way for the new castle under construction. '*portantibus meremium de domibus prius factis de Carnarnan et prostratis pro fossat' ville ibidem faciend'* or 'carrying timber from the existing demolished houses at Caernarfon for making a ditch in the same place.'
9. Ibid. 80. n3.
10. Ibid. '*ad constructionem castri et ville tunc inceptum*' and '*Pro fossura et apparatu noue mote de Caernaruan.*' Or 'the construction of the castle and town then commenced' and 'For the digging and preparation of the new moat of Caernarfon.'
11. Arnold Taylor. *Studies in Castles and Castle-Building* (London: The Hambledon Press, 1985). 26.
12. Ibid. 78–9. n4. 'It is also most curious that Caernarfon, like Constantinople, should have its own Golden Gate. As a variant name for the West or Water Gate of the walled town this now only survives in its Welsh form of *Porth yr Aur*, but its antiquity is testified by reference in 1524 to the repair 'of the kee by the gate called the Gildyn yeate.' TNA E101/488/26; it looks as if we may have the echo of a still earlier time when the idea of parallelism between Edward's recreation of the 'old city of the Emperor Constantine' in Arvon and the buildings of Constantine's own city of New Rome on the Bosporus was a known and accepted thing.'
13. Othon de la Roche became Duc d'Athènes and built a Frankish tower atop the Acropolis
14. Karystos or Carystus is a small coastal town on the Greek island of Euboea. It is the second-largest Greek island in area and population, after Crete. The Triarchy of Negroponte was a crusader state established on the island of Euboea – one element of the Triarchy was the Lordship of Karystos.
15. William Miller. *The Latins in the Levant* (New York: E. P. Dutton & Company, 1908). 115.
16. Ibid. 137.
17. Malcolm Hislop. *James of St George and the Castles of North Wales* (Barnsley: Pen & Sword Books Ltd, 2020). 140. Hislop offers examples of banded Roman masonry at Burgh Castle, Pevensey and Richborough.
18. Richard K. Morris. 'The Architecture of Arthurian Enthusiasm: Castle Symbolism in the Reigns of Edward I and his Successors.' in Late Medieval Castles (Woodbridge : The Boydell Press, 2016). 354. n10. 'The Theodosian walls are stone and tile, whereas the Caernarfon walls are two types of stone (carboniferous limestone with darker bands of carboniferous sandstone) see Royal Commission for Ancient and Historic Monuments (RCAHM) (Wales), Caernarfonshire, II, Central (1960), 190.'

19. Abigail Wheatley. 'Caernarfon Castle and its Mythology' in *The Impact of the Edwardian Castles in Wales* (Oxford: Oxbow Books, 2010). 136. Richard K. Morris. 'The Architecture of Arthurian Enthusiasm: Castle Symbolism in the Reigns of Edward I and his Successors' in *Late Medieval Castles* (Woodbridge: The Boydell Press, 2016). 360. 'it would be astonishing if contemporaries did not recognize automatically that the incontrovertible architectural links with Constantinople also implied an association with Arthur, as grandson of Constantine, following the pedigree stemming from Geoffrey of Monmouth's *Historia Regum in Britanniae*.'

20. Michael Prestwich. 'Edward I in Wales' in *The Impact of the Edwardian Castles in Wales* (Oxford: Oxbow Books, 2010). 4. 'His [Edward] main stay was at the count's [Philippe] new castle of Saint-Georges-d'Espéranche, this had concentric defences, rather like Harlech, and octagonal towers, anticipating Caernarfon.'

21. ADI. Serie L, no. 198, pacquet 1. The letters in the following report by Chabord relate to the accompanying colourwash plan (Figure 1.4) '*Le cydevant Château d'Espéranche est flanque de quatre tours A, octogones (voir le plan cyjoint figure), dont les murs ont cinq pieds d'épaisseur. Vers le sommet de ces tours, il existe quelques embrasures. Les murs extérieurs de cedit bâtiment, ainsi que le mur BC servant de clôture à la grande cour du côté du nord, ont aussi semblable épaisseur. Des fossés, comme le plan l'indique, regiment tour au tour de ce vaste bâtiment, et ont de largeur depuis trente a cinquente pieds, sur dix a dix-huit pieds de hauteur.*' Or 'The side of the Château d' Espéranche is flanked by four towers (A), octagons (see the plan attached figure), the walls of which are five feet thick. Towards the top of these towers there are a few embrasures. The exterior walls of this building, as well as the wall (B to C) serving as an enclosure for the great courtyard on the north side, are also of similar thickness. Ditches as the plan indicates, surround this vast building, and are thirty to fifty feet wide, and ten to eighteen feet high.' We thus have the best description we can now have of the Château d'Espéranche. The surviving elements of the castle in 1794 being the four towers (A), one face of the curtain wall (B-C) and the surrounding moat, which was then drained to a marsh on its northern face. But enough had survived until 1794 to identify a Carré Savoyard, but with octagonal not round towers.

22. Malcolm Hislop. *James of St George and the Castles of North Wales* (Barnsley: Pen & Sword Books Ltd, 2020). 277. n18. Hislop casts some doubt on the nature of the towers at Saint-Georges by noting the disparity in orientation of the polygonal towers of Chabord's colourwash when compared to an aerial photograph. But I think he's being a little unkind to our revolutionary functionary, the colourwash may well have been done from memory, and the disparity between reality and memory is now apparent. The colourwash remains as close as we will get to a plan of the original castle, and we should not let the orientation issue cloud the veracity of the artefact. Particularly as neither Edward nor James would have had any idea of the original orientation when planning Caernarfon.

23. Arnold Taylor. *Studies in Castles and Castle-Building* (London: The Hambledon Press, 1985). 42. 'The point that is interesting to note, in the present context, is that in north Wales, as in Savoy, not only do we have a unified group of castles in which round towers are the rule and polygonal towers the exception, but further, that the status of the principal Welsh exception, namely Caernarfon, has something in common with that of the Savoy exception, namely St Georges. For Caernarfon was essentially intended as the palace castle of the English principality of Wales, the formal, official seat of the prince's government, and it may be that in some way very similar ideas underlie the distinctive treatment accorded to both buildings.'

24. Richard K. Morris. 'The Architecture of Arthurian Enthusiasm: Castle Symbolism in the Reigns of Edward I and his Successors' in *Late Medieval Castles* (Woodbridge: The Boydell Press, 2016). 360.

25. Constantine built a new imperial residence at Byzantium and renamed the city Constantinople after himself, the laudatory epithet of 'New Rome' came a little later and was never an official title. Its first use appears in 381AD at the First Council of Constantinople. The third canon reads 'The Bishop of Constantinople, however, shall have the prerogative of honour after the Bishop of Rome because Constantinople is New Rome.' So, the epithet would have been widely known by crowned heads of the thirteenth century.

26. Abigail Wheatley. *The Idea of the Castle in Medieval England* (York: York Medieval Press, 2015). 140. 'It imitates the transfer of imperial power and resonances practised by Constantine … it signifies the geographic and symbolic relocation of imperial power and asserts the legitimate succession of the new regime.'

27. Arnold Taylor. *The Welsh Castles of King Edward I* (London: The Hambledon Press, 1986). 78.n1. cites Antiquity xxvi (1952) plate IVb

28. R. Allen Brown. *English Castles* (London: Chancellor Press, 1970). 102. And The History of Gruffydd ap Cynan; The Welsh Text. Arthur Jones. Ed. (Manchester: University Press, 1910). 132–3. 'Earl Hugh [d'Avranches] came to his domain in great force and built castles and strong places after the manner of the French, and was lord over the land. A castle he built in Anglesey, and another in Arvon in the old city of the Emperor Constantine, son of Constans the Great.'

29. Richard K. Morris. 'The Architecture of Arthurian Enthusiasm: Castle Symbolism in the Reigns of Edward I and his Successors' in *Late Medieval Castles* (Woodbridge: The Boydell Press, 2016). 361. 'Analysis of the plan of Caernarfon Castle reveals a designer playing with geometrical shapes for effect.'
30. Referred to in 1343 as the 'Gate towards the Prince's Garden'.
31. C. R. Peers. 'Carnarvan Castle.' *Transactions of the Honourable Society of Cymmrodorion* (1915-6). 15. So referred in 1343. Appendix 1. Referenced in 1343 as '*del Blaketout*'.
32. Ibid. 15. Old French for 'beautiful thing or being', So referred in 1303–4.
33. Ibid. Appendix 1. Referenced in 1343 as '*Item quod quedam Turris vocata Tour de Baner*'.
34. Ibid. 16. So referred in 1300, it would not become the Eagle Tower until 1316. Appendix 1. Referenced in 1343 '*in quadam Turri vocata Tour de Egle*'.
35. Ibid. 19. Appendix 1. Referenced in 1343 as '*quod quedam turris que vocatur le Welletour*'.
36. L. A. S. Butler. *Denbigh Castle* (Cardiff: Cadw, 2007). 9.
37. Robert J Dean. *Castles in Distant Lands: The Life and Times of Othon of Grandson* (Willingdon: Lawden Haynes Publishing, 2009). 58.
38. L. A. S. Butler. *Denbigh Castle* (Cardiff: Cadw, 2007). 27. 'the symbolism of this combination [polygonal banded towers] should not be overlooked. Although we cannot be certain of all its meanings, no doubt authority was intended. Denbigh had replaced the main castle of Dafydd ap Gruffydd and Caernarfon became the centre of Edward I's administration in north Wales, which displaced the authority of Llywelyn ap Gruffydd.'
39. J. N. Dalton. *The collegiate church of Ottery St Mary being the Ordinacio et Statuta ecclesie Sancta Marie de Otery Exon. Diocesis A.D. 1338–1339* (Cambridge: Cambridge University Press, 1917). 42. n1b.
40. Barthélémy de Grandson (1110–1158/9) had been a crusading knight, accompanying Count Amédée III de Savoie on the Second Crusade, passing from this world in Jerusalem.
41. Dressing stone was the art of masons shaping, surfacing, sculpting and finishing rough cut stone. Banker masons used a variety of chisels and a steady hand for the purpose.
42. Graham Lott. 'The Building Stones of the Edwardian Castles' in *The Impact of the Edwardian Castles in Wales* (Oxford: Oxbow Books, 2010). 117. 'The stone used for most of the fabric is pale grey, hard, occasionally fossiliferous, limestone quarried from the Lower Carboniferous (Visean) succession … Their consistent thickness reflects the regular, well-bedded character of the limestone in its natural outcrop, which probably required only minimal dressing by the masons before use. Limestones of the Lower Carboniferous age crop out … on the island of Anglesey, along both sides of the Menai Strait, at the Great Orme and in the Clwydian Hills.'
43. Ibid. 'However, the closest and therefore most accessible outcrops occur in the Penmon-Benllech area of Anglesey and along the southern shoreline of the Menai at Vaynol.'
44. Ibid. 119. 'Edward I was fortunate in that he was already familiar with the skills and experience of the 'architect/builder', James of St George, whom he was to select eventually to supervise much of this vast building project … in his role as master of the King's Works in Wales, James of St George had probably already acquired a unique understanding of the building sources available to him in north Wales and its adjacent areas.'
45. AST, Inv. Sav. 69, Fo. 69, mazzo 1, no. 1. '*Pro turre Sassonis in tascha facienda de altitudine decem teys*'
46. R. R. Davies. *The Age of Conquest: Wales 1063–1415* (Oxford: Oxford University Press, 1987). 358–9.
47. CWR Edward I 1277-1326, 352.'To Robert de Staundon, Justice of North Wales, and to Robert de Belvero, Treasurer of the Exchequer of Karnarvan. Notice that the king has pardoned Mary, late the wife of Manasser Le Fosseur of Carnarvon 23s.8d. in which Manasser was indebted to the king of the time when he was the king's bailiff in Karnarvan.'
48. Arnold Taylor. *The Welsh Castles of King Edward I* (London: The Hambledon Press, 1986). 83.n1. 'A projecting stone set on the north-west face of the North-East tower was to give a siting point for the alignment of the adjacent length of the town wall (similar siting stones were set on each of the towers of the northern stretch of Conwy town walls, also building in 1284): it therefore precedes the building of the town wall and indicates a minimum height to which the outward walls at the eastern end of the castle had been carried by October 1284.'
49. Ibid. 85.
50. CPR Edward I vol 2 1281–1292, 302. 'Protection, with clause volumus, until Michaelmas, for the following staying in Wales to fortify the castle at Karnarvan: William de Grandisono, Richard Fokeram.' Taylor suggested plausibly that 'fortify the castle' in the context of the original text '*qui in municione castri Regis de Karnarvan moratur*' taken together with a letter of May 1290 to Burnel showed the function was to audit and approve the account of the chamberlain. Arnold Taylor. *The Welsh Castles of King Edward I*. (London: The Hambledon Press. 1986). 85. n1.
51. Francis Salet. 1964. Maçons savoyards au pays de Galles. Bulletin Monumental 122: 194. "*A toutes les preuves ainsi produites des liens qui ont existé entre Savoie et pays de Galles, il faut ajouter que Philippe le Charpentier, qui apparaît à Vale Royal en 1278-1280, à Flint en 1286, à Caernarvon en 1295, 1305*

et 1320, n'était autre que Philippe de Saint-Georges, employé par Philippe de Savoie à Saint- Georges-d'Espéranche en 1274-1275."

52. TNA C47/4/5 f42 d. 'Magistro Waltero de Hereford Cementario, inagistro operis cementane ecclesie Abbath' de Valle regali ... anni xviij' or 'Master Walter of Hereford, builder, Master of the Works at the Church of Vale Royal ... in the eighteenth year [of King Edward I's reign].'

53. Arnold Taylor. Studies in Castles and Castle-Building (London: The Hambledon Press, 1985). 134. 'That the castle is on the contrary a single design, conceived as a unity, at the time work was begun on it in 1283–4 and, except for the north side, carried a considerable length towards completion within the succeeding three to four years.'

54. Nicola Coldstream, 'Architects, Advisers and Design at Edward I's Castles in Wales,' Architectural History: Journal of the Society of Architectural Historians of Great Britain 46 (2003): 29. 'Although Walter did not set out the south curtain at Caernarfon, John Maddison has isolated certain styles of moulding, that he attributed to him, so that Walter was able to influence details of design if not the whole scheme. John Harvey believed that the design of the castle was the joint responsibility of Walter of Hereford and James of St George together with Richard of Chester.'

55. Arnold Taylor. The Welsh Castles of King Edward I (London: The Hambledon Press, 1986). 86. 'resumption, from June 1295, onwards of building at Caernarfon ... At Caernarfon both the wall repairs and the ensuing phase of constructional work on the castle were entrusted to Master Walter of Hereford.' Master Walter is known to have been the Master of Works at Vale Royal in Cheshire until at least 1290, seven years into the construction of Caernarfon Castle.

56. Rick Turner. 'The Life and Career of Richard the Engineer' in The Impact of the Edwardian Castles in Wales (Oxford: Oxbow Books, 2010). 53.'He [Master Richard] was almost certainly a carpenter by training and not primarily a mason.'

57. The cloister of Vale Royal Abbey and possibly the tomb of Alianor de Provence at Amesbury being two notable examples. See Arnold Taylor. 1949. The Cloister of Vale Royal Abbey. Journal of the Chester Archaeological Society 37: 295-297. And Arnold Taylor. 1955. English Builders in Scotland during the War of Independence: A Record of 1304. The Scottish Historical Review 34: 44–6.

58. Malcolm Hislop. James of St George and the Castles of North Wales (Barnsley: Pen & Sword Books Ltd, 2020). 149. 'The more elegant Caernarfon profiles may, of course, be another example of the higher specification to which the builder of this premier castle was adhering, but equally, they may represent the hand of a different designer.'

59. A domical vault is a dome-shaped vault, where the ribs or groins are semicircular, causing the center of the vaulted bay to rise higher than the side arches.

60. Nicola Coldstream. 'James of St George' in The Impact of the Edwardian Castles in Wales (Oxford: Oxbow Books, 2010). 42. Whilst Coldstream acknowledges there is 'no evidence that Burnell gave advice on castle design', the link to the fortified Manor House, built from 1284, is put forward nonetheless. For the contrary view see Ann Darracott. The Grandisons: Their Built and Chivalric Legacy (Maidenhead: Maidenhead Civic Society, 2014). 154 n323. 'However, Burnell was close to Otho Grandison so the similarity in vaults could be due to Otho's contacts among the masons.'

61. The perche was a medieval French measure of length or height equivalent to 5.5 yards. Old French perche from Latin perticate meaning measuring rod. In England, the measurement was therefore refereed to as a rod.

62. J. G. Edwards, 'Edward I's Castle-Building in Wales,' The Proceedings of the British Academy XXXII (1944): 80. 'Scriptum apud Conewey 25 die Februarii. Memorandum quod in muro inchoato circa motam castri de Carnaruan sunt iiij turres inchoate qui quidem murus continet in longitudine xviij perticatas; et de istis perticatis viij perticate continent in altitudine xij pedes, et x perticate continent in altitudine xxiiij pedes; et iste murus continet in spissitudine xv pedes.'

63. C. R. Peers. 'Carnarvan Castle.' Transactions of the Honourable Society of Cymmrodorion (1915-6): 130.' It is to be remembered that in the wall begun round the motte of Carnarvon four towers are begun. The which wall contains in length 18 perches, and of these perches seven perches are 12 feet in height, and ten perches are 24 feet in height, and this wall is 15 feet in thickness.'

64. Arnold Taylor. Studies in Castles and Castle-Building (London: The Hambledon Press, 1985). 131.

65. Ibid. 80. n3. 'Pro fossura et apparatu noue mote de Caernaruan.' or 'For the digging and preparation of the new moat of Caernarfon.'

66. Ibid. 132.

67. Robert Liddiard. 'A Research Agenda for the Edwardian Castles' in The Impact of the Edwardian Castles in Wales (Oxford: Oxbow Books, 2010). 196. 'the design of the arrow loops at Caernarfon represents some of the most up-to-date military engineering of its day.'

68. Nicola Coldstream, 'Architects, Advisers and Design at Edward I's Castles in Wales,' Architectural History: Journal of the Society of Architectural Historians of Great Britain 46 (2003): 29. 'Although Walter did not set out the south curtain at Caernarfon, John Maddison has isolated certain styles of moulding, that he attributed to him, so that Walter was able to influence details of design if not the whole scheme.' Such moulding appears to have been a speciality of Master Walter, an ecclesiastical

mason, from his time at Vale Royal. In Arnold Taylor. 1949. The Cloister of Vale Royal Abbey. Journal of the Chester Archaeological Society 37: 295–7. Taylor translated P.R.O. Plea Rolls, no. 106, m.22d (Trinity Term, 15 Edward I). from the summer of 1287. 'the contractors are also to supply sufficient cornice moulding; the whole to be in accordance with the design and measurements contained in a specification sent to them by Master Walter of Hereford, master of the work.' A very plausible explanation of the intervening years, between 1290 and 1295, in the career of Master Walter, that is from his time at Vale Royal and his time at Caernarfon were put forward by Taylor in Arnold Taylor. 1955. English Builders in Scotland during the War of Independence: A Record of 1304. The Scottish Historical Review 34: 44–46. That he was engaged at Amesbury, the nunnery, home to Alianor de Provence, and that from 1291 he was employed in building her tomb, which sadly no longer survives. This career then, Vale Royal Abbey, Amesbury and the specific mention of moulding patterns emphasizes the ecclesiastical nature of Walter's work.'

69. Arnold Taylor. *Studies in Castles and Castle-Building* (London: The Hambledon Press, 1985). 134. 'That the castle is on the contrary a single design conceived as a unity at the time work was begun on it in 1283-4, and except on the north side, carried a considerable way towards completion within the succeeding three of four years.'

70. Arnold Taylor. *The Welsh Castles of King Edward I* (London: The Hambledon Press, 1986). 82.

71. The Saintonge and the Agenais were returned to the Duc d'Aquitaine, Edward by Philippe III, as ratified by the cousins at Amiens in 1279.

72. Michael Prestwich. *Edward I* (Yale: Yale University Press, 1997). 199.

73. The original purpose of an exchequer was to audit money paid to the Crown. It later took on other functions, such as the collection of taxes, and acted as a court of law to decide what was legally owed to the Crown. The Exchequer was named after the chequered cloth on the table where the treasurer inspected the accounts of the sheriffs, the men responsible for the King's interests in the counties.

74. TNA E101/351/9. *'Hugoni de Leominstr' clerico in partem solucionis vadiorum suorum de tempore quo fuit ultra operarios apud Caernaruan et Hardelawe annis XI et Xij'* Or 'Hugh of Leominster clerk in the payment of wages from their time at Caernarfon and Harlech in the [regnal] years 11 and 12.'

75. J. G. Edwards, 'Edward I's Castle-Building in Wales,' *The Proceedings of the British Academy* XXXII (1944): 21. n2. *'Hugoni de Leminystre, clerico Alianore nuper regine Anglie.'* Or 'Hugh of Leominster, clerk of Alianor, recently Queen of England.'

76. Arnold Taylor. *The Welsh Castles of King Edward I* (London: The Hambledon Press, 1986). 82.n8.

77. TNA E159/65 m14 v. *'Rex mandat Baronibus quod allocati faciant Magistro Roberto de Belvero. xx. li. quas per preceptum Johannis de Bonovillar defuncti super tenentis locum Ottonis de Grandisono tunc Justiciarii Regis Northwall liberavit Johanni de Haueringg nuper constabulario castri Regis de Kaernernan pro custodia eiusdem castri a festo sancti Michelis anno regni nostri xiij usque ad festum Natalitatis Domini proximum sequentem, silcut per Willelmum de Grandisono postmodum tenentem locum predicti Ottonis ibidem coram Rege est testificatum.'* Or 'The King mandates barons Twenty Pounds which were allocated to Master Robert of Belvoir. Which we note was by the command of the deceased Jean de Bonvillars, who formerly held the place of deputy to, Othon de Grandson, then King's Justiciar of North Wales, absolved by John de Havering, not long ago Constable of the King's castle of Caernarfon, for custody of the castle from the feast of Saint Michael in the Thirteenth Year of Our Reign [Michaelmas (October) 1285} to immediately following the Feast of the Nativity of our Lord {1288], as by Guillaume de Grandson, afterwards the sitting deputy of the aforesaid Othon, in that very place in the presence of and witness of the King.'

78. Michael Prestwich. Edward I (Berkeley, University of California Press, 1988), 207.

79. Arnold Taylor. *Studies in Castles and Castle-Building* (London: The Hambledon Press, 1985). 215.

80. TNA C62/66. *'Per preceptum Johannis [de Bonvillars] et dilecti et fidelis nostri Willelmi de Grandisono tenentis locum predicti Otonis in partibus predictis post mortem eiusdem Johannis.'* Or 'By the command of said Jean [de Bonvillars] and our dearly beloved and faithful Guillaume de Grandson, deputy in place of Othon in the aforesaid parts after the death of aforesaid Jean.'

81. Sara Cockerill. 2014. *Eleanor of Castile: The Shadow Queen*. Second Edition ed. (Stroud: Amberley Publishing). 343.

82. Lisa Hilton. 2008. *Queens' Consorts: England's Medieval Queens* (London: Weidenfeld & Nicolson). 246.

83. Michael Prestwich. *Edward I* (Yale: Yale University Press, 1997). 220 & 381.

84. R. R. Davies. *The Age of Conquest: Wales 1063–1415* (Oxford: Oxford University Press, 1987). 382.

Chapter Fourteen

1. Dylan Foster Evans. 'Tŵr Dewr Gwyncwewr (A Brave Conqueror's Tower): Welsh Poetic Responses to the Edwardian Castles' in *The Impact of the Edwardian Castles in Wales* (Oxford: Oxbow Books, 2010). 122.

2. Michael Prestwich. *Edward I* (Yale: Yale University Press, 1997). 220. 'Roger de Pulesdon was out to death in a manner which recalled the savagery of Dafydd's execution.'

3. Ann. Trevet, 333. *'villam et castrum de Karnervan combusserunt ... magna Anglicorum multitudine ... qui nihil tale suspicantes ad nundinas venerant, interfecta.'* Or 'a great multitude of the English' who 'without suspicion had come to the market and were slain within.'

4. CCR Edward I vol 5 1302–1307, 397.

5. Dindaethwy also appears in the name of Cynan Dindaethwy, king of Gwynedd at the start of the 9th century, as he was from this part of Anglesey.

6. Arnold Taylor, 'Scorched Earth at Flint in 1294,' *Journal of the Flintshire Historical Society* 30 (1984): 90. *'Rocardus Tirell dampnum habuit de domibus suis apud Flynt combustis per custodes ipsius castri. Qui eas combusserunt pro castro illo salvando in ultima guerra Wallie.'* Or 'Richard Tirell has lost his houses at Flint, burnt by the keepers of Flint Castle who burned them in order to safeguard the castle in the last war in Wales.'

7. John E. Morris. *The Welsh Wars of Edward I* (Oxford: Clarendon Press, 1901). 244.

8. Richard Avent. *Criccieth Castle* (Cardiff: Cadw, 1989). 5.

9. John Griffiths, 'The Revolt of Madog ap Llywelyn, 1294–5,' *Transactions of the Caernarfonshire Historical Society* 16 (1955): 15.

10. CWR 1277–1326, 291.

11. Ibid.

12. Michael Prestwich. *Edward I* (Yale: Yale University Press, 1997). 215–6.

13. John Griffiths, 'The Revolt of Madog ap Llywelyn, 1294–5,' *Transactions of the Caernarfonshire Historical Society* 16: 15.

14. J. Griffiths, 'Documents Relating to the Rebellion of Madoc, 1294-5,'. *Bulletin of the Board of Celtic Studies* VIII (1935–7).

15. John E. Morris. *The Welsh Wars of Edward I* (Oxford: Clarendon Press, 1901). 252.

16. Ibid.

17. CWR Edward I 1277–1326, 362.

18. Ibid. 355.

19. Ibid. 355.

20. Ibid. 356–9.

21. John E. Morris. *The Welsh Wars of Edward I* (Oxford: Clarendon Press, 1901). 245.

22. Ibid.

23. The dating and event are corroborated by Chron, Guisborough, 58. *'die saucti Martini.'* '11 November'.

24. Ann. Trevet, 333. *'Quibus in die sancti Martini appropinquantibus castello comitis Lincolniae de Dunbey Wallenses in magna virtute occurrerunt, et conserto gravi prælio repulerunt.'*

25. L. A. S. Butler. *Denbigh Castle* (Cardiff: Cadw, 2007). 8 & 10.

26. CWR Edward I 1277–1326, 360.

27. Ibid.

28. Ibid. 355.

29. Ibid. 352.

30. Ibid.

31. John E. Morris. *The Welsh Wars of Edward I* (Oxford: Clarendon Press, 1901). 252.

32. Arnold Taylor. *The Welsh Castles of King Edward I* (London: The Hambledon Press, 1986). 77. 'When the castle [Bere] well was excavated in 1952 late thirteenth-century pottery was found in association with charred timbers probably from the well-house. This evidence both archaeological and documentary points to the probable destruction and abandonment of the castle in 1294–95.'

33. Ibid.

34. W. W. E. Wynne. 'Castell y Bere, Merionethshire' *Archaeologia Cambrensis* vol. 16 (1861): 107.

35. Richard Avent. *Dolwyddelan Castle Dolbadarn Castle Castell y Bere*. 2010 ed. (Cardiff: Cadw, 2004). 20.

36. Ibid. 76.

37. CWR Edward I 1277–1326, 359.

38. Ibid.

39. E. B. Fryde, D. E. Greenway, S. Porter & I. Roy. (Eds). *Handbook of British Chronology*. Third ed. (London: Offices of the Royal Historical Society, 1986). 76.

40. CCR Edward I vol 3 1288–1296, 317. The King's Chamberlain (a role that would eventually evolve into that of Lord Chamberlain) was responsible for the 'chamber' or the household 'above stairs': the series of rooms used by the King to receive increasingly select visitors, ending in the royal bedchamber.

41. CWR Edward I 1277–1326, 359.

42. Ibid. 355.

43. Chron. Guisborough, 57. *'Istius autem seditonis excitatores fuerunt 'duo nominatim' Maddoch et Morgan'* or 'that is sedition was excited by 'two names' Madog and Morgan.'

44. J. Beverley Smith. *Llywellyn ap Gruffudd: Prince of Wales*. Ebook. ed. (Cardiff: The University of Wales Press, 2014). Apple.
45. Ibid.
46. J. Beverley Smith. *Llywellyn ap Gruffudd: Prince of Wales*. Ebook. ed. (Cardiff: The University of Wales Press, 2014). Apple.
47. John Griffiths, 'The Revolt of Madog ap Llywelyn, 1294–5,' *Transactions of the Caernarfonshire Historical Society* 16 (1955): 14.
48. Ann. Cestrienses, 118. '*Madokus Amereduy incepit Gwerram in Angleseye.*' Or 'Madog ap Maredudd began war in Anglesey.'
49. John Griffiths, 'The Revolt of Madog ap Llywelyn, 1294–5,' *Transactions of the Caernarfonshire Historical Society* 16 (1955): 14.
50. Formerly a steward of Leonor de Castile he would meet a sticky end at the Battle of Stirling Bridge in 1297.
51. J. G. Edwards, 'The Battle of Maes Madog and the Welsh Campaign of 1294-5,' *The English Historical Review* 39 (1924): 2. And, *Prests*. 53–4. '*Domino Hugoni de Cressingham de prestito super vadiis 124 constabulariorum et 15,909 hominum peditum de diversis comitatibus videlicet 11 constabulariorum et 2,474 peditum de comitatu Derb', 19 constabulariorum et 1,900 peditum de comitatu Cumbr', 13 constabulariorum et 1,300 peditum de Westriding' de comitatu Ebor', 37 constabulariorum et 3,700 peditum de comitatu Ebor',8 constabulariorum et 800 peditum de civitate Ebor', 3 constabulariorum et 2,340 peditum de comitatu Nottingham, 25 constabulariorum et 2,540 peditum de comitatu Lancastr', 8 constabulariorum et 855 peditum de comitatu de Westmerl.*'
52. J. G. Edwards, 'The Battle of Maes Madog and the Welsh Campaign of 1294-5,' *The English Historical Review* 39 (1924): 2.
53. Ibid. 2.
54. Ibid. 8.
55. CWR Edward I 1277–1326, 359.
56. Michael Prestwich. *Edward I* (Yale: Yale University Press, 1997). 221..
57. J. G. Edwards, 'The Battle of Maes Madog and the Welsh Campaign of 1294-5,' *The English Historical Review* 39 (1924): 3, n1. And, *Prests*. 54. '*Domino Nicholao de Okham clerico de prestito super vadiis 500 peditum et 5 constabulariorum quos domini Thomas de Berkele et W. de Pavily eligent et ducet de comitatu Wylt' ... et super vadiis 500 peditum et 5 constabulariorum Somers' et Dors' ... Eidem de prestito super vadiis 1,400 peditum et 14 constabulariorum quos dominus Alanus Plugenet et ducet de comitatu Heref' ... Eidem de prestito super vadiis 1,600 peditum et 16 constabulariorum quos domino Osbertus de Spaldington' eliget et ducet de comitatu Glouc' et Foresta de Dene.*'
58. J. G. Edwards, 'The Battle of Maes Madog and the Welsh Campaign of 1294-5,' *The English Historical Review* 39 (1924): 3
59. Ann. Cestrienses, 118-9. '*Decembris venit dominus Edwardus Rex Anglie Cestrie et die Sancti Nicholai audivit missam in ecclesia Sancte Werburge.*' Or 'on December 5, the lord Edward King of England, came to Chester, and on Saint Nicolas' Day [December 6] he heard mass in the church of Saint Werburg.'
60. Ibid. '*in crastino profectus est apud Wrutysham.*' Or 'on the morrow he set out for Wrexham.'
61. J. G. Edwards, 'The Battle of Maes Madog and the Welsh Campaign of 1294-5,' *The English Historical Review* 39 (1924): 3.
62. CPR Edward I vol 3, 1292–1301, 128.
63. John E. Morris. *The Welsh Wars of Edward I* (Oxford: Clarendon Press, 1901). 254.
64. G. Rex Smith, 'The Penmachno Letter Patent and the Welsh Uprising of 1294-95,' *Cambrian Medieval Celtic Studies* 58 (2009): 49–67.
65. John Griffiths, 'The Revolt of Madog ap Llywelyn, 1294–5,' *Transactions of the Caernarfonshire Historical Society* 16 (1955): 15.
66. *Prests*. xxxv.
67. John Griffiths, 'The Revolt of Madog ap Llywelyn, 1294–5,' *Transactions of the Caernarfonshire Historical Society* 16 (1955): 13.
68. John E. Morris. *The Welsh Wars of Edward I* (Oxford: Clarendon Press, 1901). 254.
69. CPR Edward I vol 3, 1292–1301, 127-8.
70. Ann. Trevet, 334. '*Rex autem Angliae apud Abercoun festum tenuit Nativitatis Dominicse.*' Or 'the King of England held the feast of the Nativity of our Lord at Aberconewey.'
71. Michael Prestwich. 1997. Edward I. Yale: Yale University Press. 221.
72. R. F. Walker. 1976. 'The Hagnaby Chronicle and the Battle of Maes Moydog.' *Welsh History Review* 8: 126.
73. *Prests*. 2. *apud Aberconewey 25 die Decembris'* and *apud Aberconewey ultimo die Decembris'* and '*apud Aberconewey primo de Januarii.*'
74. CFR Edward I 1272–1307, 345.

75. J. G. Edwards, 'The Battle of Maes Madog and the Welsh Campaign of 1294–5,' *The English Historical Review* 39 (1924): 4. n4. Edwards notes that 'There is one entry in the Wardrobe Accounts dated Conway, 7 January, and one in the Fine Roll dated Bangor, 7 January; so the move may actually have taken place on that day.'

76. *The Book of Prests* 1294–5 forms a key primary source, it was a novel creation of Wardrobe expenses, known when compiled as the *Liber de Hospicio* or Book of the Household. It contained the details of household income and expenditure as presented to the Exchequer. These pipe rolls, then books, were transcribed and published in 1962, edited by E. B. Fryde. Hereinafter referred to as *Prests*.

77. *Prests*. 2. '*apud Nevyn 13 die Januarii.*'

78. Ann. Trevet, 335. '*Rex Angliæ transito flumine de Coneweie ut ulterius progrederetur in Walliam , cum non dum totus comitaretur exercitus , captis bigis et curribus victualibus onustis a Wallensibus , per tempus aliquod penuria coartatur ; ita ut quousque veniret ad eum reliqua pars exercitus , aquám melle mixtam biberet , paneque cum sal sis carnibus vesceretur.*'

79. *Prests*. 2. '*apud Aberconewey 21 die Januarii.*'

80. Chron. Guisborough, vol. 2, 58. '*Unde superabundantibus aquis maris et fluctuum subitorum obsessus est a Wallensibus per tempus aliquod*' and '*bibitque aquam cum melle mixtam et panem.*'

81. Ibid. 59. '*Omnia in necessitate debent esse communia*' because '*istius et origo et causa sum*' or 'All necessary should be shared in common' because 'I am the origin and cause of this'.

82. John E. Morris. *The Welsh Wars of Edward I* (Oxford: Clarendon Press, 1901). 255. 'They rushed down and captured the whole of the commissariat train, presumably on January 9 or 10.'

83. *Prests*. 143. '*apud Aberconewey … dominus Willelmus de Cykuns constabularius …*'

84. Ibid. 148. '*Domino Petro de Chauvent … apud Abercon 9 die Februarii.*'

85. Ann. Dunstable, 386.

86. Jean-Pierre Chapuisat, '*Au service de deux rois d'Angleterre au XIIIe siècle: Pierre de Champvent,*' *Revue historique vaudoise* 72 (1964): 169. Chapuisat notes the arrow loops by example, we are frustrated from knowing more by the complete lack of building records for Champvent. Our understanding of post 1294 works there is from dendrochronology of timbers not primary sources. We can however also see this return architectural flow in the windows of Valle Crucis Abbey and the Église de St Etienne in Moudon.

87. Dr. Adam Chapman. 'Maes Moydog 1295' *The Inventory of Historic Battlefields in Wales*. Last modified Jan 2017. http://battlefields.rcahmw.gov.uk/wp-content/uploads/2017/02/Maes-Moydog-1295-Chapman-2013.pdf.

88. We can translate the word '*princeps*' in classical Latin as 'leader' or 'chief' – but given Madog's self declaration of Prince of Wales, and the Worcester Annalists likely interpretation of prince as '*princeps*', I think we should more accurately use 'prince'.

89. Chron. Worcester, 519. '*Quinto die Martii Willelmus de Bello Camp comes Warewik commisit bellum cum Wallensibus in loco quod dicitur lingua eorum Meismeidoc; et prostravit ex illis de nobilioribus septingentos viros praeter submersos et letaliter vulneratos. Sed Madocus ap Lewelin eorum princeps cum dedecore vix evasit*'

90. John E. Morris. *The Welsh Wars of Edward I* (Oxford: Clarendon Press, 1901). 256.

91. J. G. Edwards, 'The Battle of Maes Madog and the Welsh Campaign of 1294–5,' *The English Historical Review* 39 (1924): 10.

92. John E. Morris. *The Welsh Wars of Edward I* (Oxford: Clarendon Press, 1901). 257.

93. Dr. Adam Chapman. 'Maes Moydog 1295' *The Inventory of Historic Battlefields in Wales*. Last modified January 2017. http://battlefields.rcahmw.gov.uk/wp-content/uploads/2017/02/Maes-Moydog-1295-Chapman-2013.pdf.

94. Dr. Adam Chapman. 'Maes Moydog 1295' *The Inventory of Historic Battlefields in Wales*. Last modified Jan 2017. http://battlefields.rcahmw.gov.uk/wp-content/uploads/2017/02/Maes-Moydog-1295-Chapman-2013.pdf.

95. *Prests*. 60. '*Domino Roberto de Staundon*' de prestito super providenciis faciendis municione castri de Hardelagh per manus proprias apud Aberconewey 22 die Januarii. 100l.'

96. Ibid. 61, '*Magistro Ricardo de Haveringg, eunti versus partes Hibernie pro providenciis faciendis ad castrum de Hardelagh muniendum, de prestito super municione illa facienda per manus proprias ibidem dicto die.*'

97. John Griffiths, 'The Revolt of Madog ap Llywelyn, 1294–5,' *Transactions of the Caernarfonshire Historical Society* 16 (1955): 18.

98. *Prests*. 76.

99. Ibid. xxxv.

100. John Griffiths, 'The Revolt of Madog ap Llywelyn, 1294–5,' *Transactions of the Caernarfonshire Historical Society* 16 (1955): 20.

101. J. G. Edwards. Calendar of Ancient Correspondence Concerning Wales (Cardiff: University Press Board Cardiff, 1935). 108–9. '*Sachet sire qe nus moemes iceo vendirdi derrein passe vers meronnith et*'

sumes logez en les bondes de Ardodewey et merionith en un bois qui est apele Ketthlieconhan (unidentified) *en le plus fort lieu de tut Ardodewey ou la gent madoc tindrent le setiz a nus et purceo sumes logez deinz pur talir le bois.'*

102. Ann. Cestrienses, 118. *'Eodem anno dominus Edwardus Rex cepit Angleseyam et eam sibi subjugavit.'*

Chapter Fifteen

1. *Prests.* 56. *'Robert de Rye de prestito super vadiis 50 fossatorum … Micheli de Storton' de prestito super vadiis (unius) vintenarii et 20 carpentariorum'.*
2. Sir Henry Latham of Tarbock near Prescot, Lancashire.
3. *Prests.* 57. *'Domino Henrico de Lathun militi ordinato per Regem ad passandum versus Insulam de Angleseya cum 1 galia sua et 12 batellis quos secum ducet et 500 hominibus peditibus de prestito super vadiis suis per manus proprias apud Cestriam 7 die Decembris.'*
4. Ibid. 62. *'Magistro Jacobo de Sancto Georgio de prestito super factura clearum et pontium in Wirhale et super pice et aliis necessariis emendis apud Cestriam per manus proprias apud Abercon' 7 die Februarii .8 li.'*
5. CChW. 1244–1326, 53. March 4. Conway. 'Mandate to send a clerk of Chancery hastily to Master James de Seint Georg … in Wirhale or elsewhere where he makes the king's pontoons to take all the boats, he can find in Wirhale and elsewhere on the coast to carry the pontoons to the king at Aberconeway. The king has ordered his clerks at Chester, Sir Renaud . . the keeper of the forest of Wirhale and the bailiffs of Sir Roger Lestraunge of Shotwik to help with boats and other carriage and his yeoman Renaud de Assise to help with six boats. French. his lieutenant, 8 (744).'
6. Arnold Taylor. *The Welsh Castles of King Edward I* (London: The Hambledon Press, 1986). 104
7. *Prests.* 68 *'Magistro Jacobo de Sancto Georgio de prestito super meremio emendo pro pontibus faciendis apud Aberconewey ad naves 11 die Marcii. 10s.'*
8. Ibid. 155. *'Magistro Jacobo de Sancto Georgio de prestito super vadiis … 100s … Item pro Colino clerico … 16s. 8d.'*
9. *La Finanza Sabauda*, vol. 2, 123. 'In vadiis Collini' as just one example.
10. Arnold Taylor. *The Welsh Castles of King Edward I* (London: The Hambledon Press, 1986). 104. n2.
11. *Prests.* 74. *'Magistro Jacobo de Sancto Georgio de prestito super factura utensilium cementariorum apud Aberconewey tam de ferro quam de bordis per manus proprias apud Bangor. 8 die Aprilis. 10s.*
12. Henry Gough. *Itinerary of King Edward the First throughout his reign, A.D. 1272–1307, exhibiting his movements so far as they are recorded.* vol 2 (Paisley: Alexander Gardner, 1900). 128.
13. *Prests.* 75. *'Magistro Jacobo de Sancto Georgio de prestito super diversis necessariis providendis pro nova castro per manus proprias 17 die Aprilis apud Lannuais. 60s.'* Or 'Maître Jacques de Saint Georges the prest of diverse necessities for the provision of the new castle given by hand on 17 April at Llanfaes, Sixty shillings.'
14. *Prests.* 75 *'Waltero de Winton clerico de prestito super operacionibus novi castri de Beau Mareis per mantis proprias apud Lannuais 18 die Aprilis 100li.'*
15. Douglas Knoop & G. P. Jones. The Mediaeval Mason: An Economic History of English Stone Building in the Later Middle Ages and Early Modern Times (Manchester: Manchester University Press, 1933). 18.
16. *Prests.* 75. *'Waltero de Winton' clerico de prestito super operancionibus.'*
17. Eugene Mottaz, *'Note sur la construction du château d'Yverdon,' Revue historique vaudoise* 365 (1900) 'The construction of the walls and towers of the castle presented am difficulty … The foundations of this considerable work fell below the level of neighbouring rivers and even Lac de Neuchâtel.'
18. Nicola Coldstream, 'Architects, Advisers and Design at Edward I's Castles in Wales,' *Architectural History: Journal of the Society of Architectural Historians of Great Britain* 46 (2003): 24. 'it is difficult to see how Edward I could possibly have predicted that the ugly duckling at work in Savoy would turn into a swan in Wales.'
19. *Prests.* 142. *'Eidem Waltero per vices de prestito super eisdem operacionibus ut patet ex alia parte folii 6,736 li. 10s. 1d.'*
20. Arnold Taylor. *The Welsh Castles of King Edward I* (London: The Hambledon Press, 1986). 105. n4. *' facienceium fossata et motam ubi castrum de Bello Marisco situm est , ac eciam circa quoddam bretugium ibidem faciendum ex precepto Regis.'* Or 'Making the ditches and moat where the castle of Beaumaris is to be sited, as well as brattices, also ordered by the King.'
21. Henry Gough. *Itinerary of King Edward the First throughout his reign, A.D. 1272–1307, exhibiting his movements so far as they are recorded.* vol 2 (Paisley: Alexander Gardner, 1900). 129–31.
22. Arnold Taylor. *Studies in Castles and Castle-Building* (London: The Hambledon Press, 1985). 173. *'quas idem Robertus dum fuit constabularius castri regis de Hardelagh in ultima guerra Wall' recepit per preceptum regis de thesaurario nunc et tunc custode garderobe predicte ad castrum predictum de victualibus et aliis necessariis in eadem gwerra inde inueniendis. Necnon et misis et expensis quas predictus Robertus statim post eandem gwerram sedatam posuit per preceptum regis in quodam muro de petra et de calce circa quandam rupen castro predicto contiguam et in quandam porta in castro predicto versus mare admodum*

turris de novo construenda, eidem Roberto debitas allocaciones in premissis fieri faciant, prout eorum discreio melius viderit faciend' Teste R apud Westmonasterium, xxij. die Octobris anno xxxiij. Per peticionem de Consilio.' Or 'whom the same Robert, while he was constable of the king's castle of Harlech during the last war in Wales, he received by the order of the king from the treasurer, and then the keeper of the aforesaid wardrobe at the aforesaid castle, to find the supplies and other necessities in the same war. And also the expenses for the aforesaid Robert having erected immediately after the war, settled by the king's order, of a wall of rock and lime near a certain rock [castle rock] adjoining to the aforesaid castle, and into a certain gate in the aforesaid castle towards the sea, a tower of a very newly constructed tower, due to the same Robert; let them do it on the premises, according to their discretion; Witnessed by the King at Westminster, 22nd day of October in the 33rd year of his reign by request of council.'

23. Chron. Hemingburgh, 59.
24. Henry Gough. *Itinerary of King Edward the First throughout his reign, A.D. 1272–1307, exhibiting his movements so far as they are recorded.* vol 2 (Paisley: Alexander Gardner, 1900). 129–31.
25. Arnold Taylor. *The Welsh Castles of King Edward I* (London: The Hambledon Press, 1986). 106.
26. The cythara is a wide group of stringed instruments of medieval and Renaissance Europe, including not only the lyre and harp but also necked, string instruments. In fact, unless a medieval document gives an indication that it meant a necked instrument, then it likely was referring to a lyre. It was also spelled cithara or kithara and was Latin for the Greek lyre.
27. TNA E101/14/7. *'Ade de Cliderhou (Clitheroe) , cithariste , citharizanti coram Rege apud Bellum Mariscum per duas noctes de dono eiusdem Regis per manus proprias apud Bellum Mariscum , xij die Julij , -x.s.'*
28. Concentric in relation to castle design does not mean circular but come from the Old French *concentrique* which derived from the Latin *concentricus* or con and centrum, which meant together and centre.
29. R. Allen Brown. *English Castles* (London: Chancellor Press, 1970). 105. 'Beaumaris is the concentric castle par excellence'. And Charles Phillips. 2018. *The Medieval Castle* (Yeovil: Haynes Publishing). 67. 'The perfect concentric castle.'
30. Hugh Kennedy. *Crusader Castles* (Cambridge: Cambridge University Press, 1994). 112. 'The idea of putting a low outer wall in front of a higher inner wall was not new … it had been employed in the Theodosian walls of Constantinople in the fourth century.'
31. Ibid. 58. Figure. 5 has an excellent ground plan which illustrates the look of Beaumaris. Belvoir is the first dateable example in Outremer, built 1168, for the Knights Hospitaller. Krak des Chevaliers would employ lower outer and higher inner walls, but not, given its topography, water defences.
32. John. A. A. Goodall. 'The Baronial Castles of the Welsh Conquest' in *The Impact of the Edwardian Castles in Wales* (Oxford: Oxbow Books, 2010). 157–8.
33. Hugh Kennedy. Crusader Castles (Cambridge: Cambridge University Press, 1994). 106 cites an earlier example of this idea at Caesarea in Outremer.
34. Keith D. Lilley. 'The Landscape of Edward's New Towns: Their Planning and Design' in *The Impact of the Edwardian Castles in Wales* (Oxford: Oxbow Books, 2010). 106–7. 'The GIS plan of Beaumaris was reversed to create a mirror-image and reproduced at the same scale as the town plan of Conwy. When the two plans are placed beside each other, the reversed GIS plan of Beaumaris shows a remarkable coincidence of features. The castles sit in the same relative position, as do the churches and quaysides. The orientation of the T-shaped street patterns also matches. Moreover, the street dimensions of Conwy match perfectly those of Beaumaris, both sharing a slight widening on their approach towards the castle entrances. The similarities in their plans are therefore very close.'
35. Ibid. 109. 'That Master James might have had sufficient expertise or interest in laying out new towns is perhaps revealed in the common forms of Beaumaris and Conwy.'
36. Arnold Taylor. *Studies in Castles and Castle-Building* (London: The Hambledon Press, 1985). 24. 'while the ground-plans of the two towns [Yverdon and Saint-Prex are far from duplicates – they occupy very different sites and are twenty-five years apart in date – nevertheless they have certain basic characteristics in common; each has a layout based on three streets radiating from a point near the south-eastern extremity of the site; both are fully provided with water defences, Saint-Prex mainly natural and partly man-made, Yverdon's mainly man-made and partly natural; the parallelism of their orientation is striking.'
37. Arnold Taylor. *The Welsh Castles of King Edward I* (London: The Hambledon Press, 1986). 110. n9.
38. CFR Edward I vol 1 1272 - 1307. 357. "Grant for life to Master James de Sancto Georgio of the town of [Muston in Englefeld, extended at 251. 16s. Id. a year, to hold at the rent of 3s. annually at the Exchequer of Kaernarvan
39. J. G. Edwards, 'Edward I's Castle-Building in Wales,' *The Proceedings of the British Academy* XXXII (1944): 48. n2. *'vestre venerande dominacioni si placet significamus quod muri ville de Carnarvan x die Septembris fuerunt totaliter expediti.'*

40. TNA E159 / 69 m4. '*Edward par la grace de deu Rey Dengleterre seignur Dirland e Ducs Daquitaine, a sun cher clerc John de Drokeneford, saluz. Per ce qe nous amereons qe les ouerainnes de Beaumareis e de Carnaruan sespleicassent en teu manere qe les lieus peussent defensables entre cy e la sent Martin procheinement auenir, et qe hom feust en ouerant ieque a donq oue taunz ouerurs come ouerur y peussent en bon manere, vous mandoms ke par lettres de notre Escheker mandez hastiuement a Mestre Jakes de Sent George et Walter de Hereford gardeins de sites oueraines quil certefient sanz nul delai le Tresor de nostre Escheker par auisement de clers qui sunt entendaunz des oueraignes de ditz lieus coment il espleitent et ce qe il pormont faire e qe il retiegnent assez des ouerors pur faire les lieus defensables entr cy e le temps auantdit, et cumbien de deners il entendent qe peussent suffire pur les ouereignes desqe a donq. E estre ce lur enueez meintenant de deners ce qe vous porrez en bone manere sanz nul delay. Don de suz notre priue seal a Wengeham le xxix iur de Septembre, Lan de nostre regne xxiij.*'

41. Arnold Taylor. *Studies in Castles and Castle-Building* (London: The Hambledon Press, 1985). 141. '*Rex dilectis sibi Magistro Jacobo de sancto Georgio et Waltero de Wynton clerico custodibus operacionum castri nostri de Bello Marisco, salutem, Quia super statu earundem operacionum certis de causis per vos in omnibus distincte et aparte volamus quod Thesaurarius et Barones nostri de scaccario reddantur certiores, ut iidem exinde possint de eisdem operacionibus prout melius et commodius pro seisona iam instanti futura pro nobis viderint expedire, vobis mandamus firminter iniugentes quatinus eosdem Thesaurarium et Barones in premissis per prescencium portitorem sine dilacionis incomodo per litteras vestras reddatis certiores. Et hoc sicut commodum et honorem nostrum diligitis in hac parte nuilatinus omittatis. Teste J. de Cobeham etc, xiij. die Februarii anno xxiiiij. Rex scribit eodem modo et sub eisdem verbis Magistro Waltero de Hereford et Hugoni de Leyministr clerico, custodibus castri Regis et ville de Kaernaruan.*'

42. J. G. Edwards, 'Edward I's Castle-Building in Wales,' *The Proceedings of the British Academy* XXXII (1944): 79-80. *Nobilibus viris et dominis suis si placet reverentissimis dominis thesaurario et baronibus de scaccario domini regis, sui W. de Hereford et H. de Lemenistre salutem cum omni reverentia et honore. Cum dominus noster rex per breve suum de dicto scaccario nobis mandaverit quod super statu operacionum ville et castri de Carnarvan vos in omnibus distincte et aperte certificemus, vestre venerande dominacioni si placet significamus quod muri ville de Carnarvan 10 die Septembris fuerunt totaliter expediti, et a die illo usque 27 diem Novembris circa castrum ibidem fecimus operari, et a 26 die Novembris usque confectionem presencium tenuimus ibidem in opere cementarios taillantes liberam petram, carpentarios, fabros, quarreatores, minutos operarios, et batellarios cariantes petram, aliquando plures aliquando panciores, contra seisonam iam futuram, et aliqua fieri fecimus per dictum tempus ad tascam, prout melius domino nostro regi vidimus expedire. Et preter hec plures fecimus empciones veluti de ferro, calibo, plumbo, carbone marino, necnon et de multimodis victualibus pro castro domini regis inde muniendo, et pluribus aliis necessariis pro operacionibus supra dictis. Et a primo die Novembris usque nunc non recepimus de thesauro domini regis nisi solummodo £100 pro omnibus negociis prenominatis et eciam pro vadiis municonum de Carnervan et Crukyn, propter quod dominus rex modo debet ibidem plus quam £400 de tempore retroacto. Et quia circa muros dicti castri de Carnarvan faciendum cum omnibus operariis quos habere possumus 26 die Februarii pro posuimus incohasse, quod per defectum pecunie iam distulimus, excellencie vestre placuerint discrecioni voluntatem vestram nobis vestris si placet significare dignemini. Alia vobis scipsimus in quadam cedula presentibus interclusa per que super multis plenius poteritis certiorari. Valeat dominacio vestra per tempora diuturna. Scriptum apud Conewey 25 die Februarii. Memorandum quod in muro inchoato circa motam castri de Carnarvan sunt 4 turres inchoate, qui quidem murus continet in longitudine 18 perticatas, et de istis perticatis 8 perticate continent in altitudine 12 pedes, et 10 perticate continent in altitudine 24 pedes, et iste murus continet in spissitudine 15 pedes.*'

43. TNA E101/5/18. 11. The translation 'freely Englished' is Arnold Taylor from the original Norman French published in J. G. Edwards, 'Edward I's Castle-Building in Wales,' *The Proceedings of the British Academy* XXXII (1944): 80–1. '*A lour treschiers seigneurs le tresurier e as barons del escheker nostre seignur le roy Jakes de Seint George e Wauter de Wyncestre saluz e duwes reverences. Pur ce sires que nostre seignur le roy nous ad comande par ses lettres del eschekier que entotes choses suer lestat des oueraygnes de Bluumarreys apertement vous certiflens, issi que vous peussez ordiner lestat de meisme loevre pur ceste seeson qui est a venir selonc ce que vous verrez que mieutz soit a faire, vous fesoms saver que loevre qui nous fesoms est de grant coust dont il nous avoye molt. Sachez sites que nous avons tenu tot cest iver e uncore tenoms macheons tailleurs de piries, quarreurs, menutz oueriers fesantz mortier e debrisantz pirres pur chauz, carettes amenantz pirres pur chautz e merrym a edifier en chastel la ou nous sumes touz demorrantz ore, e si avoms 1,000 charpentiers, feivres, daubours e fosseurs, sanz la garenson a chivaux covertz dont ylyont to qui prenont 70s. la symeyne, e si avons 20 arblastiers qui premont 47s. 10d. e 100 hommes de pie qui prenont £6.2s.6d. la symeyne. E sachez sires quant ces lettres furent faites nous deuions quei as ouerours quei a la garneson plus de cink centz livres dont eux ont eu molt grante defaute e uncore ont, e si avons molt grant peine de les retenir pur ce quil nont dont vivre. E sachez chiers sires que si nostre seignur le roy voet que loevre se perfate vistement ausi come mestier serreit e sicome ele est commence nous ne venoms que nous*

peusseoms eschaper meyns desorenavant tant come le seeson dure que de £250 la symeyne, e ensi porroit loevre estre bien avance ceste seson. E si par aventure vous sentez que nous ne peusseoms tantz deners avoir, le nous mandez e nous mettoms overcools a vostre volunte selonc ce que vous verrez que mieutz soit pur le profit nostre seignur le roy. Endroit de lestat de loueraygne autrefoiz lavons mande a nostre seignur le roy, si vous fesoms savoir que loevre est daucinme pret de 28 piez haut e la ou ele est plus basse ele est de 20 piez haute, e si sont comence 10 tours dehors e quatre dedenz, a chescune porte deus pur les alees, e si sont quatre portes perdues qui sont closes de lok chescuine noit, e a chescune porte serront trois portes colisces. E sachez sires que un vesseal de poys de 40 toniaux porta venir a la pleine mer chargee a la porte du chastel maugre touz les Galeys tut avons nous fait. E que vous ne esmervaillez ou tantz deners soient despenduz la symeyne, vous fesons saver quilyad convenu e couendra quatre centz macheons quei tailleurs quei couchours, 2,000 menus oueriers e 100 charettes e 60 carres e 30 bateaux portanz pirres e charbon de mer, e deus centz quarreours e 30 fevres e charpentiers de mettre les gistes e les planches du chastel e autres oueres necessaries; sanz la garneson avant nomee, e ostre les achatz dont yly couendra molt. Endroit sires de lestat de la terre de Gales, nous nensavons uncore si bien nony, mais vous savez bien que Galeys sont Galeys e vous les devez bien conustre et font a duter detant le plus si les gerres de France et Descose veysent avant peynse de bien faire en touz pointz. A Dieu treschiers seignurs qui vous gard. Escrites a Aberconewey le 27 iour de Fevrier. E pur Dieu sires hastes les deners pur loueraigne tant come nostre seignur le roy le voet, car tant ilyad fait uncore poy vaut si plus mysoit fait.'

44. Henri Buathier. JEAN Ier DE GRAILLY un chevalier européen du XIIIe siècle (1995). 35.
45. Arnold Taylor. *Studies in Castles and Castle-Building* (London: The Hambledon Press, 1985). 142 '*primo die Marcii anno xxiiij.*' '1 March 1296' indeed the speed of response may well indicate the need was anticipated.
46. Ibid.
47. The Records of the Parliaments of Scotland to 1707, K. M. Brown et al eds (St Andrews, 2007–2021), A1296/2/1. Date accessed: 10 May 2021. Letters Patent issued 23 February 1296 ratifying treaty of 23 October 1295.
48. Michael Prestwich. *Edward I* (Yale: Yale University Press, 1997). 469-70.
49. Arnold Taylor. *Studies in Castles and Castle-Building* (London: The Hambledon Press, 1985). 142–3.
50. TNA E372/158, rot48.
51. Chron. Guisborough, 69.
52. A. A .M. Duncan. *The Kingship of the Scots 842–1292* (Edinburgh: Edinburgh University Press, 2002). 651–2.
53. Ibid. 652.
54. To twenty-first-century eyes what happened at Berwick sealed Edward's reputation as a 'tyrant', but this is to engage in presentism and to wilfully ignore the rules of medieval warfare. What's more Edward offered terms to the garrison of the castle, who'd seen what had happened to the town, and surrendered, the 'tyrant' allowed those inside the castle to go about their business provided they promised not to make war upon him again.
55. A. A .M. Duncan. *The Kingship of the Scots 842–1292* (Edinburgh: Edinburgh University Press, 2002). 652.
56. Ibid. 653.
57. Ibid.
58. Ibid.
59. Ibid. 'Edward moved gradually toward a position of denying the existence of a Scottish kingdom, a position he finally took up … in 1303–04.'
60. Ibid. 71.
61. Chron. Guisborough, 74.
62. Arnold Taylor. *The Welsh Castles of King Edward I* (London: The Hambledon Press, 1986). 110.
63. Joseph Bain. 1877. Calendar of Documents Relating to Scotland, vol. 4, 476 –7. '*Domino Alexandro le Convers, pro denariis per ipsum datis... carpentariis facientibus ingenium quod vocatur Lupus Guerre, et aliis operaris diversis operantibus, ..., mensibus Maii et Junii anno presenti (1304), viio die Junii, ..., 10 s.*' Or 'To Master Alexander le Convers, for money paid by him to the carpenters making the engine called "War Wolf", and other workers working (also on the engine), in May and June 1304, 10 shillings on 7 June 1304.' And *Thome de Viridi Campo, valleto regine, de dono regis in recompensacionem laboris quem sustenit circa facturem Lupus Guerre quem rex fieri ordinavit pro insultu castri de Stryvelyn, ..., xl li.*' Or 'To Thomas of Viridis Campus (i.e. Greenfield), the queen's valet, recompensed at the King's hand for his labours in the making of the 'War Wolf', which the King ordered to be made to slight Stirling Castle, £40.'
64. Arnold Taylor. 1986. *The Welsh Castles of King Edward I* (London: The Hambledon Press). 119.

Chapter Sixteen

1. Mary C. L. Salt, 'List of English Embassies to France, 1272–1307, ' *The English Historical Review* 44 (1929): 263–78.
2. Daniel de Raemy. *Le Château-Résidence d'Othon de Grandson*. Othon I de Grandson (vers 1240–1328) (Lausanne: Cahiers Lausannois d'Histoire Médiévale, 2020). 180–1.
3. www.westminster-abbey.org/about-the-abbey/history/wall-paintings retrieved 20 August 2021. 'On the stone base of her tomb, visible from the north ambulatory, are faint traces of a painting of a sepulchre, at the feet of which are four pilgrims and at the head is a knight praying before the Virgin Mary and Child. By his armorial surcoat the knight can be identified as Sir Otes de Grandison, Lord of Grandson near Lausanne, a close friend of Edward I. The background is apple green and his surcoat has blue and white stripes with a red bend and the pilgrims wear grey and red. The painter is thought to be Master Walter of Durham.' A similar image is held in the Bern Historical Museum, an altar cloth that once adorned Lausanne Cathedral (Figure 3.7)
4. Jean d'Ypres. 1456. *CRONICA siue hystoria sancti Bertini*: the Chronicle of St Bertin's Abbey, in St Omer, by Joannes Yperius, or Jean d'Ypres, abbat in 1365–1383, ending with the consecration of Abbat, British Library ref Add MS 30033. 751.
5. Clifford modified the story of Grandson's passing from that originally proposed by Maxime Reymond, a modification subsequently and recently accepted by Andenmatten. Maxime Reymond, 'Le Chevalier Othon I de Grandson,' *Revue historique vaudoise* 28 (1920): Esther Rowland Clifford. *A Knight of Great Renown: The Life and Times of Othon de Grandson* (Chicago: The University of Chicago Press, 1961). 275–6. Bernard Andenmatten. *La Part de Dieu et la Mémoire des Hommes* in Othon I de Grandson (vers 1240–1328) (Lausanne: Cahiers Lausannois d'Histoire Médiévale, 2020). 230 n40.
6. ACV C V b 53. '*meum ecclesia cathedrali beatae Mariae Laus mo eligo sepultra. Item volo et ordino quod , quando corpus meum ad ecclesiam deportabitur tumu landum , duo homines armati de armis meis et quilibet vexillum meum portans de eisdem armis precedant corpus meum super duos equos , quorum quilibet sit precii centum libre lausannensium ; et unus equorum coperiatur armis et alius ferreo et offerantur dicti equi [cum] armis et copertoriis predictis in ecclesia Lausannensi predicta , cui iure legati rema neant in remissionem peccatorum meorum.*'
7. Ibid. '*excepta parvum aurea crucis et imaginem beatae mariae virginis argentea.*'
8. Maxime Reymond., '*Le Chevalier Othon I de Grandson,*' *Revue historique vaudoise* 28 (1920). 176. Full translation of ACV C V b 53 into French was '*J'élis sépulture dans l'église cathédrale de la B. Marie. Je veux et j'ordonne que mon corps soit porté dans la tombe par deux hommes d'armes, à mes armes, précédés de ma bannière, montés sur deux chevaux, du prix de 100 livres l'un, l'un avec une couverture à mes armes, l'autre ferré et harnaché ; ces deux chevaux, armés et couverts, seront don- nés à l'église de Lausanne en rémission de mes péchés. Je veux et ordonne que l'on achète pour l'église de Lausanne 20 livrées de terre, pour que deux chapelains célèbrent` à perpétuité pour le repos de mon âme ; ces chapelains, constitués du consentement du chapitre, sont D. Thibaud, curé de Saint-Germain, mon chapelain, et D. Hugues de Ligne- rolles, prêtre. Je veux et prescris que l'on achète pour. La dite église 6. Livrées de terre pour mon anniversaire, et l'on donnera 20 sols aux clercs du cheur qui auront assisté à l'office, au jour de mon obit. Mes exécuteurs testamentaires pourront racheter ces 20 et 6 livrées de terre. Je donne et lègue à l'église de Lausanne tous mes ornements, vêtements et argenterie qui y sont maintenant déposés, à l'exception d'une petite croix d'or et d'une statue de la B. Marie Vierge, d'argent, que je porte habituellement sur moi.*' of which a reasonable English translation would be 'I elect burial in the cathedral church of B. Marie. I want and I order that my body be carried to the grave by two men at arms, with my arms, preceded by my banner, mounted on two horses, the price of 100 pounds one, one with a blanket to my arms, the other shod and harness; these two horses, armed and covered, will be donated to the church of Lausanne in remission of my sins. I want and order that we buy for the church of Lausanne 20 earthenware, so that two chaplains celebrate in perpetuity for the rest of my soul; these chaplains, made up with the consent of the chapter, are D. Thibaud, parish priest of Saint-Germain, my chaplain, and D. Hugues de Lignerolles, priest. I want and prescribe that one buys for. the said church 6. delivered of earth for my birthday, and one will give 20 sols to the clerics of the choir who will have attended the office, on the day of my obit. My executors will be able to redeem these 20 and 6 liveries. I give and bequeath to the church of Lausanne all my ornaments, clothes and silverware which are now deposited there, apart from a small gold cross and a statue of the Virgin Mary, of silver , which I usually carry with me.'
9. CPR Edward I vol 2 1281–1292, 490. 'Licence for William de Grandisono to strengthen his house of Asperton, co. Hereford, with a wall of stone and lime and to crenellate it.'
10. The current bell bears the inscription '*EX DONO IOHANNIS GRANDISON EPISCOPI EXON GVLIELMVS EVANS FECIT 1729*'.
11. J. N. Dalton. *The collegiate church of Ottery St Mary being the Ordinacio et Statuta ecclesie Sancta Marie de Otery Exon. Diocesis A.D. 1338–1339* (Cambridge: Cambridge University Press, 1917). ix.

12. CPR Edward II vol 1 1307–1311, 350. 'Grant, for life, to William Bagot of the custody of the king's castle of Aberconeway, with the same fee as William Cycouns, late constable thereof.'

13. CPR Edward I vol 3 129 –1301, 165. 'The like to John de Havering, justice of North Wales, and William Sycon [*contabulario castri sui de Aberconwey*], touching on trespasses, injuries, extortions and oppressions and grievous losses inflicted upon them since that land came into the king's hands by the sheriffs, bailiffs and other ministers of the king in those parts.'

14. CFR Edward I vol 1 1272–1307, 380. 'Commitment during pleasure to William de Cycons, constable of Aberconewey castle, of the commotes of Archleghwech Ugha and Archleghwech Issa near Aberconewey, so that he answer for the issues at the Exchequer of Karnarvan, and so that the men of those commotes do what they ought at the county of Karnarvan and else- where. Order to John de Havering, justice of North Wales, to deliver the commotes to him.'

15. CCR Edward II vol 2 1313–1318, 282 and 397.

16. Ibid. 178. 'Grant, for life, to William de Cycouns, for his good service to the late king, of 30l, a year at the Exchequer of Kaernarvan.'

17. Michael Ray . 2017. A Vaudois servant of Henry III, Ebal II de Mont (Ebulo de Montibus). www.academia.edu/31930999/A_Vaudois_servant_of_Henry_III_Ebal_II_de_Mont_ Ebulo_de_Montibus?email_work_card=view-paper. 15.

18. Michael Ray., 'The Savoyard Cousins: A Comparison of the Careers and Relative Success of the Grandson (Grandison) and Champvent (Chavent) Families in England,' *The Antiquaries Journal* 86 (2006): 152.

19. Aug. Burnand, '*Vaudois en Angleterre au XIIIe siècle, avec Othon Ier de Grandson*: (*d'après M.C.-L. Kingsford*),' *Revue historique vaudoise* 19 no 7 (1911): 213.

20. CFR Edward I vol 1 1272–1307. 357. "Grant for life to Master James de Sancto Georgio of the town of [Muston in Englefeld, extended at 251. 16s. Id. a year, to hold at the rent of 3s. annually at the Exchequer of Kaernarvan."

21. CFR Edward I vol 1 1272 - 1307. 357. "Grant for life to Master James de Sancto Georgio of the town of [Muston in Englefeld, extended at 251. 16s. Id. a year, to hold at the rent of 3s. annually at the Exchequer ofKaernarvan

22. Nicola Coldstream, 'Architects, Advisers and Design at Edward I's Castles in Wales,' *Architectural History: Journal of the Society of Architectural Historians of Great Britain* 46 (2003): 24. 'In essence, then, the context of the castles in Wales is not Savoyard but Anglo-French, a milieu that was familiar to Edward I but not to James of St George.'

23. Nicola Coldstream, 'Architects, Advisers and Design at Edward I's Castles in Wales,' *Architectural History: Journal of the Society of Architectural Historians of Great Britain* 46 (2003): 26. 'A more likely tutor to James of St George, however, although undocumented in this case, is Robert of Beverley.'

24. *La Finanza Sabauda.* vol. 1, 118. In 1266–7 '*In expensis domini Iohannis de Masoz apud Yverdunum infirmantis per xxviii dies, de mandato domini, vi lib xii den ... in acquietancia Magistri Jacobi Cementarii hoc anno et de anno preterito ... qui Jacobus percipit Yverdunum de domino in feudo, decem libras viannensium singulis annis. xv. Lib*'. in 1267–8 Arnold Taylor. *Master Bertram, Ingeniator Regis.* Studies in Medieval History presented to R. Allen Brown (Woodbridge: The Boydell Press, 1989). 294. n31. Jean de Mézos is described as '*moranti apud Salinas pro dictando opere putei de Salinas*' whilst Maître Jacques is '*euntis apud Salinas pro operibus putei per xj. dies, capientis quolibet die 3s. Pro expensis suis*.' Household roll of Count Phillip of Savoy, Archivio di Stato di Torino, Inv, Savoia 38, fo. 46, nos 3 and 4. In February 1274 '*Item domino Iohanni de Maso et Magistro Jacobo missis ad Montez, viij.s.*' In March 1274 '*In expensis domini Iohannis de Massout, Hugneti de Chillon, Magistri Jacobi, Rolleti de Cletis, qui fuerunt ad Contaminam per octo dies, iiij.lib,xvij.s.vij.d.*' In October 1274 Ibid. '*In expensis domini Petri de Langis, domini Iohannis de Massout, Magistri Jacobi et aliorum apud Burgum in Brixiam et apud Castillionem, preter centum solidos tunc eis traditos, Cv.s.*' In April 1275 Ibid. '*Domini Petro de Langis, domino Johanni de Massout, Magistro Jacobo missis apud Burgum In Bressia, vj.lib.*' In May 1275 Ibid. '*In expensis domini P.de Langis, domini Jo. de Massout et Magistri Jacobi apud Burgum per octo dies, preter sex lib. Tunc sibi traditis, lv.s.*'

25. Arnold Taylor. *Master Bertram, Ingeniator Regis.* Studies in Medieval History presented to R. Allen Brown (Woodbridge: The Boydell Press, 1989). 294. n31. Jean de Mézos is described as '*moranti apud Salinas pro dictando opere putei de Salinas*' whilst Maître Jacques is '*euntis apud Salinas pro operibus putei per xj. dies, capientis quolibet die 3s. Pro expensis suis.*'

26. Robert Liddiard. *Introduction in Late Medieval Castles* (Woodbridge: The Boydell Press, 2016). 6. 'As Nicola Coldstream explains ... the concentration of surviving castellation in north Wales is unique in the British Isles, but she questions the role of Master James of St George as a genius designer and the presence of a distinctive Savoyard connection in elements of the buildings. In preference, Master James emerges as a director of works of exceptional ability, and the castles themselves as being more English in inspiration, at least in their key structural elements.'

27. N. Pevsner, 'Terms of Architectural Planning in the Middle Ages,' *Journal of the Warburg and Courtauld Institutes* 5 (1942): 233. 'In the highly specialized civilisation of the Roman Empire the difference between planning in architecture and carrying out, between designing and actual building was clearly understood.'

28. Nicola Coldstream, 'Architects, Advisers and Design at Edward I's Castles in Wales, ' *Architectural History: Journal of the Society of Architectural Historians of Great Britain* 46 (2003): 24. 'To adapt Pevsner's famous comparison, if in Wales we have architecture, in Savoy we merely have building. Against this it could be argued that the conditions in Savoy did not allow Master James to display the talents that emerged when he came to Wales.' And 'it is difficult to see how Edward I could possibly have predicted that the ugly duckling at work in Savoy would turn into a swan in Wales.'

29. Ibid. 25' 'They [the Rhuddlan gatehouses] seem to be a less advanced type than either the Clare or London gatehouses or those of the 1280s.' And 'The inconvenient arrangement may show that the gatehouses [at Rhuddlan] were never intended for residential use, but it could alternatively be seen as an amateurish first effort by Master James.'

30. Ibid. 26. 'Master Bertram has a good claim to have inaugurated the gatehouses at Rhuddlan.'

31. Arnold Taylor. *Master Bertram Ingeniator Regis. Studies in Medieval History presented to R. Allen Brown* (Woodbridge: The Boydell Press, 1989). 303–4.

32. *'Coest le transcryt de un endenture faite deuant le Rey de le ordeynement de oueraynes de Linlyscu, de quele endenture le une partie demora vers mestre Jakes de seint Jorge, e quele partie le dyt mestre Jakes liuera as Chaumberleyns del Eschekere, e receut syz Liueres pour ses gages, Le Vinteter iour de May le an du Regne le Rey Edward Trentisme. Fait a remembrer qe le Dimenche as utaues de Pasch' lan du regne le Roi Edward Trentisme furent les choses desouz escrytes faites e ordenes deuaunt le Roi meymes en la fourme qe ensuyt. Primes le Roi ad ordine e comaunde qe le Fosse entour le Chastel de Linlithcu soit si parfund fossee e si estroit a parfound de la fosse cum len porra en mounde, E en tieu manere qe lewe du lay puysse auoir cours entour le dyt Chastel en meisme le fosse. Et si noun tote foits le facent ausi auaunt cum il perrunt. Derecheif qe par la ou le Roi auoit deuise a Mestre Jakes de seint Jorge le Machoun de fere y une porte de piere e deus Tours ausi de piere de une part e dautre de meysme la porte, et ausint deus tours de pyere en lewe chescun a chief du peel qe doit entrer en lewe dune part et dautre, le dit Roi ad eu sur coe conseil e ad chaunge son propos, e veut qe en lu de celes eoueres totes soient fetes bones portes e toreles totes de fust, si cum ly dyt Roi ad dyt sur coe plus pleinement sa volente al dyt Mestre Jakes. Et voet le Roi ausint qe le dyt peel seit fet bon e fort de fustz entiers ou de gros fustz fenduz sauns plus amenuser, Derecheif li Roi voet qe la tour del Eglise et la Eglise meysmes seit araiee et redressee e afortee si com il ad deuise al dyt Mestre Jaks. Derechif le Roi ad comaunde qe quant les dites oeures serrunt par-faites du dit fosse deuant qe lem face fere un bon fosse defensable deriere le Chastel dehors une creste pres du lay de lun bout du peel iusqes a lautre a lung' du lay. Et qe sus cele creste du fosse soit fait un bon peel mendre de lautre mes qil soit bien defensable. Derechifs Mestre Jaks y doit aler et sourueer et ordiner les dites oeueres, e prendre ses gages .xviij.d. le iour e le clerk qy irra .xij.d. Mestre Jaks receyuera sour ses gages ore al Escheker .vj.li. Et .xl.s. a la goule Aust per le Clerk qe ferra les paymentz. Et .xl.s. a la seint Michel par la Meyn meysmes le Clerk. Derechief le dyt Mestre Jaks ad dyt par eyme qe il entent qe les dites oueres cousterount entre cy en la Tous Seintz chescune symeyne .xx.li. Et ordine est qe taunt soit enuoe iloq's touz iours auauntmeyn par plus groses sommes.'*

33. TNA C47/4/1. *'Eidem Jacobo eunti in partibus Wallie ad ordinandum opera castrorum'* And *'Visitandum castra de flint et Rothelan.'* Or 'To the same Jacques going to parts in Wales for ordering the works of castle.' And 'in order to visit the castles of Flint and Rhuddlan.' N. Pevsner. 1942. Terms of Architectural Planning in the Middle Ages. Journal of the Warburg and Courtauld Institutes 5: 236. 'The word *'ordeneur'* occurs also in connection with *'architecteur'* in one of the first literary documents of Italian Renaissance influence on France, Christine of Pisan's Life of Charles V of about 1400. Here, however, the context, *'vrai architecteur, deviseur certain, et prudent ordeneur'* indicates that *'ordeneur'* is meant rather to stress the administrative side of architecture, although no other passage is known to me in which *'ordinatio'* must be taken to refer to a patron or his representative merely supervising a building job. But the sequence of *'architecteur,' 'deviseur,' 'ordeneur'* sounds very much like a sequence of architect–designer–administrator.' And 'To sum up, it can be maintained that whenever the terms *'dispositio,' 'ordinatio,' 'disegnare,'* 'deviser' and their derivatives or translations into other languages are found, they may be said to allude to architectural designing and planning and not to purely clerical work.'

34. CPR Edward II vol 1 1307–1313, 116. 'Grant, during pleasure, Adam de Stanay, king's yeoman for his good service in Scotland, of the town of Muston [Mostyn] in Englefield [Flintshire], which Master Jacques de Sancto Georgio, deceased, held for life.'

35. Nicola Coldstream, 'Architects, Advisers and Design at Edward I's Castles in Wales,' *Architectural History: Journal of the Society of Architectural Historians of Great Britain* 46 (2003): 34. 'Construction of the castles depended upon Master James' organizing skills, but their design did not'

36. Malcolm Hislop. *James of St George and the Castles of North Wales* (Barnsley: Pen & Sword Books Ltd, 2020). 264

37. Ibid. 'there is no reason to suppose that he was not consulted, nor that his advice was not taken into account.'

38. Michael Prestwich. 'Edward I in Wales' in *The Impact of the Edwardian Castles in Wales* (Oxford: Oxbow Books, 2010). 4.

39. TNA E101/351/12. *'Johanni de Byveillard militi eunti in Walliam ad supervidendum castra domini Regis ibidem precepto Regis, pro suis expensis eundo, morando et revertendo.'*

40. John E. Morris. *The Welsh Wars of Edward I* (Oxford: Clarendon Press, 1901j. 189 'Otto de Grandison, joined shortly afterwards by his old colleague John de Vescy ... took over this [Anglesey division.' And 191 'Grandison and Vescy spread out their division westwards from Bangor to Caernarvon, and soon penetrated to Harlech.' And TNA, C47/2/4. *'pacatum domino Othon de Grandisono ad sustentacionem D et lx peditum secum euncium de Castro de Bere usque Hardelach xx.li per talliam.'*

41. An ancestor of Cicon's had been with the crusade that had sacked Constantinople in 1204, one Othon de Cicon. Othon de Cicon had accompanied his uncle Othon de La Roche (who became Duc d'Athènes and built a Frankish tower atop the Acropolis) on the Fourth Crusade and became lord of Karystos from 1250 (at least) to his death around 1266. Taylor noted that Guillaume de Cicon's first arrival in the English record of 13 November 1276 follows closely on the heels of the recapture of Karystos by the Byzantines under Licario also in 1276. For full Greek history see William Miller. 1908. *The Latins in the Levant.* (New York: E. P. Dutton & Company).

42. *'la visite de tous ces lieux où le souvenir de Savoie demeure présent aujourd'hui, à sept siècles d'intervalle, m'a communiqué l'émotion du pèlerin et m'a vivement encouragé à persévérer.'*

43. Malcolm Hislop. *James of St George and the Castles of North Wales* (Barnsley: Pen & Sword Books Ltd, 2020). 267. The tide of historiography may well be rebalancing toward Taylor, the most recent work by Hislop finds 'This survey of the castles of Edward I in Wales suggests that Arnold Taylor was broadly correct in his assessment that James of St George was their principal architect.'

44. Christopher Wilson writing in *Die Kathedrale von Lausanne und ihr Marienportal im Kontext der europäischen Gotik* (Freiburg: der Universität Freiburg, 2004). 123–4. ' [Cotereel drew] heavily on contemporary English sources and thereby ... set himself apart from all of his fellow exponents of the French gothic tradition.' And Earlier Wilson had agreed with the basic English origins of the Cotereel family, writing 'Cotereel was the son of the architect who began the walls of the choir [at Lausanne] and that the latter was of English origin.' Marcel Grandjean, *'A Propos de la Construction de la Cathédrale de Lausanne (XII–XIIIe Siècle),'* Genava XI (1963): 278. *'Cotereel est un nom étranger au Pays de Vaud et aux régions avoisinantes.'* Or 'Cotereel is a foreign name in the Pays de Vaud and neighbouring regions. Malcolm Hislop. *James of St George and the Castles of North Wales* (Barnsley: Pen & Sword Books Ltd, 2020). 115–7. 'Parallels [with the Conwy window] are difficult to bring to mind, but its originality suggests that it may represent a design peculiar to Master James. In this regard it is worth considering the early thirteenth century window in the south transept of Lausanne Cathedral as a possible model ... It only takes a short flight of the imagination to see the Lausanne rose as the progenitor of the Conwy window. That there should be two references to Lausanne at Conwy seems to confirm the window tracery was determined by Master James.' Arnold Taylor. *Studies in Castles and Castle-Building* (London: The Hambledon Press, 1985). 21–2. 'Master James of St George may easily have lived to be well over 70. Let us therefore assume instead that he was at least 80 in 1309 and 32 or more in 1261. If he married at the age of 25 this would then have been no later than 1254, so that a further step into the realms of controlled conjecture would give 1255 as a likely date for the birth of his eldest child. Supposing that child to have been Tassin, and Giles to have been two years younger, they would have been 25 and 23 respectively at Saxon in 1280, and Giles would have been 25 at Aberystwyth in 1282, not too young an age to have been a 'master' if he serviced his apprenticeship from age 15 or thereabouts, particularly with so distinguished a father. Thus it is not impossible – at present we can put it no higher – that the Master James of St George and Master Giles of St George who appear briefly together at Aberystwyth in the records of 1282 were father and son, like Master John and Master James at Yverdon in 1261; if so, Giles would in all likelihood have been apprenticed to his father during the busy castle building period at StGeorges-d'Espéranche and elsewhere in the Viennois during the early 1270s.' Arnold Taylor. *Studies in Castles and Castle-Building.* (London: The Hambledon Press. 1985). 22–4. 'We may thus here be now in the presence not of two but of three generations of master masons, Master John (d. after 1261 and before 1268), Master James (d. 1309), and Master James's sons Master Tassin and Master Giles. What then can be said of the grandfather, Master John? A good deal can be said of Master John . . . his father was *magister operis* [at Lausanne] ... by 1268 he [Jean Cotereel] was no longer alive ... the possibility – to put it no higher – that he [*Maître Jean of Yverdon*, identified in primary sources as the father of Master James] is the same John as the *Magister operis* Lausannensis can hardly be excluded; clearly it would be no novelty for one with the experience of having planned

and started St Prex to be entrusted near to the end of life by Count Peter with the planning and founding of Yverdon ... Occasionally, as in the resemblance of the end hall window of the castle at Conwy to the western window of the cathedral of Lausanne, the military architect may reflect the source of his inspiration.

45. 'The Devils Brood.' *Plantagenets*. BBC, London. 17 March 2014. Television.
46. *Lettres de Rois, Reines et Autres Personnages des Cours de France et d'Angleterre*, ed. M. Champollion-Figeac (Paris: Imprimerie Royale, 1839), 1.306–07, ep. 240. Alianor also reminded Edward '*et pensés comme il vos fu ami.*' Or 'and think how he was a friend to you.'

Appendix: Key Primary Sources

1. RG i, no 2828; Close Rolls 1253–54, 194.
2. Ibid. 275 a
3. *La Finanza Sabauda*, Vol 1, 26.
4. Ibid. 41.
5. Ibid. 58–9.
6. Ibid. 63.
7. Ibid, 68.
8. Ibid.
9. Ibid. 118.
10. Archives de la Savoie, Chambéry.
11. *La Finanza Sabauda*, Vol 1, 73.
12. Ibid. 126.
13. *Viennensem* can be translated as the Viennois region.
14. Household roll of Count Phillip of Savoy, Archivio di Stato di Torino, Inv, Savoia 38, fo. 46, nos 3 and 4.
15. Ibid.
16. Ibid.
17. Ibid.
18. Gümmenen was the German name given to Contamine by the Hapsburgs once they had taken the border castle near Morat from the Savoyard.
19. Hugneti de Chillon or Hugues de Grammont, was Castellan of Chillon.
20. Household roll of Count Phillip of Savoy, Archivio di Stato di Torino, Inv, Savoia 38, fo. 46, nos 3 and 4.
21. Ibid.
22. Ibid.
23. Ibid.
24. Ibid.
25. Ibid.
26. Vien' is taken as an abbreviation of Viennois and not as an abbreviation of Vienne, since the former was the land of the Count of Savoy and the latter of the Archbishop of Vienne.
27. Household roll of Count Phillip of Savoy, Archivio di Stato di Torino, Inv, Savoia 38, fo. 46, nos 3 and 4.
28. Ibid.
29. Ibid.
30. Ibid.
31. Ibid.
32. Ibid.
33. Ibid.
34. Ibid.
35. Ibid.
36. Ibid.
37. Ibid.
38. Ibid.
39. Ibid.
40. Ibid.
41. Ibid.
42. Ibid.
43. Ibid.
44. Ibid.
45. Ibid.
46. The Valdigne is the Upper Aosta Valley, encompassing Pre'-Saint-Didier, Morgex and Courmayeur.

47. *Augusta Prætoria Salassorum* having been the Latin name for Aosta, derived from the name of the Roman colony there.
48. Household roll of Count Phillip of Savoy, Archivio di Stato di Torino, Inv, Savoia 38, fo. 46, nos 3 and 4.
49. Lully, Chablais, south-west of Evian.
50. *Augusta Prætoria Salassorum* having been the Latin name for the former Roman colony at Aosta, it seems some scribes referred to it as *Augustam* and others by a latinisation of the pre roman tribal name, *salassi* becoming *Salassorum* or *asallati*.
51. Household roll of Count Phillip of Savoy, Archivio di Stato di Torino, Inv, Savoia 38, fo. 46, nos 3 and 4'
52. Arnold Taylor. 1963. Some notes on the Savoyards in North Wales, 1277–1300. With special reference to the Savoyard element in the construction of Harlech Castle. Genava 11: 302.
53. Ibid.
54. Ibid.
55. Ibid.
56. CCR Edward I Vol 1 1272–1279. 493.
57. John Goronwy Edwards, ed. 1935. Calendar of ancient correspondence concerning Wales / by J. Goronwy Edwards. Cardiff: Cardiff, University Press Board, 1935.30–1.
58. TNA E101/3/15.
59. TNA, C 47/4/1.
60. Ibid.
61. Ibid.
62. TNA, C47/2/4
63. CWR 1277–1326, 291.
64. TNA E101/351/12
65. CPR Edward I Vol 2 1281–1292. 137.
66. TNA E372/131/26.
67. TNA E 101/485/28.
68. Ibid.
69. CWR 1277-1326, 326.
70. TNA E159/65 m14v.
71. *Prests*. 75.
72. The Perche was a medieval French measure of length or height equivalent to 5.5 yards. Old French *perche* from Latin *perticate* meaning measuring rod. In England the measurement was therefore refereed to as a rod.
73. J. G. Edwards. 1944. Edward I's Castle-Building in Wales. *The Proceedings of the British Academy* XXXII: 80.

Bibliography

Adams, Bernard. 1999. János Arany and the Bards of Wales. *The Slavonic and Eastern European Review* 77: 726–31.

Allen Brown, R. 1970. *English Castles*. London: Chancellor Press.

Allen Brown, R. 1984. *The Architecture of Castles: A Visual Guide. London*: B. T. Batsford Ltd.

Andenmatten, Bernard & Daniel de Raemy. 1990. *La Maison De Savoie En Pays De Vaud*. Lausanne: Editions Payot Lausanne.

Andenmatten, Bernard (ed.). 2020. *Othon I de Grandson (vers 1240–1328)*. Lausanne: Cahiers Lausannois d'Histoire Médiévale.

Andenmatten, Bernard. 1989. *La noblesse vaudoise face à la Maison de Savoie au XIII siècle. La Maison de Savoie et le Pays de Vaud. Bibliothèque historique vaudoise* 97: 35–50.

Ashbee, Jeremy A. 2005. 'Goodrich Castle'. London: English Heritage Guidebooks.

Ashbee, Jeremy A. 2015.' Conwy Castle and Town Walls'. Cardiff: Cadw Welsh Government.

Ashbee, Jeremy A. 2017. 'Harlech Castle'. Cardiff: Cadw Welsh Government.

Avent, Richard, 1989. 'Criccieth Castle'. Cardiff: Cadw: Welsh Historic Monuments.

Avent, Richard, 2004. *Dolwyddelan Castle Dolbadarn Castle Castell y Bere*. 2010 edition. Cardiff: Cadw.

Baker, Darren. 2015. *With All for All: The Life of Simon de Montfort*. Stroud: Amberley Publishing.

Baker, Darren. 2017. *Henry III: The Great King England Never Knew It Had*. Stroud: The History Press.

Baker, Darren. 2019. *The Two Eleanors of Henry III: The Lives of Eleanor of Provence and Eleanor de Montfort*. First ed. Barnsley: Pen & Sword Books Limited.

Bartlett, Robert. 1993. *The Making of Europe: Conquest, Colonization and Cultural Change*. London: Penguin Books Ltd.

Bartlett, Robert. 2020. *Royal Blood: Dynastic Politics in Medieval Europe*. Cambridge: Cambridge University Press.

Beverley Smith, J. 1958. 'The Lordship of Glamorgan'. Morgannwg transactions of the Glamorgan Local History Society. II: 9–37.

Beverley Smith, J. 1982/3. 'Llywelyn ap Gruffudd and the Match of Wales'. *Brycheiniog* XX: 9-22.

Beverley Smith, J. 2014. *Llywellyn ap Gruffudd: Prince of Wales*. Cardiff: The University of Wales Press.

Blomquist, Thomas W. 1971. 'Commercial Association in Thirteenth-Century Lucca'. *The Business History Review* 45: 157–78.

Blondel, Louis. 1935. *L'architecture militaire au temps de Pierre II de Savoie: Les donjons circulaires. Genava* XIII: 271–321.

Blondel, Louis. 1949. *Le château de Brignon. Vallesia* IV: 19–34.

Blondel, Louis. 1950. *Le bourg et le château de Saillon. Unsere Kunstdenkmäler* 1: 8–9.

Blondel, Louis. 1954. *Le château de Saxon. Vallesia* IX: 165–74.

Blondel, Louis. 1954. *Le château et le bourg de Conthey. Vallesia* IX: 149–64.

Blondel, Louis. 1955. *Le château de Saxon: Note Complémentaire. Vallesia* X: 87–8.

Borman, Tracy. 2015. *The Story of the Tower of London*. London: Merrell Publishers Limited.

Borrel, Étienne-Louis. 1884. *Les monuments anciens de la Tarentaise (Savoie)*. Paris: Ducher.

Buathier, Henri. 1995. *JEAN Ier DE GRAILLY un chevalier européen du XIIIe siècle*. Berne.

Burnand, Aug. 1911. *La date de la naissance d'Othon 1er, Sire de Grandson. Revue historique vaudoise* 19 no 5: 129–35.

Burnand, Aug. 1911. *Vaudois en Angleterre au XIIIe siècle, avec Othon Ier de Grandson : (d'après* M.C.-L. Kingsford). *Revue historique vaudoise* 19 no 7: 212–18.

Burt, Caroline. 2013. *Edward I and the Governance pf England, 1272–1307*. Cambridge: Cambridge University Press.

Butler, L. A. S. 2007. 'Denbigh Castle'. Cardiff: Cadw.

Butler, Lawrence & Jeremy K. Knight. 2004. 'Dolforwyn Castle Montgomery Castle'. Cardiff: Cadw.

Caple, Chris. 2007. 'Excavations at Dryslwyn Castle. Leeds': The Society for Medieval Archaeology.

Carpenter, David. 1992. 'King Henry III's 'Statute' Against Aliens: July 1263'. *The English Historical Review* 107: 925–44.

Carpenter, David. 2004. *The Struggle for Master: Britain 1066–1284*. London: Penguin Books Ltd.

Carpenter, David. 2020. *Henry III: The Rise to Power and Personal Rule 1207–1258*. New Haven: Yale University Press.

Carter Michael. 2017. 'Hailes Abbey'. London: English Heritage.

Chapman, Dr Adam 2013. 'Welsh Battlefields Historical and Documentary Research': Maes Moydog. Cardiff: Cadw, Welsh Govdrnment & CBHC.

Chapuisat, Jean-Pierre. 1960. *A Propos des Relations entre la Savoie et l'Angleterre au XIII Siècle. Bulletin Philolgique et Historique* 1: 29–34.

Chapuisat, Jean-Pierre. 1964. *Au service de deux rois d'Angleterre au XIIIe siècle: Pierre de Champvent. Revue historique vaudoise* 72: 157–75.

Chapuisat, Jean-Pierre. 1971. *Les deux faces anglaises du Grand-Saint-Bernard au moyen age. Valesia* 26: 5–14.

Chapuisat, Jean-Pierre. 1978. *Quelques variations sur un thème connue: En relisant certains comptes de châtellenies du XIII siècle. Vallesia* XXX: 107–14.

Chapuisat, Jean-Pierre. 1989. *De Mont-sur-Rolle à Windsor, de la Dullive à Dumfries ... La Maison de Savoie et le Pays de Vaud. Bibliothèque historique vaudoise* 97: 117–22.

Chapuisat, Jean-Pierre. 1992. *Un cadet vaudois en Gascogne et à Windsor. Bibliothèque historique vaudoise* 105: 27–37.

Chiaudano, Mario. 1933. *La Finanza Sabauda nel sec. XIII*. Turin: Biblioteca Della Societa Storica Subalpina.

Churchill, Winston S. 2013. *A History of the English-Speaking Peoples*. New York: Rosetta Books.

Citron, Suzanne. 1987. *Le Mythe National: L'histoire de France revisitée*. Paris: Les Éditions de l'Arelier Éditions Ouvrières.

Clifford, Esther Rowland. 1961. *A Knight of Great Renown: The Life and Times of Othon de Grandson*. Chicago: The University of Chicago Press.

Cockerill, Sara. 2014. *Eleanor of Castile: The Shadow Queen*. Second edition. Stroud: Amberley Publishing.

Coldstream, Nicola. 2003. 'Architects, Advisers and Design at Edward I's Castles in Wales'. Architectural History: *Journal of the Society of Architectural Historians of Great Britain* 46: 19–36.

Coss Peter R., P. R. Coss & Simon D. Lloyd. 1988. *King Henry III and the 'Aliens', 1236–1272*. Boydell & Brewer.

Cox, Eugene L. 1974. *The Eagles of Savoy: The House of Savoy in Thirteenth Century Europe*. Princeton: Princeton University Press.

Darracott, Ann. 2014. 'The Grandisons: Their Built and Chivalric Legacy'. Maidenhead: Maidenhead Civic Society.

Davies, R. R. 1979. 'Kings, Lords and Liberties in the March of Wales, 1066–1272'. *Transactions of the Royal Historical Society* 29: 41–61.

Davies, R. R. 1987. *The Age of Conquest: Wales 1063–1415*. Oxford: Oxford University Press.

de Gingins-La-Sarra, Frédéric. 2018. *Annales de L'Abbaye de Lac-de-Joux*. L'Orient: Imprimerie Baudat.

de Raemy, Daniel. 2004. *Châteaux, donjons et grandes tours dans les Etats de Savoie (1230–1330)*. Lausanne: Cahiers d'archéologie romande 98 et 99.

Dean, Robert J. 2009. *Castles in Distant Lands: The Life and Times of Othon of Grandson*. Willingdon: Lawden Haynes Publishing.

Demotz, Bernard. 1987. *L'État et le château au Moyen Âge : l'exemple savoyard. Journal des savants*: 27–64.

Dipartimento di Lingue e Letterature Straniere e Culture dell'Università degli Studi di Torino. Ed. 2014. A Warm Mind-Shake *Scritti in onore di Paolo Bertinetti.* Turin. *Edizioni Trauben.*

Donnet, André & Louis Blondel. 1963. *Château du Valais.* Olten: Editions Walter.

Dorens, Girart. 1909. 'Sir Otho de Grandison 1238?–1328'. *Transactions of the Royal Historical Society* 3: 125–95.

Dufour, Béatrice, Catherine Santschi, Gustave Deghilage, René Dreyfus, Bernard Golaz & Frank Perroter. 1984. 'Saint Prex 1234–1984'. Saint-Prex: Commune de Saint-Prex.

Duncan, A. A. M. 2002. *The Kingship of the Scots 842–1292.* Edinburgh: Edinburgh University Press.

Edwards, J. G. 1914. 'The Name of Flint Castle.' *The English Historical Review.* 29, no 114: 315–17.

Edwards, J. G. 1924. 'The Battle of Maes Madog and the Welsh Campaign of 1294–5'. The *English Historical Review.* 39, no 153: 1–12.

Edwards, J. G. 1931. 'The Site of the Battle of 'Meismeidoc', 1295'. *The English Historical Review.* 46, no 182: 262–5.

Edwards, J. G. 1935. *Calendar of Ancient Correspondence Concerning Wales.* Cardiff: University Press Board Cardiff.

Edwards, J. G. 1944. 'Edward I's Castle-Building in Wales'. *The Proceedings of the British Academy* XXXII.

Edwards, J. GH. 1951. 'The Building of Flin't. *The Flintshire Historical Society* XII: 5–20.

Favrod, Justin. 2000. *La nécropole du Pré de la Cure à Yverdon-Les-Bains. Cahiers d'Archéologie Romande.*

Fontannaz, Monique & Brigitte Pradervand. 2015. *Les monuments d'art et d'histoire de la Suisse.* Berne: Societe d'histoire de l'art en Suisse SHAS.

Fontannaz, Monique. 2006. *La Ville de Moudon.* Berne: Société D'Histoire de L'Art en Suisse SHAS.

Fryde, E. B. 1962. *Book of Prests of the King's Wardrobe for 1294–5.* Oxford: Clarendon Press.

Fryde, E. B. D. E. Greenway, S. Porter & I. Roy. 1986. *Handbook of British Chronology.* Third edition. London: Offices of the Royal Historical Society.

Galland, Bruno. 1988. *Un Savoyard sur le siège de Lyon au XIIIe siècle: Philippe de Savoie. Bibliothèque de l'école des chartes tome* 146 livraison 1: 31–67.

Gerald of Wales. 1978. *The Journey Through Wales and The Description of Wales.* London: Penguin Books Ltd.

Given, James. 1989. The Economic Consequences of the English Conquest of Gwynedd. *Speculum* 64: 11–45.

Goldstone, Nancy. 2010. *Four Queens: The Provençal Sisters Who Ruled Europe.* London: The Orion Publishing Group.

Goodall, John. 1999. 'Pevensey Castle'. London: English Heritage.

Gough, Henry. 1900. 'Itinerary of King Edward the First throughout his reign, A.D. 1272–1307, exhibiting his movements so far as they are recorded'. Paisley: Alexander Gardner.

Grandjean, Marcel. 1963. *A Propos de la Construction de la Cathédrale de Lausanne (XII–XIIIe Siècle). Genava* XI: 261–87.

Grandjean, Marcel. 1969. *La 'carentena' du Chapitre de Notre-Dame de Lausanne dans le cloître de la cathédrale. Revue historique vaudoise* 77: 7–13.

Gravett, Christopher. 2007. *The Castles of King Edward I in Wales 1277–1307.* Botley: Osprey Publishing Ltd.

Gravett, Christopher. 2009. *English Castles 1200–1300.* Botley: Osprey Publishing Ltd.

Griffith, Paddy. 2006. *The Vauban Fortifications of France.* Oxford: Osprey Publishing.

Griffiths, J. 1935-7. 'Documents Relating to the Rebellion of Madoc, 1294–5'. *Bulletin of the Board of Celtic Studies* VIII.

Griffiths, Ralph A.. 1966/7. 'The Revolt of Rhys ap Maredudd, 1287–8'. *Welsh History Review* 3 no. 2: 121–43.

Guy, Neil. 2015. 'Rhuddlan Castle'. *The Castle Studies Group Journal.* No. 29: 50–7.

Hislop, Malcolm. 2020. *James of St George and the Castles of North Wales*. Barnsley: Pen & Sword Books Ltd.

Howell, Margaret. 1998. *Eleanor of Provence*. Oxford: Blackwell Publishers Ltd.

Jones, Dan. 2012. *The Plantagenets: The Kings Who Made England*. Ebook edition. London: William Collins.

Kaeuper, Richard W. 1973. *Bankers to the Crown: The Riccardi of Lucca and Edward I*. Princeton: Princeton University Press.

Kennedy, Hugh. 1994. *Crusader Castles*. Cambridge: Cambridge University Press.

Knoop, Douglas & G. P. Jones. 1933. *The Mediaeval Mason: An Economic History of English Stone Building in the Later Middle Ages and Early Modern Times*. Manchester: Manchester University Press.

Liddiard, Robert (ed.) 2016. *Late Medieval Castles*. Woodbridge: The Boydell Press.

Manley, John. 1994. 'Excavations at Caergwrle Castle, Clwyd, North Wales: 1988–1990'. *Medieval Archaeology* 38: 83–133.

Martin, David & Barbara Martin. 2013. 'A Reinterpretation of the Gatehouse at Tonbridge Castle'. *Archaeologia Cantiana* 133: 235–76.

Martin, Maryline & Florian Renucci. 2016. *Guédelon: A Castle in the Making*. Rennes: Editions Ouest-France.

Ménégaldo, Silvère & Olivier Bertrand. 2016. *Vocabulaire d'ancien français* 3e éd. (Linguistique) (French edition). Malakoff: Armand Colin.

Morerod, Jean-Daniel. 2012. *La Cathédrale Notre-Dame de Lausanne: Monument européen, temple vaudois*. Lausanne: La Bibliothèque des Arts.

Morris, John E. 1901. *The Welsh Wars of Edward I*. Oxford: Clarendon Press.

Morris, Marc. 2009. *A Great and Terrible King*. London: Windmill Books.

Morris, Marc. 2012. *Castle*. London: Windmill Books.

Morris, Richard K. 2006. 'Kenilworth Castle'. Third edition. London: English Heritage.

Mottaz, Eugene. 1900. *Note sur la construction du château d'Yverdon. Revue historique vaudoise* 8: 359–67.

Mugnier, François. 1890. *Les Savoyards en Angleterre au XIIIe siècle et Pierre d'Aigueblanche évêque d'Héreford*. Chambéry: Imprimerie Ménard.

Nicoll, David. 2005. *Crusader Castles in the Holy Land 1192–1302*. Oxford: Osprey Publishing Ltd.

Palmer, Tim. 2007. 'Egryn Stone: a forgotten Welsh freestone'. Cardiff: national Museum Wales.

Peckham, John. 1884. *Registrum epistolarum fratris Johannis Peckham, Archiepiscopi Cantuariensis*: Volume 2. Cambridge: Cambridge University Press.

Peers, C. R. 1915-16. 'Carnarvon Castle'. *Transactions of the Honourable Society of Cymmrodorion*: 1–74.

Peers, C. R. 1921/2. 'Harlech Castle'. *Transactions of the Honourable Society of Cymmrodorion:* 63–82.

Perfect, Vicky. 2012. *Flint Castle: The story of Edward I's First Welsh Castle*. Mold: Alyn Books Ltd.

Pevsner, N. 1942. 'The Term 'Architect' in the Middle Ages'. *Speculum* 17: 549–62.

Pevsner, N. 1942. 'Terms of Architectural Planning in the Middle Ages'. *Journal of the Warburg and Courtauld Institutes* 5: 232–7.

Phillips, Charles. 2018. *The Medieval Castle*. Yeovil: Haynes Publishing.

Powicke, Sir Maurice. 1953. *The Thirteenth Century 1216–1307*. Oxford: Oxford University Press.

Prestwich, Michael. 1972. 'A New Account of the Welsh Campaign 1294–95'. *Welsh History Review* 6: 89–94.

Prestwich, Michael. 1997. *Edward I*. Yale: Yale University Press.

Prestwich, Michael. 2002. Document: 'Edward I's Wars in the Hagnaby Chronicle'. *Journal of Medieval Military History* X: 197–214.

Prestwich, Michael. 2005. *Plantagenet England 1225–1360*. Oxford: Oxford University Press.

Prestwich, Michael. 2010. *Knight: The Medieval Warrior's (Unofficial) Guide*. London: Thames & Hudson.

Prestwich, Michael. *Medieval People*. London: Thames & Hudson.

Previté-Orton, C.W. 1912. *The Early History of the House of Savoy (1000–1233)*. Cambridge: Cambridge University Press.

Pryce, Huw. 2001. 'National identity in Twelfth-Century Wales'. *The English Historical Review*. 116, no. 468: 775–801.

Pryce, Huw. 2005. *The Acts of Welsh Rulers: 1120 to 1283*. Cardiff: University of Wales Press.

Ray, Michael. 2006. 'The Savoyard Cousins: A Comparison of the Careers and Relative Success of the Grandson (Grandison) and Champvent (Chavent) Families in England'. *The Antiquaries Journal* 86.

Ray, Michael. 2017. 'A Vaudois servant of Henry III, Ebal II de Mont (Ebulo de Montibus)'. www.academia.edu/31930999/A_Vaudois_servant_of_Henry_III_Ebal_II_de_Mont_ Ebulo_de_Montibus?email_work_card=view-paper.

Rees, Sian E. & Chris Caple. 1999. *Dinefwr Castle Dryslwyn Castle*. Revised ed. Cardiff: Cadw.

Reeve, Matthew M. 2006. 'The Painted Chamber at Westminster, Edward I, and the Crusade'. *Viator-medieval and Renaissance Studies* 37: 189–221.

Remfry, P. M. 2014. *Harlech Castle and Its True Origins*. Ceidio: SCS Publishing.

Renn, Derek. 1989. 'Caerphilly Castle'. Revised ed. Cardiff: Cadw.

Rex Smith, G. 2009. 'The Penmachno Letter Patent and the Welsh Uprising of 1294–95'. *Cambrian Medieval Celtic Studies* 58: 49–67.

Reymond, Annick Voirol. 2013. 'Grandson Castle 1000 Years of History'. Grandson: Artgraphic Cavin SA.

Reymond, Maxime. 1920. *Le Chevalier Othon I de Grandson*. *Revue historique vaudoise* 28, no. 6: 161–79.

Roderick, A. J. 1952. 'The Feudal Relation Between the English Crown and the Welsh Princes'. *History* 37: 201–12.

Roth, Charles. 1948. *Cartulaire du Chapitre de Notre-Dame de Lausanne*. Lausanne: Librairie Payot.

Rothero, Christopher. 1984. *The Scottish and Welsh Wars 1250–1400*. 20th ed. Botley: Osprey Publishing Ltd.

Royer, Katherine. 2003. 'The Body in Parts: Reading the Execution Ritual in Late Medieval England'. *Historical Reflections / Réflexions Historiques* 29: 319–39.

Rymer, Thomas. 1816. *Fœdra, Conventiones, Litteræ, et Cujuscunque Generis Acta Publica Inter Reges Angliæ et alios quosvis Imperatores, Reges, Pontifices, bel Communitates*. London.

Salt, Mary C. L. 1929. 'List of English Embassies to France, 1272–1307'. *The English Historical Review* 44: 263-78.

Saverio Provana di Collegno. 1901. *Notizie d'alcune certose del Piemonte*, all'interno di *Miscellanea di Storia Italiana, terza serie, Tomo VI:* Turin. Fratelli Bocca Librai di S.M.

Shelby, L. R. 1964. 'The Role of the Master Mason in Mediaeval English Building'. *Speculum* 39: 387–403.

Simpson, W. Douglas. 1928. 'James de Sancto Georgio, Master of the Works to King Edward in Wales and Scotland'. *Transactions of the Anglesey Antiquarian and Field Society*: 31–41.

Snow, Dan. 2012. *Battle Castles: 500 Years of Knights and Siege Warfare*. London: HarperPress.

Spurgeon, C. J. 1978/79. 'Builth Castle'. *Brycheiniog* XVIII: 47–59.

Stevenson, Joseph. 1870. 'Documents Illustrative of the History of Scotland Volume 1'. Edinburgh: H. M. General Register House.

Tanquerey, Frédéric Joseph. 1916. *Recueil de Lettres Anglo-Françaises, 1265–1399*. Paris: Librairie Ancienne Honoré Champion.

Taylor, Arnold. 2015. 'Caernarfon Castle and Town Walls'. Cardiff: Cadw Welsh Government.

Taylor, Arnold. . 1953. 'A Letter from Lewis of Savoy to Edward I'. *The English Historical Review* LXVIII: 56–62.

Taylor, Arnold. 1949. 'The Cloister of Vale Royal Abbey'. *Journal of the Chester Archaeological Society* 37: 295–7.

Taylor, Arnold. 1950. 'Master James of St George'. *The English Historical Review* 65 no. 257: 433–57.

Taylor, Arnold. 1953. 'The Castle of St Georges d'Espéranche'. *The Antiquaries Journal* 33: 33–47.

Taylor, Arnold. 1954-55. 'Rhuddlan cathedral: a 'might-have-been' of Flintshire history'. *Journal of the Flintshire Historical Society* 15: 43–51.

Taylor, Arnold. 1955. 'English Builders in Scotland during the War of Independence: A Record of 1304'. *The Scottish Historical Review* 34: 44–6.

Taylor, Arnold. 1963. 'Some notes on the Savoyards in North Wales, 1277–1300'. With special reference to the Savoyard element in the construction of Harlech Castle. *Genava* XI: 289–315.

Taylor, Arnold. 1974. *The King's Works in Wales 1277–1330*. London: Her Majesty's Stationery Office.

Taylor, Arnold. 1976. 'Notes and Documents: Who was 'John Pennardd, leader of the men of Gwynedd'?'. *English Historical Review* 91: 79–97.

Taylor, Arnold. 1984. 'Scorched Earth at Flint in 1294'. *Journal of the Flintshire Historical Society* 30: 89-105.

Taylor, Arnold. 1985. *Studies in Castles and Castle-Building*. London: The Hambledon Press.

Taylor, Arnold. 1986. *The Welsh Castles of King Edward I*. London: The Hambledon Press.

Taylor, Arnold. 1989. 'Studies in Medieval History Presented to R. Allen Brown'. Woodbridge: The Boydell Press.

Taylor, Arnold. 2008. 'Rhuddlan Castle. 2008': Cadw Welsh Government.

Taylor, Arnold. 2015. 'Beaumaris Castle'. Cardiff: Cadw Welsh Government.

Taylor, Arnold. 2015. 'Harlech Castle'. Cardiff: Cadw Welsh Government.

Toy, Sidney. 1984. *Castles: Their Construction and History*. Mineola: Dover Publications Inc.

Tyerman, Christopher. 1996. *England and the Crusades, 1095–1588*. Chicago: University of Chicago Press.

Van Bechem, Victor. 1913. *La 'ville neuve' d'Yverdo : Foundation de Pierre de Savoie*. Festgabe fur Gerold Meyer von Kronau 205–26.

Vitruvius. 2019. *The Complete Works of Vitruvius*. Hastings: Delphi Publishing Ltd.

Walker, David. 1982/3. 'The Lordship of Builth'. *Brycheiniog* XX: 23–33.

Walker, R. F. 1976. 'The Hagnaby Chronicle and the Battle of Maes Moydog'. *Welsh History Review* 8: 125–38.

Weiler, Björn. 2006. 'Knighting, Homage, and the Meaning of Ritual: The Kings of England and their Neighbours in the Thirteenth Century'. *Viator* 37: 275–99.

Weir, Alison. 2020. *Queens of the Crusades: Eleanor of Aquitaine and her Successors*. London: Penguin Random House UK.

Wheatley, Abigail. 2015. *The Idea of the Castle in Medieval England*. York: York Medeival Press.

Williams, Diane M. & John R. Kenyon (eds.). 2010. *The Impact of the Edwardian Castles in Wales*. Oxford: Oxbow Books.

Wilson, Christopher. 1990. *The Gothic Cathedral*. London: Thames & Hobson Ltd.

Wilson, Christopher. 2004. *Die Kathedrale von Lausanne und ihr Marienportal im Kontext der europäischen Gotik*. Freiburg: der Universität Freiburg.

Wilson, Derek. 2017. *Medieval Kings and Queens*. Bristol: Immediate Media Co.

Wilson, Peter H. 2017. *The Holy Roman Empire*. Second edition. London: Penguin.

Wurstemberger, J. Ludwig. 1859. *Pierre II, Comte de Savoie, Marquis en Italie et sa Maison*. Berne: Stæmpfle.

Index

319